DERIVATIVES AND PORTFOLIO MANAGEMENT

CFA® PROGRAM CURRICULUM
2014 • Level II • Volume 6

WILEY

Photography courtesy of Hector Emanuel and Justin Runquist.

ISBN 978-1-937537-71-5 (paper)
ISBN 978-1-937537-92-0 (ebk)

10 9 8 7 6 5 4 3 2 1

Please visit our website at
www.WileyGlobalFinance.com.

CONTENTS

Derivatives

◘ indicates an optional segment

◘ indicates an optional segment

◙ indicates an optional segment

◘ indicates an optional segment

◘ indicates an optional segment

How to Use the CFA Program Curriculum

Congratulations on passing Level I of the Chartered Financial Analyst (CFA®) Program. This exciting and rewarding program of study reflects your desire to become a serious investment professional. You are embarking on a program noted for its high ethical standards and the breadth of knowledge, skills, and abilities it develops. Your commitment to the CFA Program should be educationally and professionally rewarding.

The credential you seek is respected around the world as a mark of accomplishment and dedication. Each level of the program represents a distinct achievement in professional development. Successful completion of the program is rewarded with membership in a prestigious global community of investment professionals. CFA charterholders are dedicated to life-long learning and maintaining currency with the ever-changing dynamics of a challenging profession. The CFA Program represents the first step towards a career-long commitment to professional education.

The CFA examination measures your mastery of the core skills required to succeed as an investment professional. These core skills are the basis for the Candidate Body of Knowledge (CBOK™). The CBOK consists of four components:

- A broad topic outline that lists the major top-level topic areas (CBOK Topic Outline)
- Topic area weights that indicate the relative exam weightings of the top-level topic areas
- Learning outcome statements (LOS) that advise candidates about the specific knowledge, skills, and abilities they should acquire from readings covering a topic area (LOS are provided in candidate study sessions and at the beginning of each reading)
- The CFA Program curriculum, readings, and end-of-reading questions, which candidates receive upon exam registration

Therefore, the key to your success on the CFA exam is studying and understanding the CBOK™. The following sections provide background on the CBOK, the organization of the curriculum, and tips for developing an effective study program.

CURRICULUM DEVELOPMENT PROCESS

The CFA Program is grounded in the practice of the investment profession. Using the Global Body of Investment Knowledge (GBIK) collaborative website, CFA Institute performs a continuous practice analysis with investment professionals around the world to determine the knowledge, skills, and abilities (competencies) that are relevant to the profession. Regional expert panels and targeted surveys are conducted annually to verify and reinforce the continuous feedback from the GBIK collaborative website. The practice analysis process ultimately defines the CBOK. The CBOK contains the competencies that are generally accepted and applied by investment professionals. These competencies are used in practice in a generalist context and are expected to be demonstrated by a recently qualified CFA charterholder.

A committee consisting of practicing charterholders, in conjunction with CFA Institute staff, designs the CFA Program curriculum in order to deliver the CBOK to candidates. The examinations, also written by practicing charterholders, are designed to allow you to demonstrate your mastery of the CBOK as set forth in the CFA Program curriculum. As you structure your personal study program, you should emphasize mastery of the CBOK and the practical application of that knowledge. For more information on the practice analysis, CBOK, and development of the CFA Program curriculum, please visit www.cfainstitute.org.

ORGANIZATION OF THE CURRICULUM

The Level II CFA Program curriculum is organized into 10 topic areas. Each topic area begins with a brief statement of the material and the depth of knowledge expected.

Each topic area is then divided into one or more study sessions. These study sessions—18 sessions in the Level II curriculum—should form the basic structure of your reading and preparation.

Each study session includes a statement of its structure and objective, and is further divided into specific reading assignments. An outline illustrating the organization of these 18 study sessions can be found at the front of each volume.

The reading assignments are the basis for all examination questions, and are selected or developed specifically to teach the knowledge, skills, and abilities reflected in the CBOK. These readings are drawn from CFA Institute-commissioned content, textbook chapters, professional journal articles, research analyst reports, and cases. Readings include problems and solutions to help you understand and master the topic areas.

Reading-specific Learning Outcome Statements (LOS) are listed at the beginning of each reading. These LOS indicate what you should be able to accomplish after studying the reading. The LOS, the reading, and the end-of-reading questions are dependent on each other, with the reading and questions providing context for understanding the scope of the LOS.

You should use the LOS to guide and focus your study, as each examination question is based on an assigned reading and one or more LOS. The readings provide context for the LOS and enable you to apply a principle or concept in a variety of scenarios. The candidate is responsible for the entirety of all of the required material in a study session, the assigned readings as well as the end-of-reading questions and problems.

We encourage you to review the material on LOS (www.cfainstitute.org/programs/cfaprogram/courseofstudy/Pages/study_sessions.aspx), including the descriptions of LOS "command words" (www.cfainstitute.org/programs/Documents/cfa_and_cipm_los_command_words.pdf).

FEATURES OF THE CURRICULUM

OPTIONAL SEGMENT

Required vs. Optional Segments You should read all of an assigned reading. In some cases, however, we have reprinted an entire chapter or article and marked certain parts of the reading as "optional." The CFA examination is based only on the required segments, and the optional segments are included only when they might help you to better understand the required segments (by seeing the required material in its full context). When an optional segment begins, you will see text and a dashed vertical bar in the outside margin that will continue until the optional segment ends, accompanied by another icon. *Unless the material is specifically marked as optional, you should assume it is required.* You should rely on the required segments and the reading-specific LOS in preparing for the examination.

END OPTIONAL SEGMENT

Problems/Solutions *All questions and problems in the readings as well as their solutions (which are provided directly following the problems) are part of the curriculum and are required material for the exam.* When appropriate, we have included problems within and after the readings to demonstrate practical application and reinforce your understanding of the concepts presented. The questions and problems are designed to help you learn these concepts and may serve as a basis for exam questions. Many of these questions are adapted from past CFA examinations.

Margins The wide margins in each volume provide space for your note-taking.

Six-Volume Structure For portability of the curriculum, the material is spread over six volumes.

Glossary and Index For your convenience, we have printed a comprehensive glossary in each volume. Throughout the curriculum, a **bolded** word in a reading denotes a term defined in the glossary. Each volume also contains an index specific to that volume; a combined index can be found on the CFA Institute website with the Level II study sessions.

Source Material The authorship, publisher, and copyright owners are given for each reading for your reference. We recommend that you use this CFA Institute curriculum rather than the original source materials because the curriculum may include only selected pages from outside readings, updated sections within the readings, and contains problems and solutions tailored to the CFA Program.

LOS Self-Check We have inserted checkboxes next to each LOS that you can use to track your progress in mastering the concepts in each reading.

DESIGNING YOUR PERSONAL STUDY PROGRAM

Create a Schedule An orderly, systematic approach to examination preparation is critical. You should dedicate a consistent block of time every week to reading and studying. Complete all reading assignments and the associated problems and solutions in each study session. Review the LOS both before and after you study each reading to ensure that you have mastered the applicable content and can demonstrate the knowledge, skill, or ability described by the LOS and the assigned reading. Use the LOS self-check to track your progress and highlight areas of weakness for later review.

As you prepare for your exam, we will e-mail you important exam updates, testing policies, and study tips. Be sure to read these carefully. Curriculum errata are periodically updated and posted on the study session page at www.cfainstitute.org. You may also sign up for an RSS feed to alert you to the latest errata update.

Successful candidates report an average of over 300 hours preparing for each exam. Your preparation time will vary based on your prior education and experience. For each level of the curriculum, there are 18 study sessions, so a good plan is to devote 15–20 hours per week, for 18 weeks, to studying the material. Use the final four to six weeks before the exam to review what you've learned and practice with sample and mock exams. This recommendation, however, may underestimate the hours needed for appropriate examination preparation depending on your individual circumstances, relevant experience, and academic background. You will undoubtedly adjust your study time to conform to your own strengths and weaknesses, and your educational and professional background.

You will probably spend more time on some study sessions than on others, but on average you should plan on devoting 15-20 hours per study session. You should allow ample time for both in-depth study of all topic areas and additional concentration on those topic areas for which you feel least prepared.

CFA Institute Question Bank The CFA Institute topic-based question bank is intended to assess your mastery of individual topic areas as you progress through your studies. After each test, you will receive immediate feedback noting the correct responses and indicating the relevant assigned reading so you can identify areas of weakness for further study. The topic tests reflect the question formats and level of difficulty of the actual CFA examinations. For more information on the topic tests, please visit www.cfainstitute.org.

CFA Institute Mock Examinations In response to candidate requests, CFA Institute has developed mock examinations that mimic the actual CFA examinations not only in question format and level of difficulty, but also in length and topic weight. The three-hour mock exams simulate the morning and afternoon sessions of the actual CFA exam, and are intended to be taken after you complete your study of the full curriculum so you can test your understanding of the curriculum and your readiness for the exam. You will receive feedback at the end of the mock exam, noting the correct responses and indicating the relevant assigned readings so you can assess areas of weakness for further study during your review period. We recommend that you take mock exams during the final stages of your preparation for the actual CFA examination. For more information on the mock examinations, please visit www.cfainstitute.org.

Preparatory Providers After you enroll in the CFA Program, you may receive numerous solicitations for preparatory courses and review materials. When considering a prep course, make sure the provider is in compliance with the CFA Institute Prep Provider Guidelines Program (www.cfainstitute.org/partners/examprep/Pages/cfa_prep_provider_guidelines.aspx). Just remember, there are no shortcuts to success on the CFA examinations; reading and studying the CFA curriculum is the key to success on the examination. The CFA examinations reference only the CFA Institute assigned curriculum—no preparatory course or review course materials are consulted or referenced.

SUMMARY

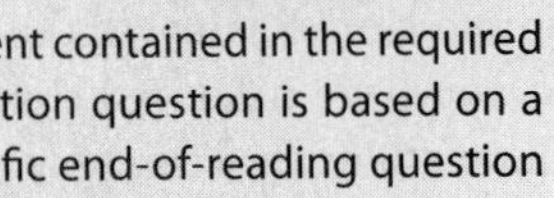

Every question on the CFA examination is based on the content contained in the required readings and on one or more LOS. Frequently, an examination question is based on a specific example highlighted within a reading or on a specific end-of-reading question and/or problem and its solution. To make effective use of the CFA Program curriculum, please remember these key points:

1 All pages printed in the curriculum are required reading for the examination except for occasional sections marked as optional. You may read optional pages as background, but you will not be tested on them.

2 All questions, problems, and their solutions - printed at the end of readings - are part of the curriculum and are required study material for the examination.

3 You should make appropriate use of the online sample/mock examinations and other resources available at www.cfainstitute.org.

4 You should schedule and commit sufficient study time to cover the 18 study sessions, review the materials, and take sample/mock examinations.

5 **Note:** Some of the concepts in the study sessions may be superseded by updated rulings and/or pronouncements issued after a reading was published. Candidates are expected to be familiar with the overall analytical framework contained in the assigned readings. Candidates are not responsible for changes that occur after the material was written.

FEEDBACK

At CFA Institute, we are committed to delivering a comprehensive and rigorous curriculum for the development of competent, ethically grounded investment professionals. We rely on candidate and member feedback as we work to incorporate content, design, and packaging improvements. You can be assured that we will continue to listen to your suggestions. Please send any comments or feedback to info@cfainstitute.org. Ongoing improvements in the curriculum will help you prepare for success on the upcoming examinations, and for a lifetime of learning as a serious investment professional.

LOFT

Derivatives

STUDY SESSIONS

Study Session 16	Forwards and Futures
Study Session 17	Options, Swaps, and Interest Rate and Credit Derivatives

TOPIC LEVEL LEARNING OUTCOME

The candidate should be able to estimate the value of futures, forwards, options, and swaps, and demonstrate how they may be used in various strategies.

LOFT
68

DERIVATIVES

STUDY SESSION 16

Derivative Investments

Forwards and Futures

This study session examines derivative investments and markets and focuses on derivative pricing, valuation, and credit risk evaluation. Assessing the relative cost/benefit of using derivative instruments or investments with embedded derivatives requires an understanding of the factors that affect valuation. This study session also addresses interest rate, equity, and currency forwards and futures.

READING ASSIGNMENTS

Reading 51	Forward Markets and Contracts *Analysis of Derivatives for the Chartered Financial Analyst® Program*, by Don M. Chance, CFA
Reading 52	Futures Markets and Contracts *Analysis of Derivatives for the Chartered Financial Analyst® Program*, by Don M. Chance, CFA

LOFT
68

READING

51

Forward Markets and Contracts

by Don M. Chance, CFA

LEARNING OUTCOMES

Mastery	The candidate should be able to:
☐	a. explain how the value of a forward contract is determined at initiation, during the life of the contract, and at expiration;
☐	b. calculate and interpret the price and value of an equity forward contract, assuming dividends are paid either discretely or continuously;
☐	c. calculate and interpret the price and value of 1) a forward contract on a fixed-income security, 2) a forward rate agreement (FRA), and 3) a forward contract on a currency;
☐	d. evaluate credit risk in a forward contract, and explain how market value is a measure of exposure to a party in a forward contract.

INTRODUCTION

1

OPTIONAL SEGMENT

Recall the definition of a forward contract: *A forward contract is an agreement between two parties in which one party, the buyer, agrees to buy from the other party, the seller, an underlying asset or other derivative, at a future date at a price established at the start of the contract.* Therefore, it is a commitment by two parties to engage in a transaction at a later date with the price set in advance. The buyer is often called the **long** and the seller is often called the **short**.[1] Although any two parties can agree on such a contract, in this book we are interested only in forward contracts that involve large corporations, financial institutions, nonprofit organizations, or governments.

As an example, a pension fund manager, anticipating the receipt of cash at a future date, might enter into a commitment to purchase a stock portfolio at a later date at a price agreed on today. By doing so, the manager's position is unaffected by any changes in the value of the stock portfolio between today and the date of the actual investment in the stock portfolio. In this sense, the manager is hedged against an

1 The derivatives industry often uses nouns, verbs, adjectives, and adverbs as parts of speech other than what they are. Hence, words like *long* and *short* are used not as adjectives but as nouns.

increase in stock prices until the cash is received and invested. The disadvantage of such a transaction is that the manager is also hedged against any decreases in stock prices. If stock prices fall between the time the commitment is established and the time the cash is received, the manager will regret having entered into the forward contract because the stock could have been acquired at a lower price. But that is the nature of a forward contract hedge: It locks in a price.

An important feature of a forward contract is that neither party pays any money at the start. The parties might require some collateral to minimize the risk of default, but we shall ignore this point. So keep in mind this very important aspect of forward contracts: *No money changes hands at the start.*

1.1 Delivery and Settlement of a Forward Contract

When a forward contract expires, there are two possible arrangements that can be used to settle the obligations of the parties. A deliverable forward contract stipulates that the long will pay the agreed-upon price to the short, who in turn will deliver the underlying asset to the long, a process called **delivery**. An alternative procedure, called **cash settlement**, permits the long and short to pay the net cash value of the position on the delivery date. For example, suppose two parties agree to a forward contract to deliver a zero-coupon bond at a price of $98 per $100 par. At the contract's expiration, suppose the underlying zero-coupon bond is selling at a price of $98.25. The long is due to receive from the short an asset worth $98.25, for which a payment to the short of $98.00 is required. In a cash-settled forward contract, the short simply pays the long $0.25. If the zero-coupon bond were selling for $97.50, the long would pay the short $0.50. Delivery of a zero-coupon bond is not a difficult thing to do, however, and cash-settled contracts are more commonly used in situations where delivery is impractical.[2] For example, if the underlying is the Russell 3000 Index, the short would have to deliver to the long a portfolio containing each of the Russell 3000 stocks proportionate to its weighting in the index. Consequently, cash settlement is much more practical. Cash-settled forward contracts are sometimes **nondeliverable forwards (NDFs)**, although this term is used predominately with respect to foreign exchange forwards.

1.2 Default Risk and Forward Contracts

An important characteristic of forward contracts is that they are subject to default. Regardless of whether the contract is for delivery or cash settlement, the potential exists for a party to default. In the zero-coupon bond example above, the long might be unable to pay the $98 or the short might be unable to buy the zero-coupon bond and make delivery of the bond to the long. Generally speaking, however, forward contracts are structured so that only the party owing the greater amount can default. In other words, if the short is obligated to deliver a zero-coupon bond selling for more than $98, then the long would not be obligated to make payment unless the short makes delivery. Likewise, in a cash settled contract, only one party—the one owing the greater amount—can default. We discuss the nature of this credit risk in the following section and in Section 5 after we have determined how to value forward contracts.

2 Be aware, however, that the choice of delivery or cash settlement is not an option available at expiration. It is negotiated between the parties at the start.

1.3 Termination of a Forward Contract

Let us note that a forward contract is nearly always constructed with the idea that the participants will hold on to their positions until the contract expires and either engage in delivery of the asset or settle the cash equivalent, as required in the specific contract. The possibility exists, however, that at least one of the participants might wish to terminate the position prior to expiration. For example, suppose a party goes long, meaning that she agrees to buy the asset at the expiration date at the price agreed on at the start, but she subsequently decides to terminate the contract before expiration. We shall assume that the contract calls for delivery rather than cash settlement at expiration.

To see the details of the contract termination, suppose it is part of the way through the life of the contract, and the long decides that she no longer wishes to buy the asset at expiration. She can then re-enter the market and create a new forward contract expiring at the same time as the original forward contract, taking the position of the seller instead. Because of price changes in the market during the period since the original contract was created, this new contract would likely have a different price at which she would have to commit to sell. She would then be long a contract to buy the asset at expiration at one price and short a contract to sell the asset at expiration at a different price. It should be apparent that she has no further exposure to the price of the asset.

For example, suppose she is long to buy at $40 and short to deliver at $42. Depending on the characteristics of the contract, one of several possibilities could occur at expiration. Everything could go as planned—the party holding the short position of the contract on which she is long at $40 delivers the asset to her, and she pays him $40. She then delivers the asset to the party who is long the contract on which she is short at $42. That party pays her $42. She nets $2. The transaction is over.

There is always a possibility that her counterparty on the long contract could default. She is still obligated to deliver the asset on the short contract, for which she will receive $42. But if her counterparty on the long contract defaults, she has to buy the asset in the market and could suffer a significant loss. There is also a possibility that the counterparty on her short contract could fail to pay her the $42. Of course, she would then not deliver the asset but would be exposed to the risk of changes in the asset's price. This type of problem illustrates the credit risk in a forward contract. We shall cover credit risk in more detail in Section 5 of this reading.

To avoid the credit risk, when she re-enters the market to go short the forward contract, she could contact the same counterparty with whom she engaged in the long forward contract. They could agree to cancel both contracts. Because she would be owed $2 at expiration, cancellation of the contract would result in the counterparty paying her the present value of $2. This termination or offset of the original forward position is clearly desirable for both counterparties because it eliminates the credit risk.[3] It is always possible, however, that she might receive a better price from another counterparty. If that price is sufficiently attractive and she does not perceive the credit risk to be too high, she may choose to deal with the other counterparty and leave the credit risk in the picture.

3 This statement is made under the assumption that the parties do not want the credit risk. Credit risk, like other risks, however, can be a risk that some parties want because of the potential for earning attractive returns by using their expertise in measuring the actual credit risk relative to the credit risk as perceived by the market. In addition, credit risk offers diversification benefits.

2 THE STRUCTURE OF GLOBAL FORWARD MARKETS

The global market for forward contracts is part of a vast network of financial institutions that make markets in these instruments as well as in other related derivatives, such as swaps and options. Some dealers specialize in certain markets and contracts, such as forward contracts on the euro or forward contracts on Japanese equity products. These dealers are mainly large global banking institutions, but many large non-banking institutions, such as Goldman Sachs and Merrill Lynch, are also big players in this market.

Dealers engage in transactions with two types of parties: end users and other dealers. An end user is typically a corporation, nonprofit organization, or government.[4] An end user is generally a party with a risk management problem that is searching for a dealer to provide it with a financial transaction to solve that problem. Although the problem could simply be that the party wants to take a position in anticipation of a market move, more commonly the end user has a risk it wants to reduce or eliminate.

As an example, Hoffman-LaRoche, the large Swiss pharmaceutical company, sells its products globally. Anticipating the receipt of a large amount of cash in U.S. dollars and worried about a decrease in the value of the dollar relative to the Swiss franc, it could buy a forward contract to sell the dollar and buy Swiss francs. It might seek out a dealer such as UBS Warburg, the investment firm affiliated with the large Swiss bank UBS, or it might approach any of the other large multinational banks with which it does business. Or it might end up dealing with a non-bank entity, like Merrill Lynch. Assume that Hoffman-LaRoche enters into this contract with UBS Warburg. Hoffman-LaRoche is the end user; UBS Warburg is the dealer.

Transactions in forward contracts typically are conducted over the phone. Each dealer has a quote desk, whose phone number is well known to the major participants in the market. If a party wishes to conduct a transaction, it simply phones the dealer for a quote. The dealer stands ready to take either side of the transaction, quoting a bid and an ask price or rate. The bid is the price at which the dealer is willing to pay for the future purchase of the asset, and the ask is the price at which the dealer is willing to sell. When a dealer engages in a forward transaction, it has then taken on risk from the other party. For example, in the aforementioned transaction of Hoffman-LaRoche and UBS Warburg, by entering into the contract, UBS Warburg takes on a risk that Hoffman-LaRoche has eliminated. Specifically, UBS Warburg has now committed to buying dollars and selling Swiss francs at a future date. Thus, UBS Warburg is effectively long the dollar and stands to gain from a strengthening dollar/weakening Swiss franc. Typically dealers do not want to hold this exposure. Rather, they find another party to offset the exposure with another derivative or spot transaction. Thus, UBS Warburg is a wholesaler of risk—buying it, selling it, and trying to earn a profit off the spread between its buying price and selling price.

One might reasonably wonder why Hoffman-LaRoche could not avoid the cost of dealing with UBS Warburg. In some cases, it might be able to. It might be aware of another party with the exact opposite needs, but such a situation is rare. The market for financial products such as forward contracts is made up of wholesalers of risk management products who use their technical expertise, their vast network of contacts, and their access to critical financial market information to provide a more efficient means for end users to engage in such risk management transactions.

4 The U.S. government does not transact in forward contracts or other derivatives, but some foreign governments and central banks do. Within the United States, however, some state and local governments do engage in forward contracts and other derivatives.

Dealers such as UBS Warburg lay off the risk they do not wish to assume by transacting with other dealers and potentially other end users. If they do this carefully, quickly, and at accurate prices, they can earn a profit from this market-making activity. One should not get the impression, however, that market making is a highly profitable activity. The competition is fierce, which keeps bid–ask spreads very low and makes it difficult to earn much money on a given transaction. Indeed, many market makers do not make much money on individual transactions—they typically make a small amount of money on each transaction and do a large number of transactions. They may even lose money on some standard transactions, hoping to make up losses on more-complicated, nonstandard transactions, which occur less frequently but have higher bid–ask spreads.

Risk magazine conducts annual surveys to identify the top dealers in various derivative products. Exhibit 1 presents the results of those surveys for two of the forward products we cover here, currency and interest rate forwards. Interest rate forwards are called forward rate agreements (FRAs). In the next section, we shall study the different types of forward contracts and note that there are some others not covered in the *Risk* surveys.

One of these surveys was sent to banks and investment banks that are active dealers in over-the-counter derivatives. The other survey was sent to end users. The tabulations are based on respondents' simple rankings of who they think are the best dealers. Although the identities of the specific dealer firms are not critical, it is interesting and helpful to be aware of the major players in these types of contracts. Most of the world's leading global financial institutions are listed, but many other big names are not. It is also interesting to observe that the perceptions of the users of these dealer firms' services differ somewhat from the dealers' self-perceptions. Be aware, however, that the rankings change, sometimes drastically, each year.

3 TYPES OF FORWARD CONTRACTS

In this section, we examine the types of forward contracts that fall within the scope of this reading. By the word "types," we mean the underlying asset groups on which these forward contracts are created. Because the CFA Program focuses on the asset management industry, our primary interest is in equity, interest rate and fixed-income, and currency forwards.

3.1 Equity Forwards

An **equity forward** is a contract calling for the purchase of an individual stock, a stock portfolio, or a stock index at a later date. For the most part, the differences in types of equity forward contracts are only slight, depending on whether the contract is on an individual stock, a portfolio of stocks, or a stock index.

Exhibit 1 ***Risk* Magazine Surveys of Banks, Investment Banks, and Corporate End Users to Determine the Top Three Dealers in Currency and Interest Rate Forwards**

	Respondents	
Currencies	**Banks and Investment Banks**	**Corporate End Users**
Currency Forwards		
$/€	UBS Warburg	Citigroup
	Deutsche Bank	Royal Bank of Scotland
	JP Morgan Chase	JP Morgan Chase/Bank of America
$/¥	UBS Warburg	Citigroup
	Citigroup	Bank of America
	JP Morgan Chase	JP Morgan Chase/UBS Warburg
$/£	UBS Warburg	Royal Bank of Scotland
	Royal Bank of Scotland	Citigroup
	Hong Kong Shanghai Banking Corporation	UBS Warburg
$/SF	UBS Warburg	UBS Warburg
	Credit Suisse First Boston	Citigroup
	BNP Paribas	Credit Suisse First Boston
Interest Rate Forwards (FRAs)		
$	JP Morgan Chase	JP Morgan Chase
	Bank of America	Royal Bank of Scotland
	Deutsche Bank	Bank of America
€	Deutsche Bank	Royal Bank of Scotland
	Intesa BCI	JP Morgan Chase
	Royal Bank of Scotland	Deutsche Bank
¥	Mizuho Securities	Citigroup
	JP Morgan Chase	Merrill Lynch
	BNP Paribas	Hong Kong Shanghai Banking Corporation
£	Royal Bank of Scotland	Royal Bank of Scotland
	Commerzbank	Bank of America/ING Barings
	Deutsche Bank	
SF	Credit Suisse First Boston	UBS Warburg
	UBS Warburg	Credit Suisse First Boston
	Deutsche Bank	Citigroup/ING Barings

Note: $ = U.S. dollar, € = euro, ¥ = Japanese yen, £ = U.K. pound sterling, SF = Swiss franc.
Source: *Risk*, September 2002, pp. 30–67 for banks and investment banking dealer respondents, and June 2002, pp. 24–34 for end user respondents. The end user survey provides responses from corporations and asset managers. The above results are for corporate respondents only.

3.1.1 *Forward Contracts on Individual Stocks*

Consider an asset manager responsible for the portfolio of a high-net-worth individual. As is sometimes the case, such portfolios may be concentrated in a small number of stocks, sometimes stocks that have been in the family for years. In many cases, the individual may be part of the founding family of a particular company. Let us say that the stock is called Gregorian Industries, Inc., or GII, and the client is so heavily invested in this stock that her portfolio is not diversified. The client notifies the portfolio manager of her need for $2 million in cash in six months. This cash can be raised by selling 16,000 shares at the current price of $125 per share. Thus, the risk exposure concerns the market value of $2 million of stock. For whatever reason, it is considered best not to sell the stock any earlier than necessary. The portfolio manager realizes that a forward contract to sell GII in six months will accomplish the client's desired objective. The manager contacts a forward contract dealer and obtains a quote of $128.13 as the price at which a forward contract to sell the stock in six months could be constructed.[5] In other words, the portfolio manager could enter into a contract to sell the stock to the dealer in six months at $128.13. We assume that this contract is deliverable, meaning that when the sale is actually made, the shares will be delivered to the dealer. Assuming that the client has some flexibility in the amount of money needed, let us say that the contract is signed for the sale of 15,600 shares at $128.13, which will raise $1,998,828. Of course when the contract expires, the stock could be selling for any price. The client can gain or lose on the transaction. If the stock rises to a price above $128.13 during the six-month period, the client will still have to deliver the stock for $128.13. But if the price falls, the client will still get $128.13 per share for the stock.

3.1.2 *Forward Contracts on Stock Portfolios*

Because modern portfolio theory and good common sense dictate that investors should hold diversified portfolios, it is reasonable to assume that forward contracts on specific stock portfolios would be useful. Suppose a pension fund manager knows that in three months he will need to sell about $20 million of stock to make payments to retirees. The manager has analyzed the portfolio and determined the precise identities of the stocks he wants to sell and the number of shares of each that he would like to sell. Thus the manager has designated a specific subportfolio to be sold. The problem is that the prices of these stocks in three months are uncertain. The manager can, however, lock in the sale prices by entering into a forward contract to sell the portfolio. This can be done one of two ways.

The manager can enter into a forward contract on each stock that he wants to sell. Alternatively, he can enter into a forward contract on the overall portfolio. The first way would be more costly, as each contract would incur administrative costs, whereas the second way would incur only one set of costs.[6] Assume that the manager chooses the second method. He provides a list of the stocks and number of shares of each he wishes to sell to the dealer and obtains a quote. The dealer gives him a quote of $20,200,000. So, in three months, the manager will sell the stock to the dealer and

5 In Section 4, we shall learn how to calculate forward prices such as this one.

6 Ignoring those costs, there would be no difference in doing forward contracts on individual stocks or a single forward contract on a portfolio. Because of the non-linearity of their payoffs, this is not true for options. A portfolio of options is not the same as an option on a portfolio, but a portfolio of forward contracts is the same as a forward contract on a portfolio, ignoring the aforementioned costs.

receive \$20,200,000. The transaction can be structured to call for either actual delivery or cash settlement, but in either case, the client will effectively receive \$20,200,000 for the stock.[7]

3.1.3 *Forward Contracts on Stock Indices*

Many equity forward contracts are based on a stock index. For example, consider a U.K. asset manager who wants to protect the value of her portfolio that is a Financial Times Stock Exchange 100 index fund, or who wants to eliminate a risk for which the FTSE 100 Index is a sufficiently accurate representation of the risk she wishes to eliminate. For example, the manager may be anticipating the sale of a number of U.K. blue chip shares at a future date. The manager could, as in our stock portfolio example, take a specific portfolio of stocks to a forward contract dealer and obtain a forward contract on that portfolio. She realizes, however, that a forward contract on a widely accepted benchmark would result in a better price quote, because the dealer can more easily hedge the risk with other transactions. Moreover, the manager is not even sure which stocks she will still be holding at the later date. She simply knows that she will sell a certain amount of stock at a later date and believes that the FTSE 100 is representative of the stock that she will sell. The manager is concerned with the systematic risk associated with the U.K. stock market, and accordingly, she decides that selling a forward contract on the FTSE 100 would be a good way to manage the risk.

Assume that the portfolio manager decides to protect £15,000,000 of stock. The dealer quotes a price of £6,000 on a forward contract covering £15,000,000. We assume that the contract will be cash settled because such index contracts are nearly always done that way. When the contract expiration date arrives, let us say that the index is at £5,925—a decrease of 1.25 percent from the forward price. Because the manager is short the contract and its price went down, the transaction makes money. But how much did it make on a notional principal of £15,000,000?

The index declined by 1.25 percent. Thus, the transaction should make 0.0125 × £15,000,000 = £187,500. In other words, the dealer would have to pay £187,500 in cash. If the portfolio were a FTSE 100 index fund, then it would be viewed as a portfolio initially worth £15,000,000 that declined by 1.25 percent, a loss of £187,500. The forward contract offsets this loss. Of course, in reality, the portfolio is not an index fund and such a hedge is not perfect, but as noted above, there are sometimes reasons for preferring that the forward contract be based on an index.

3.1.4 *The Effect of Dividends*

It is important to note the effect of dividends in equity forward contracts. Any equity portfolio nearly always has at least a few stocks that pay dividends, and it is inconceivable that any well-known equity index would not have some component stocks that pay dividends. Equity forward contracts typically have payoffs based only on the price of the equity, value of the portfolio, or level of the index. They do not ordinarily pay off any dividends paid by the component stocks. An exception, however, is that some equity forwards on stock indices are based on total return indices. For example, there are two versions of the well-known S&P 500 Index. One represents only the market value of the stocks. The other, called the S&P 500 Total Return Index, is structured so

7 If, for example, the stock is worth \$20,500,000 and the transaction calls for delivery, the manager will transfer the stocks to the dealer and receive \$20,200,000. The client effectively takes an opportunity loss of \$300,000. If the transaction is structured as a cash settlement, the client will pay the dealer \$300,000. The client would then sell the stock in the market, receiving \$20,500,000 and netting \$20,200,000 after settling the forward contract with the dealer. Similarly, if the stock is selling for less than the amount guaranteed by the forward contract, the client will deliver the stock and receive \$20,200,000 or, if the transaction is cash settled, the client will sell the stock in the market and receive a cash payment from the dealer, making the effective sale price still \$20,200,000.

that daily dividends paid by the stocks are reinvested in additional units of the index, as though it were a portfolio. In this manner, the rate of return on the index, and the payoff of any forward contract based on it, reflects the payment and reinvestment of dividends into the underlying index. Although this feature might appear attractive, it is not necessarily of much importance in risk management problems. The variability of prices is so much greater than the variability of dividends that managing price risk is considered much more important than worrying about the uncertainty of dividends.

In summary, equity forwards can be based on individual stocks, specific stock portfolios, or stock indices. Moreover, these underlying equities often pay dividends, which can affect forward contracts on equities. Let us now look at bond and interest rate forward contracts.

3.2 Bond and Interest Rate Forward Contracts

Forward contracts on bonds are similar to forward contracts on interest rates, but the two are different instruments. Forward contracts on bonds, in fact, are no more difficult to understand than those on equities. Drawing on our experience of Section 3.1, we simply extend the notion of a forward contract on an individual stock, a specific stock portfolio, or a stock index to that of a forward contract on an individual bond, a specific bond portfolio, or a bond index.[8]

3.2.1 *Forward Contracts on Individual Bonds and Bond Portfolios*

Although a forward contract on a bond and one on a stock are similar, some basic differences nonetheless exist between the two. For example, the bond may pay a coupon, which corresponds somewhat to the dividend that a stock might pay. But unlike a stock, a bond matures, and a forward contract on a bond must expire prior to the bond's maturity date. In addition, bonds often have many special features such as calls and convertibility. Finally, we should note that unlike a stock, a bond carries the risk of default. A forward contract written on a bond must contain a provision to recognize how default is defined, what it means for the bond to default, and how default would affect the parties to the contract.

In addition to forward contracts on individual bonds, there are also forward contracts on portfolios of bonds as well as on bond indices. The technical distinctions between forward contracts on individual bonds and collections of bonds, however, are relatively minor.

The primary bonds for which we shall consider forward contracts are default-free zero-coupon bonds, typically called Treasury bills or T-bills in the United States, which serve as a proxy for the risk-free rate.[9] In a forward contract on a T-bill, one party agrees to buy the T-bill at a later date, prior to the bill's maturity, at a price agreed on today. T-bills are typically sold at a discount from par value and the price is quoted in terms of the discount rate. Thus, if a 180-day T-bill is selling at a discount of 4 percent, its price per \$1 par will be \$1 – 0.04(180/360) = \$0.98. The use of 360 days is the convention in calculating the discount. So the bill will sell for \$0.98. If purchased and held to maturity, it will pay off \$1. This procedure means that the interest is deducted from the face value in advance, which is called **discount interest**.

8 It may be useful to review Chapters 1 and 3 of *Fixed Income Analysis for the Chartered Financial Analyst Program* by Frank J. Fabozzi, New Hope, PA: Frank J. Fabozzi Associates (2000).

9 A government-issued zero-coupon bond is typically used as a proxy for a risk-free asset because it is assumed to be free of default risk. It can be purchased and held to maturity, thereby eliminating any market value risk, and it has no reinvestment risk because it has no coupons. If the bond is liquidated before maturity, however, some market value risk exists in addition to the risk associated with reinvesting the market price.

The T-bill is usually traded by quoting the discount rate, not the price. It is understood that the discount rate can be easily converted to the price by the above procedure. A forward contract might be constructed that would call for delivery of a 90-day T-bill in 60 days. Such a contract might sell for \$0.9895, which would imply a discount rate of 4.2 percent because \$1 – 0.042(90/360) = \$0.9895. Later in this reading, we shall see how forward prices of T-bills are derived.

In addition to forward contracts on zero-coupon bonds/T-bills, we shall consider forward contracts on default-free coupon-bearing bonds, also called Treasury bonds in the United States. These instruments pay interest, typically in semiannual installments, and can sell for more (less) than par value if the yield is lower (higher) than the coupon rate. Prices are typically quoted without the interest that has accrued since the last coupon date, but with a few exceptions, we shall always work with the full price—that is, the price including accrued interest. Prices are often quoted by stating the yield. Forward contracts call for delivery of such a bond at a date prior to the bond's maturity, for which the long pays the short the agreed-upon price.

3.2.2 *Forward Contracts on Interest Rates: Forward Rate Agreements*

So far in Section 3.2 we have discussed forward contracts on actual fixed-income securities. Fixed-income security prices are driven by interest rates. A more common type of forward contract is the interest rate forward contract, more commonly called a **forward rate agreement (FRA)**. Before we can begin to understand FRAs, however, we must examine the instruments on which they are based.

There is a large global market for time deposits in various currencies issued by large creditworthy banks. This market is primarily centered in London but also exists elsewhere, though not in the United States. The primary time deposit instrument is called the **Eurodollar**, which is a dollar deposited outside the United States. Banks borrow dollars from other banks by issuing Eurodollar time deposits, which are essentially short-term unsecured loans. In London, the rate on such dollar loans is called the London Interbank Rate. Although there are rates for both borrowing and lending, in the financial markets the lending rate, called the **London interbank offered rate** (LIBOR), is more commonly used in derivative contracts. LIBOR is the rate at which London banks lend dollars to other London banks. Even though it represents a loan outside of the United States, LIBOR is considered to be the best representative rate on a dollar borrowed by a private, i.e., nongovernmental, high-quality borrower. It should be noted, however, that the London market includes many branches of banks from outside the United Kingdom, and these banks are also active participants in the Eurodollar market.

A Eurodollar time deposit is structured as follows. Let us say a London bank such as NatWest needs to borrow \$10 million for 30 days. It obtains a quote from the Royal Bank of Scotland for a rate of 5.25 percent. Thus, 30-day LIBOR is 5.25 percent. If NatWest takes the deal, it will owe \$10,000,000 × [1 + 0.0525 (30/360)] = \$10,043,750 in 30 days. Note that, like the Treasury bill market, the convention in the Eurodollar market is to prorate the quoted interest rate over 360 days. In contrast to the Treasury bill market, the interest is not deducted from the principal. Rather, it is added on to the face value, a procedure appropriately called **add-on interest**. The market for Eurodollar time deposits is quite large, and the rates on these instruments are assembled by a central organization and quoted in financial newspapers. The British Bankers Association publishes a semi-official Eurodollar rate, compiled from an average of the quotes of London banks.

The U.S. dollar is not the only instrument for which such time deposits exist. Eurosterling, for example, trades in Tokyo, and Euroyen trades in London. You may be wondering about Euroeuro. Actually, there is no such entity as Euroeuro, at least not by that name. The Eurodollar instrument described here has nothing to do with the European currency known as the euro. Eurodollars, Euroyen, Eurosterling, etc.

have been around longer than the euro currency and, despite the confusion, have retained their nomenclature. An analogous instrument does exist, however—a euro-denominated loan in which one bank borrows euros from another. Trading in euros and euro deposits occurs in most major world cities, and two similar rates on such euro deposits are commonly quoted. One, called EuroLIBOR, is compiled in London by the British Bankers Association, and the other, called Euribor, is compiled in Frankfurt and published by the European Central Bank. Euribor is more widely used and is the rate we shall refer to in this book.

Now let us return to the world of FRAs. FRAs are contracts in which the underlying is neither a bond nor a Eurodollar or Euribor deposit but simply an interest payment made in dollars, Euribor, or any other currency at a rate appropriate for that currency. Our primary focus will be on dollar LIBOR and Euribor, so we shall henceforth adopt the terminology LIBOR to represent dollar LIBOR and Euribor to represent the euro deposit rate.

Because the mechanics of FRAs are the same for all currencies, for illustrative purposes we shall use LIBOR. Consider an FRA expiring in 90 days for which the underlying is 180-day LIBOR. Suppose the dealer quotes this instrument at a rate of 5.5 percent. Suppose the end user goes long and the dealer goes short. The end user is essentially long the rate and will benefit if rates increase. The dealer is essentially short the rate and will benefit if rates decrease. The contract covers a given notional principal, which we shall assume is \$10 million.

The contract stipulates that at expiration, the parties identify the rate on new 180-day LIBOR time deposits. This rate is called 180-day LIBOR. It is, thus, the underlying rate on which the contract is based. Suppose that at expiration in 90 days, the rate on 180-day LIBOR is 6 percent. That 6 percent interest will be paid 180 days later. Therefore, the present value of a Eurodollar time deposit at that point in time would be

$$\frac{\$10{,}000{,}000}{1 + 0.06\left(\frac{180}{360}\right)}$$

At expiration, then, the end user, the party going long the FRA in our example, receives the following payment from the dealer, which is the party going short:

$$\$10{,}000{,}000\left[\frac{(0.06 - 0.055)\left(\frac{180}{360}\right)}{1 + 0.06\left(\frac{180}{360}\right)}\right] = \$24{,}272$$

If the underlying rate is less than 5.5 percent, the payment is calculated based on the difference between the 5.5 percent rate and the underlying rate and is paid by the long to the short. It is important to note that even though the contract expires in 90 days, the rate is on a 180-day LIBOR instrument; therefore, the rate calculation adjusts by the factor 180/360. The fact that 90 days have elapsed at expiration is not relevant to the calculation of the payoff.

Before presenting the general formula, let us review the calculations in the numerator and denominator. In the numerator, we see that the contract is obviously paying the difference between the actual rate that exists in the market on the contract expiration date and the agreed-upon rate, adjusted for the fact that the rate applies to a 180-day instrument, multiplied by the notional principal. The divisor appears because when Eurodollar rates are quoted in the market, they are based on the assumption that the rate applies to an instrument that accrues interest at that rate with the interest paid a certain number of days (here 180) later. When participants determine this rate in the London Eurodollar market, it is understood to apply to a Eurodollar time deposit that begins now and matures 180 days later. So the interest on an actual Eurodollar deposit would not be paid until 180 days later. Thus, it is necessary to adjust the FRA payoff to reflect the fact that the rate implies a payment that would occur 180 days later on a standard Eurodollar deposit. This adjustment is easily done by simply discounting the payment at the current LIBOR, which here is 6 percent, prorated over 180 days. These conventions are also followed in the market for FRAs with other underlying rates.

In general, the FRA payoff formula (from the perspective of the party going long) is

$$\text{Notional principal}\left[\frac{\left(\begin{array}{c}\text{Underlying rate at expiration}\\ -\text{Forward contract rate}\end{array}\right)\left(\dfrac{\text{Days in underlying rate}}{360}\right)}{1+\text{Underlying rate at expiration}\left(\dfrac{\text{Days in underlying rate}}{360}\right)}\right]$$

where *forward contract rate* represents the rate the two parties agree will be paid and *days in underlying rate* refers to the number of days to maturity of the instrument on which the underlying rate is based.

One somewhat confusing feature of FRAs is the fact that they mature in a certain number of days and are based on a rate that applies to an instrument maturing in a certain number of days measured from the maturity of the FRA. Thus, there are two day figures associated with each contract. Our example was a 90-day contract on 180-day LIBOR. To avoid confusion, the FRA markets use a special type of terminology that converts the number of days to months. Specifically, our example FRA is referred to as a 3 × 9, reflecting the fact that the contract expires in three months and that six months later, or nine months from the contract initiation date, the interest is paid on the underlying Eurodollar time deposit on whose rate the contract is based.[10]

FRAs are available in the market for a variety of maturities that are considered somewhat standard. Exhibit 2 presents the most common maturities. Most dealers follow the convention that contracts should expire in a given number of exact months and should be on the most commonly traded Eurodollar rates such as 30-day LIBOR, 60-day LIBOR, 90-day LIBOR, 180-day LIBOR, and so on. If a party wants a contract expiring in 37 days on 122-day LIBOR, it would be considered an exception to the standard, but most dealers would be willing to make a market in such an instrument. Such nonstandard instruments are called *off the run*. Of course, FRAs are available in all of the leading currencies.

Exhibit 2 **FRA Descriptive Notation and Interpretation**

Notation	Contract Expires in	Underlying Rate
1 × 3	1 month	60-day LIBOR
1 × 4	1 month	90-day LIBOR
1 × 7	1 month	180-day LIBOR
3 × 6	3 months	90-day LIBOR
3 × 9	3 months	180-day LIBOR
6 × 12	6 months	180-day LIBOR
12 × 18	12 months	180-day LIBOR

Note: This list is not exhaustive and represents only the most commonly traded FRAs.

10 The notation "3 × 9" is pronounced "three by nine."

The FRA market is large, but not as large as the swaps market. It is important, however, to understand FRAs before trying to understand swaps. As we will show in the reading on swap markets and contracts, a swap is a special combination of FRAs. But let us now turn to another large forward market, the market for currency forwards.

3.3 Currency Forward Contracts

Spurred by the relaxation of government controls over the exchange rates of most major currencies in the early 1970s, a currency forward market developed and grew extremely large. Currency forwards are widely used by banks and corporations to manage foreign exchange risk. For example, suppose Microsoft has a European subsidiary that expects to send it €12 million in three months. When Microsoft receives the euros, it will then convert them to dollars. Thus, Microsoft is essentially long euros because it will have to sell euros, or equivalently, it is short dollars because it will have to buy dollars. A currency forward contract is especially useful in this situation, because it enables Microsoft to lock in the rate at which it will sell euros and buy dollars in three months. It can do this by going short the forward contract, meaning that it goes short the euro and long the dollar. This arrangement serves to offset its otherwise long-euro, short-dollar position. In other words, it needs a forward contract to sell euros and buy dollars.

For example, say Microsoft goes to JP Morgan Chase and asks for a quote on a currency forward for €12 million in three months. JP Morgan Chase quotes a rate of \$0.925, which would enable Microsoft to sell euros and buy dollars at a rate of \$0.925 in three months. Under this contract, Microsoft would know it could convert its €12 million to 12,000,000 × \$0.925 = \$11,100,000. The contract would also stipulate whether it will settle in cash or will call for Microsoft to actually deliver the euros to the dealer and be paid \$11,100,000. This simplified example is a currency forward hedge.

Now let us say that three months later, the spot rate for euros is \$0.920. Microsoft is quite pleased that it locked in a rate of \$0.925. It simply delivers the euros and receives \$11,100,000 at an exchange rate of \$0.925.[11] Had rates risen, however, Microsoft would still have had to deliver the euros and accept a rate of \$0.925.

A few variations of currency forward contracts exist, but most of them are somewhat specialized and beyond the objectives of this reading. Let us now take a very brief look at a few other types of forward contracts.

3.4 Other Types of Forward Contracts

Although we focus primarily on the financial derivatives used by asset managers, we should mention here some of the other types. Commodity forwards—in which the underlying asset is oil, a precious metal, or some other commodity—are widely used. In addition, the derivatives industry has created forward contracts and other derivatives on various sources of energy (electricity, gas, etc.) and even weather, in which the underlying is a measure of the temperature or the amount of disaster damage from hurricanes, earthquakes, or tornados.

Many of these instruments are particularly difficult to understand, price, and trade. Nonetheless, through the use of derivatives and indirect investments, such as hedge funds, they can be useful for managing risk and investing in general. They are not, however, our focus.

---

11 Had the contract been structured to settle in cash, the dealer would have paid Microsoft 12,000,000 × (\$0.925 − \$0.920) = \$60,000. Microsoft would have converted the euros to dollars at the current spot exchange rate of \$0.920, receiving 12,000,000 × \$0.920 = \$11,040,000. Adding the \$60,000 payment from the dealer, Microsoft would have received \$11,100,000, an effective rate of \$0.925. risen, however, Microsoft would still have had to deliver the euros and accept a rate of \$0.925.

In the examples and illustrations used above, we have made reference to certain prices. Determining appropriate prices and fair values of financial instruments is a central objective of much of the process of asset management. Accordingly, pricing and valuation occupies a major portion of the CFA Program. As such, we turn our attention to the pricing and valuation of forward contracts.

END OPTIONAL SEGMENT

4 PRICING AND VALUATION OF FORWARD CONTRACTS

Before getting into the actual mechanics of pricing and valuation, the astute reader might wonder whether we are being a bit redundant. Are pricing and valuation not the same thing?

An equity analyst often finds that a stock is priced at more or less than its fair market value and uses this conclusion as the basis for a buy or sell recommendation.[12] In an efficient market, the price of a stock would always equal its value or the price would quickly converge to the value. Thus, for all practical purposes, pricing and valuation would be the same thing. In general, when we speak of the value and price of an *asset,* we are referring to what that asset is worth and what it sells for. With respect to certain *derivatives,* however, value and price take on slightly different meanings.

So let us begin by defining value: *Value is what you can sell something for or what you must pay to acquire something.* This applies to stocks, bonds, derivatives, and used cars.[13] Accordingly, *valuation is the process of determining the value of an asset or service.* Pricing is a related but different concept; let us explore what we mean by pricing a forward contract.

A forward contract price is the fixed price or rate at which the transaction scheduled to occur at expiration will take place. This price is agreed to on the contract initiation date and is commonly called the **forward price or forward rate**. Pricing means to determine the forward price or forward rate. Valuation, however, means to determine the amount of money that one would need to pay or would expect to receive to engage in the transaction. Alternatively, if one already held a position, valuation would mean to determine the amount of money one would either have to pay or expect to receive in order to get out of the position. Let us look at a generic example.

4.1 Generic Pricing and Valuation of a Forward Contract

Because derivative contracts have finite lives, it is important to carefully specify the time frame in which we are operating. We denote time in the following manner: Today is identified as time 0. The expiration date is time T. Time t is an arbitrary time between today and the expiration. Usually when we refer to "today," we are referring to the date on which the contract is created. Later we shall move forward to time t and time T, which will then be "today."

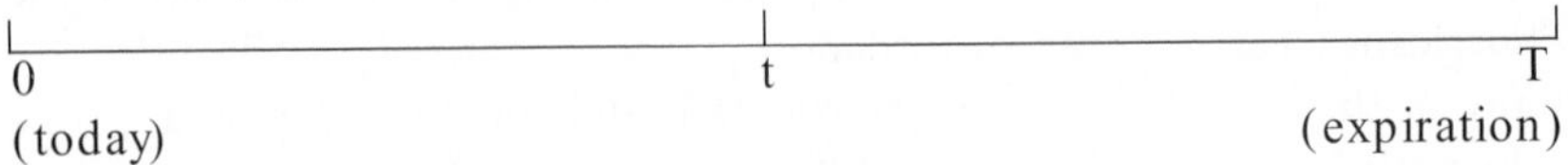

12 From your study of equity analysis, you should recall that we often use the discounted cash flow model, sometimes combined with the capital asset pricing model, to determine the fair market value of a stock.

13 Be careful. You may think the "value" of a certain used car is $5,000, but if no one will give you that price, it can hardly be called the value.

The price of the underlying asset in the spot market is denoted as S_0 at time 0, S_t at time t, and S_T at time T. The forward contract price, established when the contract is initiated at time 0, is F(0,T). This notation indicates that F(0,T) is the price of a forward contract initiated at time 0 and expiring at time T. The value of the forward contract is $V_0(0,T)$. This notation indicates that $V_0(0,T)$ is the value at time 0 of a forward contract initiated at time 0 and expiring at time T. In this reading, subscripts always indicate that we are at a specific point in time.

We have several objectives in this analysis. First, we want to determine the forward price F(0,T). We also want to determine the forward contract value today, denoted $V_0(0,T)$, the value at a point during the life of the contract such as time t, denoted $V_t(0,T)$, and the value at expiration, denoted $V_T(0,T)$. Valuation is somewhat easier to grasp from the perspective of the party holding the long position, so we shall take that point of view in this example. Once that value is determined, the value to the short is obtained by simply changing the sign.

If we are at expiration, we would observe the spot price as S_T. The long holds a position to buy the asset at the already agreed-upon price of F(0,T). Thus, the value of the forward contract at expiration should be obvious: S_T – F(0,T). If the value at expiration does not equal this amount, then an arbitrage profit can be easily made. For example, suppose the forward price established at the initiation of the contract, F(0,T), is \$20. Now at expiration, the spot price, S_T, is \$23. The contract value must be \$3. If it were more than \$3, then the long would be able to sell the contract to someone for more than \$3—someone would be paying the long more than \$3 to obtain the obligation of buying a \$23 asset for \$20. Obviously, no one would do that. If the value were less than \$3, the long would have to be willing to sell for less than \$3 the obligation of buying a \$23 asset for \$20. Obviously, the long would not do that. Thus, we state that the value at expiration of a forward contract established at time 0 is

$$V_T(0,T) = S_T - F(0,T) \tag{1}$$

Note that the value of a forward contract can also be interpreted as its profit, the difference between what the long pays for the underlying asset, F(0,T), and what the long receives, the asset price S_T. Of course, we have still not explained how F(0,T) is determined, but the above equation gives the value of the contract at expiration, at which time F(0,T) would certainly be known because it was agreed on at the initiation date of the contract.

Now let us back up to the time when the contract was originated. Consider a contract that expires in one year. Suppose that the underlying asset is worth \$100 and that the forward price is \$108. We do not know if \$108 is the correct forward price; we will simply try it and see.

Suppose we buy the asset for \$100 and sell the forward contract for \$108. We hold the position until expiration. We assume that there are no direct costs associated with buying or holding the asset, but we must recognize that we lose interest on the \$100 tied up in the asset. Assume that the interest rate is 5 percent.

Recall that no money changes hands at the start with a forward contract. Consequently, the \$100 invested in the asset is the full outlay. At the end of the year, the forward contract expires and we deliver the asset, receiving \$108 for it—not bad at all. At a 5 percent interest rate, we lose only \$5 in interest on the \$100 tied up in the asset. We receive \$108 for the asset regardless of its price at expiration. We can view \$108 – \$105 = \$3 as a risk-free profit, which more than covered the cost. In fact, if we had also borrowed the \$100 at 5 percent, we could have done this transaction without putting up any money of our own. We would have more than covered the interest on the borrowed funds and netted a \$3 risk-free profit. This profit is essentially free money—there is no cost and no risk. Thus, it is an arbitrage profit. We would certainly want to execute any transaction that would generate an arbitrage profit.

In the market, the forces of arbitrage would then prevail. Other market participants would execute this transaction as well. Although it is possible that the spot price would bear some of the adjustment, in this reading we shall always let the derivative price make the full adjustment. Consequently, the derivative price would have to come down to \$105.

If the forward price were below \$105, we could also earn an arbitrage profit, although it would be a little more difficult because the asset would have to be sold short. Suppose the forward price is \$103. If the asset were a financial asset, we could borrow it and sell it short. We would receive \$100 for it and invest that \$100 at the 5 percent rate. We would simultaneously buy a forward contract. At expiration, we would take delivery of the asset paying \$103 and then deliver it to the party from whom we borrowed it. The short position is now covered, and we still have the \$100 invested plus 5 percent interest on it. This transaction offers a clear arbitrage profit of \$2. Again, the forces of arbitrage would cause other market participants to undertake the transaction, which would push the forward price up to \$105.

If short selling is not permitted, too difficult, or too costly, a market participant who already owns the asset could sell it, invest the \$100 at 5 percent, and buy a forward contract. At expiration, he would pay \$103 and take delivery on the forward contract, which would return him to his original position of owning the asset. He would now, however, receive not only the stock but also 5 percent interest on \$100. Again, the forces of arbitrage would make this transaction attractive to other parties who held the asset, provided they could afford to part with it for the necessary period of time.[14]

Going back to the situation in which the forward contract price was \$103, an arbitrage profit could, however, be eliminated if the party going long the forward contract were required to pay some money up front. For example, suppose the party going long the forward contract paid the party going short \$1.9048. Then the party going long would lose \$1.9048 plus interest on this amount. Notice that \$1.9048 compounded at 5 percent interest equals precisely \$2, which not surprisingly is the amount of the arbitrage profit.

Thus, if the forward price were \$103, the value of the contract would be \$1.9048. With T = 1, this value equals

$$V_0(0,T) = V_0(0,1) = \$100 - \$103/1.05 = \$1.9048$$

Therefore, to enter into this contract at this forward price, one party must pay another. Because the value is positive, it must be paid by the party going long the forward contract to the party going short. Parties going long must pay positive values; parties going short pay negative values.[15]

If the forward price were \$108, the value would be

$$V_0(0,T) = \$100 - \$108/1.05 = -\$2.8571$$

In this case, the value is negative and would have to be paid from the short to the long. Doing so would eliminate the arbitrage profit that the short would have otherwise been able to make, given the forward price of \$108.

Arbitrage profits can be eliminated with an up-front payment from long to short or vice versa that is consistent with the forward price the parties select. The parties could simply negotiate a forward price, and any resulting market value could be paid from one party to the other. *It is customary, however, in the forward market for the*

14 In other words, a party holding the asset must be willing to part with it for the length of time it would take for the forces of arbitrage to bring the price back in line, thereby allowing the party to capture the risk-free profit and return the party to its original state of holding the asset. The period of time required for the price to adjust should be very short if the market is relatively efficient.

15 For example, when a stock is purchased, its value, which is always positive, is paid from the long to the short. This is true for any asset.

initial value to be set to zero. This convention eliminates the necessity of either party making a payment to the other and results in a direct and simple determination of the forward price. Specifically, setting $V_0(0,T) = 0$ and letting r represent the interest rate,

$$V_0(0,T) = S_0 - F(0,T)/(1 + r) = 0$$

which means that $F(0,T) = S_0(1 + r)$. In our example, F(0,T) = \$100(1.05) = \$105, which is the forward price that eliminates the arbitrage profit.

Our forward price formula can be interpreted as saying that the forward price is the spot price compounded at the risk-free interest rate. In our example, we had an annual interest rate of r and one year to expiration. With today being time 0 and expiration being time T, the time T − 0 = T is the number of years to expiration of the forward contract. Then we more generally write the forward price as

$$F(0,T) = S_0(1 + r)^T \quad (2)$$

Again, this result is consistent with the custom that no money changes hands at the start of a forward contract, meaning that the value of a forward contract at its start is zero.

Exhibit 3 summarizes the process of pricing a forward contract. At time 0, we buy the asset and sell a forward contract for a total outlay of the spot price of the asset.[16] Over the life of the contract, we hold the asset and forgo interest on the money. At expiration, we deliver the asset and receive the forward price for a payoff of F(0,T). The overall transaction is risk free and equivalent to investing the spot price of the asset in a risk-free bond that pays F(0,T) at time T. Therefore, the payoff at T must be the future value of the spot price invested at the risk-free rate. This equality can be true only if the forward price is the spot price compounded at the risk-free rate over the life of the asset.

Exhibit 3 Pricing a Forward Contract

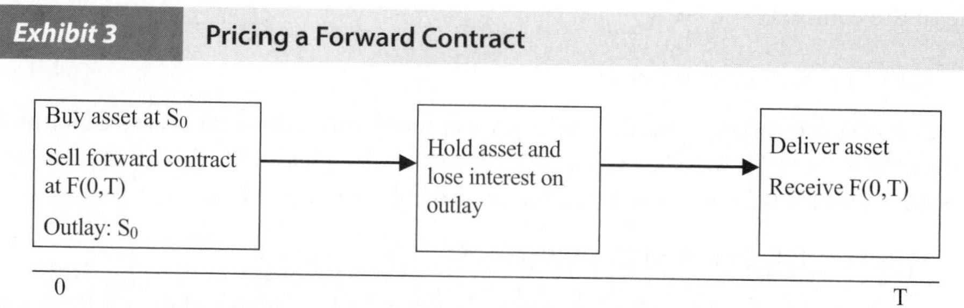

The transaction is risk free and should be equivalent to investing S_0 dollars in a risk-free asset that pays F(0,T) at time T. Thus, the amount received at T must be the future value of the initial outlay invested at the risk-free rate. For this equality to hold, the forward price must be given as

$$F(0,T) = S_0(1 + r)^T$$

Example: The spot price is \$72.50, the risk-free rate is 8.25 percent, and the contract is for five years. The forward price would be

$$F(0,T) = F(0,5) = 72.50(1.0825)^5 = 107.76$$

A contract in which the initial value is intentionally set at a nonzero value is called an **off-market FRA**. In such a contract, the forward price is set arbitrarily in the process of negotiation between the two parties. Given the chosen forward price, the

16 Remember that in a forward contract, neither party pays anything for the forward contract at the start.

contract will have a nonzero value. As noted above, if the value is positive, the long pays that amount up front to the short. If it is negative, the short pays that amount up front to the long. Although off-market FRAs are not common, we shall use them in the reading on swap markets and contracts when studying swaps.

Now suppose we are at a time t, which is a point during the life of the contract. We may want to know the value of the forward contract for several reasons. For one, it makes good business sense to know the monetary value of an obligation to do something at a later date. Also, accounting rules require that a company mark its derivatives to their current market values and report the effects of those values in income statements and balance sheets. In addition, the market value can be used as a gauge of the credit exposure. Finally, the market value can be used to determine how much money one party can pay the other to terminate the contract.

Let us start by assuming that we established a long forward contract at time 0 at the price F(0,T). Of course, its value at time 0 was zero. But now it is time t, and we want to know its new value, $V_t(0,T)$. Let us consider what it means to hold the position of being long at time t a forward contract established at time 0 at the price F(0,T) and expiring at time T:

We will have to pay F(0,T) dollars at T.

We will receive the underlying asset, which will be worth S_T, at T.

At least part of the value will clearly be the present value of a payment of F(0,T), or in other words, $-F(0,T)/(1 + r)^{T-t}$. The other part of the contract value comes from the fact that we have a claim on the asset's value at T. We do not know what S_T (the asset value at T) will be, but we do know that the market tells us its present value is S_t, the current asset price. *By definition, an asset's value today is the present value of its future value.*[17] Thus we can easily value our forward contract at time t during the life of the contract:

$$V_t(0,T) = S_t - F(0,T)/(1+r)^{(T-t)} \quad (3)$$

Consider our earlier example in which we entered into a one-year forward contract to buy the asset at \$105. Now assume it is three months later and the price of the asset is \$102. With t = 0.25 and T = 1, the value of the contract would be

$$V_t(0,T) = V_{0.25}(0,1) = \$102 - \$105/(1.05)^{0.75} = \$0.7728$$

Again, why is this the value? The contract provides the long with a claim on the asset at expiration. That claim is currently worth the current asset value of \$102. That claim also obligates the long to pay \$105 at expiration, which has a present value of $\$105/(1.05)^{0.75} = \$101.2272$. Thus, the long position has a value of \$102 – \$101.2272 = \$0.7728.

As noted above, this market value may well affect the income statement and balance sheet. In addition, it gives an idea of the contract's credit exposure, a topic we have touched on and will cover in more detail in Section 5. Finally, we noted earlier that a party could re-enter the market and offset the contract by paying the counterparty or having the counterparty pay him a cash amount. This cash amount is the market value as calculated here.[18]

Exhibit 4 summarizes how we value a forward contract. If we went long a forward contract at time 0 and we are now at time t prior to expiration, we hold a claim on the asset at expiration and are obligated to pay the forward price at expiration. The

---

17 This statement is true for any type of asset or financial instrument. It always holds by definition.

18 If the market value is positive, the value of the asset exceeds the present value of what the long promises to pay. Thus, it makes sense that the short must pay the long. If the market value is negative, then the present value of what the long promises to pay exceeds the value of the asset. Then, it makes sense that the long must pay the short.

claim on the asset is worth its current price; the obligation to pay the forward price at expiration is worth the negative of its present value. Thus, the value of the forward contract is the current spot price minus the forward price discounted from expiration back to the present.

Exhibit 4 **Valuing a Forward Contract**

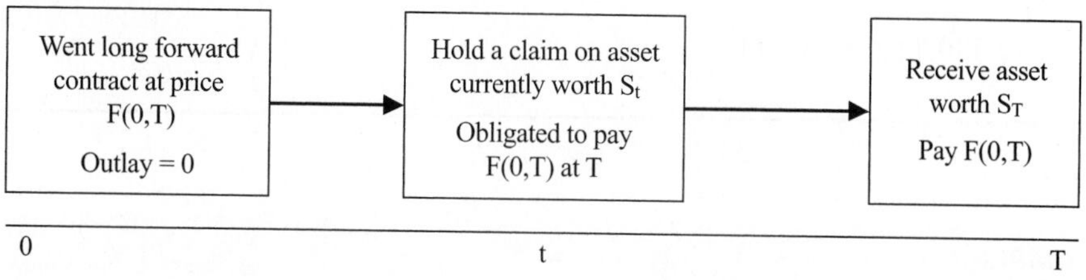

0	t	T
Went long forward contract at price F(0,T) Outlay = 0	Hold a claim on asset currently worth S_t Obligated to pay F(0,T) at T	Receive asset worth S_T Pay F(0,T)

The value of the forward contract at t must be the value of what it will produce at T:

$$V_t(0,T) = S_t - F(0,T)/(1+r)^{(T-t)}$$

Example: A two-year forward contract was established with a price of \$62.25. Now, a year and a half later (t = 1.5), the spot price is \$71.19 and the risk-free rate is 7 percent. The value of the forward contract is

$$V_t(0,T) = V_{1.5}(0,2) = 71.19 - 62.25/(1.07)^{0.5} = 11.01$$

Therefore, we have seen that the forward contract value is zero today: the asset price minus the present value of the forward price at a time prior to expiration, and the asset price minus the forward price at expiration. It may be helpful to note that in general, we can always say that *the forward contract value is the asset price minus the present value of the exercise price,* because given $V_t(0,T) = S_t - F(0,T)/(1 + r)^{(T-t)}$:

$$\text{If } t = 0, V_t(0,T) = V_0(0,T) = S_0 - F(0,T)/(1+r)^T = 0$$

$$\text{because } F(0,T) = S_0(1+r)^T$$

$$\text{If } t = T, V_t(0,T) = V_T(0,T) = S_T - F(0,T)/(1+r)^0 = S_T - F(0,T)$$

The formulas for pricing and valuation of a forward contract are summarized in Exhibit 5.

Exhibit 5 **Pricing and Valuation Formulas for a Forward Contract**

Today = time 0

Arbitrary point during the contract's life = time t

Expiration = time T

Value of a forward contract at any time t:

$$V_t(0,T) = S_t - F(0,T)/(1+r)^{(T-t)}$$

Value of a forward contract at expiration (t = T):

$$V_T(0,T) = S_T - F(0,T)$$

(continued)

Exhibit 5 (Continued)

Value of a forward contract at initiation (t = 0):

$$V_0(0,T) = S_0 - F(0,T)/(1 + r)^T$$

Customarily, no money changes hands at initiation so $V_0(0,T)$ is set equal to zero. Thus,

$$F(0,T) = S_0(1 + r)^T$$

EXAMPLE 1

An investor holds title to an asset worth €125.72. To raise money for an unrelated purpose, the investor plans to sell the asset in nine months. The investor is concerned about uncertainty in the price of the asset at that time. The investor learns about the advantages of using forward contracts to manage this risk and enters into such a contract to sell the asset in nine months. The risk-free interest rate is 5.625 percent.

A Determine the appropriate price the investor could receive in nine months by means of the forward contract.

B Suppose the counterparty to the forward contract is willing to engage in such a contract at a forward price of €140. Explain what type of transaction the investor could execute to take advantage of the situation. Calculate the rate of return (annualized), and explain why the transaction is attractive.

C Suppose the forward contract is entered into at the price you computed in Part A. Two months later, the price of the asset is €118.875. The investor would like to evaluate her position with respect to any gain or loss accrued on the forward contract. Determine the market value of the forward contract at this point in time from the perspective of the investor in Part A.

D Determine the value of the forward contract at expiration assuming the contract is entered into at the price you computed in Part A and the price of the underlying asset is €123.50 at expiration. Explain how the investor did on the overall position of both the asset and the forward contract in terms of the rate of return.

Solution to A:

$$T = 9/12 = 0.75$$
$$S_0 = 125.72$$
$$r = 0.05625$$

$$F(0,T) = 125.72(1.05625)^{0.75} = 130.99$$

Solution to B:

As found in Part A, the forward contract should be selling at €130.99, but it is selling for €140. Consequently, it is overpriced—and an overpriced contract should be sold. Because the investor holds the asset, she will be hedged by selling the forward contract. Consequently, her asset, worth €125.72 when the forward contract is sold, will be delivered in nine months and she will receive €140 for it. The rate of return will be

$$\left(\frac{140}{125.72}\right) - 1 = 0.1136$$

This risk-free return of 11.36 percent for nine months is clearly in excess of the 5.625 percent annual rate. In fact, a rate of 11.36 percent for nine months annualizes to

$$(1.1136)^{12/9} - 1 = 0.1543$$

An annual risk-free rate of 15.43 percent is clearly preferred over the actual risk-free rate of 5.625 percent. The position is not only hedged but also earns an arbitrage profit.

Solution to C:

$$t = 2/12$$
$$T - t = 9/12 - 2/12 = 7/12$$
$$S_t = 118.875$$
$$F(0,T) = 130.99$$

$$V_t(0,T) = V_{2/12}(0,9/12) = 118.875 - 130.99/(1.05625)^{7/12} = -8.0$$

The contract has a negative value. Note, however, that in this form, the answer applies to the holder of the long position. This investor is short. Thus, the value to the investor in this problem is positive 8.0.

Solution to D:

$$S_T = 123.50$$

$$V_T(0,T) = V_{9/12}(0,9/12) = 123.50 - 130.99 = -7.49$$

This amount is the value to the long. This investor is short, so the value is a positive 7.49. The investor incurred a loss on the asset of 125.72 – 123.50 = 2.22. Combined with the gain on the forward contract, the net gain is 7.49 – 2.22 = 5.27. A gain of 5.27 on an asset worth 125.72 when the transaction was initiated represents a return of 5.27/125.72 = 4.19 percent. When annualized, the rate of return equals

$$(1.0419)^{12/9} - 1 = 0.05625$$

It should come as no surprise that this number is the annual risk-free rate. The transaction was executed at the no-arbitrage forward price of €130.99. Thus, it would be impossible to earn a return higher or lower than the risk-free rate.

In our examples, there were no costs or cash flows associated with holding the underlying assets. In the specific examples below for equity derivatives, fixed-income and interest rate derivatives, and currency derivatives, we present cases in which cash flows on the underlying asset will slightly alter our results. We shall ignore any costs of holding assets. Such costs are primarily associated with commodities, an asset class we do not address in this reading.

4.2 Pricing and Valuation of Equity Forward Contracts

Equity forward contracts are priced and valued much like the generic contract described above, with one important additional feature. Many stocks pay dividends, and the effects of these dividends must be incorporated into the pricing and valuation process. Our concern is with the dividends that occur over the life of the forward contract, but not with those that may come after the contract ends. Following standard procedure, we assume that these dividends are known or are a constant percentage of the stock price.

We begin with the idea of a forward contract on either a single stock, a portfolio of stocks, or an index in which dividends are to be paid during the life of the contract. Using the time notation that today is time 0, expiration is time T, and there is an arbitrary time t during its life when we need to value the contract, assume that dividends can be paid at various times during the life of the contract between t and T.[19]

In the examples that follow, we shall calculate present and future values of this stream of dividends over the life of the forward contract. Given a series of these dividends of D_1, D_2, ... D_n, whose values are known, that occur at times t_1, t_2, ... t_n, the present value will be defined as PV(D,0,T) and computed as

$$PV(D,0,T) = \sum_{i=1}^{n} \frac{D_i}{(1+r)^{t_i}}$$

The future value will be defined as FV(D,0,T) and computed as

$$FV(D,0,T) = \sum_{i=1}^{n} D_i (1+r)^{T-t_i}$$

Recall that the forward price is established by eliminating any opportunity to arbitrage from establishing a forward contract without making any cash outlay today, as is customary with forward contracts. We found that the forward price is the spot price compounded at the risk-free interest rate. To include dividends, we adjust our formula slightly to

$$F(0,T) = [S_0 - PV(D,0,T)](1+r)^T \tag{4}$$

In other words, we simply subtract the present value of the dividends from the stock price. Note that the dividends reduce the forward price, a reflection of the fact that holders of long positions in forward contracts do not benefit from dividends in comparison to holders of long positions in the underlying stock.

For example, consider a stock priced at \$40, which pays a dividend of \$3 in 50 days. The risk-free rate is 6 percent. A forward contract expiring in six months (T = 0.5) would have a price of

$$F(0,T) = F(0,0.5) = \left[\$40 - \$3/(1.06)^{50/365}\right](1.06)^{0.5} = \$38.12$$

If the stock had more than one dividend, we would simply subtract the present value of all dividends over the life of the contract from the stock price, as in the following example.

The risk-free rate is 4 percent. The forward contract expires in 300 days and is on a stock currently priced at \$35, which pays quarterly dividends according to the following schedule:

19 Given the way dividends are typically paid, the right to the dividend leaves the stock on the ex-dividend date, which is prior to the payment date. To precisely incorporate this feature, either the dividend payment date should be the ex-dividend date or the dividend should be the present value at the ex-dividend date of the dividend to be paid at a later date. We shall ignore this point here and assume that it would be taken care of in practice.

Days to Ex-Dividend Date	Dividend ($)
10	0.45
102	0.45
193	0.45
283	0.45

The present value of the dividends is found as follows:

$$\begin{aligned}\text{PV}(\text{D},0,\text{T}) &= \$0.45/(1.04)^{10/365} + \$0.45/(1.04)^{102/365} \\ &+ \$0.45/(1.04)^{193/365} + \$0.45/(1.04)^{283/365} = \$1.77\end{aligned}$$

The time to expiration is T = 300/365. Therefore, the forward price equals

$$\text{F}(0,\text{T}) = \text{F}(0,300/365) = (\$35 - \$1.77)(1.04)^{300/365} = \$34.32$$

Another approach to incorporating the dividends is to use the future value of the dividends. With this forward contract expiring in 300 days, the first dividend is reinvested for 290 days, the second for 198 days, the third for 107 days, and the fourth for 17 days. Thus,

$$\begin{aligned}\text{FV}(\text{D},0,\text{T}) &= \$0.45(1.04)^{290/365} + \$0.45(1.04)^{198/365} \\ &+\$0.45(1.04)^{107/365} + \$0.45(1.04)^{17/365} = \$1.83\end{aligned}$$

To obtain the forward price, we compound the stock value to expiration and subtract the future value of the dividends. Thus, the forward price would be

$$\text{F}(0,\text{T}) = \text{S}_0(1 + \text{r})^{\text{T}} - \text{FV}(\text{D},0,\text{T}) \tag{5}$$

This formula will give the same answer as the one using the present value of the dividends, as shown below:

$$\text{F}(0,300/365) = \$35(1.04)^{300/365} - \$1.83 = \$34.32$$

An alternative way to incorporate dividends is to express them as a fixed percentage of the stock price. The more common version of this formulation is to assume that the stock, portfolio, or index pays dividends continuously at a rate of δ^c. By specifying the dividends in this manner, we are allowing the dividends to be uncertain and completely determined by the stock price at the time the dividends are being paid. In this case, the stock is constantly paying a dividend at the rate δ^c. In the reading on futures markets and contracts, we will again discuss how to incorporate dividends.

Because we pay dividends continuously, for consistency we must also compound the interest continuously. The continuously compounded equivalent of the discrete risk-free rate r will be denoted r^c and is found as $r^c = \ln(1 + r)$.[20] The future value of \$1 at time T is $\exp(r^cT)$. Then the forward price is given as

20 The notation "ln" stands for natural logarithm. A logarithm is the power to which its base must be raised to equal a given number. The base of the natural logarithm system is *e*, approximately 2.71828. With an interest rate of r = 0.06, we would have $r^c = \ln(1.06) = 0.058$. Then $e^{0.058} = 1.06$ is called the exponential function and often written as exp(0.058) = 1.06. The future value factor is thus $\exp(r^c)$. The present value factor is $1/\exp(r^c)$ or $\exp(-r^c)$. If the period is more or less than one year, we also multiply the rate by the number of years or fraction of a year—that is, $\exp(-r^cT)$ or $\exp(r^cT)$.

$$F(0,T) = \left(S_0 e^{-\delta^c T}\right) e^{r^c T} \quad (6)$$

The term in parentheses, the stock price discounted at the dividend yield rate, is equivalent to the stock price minus the present value of the dividends. This value is then compounded at the risk-free rate over the life of the contract, just as we have done in the other versions.

Some people attach significance to whether the forward price is higher than the spot price. It is important to note that the forward price should not be interpreted as a forecast of the future price of the underlying. This misperception is common. If the forward price is higher than the spot price, it merely indicates that the effect of the risk-free rate is greater than the effect of the dividends. In fact, such is usually the case with equity forwards. Interest rates are usually greater than dividend yields.

As an example, consider a forward contract on France's CAC 40 Index. The index is at 5475, the continuously compounded dividend yield is 1.5 percent, and the continuously compounded risk-free interest rate is 4.625 percent. The contract life is two years. With T = 2, the contract price is, therefore,

$$F(0,T) = F(0,2) = (5475 \times e^{-0.015(2)})e^{0.04625(2)} = 5828.11$$

This specification involving a continuous dividend yield is commonly used when the underlying is a portfolio or stock index. If a single stock in the portfolio pays a dividend, then the portfolio or index can be viewed as paying a dividend. Given the diversity of dividend policies and ex-dividend dates, such an assumption is usually considered a reasonable approximation for stock portfolios or stock indices, but the assumption is not as appropriate for individual stocks. No general agreement exists on the most appropriate approach, and you must become comfortable with all of them. To obtain the appropriate forward price, the most important point to remember is that one way or another, the analysis must incorporate the dividend component of the stock price, portfolio value, or index level. If the contract is not trading at the correct price, then it is mispriced and arbitrage, as described in the generic forward contract pricing section, will force an alignment between the market forward price and the theoretical forward price.

Recall that the value of a forward contract is the asset price minus the forward price discounted back from the expiration date. Regardless of how the dividend is specified or even whether the underlying stock, portfolio, or index pays dividends, the valuation formulas for a forward contract on a stock differ only in that the stock price is adjusted by removing the present value of the remaining dividends:

$$V_t(0,T) = S_t - PV(D,t,T) - F(0,T)/(1+r)^{(T-t)} \quad (7)$$

where we now note that the dividends are only those paid after time t. If we are using continuous compounding,

$$V_t(0,T) = S_t e^{-\delta^c (T-t)} - F(0,T)e^{-r^c (T-t)} \quad (8)$$

At the contract initiation date, t = 0 and $V_0(0,T)$ is set to zero because no cash changes hands. At expiration, t = T and no dividends remain, so the valuation formula reduces to $S_T - F(0,T)$.

The formulas for pricing and valuation of equity forward contracts are summarized in Exhibit 6.

Exhibit 6 Pricing and Valuation Formulas for Equity Forward Contracts

$$\text{Forward price} = (\text{Stock price} - \text{Present value of dividends over life of contract}) \times (1+r)^T$$

Exhibit 6 (Continued)

or $(\text{Stock price}) \times (1 + r)^T$ – Future value of dividends over life of contract

Discrete dividends over the life of the contract:

$$F(0,T) = \left[S_0 - PV(D,0,T)\right](1 + r)^T \text{ or } S_0(1 + r)^T - FV(D,0,T)$$

Continuous dividends at the rate δ^c:

$$F(0,T) = \left(S_0 e^{-\delta^c T}\right) e^{r^c T}$$

Value of forward contract:

$$V_t(0,T) = S_t - PV(D,t,T) - F(0,T)/(1 + r)^{(T-t)}$$

or

$$V_t(0,T) = S_t e^{-\delta^c (T-t)} - F(0,T) e^{-r^c (T-t)}$$

EXAMPLE 2

An asset manager anticipates the receipt of funds in 200 days, which he will use to purchase a particular stock. The stock he has in mind is currently selling for \$62.50 and will pay a \$0.75 dividend in 50 days and another \$0.75 dividend in 140 days. The risk-free rate is 4.2 percent. The manager decides to commit to a future purchase of the stock by going long a forward contract on the stock.

A At what price would the manager commit to purchase the stock in 200 days through a forward contract?

B Suppose the manager enters into the contract at the price you found in Part A. Now, 75 days later, the stock price is \$55.75. Determine the value of the forward contract at this point.

C It is now the expiration day, and the stock price is \$58.50. Determine the value of the forward contract at this time.

$$S_0 = \$62.50$$
$$T = 200/365$$
$$D_1 = \$0.75,\ t_1 = 50/365$$
$$D_2 = \$0.75,\ t_2 = 140/365$$
$$r = 0.042$$

Solution to A:

First find the present value of the dividends:

$$\$0.75/(1.042)^{50/365} + \$0.75/(1.042)^{140/365} = \$1.48$$

Then find the forward price:

$$F(0,T) = F(0,200/365) = (\$62.50 - \$1.48)(1.042)^{200/365} = \$62.41$$

Solution to B:

We must now find the present value of the dividends 75 days after the contract begins. The first dividend has already been paid, so it is not relevant. Because only one remains, the second dividend is now the "first" dividend. It will be paid in 65 days. Thus, $t_1 - t = 65/365$. The present value of this dividend is $\$0.75/(1.042)^{65/365} = \$0.74$. The other information is

$$t = 75/365$$
$$T - t = (200 - 75)/365 = 125/365$$
$$S_t = \$55.75$$

The value of the contract is, therefore,

$$V_t(0,T) = V_{75/365}(0,200/365) = (\$55.75 - \$0.74) - \$62.41/(1.042)^{125/365} = -\$6.53$$

Thus, the contract has a negative value.

Solution to C:

$$S_T = \$58.50$$

The value of the contract is

$$V_{200/365}(0,200/365) = V_T(0,T) = \$58.50 - \$62.41 = -\$3.91$$

Thus, the contract expires with a value of negative $3.91.

4.3 Pricing and Valuation of Fixed-Income and Interest Rate Forward Contracts

Forward contracts on fixed-income securities are priced and valued in a virtually identical manner to their equity counterparts. We can use the above formulas if S_t represents the bond price at time t and D_i represents a coupon paid at time t_i. We denote B^c as a coupon bond and then use notation to draw attention to those coupons that must be included in the forward contract pricing calculations. We will let $B_t^c(T + Y)$ represent the bond price at time t, T is the expiration date of the forward contract, Y is the remaining maturity of the bond on the forward contract expiration, and (T + Y) is the time to maturity of the bond at the time the forward contract is initiated. Consider a bond with n coupons to occur before its maturity date. Converting our formula for a forward contract on a stock into that for a forward contract on a bond and letting CI be the coupon interest over a specified period of time, we have a forward price of

$$F(0,T) = \left[B_0^c(T + Y) - PV(CI,0,T)\right](1 + r)^T \quad (9)$$

where PV(CI,0,T) is the present value of the coupon interest over the life of the forward contract. Alternatively, the forward price can be obtained as

$$F(0,T) = \left[B_0^c(T + Y)\right](1 + r)^T - FV(CI,0,T) \quad (10)$$

where FV(CI,0,T) is the future value of the coupon interest over the life of the forward contract.

The value of the forward contract at time t would be

$$V_t(0,T) = B_t^c(T + Y) - PV(CI,t,T) - F(0,T)/(1 + r)^{(T-t)} \quad (11)$$

at time t; note that the relevant coupons are only those remaining as of time t until expiration of the forward contract. As in the case for stock, this formula will reduce to the appropriate values at time 0 and at expiration. For example, at expiration, no coupons would remain, t = T, and $V_T(0,T) = B_T^c(T + Y) - F(0,T)$. At time t = 0, the contract is being initiated and has a zero value, which leads to the formula for F(0,T) above.

Consider a bond with semiannual coupons. The bond has a current maturity of 583 days and pays four coupons, each six months apart. The next coupon occurs in 37 days, followed by coupons in 219 days, 401 days, and 583 days, at which time the principal is repaid. Suppose that the bond price, which includes accrued interest, is \$984.45 for a \$1,000 par, 4 percent coupon bond. The coupon rate implies that each coupon is \$20. The risk-free interest rate is 5.75 percent. Assume that the forward contract expires in 310 days. Thus, T = 310, T + Y = 583, and Y = 273, meaning that the bond has 273 days remaining after the forward contract expires. Note that only the first two coupons occur during the life of the forward contract.

The present value of the coupons is

$$\$20/(1.0575)^{37/365} + \$20/(1.0575)^{219/365} = \$39.23$$

The forward price if the contract is initiated now is

$$F(0,T) = (\$984.45 - \$39.23)(1.0575)^{310/365} = \$991.18$$

Thus, we assume that we shall be able to enter into this contract to buy the bond in 310 days at the price of \$991.18.

Now assume it is 15 days later and the new bond price is \$973.14. Let the risk-free interest rate now be 6.75 percent. The present value of the remaining coupons is

$$\$20/(1.0675)^{22/365} + \$20/(1.0675)^{204/365} = \$39.20$$

The value of the forward contract is thus

$$\$973.14 - \$39.20 - \$991.19/(1.0675)^{295/365} = -\$6.28$$

The contract has gone from a zero value at the start to a negative value, primarily as a result of the decrease in the price of the underlying bond.

Exhibit 7 **Pricing and Valuation Formulas for Fixed-Income Forward Contracts**

$$\text{Forward price} = (\text{Bond price} - \text{Present value of coupons over life of contract})(1 + r)^T \text{ or}$$
$$(\text{Bond price})(1 + r)^T - \text{Future value of coupons over life of contract}$$

Price of forward contract on bond with coupons CI:

$$F(0,T) = \left[B_0^c(T + Y) - PV(CI,0,T)\right](1 + r)^T$$
$$\text{or}\left[B_0^c(T + Y)\right](1 + r)^T - FV(CI,0,T)$$

Value of forward contract on bond with coupons CI:

$$V_t(0,T) = B_t^c(T + Y) - PV(CI,t,T) - F(0,T)/(1 + r)^{(T-t)}$$

If the bond is a zero-coupon bond/T-bill, we can perform the same analysis as above, but we simply let the coupons equal zero.

Exhibit 7 summarizes the formulas for the pricing and valuation of forward contracts on fixed-income securities.

EXAMPLE 3

An investor purchased a bond when it was originally issued with a maturity of five years. The bond pays semiannual coupons of $50. It is now 150 days into the life of the bond. The investor wants to sell the bond the day after its fourth coupon. The first coupon occurs 181 days after issue, the second 365 days, the third 547 days, and the fourth 730 days. At this point (150 days into the life of the bond), the price is $1,010.25. The bond prices quoted here include accrued interest.

A At what price could the owner enter into a forward contract to sell the bond on the day after its fourth coupon? Note that the owner would receive that fourth coupon. The risk-free rate is currently 8 percent.

B Now move forward 365 days. The new risk-free interest rate is 7 percent and the new price of the bond is $1,025.375. The counterparty to the forward contract believes that it has received a gain on the position. Determine the value of the forward contract and the gain or loss to the counterparty at this time. Note that we have now introduced a new risk-free rate, because interest rates can obviously change over the life of the bond and any calculations of the forward contract value must reflect this fact. The new risk-free rate is used instead of the old rate in the valuation formula.

Solution to A:

First we must find the present value of the four coupons over the life of the forward contract. At the 150th day of the life of the bond, the coupons occur 31 days from now, 215 days from now, 397 days from now, and 580 days from now. Keep in mind that we need consider only the first four coupons because the owner will sell the bond on the day after the fourth coupon. The present value of the coupons is

$$\$50/(1.08)^{31/365} + \$50/(1.08)^{215/365} + \$50/(1.08)^{397/365} + \$50/(1.08)^{580/365} = \$187.69$$

Because we want the forward contract to expire one day after the fourth coupon, it expires in 731 – 150 = 581 days. Thus, T = 581/365.

$$F(0,T) = F(0,581/365) = (\$1,010.25 - \$187.69)(1.08)^{581/365} = \$929.76$$

Solution to B:

It is now 365 days later—the 515th day of the bond's life. There are two coupons to go, one occurring in 547 – 515 = 32 days and the other in 730 – 515 = 215 days. The present value of the coupons is now

$$\$50/(1.07)^{32/365} + \$50/(1.07)^{215/365} = \$97.75$$

To address the value of the forward contract and the gain or loss to the counterparty, note that 731 – 515 = 216 days now remain until the contract's expiration. Because the bondholder would sell the forward contract to hedge the future sale price of the bond, the bondholder's counterparty to the forward contract would hold a long position. The value of the forward contract is the current spot price minus the present value of the coupons minus the present value of the forward price:

$$\$1,025.375 - \$97.75 - \$929.76/(1.07)^{216/365} = \$34.36$$

Because the contract was initiated with a zero value at the start and the counterparty is long the contract, the value of $34.36 represents a gain to the counterparty.

Now let us look at the pricing and valuation of FRAs. Previously we used the notations t and T to represent the time to a given date. The expressions t or T were, respectively, the number of days to time point t or T, each divided by 365. In the FRA market, contracts are created with specific day counts. We will use the letter h to refer to the day on which the FRA expires and the letter g to refer to an arbitrary day prior to expiration. Consider the time line shown below. We shall initiate an FRA on day 0. The FRA expires on day h. The rate underlying the FRA is the rate on an m-day Eurodollar deposit. Thus, there are h days from today until the FRA expiration and h + m days until the maturity date of the Eurodollar instrument on which the FRA rate is based. The date indicated by g will simply be a date during the life of the FRA at which we want to determine a value for the FRA.

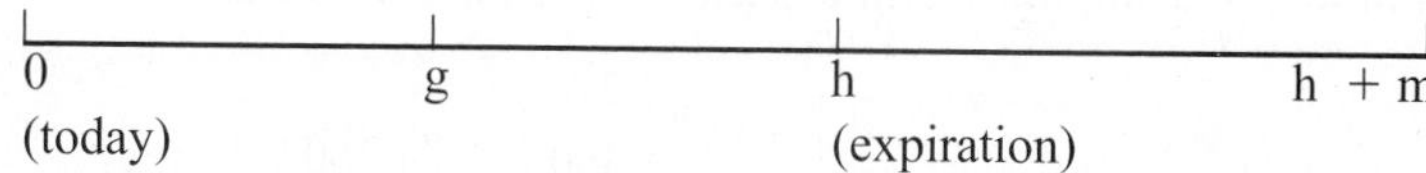

Now let us specify some notation. We let $L_i(j)$ represent the rate on a j-day LIBOR deposit on an arbitrary day i, which falls somewhere in the above period from 0 to h, inclusive. Remember that this instrument is a j-day loan from one bank to another. For example, the bank borrowing $1 on day i for j days will pay back the amount

$$\$1\left[1 + L_i(j)\left(\frac{j}{360}\right)\right]$$

in j days.

The rate for m-day LIBOR on day h, $L_h(m)$, will determine the payoff of the FRA. We denote the fixed rate on the FRA as FRA(0,h,m), which stands for the rate on an FRA established on day 0, expiring on day h, and based on m-day LIBOR. We shall use a $1 notional principal for the FRA, which means that at expiration its payoff is

$$\frac{\left[L_h(m) - \text{FRA}(0,h,m)\right]\left(\frac{m}{360}\right)}{1 + L_h(m)\left(\frac{m}{360}\right)} \quad (12)$$

The numerator is the difference between the underlying LIBOR on the expiration day and the rate agreed on when the contract was initiated, multiplied by the adjustment factor m/360. Both of these rates are annual rates applied to a Eurodollar deposit of m days; hence, multiplying by m/360 is necessary. The denominator discounts the payoff by the m-day LIBOR in effect at the time of the payoff. As noted earlier, this adjustment is necessary because the rates in the numerator apply to Eurodollar deposits created on day h and paying off m days later. If the notional principal is anything other than $1, we also must multiply the above payoff by the notional principal to determine the actual payoff.

To derive the formula for pricing an FRA, a specific arbitrage transaction involving Eurodollars and FRAs is required. We omit the details of this somewhat complex transaction, but the end result is that the FRA rate is given by the following formula:

$$\text{FRA}(0,\text{h},\text{m}) = \left[\frac{1 + \text{L}_0(\text{h}+\text{m})\left(\frac{\text{h}+\text{m}}{360}\right)}{1 + \text{L}_0(\text{h})\left(\frac{\text{h}}{360}\right)} - 1\right]\left(\frac{360}{\text{m}}\right) \quad (13)$$

This somewhat awkward-looking formula is actually just the formula for a LIBOR forward rate, given the interest payment conventions in the FRA market. The numerator is the future value of a Eurodollar deposit of h + m days. The denominator is the future value of a shorter-term Eurodollar deposit of h days. This ratio is 1 plus a rate; subtracting 1 and multiplying by 360/m annualizes the rate.[21]

Consider a 3 × 9 FRA. This instrument expires in 90 days and is based on 180-day LIBOR. Thus, the Eurodollar deposit on which the underlying rate is based begins in 90 days and matures in 270 days. Because we are on day 0, h = 90, m = 180, and h + m = 270. Let the current rates be

$$\text{L}_0(\text{h}) = \text{L}_0(90) = 0.056$$

$$\text{L}_0(\text{h}+\text{m}) = \text{L}_0(270) = 0.06$$

In other words, the 90-day rate is 5.6 percent, and the 270-day rate is 6 percent. With h = 90 and m = 180, using our formula for the FRA rate, we obtain

$$\text{FRA}(0,\text{h},\text{m}) = \text{FRA}(0,90,180) = \left[\frac{1 + 0.06\left(\frac{270}{360}\right)}{1 + 0.056\left(\frac{90}{360}\right)} - 1\right]\left(\frac{360}{180}\right) = 0.0611$$

So to enter into an FRA on day 0, the rate would be 6.11 percent.[22]

As noted, the initial outlay for entering the forward contract is zero. Thus, the initial value is zero. Later during the life of the contract, its value will rise above or fall below zero. Now let us determine the value of an FRA during its life. Specifically, we use the notation $\text{V}_\text{g}(0,\text{h},\text{m})$ to represent the value of an FRA on day g, which was established on day 0, expires on day h, and is based on m-day LIBOR. Omitting the derivation, the approximate value of the FRA will be

$$\text{V}_\text{g}(0,\text{h},\text{m}) = \frac{1}{1 + \text{L}_\text{g}(\text{h}-\text{g})\left(\frac{\text{h}-\text{g}}{360}\right)} - \frac{1 + \text{FRA}(0,\text{h},\text{m})\left(\frac{\text{m}}{360}\right)}{1 + \text{L}_\text{g}(\text{h}+\text{m}-\text{g})\left(\frac{\text{h}+\text{m}-\text{g}}{360}\right)} \quad (14)$$

This formula looks complicated, but the ideas behind it are actually quite simple. Recall that we are at day g. The first term on the right-hand side is the present value of $1 received at day h. The second term is the present value of 1 plus the FRA rate to be received on day h + m, the maturity date of the underlying Eurodollar time deposit.

Assume that we go long the FRA, and it is 25 days later. We need to assign a value to the FRA. First note that g = 25, h − g = 90 − 25 = 65, and h + m − g = 90 + 180 − 25 = 245. In other words, we are 25 days into the contract, 65 days remain until expiration, and 245 days remain until the maturity of the Eurodollar deposit on which the underlying LIBOR is based. First we need information about the new term structure. Let

21 To compare with the traditional method of calculating a forward rate, consider a two-year rate of 10 percent and a one-year rate of 9 percent. The forward rate is $[(1.10)^2/(1.09)] - 1 = 0.1101$. The numerator is the future value of the longer-term bond, and the denominator is the future value of the shorter-term bond. The ratio is 1 plus the rate. We do not need to annualize in this example, because the forward rate is on a one-year bond.

22 It is worthwhile to point out again that this rate is the forward rate in the LIBOR term structure.

$$L_g(h-g) = L_{25}(65) = 0.059$$
$$L_g(h+m-g) = L_{25}(245) = 0.065$$

We now use the formula for the value of the FRA to obtain

$$V_g(0,h,m) = V_{25}(0,90,180) = \frac{1}{1+0.059\left(\frac{65}{360}\right)} - \frac{1+0.0611\left(\frac{180}{360}\right)}{1+0.065\left(\frac{245}{360}\right)} = 0.0026$$

Thus, we went long this FRA on day 0. Then 25 days later, the term structure changes to the rates used here and the FRA has a value of $0.0026 per $1 notional principal. If the notional principal is any amount other than $1, we multiply the notional principal by $0.0026 to obtain the full market value of the FRA.

Exhibit 8 Pricing and Valuation Formulas for Interest Rate Forward Contracts (FRAs)

Forward price (rate):

$$FRA(0,h,m) = \left[\frac{1+L_0(h+m)\left(\frac{h+m}{360}\right)}{1+L_0(h)\left(\frac{h}{360}\right)} - 1\right]\left(\frac{360}{m}\right)$$

Value of FRA on day g:

$$V_g(0,h,m) = \frac{1}{1+L_g(h-g)\left(\frac{h-g}{360}\right)} - \frac{1+FRA(0,h,m)\left(\frac{m}{360}\right)}{1+L_g(h+m-g)\left(\frac{h+m-g}{360}\right)}$$

We summarize the FRA formulas in Exhibit 8. We have now looked at the pricing and valuation of equity, fixed-income, and interest rate forward contracts. One of the most widely used types of forward contracts is the currency forward. The pricing and valuation of currency forwards is remarkably similar to that of equity forwards.

EXAMPLE 4

A corporate treasurer needs to hedge the risk of the interest rate on a future transaction. The risk is associated with the rate on 180-day Euribor in 30 days. The relevant term structure of Euribor is given as follows:

30-day Euribor	5.75%
210-day Euribor	6.15%

A State the terminology used to identify the FRA in which the manager is interested.

B Determine the rate that the company would get on an FRA expiring in 30 days on 180-day Euribor.

C Suppose the manager went long this FRA. Now, 20 days later, interest rates have moved significantly downward to the following:

10-day Euribor	5.45%
190-day Euribor	5.95%

The manager would like to know where the company stands on this FRA transaction. Determine the market value of the FRA for a €20 million notional principal.

D On the expiration day, 180-day Euribor is 5.72 percent. Determine the payment made to or by the company to settle the FRA contract.

Solution to A:

This transaction would be identified as a 1 × 7 FRA.

Solution to B:

Here the notation would be h = 30, m = 180, h + m = 210. Then

$$\text{FRA}(0,\text{h},\text{m}) = \text{FRA}(0,30,180) = \left[\frac{1+0.0615\left(\frac{210}{360}\right)}{1+0.0575\left(\frac{30}{360}\right)} - 1\right]\left(\frac{360}{180}\right) = 0.0619$$

Solution to C:

Here g = 20, h − g = 30 − 20 = 10, h + m − g = 30 + 180 − 20 = 190. The value of the FRA for a €1 notional principal would be

$$\text{V}_\text{g}(0,\text{h},\text{m}) = \text{V}_{20}(0,30,180) = \frac{1}{1+0.0545\left(\frac{10}{360}\right)} - \frac{1+0.0619\left(\frac{180}{360}\right)}{1+0.0595\left(\frac{190}{360}\right)} = -0.0011$$

Thus, for a notional principal of €20 million, the value would be €20,000,000(−0.0011) = −€22,000.

Solution to D:

At expiration, the payoff is

$$\frac{\left[\text{L}_\text{h}(\text{m}) - \text{FRA}(0,\text{h},\text{m})\right]\left(\frac{\text{m}}{360}\right)}{1+\text{L}_\text{h}(\text{m})\left(\frac{\text{m}}{360}\right)} = \frac{(0.0572 - 0.0619)\left(\frac{180}{360}\right)}{1+0.0572\left(\frac{180}{360}\right)} = -0.0023$$

For a notional principal of €20 million, the payoff would then be €20,000,000(−0.0023) = −€46,000. Thus, €46,000 would be paid by the company, because it is long and the final rate was lower than the FRA rate.

4.4 Pricing and Valuation of Currency Forward Contracts

Foreign currency derivative transactions as well as spot transactions must be handled with care. The exchange rate can be quoted in terms of units of the domestic currency per unit of foreign currency, or units of the foreign currency per unit of the domestic currency. In this reading, we shall always quote exchange rates in terms of units of the domestic currency per unit of the foreign currency, which is also called a direct quote. This approach is in keeping with the way in which other underlying assets are quoted. For example, from the perspective of a U.S. investor, a stock that sells for $50 is quoted in units of the domestic currency per unit (share) of stock. Likewise, if the euro exchange rate is quoted as $0.90, then the euro sells for $0.90 per unit, which is one euro. Alternatively, we could quote that \$1 sells for 1/\$0.90 = €1.1111—that is, €1.1111 per \$1; in this case, units of foreign currency per one unit of domestic currency from the perspective of a U.S. investor. In fact, this type of quote is commonly used and is called an indirect quote. Taking that approach, however, we would quote the stock price as 1/\$50 = 0.02 shares per \$1, a very unusual and awkward way to quote a stock price.

By taking the approach of quoting prices in terms of units of the domestic currency per unit of foreign currency, we facilitate a comparison of currencies and their derivatives with equities and their derivatives—a topic we have already covered. For example, we have previously discussed the case of a stock selling for S_0, which represents units of the domestic currency per share of stock. Likewise, we shall treat the currency as having an exchange rate of S_0, meaning that it is selling for S_0. We also need the foreign interest rate, denoted as r^f, and the domestic interest rate, denoted as r.[23]

Consider the following transactions executed today (time 0), assuming a contract expiration date of T:

> *Take $S_0/(1 + r^f)^T$ units of the domestic currency and convert it to $1/(1 + r^f)^T$ units of the foreign currency.*[24]
>
> *Sell a forward contract to deliver one unit of the foreign currency at the rate F(0,T) expiring at time T.*
>
> *Hold the position until time T. The $1/(1 + r^f)^T$ units of foreign currency will accrue interest at the rate r^f and grow to one unit of the currency at T as follows:*

$$\left(\frac{1}{1+r^f}\right)^T\left(1+r^f\right)^T = 1$$

Thus, at expiration we shall have one unit of the foreign currency, which is then delivered to the holder of the long forward contract, who pays the amount F(0,T). This amount was known at the start of the transaction. Because the risk has been hedged away, the exchange rate at expiration is irrelevant. Hence, this transaction is risk-free. Accordingly, the present value of F(0,T), found by discounting at the domestic risk-free interest rate, must equal the initial outlay of $S_0/(1 + r^f)^T$. Setting these amounts equal and solving for F(0,T) gives

$$F(0,T) = \left[\frac{S_0}{\left(1+r^f\right)^T}\right](1+r)^T \tag{15}$$

The term in brackets is the spot exchange rate discounted by the foreign interest rate. This term is then compounded at the domestic interest rate to the expiration day.[25]

Recall that in pricing equity forwards, we always reduced the stock price by the present value of the dividends and then compounded the resulting value to the expiration date. We can view currencies in the same way. The stock makes cash payments that happen to be called dividends; the currency makes cash payments that happen

---

23 We do not use a superscript "d" for the domestic rate, because in all previous examples we have used r to denote the interest rate in the home country of the investor.

24 In other words, if one unit of the foreign currency costs S_0, then $S_0/(1 + r^f)^T$ units of the domestic currency would, therefore, buy $1/(1 + r^f)^T$ units of the foreign currency.

25 It is also common to see the above Equation 15 written inversely, with the spot rate divided by the domestic interest factor and compounded by the foreign interest factor. This variation would be appropriate if the spot and forward rates were quoted in terms of units of the foreign currency per unit of domestic currency (indirect quotes). As we mentioned earlier, however, it is easier to think of a currency as just another asset, which naturally should have its price quoted in units of the domestic currency per unit of the asset or foreign currency.

to be called interest. Although the time pattern of how a stock pays dividends is quite different from the time pattern of how interest accrues, the general idea is the same. After reducing the spot price or rate by any cash flows over the life of the contract, the resulting value is then compounded at the risk-free rate to the expiration day.

The formula we have obtained here is simply a variation of the formula used for other types of forward contracts. In international financial markets, however, this formula has acquired its own name: **interest rate parity** (sometimes called covered interest rate parity). It expresses the equivalence, or parity, of spot and forward exchange rates, after adjusting for differences in the interest rates in the two countries. One implication of interest rate parity is that the forward rate will exceed (be less than) the spot rate if the domestic interest rate exceeds (is less than) the foreign interest rate. With a direct quote, if the forward rate exceeds (is less than) the spot rate, the foreign currency is said to be selling at a premium (discount). One should not, on the basis of this information, conclude that a currency selling at a premium is expected to increase or one selling at a discount is expected to decrease. A forward premium or discount is merely an implication of the relationship between interest rates in the two countries. More information would be required to make any assumptions about the outlook for the exchange rate.

If the forward rate in the market does not equal the forward rate given by interest rate parity, then an arbitrage transaction can be executed. Indeed, a similar relationship is true for any of the forward rates we have studied. In the foreign exchange markets, however, this arbitrage transaction has its own name: **covered interest arbitrage**. If the forward rate in the market is higher than the rate given by interest rate parity, then the forward rate is too high. When the price of an asset or derivative is too high, it should be sold. Thus, a trader would 1) sell the forward contract at the market rate, 2) buy $1/(1 + r^f)^T$ units of the foreign currency, 3) hold the position, earning interest on the currency, and 4) at maturity of the forward contract deliver the currency and be paid the forward rate. This arbitrage transaction would earn a return in excess of the domestic risk-free rate without any risk. If the forward rate is less than the rate given by the formula, the trader does the opposite, selling the foreign currency and buying a forward contract, in a similar manner. The combined actions of many traders undertaking this transaction will bring the forward price in the market in line with the forward price given by the model.

In Equation 15, both interest rates were annual rates with discrete compounding. In dealing with equities, we sometimes assume that the dividend payments are made continuously. Similarly, we could also assume that interest is compounded continuously. If that is the case, let r^{fc} be the continuously compounded foreign interest rate, defined as $r^{fc} = \ln(1 + r^f)$, and as before, let r^c be the continuously compounded domestic interest rate. Then the forward price is given by the same formula, with appropriately adjusted symbols, as we obtained when working with equity derivatives:

$$F(0,T) = \left(S_0 e^{-r^{fc}T}\right)e^{r^cT} \quad (16)$$

Now consider how we might value a foreign currency forward contract at some point in time during its life. In fact, we already know how: We simply apply to foreign currency forward contracts what we know about the valuation of equity forwards during the contract's life. Recall that the value of an equity forward is the stock price minus the present value of the dividends over the remaining life of the contract minus the present value of the forward price over the remaining life of the contract. An analogous formula for a currency forward gives us

$$V_t(0,T) = \frac{S_t}{\left(1 + r^f\right)^{(T-t)}} - \frac{F(0,T)}{(1 + r)^{(T-t)}} \quad (17)$$

In other words, we take the current exchange rate at time t, S_t, discount it by the foreign interest rate over the remaining life of the contract, and subtract the forward price discounted by the domestic interest rate over the remaining life of the contract. Under the assumption that we are using continuous compounding and discounting, the formula would be

$$V_t(0,T) = \left(S_t e^{-r^{fc}(T-t)}\right) - F(0,T)e^{-r^{c}(T-t)} \quad (18)$$

For example, suppose the domestic currency is the U.S. dollar and the foreign currency is the Swiss franc. Let the spot exchange rate be \$0.5987, the U.S. interest rate be 5.5 percent, and the Swiss interest rate be 4.75 percent. We assume these interest rates are fixed and will not change over the life of the forward contract. We also assume that these rates are based on annual compounding and are not quoted as LIBOR-type rates. Thus, we compound using formulas like $(1 + r)^T$, where T is the number of years and r is the annual rate.[26]

Assuming the forward contract has a maturity of 180 days, we have T = 180/365. Using the above formula for the forward rate, we find that the forward price should be

$$F(0,T) = F(0,180/365) = \left[\frac{\$0.5987}{(1.0475)^{180/365}}\right](1.055)^{180/365} = \$0.6008$$

Thus, if we entered into a forward contract, it would call for us to purchase (if long) or sell (if short) one Swiss franc in 180 days at a price of \$0.6008.

Suppose we go long this forward contract. It is now 40 days later, or 140 days until expiration. The spot rate is now \$0.65. As assumed above, the interest rates are fixed. With t = 40/365 and T − t = 140/365, the value of our long position is

$$V_t(0,T) = V_{40/365}(0,180/365) = \frac{\$0.6500}{(1.0475)^{140/365}} - \frac{\$0.6008}{(1.055)^{140/365}} = \$0.0499$$

So the contract value is \$0.0499 per Swiss franc. If the notional principal were more than one Swiss franc, we would simply multiply the notional principal by \$0.0499.

If we were working with continuously compounded rates, we would have $r^c = \ln(1.055) = 0.0535$ and $r^{fc} = \ln(1.0475) = 0.0464$. Then the forward price would be $F(0,T) = F(0,180/365) = (0.5987e^{-0.0464(180/365)})e^{0.0535(180/365)} = 0.6008$, and the value 40 days later would be $V_{40/365}(0,180/365) = 0.65e^{-0.0464(140/365)} - 0.6008e^{-0.0535(140/365)} = 0.0499$. These are the same results we obtained working with discrete rates.

Exhibit 9 summarizes the formulas for pricing and valuation of currency forward contracts.

Exhibit 9 Pricing and Valuation Formulas for Currency Forward Contracts

Forward price (rate) = (Spot price discounted by foreign interest rate) compounded at domestic interest rate:

$$\text{Discrete interest: } F(0,T) = \left[\frac{S_0}{\left(1 + r^f\right)^T}\right](1 + r)^T$$

$$\text{Continuous interest: } F(0,T) = \left(S_0 e^{-r^{fc}T}\right)e^{r^c T}$$

(continued)

26 If these were LIBOR-style rates, the interest would be calculated using the factor 1 + [Rate(Days/360)].

Exhibit 9 (Continued)

Value of forward contract:

$$\text{Discrete interest: } V_t(0,T) = \left[\frac{S_t}{\left(1+r^f\right)^{(T-t)}}\right] - \frac{F(0,T)}{(1+r)^{(T-t)}}$$

$$\text{Continuous interest: } V_t(0,T) = \left[S_t e^{-r^{fc}(T-t)}\right] - F(0,T)e^{-r^c(T-t)}$$

Note: The exchange rate is quoted in units of domestic currency per unit of foreign currency.

EXAMPLE 5

The spot rate for British pounds is \$1.76. The U.S. risk-free rate is 5.1 percent, and the U.K. risk-free rate is 6.2 percent; both are compounded annually. One-year forward contracts are currently quoted at a rate of \$1.75.

A Identify a strategy with which a trader can earn a profit at no risk by engaging in a forward contract, regardless of her view of the pound's likely movements. Carefully describe the transactions the trader would make. Show the rate of return that would be earned from this transaction. Assume the trader's domestic currency is U.S. dollars.

B Suppose the trader simply shorts the forward contract. It is now one month later. Assume interest rates are the same, but the spot rate is now \$1.72. What is the gain or loss to the counterparty on the trade?

C At expiration, the pound is at \$1.69. What is the value of the forward contract to the short at expiration?

Solution to A:

The following information is given:

$S_0 = \$1.76$

$r = 0.051$

$r^f = 0.062$

$T = 1.0$

The forward price should be

$$F(0,T) = \left(\frac{\$1.76}{1.062}\right)(1.051) = \$1.7418$$

With the forward contract selling at \$1.75, it is slightly overpriced. Thus, the trader should be able to buy the currency and sell a forward contract to earn a return in excess of the risk-free rate at no risk. The specific transactions are as follows:

- Take \$1.76/(1.062) = \$1.6573. Use it to buy 1/1.062 = £0.9416.
- Sell a forward contract to deliver £1.00 in one year at the price of \$1.75.
- Hold the position for one year, collecting interest at the U.K. risk-free rate of 6.2 percent. The £0.9416 will grow to (0.9416)(1.062) = £1.00.
- At expiration, deliver the pound and receive \$1.75. This is a return of

$$\frac{1.75}{1.6573} - 1 = 0.0559$$

A risk-free return of 5.59 percent is better than the U.S. risk-free rate of 5.1 percent, a result of the fact that the forward contract is overpriced.

Solution to B:

We now need the value of the forward contract to the counterparty, who went long at \$1.75. The inputs are

$$t = 1/12$$
$$S_t = \$1.72$$
$$T - t = 11/12$$
$$F(0,T) = \$1.75$$

The value of the forward contract to the long is

$$V_t(0,T) = \frac{1.72}{(1.062)^{11/12}} - \frac{1.75}{(1.051)^{11/12}} = -0.0443$$

which is a loss of \$0.0443 to the long and a gain of \$0.0443 to the short.

Solution to C:

The pound is worth \$1.69 at expiration. Thus, the value to the long is

$$V_T(0,T) = 1.69 - 1.75 = -0.06$$

and the value to the short is + \$0.06. Note the minus sign in the equation $V_T(0,T) = -0.06$. The value to the long is always the spot value at expiration minus the original forward price. The short will be required to deliver the foreign currency and receive \$1.75, which is \$0.06 more than market value of the pound. The contract's value to the short is thus \$0.06, which is the negative of its value to the long.

We have now seen how to determine the price and value of equity, fixed-income and interest rate, and currency forward contracts. We observed that the price is determined such that no arbitrage opportunities exist for either the long or the short. We have found that the value of a forward contract is the amount we would pay or receive to enter or exit the contract. Because no money changes hands up front, the value of a forward contract when initiated is zero. The value at expiration is determined by the difference between the spot price or rate at expiration and the forward contract price or rate. The value prior to expiration can also be determined and is the present value of the claim at expiration.

Determining the value of a forward contract is important for several reasons. One, however, is particularly important: Forward contracts contain the very real possibility that one of the parties might default. By knowing the market value, one can determine the amount of money at risk if a counterparty defaults. Let us now look at how credit risk enters into a forward contract.

CREDIT RISK AND FORWARD CONTRACTS 5

To illustrate how credit risk affects a forward contract, consider the currency forward contract example we just finished in the previous section. It concerns a contract that expires in 180 days in which the long will pay a forward rate of \$0.6008 for each Swiss franc to be received at expiration. Assume that the contract covers 10 million Swiss francs. Let us look at the problem from the point of view of the holder of the long position and the credit risk faced by this party.

Assume it is the contract expiration day and the spot rate for Swiss francs is \$0.62. The long is due to receive 10 million Swiss francs and pay \$0.6008 per Swiss franc, or \$6,008,000 in total. Now suppose that perhaps because of bankruptcy or insolvency, the short cannot come up with the \$6,200,000 that it would take to purchase the Swiss francs on the open market at the prevailing spot rate.[27] In order to obtain the Swiss francs, the long would have to buy them in the open market. Doing so would incur an additional cost of \$6,200,000 – \$6,008,000 = \$192,000, which can be viewed as the credit risk at the point of expiration when the spot rate is \$0.62. Not surprisingly, this amount is also the market value of the contract at this point.

This risk is an immediate risk faced at expiration. Prior to expiration, the long faces a potential risk that the short will default. If the long wanted to gauge the potential exposure, he would calculate the current market value. In the example we used in which the long is now 40 days into the life of the contract, the market value to the long is \$0.0499 per Swiss franc. Hence, the long's exposure would be 10,000,000(\$0.0499) = \$499,000. Although no payments are due at this point, \$499,000 is the market value of the claim on the payment at expiration. Using an estimate of the probability that the short would default, the long can gauge the expected credit loss from the transaction by multiplying that probability by \$499,000.

The market value of a forward contract reflects the current value of the claim at expiration, given existing market conditions. If the Swiss franc rises significantly, the market value will increase along with it, thereby exposing the long to the potential for even greater losses. Many participants in derivatives markets estimate this potential loss by running simulations that attempt to reflect the potential market value of the contract along with the probability of the counterparty defaulting.

We have viewed credit risk from the viewpoint of the long, but what about the short's perspective? In the case in which we went to expiration and the short owed the long the greater amount, the short faces no credit risk. In the case prior to expiration in which the contract's market value was positive, the value of the future claim was greater to the long than to the short. Hence, the short still did not face any credit risk.

The short would face credit risk, however, if circumstances were such that the value of the transaction were negative to the long, which would make the value to the short positive. In that case, the scenario discussed previously in this section would apply from the short's perspective.

There are various methods of managing the credit risk of various types of derivatives transactions. At this point, however, it will be helpful to specifically examine one particular method. Let us go back to the long currency forward contract that had a market value of \$499,000. As it stands at this time, the holder of the long position has a claim on the holder of the short position that is worth \$499,000. Suppose the two parties had agreed when they entered into the transaction that in 40 days, the party owing the greater amount to the other would pay the amount owed and the contract would be repriced at the new forward rate. Now on the 40th day, the short would pay the long \$499,000. Recalling that the U.S. interest rate was 5.5 percent and the Swiss interest rate was 4.75 percent, the contract, which now has 140 days to go ($T = 140/365$), would then be repriced to the rate

27 Even if the short already holds the Swiss franc, she might be declaring bankruptcy or otherwise unable to pay debts such that the forward contract claim is combined with the claims of all of the short's other creditors.

$$F(0,T) = F(0,140/365) = \left[\frac{\$0.65}{(1.0475)^{140/365}}\right](1.055)^{140/365} = \$0.6518$$

In other words, from this point, the contract has a new rate of \$0.6518. The long now agrees to pay \$0.6518 for the currency from the short in 140 days.

What the two parties have done is called **marking to market**. They have settled up the amount owed and marked the contract to its current market rate. If the parties agree in advance, a forward contract can be marked to market at whatever dates the parties feel are appropriate. Marking to market keeps one party from becoming too deeply indebted to the other without paying up. At the dates when the contract is marked to market, the parties restructure the contract so that it remains in force but with an updated price.

Forward contracts and swaps are sometimes marked to market to mitigate credit risk. In the reading on futures markets and contracts, we will note that a distinguishing characteristic of futures contracts is that they are marked to market every day. In essence, they are forward contracts that are marked to market and repriced daily to reduce the credit risk.

THE ROLE OF FORWARD MARKETS

6

In this reading we have discussed many aspects of forward contracts and forward markets. We will conclude the reading with a brief discussion of the role that these markets play in our financial system. Although forward, futures, options, and swap markets serve similar purposes in our society, each market is unique. Otherwise, these markets would consolidate.

Forward markets may well be the least understood of the various derivative markets. In contrast to their cousins, futures contracts, forward contracts are a far less visible segment of the financial markets. Both forwards and futures serve a similar purpose: They provide a means in which a party can commit to the future purchase or sale of an asset at an agreed-upon price, without the necessity of paying any cash until the asset is actually purchased or sold. In contrast to futures contracts, forward contracts are private transactions, permitting the ultimate in customization. As long as a counterparty can be found, a party can structure the contract completely to its liking. Futures contracts are standardized and may not have the exact terms required by the party. In addition, futures contracts, with their daily marking to market, produce interim cash flows that can lead to imperfections in a hedge transaction designed not to hedge interim events but to hedge a specific event at a target horizon date. Forward markets also provide secrecy and have only a light degree of regulation. In general, forward markets serve a specialized clientele, specifically large corporations and institutions with specific target dates, underlying assets, and risks that they wish to take or reduce by committing to a transaction without paying cash at the start.

As the reading on swap markets and contracts will make clear, however, forward contracts are just miniature versions of swaps. A swap can be viewed as a series of forward contracts. Swaps are much more widely used than forward contracts, suggesting that parties that have specific risk management needs typically require the equivalent of a series of forward contracts. A swap contract consolidates a series of forward contracts into a single instrument at lower cost.

Forward contracts are the building blocks for constructing and understanding both swaps and futures. Swaps and futures are more widely used and better known, but forward contracts play a valuable role in helping us understand swaps and futures. Moreover, as noted, for some parties, forward contracts serve specific needs not met by other derivatives.

In the reading on futures markets and contracts, we shall demonstrate how similar futures contracts are to forward contracts, but the differences are important, and some of their benefits to society are slightly different and less obvious than those of forwards.

SUMMARY

OPTIONAL SEGMENT

- The holder of a long forward contract (the "long") is obligated to take delivery of the underlying asset and pay the forward price at expiration. The holder of a short forward contract (the "short") is obligated to deliver the underlying asset and accept payment of the forward price at expiration.
- At expiration, a forward contract can be terminated by having the short make delivery of asset to the long or having the long and short exchange the equivalent cash value. If the asset is worth more (less) than the forward price, the short (long) pays the long (short) the cash difference between the market price or rate and the price or rate agreed on in the contract.
- A party can terminate a forward contract prior to expiration by entering into an opposite transaction with the same or a different counterparty. It is possible to leave both the original and new transactions in place, thereby leaving both transactions subject to credit risk, or to have the two transactions cancel each other. In the latter case, the party owing the greater amount pays the market value to the other party, resulting in the elimination of the remaining credit risk. This elimination can be achieved, however, only if the counterparty to the second transaction is the same counterparty as in the first.
- A dealer is a financial institution that makes a market in forward contracts and other derivatives. A dealer stands ready to take either side of a transaction. An end user is a party that comes to a dealer needing a transaction, usually for the purpose of managing a particular risk.
- Equity forward contracts can be written on individual stocks, specific stock portfolios, or stock indices. Equity forward contract prices and values must take into account the fact that the underlying stock, portfolio, or index could pay dividends.
- Forward contracts on bonds can be based on zero-coupon bonds or on coupon bonds, as well as portfolios or indices based on zero-coupon bonds or coupon bonds. Zero-coupon bonds pay their return by discounting the face value, often using a 360-day year assumption. Forward contracts on bonds must expire before the bond's maturity. In addition, a forward contract on a bond can be affected by special features of bonds, such as callability and convertibility.
- Eurodollar time deposits are dollar loans made by one bank to another. Although the term "Eurodollars" refers to dollar-denominated loans, similar loans exist in other currencies. Eurodollar deposits accrue interest by adding it on to the principal, using a 360-day year assumption. The primary Eurodollar rate is called LIBOR.

- LIBOR stands for London Interbank Offer Rate, the rate at which London banks are willing to lend to other London banks. Euribor is the rate on a euro time deposit, a loan made by banks to other banks in Frankfurt in which the currency is the euro.
- An FRA is a forward contract in which one party, the long, agrees to pay a fixed interest payment at a future date and receive an interest payment at a rate to be determined at expiration. FRAs are described by a special notation. For example, a 3 × 6 FRA expires in three months; the underlying is a Eurodollar deposit that begins in three months and ends three months later, or six months from now.
- The payment of an FRA at expiration is based on the net difference between the underlying rate and the agreed-upon rate, adjusted by the notional principal and the number of days in the instrument on which the underlying rate is based. The payoff is also discounted, however, to reflect the fact that the underlying rate on which the instrument is based assumes that payment will occur at a later date.
- A currency forward contract is a commitment for one party, the long, to buy a currency at a fixed price from the other party, the short, at a specific date. The contract can be settled by actual delivery, or the two parties can choose to settle in cash on the expiration day.

END OPTIONAL SEGMENT

- A forward contract is priced by assuming that the underlying asset is purchased, a forward contract is sold, and the position is held to expiration. Because the sale price of the asset is locked in as the forward price, the transaction is risk free and should earn the risk-free rate. The forward price is then obtained as the price that guarantees a return of the risk-free rate. If the forward price is too high or too low, an arbitrage profit in the form of a return in excess of the risk-free rate can be earned. The combined effects of all investors executing arbitrage transactions will force the forward price to converge to its arbitrage-free level.
- The value of a forward contract is determined by the fact that a long forward contract is a claim on the underlying asset and a commitment to pay the forward price at expiration. The value of a forward contract is, therefore, the current price of the asset less the present value of the forward price at expiration. Because no money changes hands at the start, the value of the forward contract today is zero. The value of a forward contract at expiration is the price of the underlying asset minus the forward price.
- Valuation of a forward contract is important because 1) it makes good business sense to know the values of future commitments, 2) accounting rules require that forward contracts be accounted for in income statements and balance sheets, 3) the value gives a good measure of the credit exposure, and 4) the value can be used to determine the amount of money one party would have to pay another party to terminate a position.
- An off-market forward contract is established with a nonzero value at the start. The contract will, therefore, have a positive or negative value and require a cash payment at the start. A positive value is paid by the long to the short; a negative value is paid by the short to the long. In an off-market forward contract, the forward price will not equal the price of the underlying asset compounded at the risk-free rate but rather will be set in the process of negotiation between the two parties.
- An equity forward contract is priced by taking the stock price, subtracting the present value of the dividends over the life of the contract, and then compounding this amount at the risk-free rate to the expiration date of the contract. The

present value of the dividends can be found by assuming the dividends are risk-free and calculating their present value using the risk-free rate of interest. Or one can assume that dividends are paid at a constant continuously compounded rate and then discount the stock price by the exponential function using the continuously compounded dividend rate. Alternatively, an equity forward can be priced by compounding the stock price to the expiration date and then subtracting the future value of the dividends at the expiration date. The value of an equity forward contract is the stock price minus the present value of the dividends minus the present value of the forward price that will be paid at expiration.

- To price a fixed-income forward contract, take the bond price, subtract the present value of the coupons over the life of the contract, and compound this amount at the risk-free rate to the expiration date of the contract. The value of a fixed-income forward contract is the bond price minus the present value of the coupons minus the present value of the forward price that will be paid at expiration.
- The price of an FRA, which is actually a rate, is simply the forward rate embedded in the term structure of the FRA's underlying rate. The value of an FRA based on a Eurodollar deposit is the present value of $1 to be received at expiration minus the present value of $1 plus the FRA rate to be received at the maturity date of the Eurodollar deposit on which the FRA is based, with appropriate (days/360) adjustments.
- The price, which is actually an exchange rate, of a forward contract on a currency is the spot rate discounted at the foreign interest rate over the life of the contract and then compounded at the domestic interest rate to the expiration date of the contract. The value of a currency forward contract is the spot rate discounted at the foreign interest rate over the life of the contract minus the present value of the forward rate at expiration.
- Credit risk in a forward contract arises when the counterparty that owes the greater amount is unable to pay at expiration or declares bankruptcy prior to expiration. The market value of a forward contract is a measure of the net amount one party owes the other. Only one party, the one owing the lesser amount, faces credit risk at any given time. Because the market value can change from positive to negative, however, the other party has the potential for facing credit risk at a later date. Counterparties occasionally mark forward contracts to market, with one party paying the other the current market value; they then reprice the contract to the current market price or rate.
- Forward markets play an important role in society, providing a means by which a select clientele of parties can engage in customized, private, unregulated transactions that commit them to buying or selling an asset at a later date at an agreed-upon price without paying any cash at the start. Forward contracts also are a simplified version of both futures and swaps and, therefore, form a basis for understanding these other derivatives.

PRACTICE PROBLEMS

1 Consider a security that sells for $1,000 today. A forward contract on this security that expires in one year is currently priced at $1,100. The annual rate of interest is 6.75 percent. Assume that this is an off-market forward contract.

A Calculate the value of the forward contract today (at inception) $V_0(0,T)$.

B Indicate whether payment is made by the long to the short or vice versa.

2 Assume that you own a security currently worth $500. You plan to sell it in two months. To hedge against a possible decline in price during the next two months, you enter into a forward contract to sell the security in two months. The risk-free rate is 3.5 percent.

A Calculate the forward price on this contract.

B Suppose the dealer offers to enter into a forward contract at $498. Indicate how you could earn an arbitrage profit.

C After one month, the security sells for $490. Calculate the gain or loss to your position.

3 Consider an asset currently worth $100. An investor plans to sell it in one year and is concerned that the price may have fallen significantly by then. To hedge this risk, the investor enters into a forward contract to sell the asset in one year. Assume that the risk-free rate is 5 percent.

A Calculate the appropriate price at which this investor can contract to sell the asset in one year.

B Three months into the contract, the price of the asset is $90. Calculate the gain or loss that has accrued to the forward contract.

C Assume that five months into the contract, the price of the asset is $107. Calculate the gain or loss on the forward contract.

D Suppose that at expiration, the price of the asset is $98. Calculate the value of the forward contract at expiration. Also indicate the overall gain or loss to the investor on the whole transaction.

E Now calculate the value of the forward contract at expiration assuming that at expiration, the price of the asset is $110. Indicate the overall gain or loss to the investor on the whole transaction. Is this amount more or less than the overall gain or loss from Part D?

4 A security is currently worth $225. An investor plans to purchase this asset in one year and is concerned that the price may have risen by then. To hedge this risk, the investor enters into a forward contract to buy the asset in one year. Assume that the risk-free rate is 4.75 percent.

A Calculate the appropriate price at which this investor can contract to buy the asset in one year.

B Four months into the contract, the price of the asset is $250. Calculate the gain or loss that has accrued to the forward contract.

C Assume that eight months into the contract, the price of the asset is $200. Calculate the gain or loss on the forward contract.

D Suppose that at expiration, the price of the asset is $190. Calculate the value of the forward contract at expiration. Also indicate the overall gain or loss to the investor on the whole transaction.

E Now calculate the value of the forward contract at expiration assuming that at expiration, the price of the asset is \$240. Indicate the overall gain or loss to the investor on the whole transaction. Is this amount more or less than the overall gain or loss from Part D?

5 Assume that a security is currently priced at \$200. The risk-free rate is 5 percent.

A A dealer offers you a contract in which the forward price of the security with delivery in three months is \$205. Explain the transactions you would undertake to take advantage of the situation.

B Suppose the dealer were to offer you a contract in which the forward price of the security with delivery in three months is \$198. How would you take advantage of the situation?

6 Assume that you own a dividend-paying stock currently worth \$150. You plan to sell the stock in 250 days. In order to hedge against a possible price decline, you wish to take a short position in a forward contract that expires in 250 days. The risk-free rate is 5.25 percent. Over the next 250 days, the stock will pay dividends according to the following schedule:

Days to Next Dividend	Dividends per Share (\$)
30	1.25
120	1.25
210	1.25

A Calculate the forward price of a contract established today and expiring in 250 days.

B It is now 100 days since you entered the forward contract. The stock price is \$115. Calculate the value of the forward contract at this point.

C At expiration, the price of the stock is \$130. Calculate the value of the forward contract at expiration.

7 A portfolio manager expects to purchase a portfolio of stocks in 90 days. In order to hedge against a potential price increase over the next 90 days, she decides to take a long position on a 90-day forward contract on the S&P 500 stock index. The index is currently at 1145. The continuously compounded dividend yield is 1.75 percent. The discrete risk-free rate is 4.25 percent.

A Calculate the no-arbitrage forward price on this contract.

B It is now 28 days since the portfolio manager entered the forward contract. The index value is at 1225. Calculate the value of the forward contract 28 days into the contract.

C At expiration, the index value is 1235. Calculate the value of the forward contract.

8 An investor purchased a newly issued bond with a maturity of 10 years 200 days ago. The bond carries a coupon rate of 8 percent paid semiannually and has a face value of \$1,000. The price of the bond with accrued interest is currently \$1,146.92. The investor plans to sell the bond 365 days from now. The schedule of coupon payments over the first two years, from the date of purchase, is as follows:

Coupon	Days after Purchase	Amount ($)
First	181	40
Second	365	40
Third	547	40
Fourth	730	40

A Should the investor enter into a long or short forward contract to hedge his risk exposure? Calculate the no-arbitrage price at which the investor should enter the forward contract. Assume that the risk-free rate is 6 percent.

B The forward contract is now 180 days old. Interest rates have fallen sharply, and the risk-free rate is 4 percent. The price of the bond with accrued interest is now $1,302.26. Determine the value of the forward contract now and indicate whether the investor has accrued a gain or loss on his position.

9 A corporate treasurer wishes to hedge against an increase in future borrowing costs due to a possible rise in short-term interest rates. She proposes to hedge against this risk by entering into a long 6 × 12 FRA. The current term structure for LIBOR is as follows:

Term (Days)	Interest Rate (%)
30	5.10
90	5.25
180	5.70
360	5.95

A Indicate when this 6 × 12 FRA expires and identify which term of the LIBOR this FRA is based on.

B Calculate the rate the treasurer would receive on a 6 × 12 FRA.

Suppose the treasurer went long this FRA. Now, 45 days later, interest rates have risen and the LIBOR term structure is as follows:

Term (Days)	Interest Rate (%)
135	5.90
315	6.15

C Calculate the market value of this FRA based on a notional principal of $10,000,000.

D At expiration, the 180-day LIBOR is 6.25 percent. Calculate the payoff on the FRA. Does the treasurer receive a payment or make a payment to the dealer?

10 A financial manager needs to hedge against a possible decrease in short-term interest rates. He decides to hedge his risk exposure by going short on an FRA that expires in 90 days and is based on 90-day LIBOR. The current term structure for LIBOR is as follows:

Term (Days)	Interest Rate (%)
30	5.83
90	6.00
180	6.14
360	6.51

A Identify the type of FRA used by the financial manager using the appropriate terminology.

B Calculate the rate the manager would receive on this FRA.

It is now 30 days since the manager took a short position in the FRA. Interest rates have shifted down, and the new term structure for LIBOR is as follows:

Term (Days)	Interest Rate (%)
60	5.50
150	5.62

C Calculate the market value of this FRA based on a notional principal of \$15,000,000.

11 Consider a U.S.-based company that exports goods to Switzerland. The U.S. company expects to receive payment on a shipment of goods in three months. Because the payment will be in Swiss francs, the U.S. company wants to hedge against a decline in the value of the Swiss franc over the next three months. The U.S. risk-free rate is 2 percent, and the Swiss risk-free rate is 5 percent. Assume that interest rates are expected to remain fixed over the next six months. The current spot rate is \$0.5974.

A Indicate whether the U.S. company should use a long or short forward contract to hedge currency risk.

B Calculate the no-arbitrage price at which the U.S. company could enter into a forward contract that expires in three months.

C It is now 30 days since the U.S. company entered into the forward contract. The spot rate is \$0.55. Interest rates are the same as before. Calculate the value of the U.S. company's forward position.

12 The euro currently trades at \$1.0231. The dollar risk-free rate is 4 percent, and the euro risk-free rate is 5 percent. Six-month forward contracts are quoted at a rate of \$1.0225. Indicate how you might earn a risk-free profit by engaging in a forward contract. Clearly outline the steps you undertake to earn this risk-free profit.

13 Suppose that you are a U.S.-based importer of goods from the United Kingdom. You expect the value of the pound to increase against the U.S. dollar over the next 30 days. You will be making payment on a shipment of imported goods in 30 days and want to hedge your currency exposure. The U.S. risk-free rate is 5.5 percent, and the U.K. risk-free rate is 4.5 percent. These rates are expected to remain unchanged over the next month. The current spot rate is \$1.50.

A Indicate whether you should use a long or short forward contract to hedge the currency risk.

B Calculate the no-arbitrage price at which you could enter into a forward contract that expires in 30 days.

C Move forward 10 days. The spot rate is $1.53. Interest rates are unchanged. Calculate the value of your forward position.

14 Consider the following: The U.S. risk-free rate is 6 percent, the Swiss risk-free rate is 4 percent, and the spot exchange rate between the United States and Switzerland is $0.6667.

A Calculate the continuously compounded U.S. and Swiss risk-free rates.

B Calculate the price at which you could enter into a forward contract that expires in 90 days.

C Calculate the value of the forward position 25 days into the contract. Assume that the spot rate is $0.65.

15 The Japanese yen currently trades at $0.00812. The U.S. risk-free rate is 4.5 percent, and the Japanese risk-free rate is 2.0 percent. Three-month forward contracts on the yen are quoted at $0.00813. Indicate how you might earn a risk-free profit by engaging in a forward contract. Outline your transactions.

SOLUTIONS

1 **A** S_0 = \$1,000

$F(0,T)$ = \$1,100

$T = 1$

$V_0(0,T)$ = \$1,000 – \$1,100/(1.0675) = –\$30.44

B Because the value is negative, the payment is made by the short to the long.

2 **A** S_0 = \$500

$T = 2/12 = 0.1667$

$r = 0.035$

$F(0,T) = \$500 \times (1.035)^{0.1667} = \$502.88$

B Sell the security for \$500 and invest at 3.5 percent for two months. At the end of two months, you will have \$502.88. Enter into a forward contract now to buy the security at \$498 in two months.

Arbitrage profit = \$502.88 – \$498 = \$4.88

C S_t = \$490

$t = 1/12 = 0.0833$

$T = 2/12 = 0.1667$

$T - t = 0.0834$

$r = 0.035$

$V_t(0,T) = \$490.00 - \$502.88/(1.035)^{0.0834} = -\$11.44$. This represents a gain to the short position.

3 **A** S_0 = \$100

$T = 1$

$r = 0.05$

$F(0,T)$ = \$100(1.05) = \$105

B S_t = \$90

$t = 3/12 = 0.25$

$T = 1$

$T - t = 0.75$

$r = 0.05$

$V_t(0,T) = \$90 - \$105/(1.05)^{0.75} = -\$11.23$

The investor is short so this represents a gain.

C S_t = \$107

$t = 5/12 = 0.4167$

$T = 1$

$T - t = 0.5834$

$r = 0.05$

$V_t(0,T) = \$107 - \$105/(1.05)^{0.5834} = \$4.95$

The investor is short, so this represents a loss to the short position.

D S_t = \$98

$F(0,T)$ = \$105

$V_T(0,T)$ = \$98 – \$105 = –\$7

Gain to short position = \$7

Loss on asset = –\$2 (based on \$100 – \$98)

Net gain = \$5

This represents a return of 5 percent on an asset worth \$100, the same as the risk-free rate.

E S_t = \$110

F(0,T) = \$105

V_T(0,T) = 110 – 105 = \$5

Loss to short position = –\$5

Gain on asset = \$10 (based on \$110 – \$100)

Net gain = \$5

This represents a return of 5 percent on an asset worth \$100, the same as the risk-free rate. The overall gain on the transaction is the same as in Part D because the forward contract was executed at the no-arbitrage price of \$105.

4 A S_0 = \$225

T = 1

r = 0.0475

F(0,T) = \$225(1.0475) = \$235.69

B S_t = \$250

t = 4/12 = 0.3333

T = 1

T – t = 0.6667

r = 0.0475

$V_t(0,T) = \$250.00 - \$235.69/(1.0475)^{0.6667} = \$21.49$

The investor is long, so a positive value represents a gain.

C S_t = \$200

t = 8/12 = 0.6667

T = 1

T – t = 0.3333

r = 0.0475

$V_t(0,T) = \$200.00 - \$235.69/(1.0475)^{0.3333} = -\$32.07$

The investor is long, so this represents a loss to the long position.

D S_t = \$190

F(0,T) = \$235.69

V_T(0,T) = \$190.00 – \$235.69 = –\$45.69

Loss to long position = –\$45.69

Gain on asset = \$35.00 (based on \$225 – \$190)

Net loss = –\$10.69

E S_t = \$240

F(0,T) = \$235.69

V_T(0,T) = \$240.00 – \$235.69 = \$4.31

Gain to long position = \$4.31

Loss on asset = –\$15.00 (based on \$240 – \$225)

Net loss = –$10.69

This loss is the same as the loss in Part D. In fact, the loss would be the same for any other price as well, because the forward contract was executed at the no-arbitrage price of $235.69. The loss of $10.69 is the risk-free rate of 4.75 percent applied to the initial asset price of $225.

5 **A** The no-arbitrage forward price is $F(0,T) = \$200(1.05)^{3/12} = \$202.45$.

Because the forward contract offered by the dealer is overpriced, sell the forward contract and buy the security now. Doing so will yield an arbitrage profit of $2.55.

Borrow $200 and buy security. At the end of three months, repay	$202.45
At the end of three months, deliver the security for	$205.00
Arbitrage profit	$2.55

B At a price of $198.00, the contract offered by the dealer is underpriced relative to the no-arbitrage forward price of $202.45. Enter into a forward contract to buy in three months at $198.00. Short the stock now, and invest the proceeds. Doing so will yield an arbitrage profit of $4.45.

Short security for $200 and invest proceeds for three months	$202.45
At the end of three months, buy the security for	$198.00
Arbitrage profit	$4.45

6 **A** $S_0 = \$150$

$T = 250/365$

$r = 0.0525$

$PV(D,0,T) = \$1.25/(1.0525)^{30/365} + \$1.25/(1.0525)^{120/365} + \$1.25/(1.0525)^{210/365} = \$3.69$

$F(0,T) = (\$150.00 - \$3.69)(1.0525)^{250/365} = \$151.53$

B $S_t = \$115$

$F(0,T) = \$151.53$

$t = 100/365$

$T = 250/365$

$T - t = 150/365$

$r = 0.0525$

After 100 days, two dividends remain: the first one in 20 days, and the second one in 110 days.

$PV(D,t,T) = \$1.25/(1.0525)^{20/365} + \$1.25/(1.0525)^{110/365} = \$2.48$

$V_t(0,T) = \$115.00 - \$2.48 - \$151.53/(1.0525)^{150/365} = -\$35.86$

A negative value is a gain to the short.

C $S_T = \$130$

$F(0,T) = \$151.53$

$V_T(0,T) = \$130.00 - \$151.53 = -\$21.53$

The contract expires with a value of negative $21.53, a gain to the short.

7 **A** $S_0 = \$1,145$

$T = 90/365 = 0.2466$

$r = 0.0425$

$r^c = \ln(1 + 0.0425) = 0.0416$

$\delta^c = 0.0175$

$F(0,T) = (\$1{,}145 \times e^{-0.0175(0.2466)})(e^{0.0416(0.2466)}) = \$1{,}151.83$

B $S_t = \$1{,}225$

$T = 90/365 = 0.2466$

$t = 28/365 = 0.0767$

$T - t = 0.1699$

$r = 0.0425$

$r^c = \ln(1 + 0.0425) = 0.0416$

$\delta^c = 0.0175$

$V_t(0,T) = (\$1{,}225 \times e^{-0.0175(0.1699)}) - (1151.83e^{-0.0416(0.1699)}) = \$77.65$

This is a gain to the long position.

C $S_T = \$1{,}235$

$F(0,T) = \$1{,}151.83$

$V_T(0,T) = \$1{,}235.00 - \$1{,}151.83 = \$83.17$

The contract expires with a value of $83.17, a gain to the long.

8 A The investor should enter into a short forward contract, locking in the price at which he can sell the bond in 365 days.

$B_0^c(T + Y) = \$1{,}146.92$

$T = 365/365 = 1$

$r = 0.06$

Between now (i.e., 200 days since the original purchase) and the next 365 days, the investor will receive two coupons, the first 165 days from now and the second 347 days from now.

$PV(CI,0,T) = \$40/(1.06)^{165/365} + \$40/(1.06)^{347/365} = \$76.80$

$F(0,T) = (\$1{,}146.92 - \$76.81)(1.06)^{365/365} = \$1{,}134.32$

B $B_t^c(T + Y) = \$1{,}302.26$

$F(0,T) = \$1{,}134.32$

$t = 180/365$

$T = 365/365$

$T - t = 185/365$

$r = 0.04$

We are now on the 380th day of the bond's life. One more coupon payment remains until the expiration of the forward contract. The coupon payment is in 547 − 380 = 167 days.

$PV(CI,0,T) = \$40/(1.04)^{167/365} = \$39.29$

$V_t(0,T) = \$1{,}302.26 - \$39.29 - \$1{,}134.32/(1.04)^{185/365} = \$150.98$

A positive value is a loss to the short position.

9 A A 6 × 12 FRA expires in 180 days and is based on 180-day LIBOR.

B $h = 180$

$m = 180$

$h + m = 360$

$L_0(h + m) = 0.0595$

$L_0(h) = 0.057$

$$\text{FRA}(0,h,m) = \left[\frac{1 + 0.0595\left(\frac{360}{360}\right)}{1 + 0.0570\left(\frac{180}{360}\right)} - 1\right]\left(\frac{360}{180}\right) = 0.0603$$

C $h = 180$

$m = 180$

$g = 45$

$h - g = 135$

$h + m - g = 315$

$L_{45}(h - g) = 0.0590$

$L_{45}(h + m - g) = 0.0615$

$$V_t(0,h,m) = \frac{1}{1 + 0.0590\left(\frac{135}{360}\right)} - \frac{1 + 0.0603\left(\frac{180}{360}\right)}{1 + 0.0615\left(\frac{315}{360}\right)} = 0.00081$$

For \$10,000,000 notional principal, the value of the FRA would be = 0.00081 × 10,000,000 = \$8,100.

D $h = 180$

$m = 180$

$L_{180}(m) = 0.0625$

$$\text{At expiration, the payoff is} = \frac{(0.0625 - 0.0603)\left(\frac{180}{360}\right)}{1 + 0.0625\left(\frac{180}{360}\right)} = 0.001067$$

Based on a notional principal of \$10,000,000, the corporation, which is long, will receive \$10,000,000 × 0.001067 = \$10,670 from the dealer.

10 A A 3 × 6 FRA expires in 90 days and is based on 90-day LIBOR.

B $h = 90$

$m = 90$

$h + m = 180$

$L_0(h) = 0.06$

$L_0(h + m) = 0.0614$

$$\text{FRA}(0,h,m) = \left[\frac{1 + 0.0614\left(\frac{180}{360}\right)}{1 + 0.06\left(\frac{90}{360}\right)} - 1\right]\left(\frac{360}{90}\right) = 0.0619$$

C $h = 90$

$m = 90$

$g = 30$

$h - g = 60$

$h + m - g = 150$

$L_{30}(h - g) = 0.055$

$L_{30}(h + m - g) = 0.0562$

$$V_t(0,h,m) = \frac{1}{1+0.055\left(\frac{60}{360}\right)} - \frac{1+0.0619\left(\frac{90}{360}\right)}{1+0.0562\left(\frac{150}{360}\right)}$$

$= -0.001323$

For \$15,000,000 notional principal, the value of the FRA would be = −0.001323 × 15,000,000 = −\$19,845. Because the manager is short, this represents a gain to his company.

11 A The risk to the U.S. company is that the value of the Swiss franc will decline and it will receive fewer U.S. dollars on conversion. To hedge this risk, the company should enter into a contract to sell Swiss francs forward.

B S_0 = \$0.5974

T = 90/365

r = 0.02

r^f = 0.05

$$F(0,T) = \left[\frac{0.5974}{(1.05)^{90/365}}\right](1.02)^{90/365} = \$0.5931$$

C S_t = \$0.55

T = 90/365

t = 30/365

T − t = 60/365

r = 0.02

r^f = 0.05

$$V_t(0,T) = \frac{\$0.55}{(1.05)^{60/365}} - \frac{\$0.5931}{(1.02)^{60/365}} = -\$0.0456$$

This represents a gain to the short position of \$0.0456 per Swiss franc. In this problem, the U.S. company holds the short forward position.

12 First calculate the fair value or arbitrage-free price of the forward contract:

S_0 = \$1.0231

T = 180/365

r = 0.04

r^f = 0.05

$$F(0,T) = \left[\frac{1.0231}{(1.05)^{180/365}}\right](1.04)^{180/365} = \$1.0183$$

The dealer quote for the forward contract is \$1.0225; thus, the forward contract is overpriced. To earn a risk-free profit, you should enter into a forward contract to sell euros forward in six months at \$1.0225. At the same time, buy euros now.

i. Take $\frac{\$1.0231}{(1.05)^{180/365}} = \$0.9988$. Use it to buy $\frac{1}{(1.05)^{180/365}} = 0.9762$ euros.

ii. Enter a forward contract to deliver €1.00 at \$1.0225 in six months.

iii. Invest €0.9762 for six months at 5 percent per year and receive €0.9762 × $1.05^{180/365}$ = €1.00 at the end of six months.

iv. At expiration, deliver the euro and receive \$1.0225. Return over six months is $\frac{\$1.0225}{\$0.9988} - 1 = 0.0237$, or 4.74 percent a year.

This risk-free annual return of 4.74 percent exceeds the U.S. risk-free rate of 4 percent.

13 A The risk to you is that the value of the British pound will rise over the next 30 days and it will require more U.S. dollars to buy the necessary pounds to make payment. To hedge this risk you should enter a forward contract to buy British pounds.

B S_0 = \$1.50

T = 30 / 365

r = 0.055

r^f = 0.045

$$F(0,T) = \left[\frac{\$1.50}{(1.045)^{30/365}}\right](1.055)^{30/365} = \$1.5012$$

C S_t = \$1.53

T = 30/365

t = 10/365

T − t = 20/365

r = 0.055

r^f = 0.045

$$V_t(0,T) = \frac{\$1.53}{1.045^{20/365}} - \frac{\$1.5012}{1.055^{20/365}} = \$0.0295$$

Because you are long, this is a gain of \$0.0295 per British pound.

14 A $r^{fc} = \ln(1.04) = 0.0392$

$r^c = \ln(1.06) = 0.0583$

B S_0 = \$0.6667

T = 90/365

r^{fc} = 0.0392

r^c = 0.0583

$$F(0,T) = \left(\$0.6667 \times e^{-0.0392(90/365)}\right)\left(e^{0.0583(90/365)}\right) = \$0.6698$$

C S_t = \$0.65

T = 90/365

t = 25/365

T − t = 65/365

r^{fc} = 0.0392

r^c = 0.0583

$$V_t(0,T) = \left(\$0.65 \times e^{-0.0392(65/365)}\right) - \left(\$0.6698 \times e^{-0.0583(65/365)}\right) =$$

−\$0.0174

The value of the contract is −\$0.0174 per Swiss franc.

15 First, calculate the fair value or arbitrage free price of the forward contract:

S_0 = \$0.00812 per yen

T = 90/365

r = 0.045

r^f = 0.02

$$F(0,T) = \left[\frac{\$0.00812}{(1.02)^{90/365}}\right](1.045)^{90/365} = \$0.00817$$

The dealer quote for the forward contract is \$0.00813. Therefore, the forward contract is underpriced. To earn a risk-free profit, you should enter into a forward contract to buy yen in three months at \$0.00813. At the same time, sell yen now.

i. The spot rate of \$0.00812 per yen is equivalent to ¥123.15 per U.S. dollar. Take $\frac{¥123.15}{(1.045)^{90/365}} = ¥121.82$. Use it to buy $\frac{1}{(1.045)^{90/365}} = 0.9892$ U.S. dollars.

ii. Enter a forward contract to buy yen at \$0.00813 in three months. One U.S. dollar will buy $\frac{1}{\$0.00813} = ¥123.00$

iii. Invest \$0.9892 for three months at 4.5 percent a year and receive \$0.9892 × $1.045^{90/365}$ = \$1.00 at the end of three months.

iv. At expiration, deliver the dollar and receive ¥123. The return over three months is $\frac{¥123.00}{¥121.82} - 1 = 0.00969$, or 3.88 percent a year.

Because we began our transactions in yen, the relevant comparison for the return from our transactions is the Japanese risk-free rate. The 3.88 percent return above exceeds the Japanese risk-free rate of 2 percent. Therefore, we could borrow yen at 2 percent and engage in the above transactions to earn a risk-free return of 3.88 percent that exceeds the rate of borrowing.

READING

52

Futures Markets and Contracts

by Don M. Chance, CFA

LEARNING OUTCOMES

Mastery	The candidate should be able to:
☐	**a.** explain why the futures price must converge to the spot price at expiration;
☐	**b.** determine the value of a futures contract;
☐	**c.** explain why forward and futures prices differ;
☐	**d.** describe monetary and nonmonetary benefits and costs associated with holding the underlying asset, and explain how they affect the futures price;
☐	**e.** describe backwardation and contango;
☐	**f.** explain the relation between futures prices and expected spot prices;
☐	**g.** describe the difficulties in pricing Eurodollar futures and creating a pure arbitrage opportunity;
☐	**h.** calculate and interpret the prices of Treasury bond futures, stock index futures, and currency futures.

INTRODUCTION 1

OPTIONAL SEGMENT

In the reading on forward markets and contracts, we focused on forward markets. Now we explore futures markets in a similar fashion. Although we shall see a clear similarity between forward and futures contracts, critical distinctions nonetheless exist between the two.

Like a forward contract, *a futures contract is an agreement between two parties in which one party, the buyer, agrees to buy from the other party, the seller, an underlying asset or other derivative, at a future date at a price agreed on today.* Unlike a forward contract, however, a futures contract is not a private and customized transaction but rather a public transaction that takes place on an organized futures exchange. In addition, a futures contract is standardized—the exchange, rather than the individual parties, sets the terms and conditions, with the exception of price. As a result, futures contracts have a secondary market, meaning that previously created contracts can be traded. Also, parties to futures contracts are guaranteed against credit losses resulting from the counterparty's inability to pay. A clearinghouse provides this guarantee via a procedure in which it converts gains and losses that accrue on a daily basis into actual cash gains and losses. Futures contracts are regulated at the federal government level; as we noted in the reading on forward markets and contracts, forward contracts are essentially unregulated. Futures contracts are created on organized trading facilities referred to as futures exchanges, whereas forward contracts are not created in any specific location but rather initiated between any two parties who wish to enter into such a contract. Finally, each futures exchange has a division or subsidiary called a clearinghouse that performs the specific responsibilities of paying and collecting daily gains and losses as well as guaranteeing to each party the performance of the other.

In a futures transaction, one party, the long, is the buyer and the other party, the short, is the seller. The buyer agrees to buy the underlying at a later date, the expiration, at a price agreed on at the start of the contract. The seller agrees to sell the underlying to the buyer at the expiration, at the price agreed on at the start of the contract. Every day, the futures contract trades in the market and its price changes in response to new information. Buyers benefit from price increases, and sellers benefit from price decreases. On the expiration day, the contract terminates and no further trading takes place. Then, either the buyer takes delivery of the underlying from the seller, or the two parties make an equivalent cash settlement. We shall explore each of these characteristics of futures contracts in more detail. First, however, it is important to take a brief look at how futures markets came into being.

1.1 A Brief History of Futures Markets

Although vestiges of futures markets appear in the Japanese rice markets of the 18th century and perhaps even earlier, the mid-1800s marked the first clear origins of modern futures markets. For example, in the United States in the 1840s, Chicago was becoming a major transportation and distribution center for agricultural commodities. Its central location and access to the Great Lakes gave Chicago a competitive advantage over other U.S. cities. Farmers from the Midwest would harvest their grain and take it to Chicago for sale. Grain production, however, is seasonal. As a result, grain prices would rise sharply just prior to the harvest but then plunge when the grain was brought to the market. Too much grain at one time and too little at another resulted in severe problems. Grain storage facilities in Chicago were inadequate to accommodate the oversupply. Some farmers even dumped their grain in the Chicago River because prices were so low that they could not afford to take their grain to another city to sell.

To address this problem, in 1848 a group of businessmen formed an organization later named the Chicago Board of Trade (CBOT) and created an arrangement called a "to-arrive" contract. These contracts permitted farmers to sell their grain before delivering it. In other words, farmers could harvest the grain and enter into a contract to deliver it at a much later date at a price already agreed on. This transaction allowed the farmer to hold the grain in storage at some other location besides Chicago. On the other side of these contracts were the businessmen who had formed the Chicago Board of Trade.

It soon became apparent that trading in these to-arrive contracts was more important and useful than trading in the grain itself. Soon the contracts began trading in a type of secondary market, which allowed buyers and sellers to discharge their obligations by passing them on, for a price, to other parties. With the addition of the clearinghouse in the 1920s, which provided a guarantee against default, modern futures markets firmly established their place in the financial world. It was left to other exchanges, such as today's Chicago Mercantile Exchange, the New York Mercantile Exchange, Eurex, and the London International Financial Futures Exchange, to develop and become, along with the Chicago Board of Trade, the global leaders in futures markets.

We shall now explore the important features of futures contracts in more detail.

1.2 Public Standardized Transactions

A private transaction is not generally reported in the news or to any price-reporting service. Forward contracts are private contracts. Just as in most legal contracts, the parties do not publicly report that they have engaged in a contract. In contrast, a futures transaction is reported to the futures exchange, the clearinghouse, and at least one regulatory agency. The price is recorded and available from price reporting services and even on the internet.[1]

We noted that a futures transaction is not customized. Recall from the reading on forward markets and contracts that in a forward contract, the two parties establish all of the terms of the contract, including the identity of the underlying, the expiration date, and the manner in which the contract is settled (cash or actual delivery) as well as the price. The terms are customized to meet the needs of both parties. In a futures contract, the price is the only term established by the two parties; the exchange establishes all other terms. Moreover, the terms that are established by the exchange are standardized, meaning that the exchange selects a number of choices for underlyings, expiration dates, and a variety of other contract-specific items. These standardized terms are well known to all parties. If a party wishes to trade a futures contract, it must accept these terms. The only alternative would be to create a similar but customized contract on the forward market.

With respect to the underlying, for example, a given asset has a variety of specifications and grades. Consider a futures contract on U.S. Treasury bonds. There are many different Treasury bonds with a variety of characteristics. The futures exchange must decide which Treasury bond or group of bonds the contract covers. One of the most actively traded commodity futures contracts is oil, but there are many different types of oil.[2] To which type of oil does the contract apply? The exchange decides at the time it designs the contract.

The parties to a forward contract set its expiration at whatever date they want. For a futures contract, the exchange establishes a set of expiration dates. The first specification of the expiration is the month. An exchange might establish that a given futures contract expires only in the months of March, June, September, and December. The second specification determines how far the expirations go out into the future. For example, in January of a given year, there may be expirations of March, June, September, and December. Expirations might also be available for March, June, September, and December of the following year, and perhaps some months of the year after that. The exchange decides which expiration months are appropriate for trading, based on which expirations they believe would be actively traded. Treasury bond futures have expirations going out only about a year. Eurodollar futures, however, have expirations that go out about 10 years.[3] The third specification of the expiration is the specific day of expiration. Many, but not all, contracts expire some time during the third week of the expiration month.

1 The information reported to the general public does not disclose the identity of the parties to transactions but only that a transaction took place at a particular price.

2 Some of the main types are Saudi Arabian light crude, Brent crude, and West Texas intermediate crude.

3 You may be wondering why some Eurodollar futures contracts have such long expirations. Dealers in swaps and forward rate agreements use Eurodollar futures to hedge their positions. Many of those over-the-counter contracts have very long expirations.

The exchange determines a number of other contract characteristics, including the contract size. For example, one Eurodollar futures contract covers $1 million of a Eurodollar time deposit. One U.S. Treasury bond futures contract covers $100,000 face value of Treasury bonds. One futures contract on crude oil covers 1,000 barrels. The exchange also decides on the price quotation unit. For example, Treasury bond futures are quoted in points and 32nds of par of 100. Hence, you will see a price like 104 21/32, which means 104.65625. With a contract size of $100,000, the actual price is $104,656.25.

The exchange also determines what hours of the day trading takes place and at what physical location on the exchange the contract will be traded. Many futures exchanges have a trading floor, which contains octagonal-shaped pits. A contract is assigned to a certain pit. Traders enter the pits and express their willingness to buy and sell by calling out and/or indicating by hand signals their bids and offers. Some exchanges have electronic trading, which means that trading takes place on computer terminals, generally located in companies' offices. Some exchanges have both floor trading and electronic trading; some have only one or the other.

1.3 Homogenization and Liquidity

By creating contracts with generally accepted terms, the exchange standardizes the instrument. In contrast, forward contracts are quite heterogeneous because they are customized. Standardizing the instrument makes it more acceptable to a broader group of participants, with the advantage being that the instrument can then more easily trade in a type of secondary market. Indeed, the ability to sell a previously purchased contract or purchase a previously sold contract is one of the important features of futures contracts. A futures contract is therefore said to have liquidity in contrast to a forward contract, which does not generally trade after it has been created.[4] This ability to trade a previously opened contract allows participants in this market to offset the position before expiration, thereby obtaining exposure to price movements in the underlying without the actual requirement of holding the position to expiration. We shall discuss this characteristic further when we describe futures trading in Section 2.

1.4 The Clearinghouse, Daily Settlement, and Performance Guarantee

Another important distinction between futures and forwards is that the futures exchange guarantees to each party the performance of the other party, through a mechanism known as the clearinghouse. This guarantee means that if one party makes money on the transaction, it does not have to worry about whether it will collect the money from the other party because the clearinghouse ensures it will be paid. In contrast, each party to a forward contract assumes the risk that the other party will default.

An important and distinguishing feature of futures contracts is that the gains and losses on each party's position are credited and charged on a daily basis. This procedure, called **daily settlement** or marking to market, essentially results in paper gains and losses being converted to cash gains and losses each day. It is also equivalent to terminating a contract at the end of each day and reopening it the next day at that settlement price. In some sense, a futures contract is like a strategy of opening up a

4 The notion of liquidity here is only that a market exists for futures contracts, but this does not imply a high degree of liquidity. There may be little trading in a given contract, and the bid–ask spread can be high. In contrast, some forward markets can be very liquid, allowing forward contracts to be offset, as described in the reading on forward markets and contracts.

forward contract, closing it one day later, opening up a new contract, closing it one day later, and continuing in that manner until expiration. The exact manner in which the daily settlement works will be covered in more detail later in Section 3.

1.5 Regulation

In most countries, futures contracts are regulated at the federal government level. State and regional laws may also apply. In the United States, the Commodity Futures Trading Commission regulates the futures market. In the United Kingdom, the Financial Services Authority regulates both the securities and futures markets.

Federal regulation of futures markets generally arises out of a concern to protect the general public and other futures market participants, as well as through a recognition that futures markets affect all financial markets and the economy. Regulations cover such matters as ensuring that prices are reported accurately and in a timely manner, that markets are not manipulated, that professionals who offer their services to the public are qualified and honest, and that disputes are resolved. In the United States, the government has delegated some of these responsibilities to an organization called the National Futures Association (NFA). An industry self-regulatory body, the NFA was created with the objective of having the industry regulate itself and reduce the federal government's burden.

FUTURES TRADING 2

In this section, we look more closely at how futures contracts are traded. As noted above, futures contracts trade on a futures exchange either in a pit or on a screen or electronic terminal.

We briefly mentioned pit trading, also known as floor-based trading, in Section 1.2. Pit trading is a very physical activity. Traders stand in the pit and shout out their orders in the form of prices they are willing to pay or accept. They also use hand signals to indicate their bids and offers.[5] They engage in transactions with other traders in the pits by simply agreeing on a price and number of contracts to trade. The activity is fast, furious, exciting, and stressful. The average pit trader is quite young, owing to the physical demands of the job and the toll it takes on body and mind. In recent years, more trading has come off of the exchange floor to electronic screens or terminals. In electronic or screen-based trading, exchange members enter their bids and offers into a computer system, which then displays this information and allows a trader to consummate a trade electronically. In the United States, pit trading is dominant, owing to its long history and tradition. Exchange members who trade on the floor enjoy pit trading and have resisted heavily the advent of electronic trading. Nonetheless, the exchanges have had to respond to market demands to offer electronic trading. In the United States, both pit trading and electronic trading are used, but in other countries, electronic trading is beginning to drive pit trading out of business.[6]

A person who enters into a futures contract establishes either a long position or a short position. Similar to forward contracts, long positions are agreements to buy the underlying at the expiration at a price agreed on at the start. Short positions are agreements to sell the underlying at a future date at a price agreed on at the start. When the position is established, each party deposits a small amount of money, typically

5 Hand signals facilitate trading with someone who is too far away in the pit for verbal communication.

6 For example, in France electronic trading was introduced while pit trading continued. Within two weeks, all of the volume had migrated to electronic trading and pit trading was terminated.

called the margin, with the clearinghouse. Then, as briefly described in Section 1.4, the contract is marked to market, whereby the gains are distributed to and the losses collected from each party. We cover this marking-to-market process in more detail in the next section. For now, however, we focus only on the opening and closing of the position.

A party that has opened a long position collects profits or incurs losses on a daily basis. At some point in the life of the contract prior to expiration, that party may wish to re-enter the market and close out the position. This process, called **offsetting**, is the same as selling a previously purchased stock or buying back a stock to close a short position. The holder of a long futures position simply goes back into the market and offers the identical contract for sale. The holder of a short position goes back into the market and offers to buy the identical contract. It should be noted that when a party offsets a position, it does not necessarily do so with the same counterparty to the original contract. In fact, rarely would a contract be offset with the same counterparty. Because of the ability to offset, futures contracts are said to be fungible, which means that any futures contract with any counterparty can be offset by an equivalent futures contract with another counterparty. Fungibility is assured by the fact that the clearinghouse inserts itself in the middle of each contract and, therefore, becomes the counterparty to each party.

For example, suppose in early January a futures trader purchases an S&P 500 stock index futures contract expiring in March. Through 15 February, the trader has incurred some gains and losses from the daily settlement and decides that she wants to close the position out. She then goes back into the market and offers for sale the March S&P 500 futures. Once she finds a buyer to take the position, she has a long and short position in the same contract. The clearinghouse considers that she no longer has a position in that contract and has no remaining exposure, nor any obligation to make or take delivery at expiration. Had she initially gone short the March futures, she might re-enter the market in February offering to buy it. Once she finds a seller to take the opposite position, she becomes long and short the same contract and is considered to have offset the contract and therefore have no net position.

3 THE CLEARINGHOUSE, MARGINS, AND PRICE LIMITS

As briefly noted in the previous section, when a trader takes a long or short position in a futures, he must first deposit sufficient funds in a margin account. This amount of money is traditionally called the margin, a term derived from the stock market practice in which an investor borrows a portion of the money required to purchase a certain amount of stock.

Margin in the stock market is quite different from margin in the futures market. In the stock market, "margin" means that a loan is made. The loan enables the investor to reduce the amount of his own money required to purchase the securities, thereby generating leverage or gearing, as it is sometimes known. If the stock goes up, the percentage gain to the investor is amplified. If the stock goes down, however, the percentage loss is also amplified. The borrowed money must eventually be repaid with interest. The margin percentage equals the market value of the stock minus the market value of the debt divided by the market value of the stock—in other words, the investor's own equity as a percentage of the value of the stock. For example, in the United States, regulations permit an investor to borrow up to 50 percent of the initial value of the stock. This percentage is called the initial margin requirement. On any day thereafter, the equity or percentage ownership in the account, measured as the market value of the securities minus the amount borrowed, can be less than 50 percent but must be at least a percentage known as the maintenance margin requirement. A typical maintenance margin requirement is 25 to 30 percent.

In the futures market, by contrast, the word **margin** is commonly used to describe the amount of money that must be put into an account by a party opening up a futures position, but the term is misleading. When a transaction is initiated, a futures trader puts up a certain amount of money to meet the **initial margin requirement**; however, the remaining money is not borrowed. The amount of money deposited is more like a down payment for the commitment to purchase the underlying at a later date. Alternatively, one can view this deposit as a form of good faith money, collateral, or a performance bond: The money helps ensure that the party fulfills his or her obligation.[7] Moreover, both the buyer and the seller of a futures contract must deposit margin.

In securities markets, minimum margin requirements are normally set by government regulators. In the United States, minimum initial margin requirements are set by the Federal Reserve System. Maintenance margin requirements are set by securities exchanges and FINRA subject to approval by the Securities and Exchange Commission. In futures markets, margin requirements are set by the clearinghouses. In further contrast to margin practices in securities markets, futures margins are traditionally expressed in dollar terms and not as a percentage of the futures price. For ease of comparison, however, we often speak of the futures margin in terms of its relationship to the futures price. In futures markets, the initial margin requirement is typically much lower than the initial margin requirement in the stock market. In fact, futures margins are usually less than 10 percent of the futures price.[8] Futures clearinghouses set their margin requirements by studying historical price movements. They then establish minimum margin levels by taking into account normal price movements and the fact that accounts are marked to market daily. The clearinghouses thus collect and disburse margin money every day. Moreover, they are permitted to do so more often than daily, and on some occasions they have used that privilege. By carefully setting margin requirements and collecting margin money every day, clearinghouses are able to control the risk of default.

In spite of the differences in margin practices for futures and securities markets, the effect of leverage is similar for both. By putting up a small amount of money, the trader's gains and losses are magnified. Given the tremendously low margin requirements of futures markets, however, the magnitude of the leverage effect is much greater in futures markets. We shall see how this works as we examine the process of the daily settlement.

As previously noted, each day the clearinghouse conducts an activity known as the daily settlement, also called marking to market. This practice results in the conversion of gains and losses on paper into actual gains and losses. As margin account balances change, holders of futures positions must maintain balances above a level called the **maintenance margin requirement**. The maintenance margin requirement is lower than the initial margin requirement. On any day in which the amount of money in the margin account at the end of the day falls below the maintenance margin requirement, the trader must deposit sufficient funds to bring the balance back up to the initial margin requirement. Alternatively, the trader can simply close out the position but is responsible for any further losses incurred if the price changes before a closing transaction can be made.

---

7 In fact, the Chicago Mercantile Exchange uses the term "performance bond" instead of "margin." Most other exchanges use the term "margin."

8 For example, the margin requirement of the Eurodollar futures contract at the Chicago Mercantile Exchange has been less than one-tenth of one percent of the futures price. An exception to this requirement, however, is individual stock futures, which in the United States have margin requirements comparable to those of the stock market.

To provide a fair **mark-to-market** process, the clearinghouse must designate the official price for determining daily gains and losses. This price is called the **settlement price** and represents an average of the final few trades of the day. It would appear that the closing price of the day would serve as the settlement price, but the closing price is a single value that can potentially be biased high or low or perhaps even manipulated by an unscrupulous trader. Hence, the clearinghouse takes an average of all trades during the closing period (as defined by each exchange).

Exhibit 1 provides an example of the marking-to-market process that occurs over a period of six trading days. We start with the assumption that the futures price is $100 when the transaction opens, the initial margin requirement is $5, and the maintenance margin requirement is $3. In Panel A, the trader takes a long position of 10 contracts on Day 0, depositing $50 ($5 times 10 contracts) as indicated in Column 3. At the end of the day, his ending balance is $50.[9] Although the trader can withdraw any funds in excess of the initial margin requirement, we shall assume that he does not do so.[10]

Exhibit 1 Mark-to-Market Example

Initial futures price = $100, Initial margin requirement = $5, Maintenance margin requirement = $3

A. Holder of Long Position of 10 Contracts

Day (1)	Beginning Balance (2)	Funds Deposited (3)	Settlement Price (4)	Futures Price Change (5)	Gain/ Loss (6)	Ending Balance (7)
0	0	50	100.00			50
1	50	0	99.20	−0.80	−8	42
2	42	0	96.00	−3.20	−32	10
3	10	40	101.00	5.00	50	100
4	100	0	103.50	2.50	25	125
5	125	0	103.00	−0.50	−5	120
6	120	0	104.00	1.00	10	130

B. Holder of Short Position of 10 Contracts

Day (1)	Beginning Balance (2)	Funds Deposited (3)	Settlement Price (4)	Futures Price Change (5)	Gain/ Loss (6)	Ending Balance (7)
0	0	50	100.00			50
1	50	0	99.20	−0.80	8	58
2	58	0	96.00	−3.20	32	90
3	90	0	101.00	5.00	−50	40

9 Technically, we are assuming that the position was opened at the settlement price on Day 0. If the position is opened earlier during the day, it would be marked to the settlement price at the end of the day.
10 Virtually all professional traders are able to deposit interest-earning assets, although many other account holders are required to deposit cash. If the deposit earns interest, there is no opportunity cost and no obvious necessity to withdraw the money to invest elsewhere.

Exhibit 1 (Continued)

Day (1)	Beginning Balance (2)	Funds Deposited (3)	Settlement Price (4)	Futures Price Change (5)	Gain/ Loss (6)	Ending Balance (7)
4	40	0	103.50	2.50	−25	15
5	15	35	103.00	−0.50	5	55
6	55	0	104.00	1.00	−10	45

The ending balance on Day 0 is then carried forward to the beginning balance on Day 1. On Day 1, the futures price moves down to 99.20, as indicated in Column 4 of Panel A. The futures price change, Column 5, is −0.80(99.20 − 100). This amount is then multiplied by the number of contracts to obtain the number in Column 6 of −0.80 × 10 = −$8. The ending balance, Column 7, is the beginning balance plus the gain or loss. The ending balance on Day 1 of $42 is above the maintenance margin requirement of $30, so no funds need to be deposited on Day 2.

On Day 2 the settlement price goes down to $96. Based on a price decrease of $3.20 per contract and 10 contracts, the loss is $32, lowering the ending balance to $10. This amount is $20 below the maintenance margin requirement. Thus, the trader will get a margin call the following morning and must deposit $40 to bring the balance up to the initial margin level of $50. This deposit is shown in Column 3 on Day 3.

Here, we must emphasize two important points. First, additional margin that must be deposited is the amount sufficient to bring the ending balance up to the initial margin requirement, not the maintenance margin requirement.[11] This additional margin is called the **variation margin**. In addition, the amount that must be deposited the following day is determined regardless of the price change the following day, which might bring the ending balance well above the initial margin requirement, as it does here, or even well below the maintenance margin requirement. Thus, another margin call could occur. Also note that when the trader closes the position, the account is marked to market to the final price at which the transaction occurs, not the settlement price that day.

Over the six-day period, the trader in this example deposited $90. The account balance at the end of the sixth day is $130—nearly a 50 percent return over six days; not bad. But look at Panel B, which shows the position of a holder of 10 short contracts over that same period. Note that the short gains when prices decrease and loses when prices increase. Here the ending balance falls below the maintenance margin requirement on Day 4, and the short must deposit $35 on Day 5. At the end of Day 6, the short has deposited $85 and the balance is $45, a loss of $40 or nearly 50 percent, which is the same $40 the long made. Both cases illustrate the leverage effect that magnifies gains and losses.

When establishing a futures position, it is important to know the price level that would trigger a margin call. In this case, it does not matter how many contracts one has. The price change would need to fall for a long position (or rise for a short position) by the difference between the initial and maintenance margin requirements. In this example, the difference between the initial and maintenance margin requirements is $5 − $3 = $2. Thus, the price would need to fall from $100 to $98 for a long position (or rise from $100 to $102 for a short position) to trigger a margin call.

11 In the stock market, one must deposit only the amount necessary to bring the balance up to the maintenance margin requirement.

As described here, when a trader receives a margin call, he is required to deposit funds sufficient to bring the account balance back up to the initial margin level. Alternatively, the trader can choose to simply close out the position as soon as possible. For example, consider the position of the long at the end of the second day when the margin balance is $10. This amount is $20 below the maintenance level, and he is required to deposit $40 to bring the balance up to the initial margin level. If he would prefer not to deposit the additional funds, he can close out the position as soon as possible the following day. Suppose, however, that the price is moving quickly at the opening on Day 3. If the price falls from $96 to $95, he has lost $10 more, wiping out the margin account balance. In fact, if it fell any further, he would have a negative margin account balance. He is still responsible for these losses. Thus, the trader could lose more than the amount of money he has placed in the margin account. The total amount of money he could lose is limited to the price per contract at which he bought, $100, times the number of contracts, 10, or $1,000. Such a loss would occur if the price fell to zero, although this is not likely. This potential loss may not seem like a lot, but it is certainly large relative to the initial margin requirement of $50. For the holder of the short position, there is no upper limit on the price and the potential loss is theoretically infinite.

EXAMPLE 1

Consider a futures contract in which the current futures price is $82. The initial margin requirement is $5, and the maintenance margin requirement is $2. You go long 20 contracts and meet all margin calls but do not withdraw any excess margin. Assume that on the first day, the contract is established at the settlement price, so there is no mark-to-market gain or loss on that day.

A Complete the table below and provide an explanation of any funds deposited.

Day	Beginning Balance	Funds Deposited	Futures Price	Price Change	Gain/Loss	Ending Balance
0			82			
1			84			
2			78			
3			73			
4			79			
5			82			
6			84			

B Determine the price level that would trigger a margin call.

Solution to A:

Day	Beginning Balance	Funds Deposited	Futures Price	Price Change	Gain/Loss	Ending Balance
0	0	100	82			100
1	100	0	84	2	40	140
2	140	0	78	−6	−120	20
3	20	80	73	−5	−100	0

Day	Beginning Balance	Funds Deposited	Futures Price	Price Change	Gain/Loss	Ending Balance
4	0	100	79	6	120	220
5	220	0	82	3	60	280
6	280	0	84	2	40	320

On Day 0, you deposit $100 because the initial margin requirement is $5 per contract and you go long 20 contracts. At the end of Day 2, the balance is down to $20, which is $20 below the $40 maintenance margin requirement ($2 per contract times 20 contracts). You must deposit enough money to bring the balance up to the initial margin requirement of $100 ($5 per contract times 20 contracts). So on Day 3, you deposit $80. The price change on Day 3 causes a gain/loss of –$100, leaving you with a balance of $0 at the end of Day 3. On Day 4, you must deposit $100 to return the balance to the initial margin level.

Solution to B:

A price decrease to $79 would trigger a margin call. This calculation is based on the fact that the difference between the initial margin requirement and the maintenance margin requirement is $3. If the futures price starts at $82, it can fall by $3 to $79 before it triggers a margin call.

Some futures contracts impose limits on the price change that can occur from one day to the next. Appropriately, these are called **price limits**. These limits are usually set as an absolute change over the previous day. Using the example above, suppose the price limit was $4. This would mean that each day, no transaction could take place higher than the previous settlement price plus $4 or lower than the previous settlement price minus $4. So the next day's settlement price cannot go beyond the price limit and thus no transaction can take place beyond the limits.

If the price at which a transaction would be made exceeds the limits, then price essentially freezes at one of the limits, which is called a **limit move**. If the price is stuck at the upper limit, it is called **limit up**; if stuck at the lower limit, it is called **limit down**. If a transaction cannot take place because the price would be beyond the limits, this situation is called **locked limit**. By the end of the day, unless the price has moved back within the limits, the settlement price will then be at one of the limits. The following day, the new range of acceptable prices is based on the settlement price plus or minus limits. The exchanges have different rules that provide for expansion or contraction of price limits under some circumstances. In addition, not all contracts have price limits.

Finally, we note that the exchanges have the power to mark contracts to market whenever they deem it necessary. Thus, they can do so during the trading day rather than wait until the end of the day. They sometimes do so when abnormally large market moves occur.

The daily settlement procedure is designed to collect losses and distribute gains in such a manner that losses are paid before becoming large enough to impose a serious risk of default. Recall that the clearinghouse guarantees to each party that it need not worry about collecting from the counterparty. The clearinghouse essentially positions itself in the middle of each contract, becoming the short counterparty to the long and the long counterparty to the short. The clearinghouse collects funds from the parties incurring losses in this daily settlement procedure and distributes them to the parties incurring gains. By doing so each day, the clearinghouse ensures that losses cannot build up. Of course, this process offers no guarantee that counterparties will not default. Some defaults do occur, but the counterparty is defaulting to the clearinghouse, which has never failed to pay off the opposite party. In the unlikely event that the clearinghouse were unable to pay, it would turn to a reserve fund or to the exchange, or it would levy a tax on exchange members to cover losses.

4 DELIVERY AND CASH SETTLEMENT

As previously described, a futures trader can close out a position before expiration. If the trader holds a long position, she can simply enter into a position to go short the same futures contract. From the clearinghouse's perspective, the trader holds both a long and short position in the same contract. These positions are considered to offset and, therefore, there is no open position in place. Most futures contracts are offset before expiration. Those that remain in place are subject to either delivery or a final cash settlement. Here we explore this process, which determines how a futures contract terminates at expiration.

When the exchange designs a futures contract, it specifies whether the contract will terminate with delivery or cash settlement. If the contract terminates in delivery, the clearinghouse selects a counterparty, usually the holder of the oldest long contract, to accept delivery. The holder of the short position then delivers the underlying to the holder of the long position, who pays the short the necessary cash for the underlying. Suppose, for example, that two days before expiration, a party goes long one futures contract at a price of $50. The following day (the day before expiration), the settlement price is $52. The trader's margin account is then marked to market by crediting it with a gain of $2. Then suppose that the next day the contract expires with the settlement price at $53. As the end of the trading day draws near, the trader has two choices. She can attempt to close out the position by selling the futures contract. The margin account would then be marked to market at the price at which she sells. If she sells close enough to the expiration, the price she sold at would be very close to the final settlement price of $53. Doing so would add $1 to her margin account balance.

The other choice is to leave the position open at the end of the trading day. Then she would have to take delivery. If that occurred, she would be required to take possession of the asset and pay the short the settlement price of the previous day. Doing so would be equivalent to paying $52 and receiving the asset. She could then sell the asset for its price of $53, netting a $1 gain, which is equivalent to the final $1 credited to her margin account if she had terminated the position at the settlement price of $53, as described above.[12]

12 The reason she pays the settlement price of the previous day is because on the previous day when her account was marked to market, she essentially created a new futures position at a price of $52. Thus, she committed to purchase the asset at expiration, just one day later, at a price of $52. The next day when the contract expires, it is then appropriate that she buy the underlying for $52.

Exhibit 2 Closeout versus Physical Delivery versus Cash Settlement

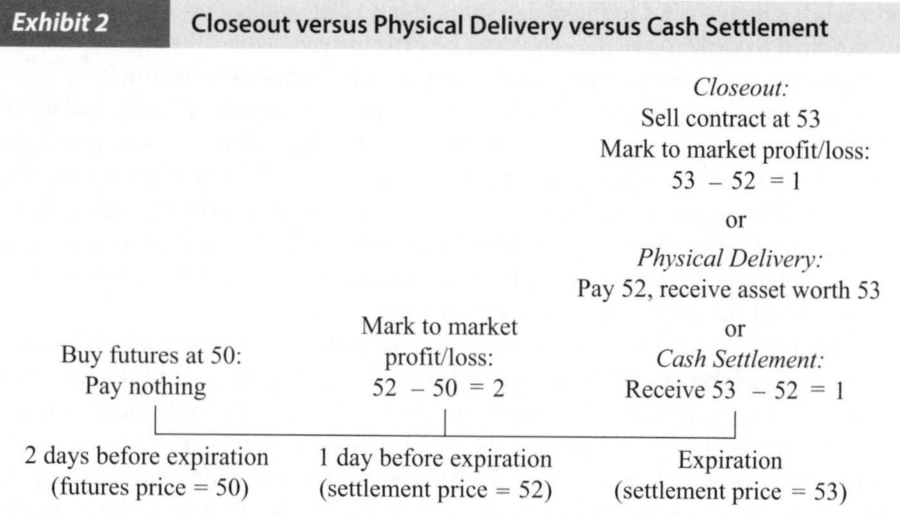

An alternative settlement procedure, which we described in the reading on forward markets and contracts, is cash settlement. The exchange designates certain futures contracts as cash-settled contracts. If the contract used in this example were cash settled, then the trader would not need to close out the position close to the end of the expiration day. She could simply leave the position open. When the contract expires, her margin account would be marked to market for a gain on the final day of $1. Cash settlement contracts have some advantages over delivery contracts, particularly with respect to significant savings in transaction costs.[13]

Exhibit 2 illustrates the equivalence of these three forms of delivery. Note, however, that because of the transaction costs of delivery, parties clearly prefer a closeout or cash settlement over physical delivery, particularly when the underlying asset is a physical commodity.

Contracts designated for delivery have a variety of features that can complicate delivery. In most cases, delivery does not occur immediately after expiration but takes place over several days. In addition, many contracts permit the short to choose when delivery takes place. For many contracts, delivery can be made any business day of the month. The delivery period usually includes the days following the last trading day of the month, which is usually in the third week of the month.

In addition, the short often has other choices regarding delivery, a major one being exactly which underlying asset is delivered. For example, a futures contract on U.S. Treasury bonds trading at the Chicago Board of Trade permits the short to deliver any of a number of U.S. Treasury bonds.[14] The wheat futures contract at the Chicago Board of Trade permits delivery of any of several types of wheat. Futures contracts calling for physical delivery of commodities often permit delivery at different locations. A given commodity delivered to one location is not the same as that commodity delivered to another because of the costs involved in transporting the commodity. The

13 Nonetheless, cash settlement has been somewhat controversial in the United States. If a contract is designated as cash settlement, it implies that the buyer of the contract never intended to actually take possession of the underlying asset. Some legislators and regulators feel that this design is against the spirit of the law, which views a futures contract as a commitment to buy the asset at a later date. Even though parties often offset futures contracts prior to expiration, the possibility of actual delivery is still present in contracts other than those settled by cash. This controversy, however, is relatively minor and has caused no serious problems or debates in recent years.

14 We shall cover this feature in more detail in Sections 6.2 and 7.2.3.

short holds the sole right to make decisions about what, when, and where to deliver, and the right to make these decisions can be extremely valuable. The right to make a decision concerning these aspects of delivery is called a **delivery option**.

Some futures contracts that call for delivery require delivery of the actual asset, and some use only a book entry. For example, in this day and age, no one physically handles U.S. Treasury bonds in the form of pieces of paper. Bonds are transferred electronically over the Federal Reserve's wire system. Other contracts, such as oil or wheat, do actually involve the physical transfer of the asset. Physical delivery is more common when the underlying is a physical commodity, whereas book entry is more common when the underlying is a financial asset.

Futures market participants use one additional delivery procedure, which is called **exchange for physicals (EFP)**. In an EFP transaction, the long and short arrange an alternative delivery procedure. For example, the Chicago Board of Trade's wheat futures contracts require delivery on certain dates at certain locations either in Chicago or in a few other specified locations in the Midwest. If the long and short agree, they could effect delivery by having the short deliver the wheat to the long in, for example, Omaha. The two parties would then report to the Chicago Board of Trade that they had settled their contract outside of the exchange's normal delivery procedures, which would be satisfactory to the exchange.

5 FUTURES EXCHANGES

A futures exchange is a legal corporate entity whose shareholders are its members. The members own memberships, more commonly called **seats**. Exchange members have the privilege of executing transactions on the exchange. Each member acts as either a **floor trader** or a **broker**. Floor traders are typically called **locals**; brokers are typically called **futures commission merchants (FCMs)**. Locals are market makers, standing ready to buy and sell by quoting a bid and an ask price. They are the primary providers of liquidity to the market. FCMs execute transactions for other parties off the exchange.

The locals on the exchange floor typically trade according to one of several distinct styles. The most common is called scalping. A **scalper** offers to buy or sell futures contracts, holding the position for only a brief period of time, perhaps just seconds. Scalpers attempt to profit by buying at the bid price and selling at the higher ask price. A **day trader** holds a position open somewhat longer but closes all positions at the end of the day.[15] A **position trader** holds positions open overnight. Day traders and position traders are quite distinct from scalpers in that they attempt to profit from the anticipated direction of the market; scalpers are trying simply to buy at the bid and sell at the ask.

Recall that futures exchanges have trading either on the floor or off the floor on electronic terminals, or in some cases, both. As previously described, floor trading in the United States takes place in pits, which are octagonal, multi-tiered areas where floor traders stand and conduct transactions. Traders wear jackets of specific colors and badges to indicate such information as what type of trader (FCM or local) they are and whom they represent.[16] As noted, to indicate a willingness to trade, a trader

15 The term "day trader" has been around the futures market for a long time but has recently acquired a new meaning in the broader financial markets. The term is now used to describe individual investors who trade stocks, often over the internet, during the day for a living or as a hobby. In fact, the term has even been used in a somewhat pejorative manner, in that day traders are often thought of as naïve investors speculating wildly with money they can ill afford to lose.

16 For example, an FCM or local could be trading for himself or could represent a company.

shouts and uses a set of standard hand signals. A trade is consummated by two traders agreeing on a price and a number of contracts. These traders might not actually say anything to each other; they may simply use a combination of hand signals and/or eye contact to agree on a transaction. When a transaction is agreed on, the traders fill out small paper forms and turn them over to clerks, who then see that the transactions are entered into the system and reported.

Exhibit 3 The World's 20 Leading Futures Exchanges

Exchange and Location	Volume in 2001 (Number of Contracts)
Eurex (Germany and Switzerland)	435,141,707
Chicago Mercantile Exchange (United States)	315,971,885
Chicago Board of Trade (United States)	209,988,002
London International Financial Futures and Options Exchange (United Kingdom)	161,522,775
Bolsa de Mercadorias & Futuros (Brazil)	94,174,452
New York Mercantile Exchange (United States)	85,039,984
Tokyo Commodity Exchange (Japan)	56,538,245
London Metal Exchange (United Kingdom)	56,224,495
Paris Bourse SA (France)	42,042,673
Sydney Futures Exchange (Australia)	34,075,508
Korea Stock Exchange (Korea)	31,502,184
Singapore Exchange (Singapore)	30,606,546
Central Japan Commodity Exchange (Japan)	27,846,712
International Petroleum Exchange (United Kingdom)	26,098,207
OM Stockholm Exchange (Sweden)	23,408,198
Tokyo Grain Exchange (Japan)	22,707,808
New York Board of Trade (United States)	14,034,168
MEFF Renta Variable (Spain)	13,108,293
Tokyo Stock Exchange (Japan)	12,465,433
South African Futures Exchange (South Africa)	11,868,242

Source: Futures Industry, January/February 2002.

Each trader is required to have an account at a clearing firm. The clearing firms are the actual members of the clearinghouse. The clearinghouse deals only with the clearing firms, which then deal with their individual and institutional customers.

In electronic trading, the principles remain essentially the same but the traders do not stand in the pits. In fact, they do not see each other at all. They sit at computer terminals, which enable them to see the bids and offers of other traders. Transactions are executed by the click of a computer mouse or an entry from a keyboard.

Exhibit 3 lists the world's 20 leading futures exchanges in 2001, ranked by trading volume. Trading volume can be a misleading measure of the size of a futures markets; nonetheless, it is the measure primarily used. The structure of global futures exchanges has changed considerably in recent years. Exchanges in the United States, primarily the Chicago Board of Trade and the Chicago Mercantile Exchange, were clearly the world leaders in the past. Note that the volume leader now, however, is Eurex, the combined German–Swiss exchange. Eurex has been so successful partly because of its decision to be an all-electronic futures exchange, whereas the Chicago exchanges are still primarily pit-trading exchanges. Note the popularity of futures trading in Japan; four of the 20 leading exchanges are Japanese.

6 TYPES OF FUTURES CONTRACTS

The different types of futures contracts are generally divided into two main groups: commodity futures and financial futures. Commodity futures cover traditional agricultural, metal, and petroleum products. Financial futures include stocks, bonds, and currencies. Exhibit 4 gives a broad overview of the most active types of futures contracts traded on global futures exchanges. These contracts are those covered by the *Wall Street Journal* on the date indicated.

Exhibit 4 Most-Active Global Futures Contracts as Covered by the *Wall Street Journal*, 18 June 2002

Commodity Futures	Financial Futures	
Corn (CBOT)	Treasury Bonds (CBOT)	Euro (CME)
Oats (CBOT)	Treasury Notes (CBOT)	Euro–Sterling (NYBOT)
Soybeans (CBOT)	10-Year Agency Notes (CBOT)	Euro–U.S. Dollar (NYBOT)
Soybean Meal (CBOT)	10-Year Interest Rate Swaps (CBOT)	Euro–Yen (NYBOT)
Soybean Oil (CBOT)	2-Year Agency Notes (CBOT)	Dow Jones Industrial Average (CBOT)
Wheat (CBOT, KCBT, MGE)	5-Year Treasury Notes (CBOT)	Mini Dow Jones Industrial Average (CBOT)
Canola (WPG)	2-Year Treasury Notes (CBOT)	S&P 500 Index (CME)
Barley (WPG)	Federal Funds (CBOT)	Mini S&P 500 Index (CME)
Feeder Cattle (CME)	Municipal Bond Index (CBOT)	S&P Midcap 400 Index (CME)
Live Cattle (CME)	Treasury Bills (CME)	Nikkei 225 (CME)
Lean Hogs (CME)	1-Month LIBOR (CME)	NASDAQ 100 Index (CME)
Pork Bellies (CME)	Eurodollar (CME)	Mini Nasdaq Index (CME)
Milk (CME)	Euroyen (CME, SGX)	Goldman Sachs Commodity Index (CME)
Lumber (CME)	Short Sterling (LIFFE)	Russell 1000 Index (CME)
Cocoa (NYBOT)	Long Gilt (LIFFE)	Russell 2000 Index (CME)
Coffee (NYBOT)	3-Month Euribor (LIFFE)	NYSE Composite Index (NYBOT)
World Sugar (NYBOT)	3-Month Euroswiss (LIFFE)	U.S. Dollar Index (NYBOT)
Domestic Sugar (NYBOT)	Canadian Bankers Acceptance (ME)	Share Price Index (SFE)
Cotton (NYBOT)	10-Year Canadian Government Bond (ME)	CAC 40 Stock Index (MATIF)
Orange Juice (NYBOT)	10-Year Euro Notional Bond (MATIF)	Xetra Dax (EUREX)
Copper (NYMEX)	3-Month Euribor (MATIF)	FTSE 200 Index (LIFFE)
Gold (NYMEX)	3-Year Commonwealth T-Bonds (SFE)	Dow Jones Euro Stoxx 50 Index (EUREX)
Platinum (NYMEX)	5-Year German Euro Government Bond (EUREX)	Dow Jones Stoxx 50 Index (EUREX)

Exhibit 4 (Continued)

Commodity Futures	Financial Futures
Palladium (NYMEX)	10-Year German Euro Government Bond (EUREX)
Silver (NYMEX)	2-Year German Euro Government Bond (EUREX)
Crude Oil (NYMEX)	Japanese Yen (CME)
No. 2 Heating Oil (NYMEX)	Canadian Dollar (CME)
Unleaded Gasoline (NYMEX)	British Pound (CME)
Natural Gas (NYMEX)	Swiss Franc (CME)
Brent Crude Oil (IPEX)	Australian Dollar (CME)
Gas Oil (IPEX)	Mexican Peso (CME)

Exchange codes: CBOT (Chicago Board of Trade), CME (Chicago Mercantile Exchange), LIFFE (London International Financial Futures Exchange), WPG (Winnipeg Grain Exchange), EUREX (Eurex), NYBOT (New York Board of Trade), IPEX (International Petroleum Exchange), MATIF (Marché a Terme International de France), ME (Montreal Exchange), MGE (Minneapolis Grain Exchange), SFE (Sydney Futures Exchange), SGX (Singapore Exchange), KCBT (Kansas City Board of Trade), NYMEX (New York Mercantile Exchange)
Note: These are not the only global futures contracts but are those covered in the *Wall Street Journal* on the date given and represent the most active contracts at that time.

Our primary focus in this reading is on financial and currency futures contracts. Within the financials group, our main interest is on interest rate and bond futures, stock index futures, and currency futures. We may occasionally make reference to a commodity futures contract, but that will primarily be for illustrative purposes. In the following subsections, we introduce the primary contracts we shall focus on. These are U.S. contracts, but they resemble most types of futures contracts found on exchanges throughout the world. Full contract specifications for these and other contracts are available on the websites of the futures exchanges, which are easy to locate with most internet search engines.

6.1 Short-Term Interest Rate Futures Contracts

The primary short-term interest rate futures contracts are those on U.S. Treasury bills and Eurodollars on the Chicago Mercantile Exchange.

6.1.1 *Treasury Bill Futures*

The Treasury bill contract, launched in 1976, was the first interest rate futures contract. It is based on a 90-day U.S. Treasury bill, one of the most important U.S. government debt instruments (described in the reading on forward markets and contracts). The Treasury bill, or T-bill, is a discount instrument, meaning that its price equals the face value minus a discount representing interest. The discount equals the face value multiplied by the quoted rate times the days to maturity divided by 360. Thus, if a 180-day T-bill is selling at a discount of 4 percent, its price per \$1 par is 1 – 0.04(180/360) = 0.98. An investor who buys the bill and holds it to maturity would receive \$1 at maturity, netting a gain of \$0.02.

The futures contract is based on a 90-day \$1,000,000 U.S. Treasury bill. Thus, on any given day, the contract trades with the understanding that a 90-day T-bill will be delivered at expiration. While the contract is trading, its price is quoted as 100 minus the rate quoted as a percent priced into the contract by the futures market. This value, 100 – Rate, is known as the IMM Index; IMM stands for International Monetary Market, a division of the Chicago Mercantile Exchange.

The IMM Index is a reported and publicly available price; however, it is not the actual futures price, which is

$$100[1 - (\text{Rate}/100)(90/360)]$$

For example, suppose on a given day the rate priced into the contract is 6.25 percent. Then the quoted price will be 100 – 6.25 = 93.75. The actual futures price would be

$$\$1,000,000[1 - 0.0625(90/360)] = \$984,375$$

Recall, however, that except for the small margin deposit, a futures transaction does not require any cash to be paid up front. As trading takes place, the rate fluctuates with market interest rates and the associated IMM Index price changes accordingly. The actual futures price, as calculated above, also fluctuates according to the above formula, but interestingly, that price is not very important. The same information can be captured more easily by referencing the IMM Index than by calculating the actual price.

Suppose, for example, that a trader had his account marked to market to the above price, 6.25 in terms of the rate, 93.75 in terms of the IMM Index, and \$984,375 in terms of the actual futures price. Now suppose the rate goes to 6.50, an increase of 0.25 or 25 basis points. The IMM Index declines to 93.50, and the actual futures price drops to

$$\$1,000,000[1 - 0.065(90/360)] = \$983,750$$

Thus, the actual futures price decreased by \$984,375 – \$983,750 = \$625. A trader who is long would have a loss of \$625; a trader who is short would have a gain of \$625.

This \$625 gain or loss can be arrived at more directly, however, by simply noting that each basis point move is equivalent to \$25.[17] This special design of the contract makes it easy for floor traders to do the necessary arithmetic in their heads. For example, if floor traders observe the IMM Index move from 93.75 to 93.50, they immediately know that it has moved down 25 basis points and that 25 basis points times \$25 per basis point is a loss of \$625. The minimum tick size is one-half basis point or \$12.50.

T-bill futures contracts have expirations of the current month, the next month, and the next four months of March, June, September, and December. Because of the small trading volume, however, only the closest expiration has much trading volume, and even that one is only lightly traded. T-bill futures expire specifically on the Monday of the week of the third Wednesday each month and settle in cash rather than physical delivery of the T-bill, as described in Section 4.

As important as Treasury bills are in U.S. financial markets, however, today this futures contract is barely active. The Eurodollar contract is considered much more important because it reflects the interest rate on a dollar borrowed by a high-quality private borrower. The rates on T-bills are considered too heavily influenced by U.S. government policies, budget deficits, government funding plans, politics, and Federal Reserve monetary policy. Although unquestionably Eurodollar rates are affected by those factors, market participants consider them much less directly influenced. But in spite of this relative inactivity, T-bill futures are useful instruments for illustrating certain principles of futures market pricing and trading. Accordingly, we shall use them on some occasions. For now, however, we turn to the Eurodollar futures contract.

17 Expressed mathematically, \$1,000,000 [0.0001(90/360)] = \$25. In other words, any move in the last digit of the rate (a basis point) affects the actual futures price by \$25.

6.1.2 *Eurodollar Futures*

Recall that in the reading on forward markets and contracts, we devoted a good bit of effort to understanding Eurodollar forward contracts, known as FRAs. These contracts pay off based on LIBOR on a given day. The Eurodollar futures contract of the Chicago Mercantile Exchange is based on $1 million notional principal of 90-day Eurodollars. Specifically, the underlying is the rate on a 90-day dollar-denominated time deposit issued by a bank in London. This deposit is called a Eurodollar time deposit, and the rate is referred to as LIBOR (London Interbank Offer Rate). On a given day, the futures contract trades based on the understanding that at expiration, the official Eurodollar rate, as compiled by the British Bankers Association (BBA), will be the rate at which the final settlement of the contract is made. While the contract is trading, its price is quoted as 100 minus the rate priced into the contract by futures traders. Like its counterpart in the T-bill futures market, this value, 100 – Rate, is also known as the IMM Index.

As in the T-bill futures market, on a given day, if the rate priced into the contract is 5.25 percent, the quoted price will be 100 – 5.25 = 94.75. With each contract based on $1 million notional principal of Eurodollars, the actual futures price is

$$\$1{,}000{,}000[1 - 0.0525(90/360)] = \$986{,}875$$

Like the T-bill contract, the actual futures price moves $25 for every basis point move in the rate or IMM Index price.

As with all futures contracts, the price fluctuates on a daily basis and margin accounts are marked to market according to the exchange's official settlement price. At expiration, the final settlement price is the official rate quoted on a 90-day Eurodollar time deposit by the BBA. That rate determines the final settlement. Eurodollar futures contracts do not permit actual delivery of a Eurodollar time deposit; rather, they settle in cash, as described in Section 4.

The Eurodollar futures contract is one of the most active in the world. Because its rate is based on LIBOR, it is widely used by dealers in swaps, FRAs, and interest rate options to hedge their positions taken in dollar-denominated over-the-counter interest rate derivatives. Such derivatives usually use LIBOR as the underlying rate.

It is important to note, however, that there is a critical distinction between the manner in which the interest calculation is built into the Eurodollar futures contract and the manner in which interest is imputed on actual Eurodollar time deposits. Recall from the reading on forward markets and contracts that when a bank borrows $1 million at a rate of 5 percent for 90 days, the amount it will owe in 90 days is

$$\$1{,}000{,}000[1 + 0.05(90/360)] = \$1{,}012{,}500$$

Interest on Eurodollar time deposits is computed on an add-on basis to the principal. As described in this section, however, it appears that in computing the futures price, interest is deducted from the principal so that a bank borrowing $1,000,000 at a rate of 5 percent would receive

$$\$1{,}000{,}000[1 - 0.05(90/360)] = \$987{,}500$$

and would pay back $1,000,000. This procedure is referred to as discount interest and is used in the T-bill market.

The discount interest computation associated with Eurodollar futures is merely a convenience contrived by the futures exchange to facilitate quoting prices in a manner already familiar to its traders, who were previously trading T-bill futures. This inconsistency between the ways in which Eurodollar futures and Eurodollar spot transactions are constructed causes some pricing problems, as we shall see in Section 7.2.2.

The minimum tick size for Eurodollar futures is 1 basis point or $25. The available expirations are the next two months plus March, June, September, and December. The expirations go out about 10 years, a reflection of their use by over-the-counter derivatives dealers to hedge their positions in long-term interest rate derivatives. Eurodollar futures expire on the second business day on which London banks are open before the third Wednesday of the month and terminate with a cash settlement.

6.2 Intermediate- and Long-Term Interest Rate Futures Contracts

In U.S. markets, the primary interest-rate-related instruments of intermediate and long maturities are U.S. Treasury notes and bonds. The U.S. government issues both instruments: Treasury notes have an original maturity of 2 to 10 years, and Treasury bonds have an original maturity of more than 10 years. Futures contracts on these instruments are very actively traded on the Chicago Board of Trade. For the most part, there are no real differences in the contract characteristics for Treasury note and Treasury bond futures; the underlying bonds differ slightly, but the futures contracts are qualitatively the same. We shall focus here on one of the most active instruments, the U.S. Treasury bond futures contract.

The contract is based on the delivery of a U.S. Treasury bond with any coupon but with a maturity of at least 15 years. If the deliverable bond is callable, it cannot be callable for at least 15 years from the delivery date.[18] These specifications mean that there are potentially a large number of deliverable bonds, which is exactly the way the Chicago Board of Trade, the Federal Reserve, and the U.S. Treasury want it. They do not want a potential run on a single issue that might distort prices. By having multiple deliverable issues, however, the contract must be structured with some fairly complicated procedures to adjust for the fact that the short can deliver whatever bond he chooses from among the eligible bonds. This choice gives the short a potentially valuable option and puts the long at a disadvantage. Moreover, it complicates pricing the contract, because the identity of the underlying bond is not clear. Although when referring to a futures contract on a 90-day Eurodollar time deposit we are relatively clear about the underlying instrument, a futures contract on a long-term Treasury bond does not allow us the same clarity.

To reduce the confusion, the exchange declares a standard or hypothetical version of the deliverable bond. This hypothetical deliverable bond has a 6 percent coupon. When a trader holding a short position at expiration delivers a bond with a coupon greater (less) than 6 percent, she receives an upward (a downward) adjustment to the price paid for the bond by the long. The adjustment is done by means of a device called the **conversion factor**. In brief, the conversion factor is the price of a $1.00 par bond with a coupon and maturity equal to those of the deliverable bond and a yield of 6 percent. Thus, if the short delivers a bond with a coupon greater (less) than 6 percent, the conversion factor exceeds (is less than) 1.0.[19] The amount the long pays the short is the futures price at expiration multiplied by the conversion factor. Thus, delivery of a bond with a coupon greater (less) than the standard amount, 6 percent, results in the short receiving an upward (a downward) adjustment to the amount received. A number of other technical considerations are also involved in determining the delivery price.[20]

18 The U.S. government no longer issues callable bonds but has done so in the past.

19 This statement is true regardless of the maturity of the deliverable bond. Any bond with a coupon in excess of its yield is worth more than its par value.

20 For example, the actual procedure for delivery of U.S. Treasury bonds is a three-day process starting with the short notifying the exchange of intention to make delivery. Delivery actually occurs several days later. In addition, as is the custom in U.S. bond markets, the quoted price does not include the accrued interest. Accordingly, an adjustment must be made.

The conversion factor system is designed to put all bonds on equal footing. Ideally, application of the conversion factor would result in the short finding no preference for delivery of any one bond over any other. That is not the case, however, because the complex relationships between bond prices cannot be reduced to a simple linear adjustment, such as the conversion factor method. As a result, some bonds are cheaper to deliver than others. When making the delivery decision, the short compares the cost of buying a given bond on the open market with the amount she would receive upon delivery of that bond. The former will always exceed the latter; otherwise, a clear arbitrage opportunity would be available. The most attractive bond for delivery would be the one in which the amount received for delivering the bond is largest relative to the amount paid on the open market for the bond. The bond that minimizes this loss is referred to as the **cheapest-to-deliver** bond.

At any time during the life of a Treasury bond futures contract, traders can identify the cheapest-to-deliver bond. Determining the amount received at delivery is straightforward; it equals the current futures price times the conversion factor for a given bond. To determine the amount the bond would cost at expiration, one calculates the forward price of the bond, positioned at the delivery date. Of course, this is just a forward computation; circumstances could change by the expiration date. But this forward calculation gives a picture of circumstances as they currently stand and identifies which bond is currently the cheapest to deliver. That bond is then considered the bond most likely to be delivered. Recall that one problem with this futures contract is that the identity of the underlying bond is unclear. Traders traditionally treat the cheapest to deliver as the bond that underlies the contract. As time passes and interest rates change, however, the cheapest-to-deliver bond can change. Thus, the bond underlying the futures contract can change, adding an element of uncertainty to the pricing and trading of this contract.

With this complexity associated with the U.S. Treasury bond futures contract, one might suspect that it is less actively traded. In fact, the opposite is true: Complexity creates extraordinary opportunities for gain for those who understand what is going on and can identify the cheapest bond to deliver.

The Chicago Board of Trade's U.S. Treasury bond futures contract covers $100,000 par value of U.S. Treasury bonds. The expiration months are March, June, September, and December. They expire on the seventh business day preceding the last business day of the month and call for actual delivery, through the Federal Reserve's wire system, of the Treasury bond. Prices are quoted in points and 32nds, meaning that you will see prices like 98 18/32, which equals 98.5625. For a contract covering $100,000 par value, for example, the price is $98,562.50. The minimum tick size is 1/32, which is $31.25.

In addition to the futures contract on the long-term government bond, there are also very similar futures contracts on intermediate-term government bonds. The Chicago Board of Trade's contracts on 2-, 5-, and 10-year Treasury notes are very actively traded and are almost identical to its long-term bond contract, except for the exact specification of the underlying instrument. Intermediate and long-term government bonds are important instruments in every country's financial markets. They give the best indication of the long-term default-free interest rate and are often viewed as a benchmark bond for various comparisons in financial markets.[21] Accordingly, futures contracts on such bonds play an important role in a country's financial markets and are almost always among the most actively traded contracts in futures markets around the world.

21 For example, the default risk of a corporate bond is often measured as the difference between the corporate bond yield and the yield on a Treasury bond or note of comparable maturity. Fixed rates on interest rate swaps are usually quoted as a spread over the rate on a Treasury bond or note of comparable maturity.

If the underlying instrument is not widely available and not actively traded, the viability of a futures contract on it becomes questionable. The reduction seen in U.S. government debt in the late 1990s has led to a reduction in the supply of intermediate and long-term government bonds, and some concern has arisen over this fact. In the United States, some efforts have been made to promote the long-term debt of Fannie Mae and Freddie Mac as substitute benchmark bonds.[22] It remains to be seen whether such efforts will be necessary and, if so, whether they will succeed.

6.3 Stock Index Futures Contracts

One of the most successful types of futures contracts of all time is the class of futures on stock indices. Probably the most successful has been the Chicago Mercantile Exchange's contract on the Standard and Poor's 500 Stock Index. Called the S&P 500 Stock Index futures, this contract premiered in 1982 and has benefited from the widespread acceptance of the S&P 500 Index as a stock market benchmark. The contract is quoted in terms of a price on the same order of magnitude as the S&P 500 itself. For example, if the S&P 500 Index is at 1183, a two-month futures contract might be quoted at a price of, say, 1187. We shall explain how to determine a stock index futures price in Section 7.3.

The contract implicitly contains a multiplier, which is (appropriately) multiplied by the quoted futures price to produce the actual futures price. The multiplier for the S&P 500 futures is \$250. Thus, when you hear of a futures price of 1187, the actual price is 1187(\$250) = \$296,750.

S&P 500 futures expirations are March, June, September, and December and go out about two years, although trading is active only in the nearest two to three expirations. With occasional exceptions, the contracts expire on the Thursday preceding the third Friday of the month. Given the impracticality of delivering a portfolio of the 500 stocks in the index combined according to their relative weights in the index, the contract is structured to provide for cash settlement at expiration.

The S&P 500 is not the only active stock index futures contract. In fact, the Chicago Mercantile Exchange has a smaller version of the S&P 500 contract, called the Mini S&P 500, which has a multiplier of \$50 and trades only electronically. Other widely traded contracts in the United States are on the Dow Jones Industrials, the S&P Midcap 400, and the NASDAQ 100. Virtually every developed country has a stock index futures contract based on the leading equities of that country. Well-known stock index futures contracts around the world include the United Kingdom's FTSE 100 (pronounced "Footsic 100"), Japan's Nikkei 225, France's CAC 40, and Germany's DAX 30.

6.4 Currency Futures Contracts

In the reading on forward markets and contracts, we described forward contracts on foreign currencies. There are also futures contracts on foreign currencies. Although the forward market for foreign currencies is much more widely used, the futures market is still quite active. In fact, currency futures were the first futures contracts not based

22 Fannie Mae is the Federal National Mortgage Association, and Freddie Mac is the Federal Home Loan Mortgage Corporation. These institutions were formerly U.S. government agencies that issued debt to raise funds to buy and sell mortgages and mortgage-backed securities. These institutions are now publicly traded corporations but are considered to have extremely low default risk because of their critical importance in U.S. mortgage markets. It is believed that an implicit Federal government guarantee is associated with their debt. Nonetheless, it seems unlikely that the debt of these institutions could take over that of the U.S. government as a benchmark. The Chicago Board of Trade has offered futures contracts on the bonds of these organizations, but the contracts have not traded actively.

on physical commodities. Thus, they are sometimes referred to as the first financial futures contracts, and their initial success paved the way for the later introduction of interest rate and stock index futures.

Compared with forward contracts on currencies, currency futures contracts are much smaller in size. In the United States, these contracts trade at the Chicago Mercantile Exchange with a small amount of trading at the New York Board of Trade. In addition there is some trading on exchanges outside the United States. The characteristics we describe below refer to the Chicago Mercantile Exchange's contract.

In the United States, the primary currencies on which trading occurs are the euro, Canadian dollar, Swiss franc, Japanese yen, British pound, Mexican peso, and Australian dollar. Each contract has a designated size and a quotation unit. For example, the euro contract covers €125,000 and is quoted in dollars per euro. A futures price such as \$0.8555 is stated in dollars and converts to a contract price of

125,000(\$0.8555) = \$106,937.50

The Japanese yen futures price is structured somewhat differently. Because of the large number of yen per dollar, the contract covers ¥12,500,000 and is quoted without two zeroes that ordinarily precede the price. For example, a price might be stated as 0.8205, but this actually represents a price of 0.008205, which converts to a contract price of

12,500,000(0.008205) = \$102,562.50

Alternatively, a quoted price of 0.8205 can be viewed as 1/0.008205 = ¥121.88 per dollar.

Currency futures contracts expire in the months of March, June, September, and December. The specific expiration is the second business day before the third Wednesday of the month. Currency futures contracts call for actual delivery, through book entry, of the underlying currency.

We have briefly examined the different types of futures contracts of interest to us. Of course there are a variety of similar instruments trading on futures exchanges around the world. Our purpose, however, is not to provide institutional details, which can be obtained at the websites of the world's futures exchanges, but rather to enhance your understanding of the important principles necessary to function in the world of derivatives.

Until now we have made reference to prices of futures contracts. Accordingly, let us move forward and examine the pricing of futures contracts.

END OPTIONAL SEGMENT

7 PRICING AND VALUATION OF FUTURES CONTRACTS

In the reading on forward markets and contracts, we devoted considerable effort to understanding the pricing and valuation of forward contracts. We first discussed the notion of what it means to *price* a forward contract in contrast to what it means to *value* a forward contract. Recall that pricing means to assign a fixed price or rate at which the underlying will be bought by the long and sold by the short at expiration. In assigning a forward price, we set the price such that the value of the contract is zero at the start. A zero-value contract means that the present value of the payments promised by each party to the other is the same, a result in keeping with the fact that neither party pays the other any money at the start. The value of the contract to the long is the present value of the payments promised by the short to the long minus the present value of the payments promised by the long to the short. Although the value is zero at the start, during the life of the contract, the value will fluctuate as market conditions change; the original forward contract price, however, stays the same.

In the reading on forward markets and contracts, we presented numerous examples of how to apply the concept of pricing and valuation when dealing with forward contracts on stocks, bonds, currencies, and interest rates. To illustrate the concepts of pricing and valuation, we started with a generic forward contract. Accordingly, we do so here in the futures reading. We assume no transaction costs.

7.1 Generic Pricing and Valuation of a Futures Contract

As we did with forward contracts, we start by illustrating the time frame within which we are working:

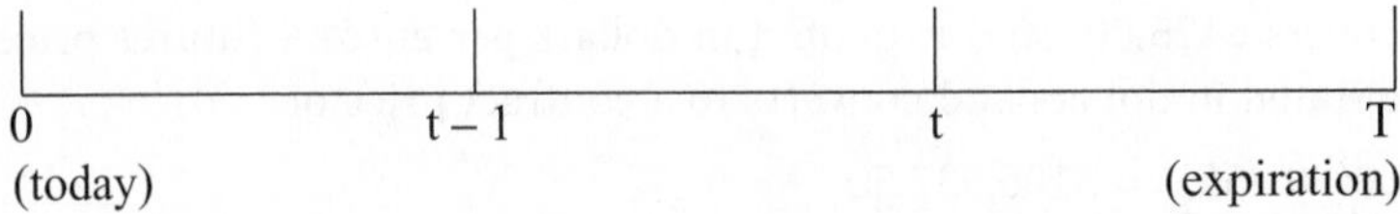

Today is time 0. The expiration date of the futures contract is time T. Times t – 1 and t are arbitrary times between today and the expiration and are the points at which the contract will be marked to market. Thus, we can think of the three periods depicted above, 0 to t – 1, t – 1 to t, and t to T, as three distinct trading days with times t – 1, t, and T being the end of each of the three days.

The price of the underlying asset in the spot market is denoted as S_0 at time 0, S_{t-1} at time t – 1, S_t at time t, and S_T at time T. We denote the futures contract price at time 0 as $f_0(T)$. This notation indicates that $f_0(T)$ is the price of a futures contract at time 0 that expires at time T. Unlike forward contract prices, however, futures prices fluctuate in an open and competitive market. The marking-to-market process results in each futures contract being terminated every day and reinitiated. Thus, we not only have a futures price set at time 0 but we also have a new one at time t – 1, at time t, and at time T. In other words,

$f_0(T)$ = price of a futures contract at time 0 that expires at time T
$f_{t-1}(T)$ = price of a futures contract at time t – 1 that expires at time T
$f_t(T)$ = price of a futures contract at time t that expires at time T
$f_T(T)$ = price of a futures contract at time T that expires at time T

Note, however, that $f_{t-1}(T)$ and $f_t(T)$ are also the prices of contracts newly established at times t – 1 and t for delivery at time T. Futures contracts are homogeneous and fungible. Any contract for delivery of the underlying at T is equivalent to any other contract, regardless of when the contracts were created.[23]

23 As an analogy from the bond markets, consider a 9 percent coupon bond, originally issued with 10 years remaining. Three years later, that bond is a 9 percent seven-year bond. Consider a newly issued 9 percent coupon bond with seven years maturity and the same issuer. As long as the coupon dates are the same and all other terms are the same, these two bonds are fungible and are perfect substitutes for each other.

The value of the futures contract is denoted as $v_0(T)$. This notation indicates that $v_0(T)$ is the value at time 0 of a futures contract expiring at time T. We are also interested in the values of the contract prior to expiration, such as at time t, denoted as $v_t(T)$, as well as the value of the contract at expiration, denoted as $v_T(T)$.[24]

7.1.1 *The Futures Price at Expiration*

Now suppose we are at time T. The spot price is S_T and the futures price is $f_T(T)$. To avoid an arbitrage opportunity, *the futures price must converge to the spot price at expiration*:

$$f_T(T) = S_T \quad (1)$$

Consider what would happen if this were not the case. If $f_T(T) < S_T$, a trader could buy the futures contract, let it immediately expire, pay $f_T(T)$ to take delivery of the underlying, and receive an asset worth S_T. The trader would have paid $f_T(T)$ and received an asset worth S_T, which is greater, at no risk. If $f_T(T) > S_T$, the trader would go short the futures, buy the asset for S_T, make delivery, and receive $f_T(T)$ for the asset, for which he paid a lesser amount. Only if $f_T(T) = S_T$ does this arbitrage opportunity go away. Thus, the futures price must equal the spot price at expiration.

Another way to understand this point is to recall that by definition, a futures contract calls for the delivery of an asset at expiration at a price determined when the transaction is initiated. If expiration is right now, a futures transaction is equivalent to a spot transaction, so the futures price must equal the spot price.

7.1.2 *Valuation of a Futures Contract*

Let us consider how to determine the value of a futures contract. We already agreed that because no money changes hands, the value of a forward contract at the initiation date is zero. For the same reason, *the value of a futures contract at the initiation date is zero*. Thus,

$$v_0(T) = 0 \quad (2)$$

Now let us determine the value of the contract during its life. Suppose we are at the end of the second day, at time t. In our diagram above, this point would be essentially at time t, but perhaps just an instant before it. So let us call it time t−. An instant later, we call the time point t+. In both cases, the futures price is $f_t(T)$. The contract was previously marked to market at the end of day t − 1 to a price of $f_{t-1}(T)$. An instant later when the futures account is marked to market, the trader will receive a gain of $f_t(T) - f_{t-1}(T)$. We can reasonably ignore the present value difference of receiving this money an instant later. Let us now state more formally that the value of a futures contract is

$v_{t-}(T) = f_t(T) - f_{t-1}(T)$ *an instant before the account is marked to market*

$v_{t+}(T) = 0$ *as soon as the account is marked to market* (3)

24 It is important at this point to make some comments about notation. First, note that in the reading on forward markets and contracts, we use an uppercase F and V for forward contracts; here we use lowercase f and v for futures contracts. Also we follow the pattern of using subscripts to indicate a price or value at a particular point in time. The arguments in parentheses refer to characteristics of a contract. Thus, in the reading on forward markets and contracts, we described the price of a forward contract as F(0,T) meaning the price of a forward contract initiated at time 0 and expiring at time T. This price does not fluctuate during the life of the contract. A futures contract, however, reprices on a daily basis. Its original time of initiation does not matter—it is reinitiated every day. Hence, futures prices are indicated by notation such as $f_0(T)$ and $f_t(T)$. We follow a similar pattern for value, using $V_0(0,T)$, $V_t(0,T)$, and $V_T(0,T)$ for forwards and $v_0(T)$, $v_t(T)$, and $v_T(T)$ for futures.

Suppose, however, that the trader is at a time j during the second trading day, between t – 1 and t. The accumulated gain or loss since the account was last marked to market is $f_j(T) - f_{t-1}(T)$. If the trader closes the position out, he would receive or be charged this amount at the end of the day. So the value at time j would be $f_j(T) - f_{t-1}(T)$ discounted back from the end of the day at time t until time j—that is, a fraction of a day. It is fairly routine to ignore this intraday interest. Thus, in general we say that *the value of a futures contract before it has been marked to market is the gain or loss accumulated since the account was last marked to market.*

So to recap, the value of a futures contract is the accumulated gain or loss since the last mark to market. The holder of a futures contract has a claim or liability on this amount. Once that claim is captured or the liability paid through the mark-to-market process, the contract is repriced to its current market price and the claim or liability goes back to a value of zero. Using these results, determining the value of a futures contract at expiration is easy. An instant before expiration, it is simply the accumulated profit since the last mark to market. At expiration, the value goes back to zero. With respect to the value of the futures, expiration is no different from any other day. Exhibit 5 summarizes the principles of valuation.

In the reading on forward markets and contracts, we devoted considerable effort toward understanding how forward contracts are valued. When holding positions in forward contracts, we are forced to assign values to instruments that do not trade in an open market with widely disseminated prices. Thus, it is important that we understand how forward contracts are valued. When dealing with futures contracts, the process is considerably simplified. Because futures contracts are generally quite actively traded, there is a market with reliable prices that provides all of the information we need. For futures contracts, we see that the value is simply the observable price change since the last mark to market.

Exhibit 5 **The Value of a Futures Contract Before and After Marking to Market**

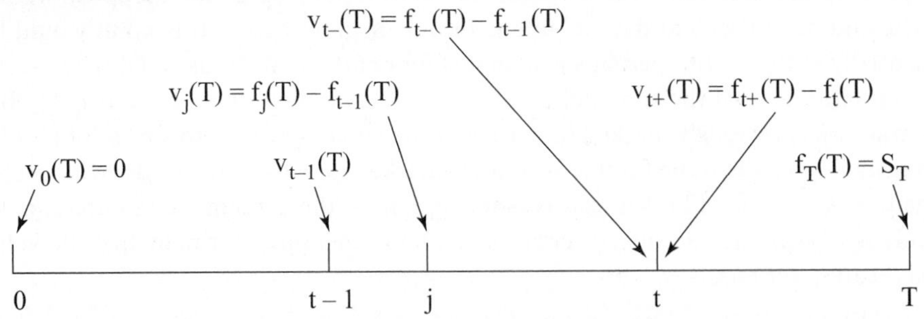

7.1.3 *Forward and Futures Prices*

For all financial instruments, it is important to be able to determine whether the price available in the market is an appropriate one. Hence, we engage in the process of "pricing" the financial instrument. A major objective of this reading is to determine the appropriate price of a futures contract. Given the similarity between futures and forward prices, however, we can benefit from studying forward contract pricing, which was covered in the reading on forward markets and contracts. But first, we must look at the similarities and differences between forward and futures contracts.

Recall that futures contracts settle daily and are essentially free of default risk. Forward contracts settle only at expiration and are subject to default risk. Yet both types of contracts allow the party to purchase or sell the underlying asset at a price agreed on in advance. It seems intuitive that futures prices and forward prices would be relatively close to each other.

The issues involved in demonstrating the relationship between futures and forward prices are relatively technical and beyond the scope of this reading. We can, however, take a brief and fairly nontechnical look at the question. First let us ignore the credit risk issue. We shall assume that the forward contract participants are prime credit risks. We focus only on the technical distinction caused by the daily marking to market.

The day before expiration, both the futures contract and the forward contract have one day to go. At expiration, they will both settle. These contracts are therefore the same. At any other time prior to expiration, futures and forward prices can be the same or different. If interest rates are constant or at least known, any effect of the addition or subtraction of funds from the marking-to-market process can be shown to be neutral. If interest rates are positively correlated with futures prices, traders with long positions will prefer futures over forwards, because they will generate gains when interest rates are going up, and traders can invest those gains for higher returns. Also, traders will incur losses when interest rates are going down and can borrow to cover those losses at lower rates. Because traders holding long positions prefer the marking to market of futures over forwards when futures prices are positively correlated with interest rates, futures will carry higher prices than forwards. Conversely, when futures prices are negatively correlated with interest rates, traders will prefer not to mark to market, so forward contracts will carry higher prices.

Because interest rates and fixed-income security prices move in opposite directions, interest rate futures are good examples of cases in which forward and futures prices should be inversely related. Alternatively, when inflation is high, interest rates are high and investors oftentimes put their money in such assets as gold. Thus, gold futures prices and interest rates would tend to be positively correlated. It would be difficult to identify a situation in which futures prices are not correlated with interest rates. Zero correlation is rare in the financial world, but we can say that when the correlation is low or close to zero, the difference between forward and futures prices would be very small.

At this introductory level of treatment, we shall make the simplifying assumption that futures prices and forward prices are the same. We do so by ignoring the effects of marking a futures contract to market. In practice, some significant issues arise related to the marking-to-market process, but they detract from our ability to understand the important concepts in pricing and trading futures and forwards.

Therefore, based on the equivalence we are assuming between futures and forwards, we can assume that the value of a futures contract at expiration, before marking to market, is

$$V_T(T) = f_T(T) - f_0(T) = S_T - f_0(T)$$

with the spot price substituted for the futures price at T, given what we know about their convergence.

7.1.4 *Pricing Futures Contracts*

Now let us proceed to the pricing of futures contracts. As we did with forward contracts, we consider the case of a generic underlying asset priced at \$100. A futures contract calls for delivery of the underlying asset in one year at a price of \$108. Let us see if \$108 is the appropriate price for this futures contract.

Suppose we buy the asset for \$100 and sell the futures contract. We hold the position until expiration. For right now, we assume no costs are involved in holding the asset. We do, however, lose interest on the \$100 tied up in the asset for one year. We assume that this opportunity cost is at the risk-free interest rate of 5 percent.

Recall that no money changes hands at the start of a futures contract. Moreover, we can reasonably ignore the rather small margin deposit that would be required. In addition, margin deposits can generally be met by putting up interest-earning securities, so there is really no opportunity cost. As discussed in the previous section, we also will assume away the daily settlement procedure; in other words, the value of the futures contract paid out at expiration is the final futures price minus the original futures price. Because the final futures price converges to the spot price, the final payout is the spot price minus the original futures price.

So at the contract expiration, we are short the futures and must deliver the asset, which we own. We do so and receive the original futures price for it. So we receive \$108 for an asset purchased a year ago at \$100. At a 5 percent interest rate, we lose only \$5 in interest, so our return in excess of the opportunity cost is 3 percent risk free. This risk-free return in excess of the risk-free rate is clearly attractive and would induce traders to buy the asset and sell the futures. This arbitrage activity would drive the futures price down until it reaches \$105.

If the futures price falls below \$105, say to \$102, the opposite arbitrage would occur. The arbitrageur would buy the futures, but either we would need to be able to borrow the asset and sell it short, or investors who own the asset would have to be willing to sell it and buy the futures. They would receive the asset price of \$100 and invest it at 5 percent interest. Then at expiration, those investors would get the asset back upon taking delivery, paying \$102. This transaction would net a clear and risk-free profit of \$3, consisting of interest of \$5 minus a \$2 loss from selling the asset at \$100 and buying it back at \$102. Again, through the buying of the futures and shorting of the asset, the forces of arbitrage would cause prices to realign to \$105.

Some difficulties occur with selling short certain assets. Although the financial markets make short selling relatively easy, some commodities are not easy to sell short. In such a case, it is still possible for arbitrage to occur. If investors who already own the asset sell it and buy the futures, they can reap similar gains at no risk. Because our interest is in financial instruments, we shall ignore these commodity market issues and assume that short selling can be easily executed.[25]

If the market price is not equal to the price given by the model, it is important to note that regardless of the asset price at expiration, the above arbitrage guarantees a risk-free profit. That profit is known at the time the parties enter the transaction. Exhibit 6 summarizes and illustrates this point.

Exhibit 6 The Risk-Free Nature of Long and Short Futures Arbitrage

Asset is priced at \$100, futures is priced at $f_0(T)$ and expires in one year. Interest rate over the life of the futures is 5 percent.

Time	Long Asset, Short Futures Arbitrage	Short Asset, Long Futures Arbitrage
Today (time 0)	Buy asset at \$100 Sell futures at $f_0(T)$	Sell short asset for \$100 Buy futures for $f_0(T)$
Expiration	Asset price is S_T	Asset price is S_T

25 Keep in mind that there are some restrictions on the short selling of financial instruments, such as uptick rules and margin requirements, but we will not concern ourselves with these impediments here.

Exhibit 6 (Continued)

Time	Long Asset, Short Futures Arbitrage	Short Asset, Long Futures Arbitrage
(time T)	Futures price converges to asset price	Futures price converges to asset price
	Deliver asset	Take delivery of asset
	Profit on asset after accounting for the 5 percent (\$5) interest lost from \$100 tied up in the investment in the asset: $S_T - 100 - 5$	Profit on asset after accounting for the 5 percent (\$5) interest earned on the \$100 received from the short sale of the asset: $100 + 5 - S_T$
	Profit on futures: $f_0(T) - S_T$	Profit on futures: $S_T - f_0(T)$
	Total profit: $f_0(T) - 100 - 5$	Total profit: $100 + 5 - f_0(T)$

Conclusion: The asset price at expiration has no effect on the profit captured at expiration for either transaction. The profit is known today. To eliminate arbitrage, the futures price today, $f_0(T)$, must equal 100 + 5 = \$105.

The transactions we have described are identical to those using forward contracts. We did note with forward contracts, however, that one can enter into an off-market forward contract, having one party pay cash to another to settle any difference resulting from the contract not trading at its arbitrage-free value up front. In the futures market, this type of arrangement is not permitted; all contracts are entered into without any cash payments up front.

So in general, through the forces of arbitrage, we say that *the futures price is the spot price compounded at the risk-free rate*:

$$f_0(T) = S_0(1 + r)$$

It is important, however, to write this result in a form we are more likely to use. In the above form, we specify r as the interest rate over the life of the futures contract. In financial markets, however, interest rates are nearly always specified as annual rates. Therefore, to compound the asset price over the life of the futures, we let r equal an annual rate and specify the life of the futures as T years. Then the futures price is found as

$$f_0(T) = S_0(1 + r)^T \quad (4)$$

The futures price is the spot price compounded over the life of the contract, T years, at the annual risk-free rate, r. From this point on, we shall use this more general specification.

As an example, consider a futures contract that has a life of 182 days; the annual interest rate is 5 percent. Then T = 182/365 and r = 0.05. If the spot price is \$100, the futures price would then be

$$\begin{aligned} f_0(T) &= S_0(1+r)^T \\ f_0(182/365) &= 100(1.05)^{182/365} \\ &= 102.46 \end{aligned}$$

If the futures is selling for more than \$102.46, an arbitrageur can buy the asset for \$100 and sell the futures for whatever its price is, hold the asset (losing interest on \$100 at an annual rate of 5 percent) and deliver it to receive the futures price. The overall strategy will net a return in excess of 5 percent a year at no risk. If the futures is selling for less than \$102.46, the arbitrageur can borrow the asset, sell it short, and buy the futures. She will earn interest on the funds obtained from the short sale and take delivery of the asset at the futures expiration, paying the original futures price. The overall transaction results in receiving \$100 up front and paying back an amount less than the 5 percent risk-free rate, making the transaction like a loan that is paid back at less than the risk-free rate. If one could create such a loan, one could use it to raise funds and invest the funds at the risk-free rate to earn unlimited gains.

7.1.5 *Pricing Futures Contracts when There Are Storage Costs*

Except for opportunity costs, we have until now ignored any costs associated with holding the asset. In many asset markets, there are significant costs, other than the opportunity cost, to holding an asset. These costs are referred to as **storage costs** or **carrying costs** and are generally a function of the physical characteristics of the underlying asset. Some assets are easy to store; some are difficult. For example, assume the underlying is oil, which has significant storage costs but a very long storage life.[26] One would not expect to incur costs associated with a decrease in quality of the oil. Significant risks do exist, however, such as spillage, fire, or explosion. Some assets on which futures are based are at risk for damage. For example, cattle and pigs can become ill and die during storage. Grains are subject to pest damage and fire. All of these factors have the potential to produce significant storage costs, and protection such as insurance leads to higher storage costs for these assets. On the other hand, financial assets have virtually no storage costs. Of course, all assets have one significant storage cost, which is the opportunity cost of money tied up in the asset, but this effect is covered in the present value calculation.

It is reasonable to assume that the storage costs on an asset are a function of the quantity of the asset to be stored and the length of time in storage. Let us specify this cost with the variable FV(SC,0,T), which denotes the value at time T (expiration) of the storage costs (excluding opportunity costs) associated with holding the asset over the period 0 to T. By specifying these costs as of time T, we are accumulating the costs and compounding the interest thereon until the end of the storage period. We can reasonably assume that when storage is initiated, these costs are known.[27]

Revisiting the example we used previously, we would buy the asset at S_0, sell a futures contract at $f_0(T)$, store the asset and accumulate costs of FV(SC,0,T), and deliver the asset at expiration to receive the futures price. The total payoff is $f_0(T) - FV(SC,0,T)$. This amount is risk free. To avoid an arbitrage opportunity, its present value should equal the initial outlay, S_0, required to establish the position. Thus,

$$[f_0(T) - FV(SC,0,T)]/(1 + r)^T = S_0$$

Solving for the futures price gives

$$f_0(T) = S_0(1 + r)^T + FV(SC,0,T) \quad (5)$$

This result says that *the futures price equals the spot price compounded over the life of the futures contract at the risk-free rate, plus the future value of the storage costs over the life of the contract.* In the previous example with no storage costs, we saw that the futures price was the spot price compounded at the risk-free rate. With storage costs, we must add the future value of the storage costs. The logic behind this adjustment should make sense. The futures price should be higher by enough to cover the storage costs when a trader buys the asset and sells a futures to create a risk-free position.[28]

26 After all, oil has been stored by nature for millions of years.

27 There may be reason to suggest that storage costs have an element of uncertainty in them, complicating the analysis.

28 We did not cover assets that are storable at significant cost when we studied forward contracts because such contracts are less widely used for these assets. Nonetheless, the formula given here would apply for forward contracts as well, given our assumption of no credit risk on forward contracts.

Consider the following example. The spot price of the asset is \$50, the interest rate is 6.25 percent, the future value of the storage costs is \$1.35, and the futures expires in 15 months. Then T = 15/12 = 1.25. The futures price would, therefore, be

$$f_0(T) = S_0(1+r)^T + FV(SC,0,T)$$

$$f_0(1.25) = 50(1.0625)^{1.25} + 1.35 = 55.29$$

If the futures is selling for more than \$55.29, the arbitrageur would buy the asset and sell the futures, holding the position until expiration, at which time he would deliver the asset and collect the futures price, earning a return that covers the 6.25 percent cost of the money and the storage costs of \$1.35. If the futures is selling for less than \$55.29, an arbitrageur who owns the asset and wishes to own the asset after expiration of the futures would sell the asset and buy the futures, reinvesting the proceeds from the short sale at 6.25 percent and saving the storage costs. The net effect would be to generate a cash inflow today plus the storage cost savings and a cash outflow at expiration that would replicate a loan with a rate less than the risk-free rate. Only if the futures sells for exactly \$55.29 do these arbitrage opportunities go away.

7.1.6 *Pricing Futures Contracts when There Are Cash Flows on the Underlying Asset*

In each case we have considered so far, the underlying asset did not generate any positive cash flows to the holder. For some assets, there will indeed be positive cash flows to the holder. Recall that in the reading on forward markets and contracts, we examined the pricing and valuation of forward contracts on stocks and bonds and were forced to recognize that stocks pay dividends, bonds pay interest, and these cash flows affect the forward price. A similar concept applies here and does so in a symmetric manner to what we described in the previous section in which the asset incurs a cash cost. As we saw in that section, a cash cost incurred from holding the asset increases the futures price. Thus, we might expect that cash generated from holding the asset would result in a lower futures price and, as we shall see in this section, that is indeed the case. But in the next section, we shall also see that it is even possible for an asset to generate nonmonetary benefits that must also be taken into account when pricing a futures contract on it.

Let us start by assuming that over the life of the futures contract, the asset generates positive cash flows of FV(CF,0,T). It is no coincidence that this notation is similar to the one we used in the previous section for the storage costs of the underlying asset over the life of the futures. Cash inflows and storage costs are just different sides of the same coin. We must remember, however, that FV(CF,0,T) represents a positive flow in this case. Now let us revisit our example.

We would buy the asset at S_0, sell a futures contract at $f_0(T)$, store the asset and generate positive cash flows of FV(CF,0,T), and deliver the asset at expiration, receiving the futures price. The total payoff is $f_0(T)$ + FV(CF,0,T). This amount is risk free and known at the start. To avoid an arbitrage opportunity, its present value should equal the initial outlay, S_0, required to establish the position. Thus,

$$[f_0(T) + FV(CF,0,T)]/(1+r)^T = S_0$$

Solving for the futures price gives

$$f_0(T) = S_0(1+r)^T - FV(CF,0,T) \tag{6}$$

In the previous example that included storage costs, we saw that the futures price was the spot price compounded at the risk-free rate plus the future value of the storage costs. With positive cash flows, we must subtract the future value of these cash flows. The logic behind this adjustment should make sense. The futures price should be reduced by enough to account for the positive cash flows when a trader buys the asset and sells a futures to create a risk-free position. Otherwise, the trader would receive risk-free cash flows from the asset *and* the equivalent amount from the sale of the asset at the futures price. Reduction of the futures price by this amount avoids overcompensating the trader.

As noted, these cash flows can be in the form of dividends from a stock or coupon interest from a bond. When we specifically examine the pricing of bond and stock futures, we shall make this specification a little more precise and work an example.

7.1.7 *Pricing Futures Contracts when There Is a Convenience Yield*

Now consider the possibility that the asset might generate nonmonetary benefits that must also be taken into account. The notion of nonmonetary benefits that could affect futures prices might sound strange, but upon reflection, it makes perfect sense. For example, a house is a common and normally desirable investment made by individuals and families. The house generates no monetary benefits and incurs significant costs. As well as being a possible monetary investment if prices rise, the house generates some nonmonetary benefits in the form of serving as a place to live. These benefits are quite substantial; many people consider owning a residence preferable to renting, and people often sell their homes for monetary gains far less than any reasonable return on a risky asset. Clearly the notion of a nonmonetary benefit to owning an asset is one most people are familiar with.

In a futures contract on an asset with a nonmonetary gain, that gain must be taken into account. Suppose, for the purpose of understanding the effect of nonmonetary benefits on a futures contract, we create a hypothetical futures contract on a house. An individual purchases a house and sells a futures contract on it. We shall keep the arguments as simple as possible by ignoring the operating or carrying costs. What should be the futures price? If the futures is priced at the spot price plus the risk-free rate, as in the original case, the homeowner receives a guaranteed sale price, giving a return of the risk-free rate *and* the use of the home. This is clearly a good deal. Homeowners would be eager to sell futures contracts, leading to a decrease in the price of the futures. Thus, any nonmonetary benefits ought to be factored into the futures price and logically would lead to a lower futures price.

Of course, in the real world of standardized futures contracts, there are no futures contracts on houses. Nonetheless, there are futures contracts on assets that have nonmonetary benefits. Assets that are often in short supply, particularly those with seasonal and highly risky production processes, are commonly viewed as having such benefits. The nonmonetary benefits of these assets are referred to as the **convenience yield**. Formally, a convenience yield is the nonmonetary return offered by an asset when in short supply. When an asset is in short supply, its price tends to be high. Holders of the asset earn an implicit incremental return from having the asset on hand. This return enables them, as commercial enterprises, to avoid the cost and inconvenience of not having their primary product or resource input on hand. Because shortages are generally temporary, the spot price can be higher than the futures price, even when the asset incurs storage costs. If a trader buys the asset, sells a futures contract, and stores the asset, the return is risk free and will be sufficient to cover the storage costs and the opportunity cost of money, but it will be reduced by an amount reflecting the benefits of holding the asset during a period of shortage or any other nonmonetary benefits.

Now, let the notation FV(CB,0,T) represent the future value of the costs of storage minus the benefits:

$$FV(CB,0,T) = \text{Costs of storage} - \text{Nonmonetary benefits (Convenience yield)}$$

where all terms are expressed in terms of their future value at time T and are considered to be known at time 0. If the costs exceed the benefits, FV(CB,0,T) is a positive number.[29] We refer to FV(CB,0,T) as the **cost of carry**.[30] The general futures pricing formula is

$$f_0(T) = S_0(1 + r)^T + FV(CB,0,T) \quad (7)$$

The futures price is the spot price compounded at the risk-free rate plus the cost of carry. This model is often called the **cost-of-carry model**.

Consider an asset priced at \$75; the risk-free interest rate is 5.15 percent, the net of the storage costs, interest, and convenience yield is \$3.20, and the futures expires in nine months. Thus, T = 9/12 = 0.75. Then the futures price should be

$$\begin{aligned} f_0(T) &= S_0(1+r)^T + FV(CB,0,T) \\ f_0(0.75) &= 75(1.0515)^{0.75} + 3.20 \\ &= 81.08 \end{aligned}$$

Exhibit 7 **Pricing a Futures Contract**

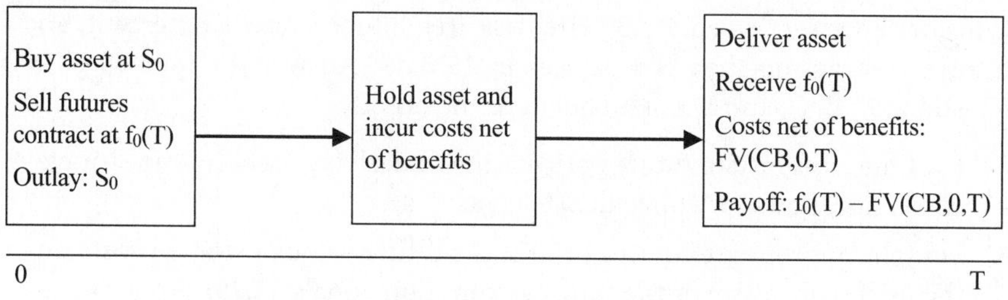

0		T
Buy asset at S_0 Sell futures contract at $f_0(T)$ Outlay: S_0	→ Hold asset and incur costs net of benefits →	Deliver asset Receive $f_0(T)$ Costs net of benefits: FV(CB,0,T) Payoff: $f_0(T)$ – FV(CB,0,T)

The transaction is risk-free and should be equivalent to investing S_0 dollars in a risk-free asset that pays $f_0(T)$ – FV(CB,0,T) at time T. Therefore, the payoff at T must be the future value of the initial outlay invested at the risk-free rate. For this relationship to hold, the futures price must be given as

$$f_0(T) = S_0(1 + r)^T + FV(CB,0,T)$$

Example: An asset is selling for \$225. A futures contract expires in 150 days (T = 150/365 = 0.411). The risk-free rate is 7.5 percent, and the net cost of carry is \$5.75. The futures price will be

$$f_0(T) = f_0(0.411) = \$225(1.075)^{0.411} + \$5.75 = \$237.54$$

As we have always done, we assume that this price will prevail in the marketplace. If it does not, the forces of arbitrage will drive the market price to the model price. If the futures price exceeds \$81.08, the arbitrageur can buy the asset and sell the futures to earn a risk-free return in excess of the risk-free rate. If the futures price is less than \$81.08, the arbitrageur can either sell the asset short or sell it if he already owns it, and then also buy the futures, creating a risk-free position equivalent to a loan that

---

29 In other words, FV(CB,0,T) has to be positive to refer to it as a "cost."

30 In some cases, such as in inventory storage, it is customary to include the opportunity cost in the definition of cost of carry; but we keep it separate in this reading.

will cost less than the risk-free rate. The gains from both of these transactions will have accounted for any nonmonetary benefits. This arbitrage activity will force the market price to converge to the model price.

The above equation is the most general form of the futures pricing formula we shall encounter. Exhibit 7 reviews and illustrates how we obtained this formula and provides another example.

Some variations of this general formula are occasionally seen. Sometimes the opportunity cost of interest is converted to dollars and embedded in the cost of carry. Then we say that $f_0(T) = S_0 + FV(CB,0,T)$; the futures price is the spot price plus the cost of carry. This is a perfectly appropriate way to express the formula if the interest is embedded in the cost of carry, but we shall not do so in this reading.

Another variation of this formula is to specify the cost of carry in terms of a rate, such as y. Then we have $f_0(T) = S_0(1 + r)^T(1 + y)^T$. Again, this variation is certainly appropriate but is not the version we shall use.[31]

Note that when we get into the specifics of pricing certain types of futures contracts, we must fine-tune the formulas a little more. First, however, we explore some general characterizations of the relationship between futures and spot prices.

EXAMPLE 2

Consider an asset priced at $50. The risk-free interest rate is 8 percent, and a futures contract on the asset expires in 45 days. Answer the following, with questions A, B, C, and D independent of the others.

A Find the appropriate futures price if the underlying asset has no storage costs, cash flows, or convenience yield.

B Find the appropriate futures price if the future value of storage costs on the underlying asset at the futures expiration equals $2.25.

C Find the appropriate futures price if the future value of positive cash flows on the underlying asset equals $0.75.

D Find the appropriate futures price if the future value of the net overall cost of carry on the underlying asset equals $3.55.

E Using Part D above, illustrate how an arbitrage transaction could be executed if the futures contract is trading at $60.

F Using Part A above, determine the value of a long futures contract an instant before marking to market if the previous settlement price was $49.

Solution to A:

First determine that T = 45/365 = 0.1233. Then the futures price is

$$f_0(0.1233) = \$50(1.08)^{0.1233} = \$50.48$$

Solution to B:

Storage costs must be covered in the futures price, so we add them:

$$f_0(0.1233) = \$50(1.08)^{0.1233} + \$2.25 = \$52.73$$

Solution to C:

A positive cash flow, such as interest or dividends on the underlying, reduces the futures price:

31 Yet another variation of this formula is to use $(1 + r + y)^T$ as an approximation for $(1 + r)^T(1 + y)^T$. We do not, however, consider this expression an acceptable way to compute the futures price as it is an approximation of a formula that is simple enough to use without approximating.

$f_0(0.1233) = \$50(1.08)^{0.1233} - \$0.75 = \$49.73$

Solution to D:

The net overall cost of carry must be covered in the futures price, so we add it:

$f_0(0.1233) = \$50(1.08)^{0.1233} + \$3.55 = \$54.03$

Solution to E:

Follow these steps:

- Sell the futures at $60.
- Buy the asset at $50.
- Because the asset price compounded at the interest rate is $50.48, the interest forgone is $0.48. So the asset price is effectively $50.48 by the time of the futures expiration.
- Incur costs of $3.55.
- At expiration, deliver the asset and receive $60. The net investment in the asset is $50.48 + $3.55 = $54.03. If the asset is sold for $60, the net gain is $5.97.

Solution to F:

If the last settlement price was $49.00 and the price is now $50.48 (our answer in Part A), the value of a long futures contract equals the difference between these prices: $50.48 – $49.00 = $1.48.

7.1.8 *Backwardation and Contango*

Because the cost of carry, FV(CB,0,T), can be either positive or negative, the futures price can be greater or less than the spot price. Because the costs plus the interest tend to exceed the benefits, it is more common for the futures price to exceed the spot price, a situation called **contango**. In contrast, when the benefits exceed the costs plus the interest, the futures price will be less than the spot price, called **backwardation**. These terms are not particularly important in understanding the necessary concepts, but they are so commonly used that they are worthwhile to remember.

7.1.9 *Futures Prices and Expected Spot Prices*

An important concept when examining futures prices is the relationship between futures prices and expected spot prices. In order to fully understand the issue, let us first consider the relationship between spot prices and expected spot prices. Consider an asset with no risk, but which incurs carrying costs. At time 0, the holder of the asset purchases it with the certainty that she will cover her opportunity cost and carrying cost. Otherwise, she would not purchase the asset. Thus, the spot price at time 0 is the present value of the total of the spot price at time T less costs minus benefits:

$$S_0 = \frac{S_T - FV(CB,0,T)}{(1+r)^T}$$

$$= \frac{S_T}{(1+r)^T} - \frac{FV(CB,0,T)}{(1+r)^T}$$

Because FV(CB,0,T) is the future value of the carrying cost, $FV(CB,0,T)/(1 + r)^T$ is the present value of the carrying cost. So on the one hand, we can say that the spot price is the future spot price minus the future value of the carrying cost, all discounted to the present. On the other hand, we can also say that the spot price is the discounted value of the future spot price minus the present value of the carrying cost.

If, however, the future price of the asset is uncertain, as it nearly always is, we must make some adjustments. For one, we do not know at time 0 what S_T will be. We must form an expectation, which we will denote as $E_0(S_T)$. But if we simply replace S_T above with $E_0(S_T)$, we would not be acting rationally. We would be paying a price today and expecting compensation only at the risk-free rate along with coverage of our carrying cost. Indeed, one of the most important and intuitive elements of all we know about finance is that risky assets require a risk premium. Let us denote this risk premium with the symbol, $\Phi_0(S_T)$. It represents a discount off of the expected value that is embedded in the current price, S_0. Specifically, the current price is now given as

$$S_0 = \frac{E_0(S_T) - FV(CB,0,T) - \Phi_0(S_T)}{(1 + r)^T}$$

where we see that the risk premium lowers the current spot price. Intuitively, investors pay less for risky assets, all other things equal.

Until now, we have worked only with the spot price, but nothing we have said so far violates the rule of no arbitrage. Hence, our futures pricing formula, $f_0(T) = S_0(1 + r)^T + FV(CB,0,T)$, still applies. If we rearrange the futures pricing formula for FV(CB,0,T), substitute this result into the formula for S_0, and solve for the futures price, $f_0(T)$, we obtain $f_0(T) = E_0(S_T) - \Phi_0(S_T)$. This equation says that the futures price equals the expected future spot price minus the risk premium.

An important conclusion to draw from this formula is that the futures price does not equal the expectation of the future spot price. The futures price would be biased on the low side. If one felt that the futures price were an unbiased predictor of the future spot price, $f_0(T) = E_0(S_T)$, one could expect on average to be able to predict the future spot price of oil by looking at the futures price of oil. But that is not likely to be the case.

The intuition behind this result is easy to see. We start with the assumption that all units of the asset must be held by someone. Holders of the asset incur the risk of its future selling price. If a holder of the asset wishes to transfer that risk by selling a futures contract, she must offer a futures contract for sale. But if the futures contract is offered at a price equal to the expected spot price, the buyer of the futures contract takes on the risk but expects to earn only a price equal to the price paid for the futures. Thus, the futures trader incurs the risk without an expected gain in the form of a risk premium. On the opposite side of the coin, the holder of the asset would have a risk-free position with an expected gain in excess of the risk-free rate. Clearly, the holder of the asset would not be able to do such a transaction. Thus, she must lower the price to a level sufficient to compensate the futures trader for the risk he is taking on. This process will lead to a futures price that equals the expected spot price minus the risk premium, as shown in the above equation. In effect, the risk premium transfers from the holder of the asset to the buyer of the futures contract.

In all fairness, however, we must acknowledge that this view is not without its opponents. Some consider the futures price an unbiased predictor of the future spot price. In such a case, the futures price would tend to overshoot and undershoot the future spot price but on average would be equal to it. For such a situation to exist would require the unreasonable assumption that there is no risk or that investors are risk neutral, meaning that they are indifferent to risk. There is, however, one other situation in which the risk premium could disappear or even turn negative. Suppose holders of the asset who want to hedge their holdings could find other parties who need to purchase the asset and who would like to hedge by going long. In that case, it should be possible for the two parties to consummate a futures transaction with the futures price equal to the expected spot price. In fact, if the parties going long exerted greater pressure than the parties going short, it might even be possible for the futures price to exceed the expected spot price.

When futures prices are lower than expected spot prices, the situation is called **normal backwardation**. When futures prices are higher than expected spot prices, it is called **normal contango**. Note the contrast with the terms backwardation and contango, which we encountered in Section 7.1.8. Backwardation means that the futures price is lower than the spot price; contango means that the futures price exceeds the spot price. Normal backwardation means that the futures price is lower than the expected spot price; normal contango means that the futures price exceeds the expected spot price.

Generally speaking, we should favor the notion that futures prices are biased predictors of future spot prices because of the transferal of the risk premium from holders of the asset to buyers of futures. Intuitively, this is the more likely case, but the other interpretations are possible. Fortunately, for our purposes, it is not critical to resolve the issue, but we do need to be aware of it.

7.2 Pricing Interest Rate Futures

OPTIONAL SEGMENT

We shall examine the pricing of three classes of interest rate futures contracts: Treasury bill futures, Eurodollar futures, and Treasury bond futures. In Section 6.1, we described the characteristics of these instruments and contracts. Now we look at their pricing, keeping in mind that we established the general foundations for pricing—the cost-of-carry model—in the previous section. Recall that in the cost-of-carry model, we buy the underlying asset, sell a futures contract, store the asset (which incurs costs and could generate benefits), and deliver the asset at expiration. To prevent arbitrage, the futures price is found in general as

$$\text{Futures price} = \text{Spot price of underlying asset} \times \text{Compounding factor} + \text{Costs net of monetary and nonmonetary benefits}$$

When the underlying is a financial instrument, there will be no nonmonetary benefits and no costs other than the opportunity cost.

7.2.1 *Pricing T-Bill Futures*

Consider the following time line of our problem:

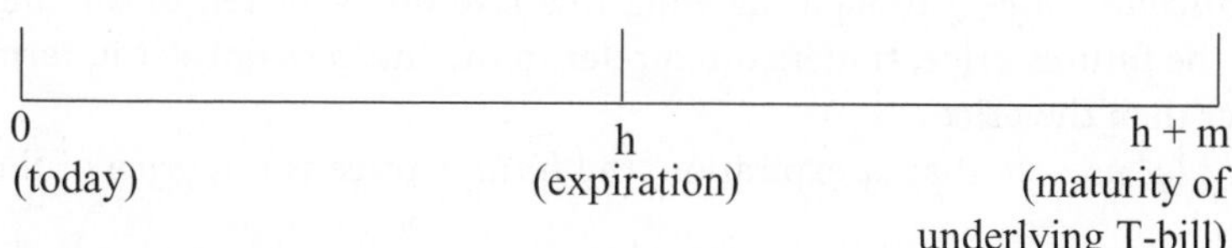

Time 0 is today, and time h is the expiration day of the futures contract. The T-bill underlying the contract is an m-day T-bill. Thus, when the futures expires, the T-bill is required to have m days to go before maturity. So from our perspective today, the underlying T-bill is an (h + m)-day T-bill.[32] As in the reading on forward markets and contracts, for FRAs, h and m represent a particular number of days. In accordance with common practice, m is traditionally 90. We now introduce some necessary notation.

32 It is common practice in the T-bill futures market to refer to the underlying as an m-day T-bill, but at time 0, the underlying must be an (h + m)-day T-bill in order for it to be an m-day T-bill at time h.

First, where necessary, we use a simple expression, r, for the risk-free interest rate. But when pricing Treasury bill futures, we need a more flexible notation. Here we need the rates for T-bills maturing on day h and on day h + m. In addition, because interest rates can change from day 0 to day h, we need notation that distinguishes rates for different maturities and rates at different points in time.[33]

To find the spot price of the underlying asset, we need the discount rate on an (h + m)-day T-bill. Suppose we have

$$r_0^d(h), r_0^d(h+m) = \text{Discount rates in effect on day 0 of h-day and } (h+m)\text{-day T-bills}$$

As described in Section 6, these are discount rates and convert to prices by the following formula: $B_0(j) = 1 - r_0^d(j)(j/360)$, where in this case j will either be h or h + m. Thus, the prices of h- and (h + m)-day spot T-bills on day 0 (assuming $1 face amounts) are

$$B_0(h) = 1 - r_0^d(h)\left(\frac{h}{360}\right)$$

$$B_0(h+m) = 1 - r_0^d(h+m)\left(\frac{h+m}{360}\right)$$

In other words, the h- or (h + m)-day discount rate is multiplied by the number of days in the life of the T-bill over 360 and subtracted from the face value of $1.

Now let us turn to the futures market. We define

$$r_0^{df}(h) = \text{implied discount rate on day 0 of futures contract expiring on day h, where the deliverable instrument is an m-day T-bill}$$

$$f_0(h) = \text{price on day 0 of futures contract expiring on day h}$$

The relationship between $r_0^{df}(h)$ and $f_0(h)$ is

$$f_0(h) = 1 - r_0^{df}(h)\left(\frac{m}{360}\right)$$

It is important to note that the futures price, not the implied discount rate, is the more important variable. Like any price, the futures price is determined in a market of buyers and sellers. Any rate is simply a way of transforming a price into a number that can be compared with rates on various other fixed-income instruments.[34] Do not think that a futures contract pays an interest rate. It is more appropriate to think of such a rate embedded in a futures price as an *implied rate*, hence our use of the term *implied discount rate*. Although knowing this rate does not tell us any more than knowing the futures price, traders often refer to the futures contract in terms of the rate rather than the price.

Finally, let us note that at expiration, the futures price is the price of the underlying T-bill

33 When we assume that the interest rates are the same for all maturities and cannot change over time, which is considered acceptable when working with stock index and currency futures, we can use the simpler notation of r for the rate.

34 To further reinforce the notion that an interest rate is just a transformation of a price, consider a zero-coupon bond selling at $95 and using 360 days as a year. The price can be transformed into a rate in the manner of 1/0.95 – 1 = 0.0526 or 5.26 percent. But using the convention of the Treasury bill market, the rate is expressed as a discount rate. Then 0.95 = 1 – Rate × (360/360), and the rate would be 0.05 or 5 percent. A price can be converted into a rate in a number of other ways, such as by assuming different compound periods. The price of any asset is determined in a market-clearing process. The rate is just a means of transforming the price so that interest rate instruments and their derivatives can be discussed in a more comparable manner.

$$f_h(h) = B_h(h + m)$$
$$= 1 - r_h^d(h + m)\left(\frac{m}{360}\right)$$

where $B_h(h + m)$ is the price on day h of the T-bill maturing on day h + m, and $r_h^d(h+m)$ is the discount rate on day h on the T-bill maturing on day h + m.

We now derive the futures price by constructing a risk-free portfolio that permits no arbitrage profits to be earned. This transaction is referred to as a cash-and-carry strategy, because the trader buys the asset in the cash (spot) market and carries (holds) it.

On day 0, we buy the (h + m)-day T-bill, investing $B_0(h + m)$. We simultaneously sell a futures contract at the price $f_0(h)$. On day h, we are required to deliver an m-day T-bill. The bill we purchased, which originally had h + m days to maturity, now has m days to maturity. We therefore deliver that bill and receive the original futures price. We can view this transaction as having paid $B_0(h + m)$ on day 0 and receiving $f_0(h)$. Because $f_0(h)$ is known on day 0, this transaction is risk free. It should thus earn the same return per dollar invested as would a T-bill purchased on day 0 that matures on day h. The return per dollar invested from the arbitrage transaction would be $f_0(h)/B_0(h + m)$, and the return per dollar invested in an h-day T-bill would be $1/B_0(h)$.[35] Consequently, we set these values equal:

$$\frac{f_0(h)}{B_0(h + m)} = \frac{1}{B_0(h)}$$

Solving for the futures price, we obtain

$$f_0(h) = \frac{B_0(h + m)}{B_0(h)}$$

In other words, the futures price is the ratio of the longer-term bill price to the shorter-term bill price. This price is, in fact, the same as the forward price from the term structure. In fact, as we noted above, futures prices and forward prices will be equal under the assumptions we have made so far and will follow throughout this book.

Recall that we previously demonstrated that the futures price should equal the spot price plus the cost of carry. Yet the above formula looks nothing like this result. In fact, however, it is consistent with the cost-of-carry formula. First, the above formula can be written as

$$f_0(h) = B_0(h + m)\left[\frac{1}{B_0(h)}\right]$$

As noted above, the expression $1/B_0(h)$ can be identified as the return per dollar invested over h days, which simplifies to $[1 + r_0(h)]^{h/365}$, which is essentially a compound interest factor for h days at the rate $r_0(h)$. Note that h is the number of days, assuming 365 in a year. For the period ending at day h, the above formula becomes

$$f_0(h) = B_0(h + m)[1 + r_0(h)]^{h/365} \quad \textbf{(8)}$$

and the futures price is seen to equal the spot price of the underlying compounded at the interest rate, which simply reflects the opportunity cost of the money tied up for h days.

Note that what we have been doing is deriving the appropriate price for a futures contract. In a market with no arbitrage opportunities, the actual futures price would be this theoretical price. Let us suppose for a moment, however, that the actual futures

35 For example, if a one-year $1 face value T-bill is selling for $0.90, the return per dollar invested is $1/$0.90 = 1.1111.

price is something else, say $f_0(h)^*$. The spot price is, of course, $B_0(h + m)$. Using these two numbers, we can infer the implied rate of return from a transaction involving the purchase of the T-bill and sale of the futures. We have

$$f_0(h)^* = B_0(h + m)[1 + r_0(h)^*]^{h/365}$$

where $r_0(h)^*$ is the implied rate of return. Solving for $r_0(h)^*$ we obtain

$$r_0(h)^* = \left[\frac{f_0(h)^*}{B_0(h + m)}\right]^{365/h} - 1 \quad (9)$$

This rate of return, $r_0(h)^*$, has a special name, the **implied repo rate**. It is the rate of return from a cash-and-carry transaction that is implied by the futures price relative to the spot price. Traders who engage in such transactions often obtain the funds to do so in the repurchase agreement (repo) market. The implied repo rate tells the trader what rate of return to expect from the strategy. If the financing rate available in the repo market is less than the implied repo rate, the strategy is worthwhile and would generate an arbitrage profit. If the trader could lend in the repo market at greater than the implied repo rate, the appropriate strategy would be to reverse the transaction—selling the T-bill short and buying the futures—turning the strategy into a source of financing that would cost less than the rate at which the funds could be lent in the repo market.[36]

The implied repo rate is the rate of return implied by the strategy of buying the asset and selling the futures. As noted above, the futures price is often expressed in terms of an implied discount rate. Remember that the buyer of a futures contract is committing to buy a T-bill at the price $f_0(h)$. In the convention of pricing a T-bill by subtracting a discount rate from par value, the implied discount rate would be

$$r_0^{df}(h) = [1 - f_0(h)]\left(\frac{360}{m}\right) \quad (10)$$

We can also determine this implied discount rate from the discount rates on the h- and (h + m)-day T-bills as follows:[37]

$$r_0^{df}(h) = \left\{1 - \left[\frac{1 - r_0^d(h + m)\left(\frac{h + m}{360}\right)}{1 - r_0^d(h)\left(\frac{h}{360}\right)}\right]\right\}\left(\frac{360}{m}\right)$$

Now let us look at an example. We are interested in pricing a futures contract expiring in 30 days. A 30-day T-bill has a discount rate of 6 percent, and a 120-day T-bill has a discount rate of 6.6 percent. With h = 30 and h + m = 120, we have

$$r_0^d(h) = r_0^d(30) = 0.06$$

$$r_0^d(h + m) = r_0^d(120) = 0.066$$

The prices of these T-bills will, therefore, be

36 The concepts of a cash-and-carry strategy and the implied repo rate are applicable to any type of futures contract, but we cover them only with respect to T-bill futures.

37 This formula is found by substituting $1 - r_0^d(h + m)[(h + m)/360]$ for $B_0(h + m)$ and $1 - r_0^d(h)(h/360)$ for $B_0(h)$ in the above equation for $r_0^{df}(h)$. This procedure expresses the spot prices in terms of their respective discount rates.

$$B_0(h) = 1 - r_0^d(h)\left(\frac{h}{360}\right)$$

$$B_0(30) = 1 - 0.06\left(\frac{30}{360}\right) = 0.9950$$

$$B_0(h + m) = 1 - r_0^d(h + m)\left(\frac{h + m)}{360}\right)$$

$$B_0(120) = 1 - 0.066\left(\frac{120}{360}\right) = 0.9780$$

Using the formula we derived, we have the price of a futures expiring in 30 days as

$$f_0(h) = \frac{B_0(h + m)}{B_0(h)}$$

$$f_0(30) = \frac{B_0(120)}{B_0(30)} = \frac{0.9780}{0.9950} = 0.9829$$

The discount rate implied by the futures price would be

$$r_0^{df}(h) = [1 - f_0(h)]\left(\frac{360}{m}\right)$$

$$r_0^{df}(30) = (1 - 0.9829)\left(\frac{360}{90}\right) = 0.0684$$

In other words, in the T-bill futures market, the rate would be stated as 6.84 percent, which would imply a futures price of 0.9829.[38] Alternatively, the implied futures discount rate could be obtained from the spot discount rates as

$$r_0^{df}(h) = \left\{1 - \left[\frac{1 - r_0^d(h + m)\left(\frac{h + m}{360}\right)}{1 - r_0^d(h)\left(\frac{h}{360}\right)}\right]\right\}\left(\frac{360}{m}\right)$$

$$r_0^{df}(30) = \left\{1 - \left[\frac{1 - 0.066\left(\frac{120}{360}\right)}{1 - 0.06\left(\frac{30}{360}\right)}\right]\right\}\left(\frac{360}{90}\right) = 0.0683$$

with a slight difference due to rounding.

To verify this result, one would buy the 120-day T-bill for 0.9780 and sell the futures at a price of 0.9829. Then, 30 days later, the T-bill would be a 90-day T-bill and would be delivered to settle the futures contract. The trader would receive the original futures price of 0.9829. The return per dollar invested would be

$$\frac{0.9829}{0.9780} = 1.0050$$

If, instead, the trader had purchased a 30-day T-bill at the price of 0.9950 and held it for 30 days, the return per dollar invested would be

$$\frac{1}{0.9950} = 1.0050$$

38 We should also probably note that the IMM Index would be 100 – 6.84 = 93.16. Thus, the futures price would be quoted in the market as 93.16.

Thus, the purchase of the 120-day T-bill with its price in 30 days hedged by the sale of the futures contract is equivalent to purchasing a 30-day T-bill and holding it to maturity. Each transaction has the same return per dollar invested and is free of risk.

Suppose in the market, the futures price is 0.9850. The implied repo rate would be

$$r_0(h)^* = \left[\frac{f_0(h)^*}{B_0(h+m)}\right]^{365/h} - 1$$

$$= \left(\frac{0.9850}{0.9780}\right)^{365/30} - 1 = 0.0906$$

Buying the 120-day T-bill for 0.9780 and selling a futures for 0.9850 generates a rate of return of 0.9850/0.9780 – 1 = 0.007157. Annualizing this rate, $(1.007157)^{365/30} - 1 =$ 0.0906. If financing could be obtained in the repo market for less than this annualized rate, the strategy would be attractive. If the trader could lend in the repo market at higher than this rate, he should buy the futures and sell short the T-bill to implicitly borrow at 9.06 percent and lend in the repo market at a higher rate.

Let us now recap the pricing of Treasury bill futures. We buy an (h + m)-day bond and sell a futures expiring on day h, which calls for delivery of an m-day T-bill. The futures price should be the price of the (h + m)-day T-bill compounded at the h-day risk-free rate. That rate is the rate of return on an h-day bill. The futures price can also be obtained as the ratio of the price of the (h + m)-day T-bill to the price of the h-day T-bill. Alternatively, we can express the futures price in terms of an implied discount rate, and we can derive the price in terms of the discount rates on the (h + m)-day T-bill and the h-day T-bill. Finally, remember that the actual futures price in the market relative to the price of the (h + m)-day T-bill implies a rate of return called the implied repo rate. The implied repo rate can be compared with the rate in the actual repo market to determine the attractiveness of an arbitrage transaction.

Exhibit 8 summarizes the important formulas involved in the pricing of T-bill futures. We then turn to the pricing of another short-term interest rate futures contract, the Eurodollar futures.

Exhibit 8 **Pricing Formulas for T-Bill Futures Contract**

Futures price = Underlying T-bill price compounded at risk-free rate

Futures price in terms of spot T-bills:

$$f_0(h) = \frac{B_0(h+m)}{B_0(h)}$$

Futures price as spot price compounded at risk-free rate:

$$f_0(h) = B_0(h+m)[1 + r_0(h)]^{h/365}$$

Discount rate implied by futures price:

$$r_0^{df}(h) = [1 - f_0(h)]\left(\frac{360}{m}\right) = \left\{1 - \left[\frac{1 - r_0^d(h+m)\left(\frac{h+m}{360}\right)}{1 - r_0^d(h)\left(\frac{h}{360}\right)}\right]\right\}\left(\frac{360}{m}\right)$$

Implied repo rate:

$$r_0(h)^* = \left[\frac{f_0(h)^*}{B_0(h+m)}\right]^{365/h} - 1$$

EXAMPLE 3

A futures contract on a Treasury bill expires in 50 days. The T-bill matures in 140 days. The discount rates on T-bills are as follows:

50-day bill:	5.0 percent
140-day bill:	4.6 percent

A Find the appropriate futures price by using the prices of the 50- and 140-day T-bills.

B Find the futures price in terms of the underlying spot price compounded at the appropriate risk-free rate.

C Convert the futures price to the implied discount rate on the futures.

D Now assume that the futures contract is trading in the market at an implied discount rate 10 basis points lower than is appropriate, given the pricing model and the rule of no arbitrage. Demonstrate how an arbitrage transaction could be executed and show the outcome. Calculate the implied repo rate and discuss how it would be used to determine the profitability of the arbitrage.

Solution to A:

First, find the prices of the 50- and 140-day bonds:

$$B_0(50) = 1 - 0.05(50/360) = 0.9931$$

$$B_0(140) = 1 - 0.046(140/360) = 0.9821$$

The futures price is, therefore,

$$f_0(50) = \frac{0.9821}{0.9931} = 0.9889$$

Solution to B:

First, find the rate at which to compound the spot price of the 140-day T-bill. This rate is obtained from the 50-day T-bill:

$$\left[1 + r_0(h)\right]^{h/365} = \frac{1}{0.9931} = 1.0069$$

We actually do not need to solve for $r_0(h)$. The above says that based on the rate $r_0(h)$, every dollar invested should grow to a value of 1.0069. Thus, the futures price should be the spot price (the price of the 140-day T-bill) compounded by the factor 1.0069:

$$f_0(50) = 0.9821(1.0069) = 0.9889$$

Annualized, this rate would equal $(1.0069)^{365/50} - 1 = 0.0515$.

Solution to C:

Given the futures price of 0.9889, the implied discount rate is

$$r_0^{df}(50) = (1 - 0.9889)\left(\frac{360}{90}\right)$$
$$= 0.0444$$

Solution to D:

If the futures is trading for 10 basis points lower, it trades at a rate of 4.34 percent, so the futures price would be

$$f_0(50) = 1 - 0.0434\left(\frac{90}{360}\right)$$
$$= 0.9892$$

Do the following:

- Buy the 140-day bond at 0.9821,
- Sell the futures at 0.9892.

This strategy provides a return per dollar invested of

$$\frac{0.9892}{0.9821} = 1.0072$$

which compares favorably with a return per dollar invested of 1.0069 if the futures is correctly priced.

The implied repo rate is simply the annualization of this rate: $(1.0072)^{365/50} - 1 = 0.0538$. The cash-and-carry transaction would, therefore, earn 5.38 percent. Because the futures appears to be mispriced, we could likely obtain financing in the repo market at less than this rate.

END OPTIONAL SEGMENT

7.2.2 *Pricing Eurodollar Futures*

Based on the T-bill case, it is tempting to argue that the interest rate implied by the Eurodollar futures price would be the forward rate in the term structure of LIBOR. Unfortunately, that is not quite the case. In fact, the unusual construction of the Eurodollar futures contract relative to the Eurodollar spot market means that no risk-free combination of a Eurodollar time deposit and a Eurodollar futures contract can be constructed. Recall that the Eurodollar time deposit is an add-on instrument. Using $L_0(j)$ as the rate (LIBOR) on a j-day Eurodollar time deposit on day 0, if one deposits \$1, the deposit will grow to a value of $1 + L_0(j)(j/360)$ j days later. So, the present value of \$1 in j days is $1/[1 + L_0(j)(j/360)]$. The Eurodollar futures contract, however, is structured like the T-bill contract—as though the underlying were a discount instrument. So its price is stated in the form of $1 - L_0(j)(j/360)$. If we try the same arbitrage with Eurodollars that we did with T-bills, we cannot get the LIBOR that determines the spot price of a Eurodollar at expiration to offset the LIBOR that determines the futures price at expiration.

In other words, suppose that on day 0 we buy an (h + m)-day Eurodollar deposit that pays \$1 on day (h + m) and sell a futures at a price of $f_0(h)$. On day h, the futures expiration, the Eurodollar deposit has m days to go and is worth $1/[1 + L_h(m)(m/360)]$. The futures price at expiration is $f_h(h) = 1 - L_h(m)(m/360)$. The profit from the futures is $f_0(h) - [1 - L_h(m)(m/360)]$. Adding this amount to the value of the m-day Eurodollar deposit we are holding gives a total position value of

$$\frac{1}{1 + L_h(m)\left(\frac{m}{360}\right)} + f_0(h) - \left[1 - L_h(m)\left(\frac{m}{360}\right)\right]$$

Although $f_0(h)$ is known when the transaction is initiated, $L_h(m)$ is not determined until the futures expiration. There is no way for the $L_h(m)$ terms to offset. This problem does not occur in the T-bill market because the spot price is a discount instrument and the futures contract is designed as a discount instrument.[39] It is, nonetheless, common for participants in the futures market to treat the Eurodollar rate as equivalent to the implied forward rate. Such an assumption would require the ability to conduct the risk-free arbitrage, which, as we have shown, is impossible. The differences are fairly small, but we shall not assume that the Eurodollar futures rate should equal the implied forward rate. In that case, it would take a more advanced model to solve the pricing problem. The essential points in pricing interest rate futures on short-term instruments can be understood by studying the T-bill futures market.

This mismatch in the design of spot and futures instruments in the Eurodollar market would appear to make the contract difficult to use as a hedging instrument. Note that in the above equation for the payoff of the portfolio combining a spot Eurodollar time deposit and a short Eurodollar futures contract, an increase (decrease) in LIBOR lowers (raises) the value of the spot Eurodollar deposit and raises (lowers) the payoff from the short Eurodollar futures. Thus, the Eurodollar futures contract can still serve as a hedging tool. The hedge will not be perfect but can still be quite effective. Indeed, the Eurodollar futures contract is a major hedging tool of dealers in over-the-counter derivatives.

We have now completed the treatment of futures contracts on short-term interest rate instruments. Now let us look at the pricing of Treasury bond futures.

7.2.3 *Pricing Treasury Note and Bond Futures*

Recall that in Section 6.2, we described the bond futures contract as one in which there are a number of deliverable bonds. When a given bond is delivered, the long pays the short the futures price times an adjustment term called the conversion factor. The conversion factor is the price of a $1 bond with coupon equal to that of the deliverable bond and yield equal to 6 percent, with calculations based on semiannual compounding. Bonds with a coupon greater (less) than 6 percent will have a conversion factor greater (less) than 1. Before we delve into the complexities added by this feature, however, let us start off by assuming a fairly generic type of contract: one in which the underlying is a single, specific bond.

When examining bond forward contracts in the reading on forward markets and contracts, we specified a time line and notation. We return to that specific time line and notation, which differs from those we used for examining short-term interest rate futures.

0	T	T + Y
(today)	(expiration)	(maturity of underlying bond)

Recall our notation from the reading on forward markets and contracts:

$B_0^c(T+Y)$ = price at time 0 of coupon bond that matures at time T + Y. The bond has a maturity of Y at the futures expiration.

39 It is not clear why the Chicago Mercantile Exchange designed the Eurodollar contract as a discount instrument when the underlying Eurodollar deposit is an add-on instrument. The most likely reason is that the T-bill futures contract was already trading, was successful, and its design was well understood and accepted by traders. The CME most likely felt that this particular design was successful and should be continued with the Eurodollar contract. Ironically, the Eurodollar contract became exceptionally successful and the T-bill contract now has virtually no trading volume.

CI_i = coupon at time t_i, where the coupons occur at times $t_1, t_2, \ldots, t_n$ Note that we care only about coupons prior to the futures expiration at T.

$f_0(T)$ = price at time 0 of futures expiring at time T.

$B_0(T)$ = price at time 0 of zero-coupon bond maturing at T.

We also need to know at time T the accumulated value of all coupons received over the period from 0 to T. We need the compound value from 0 to T of any coupons paid during the time the futures contract is alive. This value is denoted as FV(CI,0,T). We introduced this variable in the reading on forward markets and contracts, and showed how to compute it, so you may wish to review that material. It is traditionally assumed that the interest rate at which these coupons are reinvested is known. We also assume that this interest rate applies to the period from 0 to T for money borrowed or lent. We denote this rate as

$r_0(T)$ = Interest rate at time 0 for period until time T

As described in the section on T-bill futures pricing, this is the rate that determines the price of a zero-coupon bond maturing at T.[40] Hence,

$$B_0(T) = \frac{1}{\left[1 + r_0(T)\right]^T}$$

The futures price at expiration is the price of the deliverable bond at expiration:

$$f_T(T) = B_T(T + Y)$$

Now we are ready to price this bond futures contract. On day 0, we buy the bond at the price $B_0^c(T+Y)$ and sell the futures at the price $f_0(T)$. Because the futures does not require any cash up front, its initial value is zero. The current value of the overall transaction is, therefore, just the value of the bond, $B_0^c(T+Y)$. This value represents the amount of money we must invest to engage in this transaction.

We hold this position until the futures expiration. During this time, we collect and reinvest the coupons. On day T, the futures expires. We deliver the bond and receive the futures price, $f_0(T)$. We also have the reinvested coupons, which have a value at T of FV(CI,0,T). These two amounts, $f_0(T)$ and FV(CI,0,T), are known when the transaction was initiated at time 0, so the transaction is risk-free. Therefore, the current value of the transaction, $B_0^c(T+Y)$, should be the discounted value of its value at T of $f_0(T)$ + FV(CI,0,T):

$$B_0^c(T + Y) = \frac{f_0(T) + FV(CI,0,T)}{\left[1 + r_0(T)\right]^T}$$

Note that we are simply discounting the known future value at T of the transaction at the risk-free rate of $r_0(T)$.[41]

We are, of course, more interested in the futures price, which is the only unknown in the above equation. Solving, we obtain

$$f_0(T) = B_0^c(T + Y)\left[1 + r_0(T)\right]^T - FV(CI,0,T) \quad (11)$$

40 Keep in mind, however, that this rate is not the discount rate that determines the price of the zero-coupon bond maturing at T. It is the rate of return, expressed as an annual rate. When working with T-bills, the symbol "T" represented Days/365, which is consistent with its use here with T-bonds.

41 We shall not take up the topic of the implied repo rate again, but note that if the futures is selling for $f_0(T)$, then $r_0(T)$ would be the implied repo rate.

This equation is a variation of our basic cost-of-carry formula. The spot price, $B_0^c(T+Y)$, is compounded at the risk-free interest rate. We then subtract the compound future value of the reinvested coupons over the life of the contract. The coupon interest is like a negative cost of carry; it is a positive cash flow associated with holding the underlying bond.

Now let us work an example. Consider a \$1 face value Treasury bond that pays interest at 7 percent semiannually. Thus, each coupon is \$0.035. The bond has exactly five years remaining, so during that time it will pay 10 coupons, each six months apart. The yield on the bond is 8 percent. The price of the bond is found by calculating the present value of both the 10 coupons and the face value: The price is \$0.9594.

Now consider a futures contract that expires in one year and three months: T = 1.25. The risk-free rate, $r_0(T)$, is 6.5 percent. The accumulated value of the coupons and the interest on them is

$$\$0.035(1.065)^{0.75} + \$0.035(1.065)^{0.25} = \$0.0722$$

The first coupon is paid in one-half a year and reinvests for three-quarters of a year. The second coupon is paid in one year and reinvests for one-quarter of a year.

Now the futures price is obtained as

$$f_0(T) = B_0^c(T + Y)\left[1 + r_0(T)\right]^T - FV(CI,0,T)$$

$$f_0(1.25) = \$0.9594(1.065)^{1.25} - \$0.0722 = \$0.9658$$

This is the price at which the futures should trade, given current market conditions. To verify this result, buy the five-year bond for \$0.9594 and sell the futures for \$0.9658. Hold the position for 15 months until the futures expiration. Collect and reinvest the coupons. When the futures expires, deliver the bond and receive the futures price of \$0.9658. Then add the reinvested coupons of \$0.0722 for a total of \$0.9658 + \$0.0722 = \$1.0380. If we invest \$0.9594 and end up with \$1.0380 15 months later, the return is \$1.0380/\$0.9594 = 1.0819. For comparison purposes, we should determine the annual equivalent of this rate, which is found as $(1.0819)^{1/1.25} - 1 = 0.065$. This is the same 6.5 percent risk-free rate. If the futures contract trades at a higher price, the above transaction would result in a return greater than 6.5 percent. The amount available at expiration would be higher, clearly leading to a rate of return higher than 6.5 percent. If the futures trades at a lower price, the arbitrageur would sell short the bond and buy the futures, which would generate a cash inflow today. The amount paid back would be at less than the risk-free rate of 6.5 percent.[42]

Unfortunately, we now must complicate the matter a little by moving to the more realistic case with a delivery option. Bond futures contracts traditionally permit the short to choose which bond to deliver. This feature reduces the possibility of unusual price behavior of the deliverable bond caused by holders of short positions scrambling to buy a single deliverable bond at expiration. By allowing more than one bond to be deliverable, such problems are avoided. The contract is structured as though there is a standard hypothetical deliverable bond, which has a given coupon rate. The Chicago Board of Trade's contract uses a 6 percent rate. If the short delivers a bond with a higher (lower) coupon rate, the price received at delivery is adjusted upward (downward). The conversion factor is defined and calculated as the price of a \$1 face value bond with a coupon and maturity equal to that of the deliverable bond and a yield of 6 percent. Each deliverable bond has its own conversion factor. The short designates which bond he will deliver, and that bond's conversion factor is multiplied by the final futures price to determine the amount the long will pay the short for the bond.

42 Again, as in the section on T-bill futures, this analysis could be conducted in terms of the implied repo rate.

The availability of numerous deliverable bonds creates some confusion in pricing the futures contract, arising from the fact that the underlying cannot be uniquely identified, at least not on the surface. This confusion has given rise to the concept that one bond is always the best one to deliver. If a trader buys a given bond and sells the futures, he creates a risk-free hedge. If there are no arbitrage opportunities, the return from that hedge cannot exceed the risk-free rate. That return can, however, be *less* than the risk-free rate. How can this be? In all previous cases, if a return from a risk-free transaction is less than the risk-free rate, it should be a simple matter to reverse the transaction and capture an arbitrage profit. In this case, however, a reverse transaction would not work. If the arbitrageur sells short the bond and buys the futures, she must be assured that the short will deliver the bond from which the potential arbitrage profit was computed. But the short makes the delivery decision and in all likelihood would not deliver that particular bond.

Thus, the short can be long a bond and short futures and earn a return less than the risk-free rate. One bond, however, results in a return closest to the risk-free rate. Clearly that bond is the best bond to deliver. The terminology in the business is that this bond is the cheapest to deliver.

The cheapest-to-deliver bond is determined by selecting a given bond and computing the rate of return from buying that bond and selling the futures to hedge its delivery at expiration. This calculation is performed for all bonds. The one with the highest rate of return is the cheapest to deliver.[43] The cheapest-to-deliver bond can change, however, which can benefit the short and not the long. We ignore the details of determining the cheapest-to-deliver bond and assume that it has been identified. From here, we proceed to price the futures.

Let CF(T) be the conversion factor for the bond we have identified as the cheapest to deliver. Now we go back to the arbitrage transaction described for the case where there is only one deliverable bond. Recall that we buy the bond, sell a futures, and reinvest the coupons on the bond. At expiration, we deliver the bond, receive the futures price $f_0(T)$, and have the reinvested coupons, which are worth FV(CI,0,T). Now, in the case where the futures contract has many deliverable bonds, we must recognize that when the bond is delivered, the long pays $f_0(T)$ times CF(T). This adjustment does not add any risk to this risk-free transaction. Thus, the present value of the amount received at delivery, $f_0(T)CF(T) + FV(CI,0,T)$, should still equal the original price of the bond, which was the amount we invested to initiate the transaction:

$$B_0^c(T + Y) = \frac{f_0(T)CF(T) + FV(CI,0,T)}{\left[1 + r_0(T)\right]^T}$$

Solving for the futures price, we obtain

$$f_0(T) = \frac{B_0^c(T + Y)\left[1 + r_0(T)\right]^T - FV(CI,0,T)}{CF(T)} \quad (12)$$

Note that when we had only one deliverable bond, the formula did not have the CF(T) term, but a better way to look at it is that for only one deliverable bond, the conversion factor is effectively 1, so Equation 12 would still apply.

Consider the same example we previously worked, but now we need a conversion factor. As noted above, the conversion factor is the price of a $1 bond with coupon and maturity equal to that of the deliverable bond on the expiration day and yield of 6 percent, with all calculations made assuming semiannual interest payments. As noted, we shall skip the specifics of this calculation here; it is simply a present value

43 As noted, this rate of return will not exceed the risk-free rate but will be the highest rate below the risk-free rate.

calculation. For this example, the 7 percent bond with maturity of three and three-quarter years on the delivery day would have a conversion factor of 1.0505. Thus, the futures price would be

$$f_0(T) = \frac{B_0^c(T + Y)[1 + r_0(T)]^T - FV(CI,0,T)}{CF(T)}$$

$$f_0(1.25) = \frac{0.9594(1.065)^{1.25} - 0.0722}{1.0505} = 0.9193$$

If the futures is priced higher than 0.9193, one can buy the bond and sell the futures to earn more than the risk-free rate. If the futures price is less than 0.9193, one can sell short the bond and buy the futures to end up borrowing at less than the risk-free rate. As noted previously, however, this transaction has a complication: If one goes short the bond and long the futures, this bond must remain the cheapest to deliver. Otherwise, the short will not deliver this particular bond and the arbitrage will not be successful.

Exhibit 9 reviews the important formulas for pricing Treasury bond futures contracts.

EXAMPLE 4

Consider a three-year $1 par Treasury bond with a 7.5 percent annual yield and 8 percent semiannual coupon. Its price is $1.0132. A futures contract calling for delivery of this bond only expires in one year. The one-year risk-free rate is 7 percent.

A Find the future value in one year of the coupons on this bond. Assume a reinvestment rate of 3.75 percent per six-month period.

B Find the appropriate futures price.

C Now suppose the bond is one of many deliverable bonds. The contract specification calls for the use of a conversion factor to determine the price paid for a given deliverable bond. Suppose the bond described here has a conversion factor of 1.0372. Now determine the appropriate futures price.

Solution to A:

One coupon of 0.04 will be invested for half a year at 3.75 percent (half of the rate of 7.5 percent). The other coupon is not reinvested but is still counted. Thus, FV(CI,0,1) = 0.04(1.0375) + 0.04 = 0.0815.

Solution to B:

$$f_0(1) = 1.0132(1.07) - 0.0815 = 1.0026$$

Solution to C:

$$f_0(1) = \frac{1.0132(1.07) - 0.0815}{1.0372} = 0.9667$$

Exhibit 9 Pricing Formulas for Treasury Bond Futures Contract

Futures price = Underlying T-bond price compounded at risk-free rate − Compound future value of reinvested coupons.

Futures price if underlying bond is the only deliverable bond:

$$f_0(T) = B_0^c(T+Y)[1+r_0(T)]^T - FV(CI,0,T)$$

Futures price when there are multiple deliverable bonds:

$$f_0(T) = \frac{B_0^c(T+Y)[1+r_0(T)]^T - FV(CI,0,T)}{CF(T)}$$

7.3 Pricing Stock Index Futures

Now let the underlying be either a portfolio of stocks or an individual stock.[44] The former are normally referred to as stock index futures, in which the portfolio is identical in composition to an underlying index of stocks. In this material, we focus on the pricing of stock index futures, but the principles are the same if the underlying is an individual stock.

In pricing stock index futures, we must account for the fact that the underlying stocks pay dividends.[45] Recall that in our previous discussions about the generic pricing of futures, we demonstrated that the futures price is lower as a result of the compound future value of any cash flows paid on the asset. Such cash flows consist of coupon interest payments if the underlying is a bond, or storage costs if the underlying incurs costs to store.[46] Dividends work exactly like coupon interest.

Consider the same time line we used before. Today is time 0, and the futures expires at time T. During the life of the futures, there are n dividends of D_j, j = 1, 2, ..., n. We assume these dividends are all known when the futures contract is initiated. Let

FV(D,0,T) = the compound value over the period of 0 to T of all dividends collected and reinvested

We introduced this variable in the reading on forward markets and contracts and showed how to compute it, so you may wish to review that material. The other notation is the same we have previously used:

S_0 = current value of the stock index
$f_0(T)$ = futures price today of a contract that expires at T
r = risk-free interest rate over the period 0 to T

Now that we are no longer working with interest rate futures, we do not need the more flexible notation for interest rates on bonds of different maturities or interest rates at different time points. So we can use the simple notation of r as the risk-free interest rate, but we must keep in mind that it is the risk-free rate for the time period from 0 to T.

44 Futures on individual stocks have taken a long time to develop, primarily because of regulatory hurdles. They were introduced in the United States in late 2002 and, as of the publication date of this book, have achieved only modest trading volume. They currently trade in a few other countries such as the United Kingdom and Australia.

45 Even if not all of the stocks pay dividends, at least some of the stocks almost surely pay dividends.

46 We also allowed for the possibility of noncash costs, which we called the convenience yield, but there are no implicit costs or benefits associated with stock index futures.

We undertake the following transaction: On day 0, we buy the stock portfolio that replicates the index. This transaction will require that we invest the amount S_0. We simultaneously sell the futures at the price $f_0(T)$.

On day T, the futures expires. We deliver the stock and receive the original futures price $f_0(T)$.[47] We also have the accumulated value of the reinvested dividends, FV(D,0,T) for a total of $f_0(T)$ + FV(D,0,T). Because this amount is known at time 0, the transaction is risk free. Therefore, we should discount its value at the risk-free rate and set this equal to the initial value of the portfolio, S_0, as follows:

$$S_0 = \frac{f_0(T) + FV(D,0,T)}{(1+r)^T}$$

Solving for the futures price gives

$$f_0(T) = S_0(1+r)^T - FV(D,0,T) \quad (13)$$

which is the cost-of-carry formula for stock index futures. Notice that it is virtually identical to that for bond futures. Ignoring the conversion factor necessitated by the delivery option, the only difference is that we use the compound future value of the dividends instead of the compound future value of the coupon interest.

Consider the following example. A stock index is at 1,452.45, and a futures contract on the index expires in three months. Thus, T = 3/12 = 0.25. The risk-free interest rate is 5.5 percent. The value of the dividends reinvested over the life of the futures is 7.26. The futures price should, therefore, be

$$f_0(T) = S_0(1+r)^T - FV(D,0,T)$$

$$f_0(0.25) = 1{,}452.45(1.055)^{0.25} - 7.26$$

$$= 1{,}464.76$$

Thus, if the futures contract is selling for more than this price, an arbitrageur can buy the stocks and sell the futures. The arbitrageur would collect and reinvest the dividends and at expiration would receive a gain that would exceed the risk-free rate of 5.5 percent, a result of receiving more than 1,464.76 for the stocks. If the futures contract is selling for less than this price, the arbitrageur can sell short the stocks and buy the futures. After paying the dividends while holding the stocks,[48] the arbitrageur will end up buying back the stocks at a price that implies that he has borrowed money and paid it back at a rate less than the risk-free rate. The combined activities of all arbitrageurs will force the futures price to 1,464.76.

The stock index futures pricing formula has a number of variations. Suppose we define FV(D,0,T)/$(1 + r)^T$ as the present value of the dividends, PV(D,0,T):

$$FV(D,0,T) = PV(D,0,T)(1+r)^T$$

Substituting in the futures pricing formula above for FV(D,0,T), we obtain

$$f_0(T) = [S_0 - PV(D,0,T)](1+r)^T \quad (14)$$

Notice here that the stock price is reduced by the present value of the dividends. This adjusted stock price is then compounded at the risk-free rate over the life of the futures.

In the problem we worked above, the present value of the dividends is found as

47 Virtually all stock index futures contracts call for cash settlement at expiration. See the explanation of the equivalence of delivery and cash settlement in Section 4 and Exhibit 2.

48 Remember that a short seller must make restitution for any dividends paid while the position is short.

$$PV(D,0,T) = \frac{FV(D,0,T)}{(1+r)^T}$$

$$PV(D,0,0.25) = \frac{7.26}{(1.055)^{0.25}} = 7.16$$

Then the futures price would be

$$f_0(T) = [S_0 - PV(D,0,T)](1+r)^T$$

$$f_0(0.25) = (1{,}452.45 - 7.16)(1.055)^{0.25}$$
$$= 1{,}464.76$$

Another variation of the formula defines the yield as δ in the following manner:

$$\frac{1}{(1+\delta)^T} = 1 - \frac{FV(D,0,T)}{S_0(1+r)^T}$$

The exact solution for δ is somewhat complex, so we shall just leave it in the form above. Using this specification, we find that the futures pricing formula would be

$$f_0(T) = \left(\frac{S_0}{(1+\delta)^T}\right)(1+r)^T \quad (15)$$

The stock price is, thus, discounted at the dividend yield, and this adjusted stock price is then compounded at the risk-free rate over the life of the futures.[49]

In the example above, the yield calculation is

$$\frac{1}{(1+\delta)^T} = 1 - \frac{FV(D,0,T)}{S_0(1+r)^T}$$

$$\frac{1}{(1+\delta)^T} = 1 - \frac{7.26}{1{,}452.45(1.055)^{0.25}} = 0.9951$$

Then $(1 + \delta)^T$ is 1/0.9951 = 1.0049 and the futures price is

$$f_0(T) = \left(\frac{S_0}{(1+\delta)^T}\right)(1+r)^T$$

$$f_0(0.25) = \left(\frac{1{,}452.45}{1.0049}\right)(1.055)^{0.25}$$
$$= 1{,}464.84$$

The difference between this and the answer we previously obtained is strictly caused by a rounding error.

Another variation of this formula is to express the yield as

$$\delta^* = \frac{PV(D,0,T)}{S_0} = \frac{FV(D,0,T)/(1+r)^T}{S_0}$$

This means that $FV(D,0,T) = S_0(1 + r)^T\delta^*$. Substituting into our futures pricing formula for FV(D,0,T), we obtain

$$f_0(T) = S_0(1 - \delta^*)(1 + r)^T \quad (16)$$

49 Sometimes the futures price is written as $f_0(T) = S_0(1 + r - \delta)^T$ where the dividend yield is simply subtracted from the risk-free rate to give a net cost of carry. This formula is a rough approximation that we do not consider acceptable.

Here again, the stock price is reduced by the yield, and this "adjusted" stock price is compounded at the risk-free rate.

In the problem we worked above, the yield would be found as

$$\delta^* = \frac{PV(D,0,T)}{S_0}$$

$$\delta^* = \frac{7.16}{1,452.45} = 0.0049$$

Then the futures price would be

$$f_0(T) = S_0(1 - \delta^*)(1 + r)^T$$

$$f_0(0.25) = 1,452.45(1 - 0.0049)(1.055)^{0.25}$$
$$= 1,464.81$$

Again, the difference between the two prices comes from rounding.

A common variation uses the assumption of continuous compounding. The continuously compounded risk-free rate is defined as $r^c = \ln(1 + r)$. The continuously compounded dividend yield is $\delta^c = \ln(1 + \delta)$. When working with discrete dividends, we obtained the relationship

$$\frac{1}{(1 + \delta)^T} = 1 - \frac{FV(D,0,T)}{S_0(1 + r)^T}$$

We calculated $(1 + \delta)^T$. To obtain δ^c, we take the natural log of this value and divide by T: $\delta^c = (1/T)\ln[(1 + \delta)^T]$. The formula for the futures price is

$$f_0(T) = S_0 e^{(r^c - \delta^c)T}$$

In the above formula, the opportunity cost, expressed as the interest rate, is reduced by the dividend yield. Thus, the formula compounds the spot price by the interest cost less the dividend benefits. An equivalent variation of the above formula is

$$f_0(T) = \left(S_0 e^{-\delta^c T}\right) e^{r^c T} \qquad (17)$$

The expression in parentheses is the stock price discounted at the dividend yield rate. The result is an adjusted stock price with the present value of the dividends removed. This adjusted stock price is then compounded at the risk-free rate. So, as we have previously seen, the stock price less the present value of the dividends is compounded at the risk-free rate to obtain the futures price.

In the previous problem, $(1 + \delta)^T = 1.0049$. Then $\delta^c = (1/0.25)\ln(1.0049) = 0.0196$. The continuously compounded risk-free rate is $\ln(1.055) = 0.0535$. The futures price is, therefore, $f_0(0.25) = (1452.45e^{-0.0196(0.25)})e^{0.0535(0.25)} = 1464.81$; again the difference comes from rounding.

Exhibit 10 summarizes the formulas for pricing stock index futures contracts. Each of these formulas is consistent with the general formula for pricing futures. They are each based on the notion that a futures price is the spot price compounded at the risk-free rate, plus the compound future value of any other costs minus any cash flows and benefits. Alternatively, one can convert the compound future value of the costs net of benefits or cash flows of holding the asset to their current value and subtract this amount from the spot price before compounding the spot price at the interest rate. In this manner, the spot price adjusted for any costs or benefits is then compounded at the risk-free interest rate to give the futures price. These costs, benefits, and cash flows thus represent the linkage between spot and futures prices.

Exhibit 10 **Pricing Formulas for Stock Index Futures Contract**

Futures price = Stock index compounded at risk-free rate – Future value of dividends, or (Stock index – Present value of dividends) compounded at risk-free rate.

Futures price as stock index compounded at risk-free rate – Future value of dividends:

$$f_0(T) = S_0(1 + r)^T - FV(D,0,T)$$

Futures price as stock index – Present value of dividends compounded at risk-free rate:

$$f_0(T) = \left[S_0 - PV(D,0,T)\right](1 + r)^T$$

Futures price as stock index discounted at dividend yield, compounded at risk-free rate:

$$f_0(T) = \left(\frac{S_0}{(1 + \delta)^T}\right)(1 + r)^T \qquad \text{or}$$

$$f_0(T) = S_0(1 - \delta^*)(1 + r)^T$$

Futures price in terms of continuously compounded rate and yield:

$$f_0(T) = S_0 e^{(r^c - \delta^c)T} \qquad \text{or}$$

$$f_0(T) = \left(S_0 e^{-\delta^c T}\right)e^{r^c T}$$

EXAMPLE 5

A stock index is at 755.42. A futures contract on the index expires in 57 days. The risk-free interest rate is 6.25 percent. At expiration, the value of the dividends on the index is 3.94.

A Find the appropriate futures price, using both the future value of the dividends and the present value of the dividends.

B Find the appropriate futures price in terms of the two specifications of the dividend yield.

C Using your answer in Part B, find the futures price under the assumption of continuous compounding of interest and dividends.

Solution to A:

T = 57/365 = 0.1562

$f_0(0.1562) = 7.55.42(1.0625)^{0.1562} - 3.94 = 758.67$

Alternatively, we can find the present value of the dividends:

$$PV(D,0,0.1562) = \frac{3.94}{(1.0625)^{0.1562}} = 3.90$$

Then we can find the futures price as $f_0(0.1562) = (755.42 - 3.90)(1.0625)^{0.1562}$ = 758.67.

Solution to B:

Under one specification of the yield, we have

$$\frac{1}{(1+\delta)^T} = 1 - \frac{3.94}{755.42(1.0625)^{0.1562}} = 0.9948$$

We need the inverse of this amount, which is 1/0.9948 = 1.0052. Then the futures price is

$$f_0(0.1562) = \left(\frac{755.42}{1.0052}\right)(1.0625)^{0.1562} = 758.66$$

Under the other specification of the dividend yield, we have

$$\delta^* = \frac{3.90}{755.42} = 0.0052$$

The futures price is $f_0(0.1562) = 755.42(1 - 0.0052)(1.0625)^{0.1562} = 758.64$, with the difference caused by rounding.

Solution to C:

The continuously compounded risk-free rate is $r^c = \ln(1.0625) = 0.0606$. The continuously compounded dividend yield is

$$\frac{1}{0.1562}\ln(1.0052) = 0.0332$$

The futures price would then be

$$f_0(0.1562) = 755.42e^{(0.0606 - 0.0332)(0.1562)}$$
$$= 758.66$$

7.4 Pricing Currency Futures

Given our assumptions about no marking to market, it will be a simple matter to learn how to price currency futures: We price them the same as currency forwards. Recall that in the reading on forward markets and contracts we described a currency as an asset paying a yield of r^f, which can be viewed as the foreign risk-free rate. Thus, in this sense, a currency futures can also be viewed like a stock index futures, whereby the dividend yield is analogous to the foreign interest rate.

Therefore, an arbitrageur can buy the currency for the spot exchange rate of S_0 and sell a futures expiring at T for $f_0(T)$, holding the position until expiration, collecting the foreign interest, and delivering the currency to receive the original futures price. An important twist, however, is that the arbitrageur must be careful to have the correct number of units of the currency on hand to deliver.

Consider a futures contract on one unit of the currency. If the arbitrageur purchases one unit of the currency up front, the accumulation of interest on the currency will result in having more than one unit at the futures expiration. To adjust for this problem, the arbitrageur should take $S_0/(1 + r^f)^T$ units of his own currency and buy $1/(1 + r^f)^T$ units of the foreign currency.[50] The arbitrageur holds this position and collects interest at the foreign rate. The accumulation of interest is accounted for by multiplying by the interest factor $(1 + r^f)^T$. At expiration, the number of units of the currency will have grown to $[1/(1 + r^f)^T][1 + r^f]^T = 1$. So, the arbitrageur would then have 1 unit of the currency. He delivers that unit and receives the futures price of $f_0(T)$.

To avoid an arbitrage opportunity, the present value of the payoff of $f_0(T)$ must equal the amount initially invested. To find the present value of the payoff, we must discount at the domestic risk-free rate, because that rate reflects the opportunity

50 In other words, if S_0 buys 1 unit, then $S_0/(1 + r^f)^T$ buys $1/(1 + r^f)T$ units.

cost of the arbitrageur's investment of his own money. So, first we equate the present value of the future payoff, discounting at the domestic risk-free rate, to the amount initially invested:

$$\frac{f_0(T)}{(1+r)^T} = \frac{S_0}{\left(1+r^f\right)^T}$$

Then we solve for the futures price to obtain

$$f_0(T) = \left(\frac{S_0}{\left(1+r^f\right)^T}\right)(1+r)^T \tag{18}$$

This formula is the same one we used for currency forwards.

An alternative variation of this formula would apply when we use continuously compounded interest rates. The adjustment is very slight. In the formula above, dividing S_0 by $(1 + r^f)^T$ finds a present value by discounting at the foreign interest rate. Multiplying by $(1 + r)^T$ is finding a future value by compounding at the domestic interest rate. The continuously compounded analogs to those rates are $r^{fc} = \ln(1 + r^f)$ and $r^c = \ln(1 + r)$. Then the formula becomes

$$f_0(T) = \left(S_0 e^{-r^{fc}T}\right)e^{r^cT} \tag{19}$$

We also saw this formula in the reading on forward markets and contracts.

Consider a futures contract expiring in 55 days on the euro. Therefore, T = 55/365 = 0.1507. The spot exchange rate is \$0.8590. The foreign interest rate is 5.25 percent, and the domestic risk-free rate is 6.35 percent. The futures price should, therefore, be

$$f_0(T) = \left(\frac{S_0}{\left(1+r^f\right)^T}\right)(1+r)^T$$

$$f_0(0.1507) = \left(\frac{0.8590}{(1.0525)^{0.1507}}\right)(1.0635)^{0.1507} = 0.8603$$

If the futures is selling for more than this amount, the arbitrageur can buy the currency and sell the futures. He collects the foreign interest and converts the currency back at a higher rate than 0.8603, resulting in a risk-free return that exceeds the domestic risk-free rate. If the futures is selling for less than this amount, the arbitrageur can borrow the currency and buy the futures. The end result will be to receive money at the start and pay back money at a rate less than the domestic risk-free rate.

If the above problem were structured in terms of continuously compounded rates, the domestic rate would be ln(1.0635) = 0.0616 and the foreign rate would be ln(1.0525) = 0.0512. The futures price would then be

$$f_0(T) = \left(S_0 e^{-r^{fc}T}\right)e^{r^cT}$$

$$f_0(0.1507) = \left(0.85890e^{-0.0512(0.1507)}\right)e^{0.0616(0.1507)} = 0.8603$$

which, of course, is the same price we calculated above.

Exhibit 11 summarizes the formulas for pricing currency futures.

Exhibit 11 Pricing Formulas for Currency Futures Contract

Futures price = (Spot exchange rate discounted by Foreign interest rate) compounded at Domestic interest rate:

$$\text{Discrete interest: } f_0(T) = \left(\frac{S_0}{\left(1+r^f\right)^T}\right)(1+r)^T$$

$$\text{Continuous interest: } f_0(T) = \left(S_0 e^{-r^{fc}T}\right)e^{r^c T}$$

EXAMPLE 6

The spot exchange rate for the Swiss franc is \$0.60. The U.S. interest rate is 6 percent, and the Swiss interest rate is 5 percent. A futures contract expires in 78 days.

A Find the appropriate futures price.

B Find the appropriate futures price under the assumption of continuous compounding.

C Using Part A, execute an arbitrage resulting from a futures price of \$0.62.

$$T = 78/365 = 0.2137$$

Solution to A:

$$f_0(0.2137) = \frac{\$0.60}{(1.05)^{0.2137}}(1.06)^{0.2137} = \$0.6012$$

Solution to B:

The continuously compounded equivalent rates are

$$r^{fc} = \ln(1.05) = 0.0488$$

$$r^c = \ln(1.06) = 0.0583$$

The futures price is

$$f_0(0.2137) = \left(\$0.60e^{-0.0488(0.2137)}\right)e^{0.0583(0.2137)}$$

$$= \$0.6012$$

Solution to C:

At \$0.62, the futures price is too high, so we will need to sell the futures. First, however, we must determine how many units of the currency to buy. It should be

$$\frac{1}{(1.05)^{0.2137}} = 0.9896$$

So we buy this many units, which costs 0.9896(\$0.60) = \$0.5938. We sell the futures at \$0.62. We hold the position until expiration. During that time the accumulation of interest will make the 0.9896 units of the currency grow to 1.0000 unit. We convert the Swiss franc to dollars at the futures rate of \$0.62. The return per dollar invested is

$$\frac{0.62}{0.5938} = 1.0441$$

This is a return of 1.0441 per dollar invested over 78 days. At the risk-free rate of 6 percent, the return over 78 days should be $(1.06)^{0.2137} = 1.0125$. Obviously, the arbitrage transaction is much better.

7.5 Futures Pricing: A Recap

We have now examined the pricing of short-term interest rate futures, intermediate- and long-term interest rate futures, stock index futures, and currency futures. Let us recall the intuition behind pricing a futures contract and see the commonality in each of those special cases. First recall that under the assumption of no marking to market, at expiration the short makes delivery and we assume that the long pays the full futures price at that point. An arbitrageur buys the asset and sells a futures contract, holds the asset for the life of the futures, and delivers it at expiration of the futures, at which time he is paid the futures price. In addition, while holding the asset, the arbitrageur accumulates costs and accrues cash flows, such as interest, dividends, and benefits such as a convenience yield. The value of the position at expiration will be the futures price net of these costs minus benefits and cash flows. The overall value of this transaction at expiration is known when the transaction is initiated; thus, the value at expiration is risk-free. The return from a risk-free transaction should equal the risk-free rate, which is the rate on a zero-coupon bond whose maturity is the futures expiration day. If the return is indeed this risk-free rate, then the futures price must equal the spot price compounded at the risk-free rate plus the compound value of these costs net of benefits and cash flows.

It should also be noted that although we have taken the more natural approach of buying the asset and selling the futures, we could just as easily have sold short the asset and bought the futures. Because short selling is usually a little harder to do as well as to understand, the approach we take is preferable from a pedagogical point of view. It is important, nonetheless, to remember that the ability to sell short the asset or the willingness of parties who own the asset to sell it to offset the buying of the futures is critical to establishing the results we have shown here. Otherwise, the futures pricing formulas would be inequalities—limited on one side but not restricted on the other.

We should remind ourselves that this general form of the futures pricing model also applied in the reading on forward markets and contracts. Futures contracts differ from forward contracts in that the latter are subject to credit risk. Futures contracts are marked to market on a daily basis and guaranteed against losses from default by the futures clearinghouse, which has never defaulted. Although there are certain institutional features that distinguish futures from forwards, we consider those features separately from the material on pricing. Because the general economic and financial concepts are the same, for pricing purposes, we treat futures and forwards as the same.

8 THE ROLE OF FUTURES MARKETS AND EXCHANGES

We conclude this reading with a brief look at the role that futures markets and exchanges play in global financial systems and in society. Virtually all participants in the financial markets have heard of futures markets, but many do not understand the role that futures markets play. Some participants do not understand how futures markets function in global financial systems and often look at futures with suspicion, if not disdain.

Derivative markets provide price discovery and risk management, make the markets for the underlying assets more efficient, and permit trading at low transaction costs. These characteristics are also associated with futures markets. In fact, price discovery is often cited by others as the primary advantage of futures markets. Yet, all derivative markets provide these benefits. What characteristics do futures markets have that are not provided by comparable markets as forward markets?

First recall that a major distinction between futures and forwards is that futures are standardized instruments. By having an agreed-upon set of homogeneous contracts, futures markets can provide an orderly, liquid market in which traders can open and close positions without having to worry about holding these positions to expiration. Although not all futures contracts have a high degree of liquidity, an open position can nonetheless be closed on the exchange where the contract was initiated.[51] More importantly, however, futures contracts are guaranteed against credit losses. If a counterparty defaults, the clearinghouse pays and, as we have emphasized, no clearinghouse has ever defaulted. In this manner, a party can engage in a transaction to lock in a future price or rate without having to worry about the credit quality of the counterparty. Forward contracts are subject to default risk, but of course they offer the advantage of customization, the tailoring of a contract's terms to meet the needs of the parties involved.

With an open, standardized, and regulated market for futures contracts, their prices can be disseminated to other investors and the general public. Futures prices are closely watched by a vast number of market participants, many trying to discern an indication of the direction of future spot prices and some simply trying to determine what price they could lock in for future purchase or sale of the underlying asset. Although forward prices provide similar information, forward contracts are private transactions and their prices are not publicly reported. Futures markets thus provide transparency to the financial markets. They reveal the prices at which parties contract for future transactions.

Therefore, futures prices contribute an important element to the body of information on which investors make decisions. In addition, they provide opportunities to transact for future purchase or sale of an underlying asset without having to worry about the credit quality of the counterparty.

In the reading on forward markets and contracts and in this reading, we studied forward and futures contracts and showed that they have a lot in common. Both are commitments to buy or sell an asset at a future date at a price agreed on today. No money changes hands at the start of either transaction. We learned how to determine appropriate prices and values for these contracts. There are a variety of strategies and applications using forward and futures contracts. For now, however, we take a totally different approach and look at contracts that provide not the obligation but rather the right to buy or sell an asset at a later date at a price agreed on today. To obtain such a right, in contrast to agreeing to an obligation, one must pay money at the start. These instruments, called options, are the subject of the reading on option markets and contracts.

51 Recall that there is no liquid market for previously opened forward contracts to be closed, but the holder of a forward contract can re-enter the market and establish a position opposite to the one previously established. If one holds a long forward contract to buy an asset in six months, one can then do a short forward contract to sell the asset in six months, and this transaction offsets the risk of changing market prices. The credit risk on both contracts remains. In some cases, the offsetting contract can be done with the same counterparty as in the original contract, permitting the two parties to arrange a single cash settlement to offset both contracts.

SUMMARY

OPTIONAL SEGMENT

- Futures contracts are standardized instruments that trade on a futures exchange, have a secondary market, and are guaranteed against default by means of a daily settling of gains and losses. Forward contracts are customized instruments that are not guaranteed against default and are created anywhere off of an exchange.
- Modern futures markets primarily originated in Chicago out of a need for grain farmers and buyers to be able to transact for delivery at future dates for grain that would, in the interim, be placed in storage.
- Futures transactions are standardized and conducted in a public market, are homogeneous, have a secondary market giving them an element of liquidity, and have a clearinghouse, which collects margins and settles gains and losses daily to provide a guarantee against default. Futures markets are also regulated at the federal government level.
- Margin in the securities markets is the deposit of money, the margin, and a loan for the remainder of the funds required to purchase a stock or bond. Margin in the futures markets is much smaller and does not involve a loan. Futures margin is more like a performance bond or down payment.
- Futures trading occurs on a futures exchange, which involves trading either in a physical location called a pit or via a computer terminal off of the floor of the futures exchange as part of an electronic trading system. In either case, a party to a futures contract goes long, committing to buy the underlying asset at an agreed-upon price, or short, committing to sell the underlying asset at an agreed-upon price.
- A futures trader who has established a position can re-enter the market and close out the position by doing the opposite transaction (sell if the original position was long or buy if the original position was short). The party has offset the position, no longer has a contract outstanding, and has no further obligation.
- Initial margin is the amount of money in a margin account on the day of a transaction or when a margin call is made. Maintenance margin is the amount of money in a margin account on any day other than when the initial margin applies. Minimum requirements exist for the initial and maintenance margins, with the initial margin requirement normally being less than 10 percent of the futures price and the maintenance margin requirement being smaller than the initial margin requirement. Variation margin is the amount of money that must be deposited into the account to bring the balance up to the required level. The settlement price is an average of the last few trades of the day and is used to determine the gains and losses marked to the parties' accounts.
- The futures clearinghouse engages in a practice called marking to market, also known as the daily settlement, in which gains and losses on a futures position are credited and charged to the trader's margin account on a daily basis. Thus, profits are available for withdrawal and losses must be paid quickly before they build up and pose a risk that the party will be unable to cover large losses.
- The margin balance at the end of the day is determined by taking the previous balance and accounting for any gains or losses from the day's activity, based on the settlement price, as well as any money added or withdrawn.
- Price limits are restrictions on the price of a futures trade and are based on a range relative to the previous day's settlement price. No trade can take place outside of the price limits. A limit move is when the price at which two parties

would like to trade is at or beyond the price limit. Limit up is when the market price would be at or above the upper limit. Limit down is when the market price would be at or below the lower limit. Locked limit occurs when a trade cannot take place because the price would be above the limit up or below the limit down prices.

- A futures contract can be terminated by entering into an offsetting position very shortly before the end of the expiration day. If the position is still open when the contract expires, the trader must take delivery (if long) or make delivery (if short), unless the contract requires that an equivalent cash settlement be used in lieu of delivery. In addition, two participants can agree to alternative delivery terms, an arrangement called exchange for physicals.
- Delivery options are features associated with a futures contract that permit the short some flexibility in what to deliver, where to deliver it, and when in the expiration month to make delivery.
- Scalpers are futures traders who take positions for very short periods of time and attempt to profit by buying at the bid price and selling at the ask price. Day traders close out all positions by the end of the day. Position traders leave their positions open overnight and potentially longer.
- Treasury bill futures are contracts in which the underlying is $1,000,000 of a U.S. Treasury bill. Eurodollar futures are contracts in which the underlying is $1,000,000 of a Eurodollar time deposit. Treasury bond futures are contracts in which the underlying is $100,000 of a U.S. Treasury bond with a minimum 15-year maturity. Stock index futures are contracts in which the underlying is a well-known stock index, such as the S&P 500 or FTSE 100. Currency futures are contracts in which the underlying is a foreign currency.

END OPTIONAL SEGMENT

- An expiring futures contract is equivalent to a spot transaction. Consequently, at expiration the futures price must converge to the spot price to avoid an arbitrage opportunity in which one can buy the asset and sell a futures or sell the asset and buy a futures to capture an immediate profit at no risk.
- The value of a futures contract just prior to marking to market is the accumulated price change since the last mark to market. The value of a futures contract just after marking to market is zero. These values reflect the claim a participant has as a result of her position in the contract.
- The price of a futures contract will equal the price of an otherwise equivalent forward contract one day prior to expiration, or if interest rates are known or constant, or if interest rates are uncorrelated with futures prices.
- A futures price is derived by constructing a combination of a long position in the asset and a short position in the futures. This strategy guarantees that the price received from the sale of the asset is known when the transaction is initiated. The futures price is then derived as the unknown value that eliminates the opportunity to earn an arbitrage profit off of the transaction.
- Futures prices are affected by the opportunity cost of funds tied up in the investment in the underlying asset, the costs of storing the underlying asset, any cash flows paid on the underlying asset, such as interest or dividends, and nonmonetary benefits of holding the underlying asset, referred to as the convenience yield.
- Backwardation describes a condition in which the futures price is lower than the spot price. Contango describes a condition in which the futures price is higher than the spot price.

- The futures price will not equal the expected spot price if the risk premium in the spot price is transferred from hedgers to futures traders. If the risk premium is transferred, then the futures price will be biased high or low relative to the expected future spot price. When the futures price is biased low (high), it is called normal backwardation (normal contango).

OPTIONAL SEGMENT

- T-bill futures prices are determined by going short a futures contract and going long a T-bill that will have the desired maturity at the futures expiration. At expiration, the T-bill is delivered or cash settled to a price locked in when the transaction was initiated through the sale of the futures. The correct futures price is the one that prohibits this combination from earning an arbitrage profit. Under the assumptions we make, the T-bill futures price is the same as the T-bill forward price.
- The implied repo rate is the rate of return implied by a transaction of buying a spot asset and selling a futures contract. If financing can be obtained in the repo market at less than the implied repo rate, the transaction should be undertaken. If financing can be supplied to the repo market at greater than the implied repo rate, the transaction should be reversed.

END OPTIONAL SEGMENT

- Eurodollar futures cannot be priced as easily as T-bill futures, because the expiration price of a Eurodollar futures is based on a value computed as 1 minus a rate, whereas the value of the underlying Eurodollar time deposit is based on 1 divided by a rate. The difference is small but not zero. Hence, Eurodollar futures do not lend themselves to an exact pricing formula based on the notion of a cost of carry of the underlying.
- Treasury bond futures prices are determined by first identifying the cheapest bond to deliver, which is the bond that the short would deliver under current market conditions. Then one must construct a combination of a short futures contract and a long position in that bond. The bond is held, and the coupons are collected and reinvested. At expiration, the underlying bond is delivered and the futures price times the conversion factor for that bond is received. The correct futures price is the one that prevents this transaction from earning an arbitrage profit.
- Stock index futures prices are determined by constructing a combination of a long portfolio of stocks identical to the underlying index and a short futures contract. The stocks are held and the dividends are collected and reinvested. At expiration, the cash settlement results in the effective sale of the stock at the futures price. The correct futures price is the one that prevents this transaction from earning an arbitrage profit.
- Currency futures prices are determined by buying the underlying currency and selling a futures on the currency. The position is held, and the underlying currency pays interest at the foreign risk-free rate. At expiration, the currency is delivered and the futures price is received. The correct futures price is the one that prevents this transaction from earning an arbitrage profit.
- Futures markets serve our financial systems by making the markets for the underlying assets more efficient, by providing price discovery, by offering opportunities to trade at lower transaction costs, and by providing a means of managing risk. Futures markets also provide a homogeneous, standardized, and tradable instrument through which participants who might not have access to forward markets can make commitments to buy and sell assets at a future date at a locked-in price with no fear of credit risk. Because futures markets are so visible and widely reported on, they are also an excellent source of information, contributing greatly to the transparency of financial markets.

PRACTICE PROBLEMS

1 Mary Craft is expecting large-capitalization stocks to rally close to the end of the year. She is pessimistic, however, about the performance of small-capitalization stocks. She decides to go long one December futures contract on the Dow Jones Industrial Average at a price of 9,020 and short one December futures contract on the S&P Midcap 400 Index at a price of 369.40. The multiplier for a futures contract on the Dow is $10, and the multiplier for a futures contract on the S&P Midcap 400 is $500. When Craft closes her position toward the end of the year, the Dow and S&P Midcap 400 futures prices are 9,086 and 370.20, respectively. How much is the net gain or loss to Craft?

2 **A** The current price of gold is $300 per ounce. Consider the net cost of carry for gold to be zero. The risk-free interest rate is 6 percent. What should be the price of a gold futures contract that expires in 90 days?

B Using Part A above, illustrate how an arbitrage transaction could be executed if the futures contract is priced at $306 per ounce.

C Using Part A above, illustrate how an arbitrage transaction could be executed if the futures contract is priced at $303 per ounce.

3 Consider an asset priced at $90. A futures contract on the asset expires in 75 days. The risk-free interest rate is 7 percent. Answer the following questions, each of which is independent of the others, unless indicated otherwise.

A Find the appropriate futures price if the underlying asset has no storage costs, cash flows, or convenience yield.

B Find the appropriate futures price if the underlying asset's storage costs at the futures expiration equal $3.

C Find the appropriate futures price if the underlying asset has positive cash flows. The future value of these cash flows is $0.50 at the time of futures expiration.

D Find the appropriate futures price if the underlying asset's storage costs at the futures expiration equal $3.00 and the compound value at the time of the futures expiration of the positive cash flow from the underlying asset is $0.50.

E Using Part D above, illustrate how an arbitrage transaction could be executed if the futures contract is trading at $95.

F Using Part A above, determine the value of a long futures contract an instant before marking to market if the previous settlement price was $89.50.

G What happens to the value of the futures contract in Part F above as soon as it is marked to market?

4 A $1 face value bond pays an 8 percent semiannual coupon. The annual yield is 6 percent. The bond has 10 years remaining until maturity, and its price is $1.1488. Consider a futures contract calling for delivery of this bond only. The contract expires in 18 months. The risk-free rate is 5 percent.

A Compute the appropriate futures price.

B Assuming that the futures contract is appropriately priced, show the riskless strategy involving the bond and the futures contract that would earn the risk-free rate of return.

5 Consider a six-year $1 par Treasury bond. The bond pays a 6 percent semi-annual coupon, and the annual yield is 6 percent. The bond is priced at par. A futures contract expiring in 15 months calls for delivery of this bond only. The risk-free rate is 5 percent.

A Find the future value in 15 months of the coupons on this bond.

B Find the appropriate futures price.

C Now suppose that the above bond is only one of many deliverable bonds. The contract specification calls for the use of a conversion factor to determine the price paid for a given deliverable bond. Suppose the bond described here has a conversion factor of 1.0567. Find the appropriate futures price.

6 A stock index is at 1,521.75. A futures contract on the index expires in 73 days. The risk-free interest rate is 6.10 percent. The value of the dividends reinvested over the life of the futures is 5.36.

A Find the appropriate futures price.

B Find the appropriate futures price in terms of the two specifications of the dividend yield.

C Using your answer in Part B, find the futures price under the assumption of continuous compounding of interest and dividends.

7 A stock index is at 443.35. A futures contract on the index expires in 201 days. The price of the futures contract is 458.50. The risk-free interest rate is 6.50 percent. The value of the dividends reinvested over the life of the futures is 5.0.

A Show that the futures contract above is mispriced by computing what the price of this futures contract should be.

B Show how an arbitrageur could take advantage of the mispricing.

8 The spot exchange rate for the British pound is $1.4390. The U.S. interest rate is 6.3 percent, and the British interest rate is 5.8 percent. A futures contract on the exchange rate for the British pound expires in 100 days.

A Find the appropriate futures price.

B Find the appropriate futures price under the assumption of continuous compounding.

C Suppose the actual futures price is $1.4650. Is the future contract mispriced? If yes, how could an arbitrageur take advantage of the mispricing? Use discrete compounding as in Part A.

The following information relates to Questions 9–14

Uda Malquist is the chief financial officer of Axia Corporation, a global manufacturer of mobile communication devices. Axia is headquartered in Germany and reports its financial statements in euros (EUR).

Axia expects to make two major financial transactions in the coming months:

- The company will issue a note of 300 million U.S. dollars (USD) in three months (90 days) time. The note will have a six-month (180 days) term, and the proceeds will be used to meet the working capital needs of Axia's U.S. operations.
- Under a new law, Axia will have an opportunity to repatriate 900 million British pounds (GBP) of profits held in the U.K. This repatriation would be on favorable tax terms and would occur in eight months (244 days) time. Axia intends to take full advantage of this tax benefit.

Malquist must first decide whether to hedge the interest rate exposure on the U.S. borrowing with a forward rate agreement (FRA) or with futures contracts.

- Using the information in Exhibit 1 and a 30/360 day count, Malquist calculates the FRA rates implicit in the term structure. Stream Partners, a large brokerage house, offers Axia an FRA rate of 4.68 percent for the USD 300 million note in three months time (with settlement at initiation of the loan).
- Malquist believes that building a perfect hedge for the U.S. borrowing by using Eurodollar futures contracts may not be possible.

Exhibit 1 Current Term Structure of USD LIBOR Rates (Annualized)

Term (Days)	Rate (%)
30	3.10
60	3.40
90	3.71
180	3.99
270	4.12
360	4.22

Malquist must also decide whether to hedge the conversion of pounds to euros. She analyzes the GBP per euro (EUR) exchange rate using the data in Exhibit 2. She calculates the 244-day arbitrage-free forward exchange rate using a 365-day per year convention.

Malquist finds that the futures contract on the euro (quoted as GBP per EUR) is trading above the fair value and that an arbitrage opportunity exists. She also finds that the 244-day arbitrage-free futures price (GBP/EUR) is below the 244-day expected spot exchange rate, but she is confident that rates and prices will be the same in 244 days.

Exhibit 2 Interest Rate and Exchange Rate Data

U.K. interest rate*	4.17%
Euro interest rate*	3.28%
Spot exchange rate (GBP per EUR)	0.6892

*244-day interest rates, discrete and annualized

Malquist assumes that the interest rates in both exhibits are risk-free rates in her analysis.

9 The six-month FRA rate three months from now, implicit in the current term structure of USD LIBOR rates (Exhibit 1), is *closest* to:

A 4.09%.

B 4.29%.

C 5.02%.

10 Assuming a 180-day spot rate of 4.48 percent at expiration of the FRA, the payoff to Axia from the FRA offered by Stream Partners will be *closest* to:

A −$293,427.

B −$287,136.

C $287,136.

11 Is Malquist's belief about building a perfect hedge with Eurodollar futures contracts correct?

A Yes.

B No. Convexity bias allows the construction of a perfect hedge.

C No. Backwardation bias allows the construction of a perfect hedge.

12 Based on information provided in Exhibit 2, the arbitrage-free 244-day forward exchange rate (GBP per EUR) is *closest* to:

A 0.6932.

B 0.6951.

C 0.7083.

13 With respect to the futures contract on the euro, two of the transactions necessary to exploit the arbitrage opportunity include:

A Sell euros and sell euro futures contracts.

B Sell euros and buy euro futures contracts.

C Buy euros and sell euro futures contracts.

14 The difference Malquist finds between the futures price and the expected spot price for GBP in 244 days is *most likely* due to:

A contango.

B backwardation.

C normal backwardation.

SOLUTIONS

1 Her gain caused by the increase in the price of Dow Jones Industrial Average futures is \$10(9,086 – 9,020) = \$660. Because Craft had a short position in S&P Midcap 400 futures, her loss caused by the increase in the price of S&P Midcap 400 futures is \$500(370.20 – 369.40) = \$400. Craft's net gain is \$660 – \$400 = \$260.

2 A T = 90/365 = 0.2466. The futures price is

$$f_0(T) = S_0(1+r)^T$$

$$f_0(0.2466) = 300(1.06)^{0.2466} = \$304.34 \text{ per ounce}$$

B Do the following:

- Enter a short futures position—that is, sell the futures at \$306.
- Buy gold at \$300.
- At expiration, deliver an ounce of gold and receive \$306.

This amount is \$1.66 more than \$304.34, which is the sum of the cost of the asset (\$300) and the loss of interest on this amount at the rate of 6 percent a year (\$4.34). Thus, the overall strategy results in a riskless arbitrage profit of \$1.66 per futures contract. You can also look at this scenario in terms of returns: Investing \$300 and receiving \$306 90 days later is an annual return of 8.36 percent, because $300(1.0836)^{(90/365)} = 306$. This return is clearly greater than the risk-free return of 6 percent.

C The steps in this case would be the reverse of the steps in Part B above. So, do the following:

- Enter a long futures position; that is, buy the futures at \$303.
- Sell short the gold at \$300.
- At expiration, take the delivery of an ounce of gold and pay \$303.

This amount paid is \$1.34 less than \$304.34, which is the sum of the funds received from the short sale of the asset (\$300) and the interest earned on this at the rate of 6 percent per year (\$4.34). Thus, the overall strategy results in a riskless arbitrage profit of \$1.34 per futures contract. In terms of rates, receiving \$300 up front and paying \$303 90 days later represents an annual rate of 4.12 percent, because $300(1.0412)^{(90/365)} = 303$. This rate is clearly less than the risk-free rate of 6 percent. Thus, the overall transaction is equivalent to borrowing at a rate less than the risk-free rate.

3 A T = 75/365 = 0.2055. The futures price is $f_0(0.2055) = 90(1.07)^{0.2055} = 91.26$.

B Storage costs must be covered in the futures price, so we add them:

$$f_0(0.2055) = 91.26 + 3 = 94.26$$

C A positive cash flow, such as interest or dividends on the underlying, reduces the futures price:

$$f_0(0.2055) = 91.26 - 0.50 = 90.76$$

D We add the storage costs and subtract the positive cash flow:

$$f_0(0.2055) = 91.26 + 3 - 0.50 = 93.76$$

E We would do the following:

- Sell the futures at \$95.
- Buy the asset at \$90.

- Because the asset price compounded at the interest rate is \$91.26, the interest forgone is 1.26. So the asset price is effectively \$91.26 by the time of the futures expiration.
- We have incurred storage costs of \$3 on the asset. We have received \$0.50 from the asset. At expiration, we deliver the asset and receive \$95. The net investment in the asset is \$91.26 + \$3.00 – \$0.50 = \$93.76. If we sell it for \$95, we make a net gain of \$1.24. Thus, the overall strategy results in a riskless arbitrage profit of \$1.24 per futures contract. One can also look at this profit in terms of returns. Investing \$90 and receiving a net of \$95.00 – \$3.00 + \$0.50 = \$92.50 75 days later is an annual return of 14.26 percent, because $\$90(1.14264)^{(75/365)} = \$92.50$. This return is clearly greater than the risk-free return of 7 percent.

F The last settlement price was \$89.50, and the price in our answer in Part A is \$91.26. The value of a long futures contract is the difference between these prices, or \$1.76.

G When the futures contract is marked to market, the holder of the futures contract receives a gain of \$1.76, and the value of the futures contract goes back to a value of zero.

4 A Because the futures contract expires in 18 months, T = 1.5. The risk-free rate, $r_0(T)$, is 0.05. When computing the accumulated value of the coupons on the bond and the interest on them until the futures contract expires, note that the first coupon is paid in exactly six months and reinvested for the one year remaining until expiration. Also, the second coupon is paid in exactly one year and reinvested for the six months remaining until expiration, and the third coupon is paid in exactly one and a half years and not reinvested. So, the accumulated value of the coupons on the bond and the interest on them is

$$0.04(1.05)^1 + 0.04(1.05)^{0.5} + 0.04 = 0.1230$$

Because the underlying bond is the only deliverable bond in this simplistic problem, the conversion factor is 1.0, so no adjustment is required. Now the futures price is easily obtained as

$$f_0(T) = B_0^c(T+Y)\left[1 + r_0(T)\right]^T - FV(CI,0,T)$$

$$f_0(1.5) = 1.1488(1.05)^{1.5} - 0.1230$$

$$= 1.1130$$

B Buy the five-year bond for \$1.1488 and sell the futures for \$1.1130. Hold the position for one and a half years until the futures expiration. Collect and reinvest the coupons in the meantime. When the futures contract expires, deliver the bond and receive the futures price of \$1.1130. In addition, you will have the coupons and interest on them of \$0.1230 for a total of \$1.1130 + \$0.1230 = \$1.2360. You invested \$1.1488 and end up with \$1.2360 a year and a half later, so the return per dollar invested is \$1.2360/\$1.1488 = 1.0759. Because this amount is paid in 1.5 years, the annual equivalent of this is

$$1.0759^{1/1.5} = 1.05$$

This return is equivalent to the 5 percent risk-free rate.

5 A Because the futures contract expires in 15 months, T = 1.25. The risk-free rate, $r_0(T)$, is 0.05. To compute the accumulated value of the coupons on the bond and the interest on them until the futures contract expires, we note that the first coupon is paid in exactly six months and reinvested for the nine months (0.75 years) remaining until expiration. Also, the second coupon is paid in exactly one year and reinvested for the three months (0.25 years) remaining until expiration. So, the accumulated value of the coupons on the bond and the interest on them is

$$0.03(1.05)^{0.75} + 0.03(1.05)^{0.25} = 0.0615$$

B Because the underlying bond is the only deliverable bond in this part of the problem, the conversion factor is 1, and no adjustment is required. So, the futures price is

$$f_0(T) = B_0^c(T+Y)\left[1 + r_0(T)\right]^T - FV(CI,0,T)$$

$$f_0(1.25) = 1(1.05)^{1.25} - 0.0615$$

$$= 1.0014$$

C The futures price now is the price computed in Part B above divided by the conversion factor. Because the conversion factor is 1.0567, the futures price is

$$\frac{1.0014}{1.0567} = 0.9477$$

6 A T = 73/365 = 0.20. The futures price should be

$$f_0(T) = S_0(1+r)^T - FV(D,0,T)$$

$$f_0(0.20) = 1{,}521.75(1.0610)^{0.20} - 5.36$$

$$= 1{,}534.52$$

Alternatively, we can find the present value of the dividends:

$$PV(D,0,T) = \frac{FV(D,0,T)}{(1+r)^T}$$

$$PV(D,0,0.20) = \frac{5.36}{(1.0610)^{0.20}} = 5.30$$

Then the futures price would be

$$f_0(T) = \left[S_0 - PV(D,0,T)\right](1+r)^T$$

$$f_0(0.20) = (1{,}521.75 - 5.30)(1.061)^{0.20}$$

$$= 1{,}534.52$$

B One specification based on the yield δ is

$$\frac{1}{(1+\delta)^T} = 1 - \frac{FV(D,0,T)}{S_0(1+r)^T}$$

$$= 1 - \frac{5.36}{1{,}521.75(1.061)^{0.20}} = 0.9965$$

So, $(1 + \delta)^T$ is 1/0.9965 = 1.0035. Then the futures price is

$$f_0(T) = \left(\frac{S_0}{(1+\delta)^T}\right)(1+r)^T$$

$$f_0(0.20) = \left(\frac{1,521.75}{1.0035}\right)(1.061)^{0.20}$$

$$= 1,534.51$$

The difference comes from rounding.

Under the other specification, the yield would be found as

$$\delta^* = \frac{PV(D,0,T)}{S_0}$$

$$= \frac{5.30}{1,521.75} = 0.0035$$

Then the futures price would be

$$f_0(T) = S_0(1 - \delta^*)(1+r)^T$$

$$f_0(0.20) = 1,521.75(1 - 0.0035)(1.061)^{0.20}$$

$$= 1,534.49$$

The difference comes from rounding.

C The continuously compounded risk-free rate is $r^c = \ln(1 + r) = \ln(1.061) = 0.0592$. The continuously compounded dividend yield is $\delta^c = \ln(1 + \delta) = (1/T)\ln[(1 + \delta)^T] = (1/0.20)\ln(1.0035) = 0.0175$. The futures price is

$$f_0(T) = S_0 e^{(r^c - \delta^c)T}$$

$$f_0(0.20) = 1,521.75e^{(0.0592 - 0.0175)0.20}$$

$$= 1,534.49$$

The difference comes from rounding.

7 A T = 201/365 = 0.5507. The futures price should be

$$f_0(T) = S_0(1+r)^T - FV(D,0,T)$$

$$f_0(0.5507) = 443.35(1.0650)^{0.5507} - 5.0 = 454.0$$

Alternatively, we can find the present value of the dividends:

$$PV(D,0,T) = \frac{FV(D,0,T)}{(1+r)^T}$$

$$PV(D,0,0.5507) = \frac{5.0}{(1.0650)^{0.5507}} = 4.83$$

Then the futures price would be

$$f_0(T) = [S_0 - PV(D,0,T)](1+r)^T$$

$$f_0(0.5507) = (443.35 - 4.83)(1.065)^{0.5507}$$

$$= 454.0$$

Because the futures contract is selling at 458.50, which is higher than the price computed above, the futures contract is overpriced.

B The arbitrageur will buy the stocks underlying the index at their current price of \$443.35. Also, the arbitrageur will sell the futures contract at the settlement price of \$458.50. The arbitrageur will collect and reinvest the dividends, which would be worth \$5 at the time of the futures expiration. At the time of expiration, the arbitrageur will get the settlement price of \$458.50. So, the arbitrageur invests \$443.35 at the beginning and receives \$5.00 + \$458.50 = \$463.50 at the expiration 201 days later. The return per dollar invested over the 201-day period is

$$\frac{463.50}{443.35} = 1.0454$$

The annual risk-free rate is 6.5 percent, equivalent to a return per dollar invested of $(1.065)^{0.5507} = 1.0353$ over the 201-day period. Thus, the return to the arbitrageur from the transactions described above exceeds the risk-free return. Alternatively, one could see that to the arbitrageur, the return per dollar invested, over a year, is $1.0454^{365/201} = 1.0832$. This annualized return of 8.32 percent is clearly greater than the annual risk-free rate of 6.5 percent.

8 T = 100/365 = 0.274

A The futures price is

$$f_0(T) = \left(\frac{S_0}{\left(1 + r^f\right)^T}\right)(1 + r)^T$$

$$f_0(0.274) = \left(\frac{1.4390}{1.058^{0.274}}\right)(1.063)^{0.274}$$
$$= 1.4409$$

B The continuously compounded equivalent rates are

$$r^{fc} = \ln(1.058) = 0.0564$$
$$r^c = \ln(1.063) = 0.0611$$

The futures price is

$$f_0(T) = \left(S_0 e^{-r^{fc}T}\right)e^{r^c T}$$
$$f_0(T) = \left(1.4390e^{-0.0564(0.274)}\right)e^{0.0611(0.274)}$$
$$= 1.4409$$

C The actual futures price of \$1.4650 is higher than the price computed above—the futures contract is overpriced. To take advantage, the arbitrageur needs to buy the foreign currency and sell the futures contract. First, however, we must determine how many units of the currency to buy. Because we need to have 1 unit of currency, including the interest, the number of units to buy is

$$\frac{1}{(1.058)^{0.274}} = 0.9847$$

So we buy 0.9847 units, which costs 0.9847($1.4390) = $1.417. We sell the futures at $1.4650 and hold until expiration. During that time, the accumulation of interest will make the 0.9847 units of the currency grow to one unit. Using the futures contract, at expiration we convert this unit at the futures rate of $1.4650. The return per dollar invested is

$$\frac{1.4650}{1.417} = 1.0339$$

or a return of 3.39 percent over 100 days. The U.S. annual risk-free rate is 6.3 percent, which is equivalent to a return per dollar invested of $(1.063)^{0.274}$ = 1.0169, over the 100-day period. Thus, the return to the arbitrageur from the transactions described above exceeds the risk-free return. Alternatively, one could see that to the arbitrageur, the return per dollar invested, over a year, is $(1.0339)^{365/100}$ = 1.1294. This annualized return of 12.94 percent is more than double the annual risk-free rate of 6.3 percent.

9 B is correct. This requires a decomposition of the 270-day rate. The implied forward rate in this question can be found using:

$$\text{FRA}(0,h,m) = \left[\frac{1 + L_0(h+m)\left(\frac{h+m}{360}\right)}{1 + L_0(h)\left(\frac{h}{360}\right)} - 1\right]\left(\frac{360}{m}\right)$$

$$\text{For this problem, FRA} = \left[\frac{1 + 0.0412\left(\frac{270}{360}\right)}{1 + 0.0371\left(\frac{90}{360}\right)} - 1\right]\left(\frac{360}{180}\right) = 0.04285$$

10 A is correct. The payoff at expiration of an FRA (initiation of the loan) is found by solving:

$$V(0,h,m) = \frac{\left[L_h(m) - \text{FRA}(0,h,m)\right] \times \left({}^{m}/_{360}\right)}{1 + L_h(m)\left({}^{m}/_{360}\right)}$$

Then multiply the notional principal by the above calculated value. For this problem, [(0.0448 – 0.0468) × (180/360)] / [1 + 0.0448 × (180/360)] = –0.00097809. Multiply this value by the notional principal of $300,000,000 to get the answer of –$293,427. Axia will pay this to Stream Partners.

11 A is correct. Due to the design features of the Eurodollar futures contract, the rate implied by the futures contract will differ from the implied forward rate of the FRA. Thus, a "perfect" hedge cannot be accomplished.

12 A is correct. Use $F(0,T) = S_0\ [(1 + r)^T / (1 + r^f)^T]$ where F(0,T) is the futures price for the contract that expires at time T, T is the time to expiration in years, S_0 is current spot rate, r^f is the foreign interest rate, and r is the domestic interest rate. In this problem, solve $0.6892[(1.0417)^{(244/365)}/(1.0328)^{(244/365)}] = 0.6932$.

13 C is correct. By definition, to exploit an arbitrage, buy the (relatively) undervalued and sell the (relatively) overvalued. Malquist states that the futures contract on the euro is trading above its fair value. Thus, the correct answer is to buy euros and sell euro futures contract.

14 C is correct. As stated in the problem, Malquist "finds that the 244-day arbitrage-free futures price (GBP/EUR) is below the 244-day expected spot exchange rate." Normal backwardation is defined as "futures prices are lower than expected spot prices."

LOFT
68

DERIVATIVES
STUDY SESSION

17

Derivative Investments

Options, Swaps, and Interest Rate and Credit Derivatives

This study session discusses options, swaps, interest rate derivatives, and embedded derivatives and their valuation. Because derivatives are often used to reduce risk or generate additional income, it is important to understand the relative cost/benefit of derivative strategies.

READING ASSIGNMENTS

Reading 53	Option Markets and Contracts *Analysis of Derivatives for the Chartered Financial Analyst® Program,* by Don M. Chance, CFA
Reading 54	Swap Markets and Contracts *Analysis of Derivatives for the Chartered Financial Analyst® Program,* by Don M. Chance, CFA
Reading 55	Interest Rate Derivative Instruments *Fixed Income Analysis for the Chartered Financial Analyst® Program,* Second Edition, by Frank J. Fabozzi, CFA
Reading 56	Credit Default Swaps by Brian Rose and Don M. Chance, CFA

LOFT
68

READING

53

Option Markets and Contracts

by Don M. Chance, CFA

LEARNING OUTCOMES

Mastery	*The candidate should be able to:*
☐	a. calculate and interpret the prices of a synthetic call option, synthetic put option, synthetic bond, and synthetic underlying stock, and explain why an investor would want to create such instruments;
☐	b. calculate and interpret prices of interest rate options and options on assets using one- and two-period binomial models;
☐	c. explain and evaluate the assumptions underlying the Black–Scholes–Merton model;
☐	d. explain how an option price, as represented by the Black–Scholes–Merton model, is affected by a change in the value of each of the inputs;
☐	e. explain the delta of an option, and demonstrate how it is used in dynamic hedging;
☐	f. explain the gamma effect on an option's delta and how gamma can affect a delta hedge;
☐	g. explain the effect of the underlying asset's cash flows on the price of an option;
☐	h. determine the historical and implied volatilities of an underlying asset;
☐	i. demonstrate how put–call parity for options on forwards (or futures) is established;
☐	j. compare American and European options on forwards and futures, and identify the appropriate pricing model for European options.

OPTIONAL SEGMENT

1 INTRODUCTION

In the reading on forward markets and contracts and the reading on future markets and contracts, we noted how similar forward and futures contracts are: Both are commitments to buy an underlying asset at a fixed price at a later date. Forward contracts, however, are privately created, over-the-counter customized instruments that carry credit risk. Futures contracts are publicly traded, exchange-listed standardized instruments that effectively have no credit risk. Now we turn to options. Like forwards and futures, they are derivative instruments that provide the opportunity to buy or sell an underlying asset with a specific expiration date. But in contrast, buying an option gives the *right*, not the obligation, to buy or sell an underlying asset. And whereas forward and futures contracts involve no exchange of cash up front, options require a cash payment from the option buyer to the option seller.

Yet options contain several features common to forward and futures contracts. For one, options can be created by any two parties with any set of terms they desire. In this sense, options can be privately created, over-the-counter, customized instruments that are subject to credit risk. In addition, however, there is a large market for publicly traded, exchange-listed, standardized options, for which credit risk is essentially eliminated by the clearinghouse.

Just as we examined the pricing of forwards and futures, we shall now examine option pricing in this reading. We shall also see that options can be created out of forward contracts, and that forward contracts can be created out of options. With some simplifying assumptions, options can be created out of futures contracts and futures contracts can be created out of options.

Finally, we note that options also exist that have a futures or forward contract as the underlying. These instruments blend some of the features of both options and forwards/futures.

As background, we discuss the definitions and characteristics of options.

2 BASIC DEFINITIONS AND ILLUSTRATIONS OF OPTIONS CONTRACTS

An option is a financial derivative contract that provides a party the right to buy or sell an underlying at a fixed price by a certain time in the future. The party holding the right is the option buyer; the party granting the right is the option seller. There are two types of options, a **call** and a **put**. A call is an option granting the right to buy the underlying; a put is an option granting the right to sell the underlying. With the exception of some advanced types of options, a given option contract is either a call, granting the right to buy, or a put, granting the right to sell, but not both.[1] We emphasize that this right to buy or sell is held by the option buyer, also called the long or option holder, and granted by the option seller, also called the short or option writer.

To obtain this right, the option buyer pays the seller a sum of money, commonly referred to as the **option price**. On occasion, this option price is called the **option premium** or just the **premium**. This money is paid when the option contract is initiated.

1 Of course, a party could buy both a call and a put, thereby holding the right to buy *and* sell the underlying.

2.1 Basic Characteristics of Options

The fixed price at which the option holder can buy or sell the underlying is called the **exercise price, strike price, striking price**, or **strike**. The use of this right to buy or sell the underlying is referred to as **exercise** or **exercising the option**. Like all derivative contracts, an option has an **expiration date**, giving rise to the notion of an option's **time to expiration**. When the expiration date arrives, an option that is not exercised simply expires.

What happens at exercise depends on whether the option is a call or a put. If the buyer is exercising a call, she pays the exercise price and receives either the underlying or an equivalent cash settlement. On the opposite side of the transaction is the seller, who receives the exercise price from the buyer and delivers the underlying, or alternatively, pays an equivalent cash settlement. If the buyer is exercising a put, she delivers the stock and receives the exercise price or an equivalent cash settlement. The seller, therefore, receives the underlying and must pay the exercise price or the equivalent cash settlement.

As noted in the above paragraph, cash settlement is possible. In that case, the option holder exercising a call receives the difference between the market value of the underlying and the exercise price from the seller in cash. If the option holder exercises a put, she receives the difference between the exercise price and the market value of the underlying in cash.

There are two primary exercise styles associated with options. One type of option has European-style exercise, which means that the option can be exercised only on its expiration day. In some cases, expiration could occur during that day; in others, exercise can occur only when the option has expired. In either case, such an option is called a **European option**. The other style of exercise is American-style exercise. Such an option can be exercised on any day through the expiration day and is generally called an **American option**.[2]

Option contracts specify a designated number of units of the underlying. For exchange-listed, standardized options, the exchange establishes each term, with the exception of the price. The price is negotiated by the two parties. For an over-the-counter option, the two parties decide each of the terms through negotiation.

In an over-the-counter option—one created off of an exchange by any two parties who agree to trade—the buyer is subject to the possibility of the writer defaulting. When the buyer exercises, the writer must either deliver the stock or cash if a call, or pay for the stock or pay cash if a put. If the writer cannot do so for financial reasons, the option holder faces a credit loss. Because the option holder paid the price up front and is not required to do anything else, the seller does not face any credit risk. Thus, although credit risk is bilateral in forward contracts—the long assumes the risk of the short defaulting, and the short assumes the risk of the long defaulting—the credit risk in an option is unilateral. Only the buyer faces credit risk because only the seller can default. As we discuss later, in exchange-listed options, the clearinghouse guarantees payment to the buyer.

2.2 Some Examples of Options

Consider some call and put options on Sun Microsystems (SUNW). The date is 13 June and Sun is selling for $16.25. Exhibit 1 gives information on the closing prices of four options, ones expiring in July and October and ones with exercise prices of 15.00 and 17.50. The July options expire on 20 July and the October options expire on 18

2 It is worthwhile to be aware that these terms have nothing to do with Europe or America. Both types of options are found in Europe and America. The names are part of the folklore of options markets, and there is no definitive history to explain how they came into use.

October. In the parlance of the profession, these are referred to as the July 15 calls, July 17.50 calls, October 15 calls, and October 17.50 calls, with similar terminology for the puts. These particular options are American style.

Consider the July 15 call. This option permits the holder to buy SUNW at a price of $15 a share any time through 20 July. To obtain this option, one would pay a price of $2.35. Therefore, a writer received $2.35 on 13 June and must be ready to sell SUNW to the buyer for $15 during the period through 20 July. Currently, SUNW trades above $15 a share, but as we shall see in more detail later, the option holder has no reason to exercise the option right now.[3] To justify purchase of the call, the buyer must be anticipating that SUNW will increase in price before the option expires. The seller of the call must be anticipating that SUNW will not rise sufficiently in price before the option expires.

Note that the option buyer could purchase a call expiring in July but permitting the purchase of SUNW at a price of $17.50. This price is more than the $15.00 exercise price, but as a result, the option, which sells for $1.00, is considerably cheaper. The cheaper price comes from the fact that the July 17.50 call is less likely to be exercised, because the stock has a higher hurdle to clear. A buyer is not willing to pay as much and a seller is more willing to take less for an option that is less likely to be exercised.

Alternatively, the option buyer could choose to purchase an October call instead of a July call. For any exercise price, however, the October calls would be more expensive than the July calls because they allow a longer period for the stock to make the move that the buyer wants. October options are more likely to be exercised than July options; therefore, a buyer would be willing to pay more and the seller would demand more for the October calls.

Exhibit 1 Closing Prices of Selected Options on SUNW, 13 June

Exercise Price	July Calls	October Calls	July Puts	October Puts
15.00	2.35	3.30	0.90	1.85
17.50	1.00	2.15	2.15	3.20

Note: Stock price is $16.25; July options expire on 20 July; October options expire on 18 October.

Suppose the buyer expects the stock price to go down. In that case, he might buy a put. Consider the October 17.50 put, which would cost the buyer $3.20. This option would allow the holder to sell SUNW at a price of $17.50 any time up through 18 October.[4] He has no reason to exercise the option right now, because it would mean he would be buying the option for $3.20 and selling a stock worth $16.25 for $17.50. In effect, the option holder would part with $19.45 (the cost of the option of $3.20 plus the value of the stock of $16.25) and obtain only $17.50.[5] The buyer of a put obviously must be anticipating that the stock will fall before the expiration day.

3 The buyer paid $2.35 for the option. If he exercised it right now, he would pay $15.00 for the stock, which is worth only $16.25. Thus, he would have effectively paid $17.35 (the cost of the option of $2.35 plus the exercise price of $15) for a stock worth $16.25. Even if he had purchased the option previously at a much lower price, the current option price of $2.35 is the opportunity cost of exercising the option—that is, he can always sell the option for $2.35. Therefore, if he exercised the option, he would be throwing away the $2.35 he could receive if he sold it.

4 Even if the option holder did not own the stock, he could use the option to sell the stock short.

5 Again, even if the option were purchased in the past at a much lower price, the $3.20 current value of the option is an opportunity cost. Exercise of the option is equivalent to throwing away the opportunity cost.

If he wanted a cheaper option than the October 17.50 put, he could buy the October 15 put, which would cost only $1.85 but would allow him to sell the stock for only $15.00 a share. The October 15 put is less likely to be exercised than the October 17.50, because the stock price must fall below a lower hurdle. Thus, the buyer is not willing to pay as much and the seller is willing to take less.

For either exercise price, purchase of a July put instead of an October put would be much cheaper but would allow less time for the stock to make the downward move necessary for the transaction to be worthwhile. The July put is cheaper than the October put; the buyer is not willing to pay as much and the seller is willing to take less because the option is less likely to be exercised.

In observing these option prices, we have obtained our first taste of some principles involved in pricing options.

Call options have a lower premium the higher the exercise price.

Put options have a lower premium the lower the exercise price.

Both call and put options are cheaper the shorter the time to expiration.[6]

These results should be intuitive, but later in this reading we show unequivocally why they must be true.

2.3 The Concept of Moneyness of an Option

An important concept in the study of options is the notion of an option's **moneyness**, which refers to the relationship between the price of the underlying and the exercise price. We use the terms **in-the-money**, **out-of-the-money**, and **at-the-money**. We explain the concept in Exhibit 2 with examples from the SUNW options. Note that in-the-money options are those in which exercising the option would produce a cash inflow that exceeds the cash outflow. Thus, calls are in-the-money when the value of the underlying exceeds the exercise price. Puts are in-the-money when the exercise price exceeds the value of the underlying. In our example, there are no at-the-money SUNW options, which would require that the stock value equal the exercise price; however, an at-the-money option can effectively be viewed as an out-of-the-money option, because its exercise would not bring in more money than is paid out.

As explained above, *one would not necessarily exercise an in-the-money option, but one would never exercise an out-of-the-money option.*

We now move on to explore how options markets are organized.

Exhibit 2 Moneyness of an Option

In-the-Money		Out-of-the-Money	
Option	**Justification**	**Option**	**Justification**
July 15 call	16.25 > 15.00	July 17.50 call	16.25 < 17.50
October 15 call	16.25 > 15.00	October 17.50 call	16.25 < 17.50
July 17.50 put	17.50 > 16.25	July 15 put	15.00 < 16.25
October 17.50 put	17.50 > 16.25	October 15 put	15.00 < 16.25

Notes: Sun Microsystems options on 13 June; stock price is 16.25. See Exhibit 1 for more details. There are no options with an exercise price of 16.25, so no options are at-the-money.

6 There is an exception to the rule that put options are cheaper the shorter the time to expiration. This statement is always true for American options but not always for European options. We explore this point later.

3 THE STRUCTURE OF GLOBAL OPTIONS MARKETS

Although no one knows exactly how options first got started, contracts similar to options have been around for thousands of years. In fact, insurance is a form of an option. The insurance buyer pays the insurance writer a premium and receives a type of guarantee that covers losses. This transaction is similar to a put option, which provides coverage of a portion of losses on the underlying and is often used by holders of the underlying. The first true options markets were over-the-counter options markets in the United States in the 19th century.

3.1 Over-the-Counter Options Markets

In the United States, customized over-the-counter options markets were in existence in the early part of the 20th century and lasted well into the 1970s. An organization called the Put and Call Brokers and Dealers Association consisted of a group of firms that served as brokers and dealers. As brokers, they attempted to match buyers of options with sellers, thereby earning a commission. As dealers, they offered to take either side of the option transaction, usually laying off (**hedging**) the risk in another transaction. Most of these transactions were retail, meaning that the general public were their customers.

As we discuss in Section 3.2 below, the creation of the Chicago Board Options Exchange was a revolutionary event, but it effectively killed the Put and Call Brokers and Dealers Association. Subsequently, the increasing use of swaps facilitated a rebirth of the customized over-the-counter options market. Currency options, a natural extension to currency swaps, were in much demand. Later, interest rate options emerged as a natural outgrowth of interest rate swaps. Soon bond, equity, and index options were trading in a vibrant over-the-counter market. In contrast to the previous over-the-counter options market, however, the current one emerged as a largely wholesale market. Transactions are usually made with institutions and corporations and are rarely conducted directly with individuals. This market is much like the forward market described in the reading on forward markets and contracts, with dealers offering to take either the long or short position in options and hedging that risk with transactions in other options or derivatives. There are no guarantees that the seller will perform; hence, the buyer faces credit risk. As such, option buyers must scrutinize sellers' credit risk and may require some risk reduction measures, such as collateral.

As previously noted, customized options have *all* of their terms—such as price, exercise price, time to expiration, identification of the underlying, settlement or delivery terms, size of the contract, and so on—determined by the two parties.

Like forward markets, over-the-counter options markets are essentially unregulated. In most countries, participating firms, such as banks and securities firms, are regulated by the appropriate authorities but there is usually no particular regulatory body for the over-the-counter options markets. In some countries, however, there are regulatory bodies for these markets.

Exhibit 3 provides information on the leading dealers in over-the-counter currency and interest rate options as determined by *Risk* magazine in its annual surveys of banks and investment banks and also end users.

3.2 Exchange-Listed Options Markets

As briefly noted above, the Chicago Board Options Exchange was formed in 1973. Created as an extension of the Chicago Board of Trade, it became the first organization to offer a market for standardized options. In the United States, standardized options also trade on the AMEX-NASDAQ, the Philadelphia Stock Exchange, and the Pacific Stock Exchange.[7] On a worldwide basis, standardized options are widely traded on such exchanges as LIFFE (the London International Financial Futures and Options Exchange) in London, Eurex in Frankfurt, and most other foreign exchanges. Exhibit 4 (page 149) shows the 20 largest options exchanges in the world. Note, perhaps surprisingly, that the leading options exchange is in Korea.

As described in the reading on forward markets and contracts, the exchange fixes all terms of standardized instruments except the price. Thus, the exchange establishes the expiration dates and exercise prices as well as the minimum price quotation unit. The exchange also determines whether the option is European or American, whether the exercise is cash settlement or delivery of the underlying, and the contract size. In the United States, an option contract on an individual stock covers 100 shares of stock. Terminology such as "one option" is often used to refer to one option contract, which is really a set of options on 100 shares of stock. Index option sizes are stated in terms of a multiplier, indicating that the contract covers a hypothetical number of shares, as though the index were an individual stock. Similar specifications apply for options on other types of underlyings.

The exchange generally allows trading in exercise prices that surround the current stock price. As the stock price moves, options with exercise prices around the new stock price are usually added. The majority of trading occurs in options that are close to being at-the-money. Options that are far in-the-money or far out-of-the-money, called **deep-in-the-money** and **deep-out-of-the-money** options, are usually not very actively traded and are often not even listed for trading.

Most exchange-listed options have fairly short-term expirations, usually the current month, the next month, and perhaps one or two other months. Most of the trading takes place for the two shortest expirations. Some exchanges list options with expirations of several years, which have come to be called LEAPS, for **long-term equity anticipatory securities**. These options are fairly actively purchased, but most investors tend to buy and hold them and do not trade them as often as they do the shorter-term options.

Exhibit 3 ***Risk* Magazine Surveys of Banks, Investment Banks, and Corporate End Users to Determine the Top Three Dealers in Over-the-Counter Currency and Interest Rate Options**

	Respondents	
Currencies	**Banks and Investment Banks**	**Corporate End Users**
Currency Options		
$/€	UBS Warburg	Citigroup
	Citigroup/Deutsche Bank	Royal Bank of Scotland
		Deutsche Bank
$/¥	UBS Warburg	Citigroup
	Credit Suisse First Boston	JP Morgan Chase
	JP Morgan Chase/Royal Bank of Scotland	UBS Warburg
$/£	Royal Bank of Scotland	Royal Bank of Scotland
	UBS Warburg	Citigroup

(continued)

7 You may wonder why the New York Stock Exchange is not mentioned. Standardized options did trade on the NYSE at one time but were not successful, and the right to trade these options was sold to another exchange.

Exhibit 3 (Continued)

	Respondents	
Currencies	**Banks and Investment Banks**	**Corporate End Users**
	Citigroup	Hong Kong Shanghai Banking Corp.
$/SF	UBS Warburg	UBS Warburg
	Credit Suisse First Boston	Credit Suisse First Boston
	Citigroup	Citigroup
Interest Rate Options		
$	JP Morgan Chase	JP Morgan Chase
	Deutsche Bank	Citigroup
	Bank of America	Deutsche Bank/Lehman Brothers*
€	JP Morgan Chase	JP Morgan Chase
	Credit Suisse First Boston/Morgan Stanley	Citigroup UBS Warburg
¥	JP Morgan Chase/Deutsche Bank	UBS Warburg
	Bank of America	Barclays Capital
		Citigroup
£	Barclays Capital	Royal Bank of Scotland
	Societe Generale Groupe	Citigroup
	Bank of America/Royal Bank of Scotland	Hong Kong Shanghai Banking Corp.
SF	UBS Warburg	UBS Warburg
	JP Morgan Chase	JP Morgan
	Credit Suisse First Boston	Goldman Sachs

* Barclays has acquired Lehman Brothers and will maintain the family of Lehman Brothers indices and the associated index calculation, publication, and analytical infrastructure and tools.
Notes: $ = U.S. dollar, € = euro, ¥ = Japanese yen, £ = U.K. pound sterling, SF = Swiss franc. Results for Corporate End Users for Interest Rate Options are from *Risk*, July 2001, pp. 38–46. *Risk* omitted this category from its 2002 survey.
Source: Risk, September 2002, pp. 30–67, for Banks and Investment Banking dealer respondents, and June 2002, pp. 24–34, for Corporate End User respondents.

Exhibit 4 World's 20 Largest Options Exchanges

Exchange and Location	Volume in 2001
Korea Stock Exchange (Korea)	854,791,792
Chicago Board Options Exchange (United States)	306,667,851
MONEP (France)	285,667,686
Eurex (Germany and Switzerland)	239,016,516
American Stock Exchange (United States)	205,103,884
Pacific Stock Exchange (United States)	102,701,752
Philadelphia Stock Exchange (United States)	101,373,433
Chicago Mercantile Exchange (United States)	95,740,352

Exhibit 4 (Continued)

Exchange and Location	Volume in 2001
Amsterdam Exchange (Netherlands)	66,400,654
LIFFE (United Kingdom)	54,225,652
Chicago Board of Trade (United States)	50,345,068
OM Stockholm (Sweden)	39,327,619
South African Futures Exchange (South Africa)	24,307,477
MEFF Renta Variable (Spain)	23,628,446
New York Mercantile Exchange (United States)	17,985,109
Korea Futures Exchange (Korea)	11,468,991
Italian Derivatives Exchange (Italy)	11,045,804
Osaka Securities Exchange (Japan)	6,991,908
Bourse de Montreal (Canada)	5,372,930
Hong Kong Futures Exchange (China)	4,718,880

Note: Volume given is in number of contracts.
Source: Data supplied by *Futures Industry* magazine.

The exchanges also determine on which companies they will list options for trading. Although specific requirements do exist, generally the exchange will list the options of any company for which it feels the options would be actively traded. The company has no voice in the matter. Options of a company can be listed on more than one exchange in a given country.

In the reading on futures markets and contracts, we described the manner in which futures are traded. The procedure is very similar for exchange-listed options. Some exchanges have pit trading, whereby parties meet in the pit and arrange a transaction. Some exchanges use electronic trading, in which transactions are conducted through computers. In either case, the transactions are guaranteed by the clearinghouse. In the United States, the clearinghouse is an independent company called the Options Clearing Corporation or OCC. The OCC guarantees to the buyer that the clearinghouse will step in and fulfill the obligation if the seller reneges at exercise.

When the buyer purchases the option, the premium, which one might think would go to the seller, instead goes to the clearinghouse, which maintains it in a margin account. In addition, the seller must post some margin money, which is based on a formula that reflects whether the seller has a position that hedges the risk and whether the option is in- or out-of-the-money. If the price moves against the seller, the clearinghouse will force the seller to put up additional margin money. Although defaults are rare, the clearinghouse has always been successful in paying when the seller defaults. Thus, exchange-listed options are effectively free of credit risk.

Because of the standardization of option terms and participants' general acceptance of these terms, exchange-listed options can be bought and sold at any time prior to expiration. Thus, a party who buys or sells an option can re-enter the market before the option expires and offset the position with a sale or a purchase of the identical option. From the clearinghouse's perspective, the positions cancel.

As in futures markets, traders on the options exchange are generally either market makers or brokers. Some slight technical distinctions exist between different types of market makers in different options markets, but the differences are minor and do not concern us here. Like futures traders, option market makers attempt to profit by scalping (holding positions very short term) to earn the bid–ask spread and sometimes holding positions longer, perhaps closing them overnight or leaving them open for days or more.

When an option expires, the holder decides whether or not to exercise it. When the option is expiring, there are no further gains to waiting, so in-the-money options are always exercised, assuming they are in-the-money by more than the transaction cost of buying or selling the underlying or arranging a cash settlement when exercising. Using our example of the SUNW options, if at expiration the stock is at 16, the calls with an exercise price of 15 would be exercised. Most exchange-listed stock options call for actual delivery of the stock. Thus, the seller delivers the stock and the buyer pays the seller, through the clearinghouse, $15 per share. If the exchange specifies that the contract is cash settled, the seller simply pays the buyer $1. For puts requiring delivery, the buyer tenders the stock and receives the exercise price from the seller. If the option is out-of-the-money, it simply expires unexercised and is removed from the books. If the put is cash settled, the writer pays the buyer the equivalent cash amount.

Some nonstandardized exchange-traded options exist in the United States. In an attempt to compete with the over-the-counter options market, some exchanges permit some options to be individually customized and traded on the exchange, thereby benefiting from the advantages of the clearinghouse's credit guarantee. These options are primarily available only in large sizes and tend to be traded only by large institutional investors.

Like futures markets, exchange-listed options markets are typically regulated at the federal level. In the United States, federal regulation of options markets is the responsibility of the Securities and Exchange Commission; similar regulatory structures exist in other countries.

4 TYPES OF OPTIONS

Almost anything with a random outcome can have an option on it. Note that by using the word *anything*, we are implying that the underlying does not even need to be an asset. In this section, we shall discover the different types of options, identified by the nature of the underlying. Our focus in this reading is on financial options, but it is important, nonetheless, to gain some awareness of other types of options.

4.1 Financial Options

Financial options are options in which the underlying is a financial asset, an interest rate, or a currency.

4.1.1 *Stock Options*

Options on individual stocks, also called **equity options**, are among the most popular. Exchange-listed options are available on most widely traded stocks, and an option on any stock can potentially be created on the over-the-counter market. We have already given examples of stock options in an earlier section; we now move on to index options.

4.1.2 *Index Options*

Stock market indices are well known, not only in the investment community but also among many individuals who are not even directly investing in the market. Because a stock index is just an artificial portfolio of stocks, it is reasonable to expect that one could create an option on a stock index. Indeed, we have already covered forward and futures contracts on stock indices; options are no more difficult in structure.

For example, consider options on the S&P 500 Index, which trade on the Chicago Board Options Exchange and have a designated index contract multiplier of 250. On 13 June of a given year, the S&P 500 closed at 1241.60. A call option with an exercise price of $1,250 expiring on 20 July was selling for $28. The option is European style and settles in cash. The underlying, the S&P 500, is treated as though it were a share of stock worth $1,241.60, which can be bought, using the call option, for $1,250 on 20 July. At expiration, if the option is in-the-money, the buyer exercises it and the writer pays the buyer the $250 contract multiplier times the difference between the index value at expiration and $1,250.

In the United States, there are also options on the Dow Jones Industrial Average, the NASDAQ, and various other indices. There are nearly always options on the best-known stock indices in most countries.

Just as there are options on stocks, there are also options on bonds.

4.1.3 *Bond Options*

Options on bonds, usually called **bond options**, are primarily traded in the over-the-counter markets. Options exchanges have attempted to generate interest in options on bonds, but have not been very successful. Corporate bonds are not very actively traded; most are purchased and held to expiration. Government bonds, however, are very actively traded; nevertheless, options on them have not gained widespread acceptance on options exchanges. Options exchanges generate much of their trading volume from individual investors, who have far more interest in and understanding of stocks than bonds.

Thus, bond options are found almost exclusively in the over-the-counter market and are almost always options on government bonds. Consider, for example, a U.S. Treasury bond maturing in 27 years. The bond has a coupon of 5.50 percent, a yield of 5.75 percent, and is selling for $0.9659 per $1 par. An over-the-counter options dealer might sell a put or call option on the bond with an exercise price of $0.98 per $1.00 par. The option could be European or American. Its expiration day must be significantly before the maturity date of the bond. Otherwise, as the bond approaches maturity, its price will move toward par, thereby removing much of the uncertainty in its price. The option could be specified to settle with actual delivery of the bond or with a cash settlement. The parties would also specify that the contract covered a given notional principal, expressed in terms of a face value of the underlying bond.

Continuing our example, let us assume that the contract covers $5 million face value of bonds and is cash settled. Suppose the buyer exercises a call option when the bond price is at $0.995. Then the option is in-the-money by $0.995 – $0.98 = $0.015 per $1 par. The seller pays the buyer 0.015($5,000,000) = $75,000. If instead the contract called for delivery, the seller would deliver $5 million face value of bonds, which would be worth $5,000,000($0.995) = $4,975,000. The buyer would pay $5,000,000($0.98) = $4,900,000. Because the option is created in the over-the-counter market, the option buyer would assume the risk of the seller defaulting.

Even though bond options are not very widely traded, another type of related option is widely used, especially by corporations. This family of options is called **interest rate options**. These are quite different from the options we have previously discussed, because the underlying is not a particular financial instrument.

4.1.4 *Interest Rate Options*

In the reading on forward markets and contracts, we devoted considerable effort to understanding the Eurodollar spot market and forward contracts on the Eurodollar rate or LIBOR, called FRAs. In this reading, we cover options on LIBOR. Although these are not the only interest rate options, their characteristics are sufficiently general to capture most of what we need to know about options on other interest rates. First recall that a Eurodollar is a dollar deposited outside of the United States. The primary Eurodollar rate is LIBOR, and it is considered the best measure of an interest rate paid in dollars on a nongovernmental borrower. These Eurodollars represent dollar-denominated time deposits issued by banks in London borrowing from other banks in London.

Before looking at the characteristics of interest rate options, let us set the perspective by recalling that FRAs are forward contracts that pay off based on the difference between the underlying rate and the fixed rate embedded in the contract when it is constructed. For example, consider a 3 × 9 FRA. This contract expires in three months. The underlying rate is six-month LIBOR. Hence, when the contract is constructed, the underlying Eurodollar instrument matures in nine months. *When the contract expires, the payoff is made immediately*, but the rate on which it is based, 180-day LIBOR, is set in the spot market, where it is assumed that interest will be paid 180 days later. Hence, the payoff on an FRA is discounted by the spot rate on 180-day LIBOR to give a present value for the payoff as of the expiration date.

Just as an FRA is a forward contract in which the underlying is an interest rate, an **interest rate option** is an option in which the underlying is an interest rate. Instead of an exercise price, it has an **exercise rate** (or **strike rate**), which is expressed on an order of magnitude of an interest rate. At expiration, the option payoff is based on the difference between the underlying rate in the market and the exercise rate. Whereas an FRA is a *commitment* to make one interest payment and receive another at a future date, an interest rate option is the *right* to make one interest payment and receive another. And just as there are call and put options, there is also an **interest rate call** and an **interest rate put**.

An interest rate call is an option in which the holder has the right to make a known interest payment and receive an unknown interest payment. The underlying is the unknown interest rate. If the unknown underlying rate turns out to be higher than the exercise rate at expiration, the option is in-the-money and is exercised; otherwise, the option simply expires. *An interest rate put is an option in which the holder has the right to make an unknown interest payment and receive a known interest payment.* If the unknown underlying rate turns to be lower than the exercise rate at expiration, the option is in-the-money and is exercised; otherwise, the option simply expires. All interest rate option contracts have a specified size, which, as in FRAs, is called the notional principal. An interest rate option can be European or American style, but most tend to be European style. Interest rate options are settled in cash.

As with FRAs, these options are offered for purchase and sale by dealers, which are financial institutions, usually the same ones who offer FRAs. These dealers quote rates for options of various exercise prices and expirations. When a dealer takes an option position, it usually then offsets the risk with other transactions, often Eurodollar futures.

To use the same example we used in introducing FRAs, consider options expiring in 90 days on 180-day LIBOR. The option buyer specifies whatever exercise rate he desires. Let us say he chooses an exercise rate of 5.5 percent and a notional principal of $10 million.

Now let us move to the expiration day. Suppose that 180-day LIBOR is 6 percent. Then the call option is in-the-money. The payoff to the holder of the option is

$$(\$10{,}000{,}000)(0.06 - 0.055)\left(\frac{180}{360}\right) = \$25{,}000$$

This money is not paid at expiration, however; it is paid 180 days later. There is no reason why the payoff could not be made at expiration, as is done with an FRA. The delay of payment associated with interest rate options actually makes more sense, because these instruments are commonly used to hedge floating-rate loans in which the rate is set on a given day but the interest is paid later.

Note that the difference between the underlying rate and the exercise rate is multiplied by 180/360 to reflect the fact that the rate quoted is a 180-day rate but is stated as an annual rate. Also, the interest calculation is multiplied by the notional principal.

In general, the payoff of an interest rate call is

$$\begin{aligned}&(\text{Notional principal})\ \text{Max}\ (0, \text{Underlying rate at expiration}\\&- \text{Exercise rate})\left(\frac{\text{Days in underlying rate}}{360}\right)\end{aligned} \quad (1)$$

The expression Max(0,Underlying rate at expiration – Exercise rate) is similar to a form that we shall commonly see throughout this reading for all options. The payoff of a call option at expiration is based on the maximum of zero or the underlying minus the exercise rate. If the option expires out-of-the-money, then "Underlying rate at expiration – Exercise rate" is negative; consequently, zero is greater. Thus, the option expires with no value. If the option expires in-the-money, "Underlying rate at expiration – Exercise rate" is positive. Thus, the option expires worth this difference (multiplied by the notional principal and the Days/360 adjustment). The expression "Days in underlying rate," which we used in the reading on forward markets and contracts, refers to the fact that the rate is specified as the rate on an instrument of a specific number of days to maturity, such as a 90-day or 180-day rate, thereby requiring that we multiply by 90/360 or 180/360 or some similar adjustment.

For an interest rate put option, the general formula is

$$\begin{aligned}&(\text{Notional principal})\ \text{Max}\ (0, \text{Exercise rate}\\&- \text{Underlying rate at expiration})\left(\frac{\text{Days in underlying rate}}{360}\right)\end{aligned} \quad (2)$$

For an exercise rate of 5.5 percent and an underlying rate at expiration of 6 percent, an interest rate put expires out-of-the-money. Only if the underlying rate is less than the exercise rate does the put option expire in-the-money.

As noted above, borrowers often use interest rate call options to hedge the risk of rising rates on floating-rate loans. Lenders often use interest rate put options to hedge the risk of falling rates on floating-rate loans. The form we have seen here, in which the option expires with a single payoff, is not the more commonly used variety of interest rate option. Floating-rate loans usually involve multiple interest payments. Each of those payments is set on a given date. To hedge the risk of interest rates increasing, the borrower would need options expiring on each rate reset date. Thus, the borrower would require a combination of interest rate call options. Likewise, a lender needing to hedge the risk of falling rates on a multiple-payment floating-rate loan would need a combination of interest rate put options.

A combination of interest rate calls is referred to as an **interest rate cap** or sometimes just a **cap**. A combination of interest rate puts is called an **interest rate floor** or sometimes just a **floor**.[8] Specifically, *an interest rate cap is a series of call options on an interest rate, with each option expiring at the date on which the floating loan rate will be reset, and with each option having the same exercise rate.*[9] Each option is independent of the others; thus, exercise of one option does not affect the right to exercise any of the others. Each component call option is called a **caplet**. *An interest rate floor is a series of put options on an interest rate, with each option expiring at the date on which the floating loan rate will be reset, and with each option having the same exercise rate.* Each component put option is called a **floorlet**. The price of an interest rate cap or floor is the sum of the prices of the options that make up the cap or floor.

8 It is possible to construct caps and floors with options on any other type of underlying, but they are very often used when the underlying is an interest rate.

9 Technically, each option need not have the same exercise rate, but they generally do.

A special combination of caps and floors is called an **interest rate collar**. *An interest rate collar is a combination of a long cap and a short floor or a short cap and a long floor.* Consider a borrower in a floating rate loan who wants to hedge the risk of rising interest rates but is concerned about the requirement that this hedge must have a cash outlay up front: the option premium. A collar, which adds a short floor to a long cap, is a way of reducing and even eliminating the up-front cost of the cap. The sale of the floor brings in cash that reduces the cost of the cap. It is possible to set the exercise rates such that the price received for the sale of the floor precisely offsets the price paid for the cap, thereby completely eliminating the up-front cost. This transaction is sometimes called a **zero-cost collar**. The term is a bit misleading, however, and brings to mind the importance of noting the true cost of a collar. Although the cap allows the borrower to be paid from the call options when rates are high, the sale of the floor requires the borrower to pay the counterparty when rates are low. Thus, the cost of protection against rising rates is the loss of the advantage of falling rates. Caps, floors, and collars are popular instruments in the interest rate markets.

Although interest rate options are primarily written on such rates as LIBOR, Euribor, and Euroyen, the underlying can be any interest rate.

4.1.5 *Currency Options*

As we noted in the reading on forward markets and contracts, the currency forward market is quite large. The same is true for the currency options market. A **currency option** allows the holder to buy (if a call) or sell (if a put) an underlying currency at a fixed exercise rate, expressed as an exchange rate. Many companies, knowing that they will need to convert a currency X at a future date into a currency Y, will buy a call option on currency Y specified in terms of currency X. For example, say that a U.S. company will be needing €50 million for an expansion project in three months. Thus, it will be buying euros and is exposed to the risk of the euro rising against the dollar. Even though it has that concern, it would also like to benefit if the euro weakens against the dollar. Thus, it might buy a call option on the euro. Let us say it specifies an exercise rate of $0.90. So it pays cash up front for the right to buy €50 million at a rate of $0.90 per euro. If the option expires with the euro above $0.90, it can buy euros at $0.90 and avoid any additional cost over $0.90. If the option expires with the euro below $0.90, it does not exercise the option and buys euros at the market rate.

Note closely these two cases:

Euro expires above $0.90

Company buys €50 million at $0.90

Euro expires at or below $0.90

Company buys €50 million at the market rate

These outcomes can also be viewed in the following manner:

Dollar expires below €1.1111, that is, €1 > $0.90

Company sells $45 million (€50 million × $0.90) at €1.1111, equivalent to buying €50 million

Dollar expires above €1.1111, that is, €1 < $0.90

Company sells sufficient dollars to buy €50 million at the market rate

This transaction looks more like a put in which the underlying is the dollar and the exercise rate is expressed as €1.1111. Thus, the call on the euro can be viewed as a put on the dollar. Specifically, a call to buy €50 million at an exercise price of $0.90 is also a put to sell €50 million × $0.90 = $45 million at an exercise price of 1/$0.90, or €1.1111.

Most foreign currency options activity occurs on the customized over-the-counter markets. Some exchange-listed currency options trade on a few exchanges, but activity is fairly low.

4.2 Options on Futures

One of the important innovations of futures markets is options on futures. These contracts originated in the United States as a result of a regulatory structure that separated exchange-listed options and futures markets. The former are regulated by the Securities and Exchange Commission, and the latter are regulated by the Commodity Futures Trading Commission (CFTC). SEC regulations forbid the trading of options side by side with their underlying instruments. Options on stocks trade on one exchange, and the underlying trades on another or on NASDAQ.

The futures exchanges got the idea that they could offer options in which the underlying is a futures contract; no such prohibitions for side-by-side trading existed under CFTC rules. As a result, the futures exchanges were able to add an attractive instrument to their product lines. The side-by-side trading of the option and its underlying futures made for excellent arbitrage linkages between these instruments. Moreover, some of the options on futures are designed to expire on the same day the underlying futures expires. Thus, the options on the futures are effectively options on the spot asset that underlies the futures.

A call option on a futures gives the holder the right to enter into a long futures contract at a fixed futures price. A put option on a futures gives the holder the right to enter into a short futures contract at a fixed futures price. The fixed futures price is, of course, the exercise price. Consider an option on the Eurodollar futures contract trading at the Chicago Mercantile Exchange. On 13 June of a particular year, an option expiring on 13 July was based on the July Eurodollar futures contract. That futures contract expires on 16 July, a few days after the option expires.[10] The call option with exercise price of 95.75 had a price of \$4.60. The underlying futures price was 96.21. Recall that this price is the IMM index value, which means that the price is based on a discount rate of 100 – 96.21 = 3.79. The contract size is \$1 million.

The buyer of this call option on a futures would pay 0.046(\$1,000,000) = \$46,000 and would obtain the right to buy the July futures contract at a price of 95.75. Thus, at that time, the option was in the money by 96.21 – 95.75 = 0.46 per \$100 face value. Suppose that when the option expires, the futures price is 96.00. Then the holder of the call would exercise it and obtain a long futures position at a price of 95.75. The price of the underlying futures is 96.00, so the margin account is immediately marked to market with a credit of 0.25 or \$625.[11] The party on the short side of the contract is immediately set up with a short futures contract at the price of 95.75. That party will be charged the \$625 gain that the long made. If the option is a put, exercise of it establishes a short position. The exchange assigns the put writer a long futures position.

---

10 Some options on futures expire a month or so before the futures expires. Others expire very close to, if not at, the futures expiration.

11 If the contract is in-the-money by 96 – 95.75 = 0.25 per \$100 par, it is in-the-money by 0.25/100 = 0.0025, or 0.25 percent of the face value. Because the face value is \$1 million, the contract is in the money by (0.0025)(90/360)(\$1,000,000) = \$625. (Note the adjustment by 90/360.) Another way to look at this calculation is that the futures price at 95.75 is 1 – (0.0425)(90/360) = \$0.989375 per \$1 par, or \$989,375. At 96, the futures price is 1 – 0.04(90/360) = \$0.99 per \$1 par or \$990,000. The difference is \$625. So, exercising this option is like entering into a futures contract at a price of \$989,375 and having the price immediately go to \$990,000, a gain of \$625. The call holder must deposit money to meet the Eurodollar futures margin, but the exercise of the option gives him \$625. In other words, assuming he meets the minimum initial margin requirement, he is immediately credited with \$625 more.

4.3 Commodity Options

Options in which the asset underlying the option is a commodity, such as oil, gold, wheat, or soybeans, are also widely traded. There are exchange-traded as well as over-the-counter versions. Over-the-counter options on oil are widely used.

Our focus in this reading is on financial instruments so we will not spend any time on commodity options, but readers should be aware of the existence and use of these instruments by companies whose business involves the buying and selling of these commodities.

4.4 Other Types of Options

As derivative markets develop, options (and even some other types of derivatives) have begun to emerge on such underlyings as electricity, various sources of energy, and even weather. These instruments are almost exclusively customized over-the-counter instruments. Perhaps the most notable feature of these instruments is how the underlyings are often instruments that cannot actually be held. For example, electricity is not considered a storable asset because it is produced and almost immediately consumed, but it is nonetheless an asset and certainly has a volatile price. Consequently, it is ideally suited for options and other derivatives trading.

Consider weather. It is hardly an asset at all but simply a random factor that exerts an enormous influence on economic activity. The need to hedge against and speculate on the weather has created a market in which measures of weather activity, such as economic losses from storms or average temperature or rainfall, are structured into a derivative instrument. Option versions of these derivatives are growing in importance and use. For example, consider a company that generates considerable revenue from outdoor summer activities, provided that it does not rain. Obviously a certain amount of rain will occur, but the more rain, the greater the losses for the company. It could buy a call option on the amount of rainfall with the exercise price stated as a quantity of rainfall. If actual rainfall exceeds the exercise price, the company exercises the option and receives an amount of money related to the excess of the rainfall amount over the exercise price.

Another type of option, which is not at all new but is increasingly recognized in practice, is the real option. A real option is an option associated with the flexibility inherent in capital investment projects. For example, companies may invest in new projects that have the option to defer the full investment, expand or contract the project at a later date, or even terminate the project. In fact, most capital investment projects have numerous elements of flexibility that can be viewed as options. Of course, these options do not trade in markets the same way as financial and commodity options, and they must be evaluated much more carefully. They are, nonetheless, options and thus have the potential for generating enormous value.

Again, our emphasis is on financial options, but readers should be aware of the growing role of these other types of options in our economy. Investors who buy shares in companies that have real options are, in effect, buying real options. In addition, commodity and other types of options are sometimes found in investment portfolios in the form of "alternative investments" and can provide significant diversification benefits.

END OPTIONAL SEGMENT

To this point, we have examined characteristics of options markets and contracts. Now we move forward to the all-important topic of how options are priced.

PRINCIPLES OF OPTION PRICING

5

OPTIONAL SEGMENT

In the readings on forward markets and contracts and on futures markets and contracts, we discussed the pricing and valuation of forward and futures contracts. Recall that the value of a contract is what someone must pay to buy into it or what someone would receive to sell out of it. A forward or futures contract has zero value at the start of the contract, but the value turns positive or negative as prices or rates change. A contract that has positive value to one party and negative value to the counterparty can turn around and have negative value to the former and positive value to the latter as prices or rates change. The forward or futures price is the price that the parties agree will be paid on the future date to buy and sell the underlying.

With options, these concepts are different. An option has a positive value at the start. The buyer must pay money and the seller receives money to initiate the contract. Prior to expiration, the option always has positive value to the buyer and negative value to the seller. In a forward or futures contract, the two parties agree on the fixed price the buyer will pay the seller. This fixed price is set such that the buyer and seller do not exchange any money. The corresponding fixed price at which a call holder can buy the underlying or a put holder can sell the underlying is the exercise price. It, too, is negotiated between buyer and seller but still results in the buyer paying the seller money up front in the form of an option premium or price.[12]

Thus, what we called the forward or futures price corresponds more to the exercise price of an option. The option price *is* the option value: With a few exceptions that will be clearly noted, in this reading we do not distinguish between the option price and value.

In this section of the reading, we examine the principles of option pricing. These principles are characteristics of option prices that are governed by the rationality of investors. These principles alone do not allow us to calculate the option price. We do that in Section 6.

Before we begin, it is important to remind the reader that we assume all participants in the market behave in a rational manner such that they do not throw away money and that they take advantage of arbitrage opportunities. As such, we assume that markets are sufficiently competitive that no arbitrage opportunities exist.

Let us start by developing the notation, which is very similar to what we have used previously. Note that time 0 is today and time T is the expiration.

S_0, S_T = price of the underlying asset at time 0 (today) and time T (expiration)
X = exercise price
r = risk-free rate
T = time to expiration, equal to number of days to expiration divided by 365
c_0, c_T = price of European call today and at expiration
C_0, C_T = price of American call today and at expiration
p_0, p_T = price of European put today and at expiration
P_0, P_T = price of American put today and at expiration

On occasion, we will introduce some variations of the above as well as some new notation. For example, we start off with no cash flows on the underlying, but we shall discuss the effects of cash flows on the underlying in Section 5.7.

12 For a call, there is no finite exercise price that drives the option price to zero. For a put, the unrealistic example of a zero exercise price would make the put price be zero.

5.1 Payoff Values

The easiest time to determine an option's value is at expiration. At that point, there is no future. Only the present matters. An option's value at expiration is called its **payoff**. We introduced this material briefly in our basic descriptions of types of options; now we cover it in more depth.

At expiration, a call option is worth either zero or the difference between the underlying price and the exercise price, whichever is greater:

$$c_T = \text{Max}(0, S_T - X)$$
$$C_T = \text{Max}(0, S_T - X) \quad (3)$$

Note that at expiration, a European option and an American option have the same payoff because they are equivalent instruments at that point.

The expression $\text{Max}(0,S_T - X)$ means to take the greater of zero or $S_T - X$. Suppose the underlying price exceeds the exercise price, $S_T > X$. In this case, the option is expiring in-the-money and the option is worth $S_T - X$. Suppose that at the instant of expiration, it is possible to buy the option for less than $S_T - X$. Then one could buy the option, immediately exercise it, and immediately sell the underlying. Doing so would cost c_T (or C_T) for the option and X to buy the underlying but would bring in S_T for the sale of the underlying. If c_T (or C_T) $< S_T - X$, this transaction would net an immediate risk-free profit. The collective actions of all investors doing this would force the option price up to $S_T - X$. The price could not go higher than $S_T - X$, because all that the option holder would end up with an instant later when the option expires is $S_T - X$. If $S_T < X$, meaning that the call is expiring out-of-the-money, the formula says the option should be worth zero. It cannot sell for less than zero because that would mean that the option seller would have to pay the option buyer. A buyer would not pay more than zero, because the option will expire an instant later with no value.

At expiration, a put option is worth either zero or the difference between the exercise price and the underlying price, whichever is greater:

$$p_T = \text{Max}(0, X - S_T)$$
$$P_T = \text{Max}(0, X - S_T) \quad (4)$$

Suppose $S_T < X$, meaning that the put is expiring in-the-money. At the instant of expiration, suppose the put is selling for less than $X - S_T$. Then an investor buys the put for p_T (or P_T) and the underlying for S_T and exercises the put, receiving X. If p_T (or P_T) $< X - S_T$, this transaction will net an immediate risk-free profit. The combined actions of participants doing this will force the put price up to $X - S_T$. It cannot go any higher, because the put buyer will end up an instant later with only $X - S_T$ and would not pay more than this. If $S_T > X$, meaning that the put is expiring out-of-the-money, it is worth zero. It cannot be worth less than zero because the option seller would have to pay the option buyer. It cannot be worth more than zero because the buyer would not pay for a position that, an instant later, will be worth nothing.

These important results are summarized along with an example in Exhibit 5. The payoff diagrams for the short positions are also shown and are obtained as the negative of the long positions. For the special case of $S_T = X$, meaning that both call and put are expiring at-the-money, we can effectively treat the option as out-of-the-money because it is worth zero at expiration.

The value $\text{Max}(0,S_T - X)$ for calls or $\text{Max}(0,X - S_T)$ for puts is also called the option's **intrinsic value** or **exercise value**. We shall use the former terminology. Intrinsic value is what the option is worth to exercise it based on current conditions. In this section, we have talked only about the option at expiration. Prior to expiration, an option will normally sell for more than its intrinsic value.[13] The difference between the market price of the option and its intrinsic value is called its **time value** or **speculative value**. We shall use the former terminology. The time value reflects the potential for the option's intrinsic value at expiration to be greater than its current intrinsic value. At expiration, of course, the time value is zero.

Exhibit 5 **Option Values at Expiration (Payoffs)**

Option	Value	Example (X = 50)	
		$S_T = 52$	$S_T = 48$
European call	$c_T = \text{Max}(0, S_T - X)$	$c_T = \text{Max}(0, 52 - 50) = 2$	$c_T = \text{Max}(0, 48 - 50) = 0$
American call	$C_T = \text{Max}(0, S_T - X)$	$C_T = \text{Max}(0, 52 - 50) = 2$	$C_T = \text{Max}(0, 48 - 50) = 0$
European put	$p_T = \text{Max}(0, X - S_T)$	$p_T = \text{Max}(0, 50 - 52) = 0$	$p_T = \text{Max}(0, 50 - 48) = 2$
American put	$P_T = \text{Max}(0, X - S_T)$	$P_T = \text{Max}(0, 50 - 52) = 0$	$P_T = \text{Max}(0, 50 - 48) = 2$

Notes: Results for the European and American calls correspond to Graph A. Results for Graph B are the negative of Graph A. Results for the European and American puts correspond to Graph C, and results for Graph D are the negative of Graph C.

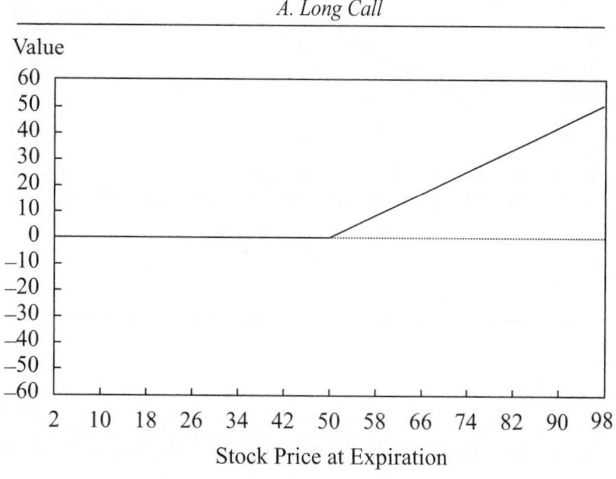

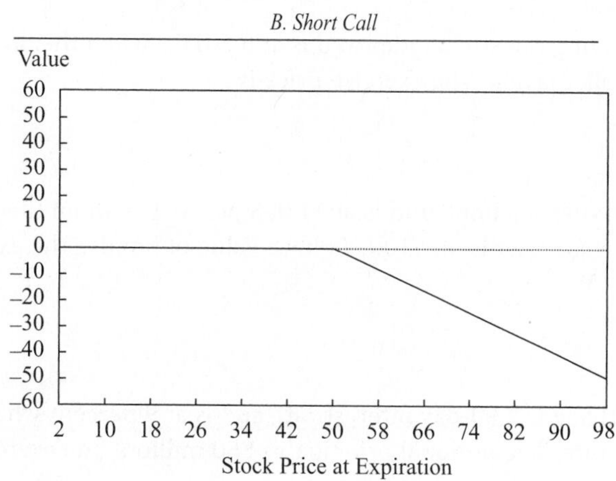

13 We shall later see an exception to this statement for European puts, but for now take it as the truth.

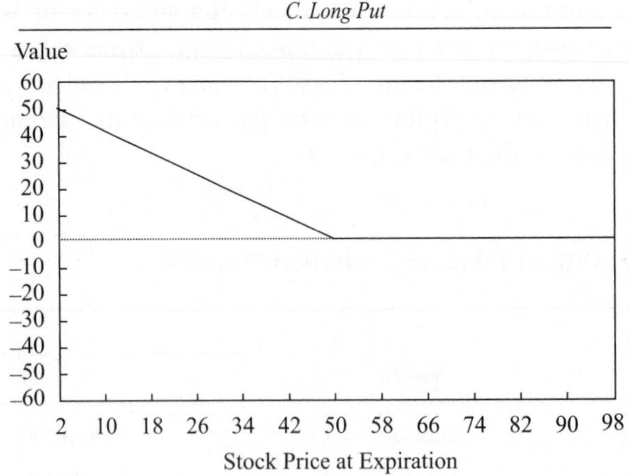

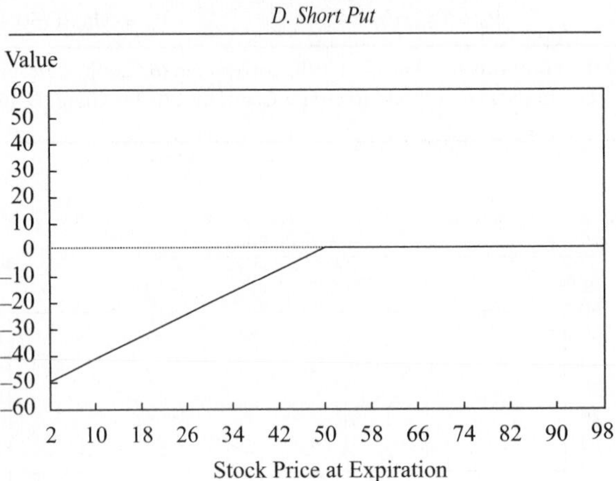

EXAMPLE 1

For Parts A through E, determine the payoffs of calls and puts under the conditions given.

A The underlying is a stock index and is at 5,601.19 when the options expire. The multiplier is 500. The exercise price is

i. 5,500.

ii. 6,000.

B The underlying is a bond and is at \$1.035 per \$1 par when the options expire. The contract is on \$100,000 face value of bonds. The exercise price is

i. \$1.00.

ii. \$1.05.

C The underlying is a 90-day interest rate and is at 9 percent when the options expire. The notional principal is \$50 million. The exercise rate is

i. 8 percent.

ii. 10.5 percent.

D The underlying is the Swiss franc and is at \$0.775 when the options expire. The options are on SF500,000. The exercise price is

  i. \$0.75.

  ii. \$0.81.

E The underlying is a futures contract and is at 110.5 when the options expire. The options are on a futures contract covering \$1 million of the underlying. These prices are percentages of par. The exercise price is

  i. 110.

  ii. 115.

For Parts F and G, determine the payoffs of the strategies indicated and describe the payoff graph.

F The underlying is a stock priced at \$40. A call option with an exercise price of \$40 is selling for \$7. You buy the stock and sell the call. At expiration, the stock price is

  i. \$52.

  ii. \$38.

G The underlying is a stock priced at \$60. A put option with an exercise price of \$60 is priced at \$5. You buy the stock and buy the put. At expiration, the stock price is

  i. \$68.

  ii. \$50.

Solution to A:

i. Calls: Max(0,5601.19 – 5500) × 500 = 50,595

Puts: Max(0,5500 – 5601.19) × 500 = 0

ii. Calls: Max(0,5601.19 – 6000) × 500 = 0

Puts: Max(0,6000 – 5601.19) × 500 = 199,405

Solution to B:

i. Calls: Max(0,1.035 – 1.00) × \$100,000 = \$3,500

Puts: Max(0,1.00 – 1.035) × \$100,000 = \$0

ii. Calls: Max(0,1.035 – 1.05) × \$100,000 = \$0

Puts: Max(0,1.05 – 1.035) × \$100,000 = \$1,500

Solution to C:

i. Calls: Max(0,0.09 – 0.08) × (90/360) × \$50,000,000 = \$125,000

Puts: Max(0,0.08 – 0.09) × (90/360) × \$50,000,000 = \$0

ii. Calls: Max(0,0.09 – 0.105) × (90/360) × \$50,000,000 = \$0

Puts: Max(0,0.105 – 0.09) × (90/360) × \$50,000,000 = \$187,500

Solution to D:

i. Calls: Max(0,0.775 – 0.75) × \$500,000 = \$12,500

Puts: Max(0,0.75 – 0.775) × \$500,000 = \$0

ii. Calls: Max(0,0.775 – 0.81) × \$500,000 = \$0

Puts: Max(0,0.81 – 0.775) × \$500,000 = \$17,500

Solution to E:

i. Calls: $\text{Max}(0,110.5 - 110) \times (1/100) \times \$1,000,000 = \$5,000$

Puts: $\text{Max}(0,110 - 110.5) \times (1/100) \times \$1,000,000 = \$0$

ii. Calls: $\text{Max}(0,110.5 - 115) \times (1/100) \times \$1,000,000 = \$0$

Puts: $\text{Max}(0,115 - 110.5) \times (1/100) \times \$1,000,000 = \$45,000$

Solution to F:

i. $52 - \text{Max}(0,52 - 40) = 40$

ii. $38 - \text{Max}(0,38 - 40) = 38$

For any value of the stock price at expiration of 40 or above, the payoff is constant at 40. For stock price values below 40 at expiration, the payoff declines with the stock price. The graph would look similar to the short put in Panel D of Exhibit 5. This strategy is known as a covered call.

Solution to G:

i. $68 + \text{Max}(0,60 - 68) = 68$

ii. $50 + \text{Max}(0,60 - 50) = 60$

For any value of the stock price at expiration of 60 or below, the payoff is constant at 60. For stock price values above 60 at expiration, the payoff increases with the stock price at expiration. The graph will look similar to the long call in Panel A of Exhibit 5. This strategy is known as a **protective put** and is covered later in this reading.

There is no question that everyone agrees on the option's intrinsic value; after all, it is based on the current stock price and exercise price. It is the time value that we have more difficulty estimating. So remembering that *Option price = Intrinsic value + Time value,* let us move forward and attempt to determine the value of an option today, prior to expiration.

5.2 Boundary Conditions

We start by examining some simple results that establish minimum and maximum values for options prior to expiration.

5.2.1 *Minimum and Maximum Values*

The first and perhaps most obvious result is one we have already alluded to: *The minimum value of any option is zero.* We state this formally as

$$c_0 \geq 0,\ C_0 \geq 0 \qquad (5)$$
$$p_0 \geq 0,\ P_0 \geq 0$$

No option can sell for less than zero, for in that case the writer would have to pay the buyer.

Now consider the maximum value of an option. It differs somewhat depending on whether the option is a call or a put and whether it is European or American. *The maximum value of a call is the current value of the underlying*:

$$c_0 \leq S_0,\ C_0 \leq S_0 \qquad (6)$$

A call is a means of buying the underlying. It would not make sense to pay more for the right to buy the underlying than the value of the underlying itself.

For a put, it makes a difference whether the put is European or American. One way to see the maximum value for puts is to consider the best possible outcome for the put holder. The best outcome is that the underlying goes to a value of zero. Then the put holder could sell a worthless asset for X. For an American put, the holder could sell it immediately and capture a value of X. For a European put, the holder would have to wait until expiration; consequently, we must discount X from the expiration day to the present. Thus, *the maximum value of a European put is the present value of the exercise price. The maximum value of an American put is the exercise price,*

$$p_0 \le X/(1+r)^T, P_0 \le X \quad (7)$$

where r is the risk-free interest rate and T is the time to expiration. These results for the maximums and minimums for calls and puts are summarized in Exhibit 6, which also includes a numerical example.

Exhibit 6 Minimum and Maximum Values of Options

Option	Minimum Value	Maximum Value	Example ($S_0 = 52, X = 50, r = 5\%, T = 1/2$ year)
European call	$c_0 \ge 0$	$c_0 \le S_0$	$0 \le c_0 \le 52$
American call	$C_0 \ge 0$	$C_0 \le S_0$	$0 \le C_0 \le 52$
European put	$p_0 \ge 0$	$p_0 \le X/(1+r)^T$	$0 \le p_0 \le 48.80$ [$48.80 = 50/(1.05)^{0.5}$]
American put	$P_0 \ge 0$	$P_0 \le X$	$0 \le P_0 \le 50$

5.2.2 *Lower Bounds*

The results we established in Section 5.2.1 do not put much in the way of restrictions on the option price. They tell us that the price is somewhere between zero and the maximum, which is either the underlying price, the exercise price, or the present value of the exercise price—a fairly wide range of possibilities. Fortunately, we can tighten the range up a little on the low side: We can establish a **lower bound** on the option price.

For American options, which are exercisable immediately, we can state that the lower bound of an American option price is its current intrinsic value:[14]

$$\begin{aligned} C_0 &\ge \text{Max}(0, S_0 - X) \\ P_0 &\ge \text{Max}(0, X - S_0) \end{aligned} \quad (8)$$

The reason these results hold today is the same reason we have already shown for why they must hold at expiration. If the option is in-the-money and is selling for less than its intrinsic value, it can be bought and exercised to net an immediate risk-free profit.[15] The collective actions of market participants doing this will force the American option price up to at least the intrinsic value.

14 Normally we have italicized sentences containing important results. This one, however, is a little different: We are stating it temporarily. We shall soon show that we can override one of these results with a lower bound that is higher and, therefore, is a better lower bound.

15 Consider, for example, an in-the-money call selling for less than $S_0 - X$. One can buy the call for C_0, exercise it, paying X, and sell the underlying netting a gain of $S_0 - X - C_0$. This value is positive and represents an immediate risk-free gain. If the option is an in-the-money put selling for less than $X - S_0$, one can buy the put for P_0, buy the underlying for S_0, and exercise the put to receive X, thereby netting an immediate risk-free gain of $X - S_0 - P_0$.

Unfortunately, we cannot make such a statement about European options—but we can show that the lower bound is either zero or the current underlying price minus the present value of the exercise price, whichever is greater. They cannot be exercised early; thus, there is no way for market participants to exercise an option selling for too little with respect to its intrinsic value. Fortunately, however, there is a way to establish a lower bound for European options. We can combine options with risk-free bonds and the underlying in such a way that a lower bound for the option price emerges.

First, we need the ability to buy and sell a risk-free bond with a face value equal to the exercise price and current value equal to the present value of the exercise price. This procedure is simple but perhaps not obvious. If the exercise price is X (say, 100), we buy a bond with a face value of X (100) maturing on the option expiration day. The current value of that bond is the present value of X, which is $X/(1 + r)^T$. So we buy the bond today for $X/(1 + r)^T$ and hold it until it matures on the option expiration day, at which time it will pay off X. We assume that we can buy or sell (issue) this type of bond. Note that this transaction involves borrowing or lending an amount of money equal to the present value of the exercise price with repayment of the full exercise price.

Exhibit 7 illustrates the construction of a special combination of instruments. We buy the European call and the risk-free bond and sell short the underlying asset. Recall that short selling involves borrowing the asset and selling it. At expiration, we shall buy back the asset. In order to illustrate the logic behind the lower bound for a European call in the simplest way, we assume that we can sell short without any restrictions.

In Exhibit 7 the two right-hand columns contain the value of each instrument when the option expires. The rightmost column is the case of the call expiring in-the-money, in which case it is worth $S_T - X$. In the other column, the out-of-the-money case, the call is worth zero. The underlying is worth $-S_T$ (the negative of its current value) in either case, reflecting the fact that we buy it back to cover the short position. The bond is worth X in both cases. The sum of all the positions is positive when the option expires out-of-the-money and zero when the option expires in-the-money. Therefore, in no case does this combination of instruments have a negative value. That means that we never have to pay out any money at expiration. We are guaranteed at least no loss at expiration and possibly something positive.

Exhibit 7 A Lower Bound Combination for European Calls

		Value at Expiration	
Transaction	**Current Value**	$S_T \le X$	$S_T > X$
Buy call	c_0	0	$S_T - X$
Sell short underlying	$-S_0$	$-S_T$	$-S_T$
Buy bond	$X/(1 + r)^T$	X	X
Total	$c_0 - S_0 + X/(1 + r)^T$	$X - S_T \ge 0$	0

If there is a possibility of a positive outcome from the combination and if we know we shall never have to pay anything out from holding a combination of instruments, the cost of that combination must be positive—it must cost us something to enter into the position. We cannot take in money to enter into the position. In that case, we would be receiving money up front and never having to pay anything out. The cost of entering the position is shown in the second column, labeled the "Current Value." Because that value must be positive, we therefore require that $c_0 - S_0 + X/(1 + r)^T \ge 0$. Rearranging this equation, we obtain $c_0 \ge S_0 - X/(1 + r)^T$. Now we have a statement about the minimum value of the option, which can serve as a lower bound. This result is solid, because if the call is selling for less than $S_0 - X/(1 + r)^T$, an investor can buy the call, sell short the underlying, and buy the bond. Doing so would bring in money up front and, as we see in Exhibit 7, an investor would not have to pay out any money at expiration and might even get a little more money. Because other investors would do the same, the call price would be forced up until it is at least $S_0 - X/(1 + r)^T$.

But we can improve on this result. Suppose $S_0 - X/(1 + r)^T$ is negative. Then we are stating that the call price is greater than a negative number. But we already know that the call price cannot be negative. So we can now say that

$$c_0 \geq \text{Max}\left[0, S_0 - X/(1+r)^T\right]$$

In other words, *the lower bound on a European call price is either zero or the underlying price minus the present value of the exercise price, whichever is greater.* Notice how this lower bound differs from the lower bound for the American call, $\text{Max}(0,S_0 - X)$. For the European call, we must wait to pay the exercise price and obtain the underlying. Therefore, the expression contains the current underlying value—the present value of its future value—as well as the present value of the exercise price. For the American call, we do not have to wait until expiration; therefore, the expression reflects the potential to immediately receive the underlying price minus the exercise price. We shall have more to say, however, about the relationship between these two values.

To illustrate the lower bound, let $X = 50$, $r = 0.05$, and $T = 0.5$. If the current underlying price is 45, then the lower bound for the European call is

$$\text{Max}\left[0, 45 - 50/(1.05)^{0.5}\right] = \text{Max}(0, 45 - 48.80) = \text{Max}(0, -3.80) = 0$$

All this calculation tells us is that the call must be worth no less than zero, which we already knew. If the current underlying price is 54, however, the lower bound for the European call is

$$\text{Max}(0, 54 - 48.80) = \text{Max}(0, 5.20) = 5.20$$

which tells us that the call must be worth no less than 5.20. With European puts, we can also see that the lower bound differs from the lower bound on American puts in this same use of the present value of the exercise price.

Exhibit 8 A Lower Bound Combination for European Puts

Transaction	Current Value	Value at Expiration	
		$S_T < X$	$S_T \geq X$
Buy put	p_0	$X - S_T$	0
Buy underlying	S_0	S_T	S_T
Issue bond	$-X/(1 + r)^T$	$-X$	$-X$
Total	$p_0 + S_0 - X/(1 + r)^T$	0	$S_T - X \geq 0$

Exhibit 8 constructs a similar type of portfolio for European puts. Here, however, we buy the put and the underlying and borrow by issuing the zero-coupon bond. The payoff of each instrument is indicated in the two rightmost columns. Note that the total payoff is never less than zero. Consequently, the initial value of the combination must not be less than zero. Therefore, $p_0 + S_0 - X/(1 + r)^T \geq 0$. Isolating the put price gives us $p_0 \geq X/(1 + r)^T - S_0$. But suppose that $X/(1 + r)^T - S_0$ is negative. Then, the put price must be greater than a negative number. We know that the put price must be no less than zero. So we can now formally say that

$$p_0 \geq \text{Max}\left[0, X/(1+r)^T - S_0\right]$$

In other words, *the lower bound of a European put is the greater of either zero or the present value of the exercise price minus the underlying price.* For the American put, recall that the expression was $\text{Max}(0,X - S_0)$. So for the European put, we adjust this value to the present value of the exercise price. The present value of the asset price is already adjusted to S_0.

Using the same example we did for calls, let X = 50, r = 0.05, and T = 0.5. If the current underlying price is 45, then the lower bound for the European put is

$$\text{Max}\left(0, 50/(1.05)^{0.5} - 45\right) = \text{Max}(0, 48.80 - 45) = \text{Max}(0, 3.80) = 3.80$$

If the current underlying price is 54, however, the lower bound is

$$\text{Max}(0, 48.80 - 54) = \text{Max}(0, -5.20) = 0$$

At this point let us reconsider what we have found. The lower bound for a European call is $\text{Max}[0,S_0 - X/(1 + r)^T]$. We also observed that an American call must be worth at least $\text{Max}(0,S_0 - X)$. But except at expiration, the European lower bound is greater than the minimum value of the American call.[16] We could not, however, expect an American call to be worth less than a European call. Thus the lower bound of the European call holds for American calls as well. Hence, we can conclude that

$$c_0 \geq \text{Max}\left[0, S_0 - X/(1+r)^T\right]$$
$$C_0 \geq \text{Max}\left[0, S_0 - X/(1+r)^T\right] \quad (9)$$

For European puts, the lower bound is $\text{Max}[0,X/(1 + r)^T - S_0]$. For American puts, the minimum price is $\text{Max}(0,X - S_0)$. The European lower bound is lower than the minimum price of the American put, so the American put lower bound is not changed to the European lower bound, the way we did for calls. Hence,

$$p_0 \geq \text{Max}\left[0, X/(1+r)^T - S_0\right]$$
$$P_0 \geq \text{Max}(0, X - S_0) \quad (10)$$

These results tell us the lowest possible price for European and American options.

Recall that we previously referred to an option price as having an intrinsic value and a time value. For American options, the intrinsic value is the value if exercised, $\text{Max}(0,S_0 - X)$ for calls and $\text{Max}(0,X - S_0)$ for puts. The remainder of the option price is the time value. For European options, the notion of a time value is somewhat murky, because it first requires recognition of an intrinsic value. Because a European option cannot be exercised until expiration, in a sense, all of the value of a European option is time value. The notion of an intrinsic value and its complement, a time value, is therefore inappropriate for European options, though the concepts are commonly applied to European options. Fortunately, understanding European options does not require that we separate intrinsic value from time value. We shall include them together as they make up the option price.

16 We discuss this point more formally and in the context of whether it is ever worthwhile to exercise an American call early in Section 5.6.

EXAMPLE 2

Consider call and put options expiring in 42 days, in which the underlying is at 72 and the risk-free rate is 4.5 percent. The underlying makes no cash payments during the life of the options.

A Find the lower bounds for European calls and puts with exercise prices of 70 and 75.

B Find the lower bounds for American calls and puts with exercise prices of 70 and 75.

Solution to A:

70 call: $\text{Max}[0,72 - 70/(1.045)^{0.1151}] = \text{Max}(0,2.35) = 2.35$

75 call: $\text{Max}[0,72 - 75/(1.045)^{0.1151}] = \text{Max}(0,-2.62) = 0$

70 put: $\text{Max}[0,70/(1.045)^{0.1151} - 72] = \text{Max}(0,-2.35) = 0$

75 put: $\text{Max}[0,75/(1.045)^{0.1151} - 72] = \text{Max}(0,2.62) = 2.62$

Solution to B:

70 call: $\text{Max}[0,72 - 70/(1.045)^{0.1151}] = \text{Max}(0,2.35) = 2.35$

75 call: $\text{Max}[0,72 - 75/(1.045)^{0.1151}] = \text{Max}(0,-2.62) = 0$

70 put: $\text{Max}(0,70 - 72) = 0$

75 put: $\text{Max}(0,75 - 72) = 3$

Exhibit 9 Portfolio Combination for European Calls Illustrating the Effect of Differences in Exercise Prices

		Value at Expiration		
Transaction	**Current Value**	$S_T \le X_1$	$X_1 < S_T < X_2$	$S_T \ge X_2$
Buy call ($X = X_1$)	$c_0(X_1)$	0	$S_T - X_1$	$S_T - X_1$
Sell call ($X = X_2$)	$-c_0(X_2)$	0	0	$-(S_T - X_2)$
Total	$c_0(X_1) - c_0(X_2)$	0	$S_T - X_1 > 0$	$X_2 - X_1 > 0$

5.3 The Effect of a Difference in Exercise Price

Now consider two options on the same underlying with the same expiration day but different exercise prices. Generally, the higher the exercise price, the lower the value of a call and the higher the price of a put. To see this, let the two exercise prices be X_1 and X_2, with X_1 being the smaller. Let $c_0(X_1)$ be the price of a European call with exercise price X_1 and $c_0(X_2)$ be the price of a European call with exercise price X_2. We refer to these as the X_1 call and the X_2 call. In Exhibit 9, we construct a combination in which we buy the X_1 call and sell the X_2 call.[17]

17 This transaction is also known as a bull spread.

Note first that the three outcomes are all non-negative. This fact establishes that the current value of the combination, $c_0(X_1) - c_0(X_2)$ has to be non-negative. We have to pay out at least as much for the X_1 call as we take in for the X_2 call; otherwise, we would get money up front, have the possibility of a positive value at expiration, and never have to pay any money out. Thus, because $c_0(X_1) - c_0(X_2) \geq 0$, we restate this result as

$$c_0(X_1) \geq c_0(X_2)$$

This expression is equivalent to the statement that *a call option with a higher exercise price cannot have a higher value than one with a lower exercise price.* The option with the higher exercise price has a higher hurdle to get over; therefore, the buyer is not willing to pay as much for it. Even though we demonstrated this result with European calls, it is also true for American calls. Thus,[18]

$$C_0(X_1) \geq C_0(X_2)$$

In Exhibit 10 we construct a similar portfolio for puts, except that we buy the X_2 put (the one with the higher exercise price) and sell the X_1 put (the one with the lower exercise price).

Observe that the value of this combination is never negative at expiration; therefore, it must be non-negative today. Hence, $p_0(X_2) - p_0(X_1) \geq 0$. We restate this result as

$$p_0(X_2) \geq p_0(X_1)$$

Exhibit 10 **Portfolio Combination for European Puts Illustrating the Effect of Differences in Exercise Prices**

		Value at Expiration		
Transaction	**Current Value**	$S_T \leq X_1$	$X_1 < S_T < X_2$	$S_T \geq X_2$
Buy put ($X = X_2$)	$p_0(X_2)$	$X_2 - S_T$	$X_2 - S_T$	0
Sell put ($X = X_1$)	$-p_0(X_1)$	$-(X_1 - S_T)$	0	0
Total	$p_0(X_2) - p_0(X_1)$	$X_2 - X_1 > 0$	$X_2 - S_T > 0$	0

Thus, *the value of a European put with a higher exercise price must be at least as great asthe value of a European put with a lower exercise price.* These results also hold for American puts. Therefore,

$$P_0(X_2) \geq P_0(X_1)$$

Even though it is technically possible for calls and puts with different exercise prices to have the same price, *generally we can say that the higher the exercise price, the lower the price of a call and the higher the price of a put.* For example, refer back to Exhibit 1 and observe how the most expensive calls and least expensive puts have the lower exercise prices.

18 It is possible to use the results from this table to establish a limit on the difference between the prices of these two options, but we shall not do so here.

5.4 The Effect of a Difference in Time to Expiration

Option prices are also affected by the time to expiration of the option. Intuitively, one might expect that the longer the time to expiration, the more valuable the option. A longer-term option has more time for the underlying to make a favorable move. In addition, if the option is in-the-money by the end of a given period of time, it has a better chance of moving even further in-the-money over a longer period of time. If the additional time gives it a better chance of moving out-of-the-money or further out-of-the-money, the limitation of losses to the amount of the option premium means that the disadvantage of the longer time is no greater. In most cases, a longer time to expiration is beneficial for an option. We will see that longer-term American and European calls and longer-term American puts are worth no less than their shorter-term counterparts.

First let us consider each of the four types of options: European calls, American calls, European puts, and American puts. We shall introduce options otherwise identical except that one has a longer time to expiration than the other. The one expiring earlier has an expiration of T_1 and the one expiring later has an expiration of T_2. The prices of the options are $c_0(T_1)$ and $c_0(T_2)$ for the European calls, $C_0(T_1)$ and $C_0(T_2)$ for the American calls, $p_0(T_1)$ and $p_0(T_2)$ for the European puts, and $P_0(T_1)$ and $P_0(T_2)$ for the American puts.

When the shorter-term call expires, the European call is worth $\text{Max}(0,S_{T1} - X)$, but we have already shown that the longer-term European call is worth *at least* $\text{Max}\left(0,S_{T1} - X/(1+r)^{(T_2-T_1)}\right)$, which is at least as great as this amount.[19] Thus, the longer-term European call is worth at least the value of the shorter-term European call. These results are not altered if the call is American. When the shorter-term American call expires, it is worth $\text{Max}(0,S_{T1} - X)$. The longer-term American call must be worth at least the value of the European call, so it is worth *at least* $\text{Max}\left[0,S - X/(1+r)^{T_2-T_1}\right]$. Thus, the longer-term call, European or American, is worth no less than the shorter-term call when the shorter-term call expires. Because this statement is always true, the longer-term call, European or American, is worth no less than the shorter-term call at any time prior to expiration. Thus,

$$\begin{aligned} c_0(T_2) &\geq c_0(T_1) \\ C_0(T_2) &\geq C_0(T_1) \end{aligned} \qquad (11)$$

Notice that these statements do not mean that the longer-term call is always worth more; it means that the longer-term call can be worth no less. With the exception of the rare case in which both calls are so far out-of-the-money or in-the-money that the additional time is of no value, the longer-term call will be worth more.

For European puts, we have a slight problem. For calls, the longer term gives additional time for a favorable move in the underlying to occur. For puts, this is also true, but there is one disadvantage to waiting the additional time. When a put is exercised, the holder receives money. The lost interest on the money is a disadvantage of the additional time. For calls, there is no lost interest. In fact, a call holder earns additional interest on the money by paying out the exercise price later. Therefore, it is not always true that additional time is beneficial to the holder of a European put. It is true, however, that the additional time is beneficial to the holder of an American put. An American put can always be exercised; there is no penalty for waiting. Thus, we have

19 Technically, we showed this calculation using a time to expiration of T, but here the time to expiration is $T_2 - T_1$.

$p_0(T_2)$ can be either greater or less than $p_0(T_1)$

$P_0(T_2) \geq P_0(T_1)$ (12)

So for European puts, either the longer-term or the shorter-term option can be worth more. The longer-term European put will tend to be worth more when volatility is greater and interest rates are lower.

Referring back to Exhibit 1, observe that the longer-term put and call options are more expensive than the shorter-term ones. As noted, we might observe an exception to this rule for European puts, but these are all American options.

END OPTIONAL SEGMENT

5.5 Put–Call Parity

So far we have been working with puts and calls separately. To see how their prices must be consistent with each other and to explore common option strategies, let us combine puts and calls with each other or with a risk-free bond. We shall put together some combinations that produce equivalent results.

5.5.1 *Fiduciary Calls and Protective Puts*

First we consider an option strategy referred to as a **fiduciary call**. It consists of a European call and a risk-free bond, just like the ones we have been using, that matures on the option expiration day and has a face value equal to the exercise price of the call. The upper part of the table in Exhibit 11 shows the payoffs at expiration of the fiduciary call. We see that if the price of the underlying is below X at expiration, the call expires worthless and the bond is worth X. If the price of the underlying is above X at expiration, the call expires and is worth S_T (the underlying price) – X. So at expiration, the fiduciary call will end up worth X or S_T, whichever is greater. This type of combination is called a fiduciary call because it allows protection against downside losses and is thus faithful to the notion of preserving capital.

Exhibit 11 Portfolio Combinations for Equivalent Packages of Puts and Calls

		Value at Expiration	
Transaction	**Current Value**	$S_T \leq X$	$S_T > X$
Fiduciary Call			
Buy call	c_0	0	$S_T - X$
Buy bond	$X/(1 + r)^T$	X	X
Total	$c_0 + X/(1 + r)^T$	X	S_T
Protective Put			
Buy put	p_0	$X - S_T$	0
Buy underlying asset	S_0	S_T	S_T
Total	$p_0 + S_0$	X	S_T

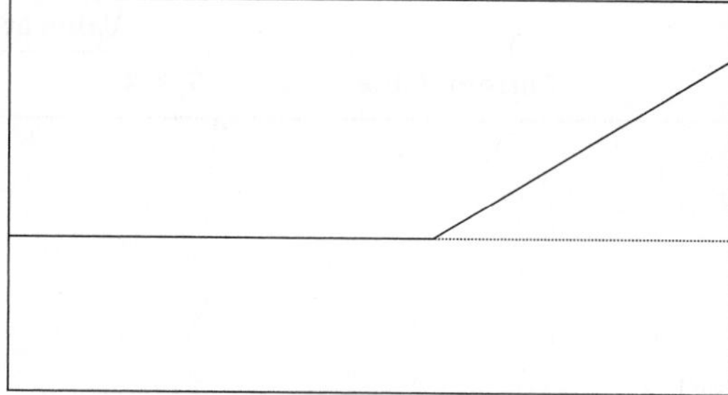

Now we construct a strategy known as a **protective put**, which consists of a European put and the underlying asset. If the price of the underlying is below X at expiration, the put expires and is worth X – S_T and the underlying is worth S_T. If the price of the underlying is above X at expiration, the put expires with no value and the underlying is worth S_T. So at expiration, the protective put is worth X or S_T, whichever is greater. The lower part of the table in Exhibit 11 shows the payoffs at expiration of the protective put.

Thus, the fiduciary call and protective put end up with the same value. They are, therefore, identical combinations. To avoid arbitrage, their values today must be the same. The value of the fiduciary call is the cost of the call, c_0, and the cost of the bond, $X/(1 + r)^T$. The value of the protective put is the cost of the put, p_0, and the cost of the underlying, S_0. Thus,

$$c_0 + X/(1 + r)^T = p_0 + S_0 \tag{13}$$

This equation is called **put–call parity** and is one of the most important results in options. It does not say that puts and calls are equivalent, but it does show an equivalence (parity) of a call/bond portfolio and a put/underlying portfolio.

Put–call parity can be written in a number of other ways. By rearranging the four terms to isolate one term, we can obtain some interesting and important results. For example,

$$c_0 = p_0 + S_0 - X/(1 + r)^T$$

means that a call is equivalent to a long position in the put, a long position in the asset, and a short position in the risk-free bond. The short bond position simply means to borrow by issuing the bond, rather than lend by buying the bond as we did in the fiduciary call portfolio. We can tell from the sign whether we should go long or short. Positive signs mean to go long; negative signs mean to go short.

5.5.2 *Synthetics*

Because the right-hand side of the above equation is equivalent to a call, we often refer to it as a **synthetic call**. To see that the synthetic call is equivalent to the actual call, look at Exhibit 12:

Exhibit 12 Call and Synthetic Call

Transaction	Current Value	Value at Expiration $S_T \le X$	$S_T > X$
Call			
Buy call	c_0	0	$S_T - X$
Synthetic Call			
Buy put	p_0	$X - S_T$	0
Buy underlying asset	S_0	S_T	S_T
Issue bond	$-X/(1 + r)^T$	$-X$	$-X$
Total	$p_0 + S_0 - X/(1 + r)^T$	0	$S_T - X$

The call produces the value of the underlying minus the exercise price or zero, whichever is greater. The synthetic call does the same thing, but in a different way. When the call expires in-the-money, the synthetic call produces the underlying value minus the payoff on the bond, which is X. When the call expires out-of-the-money, the put covers the loss on the underlying and the exercise price on the put matches the amount of money needed to pay off the bond.

Similarly, we can isolate the put as follows:

$$p_0 = c_0 - S_0 + X/(1 + r)^T$$

which says that a put is equivalent to a long call, a short position in the underlying, and a long position in the bond. Because the left-hand side is a put, it follows that the right-hand side is a **synthetic put**. The equivalence of the put and synthetic put is shown in Exhibit 13.

As you can well imagine, there are numerous other combinations that can be constructed. Exhibit 14 shows a number of the more important combinations. There are two primary reasons that it is important to understand synthetic positions in option pricing. Synthetic positions enable us to price options, because they produce the same results as options and have known prices. Synthetic positions also tell how to exploit mispricing of options relative to their underlying assets. Note that we can not only synthesize a call or a put, but we can also synthesize the underlying or the bond. As complex as it might seem to do this, it is really quite easy. First, we learn that *a fiduciary call is a call plus a risk-free bond maturing on the option expiration day with a face value equal to the exercise price of the option.* Then we learn that *a protective put is the underlying plus a put.* Then we learn the basic put–call parity equation: *A fiduciary call is equivalent to a protective put:*

$$c_0 + X/(1 + r)^T = p_0 + S_0$$

Learn the put–call parity equation this way, because it is the easiest form to remember and has no minus signs.

Exhibit 13 Put and Synthetic Put

Transaction	Current Value	Value at Expiration $S_T \le X$	Value at Expiration $S_T > X$
Put			
Buy put	p_0	$X - S_T$	0
Synthetic Put			
Buy call	c_0	0	$S_T - X$
Short underlying asset	$-S_0$	$-S_T$	$-S_T$
Buy bond	$X/(1 + r)^T$	X	X
Total	$c_0 - S_0 + X/(1 + r)^T$	$X - S_T$	0

Exhibit 14 Alternative Equivalent Combinations of Calls, Puts, the Underlying, and Risk-Free Bonds

Strategy	Consisting of	Worth	Equates to	Strategy	Consisting of	Worth
Fiduciary call	Long call + Long bond	$c_0 + X/(1 + r)^T$	=	Protective put	Long put + Long underlying	$p_0 + S_0$
Long call	Long call	c_0	=	Synthetic call	Long put + Long underlying + Short bond	$p_0 + S_0 - X/(1 + r)^T$
Long put	Long put	p_0	=	Synthetic put	Long call + Short underlying + Long bond	$c_0 - S_0 + X/(1 + r)^T$
Long underlying	Long underlying	S_0	=	Synthetic underlying	Long call + Long bond + Short put	$c_0 + X/(1 + r)^T - p_0$
Long bond	Long bond	$X/(1 + r)^T$	=	Synthetic bond	Long put + Long underlying + Short call	$p_0 + S_0 - c_0$

Next, we decide which instrument we want to synthesize. We use simple algebra to isolate that instrument, with a plus sign, on one side of the equation, moving all other instruments to the other side. We then see what instruments are on the other side, taking plus signs as long positions and minus signs as short positions. Finally, to check our results, we should construct a table like Exhibits 11 or 12, with the expiration payoffs of the instrument we wish to synthesize compared with the expiration payoffs of the equivalent combination of instruments. We then check to determine that the expiration payoffs are the same.

5.5.3 *An Arbitrage Opportunity*

In this section we examine the arbitrage strategies that will push prices to put–call parity. Suppose that in the market, prices do not conform to put–call parity. This is a situation in which price does not equal value. Recalling our basic equation, $c_0 + X/(1 + r)^T = p_0 + S_0$, we should insert values into the equation and see if the equality holds. If it does not, then obviously one side is greater than the other. We can view one side as overpriced and the other as underpriced, which suggests an arbitrage opportunity. To exploit this mispricing, we buy the underpriced combination and sell the overpriced combination.

Consider the following example involving call options with an exercise price of \$100 expiring in half a year (T = 0.5). The risk-free rate is 10 percent. The call is priced at \$7.50, and the put is priced at \$4.25. The underlying price is \$99.

The left-hand side of the basic put–call parity equation is $c_0 + X/(1 + r)^T = 7.50 + 100/(1.10)^{0.5} = 7.50 + 95.35 = 102.85$. The right-hand side is $p_0 + S_0 = 4.25 + 99 = 103.25$. So the right-hand side is greater than the left-hand side. This means that the protective put is overpriced. Equivalently, we could view this as the fiduciary call being underpriced. Either way will lead us to the correct strategy to exploit the mispricing.

We sell the overpriced combination, the protective put. This means that we sell the put and sell short the underlying. Doing so will generate a cash inflow of \$103.25. We buy the fiduciary call, paying out \$102.85. This series of transactions nets a cash inflow of \$103.25 – \$102.85 = \$0.40. Now, let us see what happens at expiration.

The options expire with the underlying above 100:

The bond matures, paying \$100.

Use the \$100 to exercise the call, receiving the underlying.

Deliver the underlying to cover the short sale.

The put expires with no value.

Net effect: No money in or out.

The options expire with the underlying below 100:

The bond matures, paying \$100.

The put expires in-the-money; use the \$100 to buy the underlying.

Use the underlying to cover the short sale.

The call expires with no value.

Net effect: No money in or out.

So we receive \$0.40 up front and do not have to pay anything out. The position is perfectly hedged and represents an arbitrage profit. The combined effects of other investors performing this transaction will result in the value of the protective put going down and/or the value of the fiduciary call going up until the two strategies are equivalent in value. Of course, it is possible that transaction costs might consume any profit, so small discrepancies will not be exploited.

It is important to note that regardless of which put–call parity equation we use, we will arrive at the same strategy. For example, in the above problem, the synthetic put (a long call, a short position in the underlying, and a long bond) is worth \$7.50 – \$99 + \$95.35 = \$3.85. The actual put is worth \$4.25. Thus, we would conclude that we should sell the actual put and buy the synthetic put. To buy the synthetic put, we would buy the call, short the underlying, and buy the bond—precisely the strategy we used to exploit this price discrepancy.

In all of these examples based on put–call parity, we used only European options. Put–call parity using American options is considerably more complicated. The resulting parity equation is a complex combination of inequalities. Thus, we cannot say that a given combination exactly equals another; we can say only that one combination is more valuable than another. Exploitation of any such mispricing is somewhat more complicated, and we shall not explore it here.

EXAMPLE 3

European put and call options with an exercise price of 45 expire in 115 days. The underlying is priced at 48 and makes no cash payments during the life of the options. The risk-free rate is 4.5 percent. The put is selling for 3.75, and the call is selling for 8.00.

A Identify the mispricing by comparing the price of the actual call with the price of the synthetic call.

B Based on your answer in Part A, demonstrate how an arbitrage transaction is executed.

Solution to A:

Using put–call parity, the following formula applies:

$$c_0 = p_0 + S_0 - X/(1 + r)^T$$

The time to expiration is T = 115/365 = 0.3151. Substituting values into the right-hand side:

$$c_0 = 3.75 + 48 - 45/(1.045)^{0.3151} = 7.37$$

Hence, the synthetic call is worth 7.37, but the actual call is selling for 8.00 and is, therefore, overpriced.

Solution to B:

Sell the call for 8.00 and buy the synthetic call for 7.37. To buy the synthetic call, buy the put for 3.75, buy the underlying for 48.00, and issue a zero-coupon bond paying 45.00 at expiration. The bond will bring in $45.00/(1.045)^{0.3151} = 44.38$ today. This transaction will bring in 8.00 – 7.37 = 0.63.

At expiration, the following payoffs will occur:

	$S_T < 45$	$S_T \geq 45$
Short call	0	$-(S_T - 45)$
Long put	$45 - S_T$	0
Underlying	S_T	S_T
Bond	–45	–45
Total	0	0

Thus there will be no cash in or out at expiration. The transaction will net a risk-free gain of 8.00 – 7.37 = 0.63 up front.

5.6 American Options, Lower Bounds, and Early Exercise

As we have noted, American options can be exercised early, and in this section we specify cases in which early exercise can have value. Because early exercise is never mandatory, the right to exercise early may be worth something but could never hurt the option holder. Consequently, the prices of American options must be no less than the prices of European options:

$$C_0 \geq c_0$$
$$P_0 \geq p_0 \quad (14)$$

Recall that we already used this result in establishing the minimum price from the lower bounds and intrinsic value results in Section 5.2.2. Now, however, our concern is understanding the conditions under which early exercise of an American option might occur.

Suppose today, time 0, we are considering exercising early an in-the-money American call. If we exercise, we pay X and receive an asset worth S_0. But we already determined that a European call is worth at least $S_0 - X/(1 + r)^T$—that is, the underlying price minus the present value of the exercise price, which is more than $S_0 - X$. Because we just argued that the American call must be worth no less than the European call, it therefore must also be worth at least $S_0 - X/(1 + r)^T$. This means that the value we could obtain by selling it to someone else is more than the value we could obtain by exercising it. Thus, there is no reason to exercise the call early.

Some people fail to see the logic behind not exercising early. Exercising a call early simply gives the money to the call writer and throws away the right to decide at expiration if you want the underlying. It is like renewing a magazine subscription before the current subscription expires. Not only do you lose the interest on the money, you also lose the right to decide later if you want to renew. Without offering an early exercise incentive, the American call would have a price equal to the European call price. Thus, we must look at another case to see the value of the early exercise option.

If the underlying makes a cash payment, there may be reason to exercise early. If the underlying is a stock and pays a dividend, there may be sufficient reason to exercise just before the stock goes ex-dividend. By exercising, the option holder throws away the time value but captures the dividend. We shall skip the technical details of how this decision is made and conclude by stating that

- *When the underlying makes no cash payments,* $C_0 = c_0$.
- *When the underlying makes cash payments during the life of the option, early exercise can be worthwhile and* C_0 *can thus be higher than* c_0.

We emphasize the word *can*. It is possible that the dividend is not high enough to justify early exercise.

For puts, there is nearly always a possibility of early exercise. Consider the most obvious case, an investor holding an American put on a bankrupt company. The stock is worth zero. It cannot go any lower. Thus, the put holder would exercise immediately. As long as there is a possibility of bankruptcy, the American put will be worth more than the European put. But in fact, bankruptcy is not required for early exercise. The stock price must be very low, although we cannot say exactly how low without resorting to an analysis using option pricing models. Suffice it to say that *the American put is nearly always worth more than the European put:* $P_0 > p_0$.

5.7 The Effect of Cash Flows on the Underlying Asset

Both the lower bounds on puts and calls and the put–call parity relationship must be modified to account for cash flows on the underlying asset. In the readings on forward markets and contracts and on futures markets and contracts, we discussed situations in which the underlying has cash flows. Stocks pay dividends, bonds pay interest, foreign currencies pay interest, and commodities have carrying costs. As we have done in the previous readings, we shall assume that these cash flows are either known or can be expressed as a percentage of the asset price. Moreover, as we did previously, we can remove the present value of those cash flows from the price of the underlying and use this adjusted underlying price in the results we have obtained above.

In the previous readings, we specified these cash flows in the form of the accumulated value at T of all cash flows incurred on the underlying over the life of the derivative contract. When the underlying is a stock, we specified these cash flows more precisely in the form of dividends, using the notation FV(D,0,T) as the future value, or alternatively PV(D,0,T) as the present value, of these dividends. When the underlying was a bond, we used the notation FV(CI,0,T) or PV(CI,0,T), where CI stands for "coupon interest." When the cash flows can be specified in terms of a yield or rate, we used the notation δ where $S_0/(1 + \delta)^T$ is the underlying price reduced by the present value of the cash flows.[20] Using continuous compounding, the rate can be specified as δ^c so that $S_0e^{-\delta_c T}$ is the underlying price reduced by the present value of the dividends. For our purposes in this reading on options, let us just write this specification as PV(CF,0,T), which represents the present value of the cash flows on the underlying over the life of the options. Therefore, we can restate the lower bounds for European options as

$$c_0 \geq \text{Max}\left\{0,\left[S_0 - \text{PV}(\text{CF},0,\text{T})\right] - X/(1+r)^T\right\}$$

$$p_0 \geq \text{Max}\left\{0, X/(1+r)^T - \left[S_0 - \text{PV}(\text{CF},0,\text{T})\right]\right\}$$

and put–call parity as

$$c_0 + X/(1+r)^T = p_0 + \left[S_0 - \text{PV}(\text{CF},0,\text{T})\right]$$

which reflects the fact that, as we said, we simply reduce the underlying price by the present value of its cash flows over the life of the option.

5.8 The Effect of Interest Rates and Volatility

It is important to know that interest rates and volatility exert an influence on option prices. *When interest rates are higher, call option prices are higher and put option prices are lower.* This effect is not obvious and strains the intuition somewhat. When investors buy call options instead of the underlying, they are effectively buying an indirect leveraged position in the underlying. When interest rates are higher, buying the call instead of a direct leveraged position in the underlying is more attractive. Moreover, by using call options, investors save more money by not paying for the underlying until a later date. For put options, however, higher interest rates are disadvantageous. When interest rates are higher, investors lose more interest while waiting to sell the underlying when using puts. Thus, the opportunity cost of waiting is higher when interest rates are higher. Although these points may not seem completely clear, fortunately they are not critical. Except when the underlying is a bond or interest rate, interest rates do not have a very strong effect on option prices.

Volatility, however, has an extremely strong effect on option prices. *Higher volatility increases call and put option prices because it increases possible upside values and increases possible downside values of the underlying.* The upside effect helps calls and does not hurt puts. The downside effect does not hurt calls and helps puts. The reasons calls are not hurt on the downside and puts are not hurt on the upside is that when options are out-of-the-money, it does not matter if they end up more out-of-the-money. But when options are in-the-money, it does matter if they end up more in-the-money.

Volatility is a critical variable in pricing options. It is the only variable that affects option prices that is not directly observable either in the option contract or in the market. It must be estimated. We shall have more to say about volatility later in this reading.

20 We actually used several specifications of the dividend yield in the reading on futures markets and contracts, but we shall use just one here.

5.9 Option Price Sensitivities

Later in this reading, we will study option price sensitivities in more detail. These sensitivity measures have Greek names:

- *Delta* is the sensitivity of the option price to a change in the price of the underlying.
- *Gamma* is a measure of how well the delta sensitivity measure will approximate the option price's response to a change in the price of the underlying.
- *Rho* is the sensitivity of the option price to the risk-free rate.
- *Theta* is the rate at which the time value decays as the option approaches expiration.
- *Vega* is the sensitivity of the option price to volatility.

6 DISCRETE-TIME OPTION PRICING: THE BINOMIAL MODEL

Until now, we have looked only at some basic principles of option pricing. Other than put–call parity, all we examined were rules and conditions, often suggesting limitations, on option prices. With put–call parity, we found that we could price a put or a call based on the prices of the combinations of instruments that make up the synthetic version of the instrument. If we wanted to determine a call price, we had to have a put; if we wanted to determine a put price, we had to have a call. What we need to be able to do is price a put or a call without the other instrument. In this section, we introduce a simple means of pricing an option. It may appear that we oversimplify the situation, but we shall remove the simplifying assumptions gradually, and eventually reach a more realistic scenario.

The approach we take here is called the **binomial model**. The word "binomial" refers to the fact that there are only two outcomes. In other words, we let the underlying price move to only one of two possible new prices. As noted, this framework oversimplifies things, but the model can eventually be extended to encompass all possible prices. In addition, we refer to the structure of this model as **discrete time**, which means that time moves in distinct increments. This is much like looking at a calendar and observing only the months, weeks, or days. Even at its smallest interval, we know that time moves forward at a rate faster than one day at a time. It moves in hours, minutes, seconds, and even fractions of seconds, and fractions of fractions of seconds. When we talk about time moving in the tiniest increments, we are talking about **continuous time**. We will see that the discrete time model can be extended to become a continuous time model. Although we present the continuous time model (Black–Scholes–Merton) in Section 7, we must point out that the binomial model has the advantage of allowing us to price American options. In addition, the binomial model is a simple model requiring a minimum of mathematics. Thus it is worthy of study in its own right.

6.1 The One-Period Binomial Model

We start off by having only one binomial period. This means that the underlying price starts off at a given level, then moves forward to a new price, at which time the option expires. Here we need to change our notation slightly from what we have been using previously. We let S be the current underlying price. One period later, it can move up to S^+ or down to S^-. Note that we are removing the time subscript, because it will not be necessary here. We let X be the exercise price of the option and r be the one period risk-free rate. The option is European style.

6.1.1 *The Model*

We start with a call option. If the underlying goes up to S^+, the call option will be worth c^+. If the underlying goes down to S^-, the option will be worth c^-. We know that if the option is expiring, its value will be the intrinsic value. Thus,

$$c^+ = \text{Max}\left(0, S^+ - X\right)$$

$$c^- = \text{Max}\left(0, S^- - X\right)$$

Exhibit 15 One-Period Binomial Model

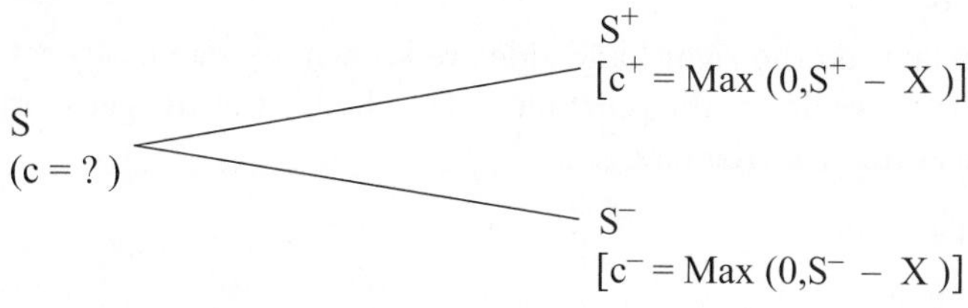

Exhibit 15 illustrates this scenario with a diagram commonly known as a **binomial tree**. Note how we indicate that the current option price, c, is unknown.

Now let us specify how the underlying moves. We identify a factor, u, as the up move on the underlying and d as the down move:

$$u = \frac{S^+}{S}$$

$$d = \frac{S^-}{S}$$

so that u and d represent 1 plus the rate of return if the underlying goes up and down, respectively. Thus, $S^+ = Su$ and $S^- = Sd$. To avoid an obvious arbitrage opportunity, we require that[21]

$$d < 1 + r < u$$

We are now ready to determine how to price the option. We assume that we have all information except for the current option price. In addition, we do not know in what direction the price of the underlying will move. We start by constructing an arbitrage portfolio consisting of one short call option. Let us now purchase an unspecified number of units of the underlying. Let that number be n. Although at the moment we do not know the value of n, we can figure it out quickly. We call this portfolio a hedge portfolio. In fact, n is sometimes called the **hedge ratio**. Its current value is H, where

21 This statement says that if the price of the underlying goes up, it must do so at a rate better than the risk-free rate. If it goes down, it must do so at a rate lower than the risk-free rate. If the underlying always does better than the risk-free rate, it would be possible to buy the underlying, financing it by borrowing at the risk-free rate, and be assured of earning a greater return from the underlying than the cost of borrowing. This would make it possible to generate an unlimited amount of money. If the underlying always does worse than the risk-free rate, one can buy the risk-free asset and finance it by shorting the underlying. This would also make it possible to earn an unlimited amount of money. Thus, the risky underlying asset cannot dominate or be dominated by the risk-free asset.

$$H = nS - c$$

This specification reflects the fact that we own n units of the underlying worth S and we are short one call.[22] One period later, this portfolio value will go to either H^+ or H^-:

$$H^+ = nS^+ - c^+$$

$$H^- = nS^- - c^-$$

Because we can choose the value of n, let us do so by setting H^+ equal to H^-. This specification means that regardless of which way the underlying moves, the portfolio value will be the same. Thus, the portfolio will be hedged. We do this by setting

$H^+ = H^-$, which means that

$$nS^+ - c^+ = nS^- - c^-$$

We then solve for n to obtain

$$n = \frac{c^+ - c^-}{S^+ - S^-} \quad (15)$$

Because the values on the right-hand side are known, we can easily set n according to this formula. If we do so, the portfolio will be hedged. A hedged portfolio should grow in value at the risk-free rate.

$H^+ = H(1 + r)$, or

$$H^- = H(1 + r)$$

We know that $H^+ = nS^+ - c^-$, $H^- = nS^- - c^-$, and $H = nS - c$. We know the values of n, S^+, S^-, c^+, and c^-, as well as r. We can substitute and solve either of the above for c to obtain

$$c = \frac{\pi c^+ + (1 - \pi)c^-}{1 + r} \quad (16)$$

where

$$\pi = \frac{1 + r - d}{u - d} \quad (17)$$

We see that the call price today, c, is a weighted average of the next two possible call prices, c^+ and c^-. The weights are π and $1 - \pi$. This weighted average is then discounted one period at the risk-free rate.

It might appear that π and $1 - \pi$ are probabilities of the up and down movements, but they are not. In fact, the probabilities of the up and down movements are not required. It is important to note, however, that π and $1 - \pi$ are the probabilities that would exist if investors were risk neutral. Risk-neutral investors value assets by computing the expected future value and discounting that value at the risk-free rate. Because we are discounting at the risk-free rate, it should be apparent that π and $1 - \pi$

22 Think of this specification as a plus sign indicating assets and a minus sign indicating liabilities.

would indeed be the probabilities if the investor were risk neutral. In fact, we shall refer to them as **risk-neutral probabilities**, and the process of valuing an option is often called **risk-neutral valuation**.[23]

6.1.2 *One-Period Binomial Example*

Suppose the underlying is a non-dividend-paying stock currently valued at \$50. It can either go up by 25 percent or go down by 20 percent. Thus, u = 1.25 and d = 0.80.

$$S^+ = Su = 50(1.25) = 62.50$$

$$S^- = Sd = 50(0.80) = 40$$

Assume that the call option has an exercise price of 50 and the risk-free rate is 7 percent. Thus, the option values one period later will be

$$c^+ = \text{Max}\left(0, S^+ - X\right) = \text{Max}\left(0, 62.50 - 50\right) = 12.50$$

$$c^- = \text{Max}\left(0, S^- - X\right) = \text{Max}\left(0, 40 - 50\right) = 0$$

Exhibit 16 depicts the situation.

Exhibit 16 One-Period Binomial Example

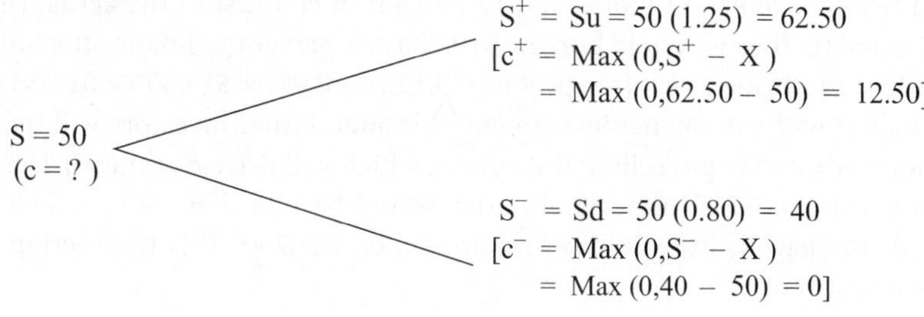

First we calculate π:

$$\pi = \frac{1 + r - d}{u - d} = \frac{1.07 - 0.80}{1.25 - 0.80} = 0.6$$

and, hence, 1 − π = 0.4. Now, we can directly calculate the option price:

$$c = \frac{0.6(12.50) + 0.4(0)}{1.07} = 7.01$$

Thus, the option should sell for \$7.01.

23 It may be helpful to contrast risk neutrality with risk aversion, which characterizes nearly all individuals. People who are risk neutral value an asset, such as an option or stock, by discounting the expected value at the risk-free rate. People who are risk averse discount the expected value at a higher rate, one that consists of the risk-free rate plus a risk premium. In the valuation of options, we are not making the assumption that people are risk neutral, but the fact that options can be valued by finding the expected value, using these special probabilities, and discounting at the risk-free rate creates the *appearance* that investors are assumed to be risk neutral. We emphasize the word "appearance," because no such assumption is being made. The terms "risk neutral probabilities" and "risk neutral valuation" are widely used in options valuation, although they give a misleading impression of the assumptions underlying the process.

6.1.3 *One-Period Binomial Arbitrage Opportunity*

Suppose the option is selling for \$8. If the option should be selling for \$7.01 and it is selling for \$8, it is overpriced—a clear case of price not equaling value. Investors would exploit this opportunity by selling the option and buying the underlying. The number of units of the underlying purchased for each option sold would be the value n:

$$n = \frac{c^+ - c^-}{S^+ - S^-} = \frac{12.50 - 0}{62.50 - 40} = 0.556$$

Thus, for every option sold, we would buy 0.556 units of the underlying. Suppose we sell 1,000 calls and buy 556 units of the underlying. Doing so would require an initial outlay of H = 556(\$50) – 1,000(\$8) = \$19,800. One period later, the portfolio value will be either

$$H^+ = nS^+ - c^+ = 556(\$62.50) - 1{,}000(\$12.50) = \$22{,}250, \text{ or}$$

$$H^- = nS^- - c^- = 556(\$40) - 1{,}000(\$0) = \$22{,}240$$

These two values are not exactly the same, but the difference is due only to rounding the hedge ratio, n. We shall use the \$22,250 value. If we invest \$19,800 and end up with \$22,250, the return is

$$\frac{\$22{,}250}{\$19{,}800} - 1 = 0.1237$$

that is, a risk-free return of more than 12 percent in contrast to the actual risk-free rate of 7 percent. Thus we could borrow \$19,800 at 7 percent to finance the initial net cash outflow, capturing a risk-free profit of (0.1237 – 0.07) × \$19,800 = \$1,063 (to the nearest dollar) without any net investment of money. Other investors will recognize this opportunity and begin selling the option, which will drive down its price. When the option sells for \$7.01, the initial outlay would be H = 556(\$50) – 1,000(\$7.01) = \$20,790. The payoffs at expiration would still be \$22,250. This transaction would generate a return of

$$\frac{\$22{,}250}{\$20{,}790} - 1 \approx 0.07$$

Thus, *when the option is trading at the price given by the model, a hedge portfolio would earn the risk-free rate,* which is appropriate because the portfolio would be risk free.

If the option sells for less than \$7.01, investors would buy the option and sell short the underlying, which would generate cash up front. At expiration, the investor would have to pay back an amount less than 7 percent. All investors would perform this transaction, generating a demand for the option that would push its price back up to \$7.01.

EXAMPLE 4

Consider a one-period binomial model in which the underlying is at 65 and can go up 30 percent or down 22 percent. The risk-free rate is 8 percent.

A Determine the price of a European call option with exercise prices of 70.

B Assume that the call is selling for 9 in the market. Demonstrate how to execute an arbitrage transaction and calculate the rate of return. Use 10,000 call options.

Solution to A:

First find the underlying prices in the binomial tree. We have u = 1.30 and d = 1 – 0.22 = 0.78.

$$S^+ = Su = 65(1.30) = 84.50$$

$$S^- = Sd = 65(0.78) = 50.70$$

Then find the option values at expiration:

$$c^+ = \text{Max}(0{,}84.50 - 70) = 14.50$$

$$c^- = \text{Max}(0{,}50.70 - 70) = 0$$

The risk-neutral probability is

$$\pi = \frac{1.08 - 0.78}{1.30 - 0.78} = 0.5769$$

and $1 - \pi = 0.4231$. The call's price today is

$$c = \frac{0.5769(14.50) + 0.4231(0)}{1.08} = 7.75$$

Solution to B:

We need the value of n for calls:

$$n = \frac{c^+ - c^-}{S^+ - S^-} = \frac{14.50 - 0}{84.50 - 50.70} = 0.4290$$

The call is overpriced, so we should sell 10,000 call options and buy 4,290 units of the underlying.

Sell 10,000 calls at 9	+ 90,000
Buy 4,290 units of the underlying at 65	– 278,850
Net cash flow	– 188,850

So we invest 188,850. The value of this combination at expiration will be If $S_T = 84.50$,

$$4{,}290(84.50) - 10{,}000(14.50) = 217{,}505$$

If $S_T = 50.70$,

$$4{,}290(50.70) - 10{,}000(0) = 217{,}503$$

These values differ by only a rounding error.

The rate of return is

$$\frac{217{,}505}{188{,}850} - 1 = 0.1517$$

Thus, we receive a risk-free return almost twice the risk-free rate. We could borrow the initial outlay of $188,850 at the risk-free rate and capture a risk-free profit without any net investment of money.

6.2 The Two-Period Binomial Model

In the example above, the movements in the underlying were depicted over one period, and there were only two outcomes. We can extend the model and obtain more-realistic results with more than two outcomes. Exhibit 17 shows how to do so with a two-period binomial tree.

Exhibit 17 Two-Period Binomial Model

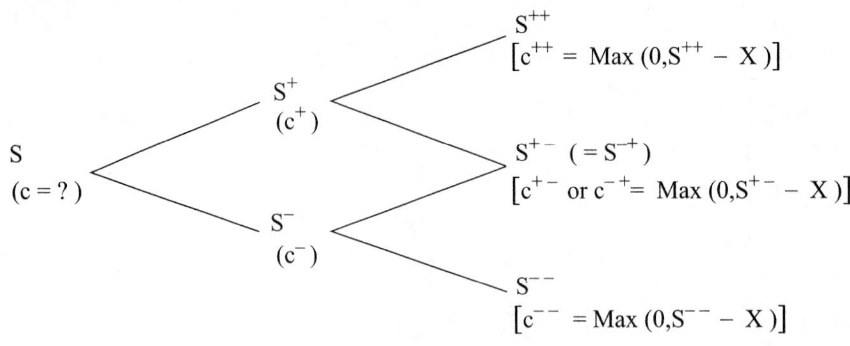

In the first period, we let the underlying price move from S to S^+ or S^- in the manner we did in the one-period model. That is, if u is the up factor and d is the down factor,

$$S^+ = Su$$

$$S^- = Sd$$

Then, with the underlying at S^+ after one period, it can either move up to S^{++} or down to S^{+-}. Thus,

$$S^{++} = S^+u$$

$$S^{+-} = S^+d$$

If the underlying is at S^- after one period, it can either move up to S^{-+} or down to S^{--}.

$$S^{-+} = S^-u$$

$$S^{--} = S^-d$$

We now have three unique final outcomes instead of two. Actually, we have four final outcomes, but S^{+-} is the same as S^{-+}. We can relate the three final outcomes to the starting price in the following manner:

$$S^{++} = S^+u = Suu = Su^2$$

$$S^{+-}\left(\text{or } S^{-+}\right) = S^+d\left(\text{or } S^-u\right) = Sud\left(\text{or } Sdu\right)$$

$$S^{--} = S^-d = Sdd = Sd^2$$

Now we move forward to the end of the first period. Suppose we are at the point where the underlying price is S^+. Note that now we are back into the one-period model we previously derived. There is one period to go and two outcomes. The call price is c^+ and can go up to c^{++} or down to c^{+-}. Using what we know from the one-period model, the call price must be

$$c^+ = \frac{\pi c^{++} + (1 - \pi)c^{+-}}{1 + r} \tag{18}$$

where again we see that the call price is a weighted average of the next two possible call prices, then discounted back one period. If the underlying price is at S^-, the call price would be

$$c^- = \frac{\pi c^{-+} + (1 - \pi)c^{--}}{1 + r} \tag{19}$$

where in both cases the formula for π is still Equation 17:

$$\pi = \frac{1 + r - d}{u - d}$$

Now we step back to the starting point and find that the option price is still given as Equation 16:

$$c = \frac{\pi c^+ + (1 - \pi)c^-}{1 + r}$$

again, using the general form that the call price is a weighted average of the next two possible call prices, discounted back to the present. Other than requiring knowledge of the formula for π, the call price formula is simple and intuitive. It is an average, weighted by the risk-neutral probabilities, of the next two outcomes, then discounted to the present.[24]

Recall that the hedge ratio, n, was given as the difference in the next two call prices divided by the difference in the next two underlying prices. This will be true in all cases throughout the binomial tree. Hence, we have different hedge ratios at each time point:

$$n = \frac{c^+ - c^-}{S^+ - S^-}$$

$$n^+ = \frac{c^{++} - c^{+-}}{S^{++} - S^{+-}} \tag{20}$$

$$n^- = \frac{c^{-+} - c^{--}}{S^{-+} - S^{--}}$$

6.2.1 *Two-Period Binomial Example*

We can continue with the example presented in Section 6.1.2 in which the underlying goes up 25 percent or down 20 percent. Let us, however, alter the example a little. Suppose the underlying goes up 11.8 percent and down 10.56 percent, and we extend the number of periods to two. So, the up factor is 1.118 and the down factor is 1 – 0.1056 = 0.8944. If the underlying goes up for two consecutive periods, it rises by a factor of 1.118(1.118) = 1.25 (25 percent). If it goes down in both periods, it falls by a factor of (0.8944)(0.8944) = 0.80 (20 percent). This specification makes the highest and lowest prices unchanged. Let the risk-free rate be 3.44 percent per period. The π becomes (1.0344 – 0.8944)/(1.118 – 0.8944) = 0.6261. The underlying prices at expiration will be

24 It is also possible to express the price today as a weighted average of the three final option prices discounted two periods, thereby skipping the intermediate step of finding c^+ and c^-; but little is gained by doing so and this approach is somewhat more technical.

Exhibit 18 Two-Period Binomial Example

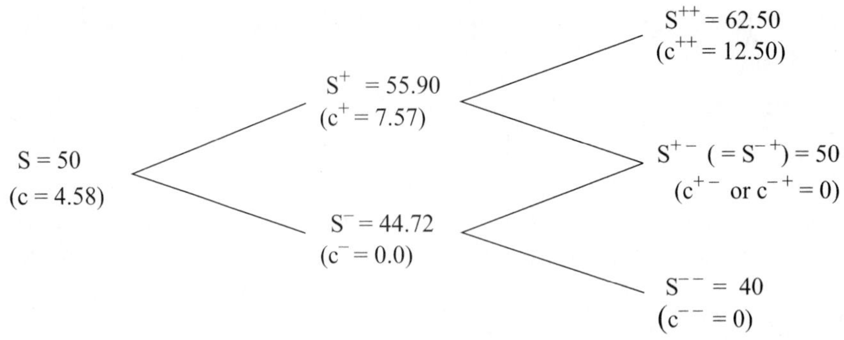

$$S^{++} = Su^2 = 50(1.118)(1.118) = 62.50$$

$$S^{+-} = Sud = 50(1.118)(0.8944) = 50$$

$$S^{--} = Sd^2 = 50(0.8944)(0.8944) = 40$$

When the options expire, they will be worth

$$c^{++} = \text{Max}\left(0, S^{++} - 50\right) = \text{Max}(0, 62.50 - 50) = 12.50$$

$$c^{+-} = \text{Max}\left(0, S^{+-} - 50\right) = \text{Max}(0, 50 - 50) = 0$$

$$c^{--} = \text{Max}\left(0, S^{--} - 50\right) = \text{Max}(0, 40 - 50) = 0$$

The option values after one period are, therefore,

$$c^{+} = \frac{\pi c^{++} + (1 - \pi)c^{+-}}{1 + r} = \frac{0.6261(12.50) + 0.3739(0)}{1.0344} = 7.57$$

$$c^{-} = \frac{\pi c^{-+} + (1 - \pi)c^{--}}{1 + r} = \frac{0.6261(0) + 0.3739(0)}{1.0344} = 0.0$$

So the option price today is

$$c = \frac{\pi c^{+} + (1 - \pi)c^{-}}{1 + r} = \frac{0.6261(7.57) + 0.3739(0)}{1.0344} = 4.58$$

These results are summarized in Exhibit 18.

We shall not illustrate an arbitrage opportunity, because doing so requires a very long and detailed example that goes beyond our needs. Suffice it to say that if the option is mispriced, one can construct a hedged portfolio that will capture a return in excess of the risk-free rate.

EXAMPLE 5

Consider a two-period binomial model in which the underlying is at 30 and can go up 14 percent or down 11 percent each period. The risk-free rate is 3 percent per period.

A Find the value of a European call option expiring in two periods with an exercise price of 30.

B Find the number of units of the underlying that would be required at each point in the binomial tree to construct a risk-free hedge using 10,000 calls.

Solution to A:

First find the underlying prices in the binomial tree: We have u = 1.14 and d = 1 – 0.11 = 0.89.

$$S^{+} = Su = 30(1.14) = 34.20$$

$$S^{-} = Sd = 30(0.89) = 26.70$$

$$S^{++} = Su^2 = 30(1.14)^2 = 38.99$$

$$S^{+-} = Sud = 30(1.14)(0.89) = 30.44$$

$$S^{--} = Sd^2 = 30(0.89)^2 = 23.76$$

Then find the option prices at expiration:

$$c^{++} = \text{Max}(0,38.99 - 30) = 8.99$$

$$c^{+-} = \text{Max}(0,30.44 - 30) = 0.44$$

$$c^{--} = \text{Max}(0,23.76 - 30) = 0$$

We will need the value of π:

$$\pi = \frac{1.03 - 0.89}{1.14 - 0.89} = 0.56$$

and 1 – π = 0.44. Then step back and find the option prices at time 1:

$$c^{+} = \frac{0.56(8.99) + 0.44(0.44)}{1.03} = 5.08$$

$$c^{-} = \frac{0.56(0.44) + 0.44(0)}{1.03} = 0.24$$

The price today is

$$c = \frac{0.56(5.08) + 0.44(0.24)}{1.03} = 2.86$$

Solution to B:

The number of units of the underlying at each point in the tree is found by first computing the values of n.

$$n = \frac{5.08 - 0.24}{34.20 - 26.70} = 0.6453$$

$$n^{+} = \frac{8.99 - 0.44}{38.99 - 30.44} = 1.00$$

$$n^{-} = \frac{0.44 - 0}{30.44 - 23.76} = 0.0659$$

The number of units of the underlying required for 10,000 calls would thus be 6,453 today, 10,000 at time 1 if the underlying is at 34.20, and 659 at time 1 if the underlying is at 26.70.

6.3 Binomial Put Option Pricing

In Section 6.2, the option was a call. It is a simple matter to make the option a put. We could step back through the entire example, changing all c's to p's and using the formulas for the payoff values of a put instead of a call. We should note, however, that if the same formula used for a call is used to calculate the hedge ratio, the minus sign should be ignored as it would suggest being long the stock (put) and short the put (stock) when the hedge portfolio should actually be long both instruments or short both instruments. The put moves opposite to the stock in the first place; hence, long or short positions in both instruments are appropriate.

EXAMPLE 6

Repeating the data from Example 4, consider a one-period binomial model in which the underlying is at 65 and can go up 30 percent or down 22 percent. The risk-free rate is 8 percent. Determine the price of a European put option with exercise price of 70.

Solution:

First find the underlying prices in the binomial tree. We have u = 1.30 and d = 1 – 0.22 = 0.78.

$$S^+ = Su = 65(1.30) = 84.50$$

$$S^- = Sd = 65(0.78) = 50.70$$

Then find the option values at expiration:

$$p^+ = \text{Max}(0, 70 - 84.50) = 0$$

$$p^- = \text{Max}(0, 70 - 50.70) = 19.30$$

The risk-neutral probability is

$$\pi = \frac{1.08 - 0.78}{1.30 - 0.78} = 0.5769$$

and 1 – π = 0.4231. The put price today is

$$p = \frac{0.5769(0) + 0.423(19.30)}{1.08} = 7.56$$

6.4 Binomial Interest Rate Option Pricing

In the examples above, the applications were appropriate for options on a stock, currency, or commodity.[25] Now we take a brief look at options on bonds and interest rates. A model for pricing these options must start with a model for the one-period interest rate and the prices of zero-coupon bonds.

We look at such a model in Exhibit 19. Note that this binomial tree is the first one we have seen with more than two time periods. At each point in the tree, we see a group of numbers. The first number is the one-period interest rate. The second set of numbers, which are in parentheses, represents the prices of $1 face value zero-coupon bonds of various maturities. At time 0, 0.9048 is the price of a one-period zero-coupon bond, 0.8106 is the price of a two-period zero-coupon bond, 0.7254 is the price of a three-period zero-coupon bond, and 0.6479 is the price of a four-period zero-coupon bond. The one-period bond price can be determined from the one-period rate—that is, 0.9048 = 1/1.1051, subject to some rounding off. The other prices cannot be determined solely from the one-period rate; we would have to see a tree of the two-, three-, and four-period rates. As we move forward in time, we lose one bond as the one-period bond matures.[26] Thus, at time 1, when the one-period rate is 13.04 percent, the two-period bond from the previous period, whose price

25 We have also been assuming that there are no cash flows on the underlying.

26 Technically we could show the bond we are losing as a bond with a price of $1.00, its face value, at its point of maturity.

was 0.8106, is now a one-period bond whose price is 1/1.1304 = 0.8846. Although we present these prices and rates here without derivation, they were determined using a model that prevents arbitrage opportunities in buying and selling bonds. We do not cover the actual derivation of the model here.

Exhibit 19 **Binomial Interest Rate Tree**

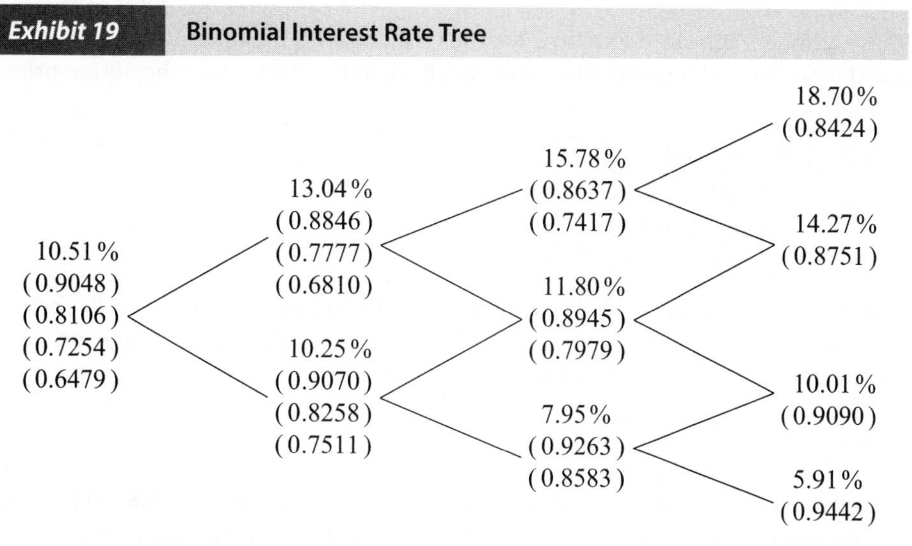

Now let us price a European option on a zero-coupon bond. First note that we need the option to expire before the bond matures, and it should have a reasonable exercise price. We shall work with the four-period zero-coupon bond. Exhibit 20 contains its price and the price of a two-period call option with an exercise price of $0.80 per $1 of par, as well as the one-period interest rate. The binomial interest rate tree in Exhibit 20 is based on the data in Exhibit 19. In parentheses in Exhibit 20 are the prices of the call option expiring at time 2.

First note that in binomial term structure models, the models are usually fit such that the risk-neutral probability, π, is 0.5. Thus we do not have to calculate π, as in the examples above. We must, however, do one thing quite differently. Whereas we have used a constant interest rate, we must now discount at a different interest rate, the one-period rate, given in Exhibit 19, depending on where we are in the tree.

Exhibit 20 **Four-Period Zero-Coupon Bond and Two-Period Call Option with Exercise Price of 0.80**

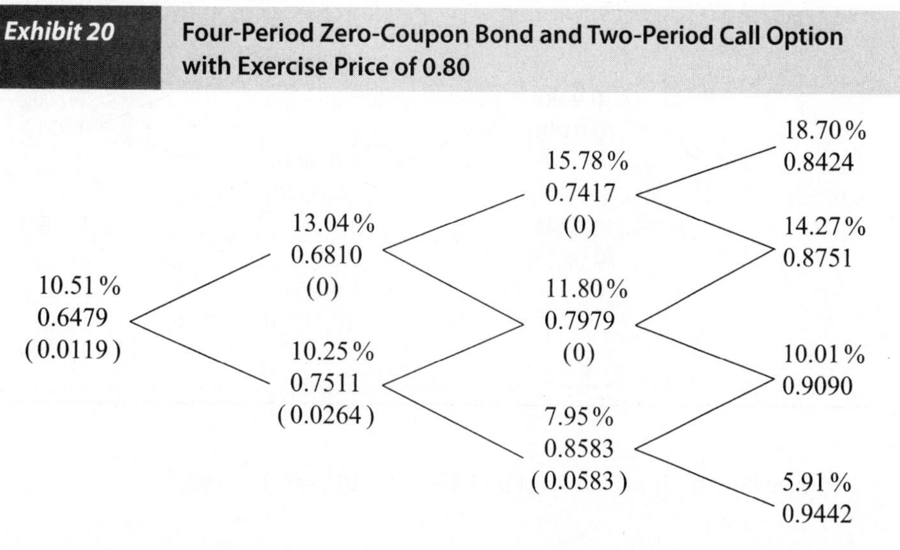

The payoff values at time 2 of the call with exercise price of 0.80 are

$$c^{++} = \text{Max}(0,0.7417 - 0.80) = 0$$

$$c^{+-} = \text{Max}(0,0.7979 - 0.80) = 0$$

$$c^{--} = \text{Max}(0,0.8583 - 0.80) = 0.0583$$

These numbers appear in Exhibit 20 at time 2 along with the underlying bond prices and the one-period interest rates. Stepping back to time 1, we find the option prices as follows:

$$c^{+} = \frac{0.5(0) + 0.5(0)}{1.1304} = 0$$

$$c^{-} = \frac{0.5(0) + 0.5(0.0583)}{1.1025} = 0.0264$$

Note how we discount by the appropriate one-period rate, which is 10.25 percent for the bottom outcome at time 1 and 13.04 percent for the top outcome at time 1. Stepping back to time 0, the option price is, therefore,

$$c = \frac{0.5(0) + 0.5(0.0264)}{1.1051} = 0.0119$$

using the one-period rate of 10.51 percent. The call option is thus worth \$0.0119 when the underlying zero-coupon bond paying \$1 at time 4 is currently worth \$0.6479.

Now let us price an option on a coupon bond. First, however, we must construct the tree of coupon bond prices. Exhibit 21 illustrates the price of a \$1 face value, 11 percent coupon bond maturing at time 4 along with a call option expiring at time 2 with an exercise price of \$0.95 per \$1 of par.

We obtain the prices of the coupon bond from the prices of zero-coupon bonds. For example, at time 0, a four-period 11 percent coupon bond is equivalent to a combination of zero-coupon bonds with face value of 0.11 maturing at times 1, 2, and 3, and a zero-coupon bond with face value of 1.11 maturing at time 4. Thus, its price can be found by multiplying these face values by the prices of one-, two-, three-, and four-period zero-coupon bonds respectively, the prices of which are taken from Exhibit 19.

Exhibit 21 **Four-Period 11 Percent Coupon Bond and Two-Period Call Option with Exercise Price of 0.95**

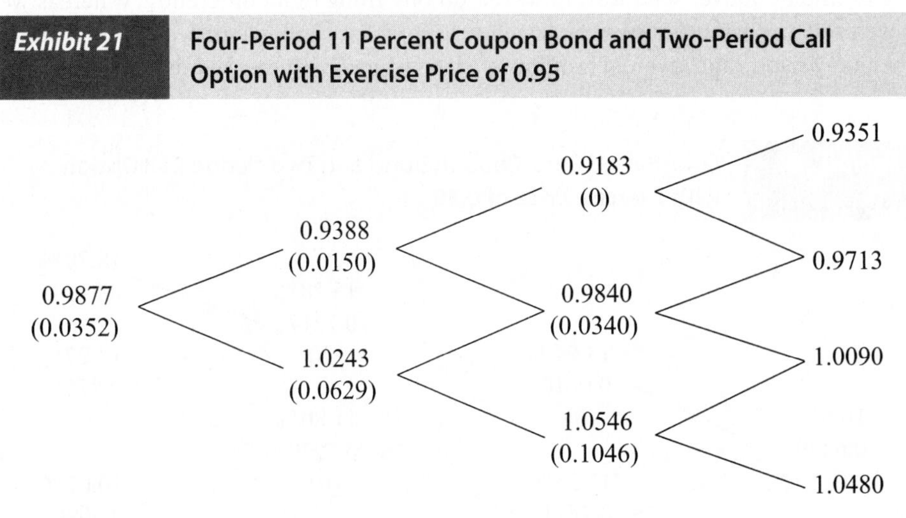

$$0.11(0.9048) + 0.11(0.8106) + 0.11(0.7254) + 1.11(0.6479) = 0.9877$$

At any other point in the tree, we use the same procedure, but of course fewer coupons remain.[27] Of course, pricing a coupon bond by decomposing it into a combination of zero-coupon bonds is basic fixed income material, which you have learned elsewhere in the CFA curriculum.

Now let us find the option prices. At time 2, the prices are

$$c^{++} = \text{Max}(0, 0.9183 - 0.95) = 0$$

$$c^{+-} = \text{Max}(0, 0.9840 - 0.95) = 0.0340$$

$$c^{--} = \text{Max}(0, 1.0546 - 0.95) = 0.1046$$

Stepping back to time 1, the prices are

$$c^{+} = \frac{0.5(0.0) + 0.5(0.0340)}{1.1304} = 0.0150$$

$$c^{-} = \frac{0.5(0.0340) + 0.5(0.1046)}{1.1025} = 0.0629$$

Stepping back to time 0, the option price is

$$c = \frac{0.5(0.0150) + 0.5(0.0629)}{1.1051} = 0.0352$$

Now let us look at options on interest rates. Recall that in Section 4.1.4, we illustrated how these options work. Their payoffs are based on the difference between the interest rate and an exercise rate. When the option expires, the payoff does not occur for one additional period. Thus, we have to discount the intrinsic value at expiration by the one-period interest rate. Recall that an interest rate cap is a set of interest rate call options expiring at various points in the life of a loan. The cap is generally set up to hedge the interest rate risk on a floating rate loan.

Exhibit 22 Two-Period Cap on One-Period Interest Rate with Exercise Rate of 10.5 Percent

A. Pricing the Two-Period Caplet

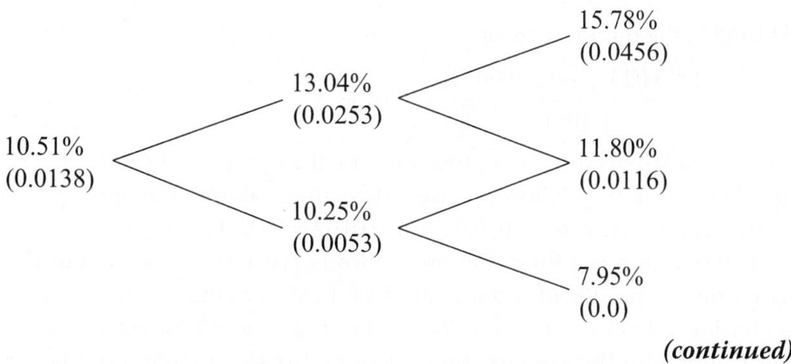

(continued)

27 For example, consider the middle **node** at time 2. The coupon bond is now a two-period bond. The one- and two-period zero-coupon bond prices are 0.8945 and 0.7979, respectively (from Exhibit 19). Thus, the coupon bond price is 0.11(0.8945) + 1.11(0.7979) = 0.9840 as shown in Exhibit 21.

Exhibit 22 (Continued)

B. Pricing the One-Period Caplet

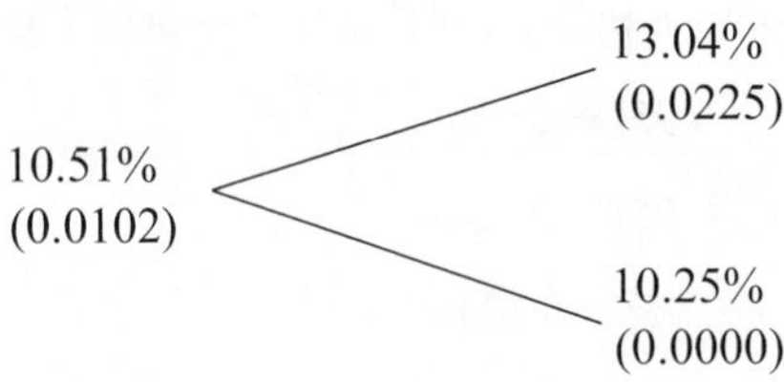

Exhibit 22 illustrates the pricing of a two-period cap with an exercise rate of 10.5 percent. This contract consists of two caplets: a one-period call option on the one-period interest rate with an exercise rate of 10.5 percent, and a two-period call option on the one-period interest rate with an exercise rate of 10.5 percent. We price the cap by pricing these two component options.

In Panel A, we price the two-period caplet. The values at time 2 are

$$c^{++} = \frac{\text{Max}(0{,}0.1578 - 0.105)}{1.1578} = 0.0456$$

$$c^{+-} = \frac{\text{Max}(0{,}0.1180 - 0.105)}{1.1180} = 0.0116$$

$$c^{--} = \frac{\text{Max}(0{,}0.0795 - 0.105)}{1.0795} = 0.0$$

Note especially that we discount the payoff one period at the appropriate one-period rate, because the payoff does not occur until one period later. Stepping back to time 1:

$$c^{+} = \frac{0.5(0.0456) + 0.5(0.0116)}{1.1304} = 0.0253$$

$$c^{-} = \frac{0.5(0.0116) + 0.5(0.0)}{1.1025} = 0.0053$$

At time 0, the option price is

$$c = \frac{0.5(0.0253) + 0.5(0.0053)}{1.1051} = 0.0138$$

Panel B illustrates the same procedure for the one-period caplet. We shall omit the details because they follow precisely the pattern above. The one-period caplet price is 0.0102; thus the cap costs 0.0138 + 0.0102 = 0.0240.

If the option is a floor, the procedure is precisely the same but the payoffs are based on the payoffs of a put instead of a call. Pricing a zero-cost collar, however, is considerably more complex. Remember that a zero-cost collar is a long cap and a short floor with the exercise rates set such that the premium on the cap equals the premium on the floor. We can arbitrarily choose the exercise rate on the cap or the floor, but the exercise rate on the other would have to be found by trial and error so that the premium offsets the premium on the other instrument.

EXAMPLE 7

The diagram below is a two-period binomial tree containing the one-period interest rate and the prices of zero-coupon bonds. The first price is a one-period zero-coupon bond, the second is a two-period zero-coupon bond, and the third is a three-period zero-coupon bond. As we move forward, one bond matures and its price is removed. The maturity of each bond is then shorter by one period.

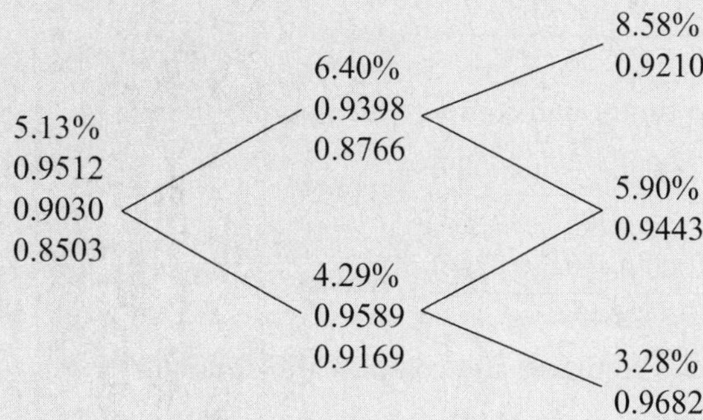

A Find the price of a European put expiring in two periods with an exercise price of 1.01 on a three-period 6 percent coupon bond with $1.00 face value.

B Find the price of a European put option expiring at time 2 with an exercise rate of 6 percent where the underlying is the one-period rate.

Solution to A:

First we have to find the price of the three-period $1.00 par, 6 percent coupon bond at expiration of the option (t = 2). We break the coupon bond up into zero-coupon bonds of one, two, and three periods to maturity. The face values of these zero-coupon bonds are 0.06, 0.06, and 1.06, respectively. The bond price at t = 2 is $1.06 discounted one period at the appropriate discount rate:

Bond prices at time 2:

+ + outcome: 1.06(0.9210) = 0.9763

+ – outcome: 1.06(0.9443) = 1.0010

–– outcome: 1.06(0.9682) = 1.0263

Now compute the put option values at expiration:

+ + outcome: Max(0,1.01 – 0.9763) = 0.0337

+ – outcome: Max(0,1.01 – 1.0010) = 0.0090

–– outcome: Max(0,1.01 – 1.0263) = 0.0000

Now step back and compute the option values at time 1:

$$+ \text{ outcome: } \frac{0.5(0.0337) + 0.5(0.0090)}{1.064} = 0.0201$$

$$- \text{ outcome: } \frac{0.5(0.0090) + 0.5(0.0000)}{1.0429} = 0.0043$$

Now step back and compute the option values at time 0:

$$\frac{0.5(0.0201) + 0.5(0.0043)}{1.0513} = 0.0116$$

Solution to B:

First compute the put option values at expiration:

$$p^{++} = \frac{\text{Max}(0,0.06 - 0.0858)}{1.0858} = 0.0000$$

$$p^{+-} = \frac{\text{Max}(0,0.06 - 0.0590)}{1.059} = 0.0009$$

$$p^{--} = \frac{\text{Max}(0,0.06 - 0.0328)}{1.0328} = 0.0263$$

Step back to time 1 and compute the option values:

$$p^{+} = \frac{0.5(0.0000) + 0.5(0.0009)}{1.064} = 0.0004$$

$$p- = \frac{0.5(0.0009) + 0.5(0.0263)}{1.0429} = 0.0130$$

Now step back to time 0 and compute the option price as

$$p = \frac{0.5(0.0004) + 0.5(0.0130)}{1.0513} = 0.0064$$

6.5 American Options

The binomial model is also well suited for handling American-style options. At any point in the binomial tree, we can see whether the calculated value of the option is exceeded by its value if exercised early. If that is the case, we replace the calculated value with the exercise value.[28]

6.6 Extending the Binomial Model

In the examples in this reading, we divided an option's life into a given number of periods. Suppose we are pricing a one-year option. If we use only one binomial period, it will give us only two prices for the underlying, and we are unlikely to get a very good result. If we use two binomial periods, we will have three prices for the underlying at expiration. This result would probably be better but still not very good. But as we increase the number of periods, the result should become more accurate. In fact, in the limiting case, we are likely to get a very good result. By increasing the number of periods, we are moving from discrete time to continuous time.

Consider the following example of a one-period binomial model for a nine-month option. The asset is priced at 52.75. It can go up by 35.41 percent or down by 26.15 percent, so u = 1.3541 and d = 1 − 0.2615 = 0.7385. The risk-free rate is 4.88 percent. A call option has an exercise price of 50 and expires in nine months. Using a one-period binomial model would obtain an option price of 10.0259. Exhibit 23 shows the results we obtain if we divide the nine-month option life into an increasing number of periods of smaller and smaller length. The manner in which we fit the binomial tree is not arbitrary, however, because we have to alter the values of u, d, and the risk-free rate so that the underlying price move is reasonable for the life of the option. How we alter u and d is related to the volatility, a topic we cover in the next section. In

28 See Chapter 4 of *An Introduction to Derivatives and Risk Management*, 6th edition, Don M. Chance (South-Western College Publishing, 2004) for a treatment of this topic.

fact, we need not concern ourselves with exactly how to alter any of these values. We need only to observe that our binomial option price appears to be converging to a value of around 8.62.

Exhibit 23 Binomial Option Prices for Different Numbers of Time Periods

Number of Time Periods	Option Price
1	10.0259
2	8.4782
5	8.8305
10	8.6983
25	8.5862
50	8.6438
100	8.6160
500	8.6162
1000	8.6190

Notes: Call option with underlying price of 52.75, up factor of 1.3541, down factor of 0.7385, risk-free rate of 4.88 percent, and exercise price of 50. The variables u, d, and r are altered accordingly as the number of time periods increases.

In the same way a sequence of rapidly taken still photographs converges to what appears to be a continuous sequence of a subject's movements, the binomial model converges to a continuous-time model, the subject of which is in our next section.

7 CONTINUOUS-TIME OPTION PRICING: THE BLACK–SCHOLES–MERTON MODEL

When we move to a continuous-time world, we price options using the famous Black–Scholes–Merton model. Named after its founders Fischer Black, Myron Scholes, and Robert Merton, this model resulted in the award of a Nobel Prize to Scholes and Merton in 1997.[29] (Fischer Black had died in 1995 and thus was not eligible for the prize.) The model can be derived either as the continuous limit of the binomial model, or through taking expectations, or through a variety of highly complex mathematical procedures. We are not concerned with the derivation here and instead simply present the model and its applications. First, however, let us briefly review its underlying assumptions.

7.1 Assumptions of the Model

7.1.1 *The Underlying Price Follows a Geometric Lognormal Diffusion Process*

This assumption is probably the most difficult to understand, but in simple terms, *the underlying price follows a lognormal probability distribution as it evolves through time.* A lognormal probability distribution is one in which the log return is normally distributed. For example, if a stock moves from 100 to 110, the return is 10 percent

29 The model is more commonly called the Black–Scholes model, but we choose to give Merton the credit he is due that led to his co-receipt of the Nobel Prize.

but the log return is ln(1.10) = 0.0953 or 9.53 percent. Log returns are often called continuously compounded returns. If the log or continuously compounded return follows the familiar normal or bell-shaped distribution, the return is said to be lognormally distributed. The distribution of the return itself is skewed, reaching further out to the right and truncated on the left side, reflecting the limitation that an asset cannot be worth less than zero.

The lognormal distribution is a convenient and widely used assumption. It is almost surely not an exact measure in reality, but it suffices for our purposes.

7.1.2 *The Risk-Free Rate Is Known and Constant*

The Black–Scholes–Merton model does not allow interest rates to be random. Generally, we assume that *the risk-free rate is constant.* This assumption becomes a problem for pricing options on bonds and interest rates, and we will have to make some adjustments then.

7.1.3 *The Volatility of the Underlying Asset Is Known and Constant*

The volatility of the underlying asset, specified in the form of the standard deviation of the log return, is assumed to be known at all times and does not change over the life of the option. This assumption is the most critical, and we take it up again in a later section. In reality, the volatility is definitely not known and must be estimated or obtained from some other source. In addition, volatility is generally not constant. Obviously, the stock market is more volatile at some times than at others. Nonetheless, the assumption is critical for this model. Considerable research has been conducted with the assumption relaxed, but this topic is an advanced one and does not concern us here.

7.1.4 *There Are No Taxes or Transaction Costs*

We have made this assumption all along in pricing all types of derivatives. Taxes and transaction costs greatly complicate our models and keep us from seeing the essential financial principles involved in the models. It is possible to relax this assumption, but we shall not do so here.

7.1.5 *There Are No Cash Flows on the Underlying*

We have discussed this assumption at great length in pricing futures and forwards and earlier in this reading in studying the fundamentals of option pricing. The basic form of the Black–Scholes–Merton model makes this assumption, but it can easily be relaxed. We will show how to do this in Section 7.4.

7.1.6 *The Options Are European*

With only a few very advanced variations, the Black–Scholes–Merton model does not price American options. Users of the model must keep this in mind, or they may badly misprice these options. For pricing American options, the best approach is the binomial model with a large number of time periods.

7.2 The Black–Scholes–Merton Formula

Although the mathematics underlying the Black–Scholes–Merton formula are quite complex, the formula itself is not difficult, although it may appear so at first glance. The input variables are some of those we have already used: S_0 is the price of the underlying, X is the exercise price, r^c is the continuously compounded risk-free rate, and T is the time to expiration. The one other variable we need is the standard deviation of the log return on the asset. We denote this as σ and refer to it as the volatility. Then, the Black–Scholes–Merton formulas for the prices of call and put options are

$$c = S_0N(d_1) - Xe^{-r^cT}N(d_2)$$
$$p = Xe^{-r^cT}[1 - N(d_2)] - S_0[1 - N(d_1)] \tag{21}$$

where

$$d_1 = \frac{\ln(S_0/X) + \left[r^c + (\sigma^2/2)\right]T}{\sigma\sqrt{T}}$$
$$d_2 = d_1 - \sigma\sqrt{T} \tag{22}$$

σ = the annualized standard deviation of the continuously compounded return on the stock

r^c = the continuously compounded risk-free rate of return

Of course, we have already seen the term "ln" and "*e*" in previous readings. We do, however, introduce two new and somewhat unusual looking terms, $N(d_1)$ and $N(d_2)$. These terms represent normal probabilities based on the values of d_1 and d_2. We compute the normal probabilities associated with values of d_1 and d_2 using the second equation above and insert these values into the formula as $N(d_1)$ and $N(d_2)$. Exhibit 24 presents a brief review of the normal probability distribution and explains how to obtain a probability value. Once we know how to look up a number in a normal probability table, we can then easily calculate d_1 and d_2, look them up in the table to obtain $N(d_1)$ and $N(d_2)$, and then insert the values of $N(d_1)$ and $N(d_2)$ into the above formula.

Consider the following example. The underlying price is 52.75 and has a volatility of 0.35. The continuously compounded risk-free rate is 4.88 percent. The option expires in nine months; therefore, T = 9/12 = 0.75. The exercise price is 50. First we calculate the values of d_1 and d_2:

$$d_1 = \frac{\ln(52.75/50) + \left(0.0488 + (0.35)^2/2\right)0.75}{0.35\sqrt{0.75}} = 0.4489$$
$$d_2 = 0.4489 - 0.35\sqrt{0.75} = 0.1458$$

To use the normal probability table in the Appendix, we must round off d_1 and d_2 to two digits to the right of the decimal. Thus we have $d_1 = 0.45$ and $d_2 = 0.15$. From the table, we obtain

$$N(0.45) = 0.6736$$
$$N(0.15) = 0.5596$$

Then we plug everything into the equation for c:

$$c = 52.75(0.6736) - 50e^{-0.0488(0.75)}(0.5596) = 8.5580$$

The value of a put with the same terms would be

$$p = 50e^{-0.0488(0.75)}(1 - 0.5596) - 52.75(1 - 0.6736) = 4.0110$$

At this point, we should note that the Black–Scholes–Merton model is extremely sensitive to rounding errors. In particular, the process of looking up values in the normal probability table is a major source of error. A number of other ways exist to obtain $N(d_1)$ and $N(d_2)$, such as using Microsoft Excel's function "=normsdist()". Using a more precise method, such as Excel, the value of the call would be 8.619. Note that this is the value to which the binomial option price converged in the example we showed with 1,000 time periods in Exhibit 23. Indeed, the Black–Scholes–Merton model is said to be the continuous limit of the binomial model.

Exhibit 24 **The Normal Probability Distribution**

The normal probability distribution, or bell-shaped curve, gives the probability that a standard normal random variable will be less than or equal to a given value. The graph below shows the normal probability distribution; note that the curve is centered around zero. The values on the horizontal axis run from $-\infty$ to $+\infty$. If we were interested in a value of x of positive infinity, we would have $N(+\infty) = 1$. This expression means that the probability is 1.0 that we would obtain a value less than $+\infty$. If we were interested in a value of x of negative infinity, then $N(-\infty) = 0.0$. This expression means that there is zero probability of a value of x of less than negative infinity. Below, we are interested in the probability of a value less than x, where x is not infinite. We want N(x), which is the area under the curve to the left of x.

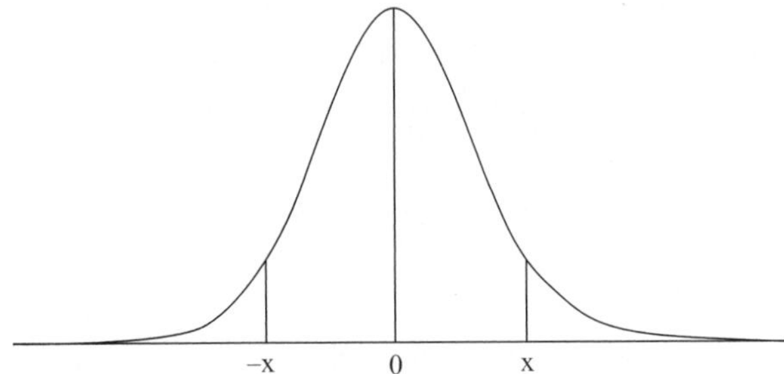

We obtain the values of N(x) by looking them up in a table. Below is an excerpt from a table of values of x (the full table is given as the Appendix). Suppose x = 1.12. Then we find the row containing the value 1.1 and move over to the column containing 0.02. The sum of the row value and the column value is the value of x. The corresponding probability is seen as the value 0.8686. Thus, N(1.12) = 0.8686. This means that the probability of obtaining a value of less than 1.12 in a normal distribution is 0.8686.

x	0	0.01	0.02	0.03	0.04	0.05	0.06	0.07	0.08	0.09
0.60	0.7257	0.7291	0.7324	0.7357	0.7389	0.7422	0.7454	0.7486	0.7517	0.7549
0.70	0.7580	0.7611	0.7642	0.7673	0.7704	**0.7734**	0.7764	0.7794	0.7823	0.7852
0.80	0.7881	0.7910	0.7939	0.7967	0.7995	0.8023	0.8051	0.8078	0.8106	0.8133
0.90	0.8159	0.8186	0.8212	0.8238	0.8264	0.8289	0.8315	0.8340	0.8365	0.8389
1.00	0.8413	0.8438	0.8461	0.8485	0.8508	0.8531	0.8554	0.8577	0.8599	0.8621
1.10	0.8643	0.8665	**0.8686**	0.8708	0.8729	0.8749	0.8770	0.8790	0.8810	0.8830
1.20	0.8849	0.8869	0.8888	0.8907	0.8925	0.8944	0.8962	0.8980	0.8997	0.9015

Now, suppose the value of x is negative. Observe in the figure above that the area to the left of –x is the same as the area to the right of +x. Therefore, if x is a negative number, N(x) is found as 1 – N(–x). For example, let x = –0.75. We simply look up N(–x) = N[–(–0.75)] = N(0.75) = 0.7734. Then N(–0.75) = 1 – 0.7734 = 0.2266.

EXAMPLE 8

Use the Black–Scholes–Merton model to calculate the prices of European call and put options on an asset priced at 68.5. The exercise price is 65, the continuously compounded risk-free rate is 4 percent, the options expire in 110 days, and the volatility is 0.38. There are no cash flows on the underlying.

Solution:

The time to expiration will be T = 110/365 = 0.3014. Then d_1 and d_2 are

$$d_1 = \frac{\ln(68.5/65) + \left(0.04 + (0.38)^2/2\right)(0.3014)}{0.38\sqrt{0.3014}} = 0.4135$$

$$d_2 = 0.4135 - 0.38\sqrt{0.3014} = 0.2049$$

Looking up in the normal probability table, we have

$$N(0.41) = 0.6591$$

$$N(0.20) = 0.5793$$

Plugging into the option price formula,

$$c = 68.5(0.6591) - 65e^{-0.04(0.3014)}(0.5793) = 7.95$$

$$p = 65e^{-0.04(0.3014)}(1 - 0.5793) - 68.5(1 - 0.6591) = 3.67$$

Let us now take a look at the various inputs required in the Black–Scholes–Merton model. We need to know where to obtain the inputs and how the option price varies with these inputs.

7.3 Inputs to the Black–Scholes–Merton Model

The Black–Scholes–Merton model has five inputs: the underlying price, the exercise price, the risk-free rate, the time to expiration, and the volatility.[30] As we have previously seen, call option prices should be higher the higher the underlying price, the longer the time to expiration, the higher the volatility, and the higher the risk-free rate. They should be lower the higher the exercise price. Put option prices should be higher the higher the exercise price and the higher the volatility. They should be lower the higher the underlying price and the higher the risk-free rate. As we saw, European put option prices can be either higher or lower the longer the time to expiration. American put option prices are always higher the longer the time to expiration, but the Black–Scholes–Merton model does not apply to American options.

These relationships are general to any European and American options and do not require the Black–Scholes–Merton model to understand them. Nonetheless, the Black–Scholes–Merton model provides an excellent opportunity to examine these relationships more closely. We can calculate and plot relationships such as those mentioned, which are usually called the option Greeks, because they are often referred to with Greek names. Let us now look at each of the inputs and the various option Greeks.

7.3.1 *The Underlying Price: Delta and Gamma*

The price of the underlying is generally one of the easiest sources of input information. Suffice it to say that if an investor cannot obtain the price of the underlying, then she should not even be considering the option. The price should generally be obtained as a quote or trade price from a liquid, open market.

The relationship between the option price and the underlying price has a special name: It is called the option **delta**. In fact, the delta can be obtained approximately from the Black–Scholes–Merton formula as the value of $N(d_1)$ for calls and $N(d_1) - 1$ for puts. More formally, the delta is defined as

30 Later we shall add one more input, cash flows on the underlying.

$$\text{Delta} = \frac{\text{Change in option price}}{\text{Change in underlying price}} \tag{23}$$

The above definition for delta is exact; the use of $N(d_1)$ for calls and $N(d_1) - 1$ for puts is approximate. Later in this section, we shall see why $N(d_1)$ and $N(d_2)$ are approximations and when they are good or bad approximations.

Let us consider the example we previously worked, where S = 52.75, X = 50, r^c = 0.0488, T = 0.75, and σ = 0.35. Using a computer to obtain a more precise Black–Scholes–Merton answer, we get a call option price of 8.6186 and a put option price of 4.0717. $N(d_1)$, the call delta, is 0.6733, so the put delta is 0.6733 – 1 = –0.3267. Given that Delta = (Change in option price/Change in underlying price), we should expect that

$$\textit{Change in option price} = \textit{Delta} \times \textit{Change in underlying price}$$

Therefore, for a $1 change in the price of the underlying, we should expect

$$\text{Change in call option price} = 0.6733(1) = 0.6733$$

$$\text{Change in put option price} = -0.3267(1) = -0.3267$$

This calculation would mean that

$$\text{Approximate new call option price} = 8.6186 + 0.6733 = 9.2919$$

$$\text{Approximate new put option price} = 4.0717 - 0.3267 = 3.7450$$

To test the accuracy of this approximation, we let the underlying price move up $1 to $53.75 and re-insert these values into the Black–Scholes–Merton model. We would then obtain

$$\text{Actual new call option price} = 9.3030$$

$$\text{Actual new put option price} = 3.7560$$

The delta approximation is fairly good, but not perfect.

Delta is important as a risk measure. *The delta defines the sensitivity of the option price to a change in the price of the underlying.* Traders, especially dealers in options, use delta to construct hedges to offset the risk they have assumed by buying and selling options. For example, recall from the reading on forward markets and contracts that FRA dealers offer to take either side of an FRA transaction. They then usually hedge the risk they have assumed by entering into other transactions. These same types of dealers offer to buy and sell options, hedging that risk with other transactions. For example, suppose we are a dealer offering to sell the call option we have been working with above. A customer buys 1,000 options for 8.619. We now are short 1,000 call options, which exposes us to considerable risk if the underlying goes up. So we must buy a certain number of units of the underlying to hedge this risk. We previously showed that the delta is 0.6733, so we would buy 673 units of the underlying at 52.75.[31] Assume for the moment that the delta tells us precisely the movement in the option for a movement in the underlying. Then suppose the underlying moves up $1:

$$\text{Change in value of 673 long units of the underlying: } 673(+\$1) = \$673$$

$$\text{Change in value of 1,000 short options: } 1{,}000(+\$1)(0.6733) \approx \$673$$

Because we are long the underlying and short the options, these values offset. At this point, however, the delta has changed. If we recalculate it, we would find it to be 0.6953. This would require that we have 695 units of the underlying, so we would need to buy an additional 22 units. We would borrow the money to do this. In some cases, we would need to sell off units of the underlying, in which case we would invest the money in the risk-free asset.

31 This transaction would require 673($52.75) = $35,500, less the 1,000($8.619) = $8,619 received from the sale of the option, for a total investment required of $26,881. We would probably borrow this money.

Let us consider how changes in the underlying price will change the delta. In fact, even if the underlying price does not change, the delta would still change as the option moves toward expiration. For a call, the delta will increase toward 1.0 as the underlying price moves up and will decrease toward 0.0 as the underlying price moves down. For a put, the delta will decrease toward –1.0 as the underlying price moves down and increase toward 0.0 as the underlying price moves up.[32] If the underlying price does not move, a call delta will move toward 1.0 if the call is in-the-money or 0.0 if the call is out-of-the-money as the call moves toward the expiration day. A put delta will move toward –1.0 if the put is in-the-money or 0.0 if the put is out-of-the-money as it moves toward expiration.

So the delta is constantly changing, which means that delta hedging is a dynamic process. In fact, delta hedging is often referred to as **dynamic hedging**. In theory, the delta is changing continuously and the hedge should be adjusted continuously, but continuous adjustment is not possible in reality. When the hedge is not adjusted continuously, we are admitting the possibility of much larger moves in the price of the underlying. Let us see what happens in that case.

Using our previous example, we allow an increase in the underlying price of $10 to $62.75. Then the call price should change by 0.6733(10) = 6.733, and the put option price should change by –0.3267(10) = –3.267. Thus, the approximate prices would be

Approximate new call option price = 8.619 + 6.733 = 15.3520

Approximate new put option price = 4.0717 – 3.267 = 0.8047

The actual prices are obtained by recalculating the option values using the Black–Scholes–Merton model with an underlying price of 62.75. Using a computer for greater precision, we find that these prices are

Actual new call option price = 16.3026

Actual new put option price = 1.7557

The approximations based on delta are not very accurate. In general, the larger the move in the underlying, the worse the approximation. This will make delta hedging less effective.

Exhibit 25 shows the relationship between the option price and the underlying price. Panel A depicts the relationship for calls and Panel B shows the corresponding relationship for puts. Notice the curvature in the relationship between the option price and the underlying price. Call option values definitely increase the greater the underlying value, and put option values definitely decrease. But the amount of change is not the same in each direction. $N(d_1)$ measures the slope of this line at a given point. As such, it measures only the slope for a very small change in the underlying. When the underlying changes by more than a very small amount, the curvature of the line comes into play and distorts the relationship between the option price and underlying price that is explained by the delta. The problem here is much like the relationship between a bond price and its yield. This first-order relationship between a bond price and its yield is called the duration; therefore, duration is similar to delta.

32 Remember that the put delta is negative; hence, its movement is down toward –1.0 or up toward 0.0.

Exhibit 25 **The Relationship between Option Price and Underlying Price**
$X = 50, r^c = 0.0488, T = 0.75, \sigma = 0.35$

A. Calls

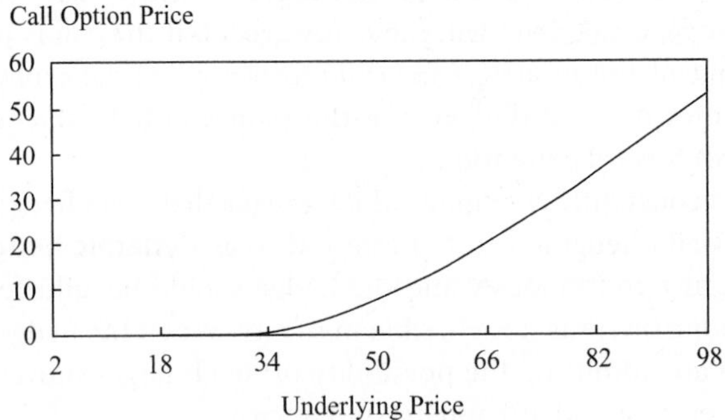

B. Puts

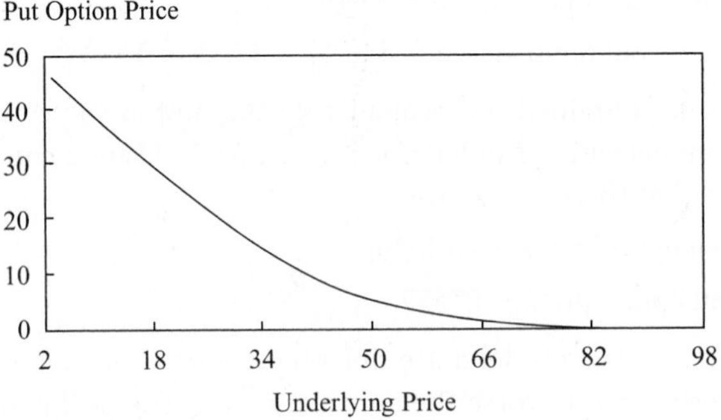

The curvature or second-order effect is known in the fixed income world as the convexity. In the options world, this effect is called **gamma**. Gamma is a numerical measure of how sensitive the delta is to a change in the underlying—in other words, how much the delta changes. When gamma is large, the delta changes rapidly and cannot provide a good approximation of how much the option moves for each unit of movement in the underlying. We shall not concern ourselves with measuring and using gamma, but we should know a few things about the gamma and, therefore, about the behavior of the delta.

Gamma is larger when there is more uncertainty about whether the option will expire in- or out-of-the-money. This means that *gamma will tend to be large when the option is at-the-money and close to expiration.* In turn, this statement means that delta will be a poor approximation for the option's price sensitivity when it is at-the-money and close to the expiration day. Thus, a delta hedge will work poorly. When the gamma is large, we may need to use a gamma-based hedge, which would require that we add a position in another option to the delta-hedge position of the underlying and the option. We shall not take up this advanced topic here.

7.3.2 *The Exercise Price*

The exercise price is easy to obtain. It is specified in the option contract and does not change. Therefore, it is not worthwhile to speak about what happens when the exercise price changes, but we can talk about how the option price would differ if we choose an option with a different exercise price. As we have previously seen, the call option price will be lower the higher the exercise price and the put option price will be higher. This relationship is confirmed for our sample option in Exhibit 26.

Exhibit 26 **The Relationship between Option Price and Exercise Price**
$S = 52.75, r^c = 0.0488, T = 0.75, \sigma = 0.35$

A. Calls

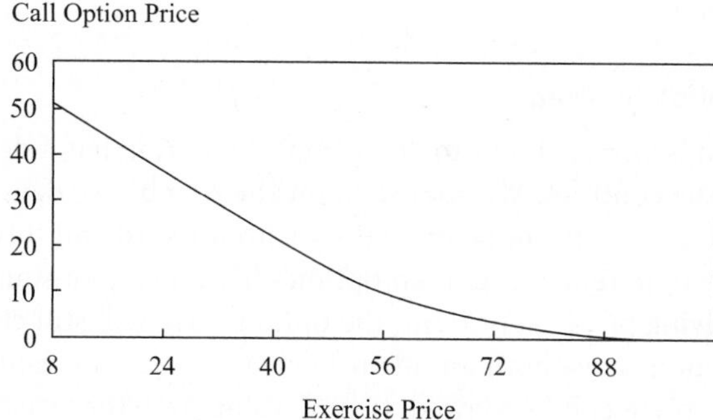

B. Puts

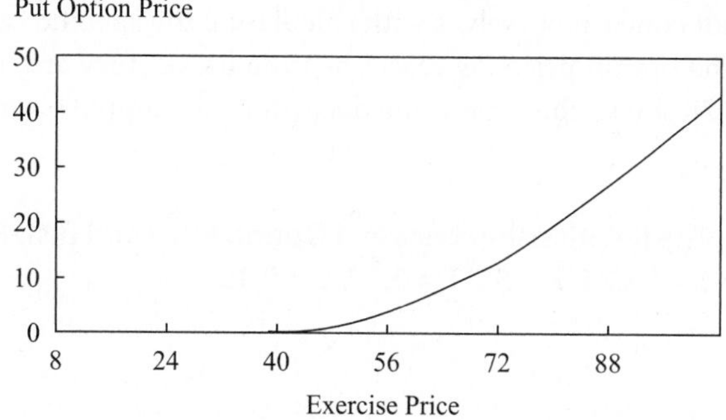

7.3.3 *The Risk-Free Rate: Rho*

The risk-free rate is the continuously compounded rate on the risk-free security whose maturity corresponds to the option's life. We have used the risk-free rate in previous readings; sometimes we have used the discrete version and sometimes the continuous version. As we have noted, the continuously compounded risk-free rate is the natural log of 1 plus the discrete risk-free rate.

For example, suppose the discrete risk-free rate quoted in annual terms is 5 percent. Then the continuous rate is

$$r^c = \ln(1 + r) = \ln(1.05) = 0.0488$$

Let us recall the difference in these two specifications. Suppose we want to find the present value of $1 in six months using both the discrete and continuous risk-free rates.

$$\text{Present value using discrete rate} = \frac{1}{(1 + r)^T} = \frac{1}{(1.05)^{0.5}} = 0.9759$$

$$\text{Present value using continuous rate} = e^{-r^c T} = e^{-0.0488(0.5)} = 0.9759$$

Obviously either specification will work. Because of how it uses the risk-free rate in the calculation of d_1, however, the Black–Scholes–Merton model requires the continuous risk-free rate.

The sensitivity of the option price to the risk-free rate is called the **rho**. We shall not concern ourselves with the calculation of rho. Technically, the Black–Scholes–Merton model assumes a constant risk-free rate, so it is meaningless to talk about the risk-free rate changing over the life of the option. We can, however, explore how the option price would differ if the current rate were different. Exhibit 27 depicts this effect. Note how little change occurs in the option price over a very broad range of the risk-free rate. Indeed, *the price of a European option on an asset is not very sensitive to the risk-free rate.*[33]

7.3.4 *Time to Expiration: Theta*

Time to expiration is an easy input to determine. An option has a definite expiration date specified in the contract. We simply count the number of days until expiration and divide by 365, as we have done previously with forward and futures contracts.

Obviously, the time remaining in an option's life moves constantly toward zero. Even if the underlying price is constant, the option price will still change. We noted that American options have both an intrinsic value and a time value. For European options, all of the price can be viewed as time value. In either case, time value is a function of the option's moneyness, its time to expiration, and its volatility. The more uncertainty there is, the greater the time value. As expiration approaches, the option price moves toward the payoff value of the option at expiration, a process known as **time value decay**. The rate at which the time value decays is called the option's **theta**. We shall not concern ourselves with calculating the specific value of theta, but be aware that if the option price decreases as time moves forward, the theta will be negative. Exhibit 28 shows the time value decay for our sample option.

Exhibit 27 **The Relationship between Option Price and Risk-Free Rate**
$S = 52.75, X = 50, T = 0.75, \sigma = 0.35$

A. Calls

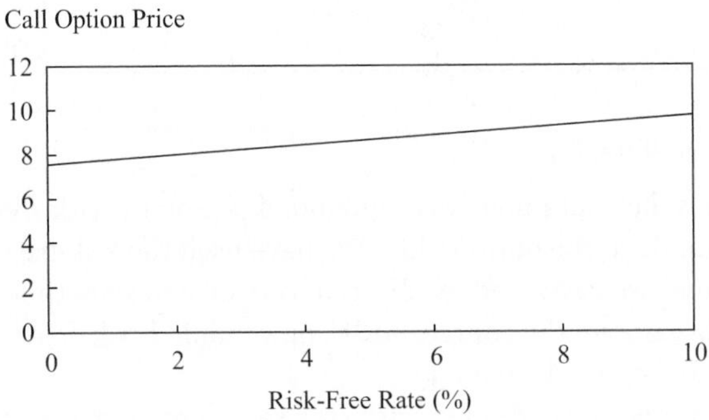

33 When the underlying is an interest rate, however, there is a strong relationship between the option price and interest rates.

Exhibit 27 (Continued)

B. Puts

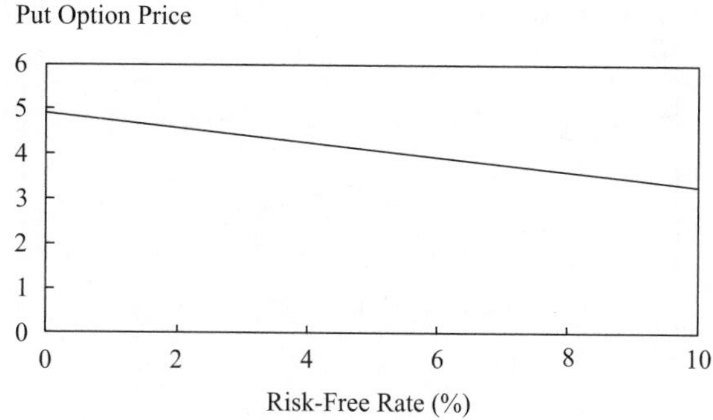

Note that both call and put values decrease as the time to expiration decreases. We previously noted that European put options do not necessarily do this. For some cases, European put options can increase in value as the time to expiration decreases, the case of a positive theta, but that is not so for our put.[34] *Most of the time, option prices are higher the longer the time to expiration. For European puts, however, some exceptions exist.*

7.3.5 *Volatility: Vega*

As we have previously noted, volatility is the standard deviation of the continuously compounded return on the stock. We have also noted that the volatility is an extremely important variable in the valuation of an option. It is the only variable that cannot be obtained easily and directly from another source. In addition, as we illustrate here, option prices are extremely sensitive to the volatility. We take up the subject of estimating volatility in Section 7.5.

Exhibit 28 **The Relationship between Option Price and Time to Expiration $S = 52.75$, $X = 50$, $r^c = 0.0488$, $\sigma = 0.35$, T Starts at 0.75 and Goes toward 0.0**

A. Calls

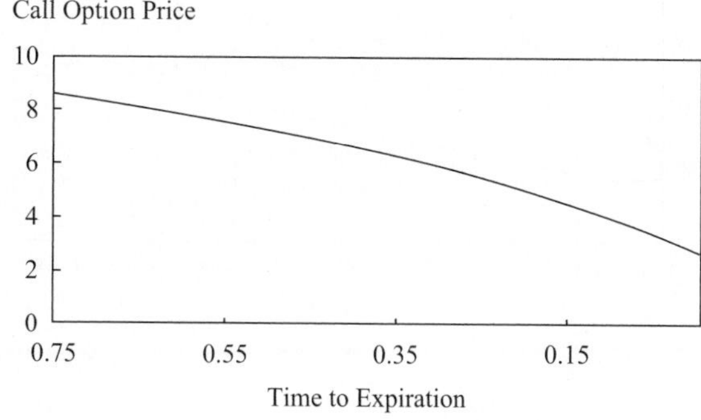

(continued)

34 Positive put thetas tend to occur when the put is deep in-the-money, the volatility is low, the interest rate is high, and the time to expiration is low.

Exhibit 28 (Continued)

B. Puts

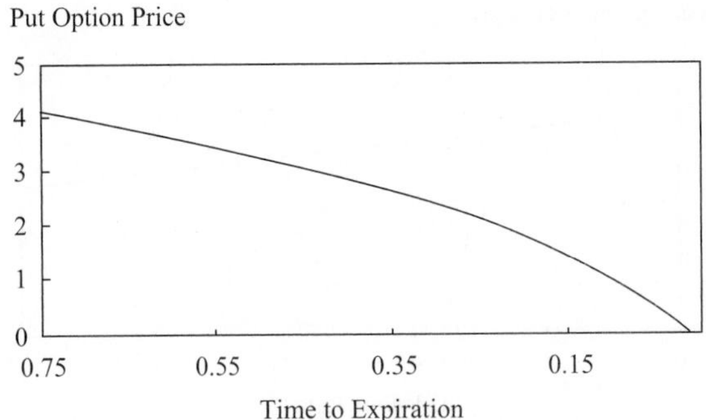

The relationship between option price and volatility is called the **vega**, which—albeit considered an option Greek—is not actually a Greek word.[35] We shall not concern ourselves with the actual calculation of the vega, but know that the vega is positive for both calls and puts, meaning that if the volatility increases, both call and put prices increase. Also, the vega is larger the closer the option is to being at-the-money.

In the problem we previously worked (S_0 = \$52.75, X = \$50, r^c = 0.0488, T = 0.75), at a volatility of 0.35, the option price was 8.619. Suppose we erroneously use a volatility of 0.40. Then the call price would be 9.446. An error in the volatility of this magnitude would not be difficult to make, especially for a variable that is not directly observable. Yet the result is a very large error in the option price.

Exhibit 29 displays the relationship between the option price and the volatility. Note that this relationship is nearly linear and that the option price varies over a very wide range, although this near-linearity is not the case for all options.

Exhibit 29 **The Relationship between Option Price and Volatility, S = 52.75, X = 50, r^c = 0.0488, T = 0.75**

A. Calls

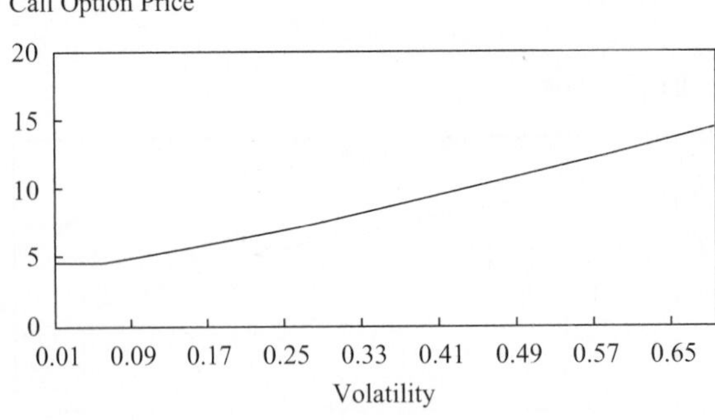

35 So that all of these effects ("the Greeks") be named after Greek words, the term *kappa* is sometimes used to represent the relationship between an option price and its volatility. As it turns out, however, vega is used far more often than kappa and is probably easier to remember, given the "v" in vega and the "v" in volatility. Vega, however, is a star, not a letter, and its origin is Latin.

Exhibit 29 (Continued)

B. Puts

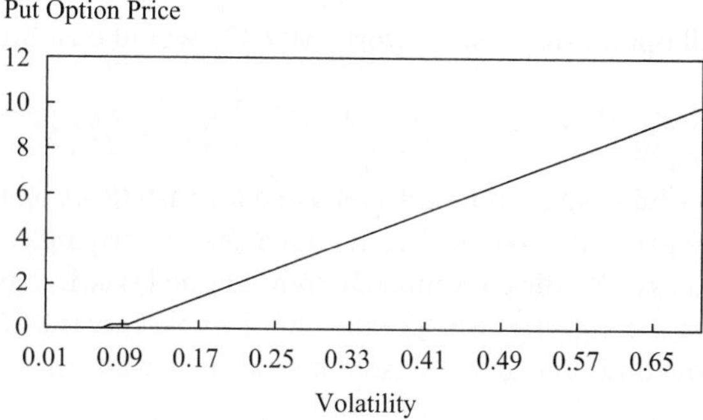

7.4 The Effect of Cash Flows on the Underlying

As we saw in the readings on forward markets and contracts and on futures markets and contracts, cash flows on the underlying affect the prices of forward and futures contracts. It should follow that they would affect the prices of options. In studying the option boundary conditions and put–call parity earlier in this reading, we noted that we subtract the present value of the dividends from the underlying price and use this adjusted price to obtain the boundary conditions or to price the options using put–call parity. We do the same using the Black–Scholes–Merton model. Specifically, we introduced the expression PV(CF,0,T) for the present value of the cash flows on the underlying over the life of the option. So, we simply use S_0 – PV(CF,0,T) in the Black–Scholes–Merton model instead of S_0.

Recall that in previous readings, we also used continuous compounding to express the cash flows. For stocks, we used a continuously compounded dividend yield; for currencies, we used a continuously compounded interest rate. In the case of stocks, we let δ^c represent the continuously compounded dividend rate. Then we substituted $S_0e^{-\delta_c T}$ for S_0 in the Black–Scholes–Merton formula. For a foreign currency, we let S_0 represent the exchange rate, which we discount using r^{fc}, the continuously compounded foreign risk-free rate. Let us work an example involving a foreign currency option.

Let the exchange rate of U.S. dollars for euros be \$0.8475. The continuously compounded U.S. risk-free rate, which in this example is r^c, is 5.10 percent. The continuously compounded euro risk-free rate, r^{fc}, is 4.25 percent. A call option expires in 125 days (T = 125/365 = 0.3425) and has an exercise price of \$0.90. The volatility of the continuously compounded exchange rate is 0.055.

The first thing we do is obtain the adjusted price of the underlying: $0.8475e^{-0.0425(0.3425)}$ = 0.8353. We then use this value as S_0 in the formula for d_1 and d_2:

$$d_1 = \frac{\ln(0.8353/0.90) + \left[0.051 + (0.055)^2/2\right](0.3425)}{0.055\sqrt{0.3425}} = -1.7590$$

$$d_2 = -1.7590 - 0.055\sqrt{0.3425} = -1.7912$$

Using the normal probability table, we find that

$$N(d_1) = N(-1.76) = 1 - 0.9608 = 0.0392$$

$$N(d_2) = N(-1.79) = 1 - 0.9633 = 0.0367$$

In discounting the exercise rate to evaluate the second term in the Black–Scholes–Merton expression, we use the domestic (here, U.S.) continuously compounded risk-free rate. The call option price would thus be

$$c = 0.8353(0.0392) - 0.90e^{-0.051(0.3425)}(0.0367) = 0.0003$$

Therefore, this call option on an asset worth $0.8475 would cost $0.0003.

EXAMPLE 9

Use the Black–Scholes–Merton model adjusted for cash flows on the underlying to calculate the price of a call option in which the underlying is priced at 225, the exercise price is 200, the continuously compounded risk-free rate is 5.25 percent, the time to expiration is three years, and the volatility is 0.15. The effect of cash flows on the underlying is indicated below for two alternative approaches:

A The present value of the cash flows over the life of the option is 19.72.

B The continuously compounded dividend yield is 2.7 percent.

Solution to A:

Adjust the price of the underlying to $S_0 = 225 - 19.72 = 205.28$. Then insert into the Black–Scholes–Merton formula as follows:

$$d_1 = \frac{\ln(205.28/200) + \left[0.0525 + (0.15)^2/2\right]3.0}{0.15\sqrt{3.0}} = 0.8364$$

$$d_2 = 0.8364 - 0.15\sqrt{3.0} = 0.5766$$

$$N(0.84) = 0.7995$$

$$N(0.58) = 0.7190$$

$$c = 205.28(0.7995) - 200e^{-0.0525(3.0)}(0.7190) = 41.28$$

Solution to B:

Adjust the price of the underlying to $S_0 = 225e^{-0.027(3.0)} = 207.49$

$$d_1 = \frac{\ln(207.49/200) + \left[0.0525 + (0.15)^2/2\right]3.0}{0.15\sqrt{3.0}} = 0.8776$$

$$d_2 = 0.8776 - 0.15\sqrt{3.0} = 0.6178$$

$$N(0.88) = 0.8106$$

$$N(0.62) = 0.7324$$

$$c = 207.49(0.8106) - 200e^{-0.0525(3.0)}(0.7324) = 43.06$$

7.5 The Critical Role of Volatility

As we have previously stressed, volatility is an extremely important variable in the pricing of options. In fact, with the possible exception of the cash flows on the underlying, it is the only variable that cannot be directly observed and easily obtained. It is, after all, the volatility over the life of the option; therefore, it is not past or current volatility but rather the future volatility. Differences in opinion on option prices nearly always result from differences of opinion about volatility. But how does one obtain a number for the future volatility?

7.5.1 *Historical Volatility*

The most logical starting place to look for an estimate of future volatility is past volatility. When the underlying is a publicly traded asset, we usually can collect some data over a recent past period and estimate the standard deviation of the continuously compounded return.

Exhibit 30 illustrates this process for a sample of 12 monthly prices of a particular stock. We convert these prices to returns, convert the returns to continuously compounded returns, find the variance of the series of continuously compounded returns, and then convert the variance to the standard deviation. In this example, the data are monthly returns, so we must annualize the variance by multiplying it by 12. Then we take the square root to obtain the historical estimate of the annual standard deviation or volatility.

Exhibit 30 Estimating Historical Volatility

Month	Price	Return	Log Return	(Log Return – Average)²
0	100			
1	102	0.020000	0.019803	0.000123
2	99	−0.029412	−0.029853	0.001486
3	97	−0.020202	−0.020409	0.000847
4	89	−0.082474	−0.086075	0.008982
5	103	0.157303	0.146093	0.018878
6	104	0.009709	0.009662	0.000001
7	102	−0.019231	−0.019418	0.000790
8	99	−0.029412	−0.029853	0.001486
9	104	0.050505	0.049271	0.001646
10	102	−0.019231	−0.019418	0.000790
11	105	0.029412	0.028988	0.000412
12	111	0.057143	0.055570	0.002197
		Sum	0.104360	0.037639
		Average	0.008697	

The variance is estimated as follows:

$$\sigma^2 = \frac{\sum_{i=1}^{N}\left(R_i^c - \overline{R}^c\right)^2}{N-1}$$

where R_i^c is the continuously compounded return for observation i (shown above in the fourth column and calculated as $\ln(1 + R_i)$, where i goes from 1 to 12) and R_i is the ith return, $\overline{R}^c$ is the average return over the entire sample, and N is the number of observations in the sample (here, N = 12). Then

$$\sigma^2 = \frac{0.037639}{11} = 0.003422$$

Because this sample consists of monthly returns, to obtain the annual variance, we must multiply this number by 12 (or 52 for weekly, or 250—the approximate number of trading days in a year—for daily). Thus

(continued)

Exhibit 30 (Continued)

$$\sigma^2 = 12(0.003422) = 0.041064$$

The annual standard deviation or volatility is, therefore,

$$\sigma = \sqrt{0.041064} = 0.2026$$

So the historical volatility estimate is 20.26 percent.

The historical estimate of the volatility is based only on what happened in the past. To get the best estimate, we must use a lot of prices, but that means going back farther in time. The farther back we go, the less current the data become, and the less reliable our estimate of the volatility. We now look at a way of obtaining a more current estimate of the volatility, but one that raises questions as well as answers them.

7.5.2 *Implied Volatility*

In a market in which options are traded actively, we can reasonably assume that the market price of the option is an accurate reflection of its true value. Thus, by setting the Black–Scholes–Merton price equal to the market price, we can work backwards to infer the volatility. This procedure enables us to determine the volatility that option traders are using to price the option. This volatility is called the **implied volatility**.

Unfortunately, determining implied volatility is not a simple task. We cannot simply solve the Black–Scholes–Merton equation for the volatility. It is a complicated function with the volatility appearing several times, in some cases as σ^2.There are some mathematical techniques that speed up the estimation of the implied volatility. Here, however, we shall look at only the most basic method: trial and error.

Recall the option we have been working with. The underlying price is 52.75, the exercise price is 50, the risk-free rate is 4.88 percent, and the time to expiration is 0.75. In our previous examples, the volatility was 0.35. Using these values in the Black–Scholes–Merton model, we obtained a call option price of 8.619. Suppose we observe the option selling in the market for 9.25. What volatility would produce this price?

We have already calculated a price of 8.619 at a volatility of 0.35. Because the call price varies directly with the volatility, we know that it would take a volatility greater than 0.35 to produce a price higher than 8.619. We do not know how much higher, so we should just take a guess. Let us try a volatility of 0.40. Using the Black–Scholes–Merton formula with a volatility of 0.40, we obtain a price of 9.446. This is too high, so we try a lower volatility. We keep doing this in the following manner:

Volatility	Black–Scholes–Merton Price
0.35	8.619
0.40	9.446
0.39	9.280
0.38	9.114

So now we know that the correct volatility lies between 0.38 and 0.39, closer to 0.39. In solving for the implied volatility, we must decide either how close to the option price we want to be or how many significant digits we want in the implied volatility. If we choose four significant digits in the implied volatility, a value of 0.3882 would produce the option price of 9.2500. Alternatively, if we decide that we want to be within 0.01 of the option price, we would find that the implied volatility is in the range of 38.76 to 38.88 percent.

Thus, if the option is selling for about 9.25, we say that the market is pricing it at a volatility of 0.3882. This number represents the market's best estimate of the true volatility of the underlying asset; it can be viewed as a more current source of volatility information than the past volatility. Unfortunately, a circularity exists in the argument. If one uses the Black–Scholes–Merton model to determine if an option is over- or underpriced, the procedure for extracting the implied volatility assumes that the market correctly prices the option. The only way to use the implied volatility in identifying mispriced options is to interpret the implied volatility as either too high or too low, which would require an estimate of true volatility. Nonetheless, the implied volatility is a source of valuable information on the uncertainty in the underlying, and option traders use it routinely.

All of this material on continuous-time option pricing has been focused on options in which the underlying is an asset. As we described earlier in this reading, there are also options on futures. Let us take a look at the pricing of options on futures, which will pave the way for a continuous-time pricing model for options on interest rates, another case in which the underlying is not an asset.

PRICING OPTIONS ON FORWARD AND FUTURES CONTRACTS AND AN APPLICATION TO INTEREST RATE OPTION PRICING 8

Earlier in this reading, we discussed how options on futures contracts are active, exchange-traded options in which the underlying is a futures contract. In addition, there are over-the-counter options in which the underlying is a forward contract. In our treatment of these instruments, we assume constant interest rates. As we learned in the readings on forward markets and contracts and on futures markets and contracts, this assumption means that futures and forward contracts will have the same prices. European options on futures and forward contracts will, therefore, have the same prices. American options on forwards will differ in price from American options on futures, and we discuss this later.

First we take a quick look at the basic rules that we previously developed for options on underlying assets. If the underlying asset is a futures contract, the payoff values of the options at expiration are

$$\begin{aligned} c_T &= \text{Max}\left[0, f_T(T) - X\right] \\ p_T &= \text{Max}\left[0, X - f_T(T)\right] \end{aligned} \tag{24}$$

where $f_T(T)$ is the price of a futures contract at T in which the contract expires at T. Thus, $f_T(T)$ is the futures price at expiration. These formulas are, of course, the same as for options when the underlying is an asset, with the futures price substituted for the asset price. When the option and the futures expire simultaneously, the futures price at expiration, $f_T(T)$, converges to the asset price, S_T, making the above payoffs precisely the same as those of the option on the underlying asset.

The minimum and maximum values for options on forwards or futures are the same as those we obtained for options on assets, substituting the futures price for the asset price. Specifically,

$$
\begin{aligned}
0 &\le c_0 \le f_0(T) \\
0 &\le C_0 \le f_0(T) \\
0 &\le p_0 \le X/(1+r)^T \\
0 &\le P_0 \le X
\end{aligned}
\tag{25}
$$

We also established lower bounds for European options and intrinsic values for American options and used these results to establish the minimum prices of these options. For options on futures, the lower bounds are

$$
\begin{aligned}
c_0 &\ge \text{Max}\left\{0,\left[f_0(T) - X\right]/(1+r)^T\right\} \\
p_0 &\ge \text{Max}\left\{0,\left[X - f_0(T)\right]/(1+r)^T\right\}
\end{aligned}
\tag{26}
$$

where $f_0(T)$ is the price at time 0 of a futures contract expiring at T. Therefore, the price of a European call or put on the futures is either zero or the difference between the futures price and exercise price, as formulated above, discounted to the present. For American options on futures, early exercise is possible. Thus, we express their lowest prices as the intrinsic values:

$$
\begin{aligned}
C_0 &\ge \text{Max}\left[0, f_0(T) - X\right] \\
P_0 &\ge \text{Max}\left[0, X - f_0(T)\right]
\end{aligned}
\tag{27}
$$

Because these values are greater than the lower bounds, we maintain these values as the minimum prices of American calls.[36]

As we have previously pointed out, with the assumption of constant interest rates, futures prices and forward prices are the same. We can treat European options on futures the same way as options on forwards. American options on futures will differ from American options on forwards. Now we explore how put–call parity works for options on forwards.

8.1 Put–Call Parity for Options on Forwards

In an earlier section, we examined put–call parity. Now we take a look at the parity between puts and calls on forward contracts and their underlying forward contracts. First recall the notation: F(0,T) is the price established at time 0 for a forward contract expiring at time T. Let c_0 and p_0 be the prices today of calls and puts on the forward contract. We shall assume that the puts and calls expire when the forward contract expires. The exercise price of the options is X. The payoff of the call is Max$(0,S_T - X)$, and the payoff of the put is Max$(0,X - S_T)$.[37] We construct a combination consisting of a long call and a long position in a zero-coupon bond with face value of X – F(0,T). We construct another combination consisting of a long position in a put and a long position in a forward contract. Exhibit 31 shows the results.

36 In other words, we cannot use the European lower bound as the lowest price of an American call or put, as we could with calls when the underlying was an asset instead of a futures.

37 Recall that the option payoffs are given by the underlying price at expiration, because the forward contract expires when the option expires. Therefore, the forward price at expiration is the underlying price at expiration.

Exhibit 31 Portfolio Combinations for Equivalent Packages of Puts, Calls, and Forward Contracts (Put–Call Parity for Forward Contracts)

		Value at Expiration	
Transaction	**Current Value**	$S_T \le X$	$S_T > X$
Call and Bond			
Buy call	c_0	0	$S_T - X$
Buy bond	$[X - F(0,T)]/(1 + r)^T$	$X - F(0,T)$	$X - F(0,T)$
Total	$c_0 + [X - F(0,T)]/(1 + r)^T$	$X - F(0,T)$	$S_T - F(0,T)$
Put and Forward			
Buy put	p_0	$X - S_T$	0
Buy forward contract	0	$S_T - F(0,T)$	$S_T - F(0,T)$
Total	p_0	$X - F(0,T)$	$S_T - F(0,T)$

As the exhibit demonstrates, both combinations produce a payoff of either $X - F(0,T)$ or $S_T - F(0,T)$, whichever is greater. The call and bond combination is thus equivalent to the put and forward contract combination. Hence, to prevent an arbitrage opportunity, the initial values of these combinations must be the same. The initial value of the call and bond combination is $c_0 + [X - F(0,T)]/(1 + r)^T$. The forward contract has zero initial value, so the initial value of the put and forward contract combination is only the initial value of the put, p_0. Therefore,

$$c_0 + \left[X - F(0,T)\right]/(1 + r)^T = p_0 \tag{28}$$

This equation is put–call parity for options on forward contracts.

Note that we seem to have implied that the bond is a long position, but that might not be the case. The bond should have a face value of $X - F(0,T)$. We learned in the reading on forward markets and contracts that $F(0,T)$ is determined in the market as the underlying price compounded at the risk-free rate.[38] Because there are a variety of options with different exercise prices, any one of which could be chosen, it is clearly possible for X to exceed or be less than $F(0,T)$. If $X > F(0,T)$, we are long the bond, because the payoff of $X - F(0,T)$ is greater than zero, meaning that we get back money from the bond. If $X < F(0,T)$, we issue the bond, because the payoff of $X - F(0,T)$ is less than zero, meaning that we must pay back money. Note the special case when $X = F(0,T)$. The bond is effectively out of the picture. Then $c_0 = p_0$.

Now recall from the reading on forward markets and contracts that with discrete interest compounding and no storage costs, the forward price is the spot price compounded at the risk-free rate. So,

$$F(0,T) = S_0(1 + r)^T$$

If we substitute this result for $F(0,T)$ in the put–call parity equation for options on forwards, we obtain

$$p_0 + S_0 = c_0 + X/(1 + r)^T$$

which is the put–call parity equation for options on the underlying that we learned earlier in this reading. Indeed, put–call parity for options on forwards and put–call parity for options on the underlying asset are the same. The only difference is that in the former, the forward contract and the bond replace the underlying. Given the

38 We are, of course, assuming no cash flows or costs on the underlying asset.

equivalence of options on the forward contract and options on the underlying, we can refer to put–call parity for options on forwards as **put–call–forward parity**. The equation

$$c_0 + \left[X - F(0,T)\right]/(1 + r)^T = p_0$$

expresses the relationship between the forward price and the prices of the options on the underlying asset, or alternatively between the forward price and the prices of options on the forward contract. We can also rearrange the equation to isolate the forward price and obtain

$$F(0,T) = (c_0 - p_0)(1 + r)^T + X$$

which shows how the forward price is related to the put and call prices and to the exercise price.

Now observe in Exhibit 32 how a synthetic forward contract can be created out of options.

Exhibit 32 Forward Contract and Synthetic Forward Contract

Transaction	Current Value	Value at Expiration $S_T \le X$	Value at Expiration $S_T > X$
Forward Contract			
Long forward contract	0	$S_T - F(0,T)$	$S_T - F(0,T)$
Synthetic Forward Contract			
Buy call	c_0	0	$S_T - X$
Sell put	$-p_0$	$-(X - S_T)$	0
Buy (or sell) bond	$[X - F(0,T)]/(1 + r)^T$	$X - F(0,T)$	$X - F(0,T)$
Total	$c_0 - p_0 + [X - F(0,T)]/(1 + r)^T$	$S_T - F(0,T)$	$S_T - F(0,T)$

In the top half of the exhibit is a forward contract. Its payoff at expiration is $S_T - F(0,T)$. In the bottom half of the exhibit is a **synthetic forward contract**, which consists of a long call, a short put, and a long risk-free bond with a face value equal to the exercise price minus the forward price. Note that this bond can actually be short if the exercise price of these options is lower than the forward price. The forward contract and synthetic forward contract have the same payoffs, so their initial values must be equal. The initial value of the forward contract is zero, so the initial value of the synthetic forward contract must be zero. Thus,

$$c_0 - p_0 + \left[X - F(0,T)\right]/(1 + r)^T = 0$$

Solving for F(0,T), we obtain the equation for the forward price in terms of the call, put, and bond that was given previously. So a synthetic forward contract is a combination consisting of a long call, a short put, and a zero-coupon bond with face value of X – F(0,T).

Consider the following example: The options and a forward contract expire in 50 days, so T = 50/365 = 0.1370. The risk-free rate is 6 percent, and the exercise price is 95. The call price is 5.50, the put price is 10.50, and the forward price is 90.72. Substituting in the above equation, we obtain

$$5.50 - 10.50 + \frac{95 - 90.72}{(1.06)^{0.1370}} = -0.7540$$

which is supposed to be zero. The left-hand side replicates a forward contract. Thus, the synthetic forward is underpriced. We buy it and sell the actual forward contract. So if we buy the call, sell the put, and buy the bond with face value 95 – 90.72 = 4.28, we bring in 0.7540. At expiration, the payoffs are as follows.

The options and forward expire with the underlying above 95:

The bond matures and pays off 95 – 90.72 = 4.28.

Exercise the call, paying 95 and obtaining the underlying.

Deliver the underlying and receive 90.72 from the forward contract.

The put expires with no value.

Net effect: No money in or out.

The options and forward expire with the underlying at or below 95:

The bond matures and pays off 95 – 90.72 = 4.28.

Buy the underlying for 95 with the short put.

Deliver the underlying and receive 90.72 from the forward contract.

The call expires with no value.

Net effect: No money in or out.

So we take in 0.7540 up front and never have to pay anything out. The pressure of other investors doing this will cause the call price to increase and the put price to decrease until the above equation equals zero or is at least equal to the transaction costs that would be incurred to exploit any discrepancy from zero.

Similarly, an option can be created from a forward contract. If a long forward contract is equivalent to a long call, short put, and zero-coupon bond with face value of X – F(0,T), then a long call is a long forward, long put, and a zero-coupon bond with face value of F(0,T) – X. A long put is a long call, short forward, and a bond with face value of X – F(0,T). These results are obtained just by rearranging what we learned here about forwards and options.

These results hold strictly for European options; some additional considerations exist for American options, but we do not cover them here.

EXAMPLE 10

Determine if a forward contract is correctly priced by using put–call–forward parity. The option exercise price is 90, the risk-free rate is 5 percent, the options and the forward contract expire in two years, the call price is 15.25, the put price is 3.00, and the forward price is 101.43.

Solution:

First note that the time to expiration is T = 2.0. There are many ways to express put–call–forward parity. We use the following specification:

$$p_0 = c_0 + [X - F(0,T)]/(1 + r)^T$$

The right-hand side is the synthetic put and consists of a long call, a short forward contract, and a bond with face value of X – F(0,T). Substituting the values into the right-hand side, we obtain

$$p_0 = 15.25 + (90 - 101.43)/(1.05)^{2.0} = 4.88$$

Because the actual put is selling for 3.00, it is underpriced. So we should buy the put and sell the synthetic put. To sell the synthetic put we should sell the call, buy the forward contract, and hold a bond with face value F(0,T) – X. Doing so will generate the following cash flow up front:

Buy put:	–3.00
Sell call:	+15.25
Buy bond:	$-(101.43 - 90)/(1.05)^{2.0} = -10.37$
Total:	+1.88

Thus the transaction brings in 1.88 up front. The payoffs at expiration are

	$S_T < 90$	$S_T \geq 90$
Long put	$90 - S_T$	0
Short call	0	$-(S_T - 90)$
Long bond	101.43 – 90	101.43 – 90
Long forward	$S_T - 101.43$	$S_T - 101.43$
Total	0	0

Therefore, no money flows in or out at expiration.

8.2 Early Exercise of American Options on Forward and Futures Contracts

As we noted earlier, the holder of an American put option may want to exercise it early. For American call options on underlying assets that make no cash payments, however, there is no justification for exercising the option early. If the underlying asset makes a cash payment, such as a dividend on a stock or interest on a bond, it may be justifiable to exercise the call option early.

For American options on futures, it may be worthwhile to exercise both calls and puts early. Even though early exercise is never justified for American calls on underlying assets that make no cash payments, early exercise can be justified for American call options on futures. Deep-in-the-money American call options on futures behave almost identically to the underlying, but the investor has money tied up in the call. If the holder exercises the call and establishes a futures position, he earns interest on the futures margin account. A similar argument holds for deep-in-the-money American put options on futures. The determination of the timing of early exercise is a specialist topic, so we do not explore it here.

If the option is on a forward contract instead of a futures contract, however, these arguments are overshadowed by the fact that a forward contract does not pay off until expiration, in contrast to the mark-to-market procedure of futures contracts. Thus, if one exercised either a call or a put on a forward contract early, doing so would only establish a long or short position in a forward contract. This position would not pay any cash until expiration. No justification exists for exercising early if one cannot generate any cash from the exercise. Therefore, an American call on a forward contract is the same as a European call on a forward contract, but American calls on futures are different from European calls on futures and carry higher prices.

8.3 The Black Model

The usual model for pricing European options on futures is called the Black model, named after Fischer Black of Black–Scholes–Merton fame. The formula is

$$c = e^{-r^c T}\left[f_0(T)N(d_1) - XN(d_2)\right]$$

$$p = e^{-r^c T}\left(X\left[1 - N(d_2)\right] - f_0(T)\left[1 - N(d_1)\right]\right)$$

where

$$d_1 = \frac{\ln\left(f_0(T)/X\right) + \left(\sigma^2/2\right)T}{\sigma\sqrt{T}}$$

$$d_2 = d_1 - \sigma\sqrt{T}$$

$$f_0(T) = \text{the futures price}$$

and the other terms are those we have previously used. The volatility, σ, is the volatility of the continuously compounded change in the futures price.[39]

Although the Black model may appear to give a somewhat different formula, it can be obtained directly from the Black–Scholes–Merton formula. Recall that the futures price in terms of the underlying spot price would be $f_0(T) = S_0 e^{r^c T}$ If we substitute the right-hand-side for $f_0(T)$ in the Black formula for d_1, we obtain the Black–Scholes–Merton formula for d_1.[40] Then if we substitute the right-hand side of the above for $f_0(T)$ in the Black formula for c_0 and p_0, we obtain the Black–Scholes–Merton formula for c_0 and p_0. These substitutions should make sense: The prices of options on futures equal the prices of options on the asset when the options and futures expire simultaneously.

The procedure should be straightforward if you have mastered substituting the asset price and other inputs into the Black–Scholes–Merton formula. Also, note that as with the Black–Scholes–Merton formula, the formula applies only to European options. As we noted in the previous section, early exercise of American options on futures is often justified, so we cannot get away with using this formula for American options on futures. We can, however, use the formula for American options on forwards, because they are never exercised early.

EXAMPLE 11

The price of a forward contract is 139.19. A European option on the forward contract expires in 215 days. The exercise price is 125. The continuously compounded risk-free rate is 4.25 percent. The volatility is 0.15.

A Use the Black model to determine the price of the call option.

B Determine the price of the underlying from the above information and use the Black–Scholes–Merton model to show that the price of an option on the underlying is the same as the price of the option on the forward.

---

39 If we were using the model to price options on forward contracts, we would insert F(0,T), the forward price, instead of the futures price. Doing so would produce some confusion because we have never subscripted the forward price, arguing that it does not change. Therefore, although we could use the formula to price options on forwards at time 0, how could we use the formula to price options on forwards at a later time, say time t, prior to expiration? In that case, we would have to use the price of a newly constructed forward contract that expires at T, F(t,T). Of course, with constant interest rates, these forward prices, F(0,T) and F(t,T), would be identical to the analogous futures price, $f_0(T)$ and $f_t(T)$. So, for ease of exposition we use the futures price.

40 This action requires us to recognize that $\ln\left(S_0 e^{r^c T}/X\right) = \ln\left(S_0/X\right) + r^c T$.

The time to expiration is T = 215/365 = 0.5890.

Solution to A:

First find d_1 and d_2, then $N(d_1)$ and $N(d_2)$, and then the call price:

$$d_1 = \frac{ln(139.19/125) + \left[(0.15)^2/2\right]0.5890}{0.15\sqrt{0.5890}} = 0.9916$$

$$d_2 = 0.9916 - 0.15\sqrt{0.5890} = 0.8765$$

$$N(0.99) = 0.8389$$

$$N(0.88) = 0.8106$$

$$c = e^{-0.0425(0.5890)}\left[139.19(0.8389) - 125(0.8106)\right] = 15.06$$

Solution to B:

We learned in the reading on forward markets and contracts that if there are no cash flows on the underlying and the interest is compounded continuously, the forward price is given by the formula $F(0,T) = S_0 e^{-r^c T}$. We can thus find the spot price as

$$S_0 = F(0,T)e^{-r^c T} = 139.19e^{-0.0425(0.5890)} = 135.75$$

Then we simply use the Black–Scholes–Merton formula:

$$d_1 = \frac{ln(135.75/125) + \left(0.0425 + (0.15)^2/2\right)(0.5890)}{0.15\sqrt{0.5890}} = 0.9916$$

$$d_2 = 0.9916 - 0.15\sqrt{0.5890} = 0.8765$$

These are the same values as in Part A, so $N(d_1)$ and $N(d_2)$ will be the same. Plugging into the formula for the call price gives

$$c = 135.75(0.8389) - 125e^{-0.0425(0.5890)}(0.8106) = 15.06$$

This price is the same as in Part A.

8.4 Application of the Black Model to Interest Rate Options

Earlier in this reading, we described options on interest rates. These derivative instruments parallel the FRAs that we covered in the reading on forward markets and contracts, in that they are derivatives in which the underlying is not a bond but rather an interest rate. Pricing options on interest rates is a challenging task. We showed how this is done using binomial trees. It would be nice if the Black–Scholes–Merton model could be easily used to price interest rate options, but the process is not so straightforward. Pricing options on interest rates requires a sophisticated model that prohibits arbitrage among interest-rate-related instruments and their derivatives. The Black–Scholes–Merton model is not sufficiently general to use in this manner. Nonetheless, practitioners often employ the Black model to price interest rate options. Somewhat remarkably, perhaps, it is known to give satisfactory results. Therefore, we provide a quick overview of this practice here.

Suppose we wish to price a one-year interest rate cap, consisting of three caplets. One caplet expires in 90 days, one 180 days, and one in 270 days.[41] The exercise rate is 9 percent. To use the Black model, we use the forward rate as though it were $f_0(T)$. Therefore, we also require its volatility and the risk-free rate for the period to the option's expiration.[42] Recalling that there are three caplets and we have to price each one individually, let us first focus on the caplet expiring in 90 days. We first specify that T = 90/365 = 0.2466. Then we need the forward rate today for the period day 90 to day 180. Let this rate be 9.25 percent. We shall assume its volatility is 0.03. We then need the continuously compounded risk-free rate for 90 days, which we assume to be 9.60 percent. So now we have the following input variables:

$$T = 0.2466$$
$$f_0(T) = 0.0925$$
$$\sigma = 0.03$$
$$X = 0.09$$
$$r^c = 0.096$$

Inserting these inputs into the Black model produces

$$d_1 = \frac{\ln(0.0925/0.09) + \left[(0.03)^2/2\right](0.2466)}{0.03\sqrt{0.2466}} = 1.8466$$
$$d_2 = 1.8466 - 0.03\sqrt{0.2466} = 1.8317$$
$$N(1.85) = 0.9678$$
$$N(1.83) = 0.9664$$
$$c_0 = e^{-0.096(0.2466)}\left[0.0925(0.9678) - 0.09(0.9664)\right] = 0.00248594$$

(Because of the order of magnitude of the inputs, we carry the answer out to eight decimal places.) But this answer is not quite what we need. The formula gives the answer under the assumption that the option payoff occurs at the option expiration. As we know, interest rate options pay off later than their expirations. This option expires in 90 days and pays off 90 days after that. Therefore, we need to discount this result back from day 180 to day 90 using the forward rate of 9.25 percent.[43] We thus have

$$0.00248594e^{-0.0925(0.2466)} = 0.00242988$$

41 A one-year cap will have three individual caplets. The first expires in 90 days and pays off in 180 days, the second expires in 180 days and pays off in 270 days, and the third expires in 270 days and pays off in 360 days. The tendency to think that a one-year cap using quarterly periods should have four caplets is incorrect because there is no caplet expiring right now and paying off in 90 days. It would make no sense to create an option that expires immediately. Also, in a one-year loan, the rate is set at the start and reset only three times; hence, only three caplets are required.

42 It is important to note here that the Black model requires that all inputs be in continuous compounding format. Therefore, the forward rate and risk-free rate would need to be the continuously compounded analogs to the discrete rates. Because the underlying is usually LIBOR, which is a discrete rate quoted on the basis of a 360-day year, some adjustments must be made to convert to a continuous rate quoted on the basis of a 365-day year. We will not address these adjustments here.

43 Be very careful in this discounting procedure. The exponent in the exponential should have a time factor of the number of days between the option expiration and its payoff. Because there are 90 days between days 90 and 180, we use 90/365 = 0.2466. This value is not quite the same as the time until the option expiration, which today is 90 but which will count down to zero.

Another adjustment is necessary. Because the underlying price and exercise price are entered as rates, the resulting answer is a rate. Moreover, the underlying rate and exercise rate are expressed as annual rates, so the answer is an annual rate. Interest rate option prices are always quoted as periodic rates (which are prices for $1 notional principal). We would adjust this rate by multiplying by 90/360.[44] The price would thus be

$$0.00242988(90/360) = 0.00060747$$

Finally, we should note that this price is valid for a $1 notional principal option. If the notional principal were $1 million, the option price would be

$$\$1{,}000{,}000(0.00060747) = \$607.47$$

We have just priced the first caplet of this cap. To price the second caplet, we need the forward rate for the period 180 days to 270 days, we would use 180/365 = 0.4932 as the time to expiration, and we need the risk-free rate for 180 days. To price the third caplet, we need the forward rate for the period 270 days to 360 days, we would use 270/365 = 0.7397 as the time to expiration, and we need the risk-free rate for 270 days. The price of the cap would be the sum of the prices of the three component caplets. If we were pricing a floor, we would price the component floorlets using the Black model for puts.

Although the Black model is frequently used to price interest rate options, binomial models, as we illustrated earlier, are somewhat more widely used in this area. These models are more attuned to deriving prices that prohibit arbitrage opportunities using any of the diverse instruments whose prices are given by the term structure. When you use the Black model to price interest rate options, there is some risk, perhaps minor, of having a counterparty be able to do arbitrage against you. Yet somehow the Black model is used often, and professionals seem to agree that it works remarkably well.

EXAMPLE 12

Use the Black model to price an interest rate put that expires in 280 days. The forward rate is currently 6.8 percent, the 280-day continuously compounded risk-free rate is 6.25 percent, the exercise rate is 7 percent, and the volatility is 0.02. The option is based on a 180-day underlying rate, and the notional principal is $10 million.

Solution:

The time to expiration is T = 280/365 = 0.7671. Calculate the value of d_1, d_2, and $N(d_1)$, $N(d_2)$, and p_0 using the Black model:

$$d_1 = \frac{\ln(0.068/0.07) + \left[(0.02)^2/2\right]0.7671}{0.02\sqrt{0.7671}} = -1.6461$$

$$d_2 = -1.6461 - 0.02\sqrt{0.7671} = -1.6636$$

$$N(-1.65) = 1 - N(1.65) = 1 - 0.9505 = 0.0495$$

$$N(-1.66) = 1 - N(1.66) = 1 - 0.9515 = 0.0485$$

$$p_0 = e^{-0.0625(0.7671)}\left[0.07(1 - 0.0485) - 0.068(1 - 0.0495)\right]$$
$$= 0.00187873$$

This formula assumes the option payoff is made at expiration. For an interest rate option, that assumption is false. This is a 180-day rate, so the payoff is made 180 days later. Therefore, we discount the payoff over 180 days using the forward rate:

44 It is customary in the interest rate options market to use 360 in the denominator to make this adjustment, even though we have used 365 in other places.

$$e^{-0.068(180/365)}(0.00187873) = 0.00181677$$

Interest rate option prices must reflect the fact that the rate used in the formula is quoted as an annual rate. So, we must multiply by 180/360 because the transaction is based on a 180-day rate:

$$0.00181677(180/360) = 0.00090839$$

Then we multiply by the notional principal:

$$\$10{,}000{,}000(0.00090839) = \$9{,}084$$

THE ROLE OF OPTIONS MARKETS

9

As we did with futures markets, we conclude the reading by looking at the important role options markets play in the financial system. Derivative markets provide price discovery and risk management, make the markets for the underlying assets more efficient, and permit trading at low transaction costs. These features are also associated with options markets. Yet, options offer further advantages that some other derivatives do not offer.

For example, forward and futures contracts have bidirectional payoffs. They have the potential for a substantial gain in one direction and a substantial loss in the other direction. The advantage of taking such a position lies in the fact that one need pay no cash up front. In contrast, options offer the feature that, if one is willing to pay cash up front, one can limit the loss in a given direction. In other words, options have unidirectional payoffs. This feature can be attractive to the holder of an option. To the writer, options offer the opportunity to be paid cash up front for a willingness to assume the risk of the unidirectional payoff. An option writer can assume the risk of potentially a large loss unmatched by the potential for a large gain. In fact, the potential gain is small. But for this risk, the option writer receives money up front.

Options also offer excellent devices for managing the risk of various exposures. An obvious one is the protective put, which we saw earlier and which can protect a position against loss by paying off when the value of the underlying is down.

Recall that futures contracts offer price discovery, the revelation of the prices at which investors will contract today for transactions to take place later. Options, on the other hand, provide volatility discovery. Through the implied volatility, investors can determine the market's assessment of how volatile it believes the underlying asset is. This valuable information can be difficult to obtain from any other source.

Futures offer advantages over forwards, in that futures are standardized, tend to be actively traded in a secondary market, and are protected by the exchange's clearinghouse against credit risk. Although some options, such as interest rate options, are available only in over-the-counter forms, many options exist in both over-the-counter and exchange-listed forms. Hence, one can often customize an option if necessary or trade it on an exchange.

In previous readings we covered forward contracts and futures contracts, and in this reading we covered option contracts. We have one more major class of derivative instruments, swaps, which we cover in the reading on swap markets and contracts.

SUMMARY

OPTIONAL SEGMENT

- Options are rights to buy or sell an underlying at a fixed price, the exercise price, for a period of time. The right to buy is a call; the right to sell is a put. Options have a definite expiration date. Using the option to buy or sell is the action of exercising it. The buyer or holder of an option pays a price to the seller or writer for the right to buy (a call) or sell (a put) the underlying instrument. The writer of an option has the corresponding potential obligation to sell or buy the underlying.
- European options can be exercised only at expiration; American options can be exercised at any time prior to expiration. Moneyness refers to the characteristic that an option has positive intrinsic value. The payoff is the value of the option at expiration. An option's intrinsic value is the value that can be captured if the option is exercised. Time value is the component of an option's price that reflects the uncertainty of what will happen in the future to the price of the underlying.
- Options can be traded as standardized instruments on an options exchange, where they are protected from default on the part of the writer, or as customized instruments on the over-the-counter market, where they are subject to the possibility of the writer defaulting. Because the buyer pays a price at the start and does not have to do anything else, the buyer cannot default.
- The underlying instruments for options are individual stocks, stock indices, bonds, interest rates, currencies, futures, commodities, and even such random factors as the weather. In addition, a class of options called real options is associated with the flexibility in capital investment projects.
- Like FRAs, which are forward contracts in which the underlying is an interest rate, interest rate options are options in which the underlying is an interest rate. However, FRAs are commitments to make one interest payment and receive another, whereas interest rate options are rights to make one interest payment and receive another.
- Option payoffs, which are the values of options when they expire, are determined by the greater of zero or the difference between underlying price and exercise price, if a call, or the greater of zero or the difference between exercise price and underlying price, if a put. For interest rate options, the exercise price is a specified rate and the underlying price is a variable interest rate.
- Interest rate options exist in the form of caps, which are call options on interest rates, and floors, which are put options on interest rates. Caps consist of a series of call options, called caplets, on an underlying rate, with each option expiring at a different time. Floors consist of a series of put options, called floorlets, on an underlying rate, with each option expiring at a different time.
- The minimum value of European and American calls and puts is zero. The maximum value of European and American calls is the underlying price. The maximum value of a European put is the present value of the exercise price. The maximum value of an American put is the exercise price.
- The lower bound of a European call is established by constructing a portfolio consisting of a long call and risk-free bond and a short position in the underlying asset. This combination produces a non-negative value at expiration, so its current value must be non-negative. For this situation to occur, the call price has to be worth at least the underlying price minus the present value of the exercise price. The lower bound of a European put is established by

constructing a portfolio consisting of a long put, a long position in the underlying, and the issuance of a zero-coupon bond. This combination produces a non-negative value at expiration so its current value must be non-negative. For this to occur, the put price has to be at least as much as the present value of the exercise price minus the underlying price. For both calls and puts, if this lower bound is negative, we invoke the rule that an option price can be no lower than zero.

- The lowest price of a European call is referred to as the lower bound. The lowest price of an American call is also the lower bound of a European call. The lowest price of a European put is also referred to as the lower bound. The lowest price of an American put, however, is its intrinsic value.
- Buying a call with a given exercise price and selling an otherwise identical call with a higher exercise price creates a combination that always pays off with a non-negative value. Therefore, its current value must be non-negative. For this to occur, the call with the lower exercise price must be worth at least as much as the other call. A similar argument holds for puts, except that one would buy the put with the higher exercise price. This line of reasoning shows that the put with the higher exercise price must be worth at least as much as the one with the lower exercise price.
- A longer-term European or American call must be worth at least as much as a corresponding shorter-term European or American call. A longer-term American put must be worth at least as much as a shorter-term American put. A longer-term European put, however, can be worth more or less than a shorter-term European put.

END OPTIONAL SEGMENT

- A fiduciary call, consisting of a European call and a zero-coupon bond, produces the same payoff as a protective put, consisting of the underlying and a European put. Therefore, their current values must be the same. For this equivalence to occur, the call price plus bond price must equal the underlying price plus put price. This relationship is called put–call parity and can be used to identify combinations of instruments that synthesize another instrument by rearranging the equation to isolate the instrument you are trying to create. Long positions are indicated by positive signs, and short positions are indicated by negative signs. One can create a synthetic call, a synthetic put, a synthetic underlying, and a synthetic bond, as well as synthetic short positions in these instruments for the purpose of exploiting mispricing in these instruments.
- Put–call parity violations exist when one side of the equation does not equal the other. An arbitrageur buys the lower-priced side and sells the higher-priced side, thereby earning the difference in price, and the positions offset at expiration. The combined actions of many arbitrageurs performing this set of transactions would increase the demand and price for the underpriced instruments and decrease the demand and price for the overpriced instruments, until the put–call parity relationship is upheld.
- American option prices must always be no less than those of otherwise equivalent European options. American call options, however, are never exercised early unless there is a cash flow on the underlying, so they can sell for the same as their European counterparts in the absence of such a cash flow. American put options nearly always have a possibility of early exercise, so they ordinarily sell for more than their European counterparts.
- Cash flows on the underlying affect an option's boundary conditions and put–call parity by lowering the underlying price by the present value of the cash flows over the life of the option.

- A higher interest rate increases a call option's price and decreases a put option's price.
- In a one-period binomial model, the underlying asset can move up to one of two prices. A portfolio consisting of a long position in the underlying and a short position in a call option can be made risk-free and, therefore, must return the risk-free rate. Under this condition, the option price can be obtained by inferring it from a formula that uses the other input values. The option price is a weighted average of the two option prices at expiration, discounted back one period at the risk-free rate.
- If an option is trading for a price higher than that given in the binomial model, one can sell the option and buy a specific number of units of the underlying, as given by the model. This combination is risk free but will earn a return higher than the risk-free rate. If the option is trading for a price lower than the price given in the binomial model, a short position in a specific number of units of the underlying and a long position in the option will create a risk-free loan that costs less than the risk-free rate.
- In a two-period binomial model, the underlying can move to one of two prices in each of two periods; thus three underlying prices are possible at the option expiration. To price an option, start at the expiration and work backward, following the procedure in the one-period model in which an option price at any given point in time is a weighted average of the next two possible prices discounted at the risk-free rate.
- To calculate the price of an option on a zero-coupon bond or a coupon bond, one must first construct a binomial tree of the price of the bond over the life of the option. To calculate the price of an option on an interest rate, one should use a binomial tree of interest rates. Then the option price is found by starting at the option expiration, determining the payoff and successively working backwards by computing the option price as the weighted average of the next two option prices discounted back one period. For the case of options on bonds or interest rates, a different discount rate is used at different parts of the tree.
- For an option of a given expiration, a greater pricing accuracy is obtained by dividing the option's life into a greater number of time periods in a binomial tree. As more time periods are added, the discrete-time binomial price converges to a stable value as though the option is being modeled in a continuous-time world.
- The assumptions under which the Black–Scholes–Merton model is derived state that the underlying asset follows a geometric lognormal diffusion process, the risk-free rate is known and constant, the volatility of the underlying asset is known and constant, there are no taxes or transaction costs, there are no cash flows on the underlying, and the options are European.
- To calculate the value of an option using the Black–Scholes–Merton model, enter the underlying price, exercise price, risk-free rate, volatility, and time to expiration into a formula. The formula will require you to look up two normal probabilities, obtained from either a table or preferably a computer routine.
- The change in the option price for a change in the price of the underlying is called the delta. The change in the option price for a change in the risk-free rate is called the rho. The change in the option price for a change in the time to expiration is called the theta. The change in the option price for a change in the volatility is called the vega.
- The delta is defined as the change in the option price divided by the change in the underlying price. The option price change can be approximated by the delta times the change in the underlying price. To construct a delta-hedged position,

a short (long) position in each call is matched with a long (short) position in delta units of the underlying. Changes in the underlying price will generate offsetting changes in the value of the option position, provided the changes in the underlying price are small and occur over a short time period. A delta-hedged position should be adjusted as the delta changes and time passes.

- If changes in the price of the underlying are large or the delta hedge is not adjusted over a longer time period, the hedge may not be effective. This effect is due to the instability of the delta and is called the gamma effect. If the gamma effect is large, option price changes will not be very close to the changes as approximated by the delta times the underlying price change.
- Cash flows on the underlying are accommodated in option pricing models by reducing the price of the underlying by the present value of the cash flows over the life of the option.
- Volatility can be estimated by calculating the standard deviation of the continuously compounded returns from a sample of recent data for the underlying. This is called the historical volatility. An alternative measure, called the implied volatility, can be obtained by setting the Black–Scholes–Merton model price equal to the market price and inferring the volatility. The implied volatility is a measure of the volatility the market is using to price the option.
- The payoffs of a call on a forward contract and an appropriately chosen zero-coupon bond are equivalent to the payoffs of a put on the forward contract and the forward contract. Thus, their current values must be the same. For this equality to occur, the call price plus the bond price must equal the put price. The appropriate zero-coupon bond is one with a face value equal to the exercise price minus the forward price. This relationship is called put–call–forward (or futures) parity.
- There is no justification for exercising American options on forward contracts early, so they are equivalent to European options on forwards. American options on futures, both calls and puts, can sometimes be exercised early, so they are different from European options on futures and carry a higher price.
- The Black model can be used to price European options on forwards or futures by entering the forward price, exercise price, risk-free rate, time to expiration, and volatility into a formula that will also require the determination of two normal probabilities.
- The Black model can be used to price European options on interest rates by entering the forward interest rate into the model for the forward or futures price and the exercise rate for the exercise price.
- Options are useful in financial markets because they provide a way to limit losses to the premium paid while permitting potentially large gains. They can be used for hedging purposes, especially in the case of puts, which can be used to limit the loss on a long position in an asset. Options also provide information on the volatility of the underlying asset. Options can be standardized and exchange-traded or customized in the over-the-counter market.

APPENDIX

Cumulative Probabilities for a Standard Normal Distribution $P(X \leq x) = N(x)$ for ≥ 0 or $1 - N(-x)$ for $x < 0$

x	0	0.01	0.02	0.03	0.04	0.05	0.06	0.07	0.08	0.09
0.00	0.5000	0.5040	0.5080	0.5120	0.5160	0.5199	0.5239	0.5279	0.5319	0.5359
0.10	0.5398	0.5438	0.5478	0.5517	0.5557	0.5596	0.5636	0.5675	0.5714	0.5753
0.20	0.5793	0.5832	0.5871	0.5910	0.5948	0.5987	0.6026	0.6064	0.6103	0.6141
0.30	0.6179	0.6217	0.6255	0.6293	0.6331	0.6368	0.6406	0.6443	0.6480	0.6517
0.40	0.6554	0.6591	0.6628	0.6664	0.6700	0.6736	0.6772	0.6808	0.6844	0.6879
0.50	0.6915	0.6950	0.6985	0.7019	0.7054	0.7088	0.7123	0.7157	0.7190	0.7224
0.60	0.7257	0.7291	0.7324	0.7357	0.7389	0.7422	0.7454	0.7486	0.7517	0.7549
0.70	0.7580	0.7611	0.7642	0.7673	0.7704	0.7734	0.7764	0.7794	0.7823	0.7852
0.80	0.7881	0.7910	0.7939	0.7967	0.7995	0.8023	0.8051	0.8078	0.8106	0.8133
0.90	0.8159	0.8186	0.8212	0.8238	0.8264	0.8289	0.8315	0.8340	0.8365	0.8389
1.00	0.8413	0.8438	0.8461	0.8485	0.8508	0.8531	0.8554	0.8577	0.8599	0.8621
1.10	0.8643	0.8665	0.8686	0.8708	0.8729	0.8749	0.8770	0.8790	0.8810	0.8830
1.20	0.8849	0.8869	0.8888	0.8907	0.8925	0.8944	0.8962	0.8980	0.8997	0.9015
1.30	0.9032	0.9049	0.9066	0.9082	0.9099	0.9115	0.9131	0.9147	0.9162	0.9177
1.40	0.9192	0.9207	0.9222	0.9236	0.9251	0.9265	0.9279	0.9292	0.9306	0.9319
1.50	0.9332	0.9345	0.9357	0.9370	0.9382	0.9394	0.9406	0.9418	0.9429	0.9441
1.60	0.9452	0.9463	0.9474	0.9484	0.9495	0.9505	0.9515	0.9525	0.9535	0.9545
1.70	0.9554	0.9564	0.9573	0.9582	0.9591	0.9599	0.9608	0.9616	0.9625	0.9633
1.80	0.9641	0.9649	0.9656	0.9664	0.9671	0.9678	0.9686	0.9693	0.9699	0.9706
1.90	0.9713	0.9719	0.9726	0.9732	0.9738	0.9744	0.9750	0.9756	0.9761	0.9767
2.00	0.9772	0.9778	0.9783	0.9788	0.9793	0.9798	0.9803	0.9808	0.9812	0.9817
2.10	0.9821	0.9826	0.9830	0.9834	0.9838	0.9842	0.9846	0.9850	0.9854	0.9857
2.20	0.9861	0.9864	0.9868	0.9871	0.9875	0.9878	0.9881	0.9884	0.9887	0.9890
2.30	0.9893	0.9896	0.9898	0.9901	0.9904	0.9906	0.9909	0.9911	0.9913	0.9916
2.40	0.9918	0.9920	0.9922	0.9925	0.9927	0.9929	0.9931	0.9932	0.9934	0.9936
2.50	0.9938	0.9940	0.9941	0.9943	0.9945	0.9946	0.9948	0.9949	0.9951	0.9952
2.60	0.9953	0.9955	0.9956	0.9957	0.9959	0.9960	0.9961	0.9962	0.9963	0.9964
2.70	0.9965	0.9966	0.9967	0.9968	0.9969	0.9970	0.9971	0.9972	0.9973	0.9974
2.80	0.9974	0.9975	0.9976	0.9977	0.9977	0.9978	0.9979	0.9979	0.9980	0.9981
2.90	0.9981	0.9982	0.9982	0.9983	0.9984	0.9984	0.9985	0.9985	0.9986	0.9986
3.00	0.9987	0.9987	0.9987	0.9988	0.9988	0.9989	0.9989	0.9989	0.9990	0.9990

PRACTICE PROBLEMS

1 Consider the following information on put and call options on a stock:

Call price, c_0 = \$4.50

Put price, p_0 = \$6.80

Exercise price, X = \$70

Days to option expiration = 139

Current stock price, S_0 = \$67.32

Risk-free rate, r = 5 percent

A Use put–call parity to calculate prices of the following:

i. Synthetic call option.

ii. Synthetic put option.

iii. Synthetic bond.

iv. Synthetic underlying stock.

B For each of the synthetic instruments in Part A, identify any mispricing by comparing the actual price with the synthetic price.

C Based on the mispricing in Part B, illustrate an arbitrage transaction using a synthetic call.

D Based on the mispricing in Part B, illustrate an arbitrage transaction using a synthetic put.

2 A stock currently trades at a price of \$100. The stock price can go up 10 percent or down 15 percent. The risk-free rate is 6.5 percent.

A Use a one-period binomial model to calculate the price of a call option with an exercise price of \$90.

B Suppose the call price is currently \$17.50. Show how to execute an arbitrage transaction that will earn more than the risk-free rate. Use 100 call options.

C Suppose the call price is currently \$14. Show how to execute an arbitrage transaction that replicates a loan that will earn less than the risk-free rate. Use 100 call options.

3 Suppose a stock currently trades at a price of \$150. The stock price can go up 33 percent or down 15 percent. The risk-free rate is 4.5 percent.

A Use a one-period binomial model to calculate the price of a put option with exercise price of \$150.

B Suppose the put price is currently \$14. Show how to execute an arbitrage transaction that replicates a loan that will earn less than the risk-free rate. Use 10,000 put options.

C Suppose the put price is currently \$11. Show how to execute an arbitrage transaction that will earn more than the risk-free rate. Use 10,000 put options.

4 Consider a two-period binomial model in which a stock currently trades at a price of $65. The stock price can go up 20 percent or down 17 percent each period. The risk-free rate is 5 percent.

   A Calculate the price of a call option expiring in two periods with an exercise price of $60.

   B Based on your answer in Part A, calculate the number of units of the underlying stock that would be needed at each point in the binomial tree to construct a risk-free hedge. Use 10,000 calls.

   C Calculate the price of a call option expiring in two periods with an exercise price of $70.

   D Based on your answer in Part C, calculate the number of units of the underlying stock that would be needed at each point in the binomial tree to construct a risk-free hedge. Use 10,000 calls.

5 Consider a two-period binomial model in which a stock currently trades at a price of $65. The stock price can go up 20 percent or down 17 percent each period. The risk-free rate is 5 percent.

   A Calculate the price of a put option expiring in two periods with exercise price of $60.

   B Based on your answer in Part A, calculate the number of units of the underlying stock that would be needed at each point in the binomial tree in order to construct a risk-free hedge. Use 10,000 puts.

   C Calculate the price of a put option expiring in two periods with an exercise price of $70.

   D Based on your answer in Part C, calculate the number of units of the underlying stock that would be needed at each point in the binomial tree in order to construct a risk-free hedge. Use 10,000 puts.

The following information relates to Questions 6–11[1]

Elsa Klein, CFA, is a hedge fund manager for Washburn Associates located in New York. One of the biotechnology companies that Klein owns, Apoth, issued a press release stating that the FDA (the U.S. regulatory body responsible for the approval of pharmaceutical products) has delayed their decision to approve or reject the latest pharmaceutical that Apoth has been developing for another six months. A junior analyst for the hedge fund, Baldev Gupta, believes that in six months the FDA will reject the new pharmaceutical and recommends selling Apoth shares. Gupta observes that, because there are many sell orders in the market for Apoth shares, the transaction cost to sell Apoth shares is greater than the transaction cost to buy Apoth shares. Gupta has prepared the data in Exhibit 1 as part of his analysis.

1 Developed by Bryan Gardiner, CFA (Richmond, Virginia).

Exhibit 1	Data Related to Apoth
Current share price	$38.00
Projected share price in six months	$26.00
Expected annual volatility of return	20%
Current annual risk-free rate	1.12%

Klein is not convinced by Gupta's analysis and is reluctant to sell their Apoth shares. Klein's expectation is that the uncertainty about the FDA's decision will increase the volatility of Apoth's shares until the decision is made.

However, Klein knows that Gupta is a good analyst and that the approval of the new drug is critical to Apoth's long-term success. She decides that it would be prudent to temporarily hedge the 100,000 shares of Apoth she owns until the outcome of the FDA's review is complete. Klein, who is very familiar with the Black–Scholes–Merton (BSM) model, decides to implement a hedging strategy using 6-month European options and gathers the data in Exhibit 2. Klein discusses the hedge strategy with Gupta, who makes the following recommendation:

"The best strategy to hedge your shares in Apoth would be to buy 6-month European put options to protect from a loss if the FDA rejects Apoth's new pharmaceutical."

Exhibit 2 Market Data for 6-month European Options on Apoth Shares

Option	W	X	Y	Z
Type of Option	Call	Call	Put	Put
Exercise Price	$38.00	$46.00	$38.00	$36.00
$N(d_1)$	0.56	0.30	0.56	0.64
$N(d_2)$	0.45	0.21	0.45	0.53

6 Based on the Black–Scholes–Merton model, Gupta's observation about the transaction cost for Apoth shares will *most likely*:

A increase the price of put options on Apoth shares.

B increase the price of call options on Apoth shares.

C have no effect on the price of options on Apoth shares.

7 Assuming Klein's expectation about the impact of the uncertainty of the FDA's decision is accurate, keeping all other factors constant, the *most likely* effect on the price of Apoth's options will be:

	Price of Call Option	Price of Put Option
A	Decrease	Decrease
B	Increase	Decrease
C	Increase	Increase

8 Using the data from Exhibit 2, the number of option X contracts that Klein would have to sell to implement the hedge strategy would be *closest to*:

A 30,000.

B 333,333.

C 476,190.

9 Based on the data in Exhibit 2, which of the following options is *most likely* to exhibit the largest gamma measure?

A Option X.

B Option Y.

C Option Z.

10 If Klein implemented Gupta's recommendation using Option Z from Exhibit 2 and Apoth's share price subsequently dropped to $36, Klein would *most likely* need to take the following action to maintain the same hedged position:

A Sell options because the put delta has become less negative.

B Sell options because the put delta has become more negative.

C Buy options because the put delta has become more negative.

11 If Apoth pays a dividend, holding all other factors constant, what would be the *most likely* effect on the price of option W?

A The price will increase.

B The price will decrease.

C The price will not change.

SOLUTIONS

1 Call price, c_0 = \$4.50

Put price, p_0 = \$6.80

Exercise price, X = \$70

Risk-free rate, r = 5 percent

Time to expiration = 139/365 = 0.3808

Current stock price, S_0 = \$67.32

Bond price = $X/(1 + r)^T = 70/(1 + 0.05)^{0.3808}$ = \$68.71

A Synthetic call = $p_0 + S_0 - X/(1 + r)^T = 6.8 + 67.32 - 68.71$ = \$5.41

Synthetic put = $c_0 + X/(1 + r)^T - S_0 = 4.5 + 68.71 - 67.32$ = \$5.89

Synthetic bond = $p_0 + S_0 - c_0 = 6.8 + 67.32 - 4.5$ = \$69.62

Synthetic underlying = $c_0 + X/(1 + r)^T - p_0 = 4.5 + 68.71 - 6.8$ = \$66.41

B

Instrument	Actual Price (\$)	Synthetic Price (\$)	Mispricing/Profit (\$)
Call	4.50	5.41	0.91
Put	6.80	5.89	0.91
Bond	68.71	69.62	0.91
Stock	67.32	66.41	0.91

Thus, the mispricing is the same regardless of the instrument used to look at it.

C The actual call is cheaper than the synthetic call. Therefore, an arbitrage transaction where you buy the call (underpriced) and sell the synthetic call (overpriced) will yield a risk-free profit of \$5.41 – \$4.50 = \$0.91.

As shown below, at expiration no cash will be received or paid out.

	Value at Expiration	
Transaction	$S_T < 70$	$S_T > 70$
Buy call	0	$S_T - 70$
Sell synthetic call		
Short put	$-(70 - S_T)$	0
Short stock	$-S_T$	$-S_T$
Long bond	70	70
Total	0	0

D The actual put is more expensive than the synthetic put. Therefore, an arbitrage transaction in which you buy the synthetic put (underpriced) and sell the put (overpriced) will yield a risk-free profit of \$6.80 – \$5.89 = \$0.91. As shown in the next table, at expiration no cash will be received or paid out.

Transaction	Value at Expiration	
	$S_T < 70$	$S_T > 70$
Sell put	$-(70 - S_T)$	
Buy synthetic put		
Long call	0	$S_T - 70$
Long bond	70	70
Short stock	$-S_T$	$-S_T$
Total	0	0

2 Current stock price, S = \$100

Up move, u = 1.1

Down move, d = 0.85

Exercise price, X = \$90

Risk-free rate, r = 6.5 percent

A Stock prices one period from now are

$$S^+ = Su = 100(1.1) = \$110$$

$$S^- = Sd = 100(0.85) = \$85$$

Call option values at expiration one period from now are

$$c^+ = \text{Max}(0,110 - 90) = \$20$$

$$c^- = \text{Max}(0,85 - 90) = \$0$$

The risk-neutral probability is

$$\pi = \frac{1.065 - 0.85}{1.1 - 0.85} = 0.86 \text{ and } 1 - \pi = 0.14$$

The call price today is

$$c = \frac{0.86(20) + 0.14(0)}{1.065} = 16.15$$

B If the current call price is \$17.50, it is overpriced. Therefore, we should sell the call and buy the underlying stock. The hedge ratio is

$$n = \frac{20 - 0}{110 - 85} = 0.8$$

For every option sold we should purchase 0.8 shares of stock. If we sell 100 calls we should buy 80 shares of stock.

Sell 100 calls at 17.50 = 1,750

Buy 80 shares at 100 = <u>–8,000</u>

Net cash flow = –6,250

At expiration the value of this combination will be

$$80(110) - 100(20) = \$6{,}800 \text{ if } S_T = 110$$
$$80(85) - 100(0) = \$6{,}800 \text{ if } S_T = 85$$

We invested \$6,250 for a payoff of \$6,800. The rate of return is (6,800/6,250) −1 = 0.088. This rate is higher than the risk-free rate of 0.065.

C If the current call price is \$14, it is underpriced. Therefore, we should buy the call and sell the underlying stock. The hedge ratio is

$$n = \frac{20 - 0}{110 - 85} = 0.8$$

For every option purchased we should sell 0.8 shares of stock. If we buy 100 calls we should sell 80 shares of stock.

Buy 100 calls at 14 = −1,400

Sell 80 shares at 100 = <u>8,000</u>

Net cash flow = 6,600

Thus, we generate \$6,600 up front.

At expiration the value of this combination will be

$$100(20) - 80(110) = -\$6{,}800 \text{ if } S_T = 110$$
$$100(0) - 80(85) = -\$6{,}800 \text{ if } S_T = 85$$

We generated \$6,600 up front and pay back \$6,800. The rate of return is (6,800/6,600) − 1 = 0.0303. This borrowing rate is lower than the risk-free rate of 0.065.

3 Current stock price, S = \$150

Up move, u = 1.33

Down move, d = 0.85

Exercise price, X = \$150

Risk-free rate, r = 4.5 percent

A Stock prices one period from now are

$$S^+ = Su = 150(1.33) = \$199.5$$
$$S^- = Sd = 150(0.85) = \$127.5$$

Put option values at expiration one period from now are

$$p^+ = \text{Max}(0{,}150 - 199.5) = \$0$$
$$p^- = \text{Max}(0{,}150 - 127.5) = \$22.5$$

The risk-neutral probability is

$$\pi = \frac{1.045 - 0.85}{1.33 - 0.85} = 0.4063, \text{ and } 1 - \pi = 0.5937$$

The put price today is

$$p = \frac{0.4063(0) + 0.5937(22.50)}{1.045} = 12.78$$

B If the current put price is \$14, it is overpriced. In order to create a hedge portfolio, we should sell the put and short the underlying stock. The hedge ratio is

$$n = \frac{p^{+} - p^{-}}{S^{+} - S^{-}} = \frac{0 - 22.5}{199.5 - 127.5} = -0.3125$$

For every option sold, we should sell 0.3125 shares of stock. If we sell 10,000 puts, we should sell 3,125 shares of stock.

Sell 10,000 puts at 14 = 140,000

Sell 3,125 shares at 150 = 468,750

Net cash flow = 608,750

Thus, we generate $608,750 up front.

At expiration, the value of this combination will be

$$-3{,}125(199.5) - 10{,}000(0) = -\$623{,}437 \text{ if } S_T = \$199.5$$
$$-3{,}125(127.5) - 10{,}000(22.5) = -\$623{,}437 \text{ if } S_T = \$127.5$$

We generated $608,750 up front and pay back $623,437. The rate of return is

$$\frac{623{,}437}{608{,}750} - 1 = 0.0241$$

This borrowing rate is lower than the risk-free rate of 0.045.

C If the current put price is $11, it is underpriced. In order to create a hedge portfolio, we should buy the put and buy the underlying stock. The hedge ratio is

$$n = \frac{p^{+} - p^{-}}{S^{+} - S^{-}} = \frac{0 - 22.5}{199.5 - 127.5} = -0.3125$$

For every option purchased we should buy 0.3125 shares of stock. If we buy 10,000 puts we should buy 3,125 shares of stock.

Buy 10,000 puts at 11 = –110,000

Buy 3,125 shares at 150 = –468,750

Net cash flow = –578,750

That is, we invest $578,750.

At expiration, the value of this combination will be

$$3{,}125(199.5) + 10{,}000(0) = \$623{,}437 \text{ if } S_T = \$199.5$$
$$3{,}125(127.5) + 10{,}000(22.5) = \$623{,}437 \text{ if } S_T = \$127.5$$

We invested $578,750 for a payoff of $623,437. The rate of return is $\frac{623{,}437}{578{,}750} - 1 = 0.0772$. This rate is higher than the risk-free rate of 0.045.

4 Current stock price, S = $65

Up move, u = 1.20

Down move, d = 0.83

Risk-free rate, r = 5 percent

A Exercise price, X = $60

Stock prices in the binomial tree one and two periods from now are

$$S^{+} = Su = 65(1.20) = \$78$$

$$S^{-} = Sd = 65(0.83) = \$53.95$$

$$S^{++} = Su^{2} = 65(1.20)(1.20) = \$93.60$$

$$S^{+-} = Sud = 65(1.20)(0.83) = \$64.74$$

$$S^{--} = Sd^{2} = 65(0.83)(0.83) = \$44.78$$

Call option values at expiration two periods from now are

$$c^{++} = \text{Max}(0{,}93.60 - 60) = \$33.6$$

$$c^{+-} = \text{Max}(0{,}64.74 - 60) = \$4.74$$

$$c^{--} = \text{Max}(0{,}44.78 - 60) = \$0$$

The risk-neutral probability is

$$\pi = \frac{1.05 - 0.83}{1.20 - 0.83} = 0.5946, \text{ and } 1 - \pi = 0.4054$$

Now find the option prices at time 1:

$$c^{+} = \frac{0.5946(33.6) + 0.4054(4.74)}{1.05} = \$20.86$$

$$c^{-} = \frac{0.5946(4.74) + 0.4054(0)}{1.05} = \$2.68$$

The call price today is

$$c = \frac{0.5946(20.86) + 0.4054(2.68)}{1.05} = \$12.85$$

B The hedge ratios at each point in the binomial tree are calculated as follows:

At the current stock price of \$65,

$$n = \frac{c^{+} - c^{-}}{S^{+} - S^{-}} = \frac{20.86 - 2.68}{78 - 53.95} = 0.7559$$

Therefore, today at time 0, the risk-free hedge would consist of a short position in 10,000 calls and a long position in 7,559 shares of the underlying stock.

At a stock price of \$78,

$$n^{+} = \frac{c^{++} - c^{+-}}{S^{++} - S^{+-}} = \frac{33.6 - 4.74}{93.6 - 64.74} = 1$$

Now the risk-free hedge would consist of a short position in 10,000 calls and a long position in 10,000 shares of the underlying stock.

At a stock price of \$53.95,

$$\frac{n^{-} = c^{+-} - c^{--}}{S^{+-} - S^{--}} = \frac{4.74 - 0}{64.74 - 44.78} = 0.2375$$

Now the risk-free hedge would consist of a short position in 10,000 calls and a long position in 2,375 shares of the underlying stock.

C Exercise price, X = \$70

Stock prices in the binomial tree one and two periods from now are

$$S^{+} = Su = 65(1.20) = \$78$$

$$S^{-} = Sd = 65(0.83) = \$53.95$$

$$S^{++} = Su^{2} = 65(1.20)(1.20) = \$93.6$$

$$S^{+-} = Sud = 65(1.20)(0.83) = \$64.74$$

$$S^{--} = Sd^{2} = 65(0.83)(0.83) = \$44.78$$

Call option values at expiration two periods from now are

$$c^{++} = \text{Max}(0{,}93.6 - 70) = \$23.6$$

$$c^{+-} = \text{Max}(0{,}64.74 - 70) = \$0$$

$$c^{--} = \text{Max}(0{,}44.78 - 70) = \$0$$

The risk-neutral probability is

$$\pi = \frac{1.05 - 0.83}{1.20 - 0.83} = 0.5946\text{, and } 1 - \pi = 0.4054$$

Now find the option prices at time 1:

$$c^{+} = \frac{0.5946(23.6) + 0.4054(0)}{1.05} = \$13.36$$

$$c^{-} = \frac{0.5946(0) + 0.4054(0)}{1.05} = \$0$$

The call price today is

$$c = \frac{0.5946(13.36) + 0.4054(0)}{1.05} = \$7.57$$

D The hedge ratios at each point in the binomial tree are calculated as follows.

At the current stock price of \$65,

$$n = \frac{c^{+} - c^{-}}{S^{+} - S^{-}} = \frac{13.36 - 0}{78 - 53.95} = 0.5555$$

Therefore, today at time 0, the risk-free hedge would consist of a short position in 10,000 calls and a long position in 5,555 shares of the underlying stock.

At a stock price of \$78,

$$n^{+} = \frac{c^{++} - c^{+-}}{S^{++} - S^{+-}} = \frac{23.6 - 0}{93.6 - 64.74} = 0.8177$$

Now, the risk-free hedge would consist of a short position in 10,000 calls and a long position in 8,177 shares of the underlying stock.

At a stock price of \$53.95,

$$n^{-} = \frac{c^{+-} - c^{--}}{S^{+-} - S^{--}} = \frac{0 - 0}{64.74 - 44.78} = 0$$

Zero shares of the underlying stock are needed for the short position in calls.

5 Current stock price, S_0 = \$65

Up move, u = 1.20

Down move, d = 0.83

Risk-free rate, r = 5 percent

A Exercise price, X = \$60

Stock prices in the binomial tree one and two periods from now are

$$S^{+} = Su = 65(1.20) = \$78$$

$$S^{-} = Sd = 65(0.83) = \$53.95$$

$$S^{++} = Su^{2} = 65(1.20)(1.20) = \$93.60$$

$$S^{+-} = Sud = 65(1.20)(0.83) = \$64.74$$

$$S^{--} = Sd^{2} = 65(0.83)(0.83) = \$44.78$$

Put option values at expiration two periods from now are

$$p^{++} = \text{Max}(0,60 - 93.6) = \$0$$

$$p^{+-} = \text{Max}(0,60 - 64.74) = \$0$$

$$p^{--} = \text{Max}(0,60 - 44.78) = \$15.22$$

The risk-neutral probability is

$$\pi = \frac{1.05 - 0.83}{1.20 - 0.83} = 0.5946 \text{ and } 1 - \pi = 0.4054$$

Now find the option prices at time 1:

$$p^{+} = \frac{0.5946(0) + 0.4054(0)}{1.05} = \$0$$

$$p^{-} = \frac{0.5946(0) + 0.4054(15.22)}{1.05} = \$5.88$$

The put price today is

$$p = \frac{0.5946(0) + 0.4054(5.88)}{1.05} = \$2.27$$

B Unlike the hedge portfolio for calls, which has the opposite positions in the two instruments (calls and underlying stock), the hedge portfolio for puts has the same positions in the two instruments. Therefore, the current value of the hedge portfolio for puts is

$$H = nS + p$$

The possible values of the hedge portfolio one period later are

$$H^{+} = nS^{+} + p^{+}$$

$$H^{-} = nS^{-} + p^{-}$$

Setting H^{+} equal to H^{-} and solving for n,

$$n = \frac{p^{-} - p^{+}}{S^{+} - S^{-}}$$

Note that the above formula is the same as that for the hedge portfolio for calls, except that the p^{+} and p^{-} have switched positions in the numerator. Similarly, the hedge ratios for the next time point are

$$n^+ = \frac{p^{+-} - p^{++}}{S^{++} - S^{+-}}$$

$$n^- = \frac{p^{--} - p^{+-}}{S^{+-} - S^{--}}$$

At the current stock price of \$65,

$$n = \frac{p^- - p^+}{S^+ - S^-} = \frac{5.88 - 0}{78 - 53.95} = 0.2445$$

Therefore, today at time 0, the risk-free hedge would consist of a long position in 10,000 puts and a long position in 2,445 shares of the underlying stock.

At a stock price of \$78,

$$n^+ = \frac{p^{+-} - p^{++}}{S^{++} - S^{+-}} = \frac{0 - 0}{93.6 - 64.74} = 0$$

Zero shares of the underlying stock are needed for the long position in puts.

At a stock price of \$53.95,

$$n^- = \frac{p^{--} - p^{+-}}{S^{+-} - S^{--}} = \frac{15.22 - 0}{64.74 - 44.78} = 0.7625$$

Now the risk-free hedge would consist of a long position in 10,000 puts and a long position in 7,625 shares of the underlying stock.

C Exercise price, X = \$70

Stock prices in the binomial tree, one and two periods from now are

$$S^+ = Su = 65(1.20) = \$78$$

$$S^- = Sd = 65(0.83) = \$53.95$$

$$S^{++} = Su^2 = 65(1.20)(1.20) = \$93.6$$

$$S^{+-} = Sud = 65(1.20)(0.83) = \$64.74$$

$$S^{--} = Sd^2 = 65(0.83)(0.83) = \$44.78$$

Put option values at expiration two periods from now are

$$p^{++} = \text{Max}(0,70 - 93.6) = \$0$$

$$p^{+-} = \text{Max}(0,70 - 64.74) = \$5.26$$

$$p^{--} = \text{Max}(0,70 - 44.78) = \$25.22$$

The risk-neutral probability is

$$\pi = \frac{1.05 - 0.83}{1.20 - 0.83} = 0.5946, \text{ and } 1 - \pi = 0.4054$$

Now find the option prices at time 1:

$$p^+ = \frac{0.5946(0) + 0.4054(5.26)}{1.05} = \$2.03$$

$$p^- = \frac{0.5946(5.26) + 0.4054(25.22)}{1.05} = \$12.72$$

The put price today is

$$p = \frac{0.5946(2.03) + 0.4054(12.72)}{1.05} = \$6.06$$

D The hedge ratios at each point in the binomial tree are calculated as follows:

At the current stock price of $65,

$$n = \frac{p^- - p^+}{S^+ - S^-} = \frac{12.72 - 2.03}{78 - 53.95} = 0.4445$$

Therefore, today at time 0, the risk-free hedge would consist of a long position in 10,000 puts and a long position in 4,445 shares of the underlying stock.

At stock price $78,

$$n^+ = \frac{p^{+-} - p^{++}}{S^{++} - S^{+-}} = \frac{5.26 - 0}{93.6 - 64.74} = 0.1823$$

Therefore, at time 1, the risk-free hedge would consist of a long position in 10,000 puts and a long position in 1,823 shares of the underlying stock.

At stock price $53.95,

$$n^- = \frac{p^{--} - p^{+-}}{S^{+-} - S^{--}} = \frac{25.22 - 5.26}{64.74 - 44.78} = 1$$

Now, the risk-free hedge would consist of a long position in 10,000 puts and a long position in 10,000 shares of the underlying stock.

6 C is correct. The BSM model assumes no transaction costs. Therefore, transaction costs should have no impact on the price of the options.

7 C is correct. Klein's expectation is that the volatility of Apoth's shares will increase. According to the BSM model, the price of an option, either a call or a put, will increase if the volatility of the underlying increases.

8 B is correct. The required number of call options to sell = Number of shares of underlying to be hedged / $N(d_1)$, where $N(d_1)$ is the estimated delta used for hedging a position with call options. There are 100,000 shares to be hedged and the $N(d_1)$ for Option X from Exhibit 2 is 0.30. Thus, the required number of call options to sell is 100,000 / 0.30 = 333,333.

9 B is correct. The gamma will tend to be large when the option is at-the-money. The exercise price of Option Y is equal to the underlying price, hence at-the-money, whereas both Option X and Option Z are out-of-the-money.

10 B is correct. The required number of put options = Number of shares of underlying to be hedged / $[N(d_1) - 1]$, where $N(d_1) - 1$ is the estimated delta used for hedging a position with put options (otherwise known as the put delta). As the share price drops to $36, the delta of a put position will decrease toward –1.0, requiring less put options than the original position.

11 B is correct. Including the effect of cash flows lowers the underlying price. Lowering the underlying price causes the price of the call option to decrease.

LOFT
68

READING

54

Swap Markets and Contracts

by Don M. Chance, CFA

LEARNING OUTCOMES

Mastery	The candidate should be able to:
□	a. distinguish between the pricing and valuation of swaps;
□	b. explain the equivalence of 1) interest rate swaps to a series of off-market forward rate agreements (FRAs) and 2) a plain vanilla swap to a combination of an interest rate call and an interest rate put;
□	c. calculate and interpret the fixed rate on a plain vanilla interest rate swap and the market value of the swap during its life;
□	d. calculate and interpret the fixed rate, if applicable, and the foreign notional principal for a given domestic notional principal on a currency swap, and estimate the market values of each of the different types of currency swaps during their lives;
□	e. calculate and interpret the fixed rate, if applicable, on an equity swap and the market values of the different types of equity swaps during their lives;
□	f. explain and interpret the characteristics and uses of swaptions, including the difference between payer and receiver swaptions;
□	g. calculate the payoffs and cash flows of an interest rate swaption;
□	h. calculate and interpret the value of an interest rate swaption at expiration;
□	i. evaluate swap credit risk for each party and during the life of the swap, distinguish between current credit risk and potential credit risk, and explain how swap credit risk is reduced by both netting and marking to market;
□	j. define swap spread and explain its relation to credit risk.

OPTIONAL SEGMENT

1 INTRODUCTION

This reading completes the survey of the main types of derivative instruments. Preceding readings covered forward contracts, futures contracts, and options. This reading covers swaps. Although swaps were the last of the main types of derivatives to be invented, they are clearly not the least important. In fact, judging by the size of the swap market, they are probably the most important. The Bank for International Settlements estimated the notional principal of the global over-the-counter derivatives market as of 30 June 2001 at $100 trillion. Of that amount, interest rate and currency swaps account for about $61 trillion, with interest rate swaps representing about $57 trillion of that total.[1] Indeed, interest rate swaps have had overwhelming success as a derivative product. They are widely used by corporations, financial institutions, and governments.

Recall first that *a swap is an agreement between two parties to exchange a series of future cash flows*. For most types of swaps, one party makes payments that are determined by a random outcome, such as an interest rate, a currency rate, an equity return, or a commodity price. These payments are commonly referred to as variable or *floating*. The other party either makes variable or floating payments determined by some other random factor or makes fixed payments. At least one type of swap involves both parties making fixed payments, but the values of those payments vary due to random factors.

In forwards, futures, and options, the terminology of *long* and *short* has been used to describe buyers and sellers. These terms are not used as often in swaps. The preferred terminology usually designates a party as being the floating- (or variable-) rate payer or the fixed-rate payer. Nonetheless, in swaps in which one party receives a floating rate and the other receives a fixed rate, the former is usually said to be long and the latter is said to be short. This usage is in keeping with the fact that parties who go long in other instruments pay a known amount and receive a claim on an unknown amount. In some swaps, however, both sides are floating or variable, and this terminology breaks down.

1.1 Characteristics of Swap Contracts

Although technically a swap can have a single payment, most swaps involve multiple payments. Thus, we refer to a swap as a *series* of payments. In fact, we have already covered a swap with one payment, which is just a forward contract. Hence, a swap is basically a series of forward contracts. We will elaborate further in Section 4.1.2, but with this idea in mind, we can see that a swap is like an agreement to buy something over a period of time. We might be paying a variable price or a price that has already been fixed: we might be paying an uncertain price, or we might already know the price we shall pay.

When a swap is initiated, neither party pays any amount to the other. Therefore, a swap has zero value at the start of the contract. Although it is not absolutely necessary for this condition to be true, swaps are typically done in this fashion. Neither party pays anything up front. There is, however, a technical exception to this point in regard to currency swaps. Each party pays the notional principal to the other, but the amounts exchanged are equivalent, though denominated in two different currencies.

Each date on which the parties make payments is called a **settlement date**, sometimes called a payment date, and the time between settlement dates is called the **settlement period**. On a given settlement date when payments are due, one party

1 Equity and commodity swaps account for less than the notional principal of currency swaps.

makes a payment to the other, which in turn makes a payment to the first party. With the exception of currency swaps and a few variations associated with other types of swaps, both sets of payments are made in the same currency. Consequently, the parties typically agree to exchange only the net amount owed from one party to the other, a practice called **netting**. In currency swaps and a few other special cases, the payments are not made in the same currency; hence, the parties usually make separate payments without netting. Note the implication that swaps are generally settled in cash. It is quite rare for swaps to call for actual physical delivery of an underlying asset.

A swap always has a **termination date**, the date of the final payment. We can think of this date as its expiration date, as we do with other derivatives. The original time to maturity is sometimes called the *tenor* of a swap.

The swap market is almost exclusively an over-the-counter market, so swaps contracts are customized to the parties' specific needs. Several of the leading futures exchanges have created futures contracts on swaps. These contracts allow participants to hedge and speculate on the rates that will prevail in the swap market at future dates. Of course, these contracts are not swaps themselves but, as derivatives of swaps, they can in some ways serve as substitutes for swaps. These futures contracts have been moderately successful, but their volume is insignificant compared with the over-the-counter market for swaps.

As we have discussed in previous readings, over-the-counter instruments are subject to default risk. Default is possible whenever a payment is due. When a series of payments is made, there is default risk potential throughout the life of the contract, depending on the financial condition of the two parties. But default can be somewhat complicated in swaps. Suppose, for example, that on a settlement date, Party A owes Party B a payment of $50,000 and Party B owes Party A a payment of $12,000. Agreeing to net, Party A owes Party B $38,000 for that particular payment. Party A may be illiquid, or perhaps even bankrupt, and unable to make the payment. But it may be the case that the market value of the swap, which reflects the present value of the remaining payments, could be positive from the perspective of Party A and negative from the perspective of Party B. In that case, Party B owes Party A more for the remaining payments. We will learn how to determine the market value of a swap in Section 4.2 of this reading.

The handling of default in swaps can be complicated, depending on the contract specifications and the applicable laws under which the contract was written. In most cases, the above situation would be resolved by having A be in default but possessing an asset, the swap, that can be used to help settle its other liabilities. We shall discuss the default risk of swaps in more detail in Section 7.

1.2 Termination of a Swap

As we noted earlier, a swap has a termination or expiration date. Sometimes, however, a party could want to terminate a swap before its formal expiration. This scenario is much like a party selling a bond before it matures or selling an exchange-traded option or futures contract before its expiration. With swaps, early termination can take place in several ways.

As we mentioned briefly and will cover in more detail later, a swap has a market value that can be calculated during its life. If a party holds a swap with a market value of $125,000, for example, it can settle the swap with the counterparty by having the counterparty pay it $125,000 in cash. This payment terminates the transaction for both parties. From the opposite perspective, a party holding a swap with a negative market value can terminate the swap by paying the market value to the counterparty. Terminating a swap in this manner is possible only if the counterparties specify in advance that such a transaction can be made, or if they reach an agreement to do so without having specified in advance. In other words, this feature is not automatically available and must be agreed to by both parties.

Many swaps are terminated early by entering into a separate and offsetting swap. For example, suppose a corporation is engaged in a swap to make fixed payments of 5 percent and receive floating payments based on LIBOR, with the payments made each 15 January and 15 July. Three years remain on the swap. That corporation can offset the swap by entering into an entirely new swap in which it makes payments based on LIBOR and receives a fixed rate with the payments made each 15 January and 15 July for three years. The swap fixed rate is determined by market conditions at the time the swap is initiated. Thus, the fixed rate on the new swap is not likely to match the fixed rate on the old swap, but the effect of this transaction is simply to have the floating payments offset; the fixed payments will net out to a known amount. Hence, the risk associated with the floating rate is eliminated. The default risk, however, is not eliminated because both swaps remain in effect.

Another way to terminate a swap early is sell the swap to another counterparty. Suppose a corporation holds a swap worth $75,000. If it can obtain the counterparty's permission, it can find another party to take over its payments. In effect, it sells the swap for $75,000 to that party. This procedure, however, is not commonly used.

A final way to terminate a swap early is by using a swaption. This instrument is an option to enter into a swap at terms that are established in advance. Thus, a party could use a swaption to enter into an offsetting swap, as described above. We shall cover swaptions in more detail in Section 6.

2 THE STRUCTURE OF GLOBAL SWAP MARKETS

The global swaps market is much like the global forward and over-the-counter options markets, which we covered in some detail in the reading on forward markets and contracts and the reading on option markets and contracts. It is made up of dealers, which are banks and investment banking firms. These dealers make markets in swaps, quoting bid and ask prices and rates, thereby offering to take either side of a swap transaction. Upon taking a position in a swap, the dealer generally offsets the risk by making transactions in other markets. The counterparties to swaps are either end users or other dealers. The end users are often corporations with risk management problems that can be solved by engaging in a swap—a corporation or other end user is usually exposed to or needs an exposure to some type of risk that arises from interest rates, exchange rates, stock prices, or commodity prices. The end user contacts a dealer that makes a market in swaps. The two engage in a transaction, at which point the dealer assumes some risk from the end user. The dealer then usually lays off the risk by engaging in a transaction with another party. That transaction could be something as simple as a futures contract, or it could be an over-the-counter transaction with another dealer.

Risk magazine conducts annual surveys of participants in various derivative products. Exhibit 1 presents the results of those surveys for currency and interest rate swaps. One survey provides opinions of banks and investment banks that are swaps dealers. In the other survey, the respondents are end users. The results give a good idea of the major players in this market. It is interesting to note the disagreement between how dealers view themselves and how end users view them. Also, note that the rankings change, sometimes drastically, from year to year.

Exhibit 1 ***Risk*** **Magazine Surveys of Banks, Investment Banks, and Corporate End Users to Determine the Top Three Dealers in Currency and Interest Rate Swaps**

	Respondents	
Currencies	**Banks and Investment Banks**	**Corporate End Users**
Currency Swaps		
$/€	UBS Warburg	Citigroup
	JP Morgan Chase	Royal Bank of Scotland
	Deutsche Bank	Bank of America
$/¥	JP Morgan Chase	Citigroup
	UBS Warburg	Bank of America
	Credit Suisse First Boston/Deutsche Bank	JP Morgan Chase
$/£	Royal Bank of Scotland	Royal Bank of Scotland
	JP Morgan Chase	Citigroup
	Goldman Sachs	Deutsche Bank
$/SF	UBS Warburg	UBS Warburg
	Goldman Sachs	Citigroup
	Credit Suisse First Boston	Credit Suisse First Boston
Interest Rate Swaps (2–10 years)		
$	JP Morgan Chase	JP Morgan Chase
	Bank of America	Bank of America
	Morgan Stanley	Royal Bank of Scotland
€	JP Morgan Chase	Royal Bank of Scotland
	Deutsche Bank	Deutsche Bank
	Morgan Stanley	Citigroup
¥	JP Morgan Chase	Royal Bank of Scotland
	Deutsche Bank	Barclays Capital
	Bank of America	Citigroup/JP Morgan Chase
£	Royal Bank of Scotland	Royal Bank of Scotland
	Barclays Capital	Barclays Capital
	UBS Warburg	Deutsche Bank
SF	UBS Warburg	UBS Warburg
	Credit Suisse First Boston	Credit Suisse First Boston
	Zürcher Kantonalbank	Zürcher Kantonalbank

Note: $ = U.S. dollar, € = euro, ¥ = Japanese yen, £ = U.K. pound sterling, SF = Swiss franc.
Source: *Risk*, September 2002, pp. 30–67 for banks and investment banking dealer respondents, and June 2002, pp. 24–34 for corporate end user respondents. Ratings for swaps with maturities less than 2 years and greater than 10 years are also provided in the September 2002 issue of *Risk*.

3 TYPES OF SWAPS

We alluded to the fact that the underlying asset in a swap can be a currency, interest rate, stock, or commodity. We now take a look at these types of swaps in more detail.

3.1 Currency Swaps

In a currency swap, each party makes interest payments to the other in different currencies.[2] Consider this example. The U.S. retailer Target Corporation (NYSE: TGT) does not have an established presence in Europe. Let us say that it has decided to begin opening a few stores in Germany and needs €9 million to fund construction and initial operations. TGT would like to issue a fixed-rate euro-denominated bond with face value of €9 million, but the company is not very well known in Europe. European investment bankers have given it a quote for such a bond. Deutsche Bank, AG (NYSE: DB), however, tells TGT that it should issue the bond in dollars and use a swap to convert it into euros.

Suppose TGT issues a five-year US$10 million bond at a rate of 6 percent. It then enters into a swap with DB in which DB will make payments to TGT in U.S. dollars at a fixed rate of 5.5 percent and TGT will make payments to DB in euros at a fixed rate of 4.9 percent each 15 March and 15 September for five years. The payments are based on a notional principal of 10 million in dollars and 9 million in euros. We assume the swap starts on 15 September of the current year. The swap specifies that the two parties exchange the notional principal at the start of the swap and at the end. Because the payments are made in different currencies, netting is not practical, so each party makes its respective payments.[3]

Thus, the swap is composed of the following transactions:

15 September:

- DB pays TGT €9 million, and
- TGT pays DB $10 million.

Each 15 March and 15 September for five years:

- DB pays TGT 0.055(180/360)$10 million = $275,000, and
- TGT pays DB 0.049(180/360) €9 million = €220,500.

15 September five years after initiation:

- DB pays TGT $10 million, and
- TGT pays DB €9 million.

Note that we have simplified the interest calculations a little. In this example, we calculated semiannual interest using the fraction 180/360. Some parties might choose to use the exact day count in the six-month period divided by 365 days. LIBOR and

2 It is important at this point to clear up some terminology confusion. Foreign currency is often called *foreign exchange* or sometimes *FX*. There is another transaction called an *FX swap*, which sounds as if it might be referring to a currency swap. In fact, an FX swap is just a long position in a forward contract on a foreign currency and a short position in a forward contract on the same currency with a different expiration. Why this transaction is called a swap is not clear, but this transaction existed before currency swaps were created. In futures markets, the analogous transaction is called a *spread*, reflecting as it does the risk associated with the spread between the prices of futures contracts with different expirations.

3 In this example, we shall assume 180 days between payment dates. In practice, exact day counts are usually used, leading to different fixed payment amounts in one six-month period from those of another. In the example here, we are only illustrating the idea behind swap cash flows, so it is convenient to keep the fixed payments the same. Later in the reading, we shall illustrate situations in which the exact day count is used, leading to fixed payments that vary slightly.

Euribor transactions, the predominant rates used in interest rate swaps, nearly always use 360 days, as mentioned in previous readings. Exhibit 2 shows the stream of cash flows from TGT's perspective.

Exhibit 2 Cash Flows to TGT on Swap with DB

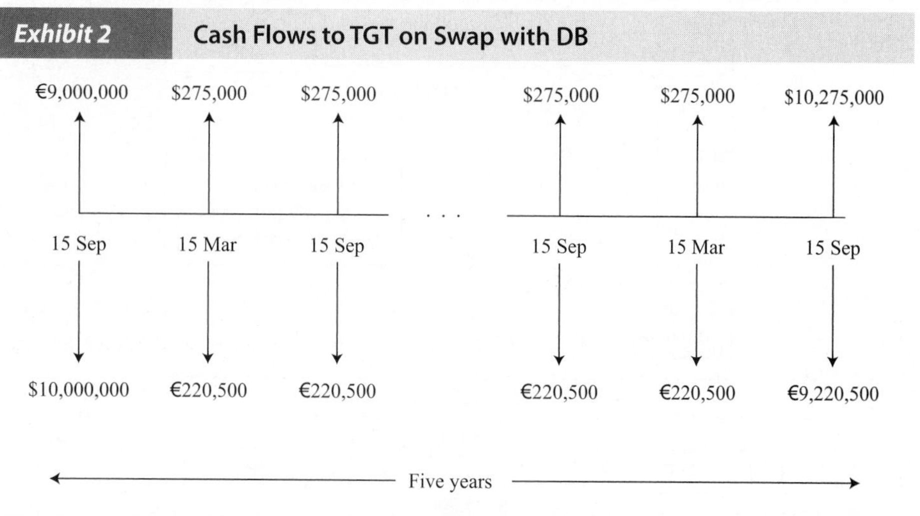

Note that the Target–Deutsche Bank transaction looks just like TGT is issuing a bond with face value of €9 million and that bond is purchased by DB. TGT converts the €9 million to $10 million and buys a dollar-denominated bond issued by DB. Note that TGT, having issued a bond denominated in euros, accordingly makes interest payments to DB in euros. DB, appropriately, makes interest payments in dollars to TGT. At the end, they each pay off the face values of the bonds they have issued. We emphasize that the Target–Deutsche Bank transaction *looks like* what we have just described. In fact, neither TGT nor DB actually issues or purchases a bond. They exchange only a series of cash flows that replicated the issuance and purchase of these bonds.

Exhibit 3 illustrates how such a combined transaction would work. TGT issues a bond in dollars (Exhibit 3, Panel A). It takes the dollars and passes them through to DB, which gives TGT the €9 million it needs. On the interest payment dates, the swap generates $275,000 of the $300,000 in interest TGT needs to pay its bondholders (Panel B). In turn, TGT makes interest payments in euros. Still, small dollar interest payments are necessary because TGT cannot issue a dollar bond at the swap rate. At the end of the transaction, TGT receives $10 million back from DB and passes it through to its bondholders (Panel C). TGT pays DB €9 million, thus effectively paying off a euro-denominated bond.

Exhibit 3 **Issuing a Dollar-Denominated Bond and Using a Currency Swap to Convert a Euro-Denominated Bond**

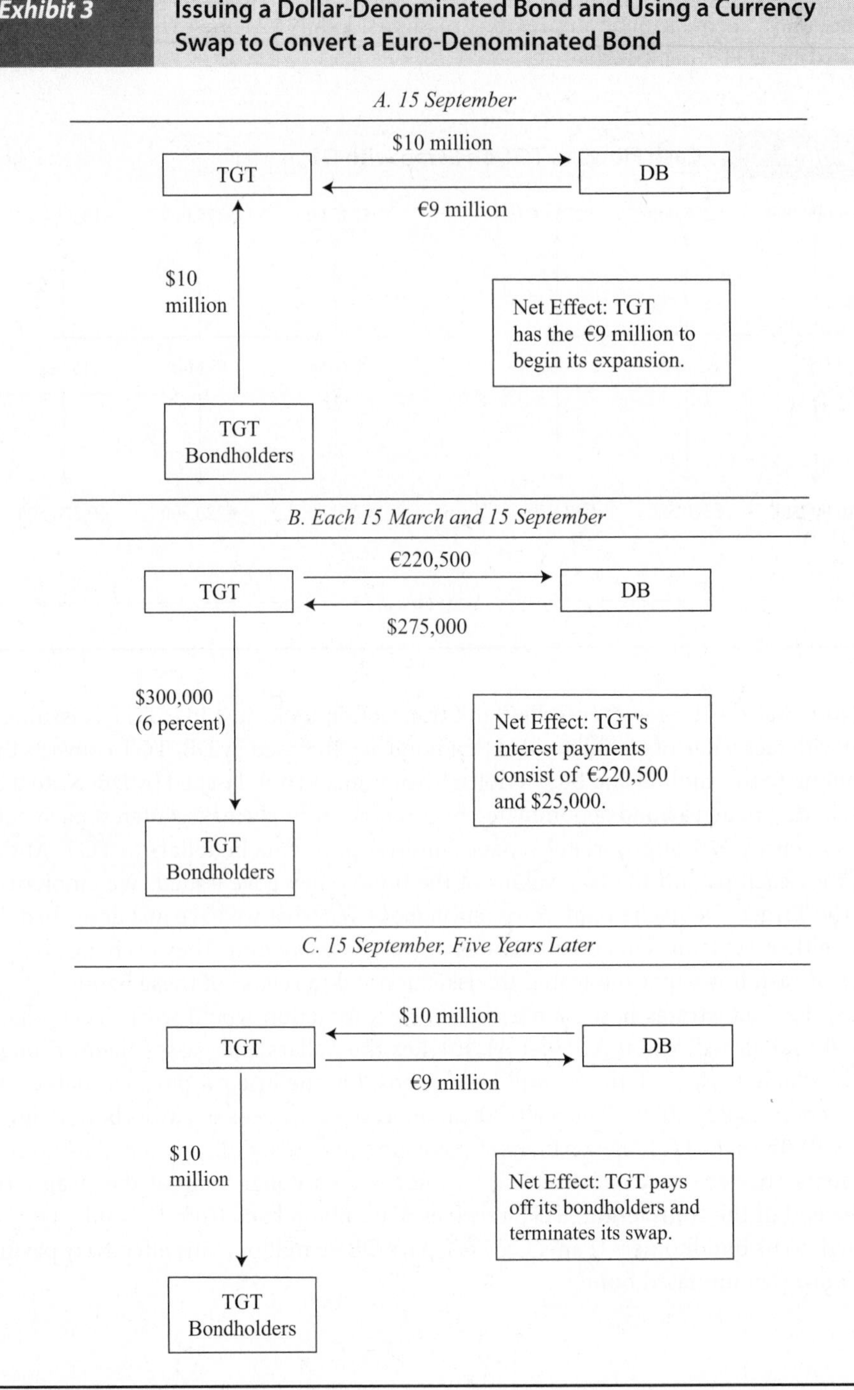

TGT has effectively issued a dollar-denominated bond and converted it to a euro-denominated bond. In all likelihood, it can save on interest expense by funding its need for euros in this way, because TGT is better known in the United States than in Europe. Its swap dealer, DB, knows TGT well and also obviously has a strong presence in Europe. Thus, DB can pass on its advantage in euro bond markets to TGT. In addition, had TGT issued a euro-denominated bond, it would have assumed no credit risk. By entering into the swap, TGT assumes a remote possibility of DB defaulting. Thus, TGT saves a little money by assuming some credit risk.

EXAMPLE 1

Consider a currency swap in which the domestic party pays a fixed rate in the foreign currency, the British pound, and the counterparty pays a fixed rate in U.S. dollars. The notional principals are \$50 million and £30 million. The fixed rates are 5.6 percent in dollars and 6.25 percent in pounds. Both sets of payments are made on the basis of 30 days per month and 365 days per year, and the payments are made semiannually.

A Determine the initial exchange of cash that occurs at the start of the swap.

B Determine the semiannual payments.

C Determine the final exchange of cash that occurs at the end of the swap.

D Give an example of a situation in which this swap might be appropriate.

Solution to A:

At the start of the swap:

Domestic party pays counterparty \$50 million.
Counterparty pays domestic party £30 million.

Solution to B:

Semiannually:

Domestic party pays counterparty £30,000,000(0.0625)(180/365) = £924,658.
Counterparty pays domestic party \$50,000,000(0.056)(180/365) = \$1,380,822.

Solution to C:

At the end of the swap:

Domestic party pays counterparty £30,000,000 + £924,658 = £30,924,658.
Counterparty pays domestic party \$50,000,000 + \$1,380,222 = \$51,380,222.

Solution to D:

This swap would be appropriate for a U.S. company that issues a dollar-denominated bond but would prefer to borrow in British pounds.

Returning to the Target swap, recall that Target effectively converted a fixed-rate loan in dollars to a fixed-rate loan in euros. Suppose instead that TGT preferred to borrow in euros at a floating rate. It then would have specified that the swap required it to make payments to DB at a floating rate. Had TGT preferred to issue the dollar-denominated bond at a floating rate, it would have specified that DB pay it dollars at a floating rate.

Although TGT and DB exchanged notional principal, some scenarios exist in which the notional principals are not exchanged. For example, suppose many years later, TGT is generating €10 million in cash semiannually and converting it back to dollars on 15 January and 15 July. It might then wish to lock in the conversion rate by entering into a currency swap that would require it to pay a dealer €10 million and receive a fixed amount of dollars. If the euro fixed rate were 5 percent, a notional principal of €400 million would generate a payment of 0.05(180/360)€400 million = €10 million. If the exchange rate is, for example, \$0.85, the equivalent dollar notional principal would be \$340 million. If the dollar fixed rate is 6 percent, TGT would receive

0.06(180/360)$340 million = $10.2 million.[4] These payments would occur twice a year for the life of the swap. TGT might then lock in the conversion rate by entering into a currency swap with notional principal amounts that would allow it to receive a fixed amount of dollars on 15 January and 15 July. There would be no reason to specify an exchange of notional principal. As we previously described, there are four types of currency swaps. Using the original Target–Deutsche Bank swap as an example, the semiannual payments would be

Swap A TGT pays euros at a fixed rate; DB pays dollars at a fixed rate.

Swap B TGT pays euros at a fixed rate; DB pays dollars at a floating rate.

Swap C TGT pays euros at a floating rate; DB pays dollars at a floating rate.

Swap D TGT pays euros at a floating rate; DB pays dollars at a fixed rate.

Or, reversing the flow, TGT could be the payer of dollars and DB could be the payer of euros:

Swap E TGT pays dollars at a fixed rate; DB pays euros at a fixed rate.

Swap F TGT pays dollars at a fixed rate; DB pays euros at a floating rate.

Swap G TGT pays dollars at a floating rate; DB pays euros at a floating rate.

Swap H TGT pays dollars at a floating rate; DB pays euros at a fixed rate.

Suppose we combine Swap A with Swap H. With TGT paying euros at a fixed rate and DB paying euros at a fixed rate, the euro payments wash out and the net effect is

Swap I TGT pays dollars at a floating rate; DB pays dollars at a fixed rate.

Suppose we combine Swap B with Swap E. Similarly, the euro payments again wash out, and the net effect is

Swap J TGT pays dollars at a fixed rate; DB pays dollars at a floating rate.

Suppose we combine Swap C with Swap F. Likewise, the euro floating payments wash out, and the net effect is

Swap K TGT pays dollars at a fixed rate; DB pays dollars at a floating rate.

Lastly, suppose we combine Swap D with Swap G. Again, the euro floating payments wash out, and the net effect is

Swap L TGT pays dollars at a floating rate; DB pays dollars at a fixed rate.

Of course, the net results of I and L are equivalent, and the net results of J and K are equivalent. What we have shown here, however, is that combinations of currency swaps eliminate the currency flows and leave us with transactions in only one currency. A swap in which both sets of interest payments are made in the same currency is an interest rate swap.

3.2 Interest Rate Swaps

As we discovered in the previous paragraph, an interest rate swap can be created as a combination of currency swaps. Of course, no one would create an interest rate swap that way; doing so would require two transactions when only one would

4 It might appear that TGT has somehow converted cash flows worth €10 million($0.085) = $8.5 million into cash flows worth $10.2 million. Recall, however, that the €10 million cash flows are generated yearly and $0.85 is the *current* exchange rate. We cannot apply the current exchange rate to a series of cash flows over various future dates. We would apply the respective forward exchange rates, not the spot rate, to the series of future euro cash flows.

suffice. Interest rate swaps evolved into their own market. In fact, the interest rate swap market is much bigger than the currency swap market, as we have seen in the notional principal statistics.

As previously noted, one way to look at an interest rate swap is that it is a currency swap in which both currencies are the same. Consider a swap to pay Currency A fixed and Currency B floating. Currency A could be dollars, and B could be euros. But what if A and B are both dollars, or A and B are both euros? The first case is a dollar-denominated plain vanilla swap; the second is a euro-denominated plain vanilla swap. *A* **plain vanilla swap** *is simply an interest rate swap in which one party pays a fixed rate and the other pays a floating rate, with both sets of payments in the same currency.* In fact, the plain vanilla swap is probably the most common derivative transaction in the global financial system.

Note that because we are paying in the same currency, there is no need to exchange notional principals at the beginning and at the end of an interest rate swap. In addition, the interest payments can be, and nearly always are, netted. If one party owes $X and the other owes $Y, the party owing the greater amount pays the net difference, which greatly reduces the credit risk (as we discuss in more detail in Section 7). Finally, we note that there is no reason to have both sides pay a fixed rate. The two streams of payments would be identical in that case. So in an interest rate swap, either one side always pays fixed and the other side pays floating, or both sides paying floating, but never do both sides pay fixed.[5]

Thus, in a plain vanilla interest rate swap, one party makes interest payments at a fixed rate and the other makes interest payments at a floating rate. Both sets of payments are on the same notional principal and occur on regularly scheduled dates. For each payment, the interest rate is multiplied by a fraction representing the number of days in the settlement period over the number of days in a year. In some cases, the settlement period is computed assuming 30 days in each month; in others, an exact day count is used. Some cases assume a 360-day year; others use 365 days.

Let us now illustrate an interest rate swap. Suppose that on 15 December, General Electric Company (NYSE: GE) borrows money for one year from a bank such as Bank of America (NYSE: BAC). The loan is for $25 million and specifies that GE will make interest payments on a quarterly basis on the 15th of March, June, September, and December for one year at the rate of LIBOR plus 25 basis points. At the end of the year, it will pay back the principal. On the 15th of December, March, June, and September, LIBOR is observed and sets the rate for that quarter. The interest is then paid at the end of the quarter.[6]

GE believes that it is getting a good rate, but fearing a rise in interest rates, it would prefer a fixed-rate loan. It can easily convert the floating-rate loan to a fixed-rate loan by engaging in a swap. Suppose it approaches JP Morgan Chase (NYSE: JPM), a large dealer bank, and requests a quote on a swap to pay a fixed rate and receive LIBOR, with payments on the dates of its loan payments. The bank prices the swap (a procedure we cover in Section 4) and quotes a fixed rate of 6.2 percent.[7] The fixed payments will be made based on a day count of 90/365, and the floating payments

---

5 The case of both sides paying floating is called a basis swap, which we shall cover in Section 5.

6 Again, we assume 90 days in each interest payment period for this example. The exact payment dates are not particularly important for illustrative purposes.

7 Typically the rate is quoted as a spread over the rate on a U.S. Treasury security with a comparable maturity. Suppose the yield on a two-year Treasury note is 6 percent. Then the swap would be quoted as 20 basis points over the two-year Treasury rate. By quoting the rate in this manner, GE knows what it is paying over the Treasury rate, a differential called the swap spread, which is a type of credit risk premium we discuss in Section 7. In addition, a quote in this form protects the bank from the rate changing drastically either during the phone conversation or shortly thereafter. Thus, the quote can stay in effect for a reasonable period of time while GE checks out quotes from other dealers.

will be made based on 90/360. Current LIBOR is 5.9 percent. Therefore, the first fixed payment, which GE makes to JPM, is \$25,000,000(0.062)(90/365) = \$382,192. This is also the amount of each remaining fixed payment.

The first floating payment, which JPM makes to GE, is \$25,000,000(0.059) (90/360) = \$368,750. Of course, the remaining floating payments will not be known until later. Exhibit 4 shows the pattern of cash flows on the swap from GE's perspective.

Exhibit 4 Cash Flows to GE on Swap with JPM

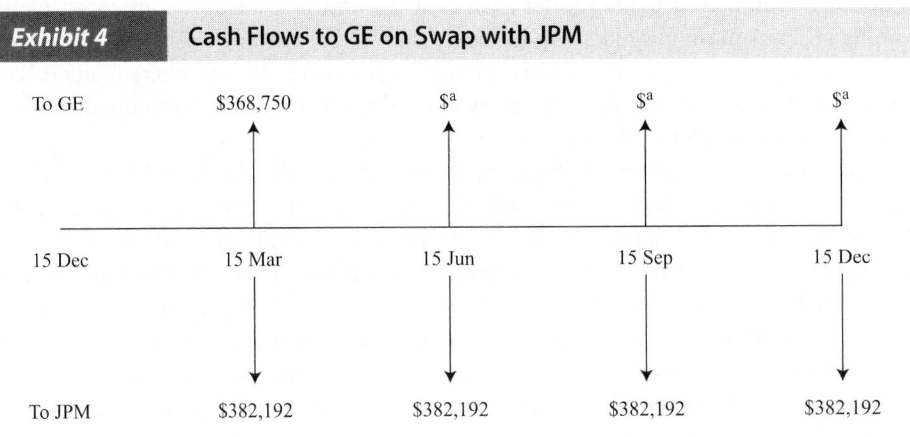

[a]Computed as \$25,000,000(L)90/360, where L is LIBOR on the previous settlement date.

EXAMPLE 2

Determine the upcoming payments in a plain vanilla interest rate swap in which the notional principal is €70 million. The end user makes semiannual fixed payments at the rate of 7 percent, and the dealer makes semiannual floating payments at Euribor, which was 6.25 percent on the last settlement period. The floating payments are made on the basis of 180 days in the settlement period and 360 days in a year. The fixed payments are made on the basis of 180 days in the settlement period and 365 days in a year. Payments are netted, so determine which party pays which and what amount.

Solution:

The fixed payments are €70,000,000(0.07)(180/365) = €2,416,438.

The upcoming floating payment is €70,000,000(0.0625)(180/360) = €2,187,500.

The net payment is that the party paying fixed will pay the party paying floating:

€2,416,438 – €2,187,500 = €228,938

Note in Exhibit 4 that we did not show the notional principal, because it was not exchanged. We could implicitly show that GE received \$25 million from JPM and paid \$25 million to JPM at the start of the swap. We could also show that the same thing happens at the end. If we look at it that way, it appears as if GE has issued a \$25 million fixed-rate bond, which was purchased by JPM, which in turn issued a \$25 million floating-rate bond, which was in turn purchased by GE. We say that *it appears* as if this is what happened: In fact, neither party actually issued a bond, but they have generated the cash flows that would occur if GE had issued such a fixed-rate bond, JPM had issued such a floating-rate bond, and each purchased the bond of the other. In other words, we could include the principals on both sides to make each set of cash flows look like a bond, yet the overall cash flows would be the same as on the swap.

So let us say that GE enters into this swap. Exhibit 5 shows the net effect of the swap and the loan. GE pays LIBOR plus 25 basis points to Bank of America on its loan, pays 6.2 percent to JPM, and receives LIBOR from JPM. The net effect is that GE pays 6.2 + 0.25 = 6.45 percent fixed.

Exhibit 5 **GE's Conversion of a Floating-Rate Loan to a Fixed-Rate Loan Using an Interest Rate Swap with JPM**

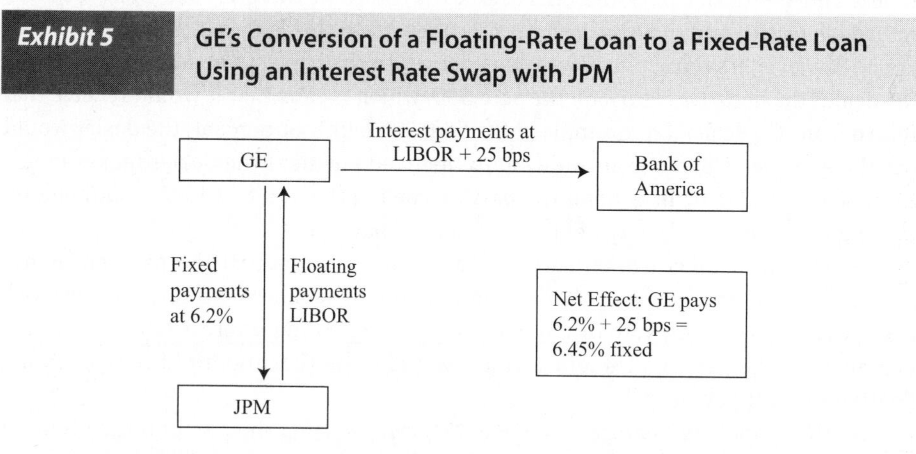

Now, JPM is engaged in a swap to pay LIBOR and receive 6.2 percent. It is exposed to the risk of LIBOR increasing. It would, therefore, probably engage in some other type of transaction to offset this risk. One transaction commonly used in this situation is to sell Eurodollar futures. As discussed in the reading on futures markets and contracts, Eurodollar futures prices move $25 in value for each basis point move in LIBOR. JPM will determine how sensitive its position is to a move in LIBOR and sell an appropriate number of futures to offset the risk. Note that Bank of America is exposed to LIBOR as well, but in the banking industry, floating-rate loans are often made because the funding that the bank obtained to make the loan was probably already at LIBOR or a comparable floating rate.

It is possible but unlikely that GE could get a fixed-rate loan at a better rate. The swap involves some credit risk: the possibility, however small, that JPM will default. In return for assuming that risk, GE in all likelihood would get a better rate than it would if it borrowed at a fixed rate. JPM is effectively a wholesaler of risk, using its powerful position as one of the world's leading banks to facilitate the buying and selling of risk for companies such as GE. Dealers profit from the spread between the rates they quote to pay and the rates they quote to receive. The swaps market is, however, extremely competitive and the spreads have been squeezed very tight, which makes it very challenging for dealers to make a profit. Of course, this competition is good for end users, because it gives them more attractive rates.

3.3 Equity Swaps

By now, it should be apparent that a swap requires at least one variable rate or price underlying it. So far, that rate has been an interest rate.[8] In an equity swap, the rate is the return on a stock or stock index. This characteristic gives the equity swap two features that distinguish it from interest rate and currency swaps.

First, the party making the fixed-rate payment could also have to make a variable payment based on the equity return. Suppose the end user pays the equity payment and receives the fixed payment, i.e., it pays the dealer the return on the S&P 500 Index, and the dealer pays the end user a fixed rate. If the S&P 500 increases, the return is positive and the end user pays that return to the dealer. If the S&P 500 goes down, however, its return is obviously negative. In that case, the end user would pay the dealer the *negative return on the S&P 500*, which means that it would receive that return from the dealer. For example, if the S&P 500 falls by 1 percent, the dealer would pay the end user 1 percent, in addition to the fixed payment the dealer makes in any case. So the dealer, or in general the party receiving the equity return, could end up making *both* a fixed-rate payment and an equity payment.

The second distinguishing feature of an equity swap is that the payment is not known until the end of the settlement period, at which time the return on the stock is known. In an interest rate or currency swap, the floating interest rate is set at the beginning of the period.[9] Therefore, one always knows the amount of the upcoming floating interest payment.[10]

Another important feature of some equity swaps is that the rate of return is often structured to include both dividends and capital gains. In interest rate and currency swaps, capital gains are not paid.[11] Finally, we note that in some equity swaps, the notional principal is indexed to change with the level of the stock, although we will not explore such swaps in this reading.[12]

Equity swaps are commonly used by asset managers. Let us consider a situation in which an asset manager might use such a swap. Suppose that the Vanguard Asset Allocation Fund (NASDAQ: VAAPX) is authorized to use swaps. On the last day of December, it would like to sell $100 million in U.S. large-cap equities and invest the proceeds at a fixed rate. It believes that a swap allowing it to pay the total return on the S&P 500, while receiving a fixed rate, would achieve this objective. It would like to hold this position for one year, with payments to be made on the last day of March, June, September, and December. It enters into such a swap with Morgan Stanley (NYSE: MWD).

Specifically, the swap covers a notional principal of $100 million and calls for VAAPX to pay MWD the return on the S&P 500 Total Return Index and for MWD to pay VAAPX a fixed rate on the last day of March, June, September, and December for one year. MWD prices the swap at a fixed rate of 6.5 percent. The fixed payments will be made using an actual day count/365 days convention. There are 90 days between 31 December and 31 March, 91 days between 31 March and 30 June, 92 days between 30 June and 30 September, and 92 days between 30 September and 31 December. Thus, the fixed payments will be

8 Currency swaps also have the element that the exchange rate is variable.

9 Technically, there are interest rate swaps in which the floating rate is set at the end of the period, at which time the payment is made. We shall briefly mention these swaps in Section 5.

10 In a currency swap, however, one does not know the exchange rate until the settlement date.

11 In some kinds of interest rate swaps, the total return on a bond, which includes dividends and capital gains, is paid. This instrument is called a **total return swap** and is a common variety of a credit derivative.

12 Some interest rate swaps also have a notional principal that changes, which we shall briefly discuss in Section 5.

31 March:	\$100,000,000(0.065)(90/365) = \$1,602,740
30 June:	\$100,000,000(0.065)(91/365) = \$1,620,548
30 September:	\$100,000,000(0.065)(92/365) = \$1,638,356
31 December:	\$100,000,000(0.065)(92/365) = \$1,638,356

Exhibit 6 shows the cash flow stream to VAAPX.

Exhibit 6 Cash Flows to VAAPX on Equity Swap with MWD

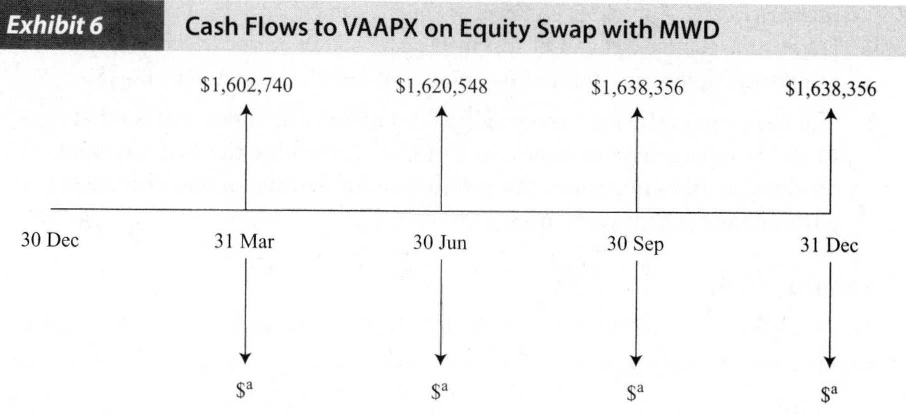

[a]Computed as \$100,000,000R, where R is the return on the S&P 500 Total Return Index from the previous settlement date.

Suppose that on the day the swap is initiated, 31 December, the S&P 500 Total Return Index is at 3,517.76. Now suppose that on 31 March, the index is at 3,579.12. The return on the index is

$$\frac{3{,}579.12}{3{,}517.76} - 1 = 0.0174$$

Thus, the return is 1.74 percent. The equity payment that VAAPX would make to MWD would be \$100,000,000(0.0174) = \$1,740,000.

Of course, this amount would not be known until 31 March, and only the difference between this amount and the fixed payment would be paid. Then on 31 March, the index value of 3,579.12 would be the base for the following period. Suppose that on 30 June, the index declines to 3,452.78. Then the return for the second quarter would be

$$\frac{3{,}452.78}{3{,}579.12} - 1 = -0.0353$$

Therefore, the loss is 3.53 percent, requiring a payment of \$100,000,000(0.0353) = \$3,530,000.

Because this amount represents a loss on the S&P 500, MWD would make a payment to VAAPX. In addition, MWD would also owe VAAPX the fixed payment of \$1,620,548. It is as though VAAPX sold out of its position in stock, thereby avoiding the loss of about \$3.5 million, and moved into a fixed-income position, thereby picking up a gain of about \$1.6 million.

EXAMPLE 3

A mutual fund has arranged an equity swap with a dealer. The swap's notional principal is $100 million, and payments will be made semiannually. The mutual fund agrees to pay the dealer the return on a small-cap stock index, and the dealer agrees to pay the mutual fund based on one of the two specifications given below. The small-cap index starts off at 1,805.20; six months later, it is at 1,796.15.

A The dealer pays a fixed rate of 6.75 percent to the mutual fund, with payments made on the basis of 182 days in the period and 365 days in a year. Determine the first payment for both parties and, under the assumption of netting, determine the net payment and which party makes it.

B The dealer pays the return on a large-cap index. The index starts off at 1155.14 and six months later is at 1148.91. Determine the first payment for both parties and, under the assumption of netting, determine the net payment and which party makes it.

Solution to A:

The fixed payment is $100,000,000(0.0675)182/365 = $3,365,753. The equity payment is

$$\left(\frac{1796.15}{1805.20} - 1\right)\$100{,}000{,}000 = -\$501{,}329$$

Because the fund pays the equity return and the equity return is negative, the dealer must pay the equity return. The dealer also pays the fixed return, so the dealer makes both payments, which add up to $3,365,753 + $501,329 = $3,867,082. The net payment is $3,867,082, paid by the dealer to the mutual fund.

Solution to B:

The large-cap equity payment is

$$\left(\frac{1148.91}{1155.14} - 1\right)\$100{,}000{,}000 = -\$539{,}329$$

The fund owes –$501,329, so the dealer owes the fund $501,329. The dealer owes –$539,329, so the fund owes the dealer $539,329. Therefore, the fund pays the dealer the net amount of $539,329 –$501,329 = $38,000.

Exhibit 7 illustrates what VAAPX has accomplished. It is important to note that the conversion of its equity assets into fixed income is not perfect. VAAPX does not hold a portfolio precisely equal to the S&P 500 Total Return Index. To the extent that VAAPX's portfolio generates a return that deviates from the index, some mismatching can occur, which can be a problem. As an alternative, VAAPX can request that MWD give it a swap based on the precise portfolio that VAAPX wishes to sell off. In that case, however, MWD would assess a charge by lowering the fixed rate it pays or raising the rate VAAPX pays to it.[13]

13 Note, however, that VAAPX is converting not its entire portfolio but simply a $100 million portion of it.

Exhibit 7 VAAPX's Conversion of an Equity Position into a Fixed-Income Position

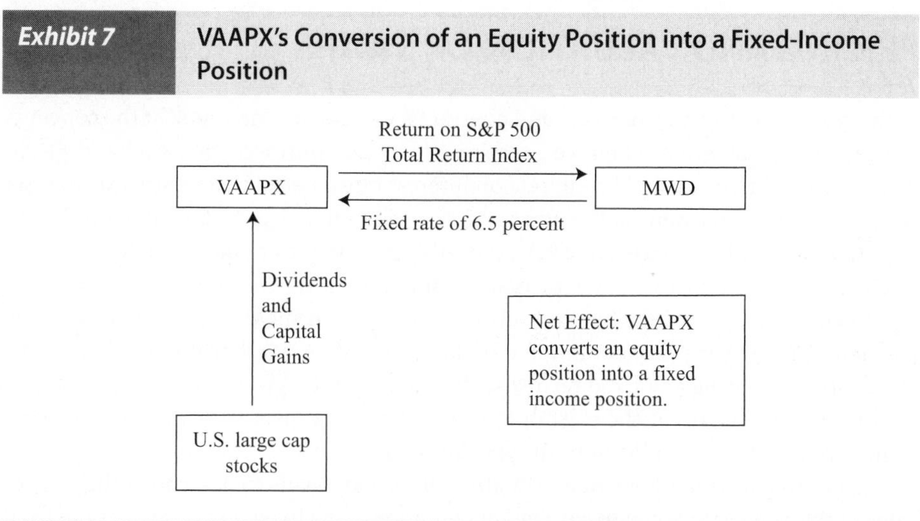

In our previous VAAPX example, the fund wanted to move some money out of a large-cap equity position and invest the proceeds at a fixed rate. Suppose instead that they do not want to move the proceeds into a fixed-rate investment. VAAPX could structure a swap to pay it a floating rate or the return on some other equity index. For example, an asset allocation from U.S. large-cap stocks to U.S. small-cap stocks could be accomplished by having MWD pay the return on the S&P 500 Small Cap 600 Index.

Suppose VAAPX wanted to move out of a position in U.S. stocks and into a position in U.K. large-cap stocks. It could structure the swap to have MWD pay it the return on the FTSE (Financial Times Stock Exchange) 100 Index. Note, however, that this index is based on the prices of U.K. stocks as quoted in pounds sterling. If VAAPX wanted the exposure in pounds—that is, it wanted the currency risk as well as the risk of the U.K. stock market—the payments from MWD to VAAPX would be made in pounds. VAAPX could, however, ask for the payments in dollars. In that case, MWD would hedge the currency risk and make payments in dollars.

Although our focus is on currency, interest rate, and equity products, we shall take a very brief look at some other types of swaps.

3.4 Commodity and Other Types of Swaps

Just as currencies, interest rates, and equities can be used to structure swaps, so too can commodities and just about anything that has a random outcome and to which a corporation, financial institution, or even an individual is exposed. Commodity swaps are very commonly used. For example, airlines enter into swaps to hedge their future purchases of jet fuel. They agree to make fixed payments to a swap dealer on regularly scheduled dates and receive payments determined by the price of jet fuel. Gold mining companies use swaps to hedge future deliveries of gold. Other parties dealing in such commodities as natural gas and precious metals often use swaps to lock in prices for future purchases and sales. In addition, swaps can be based on non-storable commodities, like electricity and the weather. In the case of the weather, payments are made based on a measure of a particular weather factor, such as amounts of rain, snowfall, or weather-related damage.

We have now introduced and described the basic structure of swaps. We have made many references to the pricing and valuation of swaps, and we now move on to explore how this is done.

END OPTIONAL SEGMENT

4 PRICING AND VALUATION OF SWAPS

In the reading on forward markets and contracts, we took our first look at the concepts of pricing and valuation when we examined forward contracts on assets and FRAs, which are essentially forward contracts on interest rates. Recall that a forward contract requires no cash payment at the start and commits one party to buy and another to sell an asset at a later date. An FRA commits one party to make a single fixed-rate interest payment and the other to make a single floating-rate interest payment. A swap extends that concept by committing one party to making a series of floating payments. The other party commits to making a series of fixed or floating payments. For swaps containing any fixed terms, such as a fixed rate, pricing the swap means to determine those terms at the start of the swap. Some swaps do not contain any fixed terms; we explore examples of both types of swaps.

All swaps have a market value. Valuation of a swap means to determine the market value of the swap based on current market conditions. The fixed terms, such as the fixed rate, are established at the start to give the swap an initial market value of zero. As we have already discussed, a zero market value means that neither party pays anything to the other at the start. Later during the life of the swap, as market conditions change, the market value will change, moving from zero from both parties' perspective to a positive value for one party and a negative value for the other. When a swap has zero value, it is neither an asset nor a liability to either party. When the swap has positive value to one party, it is an asset to that party; from the perspective of the other party, it thus has negative value and is a liability.

We begin the process of pricing and valuing swaps by learning how swaps are comparable to other instruments. If we know that one financial instrument is equivalent to another, we can price one instrument if we know or can determine the price of the other instrument.

4.1 Equivalence of Swaps and Other Instruments

In this section, we look at how swaps are similar to other instruments. Because our focus is on currency, interest rate, and equity swaps, we do not discuss commodity swaps here.

4.1.1 *Swaps and Assets*

We have already alluded to the similarity between swaps and assets. For example, a currency swap is identical to issuing a fixed- or floating-rate bond in one currency, converting the proceeds to the other currency, and using the proceeds to purchase a fixed- or floating-rate bond denominated in the other currency. An interest rate swap is identical to issuing a fixed- or floating-rate bond and using the proceeds to purchase a floating- or fixed-rate bond. The notional principal is equivalent to the face value on these hypothetical bonds.

Equity swaps appear to be equivalent to issuing one type of security and using the proceeds to purchase another, where at least one of the types of securities is a stock or stock index. For example, a pay-fixed, receive-equity swap looks like issuing a fixed-rate bond and using the proceeds to buy a stock or index portfolio. As it turns out, however, these two transactions are not exactly the same, although they are close. The stock position in the transaction is not the same as a buy-and-hold position; some adjustments are required on the settlement dates to replicate the cash flows of a swap. We shall take a look at this process of replicating an equity swap in Section 4.2.3. For now, simply recognize that an equity swap is like issuing bonds and buying stock, but not buying and holding stock.

The equivalence of a swap to transactions we are already familiar with, such as owning assets, is important because it allows us to price and value the swap using simple instruments, such as the underlying currency, interest rate, or stock. We do not require other derivatives to replicate the cash flows of a swap. Nonetheless, other derivatives can be used to replicate the cash flows of a swap, and it is worth seeing why this is true.

4.1.2 *Swaps and Forward Contracts*

Recall that a forward contract, whether on an interest rate, a currency, or an equity, is an agreement for one party to make a fixed payment to the other, while the latter party makes a variable payment to the former. A swap extends this notion by combining a series of forward contracts into a single transaction. There are, however, some subtle differences between swaps and forward contracts. For example, swaps are a series of equal fixed payments, whereas the component contracts of a series of forward contracts would almost always be priced at different fixed rates.[14] In this context we often refer to a swap as a series of off-market forward contracts, reflecting the fact that the implicit forward contracts that make up the swap are all priced at the swap fixed rate and not at the rate at which they would normally be priced in the market. In addition, in interest rate swaps, the next payment that each party makes is known. That would obviously not be the case for a single forward contract. Other subtleties distinguish currency swaps from a series of currency forwards and equity swaps from a series of equity forwards, but in general, it is acceptable to view a swap as a series of forward contracts.

4.1.3 *Swaps and Futures Contracts*

It is a fairly common practice to equate swaps to futures contracts. This practice is partially correct, but only to the extent that futures contracts can be equated to forward contracts. We saw in the reading on futures markets and contracts that futures contracts are equivalent to forward contracts only when future interest rates are known. Obviously this condition can never truly be met, and because swaps are often used to manage uncertain interest rates, the equivalence of futures with swaps is not always appropriate. Moreover, swaps are highly customized contracts, whereas futures are standardized with respect to expiration and the underlying instrument. Although it is common to equate a swap with a series of futures contracts, this equality holds true only in very limited cases.[15]

4.1.4 *Swaps and Options*

Finally, we note that swaps can be equated to combinations of options. Buying a call and selling a put would force the transacting party to make a net payment if the underlying is below the exercise rate at expiration, and would result in receipt of a payment if the underlying is above the exercise rate at expiration.

This payment will be equivalent to a swap payment if the exercise rate is set at the fixed rate on the swap. Therefore, a swap is equivalent to a combination of options with expirations at the swap payment dates. The connection between swaps and options is

14 For example, a series of FRAs would have different fixed rates unless the term structure is flat.

15 It is possible only in extremely rare circumstances for futures expirations to line up with swap settlement dates and thereby provide perfect equivalence. That does not mean, however, that futures cannot be used to hedge in a delta-hedging sense, as described in the reading on option markets and contracts. A futures price has a given sensitivity to the underlying, and futures are often highly liquid. A dealer, having entered into a swap, can determine the swap's sensitivity to the underlying and execute the appropriate number of futures transactions to balance the volatility of the swap to that of the futures. Indeed, this method is standard for hedging plain vanilla swaps using the Eurodollar futures contract.

relatively straightforward for interest rate instruments, but less so for currency and equity instruments. Nonetheless, we can generally consider swaps as equivalent to combinations of options.

In this section, we have learned that swaps can be shown to be equivalent to combinations of assets, combinations of forward contracts, combinations of futures contracts, and combinations of options. Thus, to price and value swaps we can choose any of these approaches. We choose the simplest: swaps and assets.

4.2 Pricing and Valuation

As in previous readings, our goal is to determine the market value of the derivative transaction of interest, in this case, swaps. At the start of a swap, the market value is set to zero. The process of pricing the swap involves finding the terms that force that market value to zero. To determine the market value of a swap, we replicate the swap using other instruments that produce the same cash flows. Knowing the values of these other instruments, we are able to value the swap. This value can be thought of as what the swap is worth if we were to sell it to someone else. In addition, we can think of the value as what we might assign to it on our balance sheet. The swap can have a positive value, making it an asset, or a negative value, making it a liability.

As we noted in Section 4.1, swaps are equivalent to a variety of instruments, but we prefer to use the simplest instruments to replicate the swap. The simplest instruments are the underlying assets: bonds, stocks, and currencies. Therefore, we shall use these underlying instruments to replicate the swap.

To understand the pricing of currency, interest rate, and equity swaps, we shall have to first take a brief digression to examine an instrument that plays an important role in their pricing. We shall see that the floating-rate security will have a value of 1.0, its par, at the start and on any coupon reset date. Recall that we have made numerous references to floating rates and floating payments. Accordingly, we must first obtain a solid understanding of floating-rate notes.

As we did in the reading on forward markets and contracts, let us first set up a time line that indicates where we are and where the interest payments on the floating-rate note will occur:

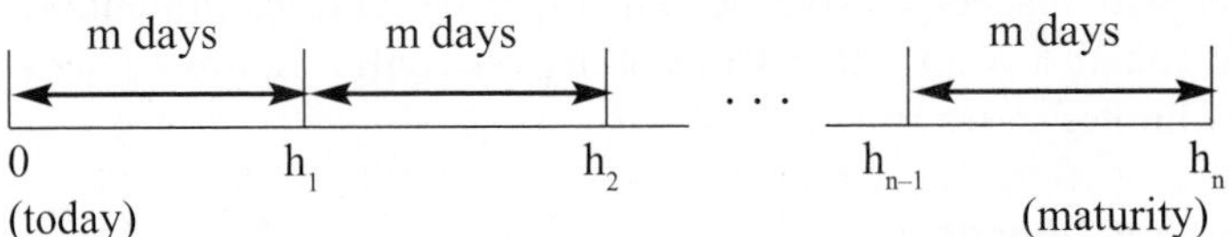

We start at time 0. The interest payments will occur on days $h_1, h_2, \ldots, h_{n-1}$, and h_n, so there are n interest payments in all. Day h_n is the maturity date of the floating-rate note. The time interval between payments is m days. The underlying rate is an m-day interest rate.

For simplicity, we will use LIBOR as the underlying rate and denote it with the symbol we have previously used, $L_i(m)$, which stands for the m-day LIBOR on day i. If i = 1, we are referring to day h_1, which might, for example, be 180 days after day 0. Thus, $h_1 = 180$. $L_0(180)$ is the 180-day LIBOR on day 0. Then h_2 would likely be 360 and $L_0(2m) = L_0(360)$, the 360-day LIBOR on day 0. We denote $B_0(h_j)$ as the present value factor on a zero-coupon instrument paying $1 at its maturity date. As an example, to discount payments 180 and 360 days later, we multiply the payment amount by the following respective factors:

$$B_0(180) = \frac{1}{1 + L_0(180) \times (180/360)}$$

$$B_0(360) = \frac{1}{1 + L_0(360) \times (360/360)}$$

We can think of these discount factors as the values of spot LIBOR deposits that pay \$1 at maturity, 180 and 360 days later.

On day 0, the floating rate is set for the first period and the interest to be paid at that rate is paid on day h_1. Then on day h_1, the rate is set for the second period and the interest is paid on day h_2. This process continues so that on day h_{n-1} the rate is set for the last period, and the final interest payment and the principal are paid on day h_n. Let the principal be 1.0.

Suppose today is day h_{n-1} and LIBOR on that day is $L_{n-1}(m)$. Remember that this rate is the m-day LIBOR in the market at that time. Therefore, looking ahead to day h_n, we anticipate receiving 1.0, the final principal payment, plus $L_{n-1}(m) \times (m/360)$. What is the value of this amount on day h_{n-1}? We would discount it by the appropriate m-day LIBOR in the following manner:

$$\begin{aligned}\text{Value at } h_{n-1} &= (\text{Payment at } h_n)(\text{One-period discount factor}) \\ &= \left[1.0 + L_{n-1}(m) \times (m/360)\right]\left[\frac{1}{1.0 + L_{n-1}(m) \times (m/360)}\right] = 1.0\end{aligned}$$

The value is 1.0, its par value. Now step back to day h_{n-2}, at which time the rate is $L_{n-2}(m)$. Looking ahead to day h_{n-1} we shall receive an interest payment of $L_{n-2}(m) \times (m/360)$. We do not receive the principal on day h_{n-1}, but it is appropriate to discount the market value on day h_{n-1}, which we just determined is 1.0.[16] Thus, the value of the floating-rate security will be

$$\begin{aligned}\text{Value at } h_{n-2} &= (\text{Payment at } h_{n-1})(\text{One-period discount factor}) \\ &= \left[1.0 + L_{n-2}(m) \times (m/360)\right]\left[\frac{1}{1.0 + L_{n-2}(m) \times (m/360)}\right] = 1.0\end{aligned}$$

We continue this procedure, stepping back until we reach time 0. The floating-rate security will have a value of 1.0, its par, at the start and on any coupon reset date.[17] We shall use this result to help us price and value swaps.

In previous material in this reading, we have covered currency swaps first. We did so because we showed that an interest rate swap is just a currency swap in which both currencies are the same. A currency swap is thus the more general instrument of the two. For the purposes of this section, however, it will be easier to price and value a currency swap if we first price and value an interest rate swap.

4.2.1 *Interest Rate Swaps*

Pricing an interest rate swap means finding the fixed rate that equates the present value of the fixed payments to the present value of the floating payments, a process that sets the market value of the swap to zero at the start. Using the time line illustrated earlier, the swap cash flows will occur on days $h_1, h_2, \ldots, h_{n-1}$, and h_n, so there are n

16 All we are doing here is discounting the upcoming cash flow and the market value of the security on the next payment date. This procedure is not unique to floating-rate securities; it is standard valuation procedure for any type of security. What is special and different for floating-rate securities is that the market value goes back to par on each payment date.

17 Floating-rate securities are designed to allow the coupon to catch up with market interest rates on a regularly scheduled basis. The price can deviate from par during the period between reset dates. In addition, if there is any credit risk and that risk changes during the life of the security, its price can deviate from par at any time, including at the coupon reset date. We are assuming no credit risk here.

cash flows in the swap. Day h_n is the expiration date of the swap. The time interval between payments is m days. We can thus think of the swap as being on an m-day interest rate, which will be LIBOR in our examples.

As previously mentioned, the payments in an interest rate swap are a series of fixed and floating interest payments. They do not include an initial and final exchange of notional principals. As we already observed, such payments would be only an exchange of the same money. But if we introduce the notional principal payments as though they were actually made, we have not done any harm. The cash flows on the swap are still the same. The advantage of introducing the notional principal payments is that we can now treat the fixed and floating sides of the swap as though they were fixed- and floating-rate bonds.

So we introduce a hypothetical final notional principal payment of \$1 on a swap starting at day 0 and ending on day h_n, in which the underlying is an m-day rate. The fixed swap interest payment *rate*, FS(0,n,m), gives the fixed payment *amount* corresponding to the \$1 notional principal. Thus, the present value of a series of fixed interest payments at the swap rate FS(0,n,m) plus a final principal payment of 1.0 is

$$\sum_{j=1}^{n} FS(0, n, m)B_0(h_j) + \$1 \times B_0(h_n), \text{ or}$$

$$FS(0, n, m)\sum_{j=1}^{n} B_0(h_j) + B_0(h_n)$$

Here the summation simply represents the sum of the present value factors for each payment. The expression $B_0(h_n)$ is the present value factor for the final hypothetical notional principal payment of 1.0.

Now we must find the present value of the floating payments, and here we use what we learned about floating-rate notes. Remember that a floating-rate note with \$1 face will have a value of \$1 at the start and at any coupon reset date. If the swap's floating payments include a final principal payment, we can treat them like a floating-rate note. Hence, we know their value is \$1.

Now all we have to do is equate the present value of the fixed payments to the present value of the floating payments

$$FS(0, n, m)\sum_{j=1}^{n} B_0(h_j) + B_0(h_n) = 1.0$$

and solve for the fixed rate FS(0,n,m) that will result in equality of these two streams of payments. The solution is as follows:

$$FS(0, n, m) = \frac{1.0 - B_0(h_n)}{\sum_{j=1}^{n} B_0(h_j)} \quad (1)$$

The swap fixed payment is 1.0 minus the last present value factor divided by the sum of the present value factors for each payment. Thus, we have priced the swap.

One can use several other ways to find the fixed payment on a swap, but this method is unquestionably the simplest. In fact, this formulation shows that the fixed rate on a swap is simply the coupon rate on a par bond whose payments coincide with those on the swap.[18]

18 Technically, bond interest payments are usually found by dividing the annual rate by 2 if the payments are semiannual, whereas swap payments do, on occasion, use day counts such as 181/365 to determine semiannual payments. When we refer to a par bond, we are assuming the payments are structured exactly like those on the swap.

Let us now work a problem. Consider a one-year swap with quarterly payments on days 90, 180, 270, and 360. The underlying is 90-day LIBOR. The annualized LIBOR spot rates today are

$$L_0(90) = 0.0345$$
$$L_0(180) = 0.0358$$
$$L_0(270) = 0.0370$$
$$L_0(360) = 0.0375$$

The present value factors are obtained as follows:

$$B_0(90) = \frac{1}{1 + 0.0345(90/360)} = 0.9914$$

$$B_0(180) = \frac{1}{1 + 0.0358(180/360)} = 0.9824$$

$$B_0(270) = \frac{1}{1 + 0.0370(270/360)} = 0.9730$$

$$B_0(360) = \frac{1}{1 + 0.375(360/360)} = 0.9639$$

The fixed payment is found as

$$FS(0, n, m) = FS(0{,}4{,}90) = \frac{1 - 0.9639}{0.9914 + 0.9824 + 0.9730 + 0.9639} = 0.0092$$

Therefore, the quarterly fixed payment will be 0.0092 for each $1 notional principal. Of course, this rate is quarterly; it is customary to quote it as an annual rate. We would thus see the rate quoted as 0.0092 × (360/90) = 0.0368, or 3.68 percent. We would also have to adjust our payment by multiplying by the actual notional principal. For example, if the actual notional principal were $30 million, the payment would be (0.0092)$30 million = $276,000.

In determining the fixed rate on the swap, we have essentially found the fixed payment that sets the present value of the floating payments plus a hypothetical notional principal of 1.0 equal to the present value of the fixed payments plus a hypothetical notional principal of 1.0. We have thus made the market value of the swap equal to zero at the start of the transaction. This equality makes sense, because neither party pays any money to the other.

Now suppose we have entered into the swap. Let us move forward into the life of the swap, at which time interest rates have changed, and determine its market value. Rather than present mathematical equations for determining its value, we shall work through this example informally. We shall see that the procedure is simple and intuitive. Suppose we have now moved 60 days into the life of the swap. At day 60, we face a new term structure of LIBORs. Because the upcoming payments occur in 30, 120, 210, and 300 days, we want the term structure for 30, 120, 210, and 300 days, which is given as follows:

$$L_{60}(30) = 0.0425$$
$$L_{60}(120) = 0.0432$$
$$L_{60}(210) = 0.0437$$
$$L_{60}(300) = 0.0444$$

The new set of discount factors is

$$B_{60}(90) = \frac{1}{1 + 0.0425(30/360)} = 0.9965$$

$$B_{60}(180) = \frac{1}{1 + 0.0432(120/360)} = 0.9858$$

$$B_{60}(270) = \frac{1}{1 + 0.0437(210/360)} = 0.9751$$

$$B_{60}(360) = \frac{1}{1 + 0.0444(300/360)} = 0.9643$$

We must value the swap from the perspective of one of the parties. Let us look at it as though we were the party paying fixed and receiving floating. Finding the present value of the remaining fixed payments of 0.0092 is straightforward. This present value, including the hypothetical notional principal, is 0.0092(0.9965 + 0.9858 + 0.9751 + 0.9643) + 1.0(0.9643) = 1.0004.

Now we must find the present value of the floating payments. Recall that on day 0, the 90-day LIBOR was 3.45 percent. Thus, the first floating payment will be 0.0345(90/360) = 0.0086. We know that we should discount this payment back 30 days, but what about the remaining floating payments? Remember that we know that the market value of the remaining payments on day 90, including the hypothetical final notional principal, is 1.0. So, we can discount 1.00 + 0.0086 = 1.0086 back 30 days to obtain 1.0086(0.9965) = 1.0051.

The present value of the remaining floating payments, plus the hypothetical notional principal, is 1.0051, and the present value of the remaining fixed payments, plus the hypothetical notional principal, is 1.0004. Therefore, the value of the swap is 1.0051 – 1.0004 = 0.0047 per $1 notional principal. If, for example, the actual swap were for a notional principal of $30 million, the market value would be $30 million(0.0047) = $141,000.

EXAMPLE 4

Consider a one-year interest rate swap with semiannual payments.

A Determine the fixed rate on the swap and express it in annualized terms. The term structure of LIBOR spot rates is given as follows:

Days	Rate (%)
180	7.2
360	8.0

B Ninety days later, the term structure is as follows:

Days	Rate (%)
90	7.1
270	7.4

Determine the market value of the swap from the perspective of the party paying the floating rate and receiving the fixed rate. Assume a notional principal of $15 million.

Solution to A:

First calculate the present value factors for 180 and 360 days:

$$B_0(180) = \frac{1}{1 + 0.072(180/360)} = 0.9653$$

$$B_0(360) = \frac{1}{1 + 0.08(360/360)} = 0.9259$$

The fixed rate is $\frac{1 - 0.9259}{0.9653 + 0.9259} = 0.0392$. The fixed payment would, therefore, be 0.0392 per $1 notional principal. The annualized rate would be 0.0392(360/180) = 0.0784.

Solution to B:

Calculate the new present value factors for 90 and 270 days:

$$B_{90}(180) = \frac{1}{1 + 0.071(90/360)} = 0.9826$$

$$B_{90}(360) = \frac{1}{1 + 0.074(270/360)} = 0.9474$$

The present value of the remaining fixed payments plus hypothetical $1 notional principal is 0.0392(0.9826 + 0.9474) + 1.0(0.9474) = 1.0231.

The 180-day rate at the start was 7.2 percent, so the first floating payment would be 0.072(180/360) = 0.036. The present value of the floating payments plus hypothetical $1 notional principal will be 1.036(0.9826) = 1.0180. The market value of a pay-floating, receive-fixed swap is, therefore, 1.0231 –1.0180 = 0.0051. For a notional principal of $15 million, the market value is $15,000,000(0.0051) = $76,500.

Note that we valued the swap from the perspective of the party paying the fixed rate. From the counterparty's perspective, the value of the swap would be the negative of the value to the fixed-rate payer.

Although an interest rate swap is like a series of FRAs, or a long position in an interest rate cap and a short position in an interest rate floor with the exercise rate set at the fixed rate on a swap, pricing and valuing an interest rate swap as either of these instruments is more difficult than what we have done here. To price the swap as a series of FRAs, we would need to calculate the forward rates, which is not difficult but would add another step. If we priced a swap as a combination of caps and floors, we would need to price these options. As we saw in the reading on option markets and contracts, interest rate option pricing can be somewhat complex. In addition, we would have to find the exercise rate on the cap and floor that equated their values, which would require trial and error. What we have seen here is the trick that if we add the notional principal to both sides of an interest rate swap, we do not change the swap payments, but we make the cash flows on each side of the swap equivalent to those of a bond. Then we can price the swap as though it were a pair of bonds, one long and the other short. One side is like a floating-rate bond, which we know is priced at par value at the time of issuance as well as on any reset date. The other side is like a fixed-rate bond. Because the value of the fixed-rate bond must equal that of the floating-rate bond at the start, we know that the coupon on a par value bond is the fixed rate on the swap.

Having discussed the pricing and valuation of interest rate swaps, we can now move on to currency swaps, taking advantage of what we know about pricing interest rate swaps. As we have already noted, an interest rate swap is just like a currency swap in which both currencies are the same.

4.2.2 *Currency Swaps*

Recall the four types of currency swaps: 1) pay one currency fixed, receive the other fixed, 2) pay one currency fixed, receive the other floating, 3) pay one currency floating, receive the other fixed, and 4) pay one currency floating, receive the other floating. In determining the fixed rate on a swap, we must keep in mind one major point: The fixed rate is the rate that makes the present value of the payments made equal the present value of the payments received. In the fourth type of currency swap mentioned here, both sides pay floating so there is no need to find a fixed rate. But all currency swaps have two notional principals, one in each currency. We can arbitrarily set the notional principal in the domestic currency at one unit. We then must determine the equivalent notional principal in the other currency. This task is straightforward: We simply convert the one unit of domestic currency to the equivalent amount of foreign currency, dividing 1.0 by the exchange rate.

Consider the first type of currency swap, in which we pay the foreign currency at a fixed rate and receive the domestic currency at a fixed rate. What are the two fixed rates? We will see that they are the fixed rates on plain vanilla interest rate swaps in the respective countries.

Because we know that the value of a floating-rate security with $1 face value is $1, we know that the fixed rate on a plain vanilla interest rate swap is the rate on a $1 par bond in the domestic currency. That rate results in the present value of the interest payments and the hypothetical notional principal being equal to 1.0 unit of the domestic currency. Moreover, for a currency swap, the notional principal is typically paid, so we do not even have to call it hypothetical. We know that the fixed rate on the domestic leg of an interest rate swap is the appropriate domestic fixed rate for a currency swap in which the domestic notional principal is 1.0 unit of the domestic currency.

What about the fixed rate for the foreign payments on the currency swap? To answer that question, let us assume the point of view of a resident of the foreign country. Given the term structure in the foreign country, we might be interested in first pricing plain vanilla interest rate swaps in that country. So, we know that the fixed rate on interest rate swaps in that country would make the present value of the interest and principal payments equal 1.0 unit of that currency.

Now let us return to our domestic setting. We know that the fixed rate on interest rate swaps in the foreign currency makes the present value of the foreign interest and principal payments equal to 1.0 unit of the foreign currency. We multiply by the spot rate, S_0, to obtain the value of those payments in our domestic currency: 1.0 times S_0 equals S_0, which is now in terms of the domestic currency. This amount does not equal the present value of the domestic payments, but if we set the notional principal on the foreign side of the swap equal to $1/S_0$, then the present value of the foreign payments will be $S_0(1/S_0) = 1.0$ unit of our domestic currency, which is what we want.

Let us now summarize this argument:

- The fixed rate on plain vanilla swaps in our country makes the present value of the domestic interest and principal payments equal 1.0 unit of the domestic currency.
- The fixed rate on plain vanilla swaps in the foreign country makes the present value of the foreign interest and principal payments equal 1.0 unit of the foreign currency.

- A notional principal of $1/S_0$ units of foreign currency makes the present value of the foreign interest and principal payments equal $1/S_0$ units of the foreign currency.
- Conversion of $1/S_0$ units of foreign currency at the current exchange rate of S_0 gives 1.0 unit of domestic currency.
- Therefore, the present value of the domestic payments equals the present value of the foreign payments.
- The fixed rates on a currency swap are, therefore, the fixed rates on plain vanilla interest rate swaps in the respective countries.

Of course, if the domestic notional principal is any amount other than 1.0, we multiply the domestic notional principal by $1/S_0$ to obtain the foreign notional principal. Then the actual swap payments are calculated by multiplying by the overall respective notional principals.

The second and third types of currency swaps each involve one side paying fixed and the other paying floating. The rate on the fixed side of each of these swaps is, again, just the fixed rate on an interest rate swap in the given country. The payments on the floating side automatically have the same present value as the payments on the fixed side. We again use 1.0 unit of domestic currency and $1/S_0$ units of foreign currency as the notional principal.

For the last type of currency swap, in which both sides pay floating, we do not need to price the swap because both sides pay a floating rate. Again, the notional principals are 1.0 unit of domestic currency and $1/S_0$ units of foreign currency.

In the example we used in pricing interest rate swaps, we were given a term structure for a one-year swap with quarterly payments. We found that the fixed payment was 0.0092, implying an annual rate of 3.68 percent. Let us now work through a currency swap in which the domestic currency is the dollar and the foreign currency is the Swiss franc. The current exchange rate is \$0.80. We shall use the same term structure used previously for the domestic term structure: $L_0(90) = 0.0345$, $L_0(180) = 0.0358$, $L_0(270) = 0.0370$, and $L_0(360) = 0.0375$. The Swiss term structure, denoted with a superscript SF, is

$$L_0^{SF}(90) = 0.0520$$
$$L_0^{SF}(180) = 0.0540$$
$$L_0^{SF}(270) = 0.0555$$
$$L_0^{SF}(360) = 0.0570$$

The present value factors are

$$B_0^{SF}(90) = \frac{1}{1 + 0.0520(90/360)} = 0.9872$$

$$B_0^{SF}(180) = \frac{1}{1 + 0.0540(180/360)} = 0.9737$$

$$B_0^{SF}(270) = \frac{1}{1 + 0.0555(270/360)} = 0.9600$$

$$B_0^{SF}(360) = \frac{1}{1 + 0.0570(360/360)} = 0.9461$$

The fixed payment is easily found as

$$FS^{SF}(0,n,m) = FS^{SF}(0,4,90) = \frac{1 - 0.9461}{0.9872 + 0.9737 + 0.9600 + 0.9461} = 0.0139$$

The quarterly fixed payment is thus SF0.0139 for each SF1.00 of notional principal. This translates into an annual rate of 0.0139(360/90) = 0.0556 or 5.56 percent, so in Switzerland we would quote the fixed rate on a plain vanilla interest rate swap in Swiss francs as 5.56 percent.

Our currency swap involving dollars for Swiss francs would have a fixed rate of 3.68 percent in dollars and 5.56 percent in Swiss francs. The notional principal would be \$1.0 and 1/\$0.80 = SF1.25. Summarizing, we have the following terms for the four swaps:

Swap 1 Pay dollars fixed at 3.68 percent, receive SF fixed at 5.56 percent.

Swap 2 Pay dollars fixed at 3.68 percent, receive SF floating.

Swap 3 Pay dollars floating, receive SF fixed at 5.56 percent.

Swap 4 Pay dollars floating, receive SF floating.

In each case, the notional principal is \$1 and SF1.25, or more generally, SF1.25 for every dollar of notional principal.

As we did with interest rate swaps, we move 60 days forward in time. We have a new U.S. term structure, given in the interest rate swap problem, and a new Swiss franc term structure, which is given below:

$$L_{60}^{SF}(30) = 0.0600$$

$$L_{60}^{SF}(120) = 0.0615$$

$$L_{60}^{SF}(210) = 0.0635$$

$$L_{60}^{SF}(300) = 0.0653$$

The new set of discount factors is

$$B_{60}^{SF}(90) = \frac{1}{1 + 0.0600(30/360)} = 0.9950$$

$$B_{60}^{SF}(180) = \frac{1}{1 + 0.0615(120/360)} = 0.9799$$

$$B_{60}^{SF}(270) = \frac{1}{1 + 0.0635(210/360)} = 0.9643$$

$$B_{60}^{SF}(360) = \frac{1}{1 + 0.0653(300/360)} = 0.9484$$

The new exchange rate is \$0.82. Now let us value each swap in turn, taking advantage of what we already know about the values of the U.S. dollar interest rate swaps calculated in the previous section. Recall we found that

Present value of dollar fixed payments = 1.0004

Present value of dollar floating payments = 1.0051

Let us find the comparable numbers for the Swiss franc payments. In other words, we position ourselves as a Swiss resident or institution and obtain the values of the fixed and floating streams of Swiss franc payments per SF1 notional principal. The present value of the remaining Swiss fixed payments is

$$0.0139(0.9950 + 0.9799 + 0.9643 + 0.9484) + 1.0(0.9484) = 1.0024$$

Recall that in finding the present value of the floating payments, we simply recognize that on the next payment date, we shall receive a floating payment of 0.052(90/360) = 0.013, and the market value of the remaining payments will be 1.0.[19] Thus, we can discount 1.0130 back 30 days to obtain 1.0130(0.9950) = 1.0079.

These two figures are based on SF1 notional principal. We convert them to the actual notional principal in Swiss francs by multiplying by SF1.25. Thus,

Present value of SF fixed payments = 1.0024(1.25) = SF1.2530

Present value of SF floating payments = 1.0079(1.25) = SF1.2599

Now we need to convert these figures to dollars by multiplying by the current exchange rate of \$0.82. Thus,

Present value of SF fixed payments in dollars = 1.2530(\$0.82) = \$1.0275

Present value of SF floating payments in dollars = 1.2599(\$0.82) = \$1.0331

Now we can value the four currency swaps:

Value of swap to receive SF fixed, pay \$ fixed = +\$1.0275 – \$1.0004 = +\$0.0271

Value of swap to receive SF floating, pay \$ fixed = +\$1.0331 – \$1.0004 = +\$0.0327

Value of swap to receive SF fixed, pay \$ floating = +\$1.0275 – \$1.0051 = +\$0.0224

Value of swap to receive SF floating, pay \$ floating = +\$1.0331 – \$1.0051 = +\$0.0280

Note that all of these numbers are positive. Therefore, our swaps are showing gains as a result of the combination of interest rate changes in the two countries as well as the exchange rate change. To the counterparty, the swaps are worth these same numerical amounts, but the signs are negative.

EXAMPLE 5

Consider a one-year currency swap with semiannual payments. The two currencies are the U.S. dollar and the euro. The current exchange rate is \$0.75.

A The term structure of interest rates for LIBOR and Euribor are

Days	LIBOR (%)	Euribor (%)
180	7.2	6.0
360	8.0	6.6

Determine the fixed rate in euros and express it in annualized terms. Note that the LIBOR rates are the same as in Example 4, in which we found that the fixed payment in dollars was 0.0392.

B Ninety days later, the term structure is as follows:

19 The first floating payment was set when the swap was initiated at the 90-day rate of 5.2 percent times 90/360.

Days	LIBOR (%)	Euribor (%)
90	7.1	5.5
270	7.4	6.0

The new exchange rate is \$0.70. Determine the market values of swaps to pay dollars and receive euros. Consider all four swaps that are covered in the reading. Assume a notional principal of \$20 million and the appropriate amount for euros. Note that the LIBOR rates are the same as in Example 4, in which we found that the present value of the fixed payments (floating payments) plus the hypothetical \$1 notional principal was \$1.0231 (\$1.0180).

Solution to A:

The fixed payment in dollars is the same as in Example 4: 0.0392. To determine the fixed rate in euros, we first compute the discount factors:

$$B_0^{€}(180) = \frac{1}{1 + 0.06(180/360)} = 0.9709$$

$$B_0^{€}(360) = \frac{1}{1 + 0.066(360/360)} = 0.9381$$

The fixed rate in euros is, therefore, $\frac{1 - 0.9381}{0.9709 + 0.9381} = 0.0324$.

On an annual basis, this rate would be 0.0324(360/180) = 0.0648.

Solution to B:

Recalculate the euro discount factors:

$$B_{90}^{€}(180) = \frac{1}{1 + 0.055(90/360)} = 0.9864$$

$$B_{90}^{€}(360) = \frac{1}{1 + 0.060(270/360)} = 0.9569$$

The present value of the fixed payments plus hypothetical €1 notional principal is €0.0324(0.9864 + 0.9569) + €1.0(0.9569) = €1.0199.

The 180-day rate at the start of the swap was 6 percent, so the first floating payment would be 0.06(180/360) = 0.03. The present value of the floating payments plus hypothetical notional principal of €1 is €1.03(0.9864) = €1.0160.

The euro notional principal, established at the start of the swap, is 1/\$0.75 = €1.3333. Converting the euro payments to dollars at the new exchange rate and multiplying by the euro notional principal, we obtain the following values for the four swaps (where we use the present values of U.S. dollar fixed and floating payments as found in Example 4, repeated in the statement of Part B above).

- Pay \$ fixed, receive € fixed = –\$1.0231 + €1.3333(\$0.70)1.0199 = –\$0.0712
- Pay \$ fixed, receive € floating = –\$1.0231 + €1.3333(\$0.70)1.0160 = –\$0.0749
- Pay \$ floating, receive € fixed = – \$1.0180 + €1.3333(\$0.70)1.0199 = –\$0.0661
- Pay \$ floating, receive € floating = –\$1.0180 + €1.3333(\$0.70)1.0160 = –\$0.0698

Now we turn to equity swaps. It is tempting to believe that we will not use any more information regarding the term structure in pricing and valuing equity swaps. In fact, for equity swaps in which one side pays either a fixed or floating rate, the results we have obtained for interest rate swaps will be very useful.

4.2.3 *Equity Swaps*

In this section, we explore how to price and value three types of equity swaps: 1) a swap to pay a fixed rate and receive the return on the equity, 2) a swap to pay a floating rate and receive the return on the equity, and 3) a swap to pay the return on one equity and receive the return on another.

To price or value an equity swap, we must determine a combination of stock and bonds that replicates the cash flows on the swap. As we saw with interest rate and currency swaps, such a replication is not difficult to create. We issue a bond and buy a bond, with one being a fixed-rate bond and the other being a floating-rate bond. If we are dealing with a currency swap, we require that one of the bonds be denominated in one currency and the other be denominated in the other currency. With an equity swap, it would appear that a replicating strategy would involve issuing a bond and buying the stock or vice versa, but this is not exactly how to replicate an equity swap. Remember that in an equity swap, we receive cash payments representing the return on the stock, and that is somewhat different from payments based on the price.

Pricing a Swap to Pay a Fixed Rate and Receive the Return on the Equity By example, we will demonstrate how to price an n-payment m-day rate swap to pay a fixed rate and receive the return on equity. Suppose the notional principal is \$1, the swap involves annual settlements and lasts for two years (n = 2), and the returns on the stock for each of the two years are 10 percent for the first year and 15 percent for the second year. The equity payment on the swap would be \$0.10 the first year and \$0.15 the second. If, however, we purchased the stock instead of doing the equity swap, we would have to sell the stock at the end of the first year or we would not generate any cash. Suppose at the end of the first year, the stock is at \$1.10. We sell the stock, withdraw \$0.10, and reinvest \$1.00 in the stock. At the end of the second year the stock would be at \$1.15. We then sell the stock, taking cash of \$0.15. But we have \$1.00 left over. To get rid of, or offset, this cash flow, suppose that when we purchased the stock we borrowed the present value of \$1.00 for two years. Then two years later, we would pay back \$1.00 on that loan. This procedure would offset the \$1.00 in cash we have from the stock. The fixed payments on the swap can be easily replicated. If the fixed payment is denoted as FS(0,n,m), we simply borrow the present value of FS(0,n,m) for one year and also borrow the present value of FS(0,n,m) for two years. When we pay those loans back, we will have replicated the fixed payments on the swap.

For the more general case of n payments, we do the following to replicate the swap whose fixed payments are FS(0,n,m):

1. Invest \$1.00 in the stock.
2. Borrow the present value of \$1.00 to be paid back at the swap expiration, day h_n. This is the amount $B_0(h_n)$.
3. Take out a series of loans requiring that we pay back FS(0,n,m) at time h_1, and also at time h_2, and at all remaining times through time h_n.

Note that this transaction is like issuing debt and buying stock. The amount of money required to do this is

$$\$1 - B_0(h_n) - FS(0,n,m)\sum_{j=1}^{n} B_0(h_j)$$

Because no money changes hands at the start, the initial value of the swap is zero. We set the expression above to zero and solve for the fixed payment FS(0,n,m) to obtain

$$FS(0,n,m) = \frac{1.0 - B_0(h_n)}{\sum_{j=1}^{n} B_0(h_j)}$$

This is precisely the formula (Equation 1) for the fixed rate on an interest rate swap or a currency swap.

Pricing a Swap to Pay a Floating Rate and Receive the Return on the Equity If, instead, the swap involves the payment of a floating rate for the equity return, no further effort is needed because there is no fixed rate for which we must solve. We know from our understanding of interest rate swaps that the present value of the floating payments equals the present value of the fixed payments, which equals the notional principal of 1.0. The market value of the swap is zero at the start, as it should be.

Pricing a Swap to Pay the Return on One Equity and Receive the Return on Another Equity Let $S_0(1)$ and $S_1(1)$ be the level of Stock Index 1 at times 0 and 1, and let $S_0(2)$ and $S_1(2)$ be the level of Stock Index 2 at times 0 and 1. Assume we pay the return on Index 2 and receive the return on Index 1. We need to replicate the cash flows on this swap by investing in these two stocks using some type of strategy. Suppose we sell short \$1.00 of Index 2, taking the proceeds and investing in \$1.00 of Index 1. Then at time 1, we liquidate the position in Index 1, as described above, withdrawing the cash and reinvesting the \$1.00 back into Index 1. We cover the short position in Index 2, taking the proceeds and reshorting Index 2. We continue in this manner throughout the life of the swap. This strategy replicates the cash flows on the swap. Thus, going long one stock and short the other replicates this swap. Of course, there is no fixed rate and thus no need to price the swap. The market value at the start is zero as it should be.

Now let us look at how to determine the market values of each of these swaps during their lives. In other words, after the swap has been initiated, we move forward in time. We must take into account where we are in the life of the swap and how interest rates and the equity price have changed.

Valuing a Swap to Pay the Fixed Rate and Receive the Return on the Equity Let us use the same U.S. term structure we have already been using for interest rate and currency swaps. Our equity swap is for one year and will involve fixed quarterly payments. Recall that the fixed payment on the interest rate swap is 0.0092, corresponding to an annual rate of 3.68 percent. This will be the rate on the swap to pay fixed and receive the equity payment.

Now let us move 60 days into the life of the swap, at which time we have a new term structure as given in the interest rate swap example. We started off with a stock price of S_0, and now the stock price is S_{60}. The stock payment we will receive at the first settlement in 30 days is $S_{90}/S_0 - 1$. Let us write this amount as

$$\left(\frac{1}{S_0}\right)S_{90} - 1$$

Sixty days into the life of the swap, we could replicate this payment by purchasing $1/S_0$ shares of stock, currently at S_{60}. Doing so will cost $(1/S_0)S_{60}$. Then at the first settlement, we shall have stock worth $(1/S_0)S_{90}$. We sell that stock, withdrawing cash of $(1/S_0)S_{90} - 1$. We then take the \$1 left over and roll it into the stock again, which will replicate the return the following period, as described above. This procedure will leave \$1 left over at the end. Thus, 60 days into the swap, to replicate the remaining cash flows, we do the following:

1 Invest $(1/S_0)S_{60}$ in the stock.

2 Borrow the present value of \$1.00 to be paid back at the swap expiration, time h_n. This is the amount $B_{60}(h_n)$.
3 Take out a series of loans requiring that we pay back FS(0,n,m) at time h_1, and also at time h_2, and at all remaining times through time h_n.

For the general case of day t, the market value of the swap is

$$\left(\frac{S_t}{S_0}\right) - B_t(h_n) - FS(0,n,m)\sum_{j=1}^{n} B_t(h_j) \quad (2)$$

The first term reflects the investment in the stock necessary to replicate the equity return. The second term is the loan for the present value of \$1.00 due at the expiration date of the swap. The third term is the series of loans of the amount FS(0,n,m) due at the various swap settlement dates. Note that all discounting is done using the new term structure. Of course, the overall market value figure would then be multiplied by the notional principal.

Let us calculate these results for our pay-fixed, receive-equity swap 60 days into its life. Suppose the stock index was at 1405.72 when the swap was initiated. Now it is at 1436.59. We use the same term structure at 60 days that we used for the interest rate swap example. The market value of the swap is

$$\left(\frac{1436.59}{1405.72}\right) - 0.9643 - (0.0092)(0.9965 + 0.9858 + 0.9751 + 0.9643)$$
$$= 0.0216$$

Thus, 60 days into its life, the market value of this fixed-for-equity swap is positive at \$0.0216 per \$1 notional principal.

Valuing a Swap to Pay a Floating Rate and Receive the Return on the Equity We can value this swap in two ways. The first will require that we discount the next floating rate and the par value, as we did with interest rate swaps. We can do this because we recognize that a floating-rate security is worth its par value on the payment date. As long as we add the notional principal, we can assume the floating payments are those of a floating-rate bond. The notional principal offsets the \$1 left over at the end from holding the stock and withdrawing all of the profits on each settlement date. The calculation of the market value of this swap is simple. We just determine the value of \$1 invested in the stock since the last settlement period, minus the present value of the floating leg. With the upcoming floating payment being 0.0086, the market value of the swap is, therefore,

$$\left(\frac{1436.59}{1405.72}\right) - (1.0086)(0.9965) = 0.0169$$

Another, and probably easier, way to arrive at this answer is to recognize that:

- a swap to pay fixed and receive the equity return is worth 0.0216, and
- a swap to pay floating and receive fixed is worth –0.0047.[20]

If we did both of these swaps, the fixed payments would offset and would leave the equivalent of the equity swap. The value would then be 0.0216 – 0.0047 = 0.0169.

Valuing a Swap to Pay One Equity Return and Receive Another Now we need to value the swap to pay the return on Index 2 and receive the return on Index 1, 60 days into the swap's life. Let the following be the values of the indices on days 0 and 60.

20 In Section 4.2.1, we found the value of a swap to pay fixed and receive floating to be 0.0047. Therefore, a swap to pay floating and receive fixed is worth –0.0047.

	Day 0	Day 60
Index 1	1405.72	1436.59
Index 2	5255.18	5285.73

As we previously described, this swap can be replicated by going long Index 1 and short Index 2. The market value calculation is simple: We find the value of $1 invested in Index 1 since the last settlement day minus the value of $1 invested in Index 2 since the last settlement day. Thus, the market value of the position is

$$\left(\frac{1436.59}{1405.72}\right) - \left(\frac{5285.73}{5255.18}\right) = 0.0161$$

Of course, all of these results are per $1 notional principal, so we would have to multiply by the actual notional principal to get the overall market value of this equity-for-equity swap.

EXAMPLE 6

Consider an equity swap that calls for semiannual payments for one year. The party will receive the return on the Dow Jones Industrial Average (DJIA), which starts off at 10033.27. The current LIBOR term structure is

Days	Rate (%)
180	7.2
360	8.0

A In Example 4, we determined that the fixed rate for a one-year interest rate swap given the above term structure was 0.0392. Given this term structure data, what is the fixed rate in an equity swap calling for the party to pay a fixed rate and receive the return on the DJIA?

B Find the market value of the swap 90 days later if the new term structure is

Days	Rate (%)
90	7.1
270	7.4

The notional principal of the swap is $60 million. The DJIA is at 9955.14. Again, these are the same rates as in Example 4, for which we computed $B_{90}(90) = 0.9826$ and $B_{90}(270) = 0.9474$.

C Recompute the market value under the assumption that the counterparty pays a floating rate instead of a fixed rate.

D Recompute the market value under the assumption that the counterparty pays the return on the Dow Jones Transportation Index, which started off at 2835.17 and 90 days later is 2842.44.

Solution to A:

Because this term structure is the same as in Example 4, the fixed rate is the same at 0.0392. The fact that the party here receives an equity return rather than a floating interest rate does not affect the magnitude of the fixed payment.

Solution to B:

Using the 180- and 360-day discount factors at 90 days from Example 4, the market value of the swap to pay a fixed rate and receive the equity return is

$$\left(\frac{9955.14}{10033.27}\right) - 0.9474 - 0.0392(0.9826 + 0.9474) = -0.0309$$

Multiplying by the notional principal of \$60 million, we obtain a market value of \$60,000,000(–0.0309) = –\$1,854,000.

Solution to C:

Because the first floating payment would be at the rate of 7.2 percent and is, therefore, 0.036, the market value of the swap to pay a floating rate and receive the equity return is

$$\left(\frac{9955.14}{10033.27}\right) - 1.036(0.9826) = -0.0258$$

Adjusting for the notional principal, the market value is \$60,000,000(–0.0258) = –\$1,548,000.

Solution to D:

The market value of the swap to pay the return on the Dow Jones Transportation Average and receive the return on the DJIA is

$$\left(\frac{9955.14}{10033.27}\right) - \left(\frac{2842.44}{2835.17}\right) = -0.0104$$

Adjusting for the notional principal, the market value is \$60,000,000(–0.0104) = –\$624,000.

4.3 Some Concluding Comments on Swap Valuation

Let us review some important results on swap valuation and pricing. Because the market value of the swap when initiated is zero, pricing the swap means to find the terms of the swap that will make its market value be zero. If the swap pays a fixed rate, we must find the fixed rate that makes the present value of the fixed payments equal the present value of the floating payments. If both sides of the swap involve floating payments, there are no terms to determine. For currency swaps, we also have to determine the notional principal in one currency that is equivalent to a given notional principal in another currency.

The market value of a swap starts off at zero but changes to either a positive or negative value as the swap evolves through its life and market conditions change. To determine the market value of a swap, we must determine the present value of the remaining stream of payments, netting one against the other.

The market value of a swap gives a number that represents what the swap is worth to each party. If the market value is positive, the swap is like an asset. The amount due to one party is worth more than the amount that party owes. If it is negative, the swap is like a liability. The amount that party owes is worth more than the amount owed to it. The market value of a swap is also sometimes known as the **replacement value**. This notion views the swap as an instrument whose value can potentially be lost through default. If a party is holding a positive value swap and the other party defaults, that value is lost and would require that amount of money to replace it. We discuss this point further in Section 7.

5 VARIATIONS OF SWAPS

So far we have covered the most common types of swaps: fixed-for-floating interest rate swaps, various combinations of fixed and floating currency swaps, and equity swaps involving fixed payments, floating payments, or the returns on another equity. We must also mention some other types of swaps.

We briefly referred to the **basis swap**, in which both sides pay a floating rate. A typical basis swap involves one party paying LIBOR and the other paying the T-bill rate. As we learned in the reading on futures markets and contracts, the term *basis* refers to the spread between two prices, usually the spot and futures prices. Here it is simply the spread between two rates, LIBOR and the T-bill rate. Because LIBOR is always more than the T-bill rate, the two parties negotiate a fixed spread such that the party paying LIBOR actually pays LIBOR minus the spread.[21] LIBOR is the borrowing rate of high-quality London banks, and the T-bill rate is the default-free borrowing rate of the U.S. government. The difference between LIBOR and the T-bill rate is thus a reflection of investors' perception of the general level of credit risk in the market. Basis swaps are usually employed for speculative purposes by end users who believe the spread between LIBOR and the T-bill rate will change.[22] A basis swap of this type is, therefore, usually a position taken in anticipation of a change in the relative level of credit risk in the market. As noted, both sides are floating, and typically both sides use 360-day years in their calculations.[23]

Another type of swap we sometimes encounter is not all that different from a plain vanilla or basis swap. In a **constant maturity swap**, one party pays a fixed rate, or a short-term floating rate such as LIBOR, and the other party pays a floating rate that is the rate on a security known as a **constant maturity treasury (CMT)** security. The transaction is also sometimes known as a CMT swap. This underlying instrument is a hypothetical U.S. Treasury note, meaning that its maturity is in the 2- to 10-year range, with a constant maturity. Obviously the reference to a particular CMT cannot be referring to a single note, because the maturity of any security decreases continuously. As mentioned, the note is hypothetical. For example, for a two-year CMT security, when there is an actual two-year note, that note is the CMT security. Otherwise, the yield on a CMT security is interpolated from the yields of securities with surrounding maturities. The distinguishing characteristic of a constant maturity swap is that the maturity of the underlying security exceeds the length of the settlement period. For example, a CMT swap might call for payments every six months, with the rate based on the one-year CMT security. In contrast, a standard swap settling every six months would nearly always be based on a six-month security. Otherwise, however, a constant maturity swap possesses the general characteristics of a plain vanilla swap.

---

21 Alternatively, the counterparty could pay the T-bill rate plus the spread.

22 The spread between LIBOR and the T-bill rate is called the TED spread. It is considered an indicator of the relative state of credit risk in the markets. LIBOR represents the rate on a private borrower (London banks); the T-bill rate is the U.S. government borrowing rate. When the global economy weakens, the TED spread tends to widen because rates based on the credit risk of private borrowers will increase while the U.S. government remains a risk-free borrower.

23 Of course, a basis swap need not be based on LIBOR and the T-bill rate, so other conventions can be used.

One interesting variant of an interest rate swap is an **overnight index swap (OIS)**. This instrument commits one party to paying a fixed rate as usual. The floating rate, however, is the cumulative value of a single unit of currency invested at an overnight rate during the settlement period. The overnight rate changes daily. This instrument is used widely in Europe but not in the United States.

Amortizing and accreting swaps are those in which the notional principal changes according to a formula related to the underlying. The more common of the two is the amortizing swap, sometimes called an **index amortizing swap**. In this type of interest rate swap, the notional principal is indexed to the level of interest rates. The notional principal declines with the level of interest rates according to a predefined schedule. This feature makes the swap similar to certain asset-backed securities, such as mortgage-backed securities, which prepay some of their principal as rates fall. An index amortizing swap is often used to hedge this type of security.

Diff swaps combine elements of interest rate, currency, and equity swaps. In a typical diff swap, one party pays the floating interest rate of one country and the other pays the floating interest rate of another country. Both sets of payments, however, are made in a single currency. So one set of payments is based on the interest rate of one country, but the payment is made in the currency of another country. This swap is a pure play on the interest rate differential between two countries and is basically a currency swap with the currency risk hedged. Alternatively, in equity diff swaps, the return on a foreign stock index is paid in the domestic currency.

An **arrears swap** is a special type of interest rate swap in which the floating payment is set at the end of the period and the interest is paid at that same time. This procedure stands in contrast to the typical interest rate swap, in which the payment is set on one settlement date and the interest is paid on the next settlement date.

In a **capped swap**, the floating payments have a limit as to how high they can be. Similarly, a **floored swap** has a limit on how low the floating payments can be.

There is no limit to the number of variations that can be found in swaps, and it is not worthwhile to examine them beyond the basic, most frequently used types. We must, however, cover an important variation of a swap that combines elements of both swaps and options.

SWAPTIONS 6

A **swaption** *is an option to enter into a swap.* Although swaptions can be designed in a variety of ways, we shall focus exclusively on the most widely used swaption, the plain vanilla interest rate swaption. This is a swaption to pay the fixed rate and receive the floating rate or the other way around. It allows the holder to establish a fixed rate on the underlying swap in advance and have the option of entering into the swap with that fixed rate or allowing the swaption to expire and entering into the swap at the fixed rate that prevails in the market.

6.1 Basic Characteristics of Swaptions

The two types of swaptions are a **payer swaption** and a **receiver swaption**. A payer swaption allows the holder to enter into a swap as the fixed-rate payer and floating-rate receiver. A receiver swaption allows the holder to enter into a swap as the fixed-rate receiver and floating-rate payer. Therefore, these terms refer to the fixed rate and are comparable to the terms *call* and *put* used for other types of options. Although it is not apparent at this point, a payer swaption is a put and a receiver swaption is a call.

Swaptions have specific expiration dates. Like ordinary options, swaptions can be European style (exercisable only at expiration) or American style (exercisable at any time prior to expiration). A swaption is based on a specific underlying swap. For example, consider a European payer swaption that expires in two years and allows the holder to enter into a three-year swap with semiannual payments every 15 January and 15 July. The payments will be made at the rate of 6.25 percent and will be computed using the 30/360 adjustment. The underlying swap is based on LIBOR, and the notional principal is $10 million. Of course, a swaption has a price or premium, which is an amount paid by the buyer to the seller up front.

Note that this swaption expires in two years and the underlying swap expires three years after that. This arrangement is called a 2 × 5 swaption, a terminology we used in explaining FRAs. The underlying can be viewed as a five-year swap at the time the swaption is initiated and will be a three-year swap when the swaption expires.

Finally, there are a number of ways to settle a swaption at expiration. Recall that ordinary options can allow for either physical delivery or cash settlement. We will explore the comparable concepts for swaptions in Section 6.3.

6.2 Uses of Swaptions

Swaptions have a variety of purposes. Now, however, we take a brief glance at why swaptions exist.

Swaptions are used by parties who anticipate the need for a swap at a later date but would like to establish the fixed rate today, while providing the flexibility to not engage in the swap later or engage in the swap at a more favorable rate in the market. These parties are often corporations that expect to need a swap later and would like to hedge against unfavorable interest rate moves while preserving the flexibility to gain from favorable moves.

Swaptions are used by parties entering into a swap to give them the flexibility to terminate the swap. In Section 1.2, we discussed why a party engaged in a swap might wish to terminate it before expiration. Suppose the party in a swap is paying fixed and receiving floating. If it owned a receiver swaption, it could exercise the swaption, thereby entering into a swap to receive a fixed rate and pay a floating rate. It would then have offset the floating parts of the swap, effectively removing any randomness from the position.[24] But the only way the party could do so would require having previously purchased a swaption. Similarly, parties engaged in a receive-fixed, pay-floating swap can effectively offset it by exercising a payer swaption.

Swaptions are used by parties to speculate on interest rates. As with any interest rate sensitive instrument, swaptions can be used to speculate. Their prices move with interest rates and, like all options, they contain significant leverage. Thus, they are appropriate instruments for interest rate speculators.

6.3 Swaption Payoffs

When a swaption is exercised, it effectively creates a stream of equivalent payments, commonly referred to in the financial world as an annuity. This stream is a series of interest payments equal to the difference between the exercise rate and the market rate on the underlying swap when the swaption is exercised.

24 Note, however, that both swaps are still in effect even though the floating sides offset. Because both swaps remain in effect, there is credit risk on the two transactions.

Consider a European payer swaption that expires in two years and is exercisable into a one-year swap with quarterly payments, using 90/360 as the day-count adjustment. The exercise rate is 3.60 percent. The notional principal is $20 million. Now, suppose we are at the swaption expiration and the term structure is the one we obtained when pricing the interest rate swap earlier in this reading. We repeat that information here:

Maturity (Days)	Rate (%)	Discount Factor
90	3.45	0.9914
180	3.58	0.9824
270	3.70	0.9730
360	3.75	0.9639

Under these conditions, we found that the swap fixed payment is 0.0092, equating to an annual fixed rate of 3.68 percent.

The holder of the swaption has the right to enter into a swap to pay 3.60 percent, whereas in the market such a swap would require payment at a rate of 3.68 percent. Therefore, here at expiration this swaption does appear to offer an advantage over the market rate. Let us consider the three possible ways to exercise this swaption.

The holder can exercise the swaption, thereby entering into a swap to pay 3.60 percent. The quarterly payment at the rate of 3.60 percent would be $20,000,000(0.0360)(90/360) = $180,000. The swaption holder would then be engaged in a swap to pay $180,000 quarterly and receive LIBOR. The first floating payment would be at 3.45 percent[25] and would be $20,000,000(0.0345)(90/360) = $172,500. The remaining floating payments would, of course, be determined later. The payment stream is illustrated in Exhibit 8, Panel A.

Alternatively, the holder can exercise the swaption, thereby entering into a swap to pay 3.60 percent, and then enter into a swap in the market to receive fixed and pay floating. The fixed rate the holder would receive is 3.68 percent, the market-determined fixed rate at the time the swaption expires. The quarterly fixed payment at 3.68 percent would be $20,000,000(0.0368)(90/360) = $184,000. Technically, the LIBOR payments are still made, but the same amount is paid and received. Hence, they effectively offset. Panel B illustrates this payment stream. This arrangement would be common if the counterparty to the second swap is not the same as the counterparty to the swaption.

The holder can arrange to receive a net payment stream of $184,000 –$180,000 = $4,000. Panel C illustrates this payment stream. In this case, the counterparty to the second swap is probably the same as the counterparty to the swap created by exercising the swaption, who would be the counterparty to the swaption. Because the floating payments are eliminated, the amount of cash passing between the parties is reduced, which mitigates the credit risk.

25 The first floating payment is at 3.45 percent because this is the 90-day rate in effect at the time the swap is initiated.

Exhibit 8 Cash Flows from Swaptions

A. Exercise of Payer Swaption, Entering into a Pay-Fixed, Receive-Floating Swap

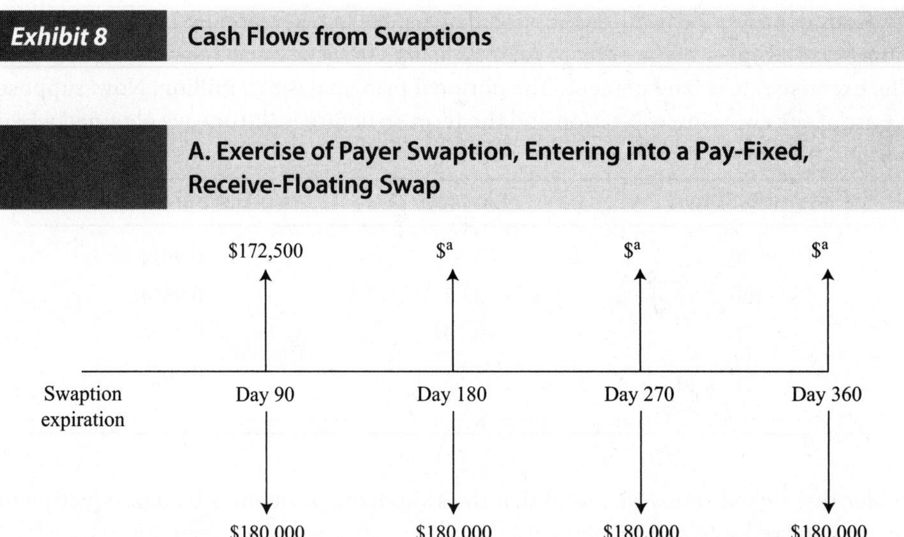

[a]Computed as $20,000,000(L)90/360, where L is LIBOR on the previous settlement date.

B. Exercise of Payer Swaption, Entering into a Pay-Fixed, Receive-Floating Swap and Entering into a Receive-Fixed, Pay-Floating Swap at the Market Rate

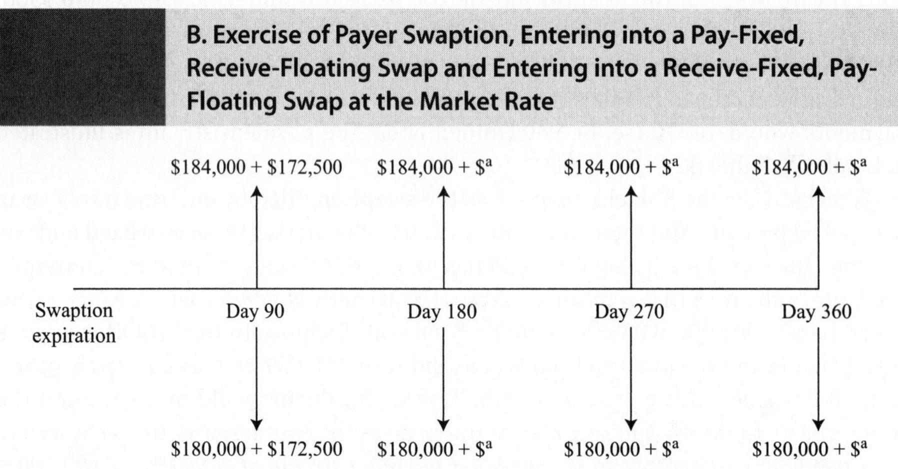

[a]Computed as $20,000,000(L)90/360, where L is LIBOR on the previous settlement date.

C. Exercise of Swaption with Offsetting Swap Netted

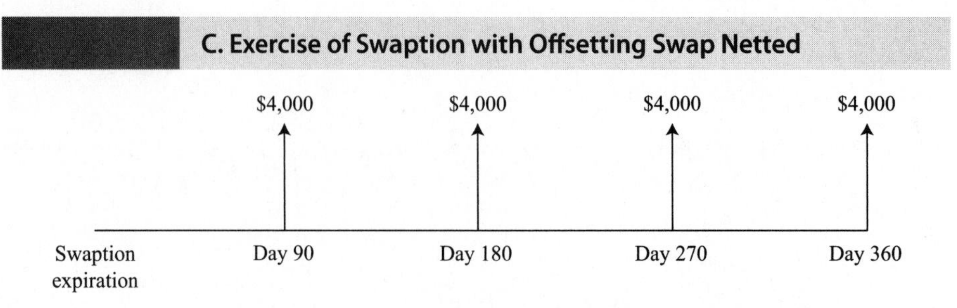

Exhibit 8 (Continued)

D. Cash Settlement

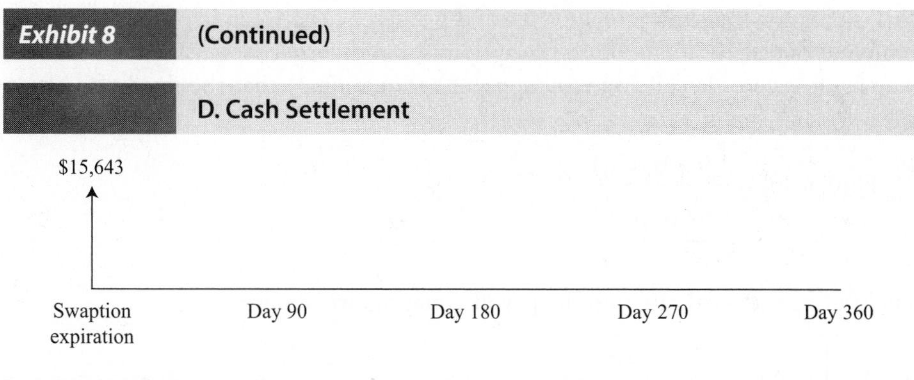

The holder can receive an up-front cash payment. We can easily determine the amount. It is simply the present value of the payment stream shown in Panel C, which we can obtain using the discount factors shown above:

$$\$4{,}000(0.9914 + 0.9824 + 0.9730 + 0.9639) = \$15{,}643$$

This pure cash settlement is illustrated in Panel D.

Other than transaction costs and the credit risk associated with the newly created swaps, each of these means of exercising a swaption has the same value. Of course, the two parties would have to agree up front which of these means to use at expiration. Cash settlement is the most common.

Therefore, the payoff of a payer swaption in which the exercise rate is x and the market rate on the underlying swap is FS(0,n,m) is

$$\text{Max}\left[0, \text{FS}(0, \text{n}, \text{m}) - \text{x}\right]\sum_{j=1}^{n} B_0(h_j) \quad (3)$$

Similarly, the payoff of a receiver swaption would be

$$\text{Max}\left[0, \text{x} - \text{FS}(0, \text{n}, \text{m})\right]\sum_{j=1}^{n} B_0(h_j) \quad (4)$$

Of course, these figures would be multiplied by the actual notional principal. So we see that a swaption effectively creates an annuity. The present value factors are not relevant in determining whether the swaption will be exercised. Exercise is determined solely on the relationship between the swap rate at expiration and the exercise rate. The present value factors are used to convert the stream of net payments obtained upon exercise of the swap into a current value. Now, let us take a brief look at how a swaption is priced.

6.4 Pricing and Valuation of Swaptions

We shall show here, perhaps somewhat surprisingly, that an interest rate swaption is like an option on a coupon bond. Restating our result given above, the payoff of a payer swaption is

$$\text{Max}\left[0, \text{FS}(0, \text{n}, \text{m}) - \text{x}\right]\sum_{j=1}^{n} B_0(h_j)$$

This expression finds the present value of the difference between the fixed rate on the swap and the exercise rate on the swaption if that difference is positive. Otherwise, the payoff is zero. Recall from Section 4.2.1 (Equation 1) that the fixed rate on an interest rate swap is

$$FS(0, n, m) = \frac{1.0 - B_0(h_n)}{\sum_{j=1}^{n} B_0(h_j)}$$

Substituting the fixed rate into the payoff equation, we obtain

$$\text{Max}\left[0, \frac{1.0 - B_0(h_n)}{\sum_{j=1}^{n} B_0(h_j)} - x\right]\sum_{j=1}^{n} B_0(h_j)$$

which can be rewritten as

$$\text{Max}\left\{0, 1.0 - \left[x\sum_{j=1}^{n} B_0(h_j) + B_0(h_N)\right]\right\}$$

Note the term in brackets,

$$x\sum_{j=1}^{n} B_0(h_j) + B_0(h_N)$$

which is the same as the market value at the swaption expiration of a coupon bond of $1.00 par value, in which the coupon is x. Thus, the swaption pay-off is effectively Max(0,1.0 –Market value of coupon bond). This amount is the payoff of a put option on a coupon bond with coupon of x, a face value of 1.0, and a maturity of the swap expiration date. The exercise price is the par value of 1.0, and the exercise rate of the swaption is the coupon rate on the bond. Hence, we can value the swaption as though it were simply a put on a bond. In a similar manner, the payoff of a receiver swaption can be shown to be that of a call option on this coupon bond.

Now you can see why, as we stated earlier, a payer swaption is a put option and a receiver swaption is a call option. More specifically, a payer swaption is a put option on a bond and a receiver swaption is a call option on a bond.

EXAMPLE 7

Calculate the market value of a receiver swaption at the expiration if the exercise rate is 8 percent and the term structure is given below:

Days	Rate (%)
180	7.2
360	8.0

These are the same rates as in Example 4. The swaption is on a swap that will make payments in 180 and 360 days, and the notional principal is $25 million. Also, show that this payoff is equivalent to that of a call option on a bond.

Solution:

Based on a fixed rate of 0.0392 from Example 4, the market value is Max(0,0.04 −0.0392)(0.9653 + 0.9259) = 0.0015.

Based on a notional principal of \$25 million, this is a market value of 25,000,000(0.0015) = \$37,500.

This payoff is equivalent to that of a call option on a bond with an exercise price of 1.0, its par value. At this point in time, the expiration of the option, the bond on which this call is based, would have a market value of 0.04(0.9653 + 0.9259) + 1.0(0.9259) = 1.0015.

Therefore, the payoff of a call on this bond is Max(0,1.0015 –1.0) = 0.0015—the same as that of the swaption.

With that result in mind, we could value the swaption using any of a number of approaches to valuing bond options. We shall not take up the pricing of swaptions here, as it is a somewhat advanced topic and the issues are somewhat complicated. It is not a straightforward matter to apply the Black–Scholes–Merton or Black models to pricing bond options. We discussed the valuation of options on bonds in the reading on option markets and contracts, noting that the binomial model is probably the best way to do so.

6.5 Forward Swaps

We have seen in this volume that options represent rights and forward contracts represent commitments. Just as there are options to enter swaps, there are also forward contracts to enter into swaps, called **forward swaps**. They are not as widely used as swaptions but do offer the advantage, as is always the case with forwards, that one does not have to pay any cash up front as with an option premium. Forward swaps are priced by pricing the swap off of the forward term structure instead of the spot term structure.

CREDIT RISK AND SWAPS

7

In this reading, we have mentioned on a few occasions that swaps are subject to credit risk. Indeed, as we have emphasized throughout the volume, *all* over-the-counter derivatives are subject to credit risk. In this section, we examine some of the issues involved in the credit risk of swaps.

Recall that a swap has zero market value at the start. It starts off as neither an asset nor a liability. Once the swap is engaged and market conditions change, the market value becomes positive for one party and negative for the other. The party holding the positive value swap effectively owns an asset, which represents a claim against the counterparty. This claim is a netting of the amount owed by the counterparty and the amount that the party owes, with the former exceeding the latter. The party holding the positive-value swap thus assumes credit risk. The counterparty could declare bankruptcy, leaving the party holding the positive-value swap with a claim that is subject to the legal process of bankruptcy. In most swap arrangements, netting is legally recognized, so the claim has a value based on the net amount. Of course, as we described in the reading, currency swaps are generally not netted, so the credit risk is greater on currency swaps.

The party to which the swap has a negative value is not subject to credit risk. It owes more than is owed to it, so the other party faces the risk.

During the life of the swap, however, the market value to a given party can change from positive to negative or vice versa. Hence, the party not facing credit risk at a given moment is not entirely free of risk, because the swap value could turn positive for it later.

The timing of credit risk is in the form of immediate or **current credit risk** and deferred or **potential credit risk**. The former arises when a payment is immediately due and cannot be made by one party. The latter reflects the ever-present possibility that, although a counterparty may currently be able to make payments, it may be unable to make future payments.

Let us work through an example illustrating these points. Consider two parties A and B who are engaged in a swap. At a given payment date, the payment of Party A to Party B is $100,000 and the payment of Party B to Party A is $35,000. As is customarily the case, Party A must pay $65,000 to Party B. Once the payment is made, we shall assume that the market value of the swap is $1,250,000, which is an asset to A and a liability to B.

Suppose Party A is unable to pay and declares bankruptcy. Then Party B does not make any payment to Party A. Party A is bankrupt, but the swap is an asset to A. Given the $65,000 owed by A to B, the claim of A against B is $1,250,000 – $65,000 = $1,185,000. We emphasize in this example that A is the bankrupt party, but the swap is an asset to A, representing its claim against B. If B were holding the positive market value of the swap, it would have a claim of $1,250,000 + $65,000 = $1,315,000 on A as A enters into the bankruptcy process.

Let us change the example a little by having A not be bankrupt on the payment date. It makes its payment of $65,000 to B and moves forward. But a few months later, before the next payment, A declares bankruptcy. Its payment is not immediately due, but it has essentially stated that it will not make its next payment or any payments thereafter. To determine the financial implications of the event, the two parties must compute the market value of the swap. Suppose the value is now $1,100,000 and is positive to A. Then A, the bankrupt party, holds a claim against B of $1,100,000. The fact that A is bankrupt does not mean that it cannot have a claim against someone else, just as a bankrupt corporation can be owed money for inventory it has sold but on which it has not yet collected payment.

Of course, A could be bankrupt and B's claim against A could be the greater. In fact, with A bankrupt, there is a very good possibility that this scenario would be the case. Then, of course, B would simply be another of A's many creditors.

Exactly what happens to resolve these claims in each of these situations is a complex legal issue and is beyond the scope of our level of treatment. In addition, the bankruptcy laws vary somewhat around the world, so the potential exists for different treatments of the same situation. Most countries do recognize the legality of netting, however, so it would be rare that a party would be able to claim the full amount owed it without netting out the amount it owes.

The credit risk in a swap varies during its life. An interest rate or equity swap has no final principal payments. The credit risk in either of these swap types is greater during the middle of its life. This occurs because near the end of the life of the swap, not many payments remain, so there is not much money at risk. And at the beginning of the life of the swap, the credit risk is usually low because the parties would probably not engage in the swap if a great deal of credit risk already were present at the start. Therefore, the greatest potential for credit losses is during the middle of the life of the swap. For currency swaps, in which the notional principals are typically exchanged at the end of the life of the swap, the credit risk is concentrated between the middle and the end of its life.

The parties that engage in swaps are generally of good credit quality, but the fear of default is still a significant concern. Yet, perhaps surprisingly, the rates that all parties pay on swaps are the same, regardless of either party's credit quality. As we have illustrated here, a plain vanilla swap, in which one party pays a floating rate and the other pays a fixed rate, has the fixed rate determined by the term structure for that underlying rate. Therefore, if a party wanted to engage in a swap to pay LIBOR and receive a fixed rate, it would get the fixed rate based on the LIBOR term structure, regardless of its credit quality or that of the counterparty, provided that the two parties agreed to do the transaction. Implicit in the fixed rate, however, is the spread between LIBOR and the default-free rate. As we described earlier in the reading, swap rates are quoted with respect to a spread over the equivalent default-free rate. Thus, a one-year swap rate of 3.68 percent as in our example might be quoted as 50 basis points over the rate on a one-year U.S. Treasury note, implying that the one-year U.S. Treasury note rate was 3.18 percent. This differential is called the **swap spread**.

It is important to note that the swap spread is not a measure of the credit risk on a given swap but rather a reflection of the general level of credit risk in the global economy. The LIBOR term structure reflects the borrowing rate for London banks, which are generally highly rated but not default free. Whenever a recession approaches or credit concerns arise, this spread widens and fixed-rate payers on swaps end up paying more. Of course, floating-rate payers end up paying more as well, but the additional cost to them is less obvious up front because the floating rates change over the life of the swap.

So all parties pay the same rate, but clearly some parties are better credit risks than others. In addition, virtually no parties are default free, and many are of lower credit quality than the typical London bank on which LIBOR is based. How do parties manage the credit risk in swaps? There are a number of methods, which we shall discuss in more detail in the reading on using credit derivatives to enhance return and manage risk. For right now, however, we cover one such method that we have seen before with respect to forward contracts and that is routinely used in the futures market: marking to market.

Reconsider the interest rate swap we covered earlier in the reading in which the payments are made quarterly in the amount of 0.0092 per $1 notional principal. The swap lasts for one year, so there are four payments. Suppose the parties agree to mark the contract to market halfway through its life—that is, in six months, immediately after the payment is made. Suppose we are at that point and the term structure is as follows:

$$L_{180}(90) = 0.0390$$

$$L_{180}(180) = 0.0402$$

Note that we are at day 180, and the upcoming payments occur in 90 and 180 days. We thus need to calculate $B_{180}(270)$ and $B_{180}(360)$. These present value factors are

$$B_{180}(270) = \frac{1}{1 + 0.039(90/360)} = 0.9903$$

$$B_{180}(360) = \frac{1}{1 + 0.0402(180/360)} = 0.9803$$

Now we can compute the market value of the swap. The present value of the remaining fixed payments, plus the hypothetical notional principal, is 0.0092(0.9903 + 0.9803) + 1.0(0.9803) = 0.9984.

Because the 90-day floating rate is 3.90 percent, the next floating payment will be 0.0390(90/360) = 0.00975. Of course, we do not know the last floating payment, but it does not matter because the present value of the remaining floating payments, plus hypothetical notional principal, is automatically 1.0 because we are on the coupon reset date. Therefore, the market value of the swap to the party receiving floating and paying fixed is the present value of the floating payments, 1.0, minus the present value of the fixed payments, 0.9984, or 1.0 – 0.9984 = 0.0016.

If the two parties marked this swap to market, the party paying floating and receiving fixed would pay the other party a lump sum cash payment of \$0.0016 per \$1 notional principal. The two parties would then reprice the swap. The new payment would be

$$FS(0, n, m) = FS(0,2,90) = \frac{1 - 0.9803}{0.9903 + 0.9803} = 0.01$$

Thus, the fixed payment would be 0.01 for the rest of the swap.

EXAMPLE 8

Consider a two-year swap to pay a fixed rate and receive a floating rate with semiannual payments. The fixed rate is 0.0462. Now, 360 days later, the term structure is

Days	Rate (%)
180	10.1
360	10.4

The next floating payment will be 0.045. The swap calls for marking to market after 180 days, and, therefore, will now be marked to market. Determine the market value, identify which party pays which, and calculate the new fixed rate.

Solution:

First find the discount factors:

$$B_{360}(540) = \frac{1}{1 + 0.101(180/360)} = 0.9519$$

$$B_{360}(720) = \frac{1}{1 + 0.104(360/360)} = 0.9058$$

The market value of the fixed payments plus \$1 hypothetical notional principal is 0.0462(0.9519 + 0.9058) + 1.0(0.9058) = 0.9916.

The market value of the floating payments plus \$1 hypothetical notional principal is 1.045(0.9519) = 0.9947.

Therefore, the market value to the party paying fixed and receiving floating is 0.9947 −0.9916 = 0.0031.

This amount would be paid by the party paying floating and receiving fixed. The new fixed rate would then be

$$\frac{1 - 0.9058}{0.9519 + 0.9058} = 0.0507$$

This rate would be quoted as an annual rate of 5.07%(360/180) = 10.14%.

As in the futures market, marking a swap contract to market results in the two parties terminating the contract and automatically engaging in a new swap. In essence, the arrangement commits the two parties to terminating the swap and reestablishing it on a predetermined schedule. This process reduces the credit risk by requiring one party to pay the other any amount due at a time prior to the expiration date of the swap. The effect is to reduce the extent to which the swap can go deeply underwater to one of the parties, who may be facing financial problems.

THE ROLE OF SWAP MARKETS

8

In each of the preceding three readings, we have discussed the role played by the markets represented by the various derivative instruments. The swap market is extremely large, consisting of dealers and end users engaging in customized transactions that involve a series of payments. As we showed in this reading, swaps can be equivalent to various other derivative instruments. Moreover, we used transactions in assets to replicate swaps. Hence, an obvious question is why swaps exist when the same results can be obtained using other instruments.

First let us ignore the obvious counter-question of why other instruments exist when swaps serve the same purpose. In the race to see which derivative instrument is more popular, swaps have clearly won. We can only surmise the reason why.

The tremendous popularity of swaps results largely from the popularity of interest rate swaps. For several reasons, these instruments have been embraced by corporations as tools for managing interest rate risk. One is that interest rate swaps, certainly the plain vanilla type, are simple instruments, rarely requiring technology, computational skills, or financial know-how beyond what exists in most corporate treasury offices. In short, they are easy to understand. In addition, interest rate swaps can easily be viewed as a pair of loans. Borrowing and lending money is second nature to corporations. Corporations view engaging in swaps as nothing more than an extension of their regular practice of borrowing and lending money. Many corporations are restricted in their use of options and futures, but they can usually justify swaps as nothing more than variations of loans. Also, swaps are so easily tailored to alter the interest rate patterns on most corporate loans that they seem to go hand in hand with the typical fixed- and floating-rate loans that corporations take out. Many corporations borrow money and combine the loan with a swap right from the start. Finally, we should note that some dealer firms have exploited the attractions of swaps by aggressive selling. In some cases, corporations entered into ill-advised and occasionally complex, exotic swaps. We do not suggest that most dealers have engaged in unethical actions (although some certainly have) but rather that, as in all sales-oriented activities, customers do not always get impartial advice from sales personnel. In some cases, corporations have used swaps to step over the line from good risk management into speculation on risks they know nothing about. In short, at least part of the success of swaps has probably not been for the right reasons.

But using swaps for the wrong reason does not sufficiently explain the success of these instruments. If it were the primary motivation for their use, swaps would die out as a risk management tool. Instead, swaps have grown in popularity. Swaps provide a mechanism for managing the risks associated with a series of payments. Although forward contracts and other instruments can manage that risk, a swap is more of a portfolio approach to managing risk—a package of risk management tools all rolled up into one. Given that risk often exists in a series, swaps are ideal instruments for managing it. Other instruments may be able to do the job, but they must be carefully constructed with a certain amount of financial ingenuity.

SUMMARY

OPTIONAL SEGMENT

- Swaps are over-the-counter contracts in which two parties agree to pay a series of cash flows to each other. At least one series is floating or variable and related to an interest rate, exchange rate, equity price, or commodity price; the other can be fixed or floating. Swaps have zero value at the start and have payments made on scheduled payment or settlement dates and a final termination or expiration date. When swap payments are made in the same currency, the payments are usually netted. Swaps are subject to default on the part of either party.

- Swaps can be terminated by having one party pay the market value of the swap to the other party, by entering into a swap in which the variable payments offset, by selling the swap to another party, or by exercising a swaption to enter into an offsetting swap.
- In a currency swap, each party makes payments to the other in different currencies. A currency swap can have one party pay a fixed rate in one currency and the other pay a fixed rate in the other currency; have both pay a floating rate in their respective currencies; have the first party pay a fixed rate in one currency and the second party pay a floating rate in the other currency; or have the first party pay a floating rate in one currency and the second pay a fixed rate in the other currency. In currency swaps, the notional principal is usually exchanged at the beginning and at the end of the life of the swap, although this exchange is not mandatory.
- The payments on a currency swap are calculated by multiplying the notional principal by the fixed or floating interest rate times a day-count adjustment. This procedure is done in each currency, and the respective parties make their separate payments to each other. The payments are not netted.
- In a plain vanilla interest rate swap, one party makes payments at a fixed rate and the other makes payments at a floating rate, with no exchange of notional principal. A typical plain vanilla swap involves one party paying a fixed rate and the other paying a floating rate such as LIBOR. Swaps are often done by a party borrowing floating at a rate tied to LIBOR; that party then uses a pay-fixed, receive-floating swap to offset the risk of its exposure to LIBOR and effectively convert its loan to a fixed-rate loan.
- The payments on an interest rate swap are calculated by multiplying the notional principal by the fixed or floating interest rate times a day-count adjustment. The respective amounts are netted so that the party owing the greater amount makes a net payment to the other.
- The three types of equity swaps involve one party paying a fixed rate, a floating rate, or the return on another equity, while the other party pays an equity return. Therefore, an equity swap is a swap in which at least one party pays the return on a stock or stock index.
- The equity payment (or payments, if both sides of the swap are related to an equity return) on an equity swap is calculated by multiplying the return on the stock over the settlement period by the notional principal. If there is a fixed or floating payment, it is calculated in the same manner as in an interest rate swap. With payments in a single currency, the two sets of payments are netted.

END OPTIONAL SEGMENT

- Swap pricing means to determine the fixed rate and any relevant terms, such as the foreign notional principal on a currency swap, at the start of the swap. Valuation means to determine the market value of the swap, which is the present value of one stream of payments less the present value of the other stream of payments. The market value of a swap is zero at the start but will change to positive for one party and negative for the other during the life of the swap, as market conditions change and time passes.
- Swaps can be viewed as combinations of assets. Currency swaps are like issuing a bond denominated in one currency and using the proceeds to buy a bond denominated in another currency. Interest rate swaps are like issuing a fixed-rate bond and using the proceeds to buy a floating-rate bond or vice versa. Equity swaps are like issuing a bond and using the proceeds to buy stock or vice

versa. Equity swaps with both sides paying an equity return are like selling short one stock and using the proceeds to buy another stock. The stock position is not, however, a buy-and-hold position and requires some rebalancing.

- An interest rate swap is like a series of off-market FRAs, meaning that the rate on each FRA is set at the swap rate, not at the rate it would be set at if priced as an FRA with zero market value at the start. In addition, the first payment on a swap is just an exchange of known amounts of cash. Currency swaps and equity swaps are similar to forward contracts, but the connection is not as straightforward as in interest rate swaps.
- Interest rate swaps are like being long (short) interest rate calls and short (long) interest rate puts. Currency swaps and equity swaps are also similar to combinations of options, but the connection is not as straightforward.
- The fixed rate on an interest rate swap equates the present value of the fixed payments plus a hypothetical notional principal to the present value of the floating payments plus a hypothetical notional principal. The notional principals offset but permit these swaps to be treated like bonds. The fixed rate is then equivalent to the fixed rate on a par bond with the same payments as on the swap. The market value of the swap during its life is found by determining the difference in the market values of the floating- and fixed-rate bonds later during their lives under the new term structure.
- The fixed rates on a currency swap are the same as the fixed rates on plain vanilla interest rate swaps in the given countries. The foreign notional principal for a domestic notional principal of one unit is the inverse of the exchange rate. In other words, it is the foreign currency equivalent of the domestic notional principal. Because a currency swap is like issuing a bond in one currency and using the proceeds to buy a bond in another currency, the market value of a currency swap during its life is found by determining the difference in the market values of the two bonds during their lives using the new term structures in the two countries. The foreign bond value must be converted to its domestic equivalent by using the new exchange rate.
- The fixed rate on an equity swap is the same as the fixed rate on a plain vanilla interest rate swap. The market value of an equity swap involving fixed or floating payments during its life is found as the present value of the equity payments less the present value of the fixed or floating payments necessary to replicate the equity swap payment. The market value of an equity swap in which both sides make equity payments is the market value of a long position in one equity and a short position in the other, assuming the positions are liquidated at each settlement date and gains and losses are paid out.
- A swaption is an option to enter into a swap. The two types of interest rate swaptions are payer swaptions, which allow the holder to enter into a swap to pay the fixed rate and receive the floating rate, and receiver swaptions, which allow the holder to enter into a swap to receive the fixed rate and pay the floating rate. Swaptions are based on a specific underlying swap and have an exercise rate and an expiration date. At expiration, they can be exercised to enter into the underlying swap. Swaptions require an up-front premium.
- Swaptions exist to allow users the flexibility to enter into swaps at later dates but establish the terms in advance. If market conditions are not favorable to exercising a swaption, the holder can allow the swaption to expire and obtain more favorable terms by entering into a swap at the market rate. Swaptions are used by parties who anticipate a need to enter into a swap at a later date, who anticipate the need to terminate an already-existing swap, or who wish to speculate on interest rates.

- The payoffs of an interest rate swaption are like those of an option on a coupon-bearing bond. The option has an exercise price of par value, and the coupon rate is the exercise rate on the swaption. A payer swaption is like a put on the bond, and a receiver swaption is like a call on the bond.
- At expiration, an interest rate payer swaption is worth the maximum of zero or the present value of the difference between the market swap rate and the exercise rate, valued as an annuity extending over the remaining life of the underlying swap. To value a receiver swaption at expiration, we take the difference between the exercise rate and the market swap rate, adjusted for its present value over the life of the underlying swap. These figures must be multiplied by the notional principal.
- The market value of a swaption at expiration can be received in one of four ways: by exercising the swaption to enter into the underlying swap, by exercising the swaption and entering into an offsetting swap that keeps both swaps in force, by exercising the swaption and entering into an offsetting swap that eliminates both swaps and pays a series of payments equal to the net difference in the fixed rates on the two swaps, or by exercising the swaption and receiving a lump sum cash payment.
- A forward swap is a forward contract to enter into a swap. It commits both parties to entering into a swap at a later date at a fixed rate agreed on today. In contrast to a swaption, which is the right to enter into a swap, a forward swap is a binding commitment to enter into a swap.
- Credit risk arises in a swap due to the possibility that a party will not be able to make its payments. Current credit risk is the risk of a party being unable to make the upcoming payment. Potential credit risk is the risk of a party being unable to make future payments. Credit risk is faced only by the party that is owed the greater amount.
- The credit risk in an interest rate or equity swap is greatest during the middle of the swap's life. The risk is small at the beginning of the swap because the parties would not engage in the swap if the credit risk were significant at the start. The risk is low at the end of the life of the swap because of the small number of remaining payments. For currency swaps, the payment of notional principal shifts the credit risk more toward the end of the life of the swap. In addition, because the payments are typically not netted, the credit risk on currency swaps is greater than on interest rate swaps.
- The swap spread is the difference between the fixed rate on a swap and the yield on a default-free security of the same maturity as the swap. The spread indicates the average credit risk in the global economy but not the credit risk in a given swap.
- Netting reduces the credit risk in a swap by reducing the amount of money passing from any one party to another. The amount owed by a party is deducted from the amount due to a party, and only the net is paid. Marking a swap to market is a process in which the parties agree to periodically calculate the market value of the swap and have the party owing the greater amount pay the market value to the other party. The fixed rate is then reset on the swap until it is marked to market again or terminates. This procedure forces the party to which the swap is losing money to pay the other party before getting too deeply in debt.
- Swaps play an important role in the financial system by providing a simple means of managing a series of risks. Their popularity has arisen largely from corporate use in managing interest rate exposure.

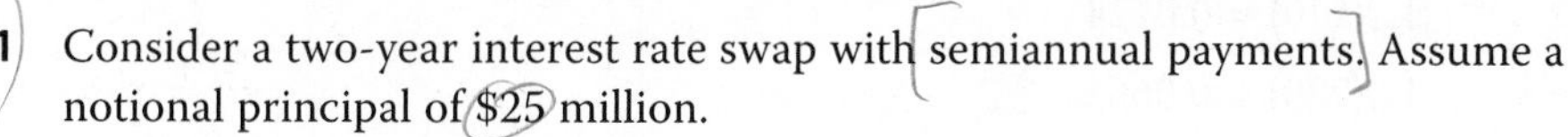

PRACTICE PROBLEMS

1 Consider a two-year interest rate swap with semiannual payments. Assume a notional principal of $25 million.

A Calculate the annualized fixed rate on the swap. The current term structure of LIBOR interest rates is as follows:

$$L_0(180) = 0.0585$$
$$L_0(360) = 0.0605$$
$$L_0(540) = 0.0624$$
$$L_0(720) = 0.0665$$

B Calculate the market value of the swap 120 days later 1) from the point of view of the party paying the floating rate and receiving the fixed rate and 2) from the point of view of the party paying the fixed rate and receiving the floating rate. The term structure 120 days later is as follows:

$$L_{120}(60) = 0.0613$$
$$L_{120}(240) = 0.0629$$
$$L_{120}(420) = 0.0653$$
$$L_{120}(600) = 0.0697$$

2 Consider a one-year interest rate swap with quarterly payments. Assume a notional principal of $15 million.

A Calculate the annualized fixed rate on the swap. The current term structure of LIBOR interest rates is as follows:

$$L_0(90) = 0.0656$$
$$L_0(180) = 0.0640$$
$$L_0(270) = 0.0621$$
$$L_0(360) = 0.0599$$

B Calculate the market value of the swap 30 days later 1) from the point of view of the party paying the floating rate and receiving the fixed rate and 2) from the point of view of the party paying the fixed rate and receiving the floating rate. The term structure 30 days later is as follows:

$$L_{30}(60) = 0.0384$$
$$L_{30}(150) = 0.0379$$
$$L_{30}(240) = 0.0382$$
$$L_{30}(330) = 0.0406$$

3 Consider a two-year currency swap with semiannual payments. The domestic currency is the U.S. dollar, and the foreign currency is the U.K. pound. The current exchange rate is $1.41 per pound.

A Calculate the annualized fixed rates for dollars and pounds. The current U.S. term structure is the same as in Problem 1, Part A:

$L_0(180) = 0.0585$
$L_0(360) = 0.0605$
$L_0(540) = 0.0624$
$L_0(720) = 0.0665$

The U.K. term structure is

$L_0^£(180) = 0.0493$
$L_0^£(360) = 0.0505$
$L_0^£(540) = 0.0519$
$L_0^£(720) = 0.0551$

B Now move forward 120 days. The new exchange rate is $1.35 per pound, and the new U.S. term structure is the same as in Problem 1, Part B:

$L_{120}(60) = 0.0613$
$L_{120}(240) = 0.0629$
$L_{120}(420) = 0.0653$
$L_{120}(600) = 0.0697$

The new U.K. term structure is

$L_{120}^£(60) = 0.0517$
$L_{120}^£(240) = 0.0532$
$L_{120}^£(420) = 0.0568$
$L_{120}^£(600) = 0.0583$

Assume that the notional principal is $1 or the corresponding amount in British pounds. Calculate the market values of the following swaps:

i. Pay £ fixed and receive $ fixed.
ii. Pay £ floating and receive $ fixed.
iii. Pay £ floating and receive $ floating.
iv. Pay £ fixed and receive $ floating.

4 Consider a one-year currency swap with quarterly payments. The domestic currency is the U.S. dollar, and the foreign currency is the euro. The current exchange rate is $0.86 per euro.

A Calculate the annualized fixed rates for dollars and euros. The current U.S. term structure is the same as in Problem 2, Part A:

$L_0(90) = 0.0656$
$L_0(180) = 0.0640$
$L_0(270) = 0.0621$
$L_0(360) = 0.0599$

The Euribor term structure is

$$L_0(90) = 0.0682$$
$$L_0(180) = 0.0673$$
$$L_0(270) = 0.0661$$
$$L_0(360) = 0.0668$$

B Now move forward 30 days. The new exchange rate is \$0.82 per euro, and the new U.S. term structure is the same as in Problem 2, Part B:

$$L_{30}(60) = 0.0384$$
$$L_{30}(150) = 0.0379$$
$$L_{30}(240) = 0.0382$$
$$L_{30}(330) = 0.0406$$

The new Euribor term structure is

$$L_{30}^{€}(60) = 0.0583$$
$$L_{30}^{€}(150) = 0.0605$$
$$L_{30}^{€}(240) = 0.0613$$
$$L_{30}^{€}(330) = 0.0651$$

Assume that the notional principal is \$1 or the corresponding amount in euros. Calculate the market values of the following swaps:

i. Pay € fixed and receive \$ fixed.

ii. Pay € floating and receive \$ fixed.

iii. Pay € floating and receive \$ floating.

iv. Pay € fixed and receive \$ floating.

5 Consider a one-year currency swap with semiannual payments. The two currencies are the U.K. pound and the euro. The current exchange rate is £0.61 per euro.

A Calculate the annualized fixed rates for pounds and euros. The current U.K. term structure is

$$L_0^{£}(180) = 0.0623$$
$$L_0^{£}(360) = 0.0665$$

The Euribor term structure is

$$L_0^{€}(180) = 0.0563$$
$$L_0^{€}(360) = 0.0580$$

B Now move forward 60 days. The new exchange rate is £0.57 per euro, and the new British term structure is

$$L_{60}^{£}(120) = 0.0585$$
$$L_{60}^{£}(300) = 0.0605$$

The new Euribor term structure is

$$L_{60}^{€}(120) = 0.0493$$
$$L_{60}^{€}(300) = 0.0505$$

Assume that the notional principal is £1 or the corresponding amount in euros. Calculate the market values in pounds of the following swaps:

i. Pay £ fixed and receive € fixed.

ii. Pay £ floating and receive € fixed.

iii. Pay £ floating and receive € floating.

iv. Pay £ fixed and receive € floating.

6 An asset manager wishes to enter into a two-year equity swap in which he will receive the rate of return on the S&P 500 Index in exchange for paying a fixed interest rate. The S&P 500 stock index is at 1150.89 at the beginning of the swap. The swap calls for semiannual payments.

A Calculate the annualized fixed rate on the swap. The current term structure of interest rates is as follows:

$$L_0(180) = 0.0458$$
$$L_0(360) = 0.0528$$
$$L_0(540) = 0.0624$$
$$L_0(720) = 0.0665$$

B Calculate the market value of the swap 160 days later if the new term structure is

$$L_{160}(20) = 0.0544$$
$$L_{160}(200) = 0.0629$$
$$L_{160}(380) = 0.0679$$
$$L_{160}(560) = 0.0697$$

The S&P 500 is at 1204.10. The notional principal of the swap is $100 million.

7 Assume an asset manager enters into a one-year equity swap in which he will receive the return on the NASDAQ 100 Index in return for paying a floating interest rate. The swap calls for quarterly payments. The NASDAQ 100 is at 1561.27 ninety days later, and the rate $L_{90}(90)$ is 0.0432. Calculate the market value of the swap 100 days from the beginning of the swap if the NASDAQ 100 is at 1595.72 and the term structure is

$$L_{100}(80) = 0.0427$$
$$L_{100}(170) = 0.0481$$
$$L_{100}(260) = 0.0544$$

The notional principal of the swap is $50 million.

8 Consider an equity swap in which the asset manager receives the return on the Russell 2000 Index in return for paying the return on the DJIA. At the inception of the equity swap, the Russell 2000 is at 478.19 and the DJIA is at 9867.33. Calculate the market value of the swap a few months later when the Russell 2000 is at 524.29 and the DJIA is at 10016. The notional principal of the swap is $15 million.

9 Consider a European receiver swaption that expires in one year and is on a two-year swap that will make semiannual payments. The swaption has an exercise rate of 7 percent. The notional principal is $50 million. At expiration, the term structure of interest rates is as follows:

$L_0(180) = 0.0420$
$L_0(360) = 0.0474$
$L_0(540) = 0.0544$
$L_0(720) = 0.0661$

A List the four possible ways this swaption could be exercised, and indicate the relevant cash flows in each case.

B Show that the payoff on the swaption is equivalent to that of a call option on a bond with exercise price of $1 (the par value of the bond).

10 Consider a European payer swaption that expires in one year and is on a two-year swap that will make semiannual payments. The swaption has an exercise rate of 5 percent. The notional principal is $10 million. At expiration, the term structure of interest rates is as follows:

$L_0(180) = 0.0583$
$L_0(360) = 0.0605$
$L_0(540) = 0.0614$
$L_0(720) = 0.0651$

A List the four possible ways this swaption could be exercised, and indicate the relevant cash flows in each case.

B Show that the payoff on the swaption is equivalent to that of a put option on a bond with exercise price of $1 (the par value of the bond).

11 Consider a European receiver swaption that expires in two years and is on a one-year swap that will make quarterly payments. The swaption has an exercise rate of 6.5 percent. The notional principal is $100 million. At expiration, the term structure of interest rates is as follows:

$L_0(90) = 0.0373$
$L_0(180) = 0.0429$
$L_0(270) = 0.0477$
$L_0(360) = 0.0538$

A Calculate the market value of the swaption at expiration.

B Show that the payoff is equivalent to that of a call option on a bond with exercise price of $1 (the par value of the bond).

12 A two-year swap with semiannual payments pays a floating rate and receives a fixed rate. The term structure at the beginning of the swap is

$L_0(180) = 0.0583$
$L_0(360) = 0.0616$
$L_0(540) = 0.0680$
$L_0(720) = 0.0705$

In order to mitigate the credit risk of the parties engaged in the swap, the swap will be marked to market in 180 days. Suppose it is now 180 days later and the swap is being marked to market. The new term structure is

$$L_{180}(180) = 0.0429$$
$$L_{180}(360) = 0.0538$$
$$L_{180}(540) = 0.0618$$

A Calculate the market value of the swap per \$1 notional principal and indicate which party pays which.

B Calculate the new fixed rate on the swap at which the swap would proceed after marking to market.

13 A one-year swap with quarterly payments pays a fixed rate and receives a floating rate. The term structure at the beginning of the swap is

$$L_0(90) = 0.0252$$
$$L_0(180) = 0.0305$$
$$L_0(270) = 0.0373$$
$$L_0(360) = 0.0406$$

In order to mitigate the credit risk of the parties engaged in the swap, the swap will be marked to market in 90 days. Suppose it is now 90 days later and the swap is being marked to market. The new term structure is

$$L_{90}(90) = 0.0539$$
$$L_{90}(180) = 0.0608$$
$$L_{90}(270) = 0.0653$$

A Calculate the market value of the swap per \$1 notional principal and indicate which party pays which.

B Calculate the new fixed rate on the swap at which the swap would proceed after marking to market.

The following information relates to Questions 14–19

Meredith Gale, an analyst at a money management firm, is preparing for a meeting with clients to discuss using equity options and interest rate swaptions as investment and hedging vehicles. Gale plans to focus on three major issues: 1) the implications of put–call parity for identifying and exploiting arbitrage opportunities, 2) valuing options by using binomial pricing models, and 3) the application and pricing of interest rate swaptions.

Allison Burke, a summer intern, is helping Gale prepare for the meeting. Based on her research on put–call parity and swaption valuation, Burke makes the following statements:

Statement #1 "Based on put–call parity, an arbitrage opportunity is indicated when the price of the protective put is greater than the price of the fiduciary call."

Statement #2 "Using put–call parity, you can create a long position in a synthetic underlying asset by combining long positions in a call option, a risk-free bond, and a put option."

Statement #3 "Using put–call parity, you can also create synthetic options on forward contracts. The data in Exhibit 1 can be used to establish the price of such a synthetic put."

Exhibit 1 Market Data for Options on Forward Contracts

Call price	$7.50
Put price	$18.00
Exercise price	$55.00
Days to option expiration	175
Days in year	365
Forward price	$46.00
Annualized risk-free rate	4.00%
Market value of forward contract	$0.00

Burke also examines the valuation of call options with a one-period binomial pricing model. She uses the information in Exhibit 2, which applies to a non-dividend-paying stock whose price could rise by 12 percent or fall by 15 percent over one year. Based on a one-period binomial model, she calculates the price of a call option on this stock to be $7.44 and concludes that an arbitrage opportunity is available.

Exhibit 2 Market Data for Option on Non-Dividend-Paying Stock

Annualized risk-free rate	4.00%
Exercise price	$45
Current stock market price	$50
Current call option market price	$7.75

Note: One call is exercisable for one share.

In addition, Gale must address the following situations of two clients:

Client 1 has asked Gale to value the following European-style, interest rate payer swaption:

- The payer swaption was entered into one year ago and is maturing today.
- The payer swaption is on a two-year swap that will make semi-annual payments.
- The payer swaption has an exercise rate of 5.10 percent and a notional principal of $15 million.
- Based on the data in Exhibit 3, the annualized fixed payment on the swap underlying the payer swaption is 6.20 percent.

Exhibit 3 Term Structure of Interest Rates at Expiration of Swaptions

Days	Rate	Discount Factor
180	0.0583	0.9717
360	0.0605	0.9430
540	0.0614	0.9157
720	0.0651	0.8848

Finally, Gale meets with Client 2, who last year purchased an interest rate swap in which he pays fixed and receives floating. Now, Client 2 would like to know the type of interest rate swaption contract to buy in order to have the flexibility to remove interest rate uncertainty from his interest rate swap position.

14 To exploit the arbitrage condition described in Burke's Statement #1, two of the actions that are necessary, but not sufficient, are:

A sell the put and sell the underlying asset.

B sell the put and sell the appropriate risk-free bond.

C buy the call and buy the underlying asset.

15 Is Burke's Statement #2 correct?

A Yes.

B No, because the appropriate combination is a long position in a call option, a long position in a risk-free bond, and a short position in a put option.

C No, because the appropriate combination is a long position in a put option, a short position in a risk-free bond, and a short position in a call option.

16 The price of the synthetic put in Statement #3 is *closest* to:

A $15.48.

B $16.33.

C $18.00.

17 Based on Exhibit 2 and Burke's valuation of the call option, an appropriate set of arbitrage transactions is to:

A sell 1,000 calls and buy 815 shares.

B sell 815 calls and buy 1,000 shares.

C buy 1,000 calls and sell 815 shares.

18 Based on the data in Exhibit 3, the market value of the European-style, interest rate payer swaption at expiration is *closest* to:

A $307,000.

B $330,000.

C $465,000.

19 To remove Client 2's interest rate uncertainty, Gale is *most likely* to recommend buying a:

A payer swaption that would allow Client 2 the option to enter into a swap to pay floating and receive fixed.

B receiver swaption that would allow Client 2 the option to enter into a swap to receive floating and pay fixed.

C receiver swaption that would allow Client 2 the option to enter into a swap to receive fixed and pay floating.

SOLUTIONS

1 A The present value factors for 180, 360, 540, and 720 days are as follows:

$$B_0(180) = \frac{1}{1 + 0.0585(180/360)} = 0.9716$$

$$B_0(360) = \frac{1}{1 + 0.0605(360/360)} = 0.9430$$

$$B_0(540) = \frac{1}{1 + 0.0624(540/360)} = 0.9144$$

$$B_0(720) = \frac{1}{1 + 0.0665(720/360)} = 0.8826$$

The semiannual fixed rate (or payment per \$1 of notional principal) is calculated as

$$FS(0, n, m) = FS(0,4,180) = \frac{1 - 0.8826}{0.9716 + 0.9430 + 0.9144 + 0.8826}$$
$$= 0.0316$$

The annualized fixed rate (or payment per \$1 of notional principal) is 0.0316(360/180) = 0.0632. Because the notional principal is \$25,000,000, the semiannual fixed payment is 25,000,000(0.0316) = \$790,000.

B The new present value factors for 60, 240, 420, and 600 days are as follows:

$$B_{120}(180) = \frac{1}{1 + 0.0613(60/360)} = 0.9899$$

$$B_{120}(360) = \frac{1}{1 + 0.0629(240/360)} = 0.9598$$

$$B_{120}(540) = \frac{1}{1 + 0.0653(420/360)} = 0.9292$$

$$B_{120}(720) = \frac{1}{1 + 0.0697(600/360)} = 0.8959$$

The present value of the remaining fixed payments plus the \$1 hypothetical notional principal is 0.0316(0.9899 + 0.9598 + 0.9292 + 0.8959) + 1(0.8959) = 1.0152.

The present value of the floating payments plus the hypothetical \$1 notional principal is 1.0293(0.9899) = 1.0189, where

- 1.0293 is the first floating payment, 0.0585(180/360) + 1, which is the market value of the remaining payments plus the \$1 notional principal, and
- 0.9899 is the discount factor.

Based on a notional principal of \$25,000,000, the market value of the swap to the pay-floating, receive-fixed party is (1.0152 – 1.0189) 25,000,000 = –\$92,500. Thus, the market value of the swap to opposite party that pays fixed and receives floating is \$92,500.

2 A The present value factors for 90, 180, 270, and 360 days are as follows:

$$B_0(90) = \frac{1}{1 + 0.0656(90/360)} = 0.9839$$

$$B_0(180) = \frac{1}{1 + 0.0640(180/360)} = 0.9690$$

$$B_0(270) = \frac{1}{1 + 0.0621(270/360)} = 0.9555$$

$$B_0(360) = \frac{1}{1 + 0.0599(360/360)} = 0.9435$$

The quarterly fixed rate (or payment per $1 of notional principal) is calculated as

$$FS(0, n, m) = FS(0{,}4{,}90) = \frac{1 - 0.9435}{0.9839 + 0.9690 + 0.9555 + 0.9435}$$
$$= 0.0147$$

The annualized fixed rate (or payment per $1 of notional principal) is 0.0147(360/90) = 0.0588. Because the notional principal is $15,000,000, the quarterly fixed payment is 15,000,000(0.0147) = $220,500.

B The new present value factors for 60, 150, 240, and 330 days are as follows:

$$B_{30}(90) = \frac{1}{1 + 0.0384(60/360)} = 0.9936$$

$$B_{30}(180) = \frac{1}{1 + 0.0379(150/360)} = 0.9845$$

$$B_{30}(270) = \frac{1}{1 + 0.0382(240/360)} = 0.9752$$

$$B_{30}(360) = \frac{1}{1 + 0.0406(330/360)} = 0.9641$$

The present value of the remaining fixed payments plus the $1 notional principal is 0.0147(0.9936 + 0.9845 + 0.9752 + 0.9641) + 1(0.9641) = 1.0217.

The present value of the floating payments plus hypothetical $1 notional principal is 1.0164(0.9936) = 1.0099, where

- 1.0164 is the first floating payment, 0.0656(90/360) + 1, which is the market value of the remaining payments plus the $1 notional principal, and
- 0.9936 is the discount factor.

Based on a notional principal of $15,000,000, the market value of the swap to the pay-floating, receive-fixed party is (1.0217 – 1.0099)15,000,000 = $177,000. Thus, the market value of the swap to the pay-fixed, receive-floating party is –$177,000.

3 A First calculate the fixed payment in dollars. The dollar present value factors for 180, 360, 540, and 720 days are as follows:

$$B_0(180) = \frac{1}{1 + 0.0585(180/360)} = 0.9716$$

$$B_0(360) = \frac{1}{1 + 0.0605(360/360)} = 0.9430$$

$$B_0(540) = \frac{1}{1 + 0.0624(540/360)} = 0.9144$$

$$B_0(720) = \frac{1}{1 + 0.0665(720/360)} = 0.8826$$

The semiannual fixed payment per $1 of notional principal is calculated as

$$FS(0, n, m) = FS(0,4,180) = \frac{1 - 0.8826}{0.9716 + 0.9430 + 0.9144 + 0.8826}$$
$$= 0.0316$$

The annualized fixed payment per $1 of notional principal is calculated as 0.0316(360/180) = 0.0632.

Now calculate the fixed payment in pounds. The pound present value factors for 180, 360, 540, and 720 days are as follows:

$$B_0^{£}(180) = \frac{1}{1 + 0.0493(180/360)} = 0.9759$$

$$B_0^{£}(360) = \frac{1}{1 + 0.0505(360/360)} = 0.9519$$

$$B_0^{£}(540) = \frac{1}{1 + 0.0519(540/360)} = 0.9278$$

$$B_0^{£}(720) = \frac{1}{1 + 0.0551(720/360)} = 0.9007$$

The semiannual fixed payment per £1 of notional principal is calculated as

$$FS(0, n, m) = FS(0,4,180) = \frac{1 - 0.9007}{0.9759 + 0.9519 + 0.9278 + 0.9007}$$
$$= 0.0264$$

The annualized fixed payment per £1 of notional principal is calculated as 0.0264(360/180) = 0.0528.

B The new dollar discount factors for 60, 240, 420, and 600 days are as follows:

$$B_{120}(180) = \frac{1}{1 + 0.0613(60/360)} = 0.9899$$

$$B_{120}(360) = \frac{1}{1 + 0.0629(240/360)} = 0.9598$$

$$B_{120}(540) = \frac{1}{1 + 0.0653(420/360)} = 0.9292$$

$$B_{120}(720) = \frac{1}{1 + 0.0697(600/360)} = 0.8959$$

The present value of the remaining fixed payments plus the $1 notional principal is 0.0316(0.9899 + 0.9598 + 0.9292 + 0.8959) + 1(0.8959) = 1.0152.

The present value of the floating payments plus hypothetical $1 notional principal discounted back 120 days is 1.0293(0.9899) = 1.0189, where

- 1.0293 is the first floating payment, 0.0585(180/360) + 1, which is the market value of the remaining payments plus the \$1 notional principal, and
- 0.9899 is the discount factor.

The new pound discount factors for 60, 240, 420, and 600 days are as follows:

$$B_{120}^{\pounds}(180) = \frac{1}{1 + 0.0517(60/360)} = 0.9915$$

$$B_{120}^{\pounds}(360) = \frac{1}{1 + 0.0532(240/360)} = 0.9657$$

$$B_{120}^{\pounds}(540) = \frac{1}{1 + 0.0568(420/360)} = 0.9379$$

$$B_{120}^{\pounds}(720) = \frac{1}{1 + 0.0583(600/360)} = 0.9114$$

The present value of the remaining fixed payments plus the £1 notional principal is 0.0264(0.9915 + 0.9657 + 0.9379 + 0.9114) + 1(0.9114) = 1.0119. Convert this amount to the equivalent of \$1 notional principal; that is, 1/\$1.41: 1.0119(1/1.41) = £0.7177. Now convert to dollars at the current exchange rate \$1.35/£: 0.7177(1.35) = \$0.9688.

The present value of the floating payments plus hypothetical £1 notional principal is 1.0247(0.9915) = 1.016, where

- 1.0247 is the first floating payment, 0.0493(180/360) + 1, which is the market value of the remaining payments plus the £1 notional principal, and
- 0.9915 is the discount factor.

Convert this amount to the equivalent of \$1 notional principal; that is, 1/\$1.41: 1.016(1/1.41) = £0.7206. Now convert to dollars at the current exchange rate \$1.35/£: 0.7206(1.35) = \$0.9728.

The market values based on notional principal of \$1 are as follows:

i. Pay £ fixed and receive \$ fixed = \$0.0464 = 1.0152 – 0.9688

ii. Pay £ floating and receive \$ fixed = \$0.0424 = 1.0152 – 0.9728

iii. Pay £ floating and receive \$ floating = \$0.0461 – 1.0189 – 0.9728

iv. Pay £ fixed and receive \$ floating = \$0.0501 = 1.0189 – 0.9688

4 A First calculate the fixed payment in dollars. The dollar present value factors for 90, 180, 270, and 360 days are as follows:

$$B_0(90) = \frac{1}{1 + 0.0656(90/360)} = 0.9839$$

$$B_0(180) = \frac{1}{1 + 0.0640(180/360)} = 0.9690$$

$$B_0(270) = \frac{1}{1 + 0.0621(270/360)} = 0.9555$$

$$B_0(360) = \frac{1}{1 + 0.0599(360/360)} = 0.9435$$

The quarterly fixed payment per \$1 of notional principal is calculated as

$$FS(0, n, m) = FS(0,4,90) = \frac{1 - 0.9435}{0.9839 + 0.9690 + 0.9555 + 0.9435}$$
$$= 0.0147$$

The annualized fixed payment per $1 of notional principal is 0.0147(360/90) = 0.0588.

Now calculate the fixed payment in euros. The euro present value factors for 90, 180, 270, and 360 days are as follows:

$$B_0^{€}(90) = \frac{1}{1 + 0.0682(90/360)} = 0.9832$$

$$B_0^{€}(180) = \frac{1}{1 + 0.0673(180/360)} = 0.9674$$

$$B_0^{€}(270) = \frac{1}{1 + 0.0661(270/360)} = 0.9528$$

$$B_0^{€}(360) = \frac{1}{1 + 0.0668(360/360)} = 0.9374$$

The quarterly fixed payment per €1 of notional principal is calculated as

$$FS(0, n, m) = FS(0,4,90) = \frac{1 - 0.9374}{0.9832 + 0.9674 + 0.9528 + 0.9374}$$
$$= 0.0163$$

The annualized fixed payment per €1 of notional principal is 0.0163(360/90) = 0.0652.

B The new dollar discount factors for 60, 150, 240, and 330 days are as follows:

$$B_{30}(90) = \frac{1}{1 + 0.0384(60/360)} = 0.9936$$

$$B_{30}(180) = \frac{1}{1 + 0.0379(150/360)} = 0.9845$$

$$B_{30}(270) = \frac{1}{1 + 0.0382(240/360)} = 0.9752$$

$$B_{30}(360) = \frac{1}{1 + 0.0406(330/360)} = 0.9641$$

The present value of the remaining fixed payments plus the $1 notional principal is 0.0147(0.9936 + 0.9845 + 0.9752 + 0.9641) + 1(0.9641) = 1.0217.

The present value of the floating payments plus hypothetical $1 notional principal is 1.0164(0.9936) = 1.0099, where

- 1.0164 is the first floating payment, 0.0656(90/360) + 1, which is the market value of the remaining payments plus the $1 notional principal, and
- 0.9936 is the discount factor.

The new euro discount factors for 60, 150, 240, and 330 days are as follows:

$$B_{30}^{€}(90) = \frac{1}{1 + 0.0583(60/360)} = 0.9904$$

$$B_{30}^{€}(180) = \frac{1}{1 + 0.0605(150/360)} = 0.9754$$

$$B_{30}^{€}(270) = \frac{1}{1 + 0.0613(240/360)} = 0.9607$$

$$B_{30}^{€}(360) = \frac{1}{1 + 0.0651(330/360)} = 0.9437$$

The present value of the remaining fixed payments plus the €1 notional principal is 0.0163(0.9904 + 0.9754 + 0.9607 + 0.9437) + 1(0.9437) = 1.0068. Convert this amount to the equivalent of $1 notional principal; that is, 1/$0.86: 1.0068(1/0.86) = €1.1707. Now convert to dollars at the current exchange rate of $0.82 per euro: 1.1707(0.82) = $0.96.

The present value of the floating payments plus hypothetical €1 notional principal is 1.0171(0.9904) = 1.0073, where

- 1.0171 is the first floating payment, 0.0682(90/360) + 1, which is the market value of the remaining payments plus the €1 notional principal, and
- 0.9904 is the discount factor.

Convert this amount to the equivalent of $1 notional principal; that is, 1/$0.86: 1.0073(1/0.86) = €1.1713. Now convert to dollars at the current exchange rate of $0.82 per euro: 1.1713(0.82) = $0.9605. The market values based on notional principal of $1 are:

i. Pay € fixed and receive $ fixed = $0.0617 = 1.0217 – 0.96

ii. Pay € floating and receive $ fixed = $0.0612 = 1.0217 – 0.9605

iii. Pay € floating and receive $ floating = $0.0494 = 1.0099 – 0.9605

iv. Pay € fixed and receive $ floating = $0.0499 = 1.0099 – 0.96

5 A First calculate the fixed payment in pounds. The pound present value factors for 180 and 360 days are as follows:

$$B_{0}^{£}(180) = \frac{1}{1 + 0.0623(180/360)} = 0.9698$$

$$B_{0}^{£}(360) = \frac{1}{1 + 0.0665(360/360)} = 0.9376$$

The semiannual fixed payment per £1 of notional principal is calculated as

$$FS(0, n, m) = FS(0,2,180) = \frac{1 - 0.9376}{0.9698 + 0.9376} = 0.0327$$

The annualized fixed payment per £1 of notional principal is calculated as 0.0327(360/180) = 0.0654.

Now calculate the fixed payment in euros. The euro present value factors for 180 and 360 days are as follows:

$$B_{0}^{€}(180) = \frac{1}{1 + 0.0563(180/360)} = 0.9726$$

$$B_{0}^{€}(360) = \frac{1}{1 + 0.0580(360/360)} = 0.9452$$

The quarterly fixed payment per €1 of notional principal is calculated as

$$FS(0, n, m) = FS(0,2,180) = \frac{1 - 0.9452}{0.9726 + 0.9452} = 0.0286$$

The annualized fixed payment per €1 of notional principal is 0.0286(360/180) = 0.0572.

B The new pound present value factors for 120 and 300 days are as follows:

$$B_{60}^{£}(180) = \frac{1}{1 + 0.0585(120/360)} = 0.9809$$

$$B_{60}^{£}(360) = \frac{1}{1 + 0.0605(300/360)} = 0.9520$$

The present value of the remaining fixed payments plus the £1 notional principal is 0.0327(0.9809 + 0.9520) + 1(0.9520) = 1.0152.

The present value of the floating payments plus hypothetical £1 notional principal is 1.0312(0.9809) = 1.0115, where

- 1.0312 is the first floating payment, 0.0623(180/360) + 1, which is the market value of the remaining payments plus the £1 notional principal, and
- 0.9809 is the discount factor.

The new euro discount factors for 120 and 300 days are as follows:

$$B_{60}^{€}(180) = \frac{1}{1 + 0.0493(120/360)} = 0.9838$$

$$B_{60}^{€}(360) = \frac{1}{1 + 0.0505(300/360)} = 0.9596$$

The present value of the remaining fixed payments plus the €1 notional principal is 0.0286(0.9838 + 0.9596) + 1(0.9596) = 1.0152. Convert this to the equivalent of £1 notional principal; that is, 1/£0.61: 1.0152(1/0.61) = €1.6643.

Now convert to pounds at the current exchange rate of £0.57 per euro: 1.6643(0.57) = £0.9487. The present value of the floating payments plus hypothetical €1 notional principal is 1.0282(0.9838) = 1.0115, where

- 1.0282 is the first floating payment, 0.0563(180/360) + 1, which is the market value of the remaining payments plus the €1 notional principal, and
- 0.9838 is the discount factor.

Convert this amount to the equivalent of £1 notional principal; that is, 1/£0.61: 1.0115(1/0.61) = €1.6582. Now convert to pounds at the current exchange rate of £0.57 per euro: 1.6582(0.57) = £0.9452. The market values based on notional principal of £1 are:

i. Pay £ fixed and receive € fixed = –£0.0665 = 0.9487 – 1.0152

ii. Pay £ floating and receive € fixed = –£0.0628 = 0.9487 – 1.0115

iii. Pay £ floating and receive € floating = –£0.0663 = 0.9452 – 1.0115

iv. Pay £ fixed and receive € floating = –£0.07 = 0.9452 – 1.0152

6 A The present value factors for 180, 360, 540, and 720 days are as follows:

$$B_0(180) = \frac{1}{1 + 0.0458(180/360)} = 0.9776$$

$$B_0(360) = \frac{1}{1 + 0.0528(360/360)} = 0.9499$$

$$B_0(540) = \frac{1}{1 + 0.0624(540/360)} = 0.9144$$

$$B_0(720) = \frac{1}{1 + 0.0665(720/360)} = 0.8826$$

The semiannual fixed payment per $1 of notional principal is calculated as

$$FS(0, n, m) = FS(0,4,180) = \frac{1 - 0.8826}{0.9776 + 0.9499 + 0.9144 + 0.8826}$$
$$= 0.0315$$

The annualized fixed payment per $1 of notional principal is 0.0315(360/180) = 0.0630.

B The new present value factors for 20, 200, 380, and 560 days are as follows:

$$B_{160}(180) = \frac{1}{1 + 0.0544(20/360)} = 0.9970$$

$$B_{160}(360) = \frac{1}{1 + 0.0629(200/360)} = 0.9662$$

$$B_{160}(540) = \frac{1}{1 + 0.0679(380/360)} = 0.9331$$

$$B_{160}(720) = \frac{1}{1 + 0.0697(560/360)} = 0.9022$$

The present value of the remaining fixed payments plus the $1 notional principal is 0.0315(0.9970 + 0.9662 + 0.9331 + 0.9022) + 1(0.9022) = 1.0219. The value of the equity payment is

$$\left(\frac{1204.10}{1150.89}\right) = 1.0462$$

Based on a notional principal of $100,000,000, the market value of a swap to pay the fixed and receive the equity return is (1.0462 – 1.0219)100,000,000 = $2,430,000.

7 The asset manager enters into the swap at time t = 0. After moving forward 100 days, the next floating payment is due on day 180—that is, 80 days from now. Based on the rate in effect on day 100, the present value factor is

$$B_{100}(180) = \frac{1}{1 + 0.0427(80/360)} = 0.9906$$

The next floating payment, based on the rate in effect on day 90, will be 0.0432(90/360) = 0.0108. The present value of the next floating payment plus the $1 market value of the remaining floating payments is 0.9906(1.0108) = 1.0013. The value of the equity payment is

$$\left(\frac{1595.72}{1561.27}\right) = 1.0221$$

Based on a notional principal of \$50 million, the market value of the swap to the party that pays floating and receives the equity return is (1.0221 – 1.0013)50,000,000 = \$1,040,000.

8 The value of the equity payment received on the Russell 2000 is

$$\left(\frac{524.29}{478.19}\right) = 1.0964$$

The value of the equity payment made on the DJIA is

$$\left(\frac{10016}{9867.33}\right) = 1.0151$$

Based on a notional principal of \$15 million, the market value of the swap to pay the return on the DJIA and receive the return on the Russell 2000 is (1.0964 – 1.0151)15,000,000 = \$1,219,500.

9 **A** The present value factors for 180, 360, 540, and 720 days are as follows:

$$B_0(180) = \frac{1}{1 + 0.042(180/360)} = 0.9794$$

$$B_0(360) = \frac{1}{1 + 0.0474(360/360)} = 0.9547$$

$$B_0(540) = \frac{1}{1 + 0.0554(540/360)} = 0.9246$$

$$B_0(720) = \frac{1}{1 + 0.0661(720/360)} = 0.8832$$

The semiannual fixed payment per \$1 of notional principal is calculated as

$$FS(0, n, m) = FS(0,4,180) = \frac{1 - 0.8832}{0.9794 + 0.9547 + 0.9246 + 0.8832}$$
$$= 0.0312$$

The annualized fixed payment per \$1 of notional principal is 0.0312(360/180) = 0.0624. Based on a notional principal of \$50,000,000, the four possible ways to exercise this swaption are:

i. Exercise the swaption, entering into a receive-fixed, pay-floating swap. The fixed receipt is (based on the exercise rate of 7 percent) \$50,000,000(0.07 × 180/360) \$1,750,000.

The first floating payment is (based on the 180-day rate of 4.20 percent in effect at the time the swap is initiated) \$50,000,000(0.0420 × 180/360) = \$1,050,000.

ii. Exercise the swaption, entering into a receive-fixed, pay-floating swap *and* entering into a pay-fixed, receive-floating swap at the market rate.

The fixed receipt is (based on the exercise rate of 7 percent) \$1,750,000.

The fixed payment is (based on the rate of 6.24 percent) \$50,000,000 (0.0624 × 180/360) = \$1,560,000.

The first floating payment and receipt of \$1,050,000 offset each other.

iii. Exercise the swaption with offsetting swap netted.

The holder would receive a net payment stream of \$1,750,000 – \$1,560,000 = \$190,000.

iv. The holder can choose to receive an up-front cash payment now of \$190,000 (0.9794 + 0.9547 + 0.9246 + 0.8832) = \$710,961.

B At expiration, the market value of a bond with face (exercise price) of \$1 and annual coupon 7 percent = (0.07 × 180/360)(0.9794 + 0.9547 + 0.9246 + 0.8832) + 1(0.8832) = 1.0142. The payoff on a call option on this bond with exercise price \$1 is Max [0,(1.0142 – 1)] = 0.0142. Based on notional principal of \$50,000,000, the payoff is \$50,000,000(0.0142) = \$710,000. This amount is the same as the payoff on the swaption computed in Part A (iv) above (the difference comes from rounding).

10 A The present value factors for 180, 360, 540, and 720 days are as follows:

$$B_0(180) = \frac{1}{1 + 0.0583(180/360)} = 0.9717$$

$$B_0(360) = \frac{1}{1 + 0.0605(360/360)} = 0.9430$$

$$B_0(540) = \frac{1}{1 + 0.0614(540/360)} = 0.9157$$

$$B_0(720) = \frac{1}{1 + 0.0651(720/360)} = 0.8848$$

The semiannual fixed payment per \$1 of notional principal is calculated as

$$FS(0, n, m) = FS(0,4,180) = \frac{1 - 0.8848}{0.9717 + 0.9430 + 0.9157 + 0.8848}$$
$$= 0.031$$

The annualized fixed payment per \$1 of notional principal is 0.031 (360/180) = 0.062.

Based on a notional principal of \$10,000,000, the four possible ways to exercise this payer swaption are:

i. Exercise the swaption, entering into pay-fixed and receive-floating swap.

The fixed payment is (based on the exercise rate of 5 percent) \$10,000,000 (0.05 × 180/360) = \$250,000.

The first floating receipt is (based on the 180-day rate in effect at the time the swap is initiated of 5.83 percent) \$10,000,000(0.0583 × 180/360) = \$291,500.

ii. Exercise the swaption, entering into pay-fixed and receive-floating swap, and entering into receive-fixed pay-floating swap at the market rate.

The fixed payment is (based on the exercise rate of 5 percent) \$250,000.

The fixed receipt is (based on the rate of 6.2 percent) \$10,000,000(0.062 × 180/360) = \$310,000.

The first floating payment and receipt of \$291,500 offset each other.

iii. Exercise the swaption with offsetting swap netted.

The holder would receive a net payment stream of \$310,000 – \$250,000 = \$60,000.

iv. The holder can choose to receive an up-front cash payment now of 60,000 (0.9717 + 0.9430 + 0.9157 + 0.8848) = \$222,912.

B At expiration, the market value of a bond with face (exercise price) of \$1 and annual coupon 5 percent = (0.05 × 180/360) (0.9717 + 0.9430 + 0.9157 + 0.8848) + 1(0.8848) = 0.9777. The payoff on a put option on this bond with exercise price \$1 is Max [0,(1 – 0.9777)] = 0.0223. The payoff based on a notional principal of \$10,000,000 is 0.0223 (10,000,000) = \$223,000. This amount is the same as the payoff on the swaption as computed in Part A (iv) above (the difference comes from rounding).

11 A The present value factors for 90, 180, 270, and 360 days are as follows:

$$B_0(90) = \frac{1}{1 + 0.0373(90/360)} = 0.9908$$

$$B_0(180) = \frac{1}{1 + 0.0429(180/360)} = 0.9790$$

$$B_0(270) = \frac{1}{1 + 0.0477(270/360)} = 0.9655$$

$$B_0(360) = \frac{1}{1 + 0.0538(360/360)} = 0.9489$$

The quarterly fixed payment per \$1 of notional principal is calculated as

$$FS(0, n, m) = FS(0,4,180) = \frac{1 - 0.9489}{0.9908 + 0.9790 + 0.9655 + 0.9489}$$
$$= 0.0132$$

The annualized fixed payment per \$1 of notional principal is 0.0132(360/90) = 0.0528. The market value at expiration of the receiver swaption is Max [0, [0.065 × (90/360) – 0.0132] (0.9908 + 0.9790 + 0.9655 + 0.9489) = 0.012. Based on notional principal of \$100,000,000, the market value is 100,000,000(0.012) = \$1,200,000.

B At expiration, the market value of a bond with face (exercise price) of \$1 and annual coupon of 6.5 percent is (0.065 × 90/360)(0.9908 + 0.9790 + 0.9655 + 0.9489) + 1(0.9489) = 1.012. The payoff on a call option on this bond with exercise price \$1 is Max [0, (1.012 – 1)] = 0.012. This is the same as the payoff on the swaption.

12 A The present value factors for 180, 360, 540, and 720 days are as follows:

$$B_0(180) = \frac{1}{1 + 0.0583(180/360)} = 0.9717$$

$$B_0(360) = \frac{1}{1 + 0.0616(360/360)} = 0.9420$$

$$B_0(540) = \frac{1}{1 + 0.0680(540/360)} = 0.9074$$

$$B_0(720) = \frac{1}{1 + 0.0705(720/360)} = 0.8764$$

The semiannual fixed payment per \$1 of notional principal is calculated as

$$FS(0, n, m) = FS(0,4,180) = \frac{1 - 0.8764}{0.9717 + 0.9420 + 0.9074 + 0.8764}$$
$$= 0.0334$$

The annualized fixed payment per \$1 of notional principal is calculated as 0.0334(360/180) = 0.0668.

The new present value factors for 180, 360, and 540 days are as follows:

$$B_{180}(360) = \frac{1}{1 + 0.0429(180/360)} = 0.9790$$

$$B_{180}(540) = \frac{1}{1 + 0.0583(360/360)} = 0.9489$$

$$B_{180}(720) = \frac{1}{1 + 0.0618(540/360)} = 0.9152$$

The present value of the remaining fixed payments plus the \$1 notional principal is 0.0334(0.9790 + 0.9489 + 0.9152) + 1(0.9152) = 1.0102.

Because we are on the payment date, the present value of the remaining floating payments plus hypothetical \$1 notional principal is automatically 1.0.

The market value of the swap to the pay-floating, receive-fixed party is (1.0102 – 1) = \$0.0102. So the market value of the swap to the pay-fixed, receive-floating party is –\$0.0102. Because the swap is marked to market, the party that pays floating will now receive \$0.0102 per \$1 of notional principal from the party that pays fixed. The two parties would then reprice the swap.

B The new fixed-rate payment per \$1 of notional principal is

$$FS(0, n, m) = FS(0,3,180) = \frac{1 - 0.9152}{0.9790 + 0.9489 + 0.9152}$$
$$= 0.0298$$

13 A The present value factors for 90, 180, 270, and 360 days are as follows:

$$B_0(90) = \frac{1}{1 + 0.0252(90/360)} = 0.9937$$

$$B_0(180) = \frac{1}{1 + 0.0305(180/360)} = 0.9850$$

$$B_0(270) = \frac{1}{1 + 0.0373(270/360)} = 0.9728$$

$$B_0(360) = \frac{1}{1 + 0.0406(360/360)} = 0.9610$$

The quarterly fixed payment per \$1 of notional principal is calculated as

$$FS(0, n, m) = FS(0,4,90) = \frac{1 - 0.9610}{0.9937 + 0.9850 + 0.9728 + 0.9610}$$
$$= 0.01$$

The annualized fixed payment per \$1 of notional principal is calculated as 0.01(360/90) = 0.04.

The new present value factors for 90, 180, and 270 days are as follows:

$$B_{90}(180) = \frac{1}{1 + 0.0539(90/360)} = 0.9867$$

$$B_{90}(270) = \frac{1}{1 + 0.0608(180/360)} = 0.9705$$

$$B_{90}(360) = \frac{1}{1 + 0.0653(270/360)} = 0.9533$$

The present value of the remaining fixed payments plus the \$1 notional principal is 0.01(0.9867 + 0.9705 + 0.9533) + 1(0.9533) = 0.9824.

Because we are on the payment date, the present value of the remaining floating payments plus hypothetical \$1 notional principal is automatically 1.0.

The market value of the swap to the pay-floating, receive-fixed party is (0.9824 – 1) = –\$0.0176. So, the market value of the swap to the pay-fixed, receive-floating party is \$0.0176. Because the swap is marked to market, the party that pays floating will now pay \$0.0176 per \$1 of notional principal to the party that pays fixed. The two parties would then reprice the swap.

B The new fixed-rate payment per \$1 of notional principal is

$$\mathrm{FS}(0,\mathrm{n},\mathrm{m}) = \mathrm{FS}(0,3,90) = \frac{1-0.9533}{0.9867+0.9705+0.9533} = 0.0160$$

14 A is correct. Burke's Statement #1 has the price of the protective put above that of the fiduciary call. Put–call parity establishes that the two should be equal. To exploit an arbitrage condition, one buys the (relatively) undervalued and sells the (relatively) overvalued. Thus, in this problem, one would sell the overvalued protective put (sell the put and sell the asset) and buy the undervalued fiduciary call (buy the call and buy the appropriate risk-free bond). Only answer A is a correct statement in exploiting this arbitrage.

15 B is correct. In Statement #2, Burke mischaracterizes put–call parity. Put–call parity is

$$P_0 + S_0 = C_0 + X/(1+r)^T$$

Solving for the underlying asset, $S_0 = C_0 + [X/(1 + r)^T] - P_0$.

Therefore, the synthetic long asset is a combination of long the call, long the risk-free bond, and short the put option.

16 B is correct. When dealing with forward contracts, as in Burke's Statement #3, put–call parity must be modified. Rather than shorting the stock, a forward contract is used. The current stock price, S_0, drops out of the formula and is replaced by the present value of the forward price. That is:

$$P_0 = C_0 + [X - F(0,T)]/(1+r)^T$$

Substituting the values from Exhibit 1:

$$P_0 = 7.5 + (55 - 46)/(1.04)^{(175/365)} = \$16.33$$

17 A is correct. Burke has valued the call at \$7.44. Exhibit 2 reports the market price of the call is \$7.75. The call is overvalued from Burke's perspective. To arbitrage this difference, Burke should sell calls and buy the underlying shares. Thus, the answer is either A or B. Next, consider the question of how many calls per share to form the arbitrage. Note these facts: the delta of a call is the change in value of the call for a unit (\$1.00) change in the value of the stock. Deltas range from + 1.00 (very deep in the money) to 0.00 (very far out of the money). Ignoring very deep in the money options where the hedge is one underlying asset to one call, in order to form a delta-neutral hedge, one needs more calls (on a per unit basis) than underlying assets.

Confirmation comes from solving the binomial model for the given values. The expiration date values for the stock are \$56 (up 12%) or \$42.5 (down 15%). Assume one borrows the present value of \$42.50 at time zero. The payoffs at expiration from a portfolio of long the stock and short the bond are zero in the down state (42.50 – 42.50) when the stock is sold and the bond (loan) paid off and $13.50 in the up state (56 – 42.50). The terminal values of the call with a strike of $45 are $11.00 in the up-state and $0.00 in the down-state. To make the expiration payoffs match, multiply the call payoffs by 13.50/11. To avoid arbitrage, for each share of stock bought one should sell 13.50/11 calls or for each call sold one should buy 11/13.50 stocks. For 1,000 calls, the replicating portfolio would need 815 shares of stock [(11/13.5) × 1,000].

18 A is correct. The value of the swaption is the sum of the present values of the related cash flows. The net cash flows reflect the fixed rate of 6.20%, adjusted for semi-annual payments, minus the exercise rate of 5.10%, adjusted for semi-annual payments, times the notional principal of $15 million. Thus, the semi-annual payments are [(0.062/2) – (0.051/2)] × $15,000,000 = $82,500. Find the PV of these cash flows at the given interest rates: $82,500 × (0.9717 + 0.9430 + 0.9157 + 0.8848) = $306,504.

19 C is correct. Under the terms of the swap Client 2 entered into last year, Client 2 is currently committed to paying fixed and receiving floating. By entering into a receiver swaption to receive fixed and pay floating, the client can offset the current swap commitment if future conditions make it attractive to do so.

READING

55

Interest Rate Derivative Instruments

by Frank J. Fabozzi, CFA

LEARNING OUTCOMES

Mastery	*The candidate should be able to:*
☐	**a.** demonstrate how both a cap and a floor are packages of 1) options on interest rates and 2) options on fixed-income instruments;
☐	**b.** calculate the payoff for a cap and a floor, and explain how a collar is created.

INTRODUCTION

1

OPTIONAL SEGMENT

In this reading we turn our attention to financial contracts that are popularly referred to as interest rate derivative instruments because they derive their value from some cash market instrument or reference interest rate. These instruments include futures, forwards, options, swaps, caps, and floors. In this reading we will discuss the basic features of these instruments and in the next we will see how they are valued.

Why would a portfolio manager be motivated to use interest rate derivatives rather than the corresponding cash market instruments? There are three principal reasons for doing this when there is a well-developed interest rate derivatives market for a particular cash market instrument. First, typically it costs less to execute a transaction or a strategy in the interest rate derivatives market in order to alter the interest rate risk exposure of a portfolio than to make the adjustment in the corresponding cash market. Second, portfolio adjustments typically can be accomplished faster in the interest rate derivatives market than in the corresponding cash market. Finally, interest rate derivatives may be able to absorb a greater dollar transaction amount without an adverse effect on the price of the derivative instrument compared to the price effect on the cash market instrument; that is, the interest rate derivative may be more liquid than the cash market. To summarize: There are three potential advantages that motivate the use of interest rate derivatives: cost, speed, and liquidity.

2 INTEREST RATE FUTURES

A **futures contract** is an agreement that requires a party to the agreement either to buy or sell something at a designated future date at a predetermined price. Futures contracts are products created by exchanges. Futures contracts based on a financial instrument or a financial index are known as **financial futures**. Financial futures can be classified as 1) stock index futures, 2) interest rate futures, and 3) currency futures. Our focus in this reading is on interest rate futures.

A. Mechanics of Futures Trading

A futures contract is an agreement between a buyer (seller) and an established exchange or its clearinghouse in which the buyer (seller) agrees to take (make) delivery of something (the **underlying**) at a specified price at the end of a designated period of time. The price at which the parties agree to transact in the future is called the futures price. The designated date at which the parties must transact is called the **settlement date** or delivery date.

1 *Liquidating a Position*

Most financial futures contracts have settlement dates in the months of March, June, September, and December. This means that at a predetermined time in the contract settlement month the contract stops trading, and a price is determined by the exchange for settlement of the contract. The contract with the closest settlement date is called the nearby futures contract. The next futures contract is the one that settles just after the nearby futures contract. The contract farthest away in time from settlement is called the most distant futures contract.

A party to a futures contract has two choices on liquidation of the position. First, the position can be liquidated prior to the settlement date. For this purpose, the party must take an offsetting position in the same contract. For the buyer of a futures contract, this means selling the same number of the identical futures contracts; for the seller of a futures contract, this means buying the same number of identical futures contracts.

The alternative is to wait until the settlement date. At that time the party purchasing a futures contract accepts delivery of the underlying at the agreed-upon price; the party that sells a futures contract liquidates the position by delivering the underlying at the agreed-upon price. For some interest rate futures contracts, settlement is made in cash only. Such contracts are referred to as cash settlement contracts.

2 *The Role of the Clearinghouse*

Associated with every futures exchange is a clearinghouse, which performs several functions. One of these functions is to guarantee that the two parties to the transaction will perform.

When an investor takes a position in the futures market, the clearinghouse takes the opposite position and agrees to satisfy the terms set forth in the contract. Because of the clearinghouse, the investor need not worry about the financial strength and integrity of the party taking the opposite side of the contract. After initial execution of an order, the relationship between the two parties ends. The clearinghouse interposes itself as the buyer for every sale and the seller for every purchase. Thus investors are free to liquidate their positions without involving the other party in the original contract, and without worrying that the other party may default. This is the reason that we define a futures contract as an agreement between a party and a clearinghouse associated with an exchange. Besides its guarantee function, the clearinghouse makes it simple for parties to a futures contract to unwind their positions prior to the settlement date.

3 *Margin Requirements*

When a position is first taken in a futures contract, the investor must deposit a minimum dollar amount per contract as specified by the exchange. This amount is called initial margin and is required as deposit for the contract. The initial margin may be in the form of an interest-bearing security such as a Treasury bill. As the price of the futures contract fluctuates, the value of the margin account changes. Marking to market means effectively replacing the initiation price with a current settlement price. The contract thus has a new settlement price. At the end of each trading day, the exchange determines the current settlement price for the futures contract. This price is used to mark to market the investor's position, so that any gain or loss from the position is reflected in the margin account.[1]

Maintenance margin is the minimum level (specified by the exchange) to which the margin account may fall to as a result of an unfavorable price movement before the investor is required to deposit additional margin. The additional margin deposited is called **variation margin**, and it is an amount necessary to bring the account back to its initial margin level. This amount is determined from the process of marking the position to market. Unlike initial margin, variation margin must be in cash, not interest-bearing instruments. Any excess margin in the account may be withdrawn by the investor. If a party to a futures contract who is required to deposit variation margin fails to do so within 24 hours, the futures position is closed out.

Although there are initial and maintenance margin requirements for buying securities on margin, the concept of margin differs for securities and futures. When securities are acquired on margin, the difference between the price of the security and the initial margin is borrowed from the broker. The security purchased serves as collateral for the loan, and the investor pays interest. For futures contracts, the initial margin, in effect, serves as "good faith" money, an indication that the investor will satisfy the obligation of the contract.

B. Forward Contracts

A **forward contract**, just like a futures contract, is an agreement for the future delivery of something at a specified price at the end of a designated period of time. Futures contracts are standardized agreements as to the delivery date (or month) and quality of the deliverable, and are traded on organized exchanges. A forward contract differs in that it is usually non-standardized (that is, the terms of each contract are negotiated individually between buyer and seller), there is no clearinghouse, and secondary markets are often non-existent or extremely thin. Unlike a futures contract, which is an exchange-traded product, a forward contract is an over-the-counter instrument.

Futures contracts are marked to market at the end of each trading day. Consequently, futures contracts are subject to interim cash flows as additional margin may be required in the case of adverse price movements, or as cash is withdrawn in the case of favorable price movements. A forward contract *may* or *may not be marked to market*, depending on the wishes of the two parties. For a forward contract that is *not* marked to market, there are no interim cash flow effects because no additional margin is required.

Finally, the parties in a forward contract are exposed to credit risk because either party may default on its obligation. This risk is called counterparty risk. This risk is minimal in the case of futures contracts because the clearinghouse associated with the exchange guarantees the other side of the transaction. In the case of a forward contract, both parties face counterparty risk. Thus, there exists bilateral counterparty risk.

1 For a further discussion of margin requirements and illustrations of how the margin account changes as the futures price changes, see Don M. Chance, *Analysis of Derivatives for the CFA Program* (Charlottesville, VA: Association for Investment Management and Research, 2003), pp. 86–91.

Other than these differences, most of what we say about futures contracts applies equally to forward contracts.

C. Risk and Return Characteristics of Futures Contracts

When an investor takes a position in the market by buying a futures contract, the investor is said to be in a long position or to be long futures. The buyer of the futures contract is also referred to as the "long." If, instead, the investor's opening position is the sale of a futures contract, the investor is said to be in a short position or to be short futures. The seller of the futures contract is also referred to as the "short." The buyer of a futures contract will realize a profit if the futures price increases; the seller of a futures contract will realize a profit if the futures price decreases.

When a position is taken in a futures contract, the party need not put up the entire amount of the investment. Instead, only initial margin must be put up. Consequently, an investor can effectively create a leveraged position by using futures. At first, the leverage available in the futures market may suggest that the market benefits only those who want to speculate on price movements. This is not true. As we shall see in Level III, futures markets can be used to control interest rate risk. Without the effective leverage possible in futures transactions, the cost of reducing price risk using futures would be too high for many market participants.

D. Exchange-Traded Interest Rate Futures Contracts

Interest rate futures contracts can be classified by the maturity of their underlying security. Short-term interest rate futures contracts have an underlying security that matures in less than one year. Examples of these are futures contracts in which the underlying is a 3-month Treasury bill and a 3-month Eurodollar certificate of deposit. The maturity of the underlying security of long-term futures contracts exceeds one year. Examples of these are futures contracts in which the underlying is a Treasury coupon security, a 10-year agency note, and a municipal bond index. Our focus will be on futures contracts in which the underlying is a Treasury coupon security (a Treasury bond or a Treasury note). These contracts are the most widely used by managers of bond portfolios, and we begin with the specifications of the Treasury bond futures contract. We will also discuss the agency note futures contracts.

There are futures contracts on non-U.S. government securities traded throughout the world. Many of them are modeled after the U.S. Treasury futures contracts and consequently, the concepts discussed below apply directly to those futures contracts.

1 *Treasury Bond Futures*

The Treasury bond futures contract is traded on the Chicago Board of Trade (CBOT). The underlying instrument for a Treasury bond futures contract is $100,000 par value of a hypothetical 20-year coupon bond. The coupon rate on the hypothetical bond is called the notional coupon.

The futures price is quoted in terms of par being 100. Quotes are in 32nds of 1%. Thus a quote for a Treasury bond futures contract of 97-16 means 97 and $^{16}/_{32}$ or 97.50. So, if a buyer and seller agree on a futures price of 97-16, this means that the buyer agrees to accept delivery of the hypothetical underlying Treasury bond and pay 97.50% of par value and the seller agrees to accept 97.50% of par value. Since the par value is $100,000, the futures price that the buyer and seller agree to for this hypothetical Treasury bond is $97,500.

The minimum price fluctuation for the Treasury bond futures contract is 1/32 of 1%, which is referred to as "a 32nd." The dollar value of a 32nd for $100,000 par value (the par value for the underlying Treasury bond) is $31.25. Thus, the minimum price fluctuation is $31.25 for this contract.

We have been referring to the underlying as a hypothetical Treasury bond. The seller of a Treasury bond futures contract who decides to make delivery rather than liquidate the position by buying back the contract prior to the settlement date must deliver some Treasury bond issue. But what Treasury bond issue? The CBOT allows the seller to deliver one of several Treasury bonds that the CBOT designates as acceptable for delivery. The specific issues that the seller may deliver are published by the CBOT for all contracts by settlement date. The CBOT makes its determination of the Treasury bond issues that are acceptable for delivery from all outstanding Treasury bond issues that have at least 15 years to maturity from the date of delivery.

Exhibit 1 shows the Treasury bond issues that the seller could have selected to deliver to the buyer of the CBOT Treasury bond futures contract as of May 29, 2002. Should the U.S. Department of the Treasury issue any Treasury bonds that meet the CBOT criteria for eligible delivery, those issues would be added to the list. Notice that for the Treasury bond futures contract settling (i.e., maturing) in March 2005, there are 25 eligible issues. For contracts settling after March 2005, there are fewer than 25 eligible issues due to the shorter maturity of each previous eligible issue that results in a maturity of less than 15 years.

Although the underlying Treasury bond for this contract is a hypothetical issue and therefore cannot itself be delivered into the futures contract, the contract is not a cash settlement contract. The only way to close out a Treasury bond futures contract is to either initiate an offsetting futures position, or to deliver a Treasury bond issue satisfying the above-mentioned criteria into the futures contract.

a. Conversion Factors The delivery process for the Treasury bond futures contract makes the contract interesting. At the settlement date, the seller of a futures contract (the short) is now required to deliver to the buyer (the long) $100,000 par value of a 6% 20-year Treasury bond. Since no such bond exists, the seller must choose from one of the acceptable deliverable Treasury bonds that the CBOT has specified. Suppose the seller is entitled to deliver $100,000 of a 5% 20-year Treasury bond to settle the futures contract. The value of this bond is less than the value of a 6% 20-year bond. If the seller delivers the 5% 20-year bond, this would be unfair to the buyer of the futures contract who contracted to receive $100,000 of a 6% 20-year Treasury bond. Alternatively, suppose the seller delivers $100,000 of a 7% 20-year Treasury bond. The value of a 7% 20-year Treasury bond is greater than that of a 6% 20-year bond, so this would be a disadvantage to the seller.

Exhibit 1 **U.S. Treasury Bond Issues Acceptable for Delivery and Conversion Factors**

Eligible for Delivery as of May 29, 2002.

		Conversion Factors									
Issue		**Mar. 2005**	**Jun. 2005**	**Sep. 2005**	**Dec. 2005**	**Mar. 2006**	**Jun. 2006**	**Sep. 2006**	**Dec. 2006**	**Mar. 2007**	**Jun. 2007**
5¼	11/15/28	0.9062	0.9065	0.9071	0.9075	0.9081	0.9084	0.9090	0.9095	0.9101	0.9105
5¼	02/15/29	0.9056	0.9062	0.9065	0.9071	0.9075	0.9081	0.9084	0.9090	0.9095	0.9101
5⅜	02/15/31	0.9185	0.9189	0.9191	0.9196	0.9198	0.9203	0.9206	0.9210	0.9213	0.9218
5	08/15/28	0.9376	0.9381	0.9383	0.9387	0.9389	0.9394	0.9396	0.9400	0.9403	0.9407

(continued)

Exhibit 1 (Continued)

Issue		Conversion Factors									
		Mar. 2005	Jun. 2005	Sep. 2005	Dec. 2005	Mar. 2006	Jun. 2006	Sep. 2006	Dec. 2006	Mar. 2007	Jun. 2007
6	02/15/26	0.9999	1.0000	0.9999	1.0000	0.9999	1.0000	0.9999	1.0000	0.9999	1.0000
6⅛	11/15/27	1.0153	1.0151	1.0152	1.0150	1.0150	1.0148	1.0148	1.0146	1.0146	1.0144
6⅛	08/15/29	1.0158	1.0158	1.0156	1.0156	1.0154	1.0155	1.0153	1.0153	1.0151	1.0152
6¼	08/15/23	1.0274	1.0273	1.0270	1.0269	1.0265	1.0264	1.0261	1.0260	1.0256	1.0255
6¼	05/15/30	1.0322	1.0319	1.0319	1.0316	1.0316	1.0313	1.0313	1.0310	1.0310	1.0307
6⅜	08/15/27	1.0456	1.0455	1.0451	1.0450	1.0446	1.0444	1.0441	1.0439	1.0435	1.0433
6	11/15/26	1.0600	1.0595	1.0593	1.0588	1.0585	1.0580	1.0578	1.0573	1.0570	1.0565
6⅝	02/15/27	1.0752	1.0749	1.0744	1.0741	1.0735	1.0732	1.0726	1.0722	1.0716	1.0713
6¾	08/15/26	1.0893	1.0889	1.0882	1.0878	1.0871	1.0867	1.0860	1.0855	1.0848	1.0843
6⅞	08/15/25	1.1017	1.1011	1.1003	1.0998	1.0990	1.0984	1.0976	1.0970	1.0961	1.0955
7⅛	02/15/23	1.1217	1.1209	1.1197	1.1189	1.1177	1.1168	1.1156	1.1147	1.1135	1.1125
7	08/15/22	1.1331	1.1321	1.1308	1.1298	1.1285	1.1274	1.1261	1.1250	1.1236	1.1225
7	11/15/24	1.1711	1.1697	1.1687	1.1673	1.1663	1.1649	1.1637	1.1623	1.1612	1.1597
7⅝	11/15/22	1.1746	1.1730	1.1717	1.1701	1.1687	1.1671	1.1657	1.1640	1.1625	1.1607
7⅝	02/15/25	1.1864	1.1853	1.1839	1.1828	1.1813	1.1801	1.1786	1.1774	1.1759	1.1746
7⅞	02/15/21	1.1892	1.1875	1.1855	1.1838	—	—	—	—	—	—
8	11/15/21	1.2077	1.2056	1.2039	1.2018	1.2000	1.1979	1.1960	—	—	—
8⅛	05/15/21	1.2166	1.2144	1.2125	1.2102	1.2083	—	—	—	—	—
8⅛	08/15/21	1.2185	1.2166	1.2144	1.2125	1.2102	1.2083	—	—	—	—
8¾	05/15/20	1.2695	—	—	—	—	—	—	—	—	—
8¾	08/15/20	1.2721	1.2695	—	—	—	—	—	—	—	—
No. of Eligible issues		25	24	23	23	22	21	20	19	19	19

Source: Chicago Board of Trade.

How can this problem be resolved? To make delivery equitable to both parties, the CBOT has introduced conversion factors for adjusting the price of each Treasury issue that can be delivered to satisfy the Treasury bond futures contract. The conversion factor is determined by the CBOT before a contract with a specific settlement date begins trading.[2] The adjusted price is found by multiplying the conversion factor by the futures price. The adjusted price is called the converted price.

Exhibit 1 shows conversion factors as of May 29, 2002. The conversion factors are shown by contract settlement date. Note that the conversion factor depends not only on the issue delivered but also on the settlement date of the contract. For example, look at the first issue in Exhibit 1, the 5¼% coupon bond maturing 11/15/28. For the Treasury bond futures contract settling (i.e., maturing) in March 2005, the conversion factor is 0.9062. For the December 2005 contract, the conversion factor is 0.9075.

2 The conversion factor is based on the price that a deliverable bond would sell for at the beginning of the delivery month if it were to yield 6%.

The price that the buyer must pay the seller when a Treasury bond is delivered is called the invoice price. The invoice price is the futures settlement price plus accrued interest. However, as just noted, the seller can deliver one of several acceptable Treasury issues and to make delivery fair to both parties, the invoice price must be adjusted based on the actual Treasury issue delivered. It is the conversion factors that are used to adjust the invoice price. The invoice price is:

$$\text{Invoice price} = \text{Contract size} \times \text{Futures settlement price} \times \text{Conversion factor} + \text{Accrued interest}$$

Suppose the Treasury March 2006 futures contract settles at 105-16 and that the issue delivered is the 8% of 11/15/21. The futures contract settlement price of 105-16 means 105.5% of par value or 1.055 times par value. As indicated in Exhibit 1, the conversion factor for this issue for the March 2006 contract is 1.2000. Since the contract size is \$100,000, the invoice price the buyer pays the seller is:

$$\$100{,}000 \times 1.055 \times 1.2000 + \text{Accrued interest} = \$126{,}600 + \text{Accrued interest}$$

b. Cheapest-to-Deliver Issue As can be seen in Exhibit 1, there can be more than one issue that is permitted to be delivered to satisfy a futures contract. In fact, for the March 2005 contract, there are 25 deliverable or eligible bond issues. It is the short that has the option of selecting which one of the deliverable bond issues if he decides to deliver.[3] The decision of which one of the bond issues a short will elect to deliver is *not* made arbitrarily. There is an economic analysis that a short will undertake in order to determine the best bond issue to deliver. In fact, as we will see, all of the elements that go into the economic analysis will be the same for all participants in the market who are either electing to deliver or who are anticipating delivery of one of the eligible bond issues. In this section, how the best bond issue to deliver is determined will be explained.

PRACTICE QUESTION 1

Suppose that the June 200X Treasury bond futures contract settles at 97-24 and the issue delivered has a conversion factor of 1.17. Assume that the accrued interest for the issue delivered is \$3,800 per \$100,000 par value. What is the invoice price the buyer pays the seller?

The economic analysis is not complicated. The basic principle is as follows. Suppose that an investor enters into the following two transactions *simultaneously*:

1 buys one of the deliverable bond issues today with borrowed money and
2 sells a futures contract.

The two positions (i.e., the long position in the deliverable bond issue purchased and the short position in the futures contract) will be held to the delivery date. At the delivery date, the bond issue purchased will be used to satisfy the short's obligation to deliver an eligible bond issue. The simultaneous transactions above and the delivery of the acceptable bond issue purchased to satisfy the short position in the futures contract is called a cash and carry trade.

Let's look at the economics of this cash and carry trade. The investor (who by virtue of the fact that he sold a futures contract is the short), has synthetically created a short-term investment vehicle. The reason is that the investor has purchased a bond

3 Remember that the short can always unwind his position by buying the same futures contract before the settlement date.

issue (one of the deliverable bond issues) and at the delivery date delivers that bond issue and receives the futures price. So, the investor knows the cost of buying the bond issue and knows how much will be received from the investment. The amount received is the coupon interest until the delivery date, any reinvestment income from reinvesting coupon payments, and the futures price at the delivery date. (Remember that the futures price at the delivery date for a given deliverable bond issue will be its converted price.) Thus, the investor can calculate the rate of return that will be earned on the investment. In the futures market, this rate of return is called the **implied repo rate**.

An implied repo rate can be calculated for *every* deliverable bond issue. For example, suppose that there are N deliverable bond issues that can be delivered to satisfy a bond futures contract. Market participants who want to know either the best issue to deliver or what issue is likely to be delivered will calculate an implied repo rate for all N eligible bond issues. Which would be the best issue to deliver by a short? Since the implied repo rate is the rate of return on an investment, the best bond issue is the one that has the *highest* implied repo rate (i.e., the highest rate of return). The bond issue with the highest implied repo rate is called the cheapest-to-deliver issue.

Now that we understand the economic principle for determining the best bond issue to deliver (i.e., the cheapest-to-deliver issue), let's look more closely at how one calculates the implied repo rate for each deliverable bond issue. This rate is computed using the following information for a given deliverable bond issue:

1 the price plus accrued interest at which the Treasury issue could be purchased

2 the converted price plus the accrued interest that will be received upon delivery of that Treasury bond issue to satisfy the short futures position

3 the coupon payments that will be received between today and the date the issue is delivered to satisfy the futures contract.

4 the reinvestment income that will be realized on the coupon payments between the time the interim coupon payment is received and the date that the issue is delivered to satisfy the Treasury bond futures contract.

The first three elements are known. The last element will depend on the reinvestment rate that can be earned. While the reinvestment rate is unknown, typically this is a small part of the rate of return and not much is lost by assuming that the implied repo rate can be predicted with certainty.

The general formula for the implied repo rate is as follows:

$$\text{Implied repo rate} = \frac{\text{Dollar return}}{\text{Cost of the investment}} \times \frac{360}{\text{Days}_1}$$

where days_1 is equal to the number of days until settlement of the futures contract. Below we will explain the other components in the formula for the implied repo rate.

Let's begin with the dollar return. The dollar return for an issue is the difference between the proceeds received and the cost of the investment. The proceeds received are equal to the proceeds received at the settlement date of the futures contract and any interim coupon payment plus interest from reinvesting the interim coupon payment. The proceeds received at the settlement date include the converted price (i.e., futures settlement price multiplied by the conversion factor for the issue) and the accrued interest received from delivery of the issue. That is,

$$\begin{aligned}\text{Proceeds received} = {} & \text{Converted price} + \text{Accrued interest received} \\ & + \text{Interim coupon payment} + \text{Interest from} \\ & \text{reinvesting the interim coupon payment}\end{aligned}$$

As noted earlier, all of the elements are known except the interest from reinvesting the interim coupon payment. This amount is estimated by assuming that the coupon payment can be reinvested at the term repo rate. At Level III we describe the repo market and the term repo rate. The term repo rate is not only a borrowing rate for an investor who wants to borrow in the repo market but also the rate at which an investor can invest proceeds on a short-term basis. For how long is the reinvestment of the interim coupon payment? It is the number of days from when the interim coupon payment is received and the actual delivery date to satisfy the futures contract. The reinvestment income is then computed as follows:

$$\text{Interest from reinvesting the interim coupon payment} = \text{Interim coupon} \times \text{Term repo rate} \times (\text{Days}_2/360)$$

where

Days_2 = Number of days between when the interim coupon payment is received and the actual delivery date of the futures contract

The reason for dividing days_2 by 360 is that the ratio represents the number of days the interim coupon is reinvested as a percentage of the number of days in a year as measured in the money market.

The cost of the investment is the amount paid to purchase the issue. This cost is equal to the purchase price plus accrued interest paid. That is,

$$\text{Cost of the investment} = \text{Purchase price} + \text{Accrued interest paid}$$

Thus, the dollar return for the numerator of the formula for the implied repo rate is equal to

$$\text{Dollar return} = \text{Proceeds received} - \text{Cost of the investment}$$

The dollar return is then divided by the cost of the investment.[4]

So, now we know how to compute the numerator and the denominator in the formula for the implied repo rate. The second ratio in the formula for the implied repo rate simply involves annualizing the return using a convention in the money market for the number of days. (Recall that in the money market the convention is to use a 360 day year.) Since the investment resulting from the cash and carry trade is a synthetic money market instrument, 360 days are used.

Let's compute the implied repo rate for a hypothetical issue that may be delivered to satisfy a hypothetical Treasury bond futures contract. Assume the following for the deliverable issue and the futures contract:

Futures contract:

futures price = 96
days to futures delivery date (days_1) = 82 days

Deliverable issue:

price of issue = 107

accrued interest paid = 3.8904

coupon rate = 10%

days remaining before interim coupon paid = 40 days

interim coupon = $5

number of days between when the interim coupon payment is received and the actual delivery date of the futures contract (days_2) = 42

4 Actually, the cost of the investment should be adjusted because the amount that the investor ties up in the investment is reduced if there is an interim coupon payment. We will ignore this adjustment here.

conversion factor = 1.1111

accrued interest received at futures settlement date = 1.1507

Other information:

42-day term repo rate = 3.8%

Let's begin with the proceeds received. We need to compute the converted price and the interest from reinvesting the interim coupon payment. The converted price is:

$$\text{Converted price} = \text{Futures price} \times \text{Conversion factor}$$
$$= 96 \times 1.1111 = 106.6656$$

The interest from reinvesting the interim coupon payment depends on the term repo rate. The term repo rate is assumed to be 3.8%. Therefore,

$$\text{Interest from reinvesting the interim coupon payment} = \$5 \times 0.038 \times \left(\frac{42}{360}\right) = 0.0222$$

To summarize:

Converted price	=	106.6656
Accrued interest received at futures settlement date	=	1.1507
Interim coupon payment	=	5.0000
Interest from reinvesting the interim coupon payment	=	0.0222
Proceeds received	=	112.8385

The cost of the investment is the purchase price for the issue plus the accrued interest paid, as shown below:

$$\text{Cost of the investment} = 107 + 3.8904 = 110.8904$$

The implied repo rate is then:

$$\text{Implied repo rate} = \frac{112.8385 - 110.8904}{110.8904} \times \frac{360}{82} = 0.0771 = 7.71\%$$

Once the implied repo rate is calculated for each deliverable issue, the cheapest-to-deliver issue will be the one that has the highest implied repo rate (i.e., the issue that gives the maximum return in a cash-and-carry trade). As explained in the reading on using credit derivatives to enhance return and manage risk, this issue plays a key role in the pricing of a Treasury bond futures contract.

While an eligible bond issue may be the cheapest to deliver today, changes in factors may cause some other eligible bond issue to be the cheapest to deliver at a future date. A sensitivity analysis can be performed to determine how a change in yield affects the cheapest to deliver.

PRACTICE QUESTION 2

Calculate the implied repo rate for a hypothetical issue that is deliverable for a Treasury bond futures contract assuming the following for the deliverable issue and the futures contract:

Futures contract:

Futures price = 97
days to futures delivery date (days_1) = 62 days

Deliverable issue:

price of issue = 95

accrued interest paid = 3.0110

coupon rate = 7%

days remaining before interim coupon made = 25 days

interim coupon = \$3.50

number of days between when the interim coupon payment is received and the actual delivery date of the futures contract (day_2) = 37 days

conversion factor = 0.9710

accrued interest received at futures settlement date = 0.7096

Other information:

37-day repo rate = 4.7%

c. Other Delivery Options In addition to the choice of which acceptable Treasury issue to deliver—sometimes referred to as the quality option or swap option—the short has at least two more options granted under CBOT delivery guidelines. The short is permitted to decide when in the delivery month delivery actually will take place. This is called the timing option. The other option is the right of the short to give notice of intent to deliver up to 8:00 p.m. Chicago time after the closing of the exchange (3:15 p.m. Chicago time) on the date when the futures settlement price has been fixed. This option is referred to as the wild card option. The quality option, the timing option, and the wild card option (in sum referred to as the **delivery options**), mean that the long position can never be sure which Treasury bond will be delivered or when it will be delivered. These three delivery options are summarized in Exhibit 2.

Exhibit 2 **Delivery Options Granted to the Short (Seller) of a CBOT Treasury Bond Futures Contract**

Delivery Option	Description
Quality or swap option	Choice of which acceptable Treasury issue to deliver
Timing option	Choice of when in delivery month to deliver
Wild card option	Choice to deliver after the closing price of the futures contract is determined

d. Delivery Procedure For a short who wants to deliver, the delivery procedure involves three days. The first day is the position day. On this day, the short notifies the CBOT that it intends to deliver. The short has until 8:00 p.m. central standard time to do so. The second day is the notice day. On this day, the short specifies which particular issue will be delivered. The short has until 2:00 p.m. central standard time to make this declaration. (On the last possible notice day in the delivery month, the short has until 3:00 p.m.) The CBOT then selects the long to whom delivery will be made. This is the long position that has been outstanding for the greatest period of time. The long is then notified by 4:00 p.m. that delivery will be made. The third day is the delivery day. By 10:00 a.m. on this day the short must have in its account the Treasury issue that it specified on the notice day and by 1:00 p.m. must deliver that bond to the long that was assigned by the CBOT to accept delivery. The long pays the short the invoice price upon receipt of the bond.

2 *Treasury Note Futures*

The three Treasury note futures contracts are 10-year, 5-year, and 2-year note contracts. All three contracts are modeled after the Treasury bond futures contract and are traded on the CBOT.

The underlying instrument for the 10-year Treasury note futures contract is $100,000 par value of a hypothetical 10-year, 6% Treasury note. Several acceptable Treasury issues may be delivered by the short. An issue is acceptable if the maturity is not less than 6.5 years and not greater than 10 years from the first day of the delivery month. Delivery options are granted to the short position.

For the 5-year Treasury note futures contract, the underlying is $100,000 par value of a 6% notional coupon U.S. Treasury note that satisfies the following conditions: 1) an original maturity of not more than 5 years and 3 months, 2) a remaining maturity no greater than 5 years and 3 months, and 3) a remaining maturity not less than 4 years and 2 months.

The underlying for the 2-year Treasury note futures contract is $200,000 par value of a 6% notional coupon U.S. Treasury note with a remaining maturity of not more than 2 years and not less than 1 year and 9 months. Moreover, the original maturity of the note delivered to satisfy the 2-year futures cannot be more than 5 years and 3 months.

3 *Agency Note Futures Contract*

In 2000, the CBOT and the Chicago Mercantile Exchange (CME) began trading in futures contracts in which the underlying is a Fannie Mae or Freddie Mac agency debenture security. (Agency debentures are explained at Level I.) The underlying for the CBOT 10-year agency note futures contract is a Fannie Mae benchmark note or Freddie Mac reference note having a par value of $100,000 and a notional coupon of 6%. The 10-year agency note futures contract of the CME is similar to that of the CBOT, but has a notional coupon of 6.5% instead of 6%.

As with the Treasury futures contract, more than one issue is deliverable for both the CBOT and CME agency note futures contract. The contract delivery months are March, June, September, and December. As with the Treasury futures contract, a conversion factor applies to each eligible issue for each contract settlement date. Because many issues are deliverable, one issue is the cheapest-to-deliver issue. This issue is found in exactly the same way as with the Treasury futures contract.

3 INTEREST RATE OPTIONS

An **option** is a contract in which the writer of the option grants the buyer of the option the right, but not the obligation, to purchase from or sell to the writer something at a specified price within a specified period of time (or at a specified date). The writer, also referred to as the seller, grants this right to the buyer in exchange for a certain sum of money, called the **option price** or **option premium**. The price at which the underlying for the contract may be bought or sold is called the **exercise price** or **strike price**. The date after which an option is void is called the **expiration date**. Our focus is on options where the “something” underlying the option is an interest rate instrument or an interest rate.

When an option grants the buyer the right to purchase the designated instrument from the writer (seller), it is referred to as a call option, or **call**. When the option buyer has the right to sell the designated instrument to the writer, the option is called a put option, or **put**.

An option is also categorized according to when the option buyer may exercise the option. There are options that may be exercised at any time up to and including the expiration date. Such an option is referred to as an **American option**. There are options that may be exercised only at the expiration date. An option with this feature is called a **European option**. An option that can be exercised prior to maturity but only on designated dates is called a modified American, Bermuda, or Atlantic option.

A. Risk and Return Characteristics of Options

The maximum amount that an option buyer can lose is the option price. The maximum profit that the option writer can realize is the option price at the time of sale. The option buyer has substantial upside return potential, while the option writer has substantial downside risk.

It is assumed in this reading that the reader has an understanding of the basic positions that can be created with options. These positions include:

1 long call position (buying a call option)
2 short call position (selling a call option)
3 long put position (buying a put option)
4 short put position (selling a put option)

Exhibit 3 shows the payoff profile for these four option positions *assuming that each option position is held to the expiration date and not exercised early.*

B. Differences between Options and Futures Contracts

Unlike a futures contract, one party to an option contract is not obligated to transact. Specifically, the option buyer has the right, but not the obligation, to transact. The option writer does have the obligation to perform. In the case of a futures contract, both buyer and seller are obligated to perform. Of course, a futures buyer does not pay the seller to accept the obligation, while an option buyer pays the option seller an option price.

Consequently, the risk/reward characteristics of the two contracts are also different. In the case of a futures contract, the buyer of the contract realizes a dollar-for-dollar gain when the price of the futures contract increases and suffers a dollar-for-dollar loss when the price of the futures contract drops. The opposite occurs for the seller of a futures contract. Options do not provide this symmetric risk/reward relationship. The most that the buyer of an option can lose is the option price. While the buyer of an option retains all the potential benefits, the gain is always reduced by the amount of the option price. The maximum profit that the writer may realize is the option price; this is compensation for accepting substantial downside risk.

Exhibit 3 Payoff of Basic Option Positions if Held to Expiration Date

A. Long Call Position

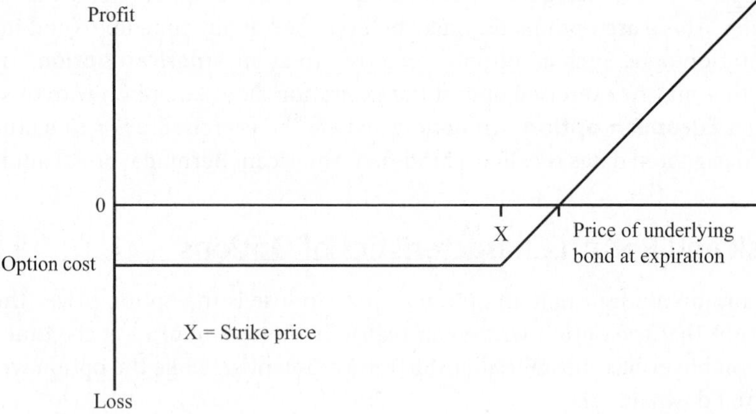

B. Short Call Position

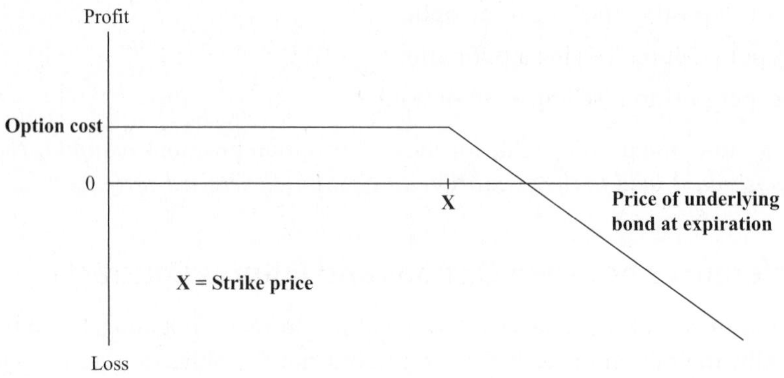

C. Long Put Position

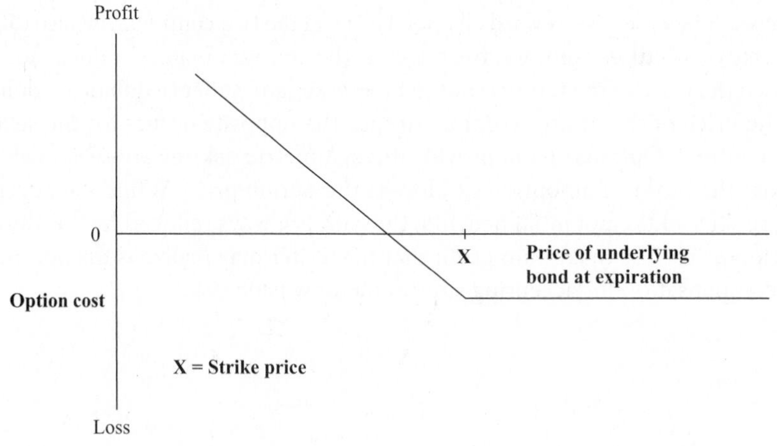

Exhibit 3 (Continued)

D. Short Put Position

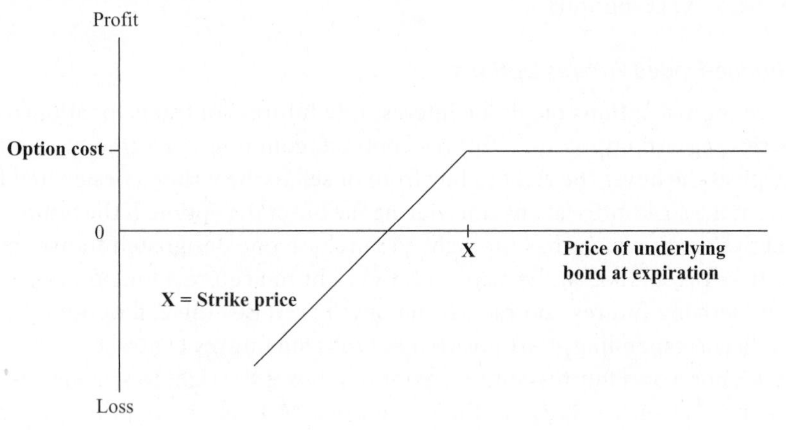

Both parties to a futures contract are required to post margin. There are no margin requirements for the buyer of an option once the option price has been paid in full. Because the option price is the maximum amount that the investor can lose, no matter how adverse the price movement of the underlying, there is no need for margin. Because the writer of an option has agreed to accept all of the risk (and none of the reward) of the position in the underlying, the writer is generally required to put up the option price received as margin. In addition, as price changes occur that adversely affect the writer's position, the writer is required to deposit additional margin (with some exceptions) as the position is marked to market.

C. Exchange-Traded versus OTC Options

Options, like other financial instruments, may be traded either on an organized exchange or in the over-the-counter (OTC) market. An exchange that wants to create an options contract must obtain approval from regulators. Exchange-traded options have three advantages. First, the strike price and expiration date of the contract are standardized.[5] Second, as in the case of futures contracts, the direct link between buyer and seller is severed after the order is executed because of the interchangeability of exchange-traded options. The clearinghouse performs the same guarantor function in the options market that it does in the futures market. Finally, transaction costs are lower for exchange-traded options than for OTC options.

The higher cost of an OTC option reflects the cost of customizing the option for the many situations where an institutional investor needs to have a tailor-made option because the standardized exchange-traded option does not satisfy its investment objectives. Investment banking firms and commercial banks act as principals as well as brokers in the OTC options market. While an OTC option is less liquid than an exchange-traded option, this is typically not of concern to an institutional investor—most institutional investors use OTC options as part of an asset/liability strategy and intend to hold them to expiration.

5 Exchanges have developed put and call options issued by their clearinghouse that are customized with respect to expiration date, exercise style, and strike price. These options are called *flexible exchange options* and are nicknamed "Flex" options.

Exchange-traded interest rate options can be written on a fixed income security or an interest rate futures contract. The former options are called *options on physicals.* For reasons to be explained later, options on interest rate futures are more popular than options on physicals. However, portfolio managers have made increasingly greater use of OTC options.

1 *Exchange-Traded Futures Options*

There are futures options on all the interest rate futures contracts mentioned earlier in this reading. An option on a futures contract, commonly referred to as a futures option, gives the buyer the right to buy from or sell to the writer a designated futures contract at the strike price at any time during the life of the option. If the futures option is a call option, the buyer has the right to purchase one designated futures contract at the strike price. That is, the buyer has the right to acquire a long futures position in the underlying futures contract. If the buyer exercises the call option, the writer acquires a corresponding short position in the same futures contract.

A put option on a futures contract grants the buyer the right to sell one designated futures contract to the writer at the strike price. That is, the option buyer has the right to acquire a short position in the designated futures contract. If the put option is exercised, the writer acquires a corresponding long position in the designated futures contract.

As the parties to the futures option will realize a position in a futures contract when the option is exercised, the question is: what will the futures price be? What futures price will the long be required to pay for the futures contract, and at what futures price will the short be required to sell the futures contract?

Upon exercise, the futures price for the futures contract will be set equal to the strike price. The position of the two parties is then immediately marked-to-market in terms of the then-current futures price. Thus, the futures position of the two parties will be at the prevailing futures price. At the same time, the option buyer will receive from the option seller the economic benefit from exercising. In the case of a call futures option, the option writer must pay the difference between the current futures price and the strike price to the buyer of the option. In the case of a put futures option, the option writer must pay the option buyer the difference between the strike price and the current futures price.

For example, suppose an investor buys a call option on some futures contract in which the strike price is 85. Assume also that the futures price is 95 and that the buyer exercises the call option. Upon exercise, the call buyer is given a long position in the futures contract at 85 and the call writer is assigned the corresponding short position in the futures contract at 85. The futures positions of the buyer and the writer are immediately marked-to-market by the exchange. Because the prevailing futures price is 95 and the strike price is 85, the long futures position (the position of the call buyer) realizes a gain of 10, while the short futures position (the position of the call writer) realizes a loss of 10. The call writer pays the exchange 10 and the call buyer receives from the exchange 10. The call buyer, who now has a long futures position at 95, can either liquidate the futures position at 95 or maintain a long futures position. If the former course of action is taken, the call buyer sells his futures contract at the prevailing futures price of 95. There is no gain or loss from liquidating the position. Overall, the call buyer realizes a gain of 10 (less the option purchase price). The call buyer who elects to hold the long futures position will face the same risk and reward of holding such a position, but still realizes a gain of 10 from the exercise of the call option.

Suppose instead that the futures option with a strike price of 85 is a put rather than a call, and the current futures price is 60 rather than 95. Then, if the buyer of this put option exercises it, the buyer would have a short position in the futures contract at 85; the option writer would have a long position in the futures contract at 85.

The exchange then marks the position to market at the then-current futures price of 60, resulting in a gain to the put buyer of 25 and a loss to the put writer of the same amount. The put buyer now has a short futures position at 60 and can either liquidate the short futures position by buying a futures contract at the prevailing futures price of 60 or maintain the short futures position. In either case the put buyer realizes a gain of 25 (less the option purchase price) from exercising the put option.

There are no margin requirements for the buyer of a futures option once the option price has been paid in full. Because the option price is the maximum amount that the buyer can lose regardless of how adverse the price movement of the underlying instrument, there is no need for margin. Because the writer (seller) of a futures option has agreed to accept all of the risk (and none of the reward) of the position in the underlying instrument, the writer (seller) is required to deposit not only the margin required on the interest rate futures contract position but also (with certain exceptions) the option price that is received from writing the option.

The price of a futures option is quoted in 64ths of 1% of par value. For example, a price of 24 means $^{24}\!/_{64}$ of 1% of par value. Since the par value of a Treasury bond futures contract is \$100,000, an option price of 24 means: [(24/64)/100] × \$100,000 = \$375. In general, the price of a futures option quoted at Q is equal to:

$$\text{Option price} = \left[\frac{Q/64}{100}\right] \times \$100{,}000$$

There are three reasons that futures options have largely supplanted options on fixed income securities as the options vehicle of choice for institutional investors who want to use exchange-traded options. First, unlike options on fixed income securities, options on Treasury coupon futures do not require payments for accrued interest to be made. Consequently, when a futures option is exercised, the call buyer and the put writer need not compensate the other party for accrued interest. Second, futures options are believed to be "cleaner" instruments because of the reduced likelihood of delivery squeezes. Market participants who must deliver an instrument are concerned that at the time of delivery the instrument to be delivered will be in short supply, resulting in a higher price to acquire the instrument. As the deliverable supply of futures contracts is infinite for futures options currently traded, there is no concern about a delivery squeeze. Finally, in order to price any option, it is imperative to know at all times the price of the underlying instrument. In the bond market, current prices are not as easily available as price information on the futures contract. The reason is that as bonds trade in the OTC market there is no single reporting system with recent price information. Thus, an investor who wanted to purchase an option on a Treasury bond would have to call several dealer firms to obtain a price. In contrast, futures contracts are traded on an exchange and, as a result, price information is reported.

2 *Over-the-Counter Options*

Institutional investors who want to purchase an option on a specific Treasury security or a Ginnie Mae passthrough security can do so on an over-the-counter basis. There are government and mortgage-backed securities dealers who make a market in options on specific securities. OTC options, also called dealer options, usually are purchased by institutional investors who want to hedge the risk associated with a specific security. For example, a thrift may be interested in hedging its position in a specific mortgage passthrough security. Typically, the maturity of the option coincides with the time period over which the buyer of the option wants to hedge, so the buyer is not concerned with the option's liquidity.

PRACTICE QUESTION 3

A Suppose an investor purchases a call option on a Treasury bond futures contract with a strike price of 98. Also assume that at the expiration date the price of the Treasury bond futures contract is 103. Will the investor exercise the call option and, if so, what will the investor and the writer of the call option receive?

B Suppose an investor purchases a put option on a Treasury bond futures contract with a strike price of 105. Also assume that at the expiration date the price of the Treasury bond futures contract is 96. Will the investor exercise the put option and, if so, what will the investor and the writer of the put option receive?

In the absence of a clearinghouse the parties to any over-the-counter contract are exposed to counterparty risk.[6] In the case of forward contracts where both parties are obligated to perform, both parties face counterparty risk. In contrast, in the case of an option, once the option buyer pays the option price, it has satisfied its obligation. It is only the seller that must perform if the option is exercised. Thus, the option buyer is exposed to counterparty risk—the risk that the option seller will fail to perform.

OTC options can be customized in any manner sought by an institutional investor. Basically, if a dealer can reasonably hedge the risk associated with the opposite side of the option sought, it will create the option desired by a customer. OTC options are not limited to European or American type. Dealers also create modified American (Bermuda or Atlantic) type options.

4 INTEREST RATE SWAPS

In an interest rate swap, two parties agree to exchange periodic interest payments. The dollar amount of the interest payments exchanged is based on some predetermined dollar principal, which is called the notional principal or notional amount. The dollar amount each counterparty pays to the other is the agreed-upon periodic interest rate times the notional principal. The only dollars that are exchanged between the parties are the interest payments, not the notional principal. In the most common type of swap, one party agrees to pay the other party fixed interest payments at designated dates for the life of the contract. This party is referred to as the fixed-rate payer. The fixed rate that the fixed-rate payer must make is called the swap rate. The other party, who agrees to make interest rate payments that float with some reference rate, is referred to as the fixed-rate receiver.

The reference rates that have been used for the floating rate in an interest rate swap are those on various money market instruments: Treasury bills, the London interbank offered rate, commercial paper, bankers acceptances, certificates of deposit, the federal funds rate, and the prime rate. The most common is the London interbank offered rate (LIBOR). LIBOR is the rate at which prime banks offer to pay on Eurodollar deposits

6 There are well-established institutional arrangements for mitigating counterparty risk in not only OTC options but also the other OTC derivatives described in this reading (swaps, caps, and floors). These arrangements include limiting exposure to a specific counterparty, marking to market positions, collateralizing trades, and netting arrangement. For a discussion of these arrangements, see Chance, *Analysis of Derivatives for the CFA Program*, pp. 595–598.

available to other prime banks for a given maturity. Basically, it is viewed as the global cost of bank borrowing. There is not just one rate but a rate for different maturities. For example, there is a 1-month LIBOR, 3-month LIBOR, 6-month LIBOR, etc.

To illustrate an interest rate swap, suppose that for the next five years party X agrees to pay party Y 6% per year (the swap rate), while party Y agrees to pay party X 6-month LIBOR (the reference rate). Party X is the fixed-rate payer, while party Y is the fixed-rate receiver. Assume that the notional principal is $50 million, and that payments are exchanged every six months for the next five years. This means that every six months, party X (the fixed-rate payer) will pay party Y $1.5 million (6% times $50 million divided by 2). The amount that party Y (the fixed-rate receiver) will pay party X will be 6-month LIBOR times $50 million divided by 2. If 6-month LIBOR is 5% at the beginning of the 6-month period, party Y will pay party X $1.25 million (5% times $50 million divided by 2). Mechanically, the floating rate is determined at the beginning of a period and paid in arrears—that is, it is paid at the end of the period. The two payments are actually netted out so that $0.25 million will be paid from party X to party Y. Note that we divide by two because one-half year's interest is being paid. This is illustrated in panel A of Exhibit 4.

PRACTICE QUESTION 4

Suppose that party G and party H enter into a 4-year interest rate swap. The notional amount for the swap is $100 million and the reference rate is 3-month LIBOR. Suppose that the payments are made quarterly by both the fixed-rate payer and the fixed-rate receiver. Also assume that the swap rate is 4.4%.

A What are the payments that must be made by the fixed-rate payer every quarter?

B Suppose for the first floating-rate payment 3-month LIBOR is 7.2%. What is the amount of the first floating-rate payment that must be made by the fixed-rate receiver?

The convention that has evolved for quoting a swap rate is that a dealer sets the floating rate equal to the reference rate and then quotes the fixed rate that will apply. The fixed rate is the swap rate and reflects a "spread" above the Treasury yield curve with the same term to maturity as the swap. This spread is called the **swap spread**.

A. Entering into a Swap and Counterparty Risk

Interest rate swaps are OTC instruments. This means that they are not traded on an exchange. An institutional investor wishing to enter into a swap transaction can do so through either a securities firm or a commercial bank that transacts in swaps.[7] These entities can do one of the following. First, they can arrange or broker a swap between two parties that want to enter into an interest rate swap. In this case, the securities firm or commercial bank is acting in a brokerage capacity. The broker is not a party to the swap.

The second way in which a securities firm or commercial bank can get an institutional investor into a swap position is by taking the other side of the swap. This means that the securities firm or the commercial bank is a dealer rather than a broker in

7 Don't get confused here about the role of commercial banks. A bank can use a swap in its asset/liability management. Or, a bank can transact (buy and sell) swaps to clients to generate fee income. It is in the latter sense that we are discussing the role of a commercial bank in the swap market here.

the transaction. Acting as a dealer, the securities firm or the commercial bank must hedge its swap position in the same way that it hedges its position in other securities that it holds. Also it means that the dealer (which we refer to as a swap dealer) is the counterparty to the transaction. If an institutional investor entered into a swap with a swap dealer, the institutional investor will look to the swap dealer to satisfy the obligations of the swap; similarly, that same swap dealer looks to the institutional investor to fulfill its obligations as set forth in the swap.

Exhibit 4 Summary of How the Value of a Swap to Each Counterparty Changes when Interest Rates Change

A. Initial Position

Swap rate	= 6%	Settlement	= semiannual
Reference rate	= 6-month LIBOR	Term of swap	= 5 years
Notional amount	= $50 million	Payment by fixed-rate payer	= $1.5 million

Every six months

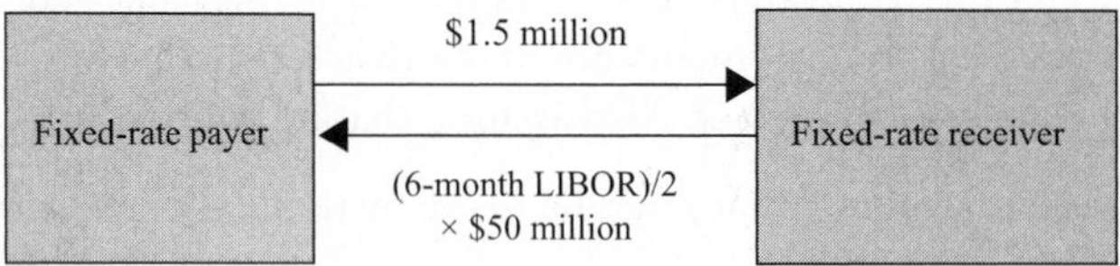

B. Interest Rates Increase Such That Swap Rate Is 7% for New Swaps

Fixed-rate payer pays initial swap rate of 6% to obtain 6-month LIBOR.

Advantage to fixed-rate payer: pays only 6%, not 7%, to obtain 6-month LIBOR.

Fixed-rate receiver pays 6-month LIBOR.

Disadvantage to fixed-rate receiver: receives only 6% in exchange for 6-month LIBOR, not 7%.

Results of a rise in interest rates:

Party	Value of Swap
Fixed-rate payer	Increases
Fixed-rate receiver	Decreases

C. Interest Rates Decrease Such That Swap Rate Is 5% for New Swaps

Fixed-rate payer pays initial swap rate of 6% to obtain 6-month LIBOR.

Disadvantage to fixed-rate payer: must pay 6%, not 5%, to obtain 6-month LIBOR.

Fixed-rate receiver pays 6-month LIBOR.

Advantage to fixed-rate receiver: receives 6% in exchange for 6-month LIBOR, not 5%.

Results of a decrease in interest rates:

Exhibit 4 (Continued)

Party	Value of Swap
Fixed-rate payer	Decreases
Fixed-rate receiver	Increases

The risk that the two parties take on when they enter into a swap is that the other party will fail to fulfill its obligations as set forth in the swap agreement. That is, each party faces default risk and therefore there is bilateral counterparty risk.

B. Risk/Return Characteristics of an Interest Rate Swap

The value of an interest rate swap will fluctuate with market interest rates. As interest rates rise, the fixed-rate payer is receiving a higher 6-month LIBOR (in our illustration). He would need to pay more for a new swap. Let's consider our hypothetical swap. Suppose that interest rates change immediately after parties X and Y enter into the swap. Panel A in Exhibit 4 shows the transaction. First, consider what would happen if the market demanded that in any 5-year swap the fixed-rate payer must pay 7% in order to receive 6-month LIBOR. If party X (the fixed-rate payer) wants to sell its position to party A, then party A will benefit by having to pay only 6% (the original swap rate agreed upon) rather than 7% (the current swap rate) to receive 6-month LIBOR. Party X will want compensation for this benefit. Consequently, the value of party X's position has increased. Thus, if interest rates increase, the fixed-rate payer will realize a profit and the fixed-rate receiver will realize a loss. Panel B in Exhibit 4 summarizes the results of a rise in interest rates.

Next, consider what would happen if interest rates decline to, say, 5%. Now a 5-year swap would require a new fixed-rate payer to pay 5% rather than 6% to receive 6-month LIBOR. If party X wants to sell its position to party B, the latter would demand compensation to take over the position. In other words, if interest rates decline, the fixed-rate payer will realize a loss, while the fixed-rate receiver will realize a profit. Panel C in Exhibit 4 summarizes the results of a decline in interest rates.

C. Interpreting a Swap Position

There are two ways that a swap position can be interpreted: 1) a package of forward (futures) contracts and 2) a package of cash flows from buying and selling cash market instruments.

1 *Package of Forward (Futures) Contracts*

Contrast the position of the counterparties in an interest rate swap summarized above to the position of the long and short interest rate futures (forward) contract. The long futures position gains if interest rates decline and loses if interest rates rise—this is similar to the risk/return profile for a floating-rate payer. The risk/return profile for a fixed-rate payer is similar to that of the short futures position: a gain if interest rates increase and a loss if interest rates decrease. By taking a closer look at the interest rate swap we can understand why the risk/return relationships are similar.

Consider party X's position in our previous swap illustration. Party X has agreed to pay 6% and receive 6-month LIBOR. More specifically, assuming a $50 million notional principal, X has agreed to buy a commodity called "6-month LIBOR" for $1.5 million. This is effectively a 6-month forward contract where X agrees to pay $1.5 million in exchange for delivery of 6-month LIBOR. If interest rates increase to 7%, the price of that commodity (6-month LIBOR) is higher, resulting in a gain for the fixed-rate payer, who is effectively long a 6- month forward contract on 6-month LIBOR. The floating-rate payer is effectively short a 6-month forward contract on 6-month LIBOR. There is therefore an implicit forward contract corresponding to each exchange date.

Now we can see why there is a similarity between the risk/return relationship for an interest rate swap and a forward contract. If interest rates increase to, say, 7%, the price of that commodity (6-month LIBOR) increases to $1.75 million (7% times $50 million divided by 2). The long forward position (the fixed-rate payer) gains, and the short forward position (the floating-rate payer) loses. If interest rates decline to, say, 5%, the price of our commodity decreases to $1.25 million (5% times $50 million divided by 2). The short forward position (the floating-rate payer) gains, and the long forward position (the fixed-rate payer) loses.

Consequently, interest rate swaps can be viewed as a package of more basic interest rate derivatives, such as forwards.[8] The pricing of an interest rate swap will then depend on the price of a package of forward contracts with the same settlement dates in which the underlying for the forward contract is the same reference rate. We will make use of this principle when we explain how to value swaps in the reading on using derivatives to enhance return and manage risk.

While an interest rate swap may be nothing more than a package of forward contracts, it is not a redundant contract for several reasons. First, maturities for forward or futures contracts do not extend out as far as those of an interest rate swap; an interest rate swap with a term of 15 years or longer can be obtained. Second, an interest rate swap is a more transactionally efficient instrument. By this we mean that in one transaction an entity can effectively establish a payoff equivalent to a package of forward contracts. The forward contracts would each have to be negotiated separately. Third, the interest rate swap market has grown in liquidity since its introduction in 1981; interest rate swaps now provide more liquidity than forward contracts, particularly long-dated (i.e., long-term) forward contracts.

2 *Package of Cash Market Instruments*

To understand why a swap can also be interpreted as a package of cash market instruments, consider an investor who enters into the transaction below:

- buy $50 million par of a 5-year floating-rate bond that pays 6-month LIBOR every six months, and
- finance the purchase by borrowing $50 million for five years on terms requiring a 6% annual interest rate payable every six months.

As a result of this transaction, the investor

- receives a floating rate every six months for the next five years, and
- pays a fixed rate every six months for the next five years.

8 More specifically, an interest rate swap is equivalent to a package of forward rate agreements. A **forward rate agreement (FRA)** is the over-the-counter equivalent of the exchange-traded futures contracts on short-term rates. Typically, the short-term rate is LIBOR. The elements of an FRA are the contract rate, reference rate, settlement rate, notional amount, and settlement date.

Exhibit 5 **Cash Flow for the Purchase of a 5-Year Floating-Rate Bond Financed by Borrowing on a Fixed-Rate Basis**

Transaction:

- Purchase for \$50 million a 5-year floating-rate bond: floating rate = LIBOR, semiannual payments
- Borrow \$50 million for five years: fixed rate = 6%, semiannual payments

Cash Flow (in Millions of Dollars) from:			
Six Month Period	**Floating-Rate Bond**[a]	**Borrowing at 5%**	**Net = Same as Swap**
0	–\$50	+ \$50.0	\$0
1	+ $(LIBOR_1/2) \times 50$	−1.5	+ $(LIBOR_1/2) \times 50 - 1.5$
2	+ $(LIBOR_2/2) \times 50$	−1.5	+ $(LIBOR_2/2) \times 50 - 1.5$
3	+ $(LIBOR_3/2) \times 50$	−1.5	+ $(LIBOR_3/2) \times 50 - 1.5$
4	+ $(LIBOR_4/2) \times 50$	−1.5	+ $(LIBOR_4/2) \times 50 - 1.5$
5	+ $(LIBOR_5/2) \times 50$	−1.5	+ $(LIBOR_5/2) \times 50 - 1.5$
6	+ $(LIBOR_6/2) \times 50$	−1.5	+ $(LIBOR_6/2) \times 50 - 1.5$
7	+ $(LIBOR_7/2) \times 50$	−1.5	+ $(LIBOR_7/2) \times 50 - 1.5$
8	+ $(LIBOR_8/2) \times 50$	−1.5	+ $(LIBOR_8/2) \times 50 - 1.5$
9	+ $(LIBOR_9/2) \times 50$	−1.5	+ $(LIBOR_9/2) \times 50 - 1.5$
10	+ $(LIBOR_{10}/2) \times 50 + 50$	−51.5	+ $(LIBOR_{10}/2) \times 50 - 1.5$

[a] The subscript for LIBOR indicates the 6-month LIBOR as per the terms of the floating-rate bond at time *t*.

The cash flows for this transaction are set forth in Exhibit 5. The second column of the exhibit shows the cash flow from purchasing the 5-year floating-rate bond. There is a \$50 million cash outlay and then ten cash inflows. The amount of the cash inflows is uncertain because they depend on future LIBOR. The next column shows the cash flow from borrowing \$50 million on a fixed-rate basis. The last column shows the net cash flow from the entire transaction. As the last column indicates, there is no initial cash flow (no cash inflow or cash outlay). In all ten 6-month periods, the net position results in a cash inflow of LIBOR and a cash outlay of \$1.5 million. This net position, however, is identical to the position of a fixed-rate payer/floating-rate receiver.

It can be seen from the net cash flow in Exhibit 5 that a fixed-rate payer has a cash market position that is equivalent to a long position in a floating-rate bond and a short position in a fixed-rate bond—the short position being the equivalent of borrowing by issuing a fixed-rate bond.

What about the position of a floating-rate payer? It can be easily demonstrated that the position of a floating-rate payer is equivalent to purchasing a fixed-rate bond and financing that purchase at a floating rate, where the floating rate is the reference rate for the swap. That is, the position of a floating-rate payer is equivalent to a long position in a fixed-rate bond and a short position in a floating-rate bond.

Exhibit 6 Describing the Parties to a Swap Agreement

Fixed-Rate Payer	Fixed-Rate Receiver
■ pays fixed rate in the swap	■ pays floating rate in the swap
■ receives floating in the swap	■ receives fixed in the swap
■ is short the bond market	■ is long the bond market
■ has bought a swap	■ has sold a swap
■ is long a swap	■ is short a swap
■ has established the price sensitivities of a longer-term fixed-rate liability and a floating-rate asset	■ has established the price sensitivities of a longer-term fixed-rate asset and a floating-rate liability

D. Describing the Counterparties to a Swap Agreement

The terminology used to describe the position of a party in the swap markets combines cash market jargon and futures market jargon, given that a swap position can be interpreted as a position in a package of cash market instruments or a package of futures/forward positions. As we have said, the counterparty to an interest rate swap is either a fixed-rate payer or floating-rate payer.

Exhibit 6 lists how the counterparties to an interest rate swap agreement are described.[9] To understand why the fixed-rate payer is viewed as "short the bond market," and the floating-rate payer is viewed as "long the bond market," consider what happens when interest rates change. Those who borrow on a fixed-rate basis will benefit if interest rates rise because they have locked in a lower interest rate. But those who have a short bond position will also benefit if interest rates rise. Thus, a fixed-rate payer can be said to be short the bond market. A floating-rate payer benefits if interest rates fall. A long position in a bond also benefits if interest rates fall, so terminology describing a floating-rate payer as long the bond market is not surprising. From our discussion of the interpretation of a swap as a package of cash market instruments, describing a swap in terms of the sensitivities of long and short cash positions follows naturally.[10]

END OPTIONAL SEGMENT

5 INTEREST RATE CAPS AND FLOORS

There are agreements between two parties whereby one party for an upfront premium agrees to compensate the other at specific time periods if the reference rate is different from a predetermined level. If one party agrees to pay the other when the reference rate exceeds a predetermined level, the agreement is referred to as an **interest rate cap** or ceiling. The agreement is referred to as an **interest rate floor** if one party

9 Robert F. Kopprasch, John Macfarlane, Daniel R. Ross, and Janet Showers, "The Interest Rate Swap Market: Yield Mathematics, Terminology, and Conventions," Chapter 58 in Frank J. Fabozzi and Irving M. Pollack (eds.), *The Handbook of Fixed Income Securities* (Homewood, IL: Dow Jones-Irwin, 1987).

10 It is common for market participants to refer to one leg of a swap as the "funding leg" and the other as the "asset leg." This jargon is the result of the interpretation of a swap as a leveraged position in the asset. The payment of the floating-rate is referred to as the "funding leg" and the fixed-rate side is referred to as the "asset side."

agrees to pay the other when the reference rate falls below a predetermined level. The predetermined level is called the strike rate. The strike rate for a cap is called the cap rate; the strike rate for a floor is called the floor rate.

The terms of a cap and floor agreement include:

1 the reference rate
2 the strike rate (cap rate or floor rate) that sets the ceiling or floor
3 the length of the agreement
4 the frequency of settlement
5 the notional principal

For example, suppose that C buys an interest rate cap from D with the following terms:

1 the reference rate is 3-month LIBOR.
2 the strike rate is 6%.
3 the agreement is for four years.
4 settlement is every three months.
5 the notional principal is $20 million.

Under this agreement, every three months for the next four years, D will pay C whenever 3-month LIBOR exceeds 6% at a settlement date. The payment will equal the dollar value of the difference between 3-month LIBOR and 6% times the notional principal divided by 4. For example, if three months from now 3-month LIBOR on a settlement date is 8%, then D will pay C 2% (8% minus 6%) times $20 million divided by 4, or $100,000. If 3-month LIBOR is 6% or less, D does not have to pay anything to C.

In the case of an interest rate floor, assume the same terms as the interest rate cap we just illustrated. In this case, if 3-month LIBOR is 8%, C receives nothing from D, but if 3-month LIBOR is less than 6%, D compensates C for the difference. For example, if 3-month LIBOR is 5%, D will pay C $50,000 (6% minus 5% times $20 million divided by 4).[11]

A. Risk/Return Characteristics

In an interest rate agreement, the buyer pays an upfront fee which represents the maximum amount that the buyer can lose and the maximum amount that the seller (writer) can gain. The only party that is required to perform is the seller of the interest rate agreement. The buyer of an interest rate cap benefits if the reference rate rises above the strike rate because the seller must compensate the buyer. The buyer of an interest rate floor benefits if the reference rate falls below the strike rate, because the seller must compensate the buyer.

The seller of an interest rate cap or floor does not face counterparty risk once the buyer pays the fee. In contrast, the buyer faces counterparty risk. Thus, as with options, there is unilateral counterparty risk.

PRACTICE QUESTION 5

Suppose that a 4-year cap has a cap rate of 7% and a notional amount of $100 million. The frequency of settlement is quarterly and the reference rate is 3-month LIBOR. Assume that 3-month LIBOR for the next four quarters is as shown below. What is the payoff for each quarter?

11 Interest rate caps and floors can be combined to create an *interest rate collar*. This is done by buying an interest rate cap and selling an interest rate floor. The purchase of the cap sets a maximum rate; the sale of the floor sets a minimum rate. The range between the maximum and minimum rate is called the collar.

Period	3-Month LIBOR (%)
1	6.7
2	7.0
3	7.4
4	7.6

B. Interpretation of a Cap and Floor Position

In an interest rate cap and floor, the buyer pays an upfront fee, which represents the maximum amount that the buyer can lose and the maximum amount that the seller of the agreement can gain. The only party that is required to perform is the seller of the interest rate agreement. The buyer of an interest rate cap benefits if the reference rate rises above the strike rate because the seller must compensate the buyer. The buyer of an interest rate floor benefits if the reference rate falls below the strike rate because the seller must compensate the buyer.

How can we better understand interest rate caps and interest rate floors? In essence these contracts are equivalent to a *package of interest rate options* at different time periods. As with a swap, a complex contract can be seen to be a package of basic contracts—options in the case of caps and floors. Each of the interest rate options comprising a cap are called **caplets**; similarly, each of the interest rate options comprising a floor are called **floorlets**.

The question is what type of package of options is a cap and a floor. Note the following very carefully! It depends on whether the underlying is a rate or a fixed-income instrument. If the underlying is considered a fixed-income instrument, its value changes inversely with interest rates. Therefore:

- for a call option on a fixed-income instrument:
  1 interest rates increase → fixed-income instrument's price decreases → call option value decreases

    and

  2 interest rates decrease → fixed-income instrument's price increases → call option value increases
- for a put option on a fixed-income instrument:
  1 interest rates increase → fixed-income instrument's price decreases → put option value increases

    and

  2 interest rates decrease → fixed-income instrument's price increases → put option value decreases

To summarize the situation for call and put options on a fixed-income instrument:

Value of	When Interest Rates Increase	When Interest Rates Decrease
long call	decrease	increase
short call	increase	decrease
long put	increase	decrease
short put	decrease	increase

For a cap and floor, the situation is as follows:

Value of	When Interest Rates Increase	When Interest Rates Decrease
short cap	decrease	increase
long cap	increase	decrease
short floor	increase	decrease
long floor	decrease	increase

Therefore, buying a cap (long cap) is equivalent to buying a package of puts on a fixed-income instrument, and buying a floor (long floor) is equivalent to buying a package of calls on a fixed-income instrument.

Caps and floors can also be seen as packages of options on interest rates. In the over-the-counter market one can purchase an option on an interest rate. These options work as follows in terms of their payoff. There is a strike rate. For a call option on an interest rate, there is a payoff if the reference rate is greater than the strike rate. This means that when interest rates increase, the call option's value increases and when interest rates decrease, the call option's value decreases. As can be seen from the payoff for a cap and a floor summarized above, this is the payoff of a long cap. Consequently, a cap is equivalent to a package of call options on an interest rate. For a put option on an interest rate, there is a payoff when the reference rate is less than the strike rate. When interest rates increase, the value of the put option on an interest rate decreases, as does the value of a long floor position (see the summary above); when interest rates decrease, the value of the put on an interest rate increases, as does the value of a long floor position (again, see the summary above). Thus, a floor is equivalent to a package of put options on an interest rate.

When market participants talk about the equivalency of caps and floors in terms of put and call options, they must specify the underlying. For example, a long cap is equivalent to a package of call options on interest rates or a package of put options on a fixed-income instrument.

C. Creation of an Interest Rate Collar

Interest rate caps and floors can be combined by borrowers to create an **interest rate collar**. This is done by buying an interest rate cap and selling an interest rate floor. The purchase of the cap sets a maximum interest rate that a borrower would have to pay if the reference rate rises. The sale of a floor sets the minimum interest rate that a borrower can benefit from if the reference rate declines. Therefore, there is a range for the interest rate that the borrower must pay if the reference rate changes. The net premium that a borrower who wants to create a collar must pay is the difference between the premium paid to purchase the cap and the premium received to sell the floor.

For example, consider the following collar created by a borrower: a cap purchased with a strike rate of 7% and a floor sold with a strike rate of 4%. If the reference rate exceeds 7%, the borrower receives a payment; if the reference rate is less than 4%, the borrower makes a payment. Thus, the borrower's cost will have a range from 4% to 7%. Note, however, that the borrower's effective interest cost is adjusted by the net premium that the borrower must pay.

SOLUTIONS FOR PRACTICE QUESTIONS FOUND IN READING

1 The invoice price is equal to

Contract size × Futures settlement price × Conversion factor + Accrued interest

The futures settlement price is 97-24 or 97.75 (= 97 + 24/32). The futures settlement price per $1 of par value is therefore 0.9775. The invoice price is then:

$$\$100{,}000 \times 0.9775 \times 1.17 + \$3{,}800 = \$118{,}167.50$$

2 The proceeds received are:

$$\text{Converted price} = \text{Futures price} \times \text{Conversion factor}$$
$$= \$97 \times 0.9710 = \$94.1870$$

The term repo rate is 4.7%, so the interest from reinvesting the interim coupon payment is

Interest from reinvesting the interim coupon payment

$$= \$3.5 \times 0.047 \times \left(\frac{37}{360}\right) = \$0.0169$$

Summary:

converted price	=	$94.1870
accrued interest received	=	0.7096
interim coupon payment	=	3.5000
interest from reinvesting the interim coupon payment	=	0.0169
proceeds received	=	$98.4135

The cost of the investment is the purchase price for the issue plus the accrued interest paid, as shown below:

$$\text{Cost of the investment} = \$95 + \$3.0110 = \$98.0110$$

The implied repo rate is then:

$$\text{Implied repo rate} = \frac{\$98.4135 - \$98.0110}{\$98.0110} \times \frac{360}{62} = 0.0238 = 2.38\%$$

3 **A** The investor will exercise the call option because the price of the futures contract exceeds the strike price. By exercising, the investor receives a long position in the Treasury bond futures contract and the call option writer receives the corresponding short position. The futures price for both parties is the strike price of \$98. The positions are then marked-to-market using the futures price of \$103, and the option writer must pay the option buyer \$5 (the difference between the futures price of \$103 and the strike price of \$98).

After this, the positions look as follows:

- the investor (the buyer of the call option) has a long position in the Treasury bond futures contract at \$103 and cash of \$5, and
- the writer of the call option has a short position in the Treasury bond futures contract at \$103 and has paid cash of \$5.

B The investor will exercise the put option because the price of the futures contract is less than the strike price. By exercising, the investor receives a short position in the Treasury bond futures contract and the put option writer receives the corresponding long position. The futures price for both parties is the strike price of \$105. The positions are then marked-to-market using the futures price of \$105 and the option writer must pay the option buyer \$9 (the difference between the strike price of \$105 and the futures price of \$96).

After this, the positions look as follows:

- the investor (the buyer of the put option) has a short position in the Treasury bond futures contract at \$105 and cash of \$9, and
- the writer of the call option has a long position in the Treasury bond futures contract at \$105 and has paid cash of \$9.

4 Although the payments are quarterly rather than semiannual as illustrated in the text illustration, the concept is the same.

A Since the swap rate is 4.4%, the fixed-rate payment each quarter will be:

$$\$100 \text{ million} \times (0.044/4) = \$1.1 \text{ million}$$

B Since 3-month LIBOR is 7.2%, the first quarterly payment will be:

$$\$100 \text{ million} \times (0.072/4) = \$1.8 \text{ million}$$

5 There is a payoff to the cap if the cap rate exceeds 3-month LIBOR. For Periods 1 and 2, there is no payoff because the 3-month LIBOR is below the cap rate. For Periods 3 and 4, there is a payoff and the payoff is determined by:

$$\$100 \text{ million} \times (\text{3-month LIBOR} - \text{Cap rate})/4$$

The payoffs are summarized below:

Period	3-Month LIBOR (%)	Payoff (\$)
1	6.7	0
2	7.0	0
3	7.4	100,000
4	7.6	150,000

SUMMARY

OPTIONAL SEGMENT

- A futures contract is an agreement between a buyer (seller) and an established exchange or its clearinghouse in which the buyer (seller) agrees to take (make) delivery of something at a specified price at the end of a designated period of time.
- A forward contract is an agreement for the future delivery of something at a specified price at a designated time, but differs from a futures contract in that it is usually non-standardized and traded in the over-the-counter market.
- An investor who takes a long futures position realizes a gain when the futures price increases; an investor who takes a short futures position realizes a gain when the futures price decreases.
- The parties to a futures contract are required to satisfy margin requirements.
- Parties to over-the-counter interest rate contracts are exposed to counterparty risk, which is the risk that the counterparty will not satisfy its contractual obligations.
- For the Treasury bond futures contract the underlying instrument is $100,000 par value of a hypothetical 20-year 6% coupon Treasury bond.
- Conversion factors are used to adjust the invoice price of a Treasury bond futures contract to make delivery equitable to both parties.
- The short in a Treasury bond futures contract has several delivery options: quality option (or swap option), timing option, and wildcard option.
- For all the issues that may be delivered to satisfy a Treasury futures contract, a rate of return can be computed in a cash and carry trade; the rate of return is called the implied repo rate.
- For all the issues that may be delivered to satisfy a Treasury futures contract, the cheapest-to-deliver issue is the one with the highest implied repo rate.
- By varying the yield on Treasury bonds, it can be determined which issue will become the new cheapest-to-deliver issue.
- There are futures contracts in which the underlying is a Fannie Mae and Freddie Mac debenture.
- An option is a contract in which the writer of the option grants the buyer of the option the right, but not the obligation, to purchase from or sell to the writer something at a specified price within a specified period of time (or at a specified date).
- The option buyer pays the option writer (seller) a fee, called the option price (or premium).
- A call option allows the option buyer to purchase the underlying from the option writer at the strike price; a put option allows the option buyer to sell the underlying to the option writer at the strike price.
- Interest rate options include options on fixed income securities and options on interest rate futures contracts; the latter, called futures options, are the preferred exchange-traded vehicle for implementing investment strategies.
- Because of the difficulties of hedging particular fixed income securities, some institutional investors have found over-the-counter options more useful.

- An interest rate swap is an agreement specifying that the parties exchange interest payments at designated times, with a generic or vanilla swap calling for one party to make fixed-rate payments and the other to make floating-rate payments based on a notional principal.
- The swap rate is the interest rate paid by the fixed-rate payer.
- The swap spread is the spread paid by the fixed-rate payer over the on-the-run Treasury rate with the same maturity as the swap agreement.
- The convention in quoting swaps is to quote the payments made by the floating-rate payer flat (that is, without a spread) and the fixed-rate payer payments as a spread to the on-the-run Treasury with the same maturity as the swap (the swap spread).
- A swap position can be interpreted as either a package of forward/futures contracts or a package of cash flows from buying and selling cash market instruments.

END OPTIONAL SEGMENT

- An interest rate cap specifies that one party receive a payment if the reference rate is above the cap rate; an interest rate floor specifies that one party receive a payment if a reference rate is below the floor rate.
- The terms of a cap and floor set forth the reference rate, the strike rate, the length of the agreement, the frequency of reset, and the notional amount.
- In an interest rate cap and floor, the buyer pays an upfront fee, which represents the maximum amount that the buyer can lose and the maximum amount that the seller of the agreement can gain.
- Buying a cap is equivalent to buying a package of puts on a fixed income security and buying a floor is equivalent to buying a package of calls on a fixed income security.
- If an option is viewed as one in which the underlying is an interest rate, then buying a cap is equivalent to buying a package of calls on interest rates and buying a floor is equivalent to buying a package of puts on interest rates.
- An interest collar is created by buying an interest rate cap and selling an interest rate floor.
- Forward contracts and swaps expose the parties to bilateral counterparty risk while buyers of OTC options, caps, and floors face unilateral counterparty risk.

PRACTICE PROBLEMS

1 Suppose that a 1-year cap has a cap rate of 8% and a notional amount of $10 million. The frequency of settlement is quarterly and the reference rate is 3-month LIBOR. Assume that 3-month LIBOR for the next four quarters is as shown below. What is the payoff for each quarter?

Period	3-Month LIBOR (%)
1	8.7
2	8.0
3	7.8
4	8.2

2 Suppose that a 1-year floor has a floor rate of 4% and a notional amount of $20 million. The frequency of settlement is quarterly and the reference rate is 3-month LIBOR. Assume that 3-month LIBOR for the next four quarters is as shown below. What is the payoff for each quarter?

Period	3-Month LIBOR (%)
1	4.7
2	4.4
3	3.8
4	3.4

3 What counterparty risk is the seller of an interest rate floor exposed to?

4 A What is an interest rate cap or floor equivalent to?

B What is a caplet and a floorlet?

SOLUTIONS

1 There is no payoff to the cap if the cap rate exceeds 3-month LIBOR. For Periods 2 and 3, there is no payoff because 3-month LIBOR is below the cap rate. For Periods 1 and 4, there is a payoff and the payoff is determined by:

$$\$10 \text{ million} \times (\text{3-month LIBOR} - \text{Cap rate})/4$$

The payoffs are summarized below:

Period	3-Month LIBOR (%)	Payoff ($)
1	8.7	17,500
2	8.0	0
3	7.8	0
4	8.2	5,000

2 There is a payoff to the floor if 3-month LIBOR is less than the floor rate. For Periods 1 and 2, there is no payoff because 3-month LIBOR is greater than the floor rate. For Periods 3 and 4, there is a payoff and the payoff is determined by:

$$\$20 \text{ million} \times (\text{Floor rate} - \text{3-month LIBOR})/4$$

The payoffs are summarized below:

Period	3-Month LIBOR (%)	Payoff ($)
1	4.7	0
2	4.4	0
3	3.8	10,000
4	3.4	30,000

3 Once the fee for the interest rate floor is paid, the seller of an interest rate floor is not exposed to counterparty risk. Only the seller, not the buyer, must perform.

4 **A** An interest rate cap or floor is equivalent to a package of interest rate options.

B Since a cap is equivalent to a package of interest rate options, each option in the package is called a caplet. Similarly, since a floor is equivalent to a package of interest rate options, each interest rate option in the package is called a floorlet.

LOFT
68

READING

56

Credit Default Swaps

by Brian Rose and Don M. Chance, CFA

LEARNING OUTCOMES

Mastery	The candidate should be able to:
☐	a. describe credit default swaps (CDS), single-name and index CDS, and the parameters that define a given CDS product;
☐	b. describe credit events and settlement protocols with respect to CDS;
☐	c. explain the principles underlying, and factors that influence, the market's pricing of CDS;
☐	d. describe the use of CDS to manage credit exposures and to express views regarding changes in shape and/or level of the credit curve;
☐	e. describe the use of CDS to take advantage of valuation differences among separate markets, such as bonds, loans, and equities.

INTRODUCTION

1

A **credit derivative** is a derivative instrument in which the underlying is a measure of a borrower's credit quality. Four types of credit derivatives are (1) total return swaps, (2) credit spread options, (3) credit-linked notes, and (4) credit default swaps, or CDS.[1] The first three are not frequently encountered. CDS have clearly emerged as the primary type of credit derivative and, as such, are the topic of this reading. In a CDS, one party makes payments to the other and receives in return the promise of compensation if a third party defaults.

In any derivative, the payoff is based on (*derivedfrom*) the performance of an underlying instrument, rate, or asset that we call the underlying.[2] For a CDS, the underlying is the credit quality of a borrower. At its most fundamental level, a CDS provides protection against default, but it also protects against changes in the market's

1 We use the expression CDS in both singular and plural form, as opposed to CDSs or CDS's.

2 Consistent with industry practice, we use the word underlying as a noun even though it generally requires a follower, such as in underlying asset. Because derivatives exist on credit and other non-assets, the word underlying has taken on the properties of a noun in the world of derivatives.

perception of a borrower's credit quality well in advance of default. The value of a CDS will rise and fall as opinions change about the likelihood of default. The actual event of default might never occur.

Derivatives are characterized as *contingent claims*, meaning that their payoffs are dependent on the occurrence of a specific event or outcome. For an equity option, the event is that the stock price is above (for a call) or below (for a put) the exercise price at expiration. For a CDS, the credit event is more difficult to identify. In financial markets, whether a default has occurred is sometimes not clear. Bankruptcy would seem to be a default, but many companies declare bankruptcy and some ultimately pay all of their debts. Some companies restructure their debts, usually with creditor approval but without formally declaring bankruptcy. Creditors are clearly damaged when debts are not paid, not paid on time, or paid in a form different from what was promised, but they are also damaged when there is simply an increase in the likelihood that the debt will not be paid. The extent of damage to the creditor can be difficult to determine. A decline in the price of a bond when investors perceive an increase in the likelihood of default is a very real loss to the bondholder. Credit default swaps are designed to protect creditors against such credit events. As a result of the complexity of defining what constitutes default, the industry has expended great effort to provide clear guidance on what credit events are covered by a CDS contract. As with all efforts to write a perfect contract, however, no such device exists and disputes do occasionally arise. We will take a look at these issues later.

This reading is organized as follows: Section 2 explores basic definitions and concepts, and Section 3 covers the elements of valuation and pricing. Section 4 discusses applications. Section 5 provides a summary.

2 BASIC DEFINITIONS AND CONCEPTS

We start by defining a **credit default swap**:

> *A credit default swap is a derivative contract between two parties, a credit protection buyer and credit protection seller, in which the buyer makes a series of cash payments to the seller and receives a promise of compensation for credit losses resulting from the default—that is, a pre-defined credit event—of a third party.*

In a CDS contract there are two counterparties, the **credit protection buyer** and the **credit protection seller**. The buyer agrees to make a series of periodic payments to the seller over the life of the contract (which are determined and fixed at contract initiation) and receives in return a promise that if default occurs, the protection seller will compensate the protection buyer. If default occurs, the periodic payments made by the protection buyer to the protection seller terminate. Exhibit 1 shows the structure of payment flows.

Exhibit 1 Payment Structure of a CDS

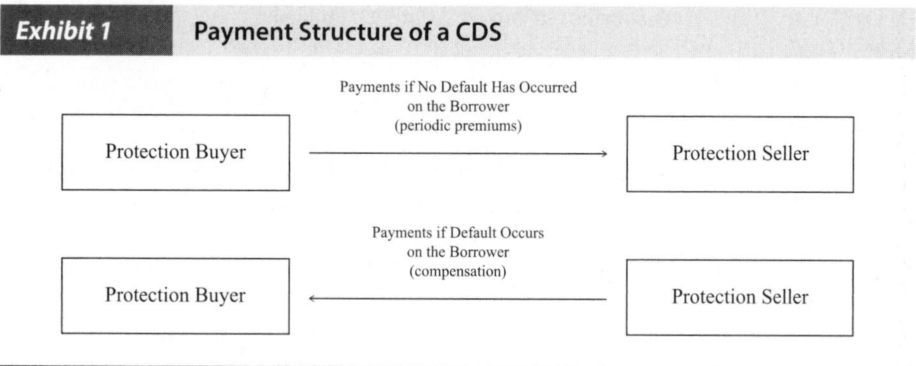

Credit default swaps are somewhat similar to put options. Put options effectively enable the option holder to sell (put) the underlying to the option seller if the underlying performs poorly relative to the exercise price. The option holder is thus compensated for the poor performance of the underlying. CDS act in a similar manner. If a default occurs, a loan or bond has clearly performed badly. The protection buyer is then compensated by the protection seller. How that compensation occurs and how much protection it provides are some points we will discuss.[3]

The majority of CDS are written on debt issued by corporate borrowers, which will be our focus in this reading. But note that CDS can be written on the debt of sovereign governments and state and local governments. In addition, CDS can be written on portfolios of loans, mortgages, or debt securities.

2.1 Types of CDS

There are three types of CDS; single-name CDS, index CDS, and tranche CDS.[4] A CDS on one specific borrower is called a **single-name CDS**. The borrower is called the **reference entity**, and the contract specifies a **reference obligation**, a particular debt instrument issued by the borrower that is the designated instrument being covered. The designated instrument is usually a senior unsecured obligation, which is often referred to as a senior CDS, but the reference obligation is not the only instrument covered by the CDS. Any debt obligation issued by the borrower that is *pari passu* (ranked equivalently in priority of claims) or higher relative to the reference obligation is covered. The payoff of the CDS is determined by the **cheapest-to-deliver** obligation, which is the debt instrument that can be purchased and delivered at the lowest cost but has the same seniority as the reference obligation.

EXAMPLE 1

Cheapest-to-Deliver Obligation

Assume that a company with several debt issues trading in the market files for bankruptcy (i.e., a credit event takes place). What is the cheapest-to-deliver obligation for a senior CDS contract?

A A subordinated unsecured bond trading at 20% of par

3 Note that a CDS does not eliminate credit risk. It eliminates the credit risk of one party but substitutes the credit risk of the CDS seller. Although there are no guarantees that the CDS seller will not default, as was seen with several large financial institutions in the crisis that started in 2007, most CDS sellers are relatively high-quality borrowers. If they were not, they could not be active sellers of CDS.

4 In addition to CDS, there are also options on CDS, which are called CDS swaptions. We will not cover this instrument here. Swaptions in general are covered elsewhere in the derivatives material.

B A five-year senior unsecured bond trading at 50% of par

C A two-year senior unsecured bond trading at 45% of par

Solution:

C is correct. The cheapest-to-deliver, or lowest-priced, instrument is the two-year senior unsecured bond trading at 45% of par. Although the bond in A trades at a lower dollar price, it is subordinated and, therefore, does not qualify for coverage under the senior CDS. Note that even if the CDS holder also held the five-year bonds, he would still receive payment on the CDS based on the cheapest-to-deliver obligation, not the specific obligations he holds.

A second type of credit default swap, an **index CDS**, involves a combination of borrowers. These instruments have been created such that it is possible to trade indices of CDS. This type of instrument allows participants to take positions on the credit risk of a combination of companies, in much the same way that investors can trade index or exchange-traded funds that are combinations of the equities of companies. Correlation of returns is a strong determinant of a portfolio's behavior. For index CDS, this concept takes the form of a factor called **credit correlation**, and it is a key determinant of the value of an index CDS. Analyzing the effects of those correlations is a highly specialized subject beyond the CFA Program, but the reader should be aware that much effort is placed on modeling how defaults by certain companies are connected to defaults by other companies. The more correlated the defaults, the more costly it is to purchase protection for a combination of the companies. In contrast, for a diverse combination of companies whose defaults have low correlations, it will be much less expensive to purchase protection.

A third type of CDS is the **tranche CDS**, which covers a combination of borrowers but only up to pre-specified levels of losses—much in the same manner that asset-backed securities are divided into tranches, each covering particular levels of losses. The tranche CDS is only a small portion of the CDS market, and we will not cover it any further.

2.2 Important Features of CDS Markets and Instruments

As we will describe in more detail later, the CDS market is large, global, and well organized. The unofficial industry governing body is the International Swaps and Derivatives Association (ISDA), which publishes industry-supported conventions that facilitate the functioning of the market. Parties to CDS contracts generally agree that their contracts will conform to ISDA specifications. These terms are specified in a document called the **ISDA Master Agreement**, which the parties to a CDS sign. In Europe, the standard CDS contract is called the Standard Europe Contract, and in the United States and Canada, it is called the Standard North American Contract. Other standardized contracts exist for Asia, Australia, Latin America, and a few specific countries.

Each CDS contract specifies a **notional amount**, or "notional" for short, which is the amount of protection being purchased. For example, if a company has a bond issue of €100 million, a CDS could be constructed for any amount up to €100 million. The notional amount can be thought of as the *size* of the contract. It is important to understand that the total amount of CDS notional can exceed the amount of debt outstanding of the reference entity.[5] As we will discuss later, the credit protection buyer does not have to be an actual creditor holding exposure (i.e., owing a loan, bond, or other debt instrument). It can be simply a party that believes that there will be a change in the credit quality of the reference entity.

As with all derivatives, the CDS contract has an expiration or maturity date, and coverage is provided up to that date. The typical maturity range is 1 to 10 years, with 5 years being the most common and actively traded maturity, but the two parties can negotiate any maturity. Maturity dates are typically the last day of March, June, September, or December, with June and December being the most popular. As with bonds, a CDS contract of a particular maturity is really that maturity only for an instant. For example, a five-year CDS is technically no longer a five-year CDS just a day later. As the maturity of that CDS decreases, a new five-year CDS is created, and it begins to be referred to as the five-year CDS. Of course, this point is no different from ordinary bonds.

The buyer of a CDS pays a periodic premium to the seller, referred to as the **CDS spread**, which is a return over LIBOR required to protect against credit risk. It is sometimes referred to as a credit spread. Conceptually, it is the same as the credit spread on a bond, the compensation for bearing credit risk. This premium is determined based on valuation models that are beyond the scope of the CFA program. Nonetheless, it is important to understand the concept of the credit spread on a CDS, and we will have much more to say about it later in this reading.

An important advancement in the development of CDS in recent years has been in establishing standard annual coupon rates on CDS contracts.[6] Formerly, the rate was set at the credit spread. If a CDS required a rate of 4% to compensate the protection seller for the assumption of credit risk, the protection buyer made quarterly payments amounting to 4% annually. Now CDS rates are standardized, with the most common coupons being either 1% or 5%. The 1% rate typically is used for a CDS on an investment-grade company or index, and the 5% rate is used for a CDS on a high-yield company or index. Obviously, either standardized rate might not be the appropriate rate to compensate the seller. Clearly, not all investment-grade companies have equivalent credit risk, and not all high-yield companies have equivalent credit risk. In effect, the standard rate may be too high or too low. This discrepancy is accounted for by an **upfront payment**, commonly called the **upfront premium**. The differential between the credit spread and the standard rate is converted to a present value basis. Thus, a protection buyer paying a standard rate that is insufficient to compensate the protection seller will make a cash upfront payment. Similarly, a credit spread less than the standard rate would result in a cash payment from the protection seller to the protection buyer.

Regardless of whether either party makes an upfront payment, the reference entity's credit quality could change during the life of the contract, thereby resulting in changes in the value of the CDS. These changes are reflected in the price of the CDS in the market. Consider a high-yield company with a 5% credit spread and its CDS bears a coupon of 5%. Therefore, there is no upfront payment. The protection buyer

---

5 This point will be discussed in more detail later, but here we will address the obvious question of how the aggregate amount of protection can exceed the aggregate risk. As an analogy, consider the exercise of an option. Given the number of options created, at exercise the call option holders could have the right to buy more shares than exist or put option holders could have the right to sell more shares than exist. Such an event has never come close to happening. In the CDS market, the cash settlement feature, which is typically not used for options on stocks, solves this problem. We will describe how cash settlement works later.

6 The reader should be aware of the potential confusion over the term "coupon." The reference bond will make payments that are referred to collectively as the coupon. A CDS on the reference bond will have its own coupon rate, which is calculated based on the expected payoff. Furthermore, with standardization of CDS coupons, there is likely to be a third payment referred to as a coupon. The reader must be alert to the context.

simply agrees to make 5% payments over the life of the CDS. Now suppose that at some later date, the reference entity experiences a decrease in its credit quality. The credit protection buyer is thus paying 5% for risk that now merits a rate higher than 5%. The coverage and cost of protection are the same, but the risk being covered is greater. The value of the CDS to the credit protection buyer has, therefore, increased, and if desired, he could unwind the position to capture the gain. The credit protection seller has experienced a loss in value of the instrument because he is receiving 5% to cover a risk that is higher than it was when the contract was initiated. It should be apparent that absent any other exposure to the reference entity, if the credit quality of the reference entity decreases, the credit protection buyer gains and the credit protection seller loses.[7] The market value of the CDS reflects these gains and losses.

Because of these CDS characteristics, there is potential confusion regarding which party is long and which is short. Normally, we think of buyers as being long and sellers as being short, but in the CDS world, it is the opposite. Because the credit protection buyer promises to make a series of future payments, it is regarded as being short. This is consistent with the fact that in the financial world, "shorts" are said to benefit when things go badly. Credit quality is based on the underlying debt obligation, and when it improves, the credit protection seller benefits. When credit quality deteriorates, the credit protection buyer benefits. Hence, the CDS industry views the credit protection seller as the long and the buyer as the short. This point can lead to confusion because we effectively say the credit protection buyer is short and the credit protection seller is long.

2.3 Credit and Succession Events

The **credit event** is what defines default by the reference entity—that is, the outcome that triggers a payment from the credit protection seller to the credit protection buyer. This event must be unambiguous: Did it occur, or did it not? For the market to function well, the answer to this question must be clear.

There are three general types of credit events: bankruptcy, failure to pay, and restructuring. **Bankruptcy** is a declaration provided for by a country's laws that typically involves the establishment of a legal procedure that forces creditors to defer their claims. Bankruptcy essentially creates a temporary fence around the company through which the creditors cannot pass. During the bankruptcy process, the defaulting party works with its creditors and the court to attempt to establish a plan for repaying the debt. If that plan fails, there is likely to be a full liquidation of the company, at which time the court determines the payouts to the various creditors. Until liquidation occurs, the company normally continues to operate. Many companies do not liquidate and are able to emerge from bankruptcy. A bankruptcy filing by the reference entity is universally regarded as a credit event in CDS contracts.

Another credit event recognized in standard CDS contracts is **failure to pay**, which occurs when a borrower does not make a scheduled payment of principal or interest on any outstanding obligations after a grace period, without a formal bankruptcy filing. The third type of event, **restructuring**, refers to a number of possible events, including reduction or deferral of principal or interest, change in seniority or priority of an obligation, or change in the currency in which principal or interest is scheduled to be paid. To qualify as a credit event, the restructuring must be involuntary, meaning that it is forced on the borrower by the creditors who must accept the restructured

7 A key element of this point is the absence of any other exposure to the reference entity. The credit protection buyer could be holding the debt itself, and the CDS might cover only a portion of the debt. Thus, the credit protection buyer might be gaining on the CDS, as described in the text, but be losing on its overall position.

terms.[8] In the United States, restructuring is not considered a credit event because bankruptcy is typically the preferred route for U.S. companies. Outside the United States, restructuring is more commonly used and is considered a credit event. The Greek debt crisis is a good example of a restructuring that triggered a credit event.

Determination of whether a credit event occurs is done by a 15-member group within the ISDA called the Determinations Committee (DC). Each region of the world has a Determinations Committee, which consists of 10 CDS dealer banks and 5 non-bank end users. To declare a credit event, there must be a supermajority vote of 12 members.

The determinations committees also play a role in determining whether a **succession event** occurred. A succession event arises when there is a change in the corporate structure of the reference entity, such as through a merger, divestiture, spinoff, or any similar action in which ultimate responsibility for the debt in question becomes unclear. For example, if a company acquires all of the shares of a target company, it ordinarily assumes the target company's debt as well. Many mergers, however, are more complicated and can involve only partial acquisition of shares. Spinoffs and divestitures can also involve some uncertainty about who is responsible for certain debts. When such a question arises, it becomes critical for CDS holders. The question is ordinarily submitted to a DC, and its resolution often involves complex legal interpretations of contract provisions and country laws. If a succession event is declared, the CDS contract is modified to reflect the DC's interpretation of whoever it believes becomes the obligor for the original debt. Ultimately, the CDS contract could be split among multiple entities.

2.4 Settlement Protocols

If the DC declares that a credit event has occurred, the two parties to a CDS have the right, but not the obligation, to settle. **Settlement** typically occurs 30 days after declaration of the credit event by the DC. CDS can be settled by **physical settlement** or by **cash settlement**. The former is less common and involves actual delivery of the debt instrument in exchange for a payment by the credit protection seller of the notional amount of the contract. In cash settlement, the credit protection seller pays cash to the credit protection buyer. Determining the amount of that payment is a critical factor because opinions can differ about how much money has actually been lost. The payment should essentially be the loss that the credit protection buyer has incurred, but determining that amount is not straightforward. Default on a debt does not mean that the creditor will lose the entire amount owed. A portion of the loss could be recovered. The percentage of the loss recovered is called the **recovery rate**. It then becomes the percentage received by the protection buyer relative to the amount owed. The complement is called the **payout ratio**, which is essentially an estimate of the expected credit loss. The **payout amount** is determined as the payout ratio multiplied by the notional.[9]

Payout ratio = 1 – Recovery rate (%)

Payout amount = Payout ratio × Notional

Actual recovery can be a very long process, however, and can occur much later than the payoff date of the CDS. To determine an appropriate payout ratio, the industry conducts an auction in which major banks and dealers submit bids and offers for the

8 Although our focus is on corporate debt, sovereign and municipal governments sometimes declare a moratorium or, more drastically, a repudiation of debt, both of which typically qualify as credit events.

9 Do not confuse this payout ratio with the payout ratio in equity analysis, which is the percentage of earnings paid out as dividends.

cheapest-to-deliver defaulted debt. This process identifies the market's expectation for the recovery rate and the complementary payout ratio, and the CDS parties agree to accept the outcome of the auction, even though the actual recovery rate can ultimately be quite different, which is an important point if the CDS protection buyer also holds the underlying debt.

EXAMPLE 2

Settlement Preference

A French company files for bankruptcy, triggering various CDS contracts. It has two series of senior bonds outstanding: Bond A trades at 30% of par, and Bond B trades at 40% of par. Investor X owns €10 million of Bond A and owns €10 million of CDS protection. Investor Y owns €10 million of Bond B and owns €10 million of CDS protection.

1 Determine the recovery rate for both CDS contracts.
2 Explain whether Investor X would prefer to cash settle or physically settle her CDS contract or whether she is indifferent.
3 Explain whether Investor Y would prefer to cash settle or physically settle his CDS contract or whether he is indifferent.

Solution to 1:

Bond A is the cheapest-to-deliver obligation, trading at 30% of par, so the recovery rate for both CDS contracts is 30%.

Solution to 2:

Investor X has no preference between settlement methods. She can cash settle for €7 million [(1 – 30%) × €10 million] and sell her bond for €3 million, for total proceeds of €10 million. Alternatively, she can physically deliver her entire €10 million face amount of bonds to the counterparty in exchange for €10 million in cash.

Solution to 3:

Investor Y would prefer a cash settlement because he owns Bond B, which is worth more than the cheapest-to-deliver obligation. He will receive the same €7 million payout on his CDS contract, but can sell Bond B for €4 million, for total proceeds of €11 million. If he were to physically settle his contract, he would receive only €10 million, the face amount of his bond.

2.5 CDS Index Products

So far, we have mostly been focusing on single-name CDS. As noted, there are also index CDS products. A company called Markit has been instrumental in producing CDS indices. Of course, a CDS index is not in itself a traded instrument any more than a stock index is a traded product. As with the major stock indices, however, the industry has created traded instruments based on the Markit indices. These instruments are CDS that generate a payoff based on any default that occurs on any entity covered by the index.

The Markit indices are classified by region and further classified (or divided) by credit quality. The two most commonly traded regions are North America and Europe. North American indices are identified by the symbol CDX, and European, Asian, and Australian indices are identified as iTraxx. Within each geographic category are investment-grade and high-yield indices. The former are identified as CDX

IG and iTraxx Main, each comprising 125 entities. The latter are identified as CDX HY, consisting of 100 entities, and iTraxx Crossover, consisting of up to 50 high-yield entities.[10] Investment-grade index CDS are typically quoted in terms of spreads, whereas high-yield index CDS are quoted in terms of prices. Both types of products use standardized coupons. All CDS indices are equally weighted. Thus, if there are 125 entities, the settlement on one entity is 1/125 of the notional.[11]

Markit updates the components of each index every six months by creating new series while retaining the old series. The latest created series is called the **on-the-run** series, whereas the older series are called **off-the-run** series. When an investor moves from one series to a new one, the move is called a **roll**. When an entity within an index defaults, that entity is removed from the index and settled as a single-name CDS based on its relative proportion in the index. The index then moves forward with a smaller notional.

Index CDS are typically used to take positions on the credit risk of the sectors covered by the indices as well as to protect bond portfolios that consist of or are similar to the components of the indices. Standardization is generally undertaken to increase trading volume, which is somewhat limited in the single-name market with so many highly diverse entities. With CDS indices on standardized portfolios based on the credit risk of well-identified companies, market participants have responded by trading them in large volumes. Indeed, index CDS are typically more liquid than single-name CDS with average daily trading volume several times that of single-name CDS.

EXAMPLE 3

Hedging and Exposure Using Index CDS

Assume that an investor sells $500 million of protection on the CDX IG index. Concerned about the creditworthiness of a few of the components, the investor hedges a portion of the credit risk in each. For Company A, he purchases $3 million of single-name CDS protection, and Company A subsequently defaults.

1 What is the investor's net notional exposure to Company A?

2 What proportion of his exposure to Company A has he hedged?

3 What is the remaining notional on his index CDS trade?

Solution to 1:

The investor is long $4 million notional ($500 million/125) through the index CDS and is short $3 million notional through the single-name CDS. His net notional exposure is $1 million.

Solution to 2:

He has hedged 75% of his exposure ($3 million out of $4 million).

Solution to 3:

His index CDS has $496 million remaining notional.

10 Markit also creates other categories of CDS indices, including emerging markets, sovereigns, municipals, high-yield/high-beta companies, and high-volatility companies.

11 Some confusion might arise from quoting certain CDS as prices and some as spreads, but keep in mind that the bond market often quotes bonds as prices and sometimes as yields. For example, a Treasury bond can be described as having a price of 120 or a yield of 2¾%. Both terms, combined with the other characteristics of the bond, imply the same concept.

2.6 Market Characteristics

Credit default swaps trade in the over-the-counter market in a network of banks and other financial institutions. To better understand this market, we will first review how credit derivatives and specifically CDS were started.

As financial intermediaries, banks draw funds from savings-surplus sectors, primarily consumers, and channel them to savings-deficit sectors, primarily businesses. Corporate lending is indeed the core element of banking. When a bank makes a corporate loan, it assumes two primary risks. One is that the borrower will not repay principal and interest, and the other is that interest rates will change such that the return the bank is earning is not commensurate with returns on comparable instruments in the marketplace. The former is called **credit risk** or **default risk**, and the latter is called **interest rate risk**. There are many ways to manage interest rate risk.[12] Until around the mid-1990s, credit risk could be managed only by using traditional methods, such as analysis of the borrower, its industry, and the macroeconomy, as well as control methods, such as credit limits, monitoring, and collateral. These two groups of techniques defined what amounted only to internal credit risk management. In effect, the only defenses against credit risk were to not make a loan, to lend but require collateral (the value of which is also at risk), or to lend and closely monitor the borrower, hoping that any problems could be foreseen and dealt with before a default occurred.

Around 1995, credit derivatives were created to provide a new and potentially more effective method of managing credit risk.[13] They allow credit risk to be transferred from the lender to another party. In so doing, they facilitate the separation of interest rate risk from credit risk. Banks can then provide their most important service—lending—knowing that the credit risk can be transferred to another party if so desired. This ability to easily transfer credit risk allows banks to greatly expand their loan business. Given that lending is such a large and vital component of any economy, credit derivatives facilitate economic growth and have expanded to cover, and indeed are primarily focused on, the short-, intermediate-, and long-term bond markets. In fact, credit derivatives are more effective in the bond market, in which terms and conditions are far more standard, than in the bank loan market. Of the four types of credit derivatives, credit default swaps have clearly established themselves as the most widely used instrument. Indeed, in today's markets CDS are nearly the only credit derivative used to any great extent.

In principle, insurance contracts could be written that would allow the transfer of credit risk from one party to another. Credit insurance has existed for many years, but its growth has been constrained by the fact that insurance products are typically more consumer focused than commercially focused. Because it is such an important consumer product, insurance is very heavily regulated. It is very costly for insurance products to expand into new areas with different regulatory authorities. Thus, the ability of a relatively standard product to expand in similar form beyond its regulatory borders is limited. The CDS instrument arose and grew partly in response to this problem. By distinguishing CDS from insurance, the industry was able to effectively

12 These methods include duration-based strategies, gap management, and the use of interest rate derivatives.

13 There is some evidence that the first credit derivative was created by Blythe Masters, a managing director of J.P. Morgan, and was used to manage the potential risk of Exxon defaulting following its oil spill near Valdez, Alaska.

offer a product that entailed a buyer making a series of promised payments in return for which it received a promise of compensation for losses, a product almost economically identical to insurance but legally distinct.[14]

CDS transactions are executed in the over-the-counter market by phone, instant message, or the Bloomberg message service. Trade information is reported to the **Depository Trust and Clearinghouse Corporation**, which is a U.S.-headquartered entity providing post-trade clearing, settlement, and information services for many kinds of securities in addition to asset custody and asset servicing. New regulations require that almost all CDS be centrally cleared, meaning that parties will send their contracts through clearinghouses that collect and distribute payments and impose margin requirements, as well as mark positions to market. In so doing, a considerable amount of systemic risk is eliminated.[15]

The Bank for International Settlements reported that as of June 2012, the gross notional amount of CDS was about \$26.9 trillion with a market value of \$1.2 trillion.[16] A rough estimate of the net notional, or promised payments if all possible defaults occur, is about 10% of the gross notional. Single-name CDS are about 60% of the credit derivatives market.

The size of the market today is considerably smaller than it was just a few years ago. For example, in December 2007 CDS gross notional was \$57.9 trillion, about twice the size as in December 2011. The decline is accounted for by the fact that the use of CDS fell following the 2008 financial crisis. CDS had been widely used, and indeed overused and mismanaged, by many financial institutions that were ultimately bailed out by governments and central banks. Many of these institutions took credit risk exposures that they thought were diversified or controlled by complex models they had spent millions of dollars and many years developing. Notably, the financial crisis was largely brought about by a real estate crash and the widespread use of subprime mortgages. Credit risk proved to be globally systemic, a possibility not envisioned by risk managers of many well-known institutions, such as AIG. With so many of the large participants in the CDS market effectively out of business, bailed out or taken over, or having to pull back their lending substantially, the use of CDS declined greatly. Nonetheless, the CDS global market is extremely large and well worth our attention.

Until 2010, CDS were essentially unregulated over-the-counter financial instruments. Because of some of the problems discussed earlier, they are now under government regulations or securities and derivatives guidelines in virtually all countries. These regulations require that most CDS transactions be centrally reported and, as noted, most have to be cleared through an authorized clearinghouse.

3 BASICS OF VALUATION AND PRICING

Derivatives are typically valued by constructing a hedge between the derivative and the underlying that produces a risk-free position and merits a return of the risk-free rate. The price of the underlying and certain other variables jointly imply the price of

---

14 Probably the most important step in the development of credit default swaps was not calling them "insurance," which would have almost surely triggered a different set of regulations. It is unclear why they are called *swaps*. As presented elsewhere in the curriculum on the subject of derivatives, swaps involve a series of bilateral payments in which parties exchange a series of cash flows. A CDS is clearly a variation of an option and is not at all a swap.

15 The use and operations of clearinghouses are covered in Level I readings on derivatives.

16 By comparison, interest rate swap notional at that same time was about \$379 trillion. These figures are obtained from the Bank for International Settlements' semi-annual surveys of derivatives usage.

the derivative that guarantees a risk-free return on the hedged position. In the context of CDS, pricing means determining the CDS spread or upfront payment given a particular coupon rate for a contract. In turn, this process implies the CDS price.[17]

This principle is fairly easy to apply for conventional derivatives but somewhat more difficult for credit derivatives. For conventional derivatives, the underlying is usually traded in active markets. For example, options on Royal Dutch Shell, futures on a German government bond, and swaps on the yen are relatively easy to value because the underlying instruments trade actively. But the underlying of a CDS is credit, which is a somewhat vague concept. Credit does not "trade" in the traditional sense but exists implicitly within the bond and loan market. The actual valuation of credit, which reveals the price at which credit risk can be sold, is much more difficult to obtain in relation to the valuation of derivatives driven by equities, interest rates, and currencies.

The exact application of these concepts in CDS pricing models is an advanced topic beyond the scope of the CFA Program. It is important, nonetheless, that CFA charterholders have a good grasp of the factors that determine CDS pricing, but the details are not necessary. Thus, we will cover this material at a high level.

3.1 Basic Pricing Concepts

The most important element of CDS pricing is the **probability of default**. With a few exceptions, a loan or bond involves a series of promised payments. Non-payment on any one of these obligations is a default. To illustrate, consider a simple example of a two-year, 5%, $1,000 loan, with one interest payment of $50 due in one year and a final interest and principal payment of $1,050 due in two years. Each of these payments is subject to the possibility of default.

It can be a bit confusing to refer to a general probability of default. There might be a 2% chance of defaulting on the first interest payment but a greater probability of default on the final interest and principal payment because the amount owed is larger and there is a longer period of time until the second payment. The probability of default is normally greater over a longer period of time.[18]

The relevant probability of default is referred to as a concept from statistics called the **hazard rate**. The hazard rate is the probability that an event will occur *given that it has not already occurred*. Once the event occurs, there is no further likelihood of its occurrence. A hazard rate can also be viewed as a conditional probability. It is the probability that something will occur, with the condition that it has not already occurred.

In the life insurance industry, the probability of death clearly meets the concept of a hazard rate. One cannot die if one has already died. Analogously, in the credit industry, default is treated this way.[19] In our example, let the hazard rates be 2% for the first interest payment and 4% for the final interest and principal payment. The 4% rate is the probability that default occurs in Year 2, given that it has not occurred in Year 1. We will assume a 40% recovery rate, which is a common assumption for

17 Recall that we have sometimes distinguished between valuation and pricing for forward, futures, and swaps but not options. Although credit default swaps may be called "swaps," they are really options. Valuation and pricing are, thus, the same concept.

18 The probability of default is typically greater over a longer period of time, because there is more time for the borrower's financial condition to worsen. But there are some exceptions. A borrower could be struggling financially in the short run but might have better prospects in the long run.

19 Technically, a company can default more than once. It can declare bankruptcy, reorganize, continue to operate and even emerge from bankruptcy only to default again, perhaps years later. For example, there are many instances of this occurring in the U.S. airline and auto industries. Credit risk modeling typically does not consider such possibilities because they are fairly uncommon. For our purposes, a CDS terminates with the first credit event, so this event is the principal focus.

senior unsecured debt. Thus, if default occurs on the \$50 payment, the bondholder will receive \$20 (\$50 × 40%), and if default occurs on the final \$1,050 payment, the bondholder receives \$420 (\$1,050 × 40%). Exhibit 2 shows the possibilities. Note that there are three outcomes: the bondholder receives (1) \$50 at Year 1 and \$1,050 at Year 2 with a probability of 98% × 96% = 94.08%, (2) \$50 at Year 1 and \$420 at Year 2 with probability 98% × 4% = 3.92%, and (3) \$20 at Year 1 and \$420 at Year 2 with probability 2%.[20] These probabilities add up to 100%.

Exhibit 2 **Default Possibilities on a Two-Year \$1,000 Loan with Annual Payments at 5% Interest**

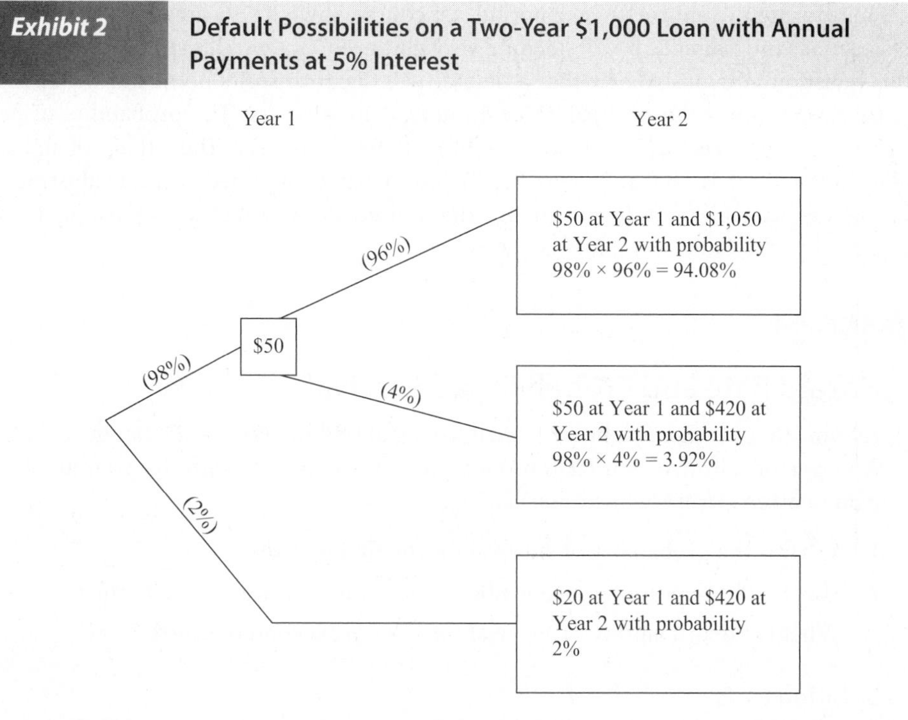

Now, suppose we ask the question, "what is the probability of default?" There are several possible answers because there are really several questions. The probability of default is 2% on the first payment but 4% on the second. In a more general sense, we might like to know the probability of *any* default occurring or, in a complementary sense, the **probability of survival**. In this problem, the probability of survival is 0.98 multiplied by 0.96, approximately 94.08%. Thus, the probability of default occurring at some time in the life of the loan is 100% – 94.08% = 5.92%.

An important concept in credit analysis is the **loss given default**, which is the amount that will be lost if a default occurs. In the example, that amount cannot be precisely specified because it must refer to a particular default. If the borrower defaults on the first payment, the amount lost is \$50 – \$20 = \$30 on the first payment and \$1,050 – \$420 = \$630 on the second, for a total loss given default of \$660. If the borrower defaults only on the second payment, the loss given default is \$630. From the loss given default, it is possible to calculate the **expected loss**, which is simply the full amount owed minus the expected recovery, or the loss given default, multiplied by the probability of default:

20 Although we say "at Year 1" and "at Year 2," we do not really know when during a year recovery will occur. In the exhibit, we simply assume that the cash flow occurs "at Year 1 (or 2)," but it could occur earlier in the year. Also, for the third outcome, we assume that if default occurs on the first payment, it will also occur on the second but that recovery on the second will be the same as if the first were made in full. This might not be the case in practice, but other estimates can be easily inserted.

Expected loss = Loss given default × Probability of default

In the example, there is a 2% chance of losing \$660 and a (0.98) × (0.04) = 0.0392, or 3.92%, chance of losing \$630. Thus, unadjusted for time value of money, the expected loss is (0.02) × (\$660) + (0.0392) × (\$630) = \$37.90. This calculation shows that the expected loss is obtained by multiplying the losses given defaults (\$660 and \$630, respectively) by the probabilities of default (2% and 3.92%, respectively).

Now consider another possibility, a 10-year bond with an equivalent hazard rate of 2% each year.[21] Suppose we want to know the probability that the borrower will not default during the entire 10-year period. Of course, if we try to draw a 10-year tree diagram, as in Exhibit 2, it will become very cluttered, but we can still easily answer this question. The probability that a default will occur at some point during the 10 years is one minus the probability of no default in 10 years. The probability of no default in 10 years is (0.98) × (0.98) ... (0.98) = $(0.98)^{10}$ = 0.p817. Thus, the probability of default is 1 – 0.817 = 0.183, or 18.3%. This somewhat simplified example illustrates how a low probability of default in any one period can turn into a surprisingly high probability of default over a longer period of time.

EXAMPLE 4

Hazard Rate and Probability of Survival

Assume that a company's hazard rate is a constant 8% per year, or 2% per quarter. An investor sells five-year CDS protection on the company with the premiums paid quarterly over the next five years.

1 What is the probability of survival for the first quarter?

2 What is the conditional probability of survival for the second quarter?

3 What is the probability of survival through the second quarter?

Solution to 1:

The probability of survival for the first quarter is 98% (100% minus the 2% hazard rate).

Solution to 2:

The conditional probability of survival for the second quarter is also 98%, because the hazard rate is constant at 2%. In other words, *conditional on the company having survived the first quarter,* there is a 2% probability of default in the second quarter.

Solution to 3:

The probability of survival through the second quarter is 96.04%. The probability of survival through the first quarter is 98%, and the conditional probability of survival through the second quarter is also 98%. The probability of survival through the second quarter is thus 98% × 98% = 96.04%. Alternatively, 1 – 96.04% = 3.96% is the probability of default sometime during the first two quarters.

21 The hazard rate is unlikely to be the same each year, but we will use a simple case here to minimize the computations.

Understanding the concept of pricing a CDS is facilitated by recognizing that there are essentially two sides, or legs, of a contract. There is the **protection leg**, which is the contingent payment that the credit protection seller may have to make to the credit protection buyer, and the **premium leg**, which is the series of payments the credit protection buyer promises to make to the credit protection seller.

To estimate the value of the protection leg, the probability of each payment, the timing of each payment, and the discount rate must be taken into account.[22] In essence, we need to determine the expected payoff of each promised payment on the reference entity. Having estimated the probability of default for each payment, we find the expected payoff of a given payment on the reference entity by multiplying the payment adjusted for the expected recovery rate by the probability of survival and then discounted at an appropriate rate. The sum of all of these amounts is the expected payoff of the bond or loan, which should, of course, be the price at which the bond is trading in the market. Then, suppose we assume there is no default possibility on the bond. We could then discount all payments at the risk-free rate to obtain the hypothetical value of the bond if it had no credit risk. The difference between these two figures is the value of the credit exposure. In other words, what an investor would pay for the bond, which contains credit risk, minus what the investor would pay if the bond had no credit risk is what it would cost to eliminate the credit risk. This amount is, therefore, the value of the protection leg and is the present value of the contingent obligation of the credit protection seller to the credit protection buyer. Although we could obtain the value of the bond and implicitly the credit premium from the bond's price in the market, we would have to trust that the bond market is properly pricing the credit risk. That may not be the case, as we will discuss later.

Now, we must evaluate the premium leg or present value of the payments made by the protection buyer to the protection seller. With a fixed standardized coupon rate, this calculation would seem simple, but one complication must be considered. For example, for a five-year CDS, the credit protection buyer promises a set of payments over five years, but if the credit event occurs any time during that five-year period, the payments terminate. Hence, the various hazard rates must also be applied to the premium leg to obtain the expected payments promised by the CDS buyer to the seller.

The difference in value of the protection leg and premium leg determines the upfront payment. The party having a claim on the greater present value must make up the cash difference at the initiation date of the contract. Thus, we have

Upfront payment = Present value of protection leg – Present value of premium leg

and if the result is greater (less) than zero, the protection buyer (seller) pays the protection seller (buyer). The actual mechanics of these calculations are somewhat more complex than described here. As noted, for the CFA Program, we take a high-level view of credit default swaps and leave the details to credit derivatives specialists.

3.2 The Credit Curve

The credit spread of a debt instrument is the rate in excess of LIBOR that investors expect to receive to justify holding the instrument.[23] The credit spread can be expressed roughly as the probability of default multiplied by the loss given default, with the latter

22 There is a technical distinction between the true probability of default and the risk-neutral probability of default. Pricing is done using the risk-neutral probability of default, not the true probability of default. Risk-neutral probability is covered in the Level I readings on derivatives. In this reading, we will not make the distinction explicitly but it should be kept in mind.

23 LIBOR is not a risk-free rate and contains some credit risk itself. LIBOR is the rate on loans made from one London bank to another. Given that London banks bear some default risk, LIBOR is typically higher than the rate on government debt.

in terms of a percentage.[24] The credit spreads for a range of maturities of a company's debt make up its **credit curve**. The credit curve is somewhat analogous to the term structure of interest rates, which is the set of rates on default-free debt over a range of maturities, but the credit curve applies to non-government borrowers and incorporates credit risk into each rate.

The CDS market for a given borrower is integrated with the credit curve of that borrower. In fact, given the evolution and high degree of efficiency of the CDS market, the credit curve is essentially determined by the CDS rates. The curve is affected by a number of factors, a key one of which is the set of aforementioned hazard rates. A constant hazard rate will tend to flatten the credit curve.[25] Upward-sloping credit curves imply a greater likelihood of default in later years, whereas downward-sloping credit curves imply a greater probability of default in the earlier years. Downward-sloping curves are less common and often a result of severe near-term stress in the financial markets.

EXAMPLE 5

Change in Credit Curve

A company's 5-year CDS trades at a credit spread of 300 bps, and its 10-year CDS trades at a credit spread of 500 bps.

1 The company's 5-year spread is unchanged, but the 10-year spread widens by 100 bps. Describe the implication of this change in the credit curve.

2 The company's 10-year spread is unchanged, but the 5-year spread widens by 500 bps. Describe the implication of this change in the credit curve.

Solution to 1:

This change implies that although the company is not any riskier in the short term, its longer-term creditworthiness is less attractive. Perhaps the company has adequate liquidity for the time being, but after five years it must begin repaying debt or it will be expected to have cash flow difficulties.

Solution to 2:

This change implies that the company's near-term credit risk is now much greater. In fact, the probability of default will decrease if the company can survive for the next five years. Perhaps the company has run into liquidity issues that must be resolved soon, and if not resolved, the company will default.

3.3 CDS Pricing Conventions

With corporate bonds, we typically refer to their values in terms of prices or spreads. The spread is a somewhat more informative measure than price. People are relatively familiar with a normal range of interest rates, so spreads can be easily compared with

24 We previously showed that the expected loss is also the loss given default times the probability of default expressed in currency units. When expressed as a percentage of notional, this relationship is the credit spread. These are all rough approximations because the true relationships are complicated by multiple payments and discounting.

25 Because of discounting, the credit curve would not be completely flat even if the hazard rates are constant. For example, for a company issuing 5- and 10-year zero-coupon bonds, there could be equally likely probabilities of default and hence equal expected payoffs. But the present values of the payoffs are not the same and hence the discount rates that equate the present value to the expected payoffs will not be the same. Constant hazard rates tend to flatten a curve but would not flatten it completely unless all rates were zero.

interest rates. It is more difficult to compare prices. A high-yield bond can be offered with a coupon equal to its yield and, therefore, a price of par value. At the same time, a low-yield bond with the same maturity can likewise be offered with a coupon equal to its yield, and therefore, its price is at par. These two bonds would have identical prices at the offering date, and their prices might even be close through much of their lives, but they are quite different bonds. Focusing on their prices would, therefore, provide little information. Their spreads are much more informative. With LIBOR or the risk-free rate as a benchmark, investors can get a sense for the amount of credit risk implied by their prices, maturities, and coupons. The same is true for CDS. Although CDS have their own prices, their spreads are far more informative.

As we briefly described earlier, the convention in the CDS market starting in recent years is for standardized coupons of 1% for investment-grade debt or 5% for high-yield debt. Clearly, the reference entity need not have debt that implies a credit spread of either of these rates. As such, the present value of the promised payments from the credit protection buyer to the credit protection seller can either exceed or be less than the expected payoff. In effect, the payments are either too large or too small for the risk. The present value difference is the upfront premium paid from one party to the other. Hence, the upfront premium is the present value of the credit spread minus the present value of the fixed coupon. Of course, this specification is quite general. A good rough approximation used by the industry is that the upfront premium is the (Credit spread – Fixed coupon) × Duration of the CDS.[26] Moreover, this specification is in terms of rates. The upfront premium must ultimately be converted to a price, which is done by subtracting the percentage premium from 100.

These relationships are summarized as follows:

Present value of credit spread = Upfront premium + Present value of fixed coupon

A good approximation of the present value of a stream of payments can be made by multiplying the payment rate by the duration:

Upfront premium ≈ (Credit spread – Fixed coupon) × Duration

Credit spread ≈ (Upfront premium/Duration) + Fixed coupon

Price of CDS in currency per 100 par = 100 – Upfront premium %

Upfront premium % = 100 – Price of CDS in currency per 100 par

EXAMPLE 6

Premiums and Credit Spreads

1 Assume a high-yield company's 10-year credit spread is 600 bps, and the duration of the CDS is eight years. What is the approximate upfront premium required to buy 10-year CDS protection? Assume high-yield companies have 5% coupons on their CDS.

2 Imagine an investor sold five-year protection on an investment-grade company and had to pay a 2% upfront premium to the buyer of protection. Assume the duration of the CDS to be four years. What are the company's credit spreads and the price of the CDS per 100 par?

26 Recall that duration is a type of cash flow weighted-average maturity for a bond. For a CDS, if default occurs, the payments terminate. Thus, we cannot assume that all payments are made with certainty, and the duration must take this possibility into account for every payment. Normally, one should adjust the duration of a bond for credit losses, but it is not usually done unless the bond pricing model used takes into account the stochastic nature of the credit spread.

Solution to 1:

To buy 10-year CDS protection, an investor would have to pay a 500 bps coupon plus the present value of the difference between that coupon and the current market spread (600 bps). In this case, the upfront premium would be approximately 100 bps × 8 (duration), or 8% of the notional.

Solution to 2:

The value of the upfront premium is equal to the premium (–2%) divided by the duration (4), or –50 bps. The sign of the upfront premium is negative because the seller is paying the premium rather than receiving it. The credit spread is equal to the fixed coupon (100 bps) plus the running value of the upfront premium (–50 bps), or 50 bps. As a reminder, because the company's credit spread is less than the fixed coupon, the protection seller must pay the upfront premium to the protection buyer. The price in currency would be 100 minus the upfront premium, but the latter is negative, so the price is 100 – (–2) = 102.

3.4 Valuation Changes in CDS during Their Lives

As with any traded financial instrument, a CDS has a value that fluctuates during its lifetime. That value is determined in the competitive marketplace. Market participants constantly assess the current credit quality of the reference entity to determine its current value and (implied) credit spread. Clearly, many factors can change over the life of the CDS. By definition, the duration shortens through time. Likewise, the probability of default, the expected loss given default, and the shape of the credit curve will all change as new information is received. The exact valuation procedure of the CDS is precisely the same as it is when the CDS is first issued and simply incorporates the new inputs. The new market value of the CDS reflects gains and losses to the two parties.

Consider the following example of a five-year CDS with a fixed 1% coupon. The credit spread on the reference entity is 2.5%. In promising to pay 1% coupons to receive coverage on a company whose risk justifies 2.5% coupons, the present value of the protection leg exceeds the present value of the payment leg. The difference is the upfront premium, which will be paid by the CDS buyer to the CDS seller. During the life of the CDS, assume that the credit quality of the reference entity improves, such that the credit spread is now 2.1%. Now, consider a newly created CDS with the same remaining maturity and 1% coupon. The present value of the payment leg would still be less than the present value of the protection leg, but the difference would be less than it was when the original CDS was created because the risk is now less. Logically, it should be apparent that for the original CDS, the seller has gained and the buyer has lost. The difference between the original upfront premium and the new value is the seller's gain and buyer's loss. A rough approximation of the change in value of the CDS for a given change in spread is as follows:[27]

Profit for the buyer of protection ≈ Change in spread in bps × Duration × Notional

Alternatively, we might be interested in the CDS percentage price change, which is obtained as

27 The relationships expressed in the two equations should be somewhat known to candidates from the fixed-income readings, which illustrate that the percentage change in the price of a bond is approximately the change in yield multiplied by the modified duration. In this case, the change in yield is analogous to the change in spread, measured in basis points. The duration of the CDS is analogous to the duration of the bond on which the CDS is written. The use of the term "modified" with respect to duration is a small adjustment requiring division by one plus the yield.

% Change in CDS price = Change in spread in bps × Duration

EXAMPLE 7

Profit and Loss from Change in Credit Spread

An investor buys $10 million of five-year CDS protection, and the CDS contract has a duration of four years. The company's credit spread was originally 500 bps and widens to 800 bps.

1 Does the investor (credit protection buyer) benefit or lose from the change in credit spread?
2 Estimate the CDS price change and estimated profit to the investor.

Solution to 1:

The investor owns protection, so he is economically short and benefits from an increase in the company's credit spread. He can sell the protection for a higher premium.

Solution to 2:

The percentage price change is estimated as the change in spread (300 bps) multiplied by the duration (4) or 12%. The profit to the investor is 12% times the notional ($10 million), or $1.2 million.

3.5 Monetizing Gains and Losses

As with any financial instrument, changes in the price of a CDS gives rise to opportunities to unwind the position, and either capture a gain or realize a loss. This process is called **monetizing** a gain or loss. Keep in mind that the protection seller is effectively long the reference entity. He has entered into a contract to insure the debt of the reference entity, for which he receives a series of promised payments and possibly an upfront premium. He clearly benefits if the reference entity's credit quality improves because he continues to receive the same compensation but bears less risk. Using the opposite argument, the credit protection buyer benefits from a deterioration of the reference entity's credit quality.[28] Thus, the seller is more or less long the company and the buyer is more or less short the company. As the company's credit quality changes through time, the market value of the CDS changes, giving rise to gains and losses for the CDS counterparties. The counterparties can realize those gains and losses by entering into new offsetting contracts, effectively selling their CDS positions to other parties.

Going back to the example in the previous section, assume that during the life of the CDS, the credit quality of the reference entity improves. The implied upfront premium on a new CDS that matches the terms of the original CDS with adjusted maturity is now the market value of the original CDS. In our example, this new CDS has an upfront premium that would be paid by the buyer to the seller, but that premium is smaller than on the original CDS.

Now, suppose that the buyer of the original CDS wants to unwind his position. He would then enter into this new CDS as a protection seller and receive the newly calculated upfront premium. As we noted, this value is less than what he paid originally. Likewise, the seller could offset his original position by entering into this new

28 Again, it is important to remember that these statements are limited to the buyer or seller's position in the CDS and not any other instruments held by either party.

CDS as a protection buyer. He would pay an upfront premium that is less than what he originally received. The original protection buyer monetizes a loss and the seller monetizes a gain. The transaction to unwind the CDS does not need to be done with the same original party, although doing so offers some advantages. As clearinghouses begin to be more widely used with CDS, unwind transactions should become even more common and easier to do.

At this point, we have identified two ways of realizing a profit or loss on a CDS. One is to effectively exercise the CDS in response to a default. The other is to unwind the position by entering into a new offsetting CDS in the market. A third, and the least common, method occurs if there is no default. A party can simply hold the position until expiration, at which time the credit protection seller has captured all of the premiums and has not been forced to make any payments, and the seller's obligation for any further payments is terminated. The spread of the CDS will go to zero, in much the same manner as a bond converges toward par as it approaches maturity. The CDS seller clearly gains, having been paid to bear the risk of default that is becoming increasingly unlikely, and the CDS buyer loses.[29]

4 APPLICATIONS OF CDS

Credit default swaps, as demonstrated, facilitate the transfer of credit risk. As simple as that concept seems, there are many different circumstances under which CDS are used. In this section, we consider some applications of this instrument.

Any derivative instrument has two general uses. One is to exploit an expected movement in the underlying. The derivative typically requires less capital and is usually an easier instrument in which to create a short economic exposure as compared with the underlying. The derivatives market can also be more efficient, meaning that it can react to information more rapidly and have more liquidity than the market for the underlying. Thus, information or an expectation of movement in the underlying can often be exploited much better with the derivative than with the underlying directly.

The other trading opportunity facilitated by derivatives is in valuation differences between the derivative and the underlying. If the derivative is mispriced relative to the underlying, one can take the appropriate position in the derivative and an offsetting position in the underlying. If the valuation assessment is correct and other investors come to the same conclusion, the values of the derivative and underlying will converge, and the investor will earn a return that is essentially free of risk because the risk of the underlying has been hedged away by the holding of long and short positions. Whether this happens as planned depends on both the efficiency of the market and the quality of the valuation model. Differences can also exist between the derivative and other derivatives on the same underlying.

These two general types of uses are also the major applications of CDS. We will refer to them as managing credit exposures, meaning the taking on or shedding of credit risk in light of changing expectations and/or valuation disparities. With valuation disparities, the focus is on differences in the pricing of credit risk in the CDS market relative to that of the underlying bonds.

29 Indeed, the buyer loses on the CDS because it paid premiums to receive protection in the event of a default, which did not occur. Although technically a loss, the buyer might well be a creditor of the reference entity, so the buyer's overall position is not a loss. The CDS is, as we have mentioned, somewhat like insurance, so the buyer may not look at it as a loss in the same manner that an individual might not look at an expiring insurance contract on his house as a loss simply because it did not burn down.

4.1 Managing Credit Exposures

The most basic application of a CDS is to increase or decrease credit exposure. The most obvious such application is for a lender to buy a CDS to reduce its credit exposure to a borrower. For the CDS seller, the trade adds credit exposure. A lender's justification for using a CDS seems obvious. The lender may have assumed too much credit risk but does not want to sell the bond or loan because there can be significant transaction costs, because later it may want the bond or loan back, or because the market for the bond or loan is relatively illiquid. If the risk is temporary, it is almost always easier to temporarily reduce risk by using a CDS. Beyond financial institutions, any organization exposed to credit is potentially a candidate for using CDS.

The justification for selling credit protection is somewhat less obvious. The seller can be a CDS dealer, whose objective is to profit from making markets in CDS. A dealer typically attempts to manage its exposure by either diversifying its credit risks or hedging the risk by entering into a transaction with yet another party, such as by shorting the debt or equity of the reference entity, often accompanied by investment of the funds in a repurchase agreement, or repo. If the dealer manages the risk effectively, the risk assumed in selling the CDS is essentially offset when the payment for assuming the risk exceeds the cost of removing the risk. Achieving this outcome successfully requires sophisticated credit risk modeling, a topic beyond the scope of the CFA Program.

Although dealers make up a large percentage of CDS sellers, not all are dealers. Consider that any bondholder is a buyer of credit and interest rate risk. If the bondholder wants only credit risk, it can obtain it by selling a CDS, which would require far less capital and incur potentially lower overall transaction costs than buying the bond. Moreover, the CDS can easily be more liquid than the bond, so the position can be unwound much more easily.

As noted, it is apparent why a party making a loan might want credit protection. Consider, however, that a party with no exposure to the reference entity might also purchase credit protection. Such a position is called a **naked credit default swap**, and it has resulted in some controversy in regulatory and political circles. In buying a naked CDS, the investor is taking a position that the entity's credit quality will deteriorate, whereas the seller of a naked CDS is taking the position that the entity's credit quality will improve.[30] It is the position of the buyer that has caused some controversy. Some regulators and politicians believe it is inappropriate for a party with no exposure to a borrower to speculate that the borrower's financial condition will deteriorate. This controversy accelerated during the financial crises of 2008–2009 because many investors held these naked CDS and benefited from the crisis.

The counterargument, however, is that elsewhere in the financial markets, such bets are made all of the time in the form of long puts, short futures, and short sales of stocks and bonds. These instruments are generally accepted as a means of protecting oneself against weak if not bad performance in the financial markets. Likewise, a CDS is a means of protecting oneself against terrible economic conditions. Must everyone suffer during a financial crisis? Are there not ways to trade that would reward investors who go against the majority of investors and ultimately are proven correct? Moreover, not having a position in an entity does not mean one does not have exposure. In particular, the default of a sovereign entity or municipality imposes costs on

30 To be clear, a naked CDS does not mean that *both* parties have no exposure to the underlying. Either or both could have no exposure. A naked CDS simply refers to the position of one party. The counterparty may or may not have exposure.

many citizens and organizations.[31] Other proponents of naked CDS argue that they bring liquidity to the credit market, potentially providing more stability, not less. Nonetheless, naked CDS trading is banned in Europe for sovereign debt, although generally permitted otherwise.

CDS trading strategies, with or without naked exposure, can take several forms. A party can take an outright long or short position, as we have previously discussed. Alternatively, the party can take a long position in one CDS and a short position in another, called a **long/short trade.**[32] One CDS would be on one reference entity, and the other would be on a different entity. This transaction is a bet that the credit position of one entity will improve relative to that of another. The two entities might be related in some way or might produce substitute goods. For example, one might take a position that because of competition and changes in the luxury car industry, the credit quality of Daimler will improve and that of BMW will weaken, so going long a Daimler CDS and short a BMW CDS would be appropriate. Another similar trade would be to take a long position in one CDS index and a short position in another. For example, the anticipation of a weakening economy could make one go short a high-yield CDS index and long an investment-grade CDS index. As another example, the expectation of strengthening in the Asian economy relative to the European economy could induce one to go short a European CDS index and long an Asian CDS index.[33]

Another type of long/short trade, called a **curve trade**, involves buying a CDS of one maturity and selling a CDS on the same reference entity with a different maturity. Consider two CDS maturities, which we will call the short term and the long term to keep things simple. We will assume the more common situation of an upward-sloping credit curve, meaning that long-term CDS rates are higher than short-term rates. If the curve changes shape, it becomes either steeper or flatter. A steeper (flatter) curve means that long-term credit risk increases (decreases) relative to short-term credit risk.[34] An investor who believes that long-term credit risk will increase relative to short-term credit risk (credit curve steepening) can go short a long-term CDS and long a short-term CDS. In the short run, a curve-steepening trade is bullish. It implies that the short-term outlook for the reference entity is better than the long-term outlook. In the short run, a curve-flattening trade is bearish. It implies that the short-run outlook for the reference entity looks worse than the long-run outlook and reflects the expectation of near-term problems for the reference entity.

31 Another apparent naked exposure to the reference entity arises from simply having large commercial deposits at a bank, either traditional deposits or collateral for another transaction. If the bank defaults, the funds could be at risk. Technically, this is not naked exposure, but it does not take the form of a traditional loan or bond.

32 In the world of options and futures trading, such a transaction is typically called a spread.

33 As a reminder, the CDS seller is long credit and the buyer is short credit. Improvements in credit quality benefit (hurt) the CDS seller (buyer).

34 The considerably less common starting scenario of a downward-sloping credit curve has the opposite interpretation. A steeper curve means that short-term credit risk increases relative to long-term credit risk. Even less common is that of a flat credit curve, in which case a steeper curve can occur either from an increase or decrease in long-term credit risk relative to short-term credit risk.

EXAMPLE 8

Curve Trading

An investor owns some intermediate-term bonds issued by a company and has become concerned about the risk of a near-term default, although he is not very concerned about a default in the long term. The company's two-year duration CDS currently trades at 350 bps, and the four-year duration CDS is at 600 bps.

1 Describe a potential curve trade that the investor could use to hedge the default risk.

2 Explain why an investor may prefer to use a curve trade as a hedge against the company's default risk rather than a straight short position in one CDS.

Solution to 1:

The investor anticipates a flattening curve and can exploit this possibility by positioning himself short (buying protection) in the two-year CDS while going long in the four-year CDS (selling protection).

Solution to 2:

Going short one CDS and long another reduces some of the risk because both positions will react similarly, although not equally, to information about the reference entity's default risk. Moreover, the cost of one position will be partially or more than wholly offset by the premium on the other.

Of course, there can be changes to the credit curve that take the form of simply shifts in the general level of the curve, whereby all rates go up or down by roughly equal amounts. As with long-duration bonds relative to short-duration bonds, the values of longer-term CDS will be more sensitive than those of shorter-term CDS. As an example, a trader who believes that all rates will go up will want to be short CDS but will realize that long-term CDS will move more than short-term CDS. Thus, he might want to be short in long-term CDS and hedge by going long in short-term CDS. He will balance the sizes of the positions so that the volatility of the position he believes will gain in value will be more than the other position. If more risk is desired, he might choose to trade only one leg, the more volatile one.

4.2 Valuation Differences and Basis Trading

Different investors will have different assessments of the price of credit risk. Such differences of opinion will lead to valuation disparities. Clearly, there can be only one appropriate price at which credit risk can be eliminated, but that price is not easy to determine. The party that has the best estimate of the appropriate price of credit risk can capitalize on its knowledge or ability at the expense of another party. Any such comparative advantage can be captured by trading the CDS against either the reference entity's debt or equity or derivatives on its debt or equity, but such trading is critically dependent on the accuracy of models that isolate the credit risk component of the debt or equity return. As noted, those models are beyond the scope of the CFA Program, but it is important to understand the basic ideas.

The yield on the bond issued by the reference entity to a CDS contains a factor that reflects the credit risk. In principle, the amount of yield attributable to credit risk on the bond should be the same as the credit spread on a CDS. It is, after all, the compensation paid to the party assuming the credit risk, regardless of whether that risk is borne by a bondholder or a CDS seller. But there may be a difference in the credit risk compensation in the bond market and CDS market. This differential pricing can arise from mere differences of opinions, differences in models used by participants in the two markets, differences in liquidity in the two markets, and supply and demand conditions in the repo market, which is a primary source of financing for bond purchases. A difference in the credit spreads in these two markets is the foundation of a strategy known as a **basis trade**.

The general idea behind most basis trades is that any such mispricing is likely to be temporary and the spreads should return to equivalence when the market recognizes the disparity. For example, suppose the bond market implies a 5% credit risk premium whereas the CDS market implies a 4% credit risk premium. The trader does not know which is correct but believes these two rates will eventually converge. From the perspective of the CDS, its premium is too low relative to the bond credit risk premium. From the perspective of the bond, its premium is too high relative to the CDS market, which means its price is too low. So, the CDS market could be pricing in too little credit risk, and/or the bond market could be pricing in too much credit risk. Either market could be correct, but it does not matter. The investor would buy the CDS, thereby purchasing credit protection at what appears to be an unjustifiably low rate, and buy the bond, thereby assuming credit risk and paying an unjustifiably low price for the bond. The risk is balanced because the default potential on the bond is protected by the CDS.[35] If convergence occurs, the trade would capture the 1% differential in the two markets.

To determine the profit potential of such a trade, it is necessary to decompose the bond yield into the risk-free rate plus the funding spread plus the credit spread.[36] The risk-free rate plus the funding spread is essentially LIBOR. The credit spread is then the excess of the yield over LIBOR and can be compared with the credit spread in the CDS market. If the spread is higher in the bond (CDS) market than the CDS (bond) market, it is said to be a negative (positive) basis.

EXAMPLE 9

Bonds vs. Credit Default Swaps

An investor wants to be long the credit risk of a given company. The company's bond currently yields 6% and matures in five years. A comparable five-year CDS contract has a credit spread of 3.25%. The investor can borrow in the market at a 2.5% interest rate.

1 Calculate the bond's credit spread.

2 Identify a basis trade that would exploit the current situation.

Solution to 1:

The bond's credit spread is equal to the yield (6%) minus the investor's cost of funding (2.5%). Therefore, the bond's credit spread is currently 3.5%.

35 The bondholder does bear interest rate risk on the bond, but this risk can be hedged with a duration strategy or interest rate derivatives. The general idea is to eliminate all risks and capitalize on the disparity between the price of credit risk in the bond and CDS markets.

36 In practice, this decomposition can be complicated by the existence of embedded options, such as with callable and convertible bonds or when the bond is not selling near par. Those factors would need to be removed in the calculations.

Solution to 2:

The bond and CDS markets imply different credit spreads. Credit risk is cheap in the CDS market (3.25%) relative to the bond market (3.5%). The investor should buy protection in the CDS market at 3.25% and go long the bond, thereby earning 3.5% for assuming the credit risk.

Another type of trade using CDS can occur within the instruments issued by a single entity. Credit risk is an element of virtually every unsecured debt instrument or the capital leases issued by a company. Each of these instruments is priced to reflect the appropriate credit risk. Investors can use the CDS market to first determine whether any of these instruments is incorrectly priced relative to the CDS and then buy the cheaper one and sell the more expensive one. Again, there is the assumption that the market will adjust. This type of trading is much more complex, however, because priority of claims means that not all of the instruments pay off equally if default occurs.

EXAMPLE 10

Using CDS to Trade on a Leveraged Buyout

An investor believes that a company will undergo a leveraged buyout (LBO) transaction, whereby it will issue large amounts of debt and use the proceeds to repurchase all of the publicly traded equity, leaving the company owned by management and a few insiders.

1 Why might the CDS spread change?

2 What equity-versus-credit trade might an investor execute in anticipation of such a corporate action?

Solution to 1:

Taking on the additional debt will almost surely increase the probability of default, thereby increasing the CDS spread.

Solution to 2:

The investor might consider buying the stock and buying CDS protection. Both legs will profit if the LBO occurs because the stock price rises and the CDS price rises as its spread widens to reflect the increased probability of default.

The CDS indices also permit some opportunities for a type of arbitrage trade. If the cost of the index is not equivalent to the aggregate cost of the index components, the opportunity exists to go long the cheaper instrument and short the more expensive instrument. Again, there is the implicit assumption that convergence will occur. Assuming it does, the investor gains the benefit while basically having neutralized the risk.

A collateralized debt obligation (CDO) is created by assembling a portfolio of debt securities and issuing claims against the portfolio in the form of tranches. These tranches have different priorities of claims, with some tranches responsible for credit losses before others. Yet another type of instrument, called a **synthetic CDO**, is created by combining a portfolio of default-free securities with a combination of credit default swaps undertaken as protection sellers. The default-free securities plus the CDS holdings are, thus, a synthetic CDO because they effectively contain securities subject to default. If an institution can assemble the synthetic CDO at a lower cost than the actual CDO, it can then buy the former and sell the latter, capturing a type of arbitrage profit.

SUMMARY

This reading on credit default swaps provides a basic introduction to these instruments and their markets. The following key points are covered:

- A credit default swap (CDS) is a contract between two parties in which one party purchases protection from another party against losses from the default of a borrower for a defined period of time.
- A CDS is written on the debt of a third party, called the reference entity, whose relevant debt is called the reference obligation, typically a senior unsecured bond.
- A CDS written on a particular reference obligation normally provides coverage for all obligations of the reference entity that have equal or higher seniority.
- The two parties to the CDS are the credit protection buyer, who is said to be short the reference entity's credit, and the credit protection seller, who is said to be long the reference entity's credit. The seller (buyer) is said to be long (short) because the seller is bullish (bearish) on the financial condition of the reference entity.
- The CDS pays off upon occurrence of a credit event, which includes bankruptcy, failure to pay, and, in some countries, restructuring.
- Settlement of a CDS can occur through a cash payment from the credit protection seller to the credit protection buyer as determined by the cheapest-to-deliver obligation of the reference entity, or by physical delivery of the reference obligation from the protection buyer to the protection seller in exchange for the CDS notional.
- A cash settlement payoff is determined by an auction of the reference entity's debt, which gives the market's assessment of the likely recovery rate. The credit protection buyer must accept the outcome of the auction even though the ultimate recovery rate could differ.
- CDS can be constructed on a single entity or as indices containing multiple entities.
- The fixed payments made from CDS buyer to CDS seller are customarily set at a fixed annual rate of 1% for investment-grade debt or 5% for high-yield debt.
- Valuation of a CDS is determined by estimating the present value of the protection leg, which is the payment from the protection seller to the protection buyer in event of default, and the present value of the payment leg, which is the series of payments made from the protection buyer to the protection seller. Any difference in the two series results in an upfront payment from the party having the greater present value to the counterparty.
- An important determinant of the value of the expected payments is the hazard rate, the probability of default given that default has not already occurred.
- CDS prices are often quoted in terms of credit spreads, the implied number of basis points that the credit protection seller receives from the credit protection buyer to justify providing the protection.

- Credit spreads are often expressed in terms of a credit curve, which expresses the relationship between the credit spreads on bonds of different maturities for the same borrower.
- CDS change in value over their lives as the credit quality of the reference entity changes, which leads to gains and losses for the counterparties, even though default may not have occurred or may never occur.
- Either party can monetize an accumulated gain or loss by entering into an offsetting position that matches the terms of the original CDS.
- CDS are used to increase or decrease credit exposures or to capitalize on different assessments of the cost of credit among different instruments tied to the reference entity, such as debt, equity, and derivatives of debt and equity.

Portfolio Management

STUDY SESSION

Study Session 18	Capital Market Theory and the Portfolio Management Process

TOPIC LEVEL LEARNING OUTCOME

The candidate should be able to explain and demonstrate the use of portfolio theory in risk and return estimation, security selection, and international asset pricing. The candidate should also be able to explain the portfolio management process.

PORTFOLIO MANAGEMENT

STUDY SESSION 18

Portfolio Management

Capital Market Theory and the Portfolio Management Process

The first readings in this study session reviews the CAPM (the capital asset pricing model)—a foundation for this study session and one of the first rigorous models for the expected returns on risky assets in equilibrium. The second and third readings discuss active portfolio management and apply concepts from the first reading to it. The final reading summarizes the portfolio management process, introducing topics that will be covered in more detail at Level III.

READING ASSIGNMENTS

Reading 57 Portfolio Concepts
Quantitative Methods for Investment Analysis, Second Edition,
by Richard A. DeFusco, CFA, Dennis W. McLeavey, CFA, Jerald E. Pinto, CFA, and David E. Runkle, CFA

Reading 58 Residual Risk and Return: The Information Ratio
Active Portfolio Management: A Quantitative Approach for Providing Superior Returns and Controlling Risk,
by Richard C. Grinold and Ronald N. Kahn

Reading 59 The Fundamental Law of Active Management
Active Portfolio Management: A Quantitative Approach for Providing Superior Returns and Controlling Risk,
by Richard C. Grinold and Ronald N. Kahn

(continued)

Reading 60	The Portfolio Management Process and the Investment Policy Statement *Managing Investment Portfolios: A Dynamic Process*, Third Edition, John L. Maginn, CFA, Donald L. Tuttle, CFA, Dennis W. McLeavey, CFA, and Jerald E. Pinto, CFA, editors

A NOTE ON THE TERMINOLOGY OF *ACTIVE PORTFOLIO MANAGEMENT*

The following list defines terms as they are used in Readings 58 and 59 (Chapters 5 and 6 of Grinold and Kahn's *Active Portfolio Management*). Although some of the terms and definitions are discussed elsewhere in the CFA Program Curriculum, terminology in Grinold and Kahn's book is in some cases distinctive. They focus on equities, but the analysis applies to bonds, currencies, and other asset classes as well.

Risk	the standard deviation of return.
Benchmark portfolio	a portfolio with risk and return characteristics representative of the investment universe and style of an investment manager; the portfolio is used for performance measurement of investment efforts.
Excess return	the return on an asset (or a portfolio of assets) in excess of the risk-free rate.
Active return	the return on a portfolio in excess of its benchmark.
Active risk	the standard deviation of active return. This risk is also often referred to as the "tracking error."
Residual risk	the portion of active risk that cannot be attributed to the beta (systematic risk) of the portfolio.
Residual return	the return of a portfolio in excess of its benchmark, adjusted for the difference in beta.
Active position	the difference between portfolio and benchmark holdings of a security.
Value added	the (active) return on an investment.
Benchmark timing	the choice of an active beta, period by period.
MMI	refers to the New York Stock Exchange (NYSE) Arca Major Market Index, previously known as the American Stock Exchange (AMEX) Major Market Index (ticker code XMI or MMI). It is a price-weighted average of 20 Blue Chip industrial stocks of major U.S. Corporations; several of the stocks are also components of the Dow Jones Industrial Average (DJIA).

READING

57

Portfolio Concepts

by Richard A. DeFusco, CFA, Dennis W. McLeavey, CFA, Jerald E. Pinto, CFA, and David E. Runkle, CFA

LEARNING OUTCOMES

Mastery	The candidate should be able to:
☐	**a.** explain mean–variance analysis and its assumptions, and calculate the expected return and the standard deviation of return for a portfolio of two or three assets;
☐	**b.** describe the minimum-variance and efficient frontiers, and explain the steps to solve for the minimum-variance frontier;
☐	**c.** explain the benefits of diversification and how the correlation in a two-asset portfolio and the number of assets in a multi-asset portfolio affect the diversification benefits;
☐	**d.** calculate the variance of an equally weighted portfolio of *n* stocks, explain the capital allocation and capital market lines (CAL and CML) and the relation between them, and calculate the value of one of the variables given values of the remaining variables;
☐	**e.** explain the capital asset pricing model (CAPM), including its underlying assumptions and the resulting conclusions;
☐	**f.** explain the security market line (SML), the beta coefficient, the market risk premium, and the Sharpe ratio, and calculate the value of one of these variables given the values of the remaining variables;
☐	**g.** explain the market model, and state and interpret the market model's predictions with respect to asset returns, variances, and covariances;
☐	**h.** calculate an adjusted beta, and explain the use of adjusted and historical betas as predictors of future betas;
☐	**i.** explain reasons for and problems related to instability in the minimum-variance frontier;
☐	**j.** describe and compare macroeconomic factor models, fundamental factor models, and statistical factor models;
☐	**k.** calculate the expected return on a portfolio of two stocks, given the estimated macroeconomic factor model for each stock;

(continued)

LEARNING OUTCOMES	
Mastery	*The candidate should be able to:*
☐	l. describe the arbitrage pricing theory (APT), including its underlying assumptions and its relation to the multifactor models, calculate the expected return on an asset given an asset's factor sensitivities and the factor risk premiums, and determine whether an arbitrage opportunity exists, including how to exploit the opportunity;
☐	m. explain sources of active risk, interpret tracking error, tracking risk, and the information ratio, and explain factor portfolio and tracking portfolio;
☐	n. compare underlying assumptions and conclusions of the CAPM and APT model, and explain why an investor can possibly earn a substantial premium for exposure to dimensions of risk unrelated to market movements.

1 INTRODUCTION

No aspect of quantitative investment analysis is as widely studied or as vigorously debated as portfolio theory. Issues that portfolio managers have studied during the last 50 years include the following:

- What characteristics of a portfolio are important, and how may we quantify them?
- How do we model risk?
- If we could know the distribution of asset returns, how would we select an optimal portfolio?
- What is the optimal way to combine risky and risk-free assets in a portfolio?
- What are the limitations of using historical return data to predict a portfolio's future characteristics?
- What risk factors should we consider in addition to market risk?

In this reading, we present key quantitative methods to support the management of portfolios. In Section 2, we focus on mean–variance analysis and related models and issues. Then in Section 3, we address some of the problems encountered using mean–variance analysis and how we can respond to them. We introduce a single-factor model, the market model, which explains the return on assets in terms of a single variable, a market index. In Section 4, we present models that explain the returns on assets in terms of multiple factors, and we illustrate some important applications of these models in current practice.

2 MEAN–VARIANCE ANALYSIS

When does portfolio diversification reduce risk? Are there some portfolios that all risk-averse investors would avoid? These are some of the questions that Harry Markowitz addressed in the research for which he shared the 1990 Nobel Prize in Economics.

Mean–variance portfolio theory, the oldest and perhaps most accepted part of modern portfolio theory, provides the theoretical foundation for examining the roles of risk and return in portfolio selection. In this section, we describe Markowitz's theory, illustrate the principles of portfolio diversification with several examples, and discuss several important issues in implementation.

Mean–variance portfolio theory is based on the idea that the value of investment opportunities can be meaningfully measured in terms of mean return and variance of return. Markowitz called this approach to portfolio formation **mean–variance analysis**. Mean–variance analysis is based on the following assumptions:

1 All investors are risk averse; they prefer less risk to more for the same level of expected return.[1]

2 Expected returns for all assets are known.

3 The variances and covariances of all asset returns are known.

4 Investors need only know the expected returns, variances, and covariances of returns to determine optimal portfolios. They can ignore skewness, kurtosis, and other attributes of a distribution.[2]

5 There are no transaction costs or taxes.

Note that the first assumption does not mean that all investors have the same tolerance for risk. Investors differ in the level of risk they are willing to accept; however, risk-averse investors prefer as little risk as possible for a given level of expected return. In practice, expected returns and variances and covariances of returns for assets are not known but rather estimated. The estimation of those quantities may be a source of mistakes in decision-making when we use mean–variance analysis.

The fourth assumption is a key one, as it says that we may rely on certain summary measures of assets' return distributions—expected returns, variances, and covariances—to determine which combinations of assets make an optimal portfolio.

2.1 The Minimum-Variance Frontier and Related Concepts

An investor's objective in using a mean–variance approach to portfolio selection is to choose an efficient portfolio. An **efficient portfolio** is one offering the highest expected return for a given level of risk as measured by variance or standard deviation of return. Thus if an investor quantifies her tolerance for risk using standard deviation, she seeks the portfolio that she expects will deliver the greatest return for the standard deviation of return consistent with her risk tolerance. We begin the exploration of portfolio selection by forming a portfolio from just two asset classes, government bonds and large-cap stocks.

Table 1 shows the assumptions we make about the expected returns of the two assets, along with the standard deviation of return for the two assets and the correlation between their returns.

To begin the process of finding an efficient portfolio, we must identify the portfolios that have minimum variance for each given level of expected return. Such portfolios are called **minimum-variance portfolios**. As we shall see, the set of efficient portfolios is a subset of the set of minimum variance portfolios.

1 For more on risk aversion and its role in portfolio theory, see, for example, Sharpe, Alexander, and Bailey (1999) or Reilly and Brown (2003).

2 This assumption could follow either from assuming that returns follow a normal distribution or from assuming that investors' attitudes toward risk and return can be mathematically represented in terms of mean and variance only.

Table 1 Assumed Expected Returns, Variances, and Correlation: Two-Asset Case

	Asset 1 Large-Cap Stocks	Asset 2 Government Bonds
Expected return	15%	5%
Variance	225	100
Standard deviation	15%	10%
Correlation	0.5	

We see from Table 1 that the standard deviation of the return to large-cap stocks (Asset 1) is 15 percent, the standard deviation of the return to government bonds (Asset 2) is 10 percent, and the correlation between the two assets' returns is 0.5. Therefore, we can compute the variance of a portfolio's returns as a function of the fraction of the portfolio invested in large-cap stocks (w_1) and the fraction of the portfolio invested in government bonds (w_2). Because the portfolio contains only these two assets, we have the relationship $w_1 + w_2 = 1$. When the portfolio is 100 percent invested in Asset 1, w_1 is 1.0 and w_2 is 0; and when w_2 is 1.0, then w_1 is 0 and the portfolio is 100 percent invested in Asset 2. Also, when w_1 is 1.0, we know that our portfolio's expected return and variance of return are those of Asset 1. Conversely, when w_2 is 1.0, the portfolio's expected return and variance are those of Asset 2. In this case, the portfolio's maximum expected return is 15 percent if 100 percent of the portfolio is invested in large-cap stocks; its minimum expected return is 5 percent if 100 percent of the portfolio is invested in government bonds.

Before we can determine risk and return for all portfolios composed of large-cap stocks and government bonds, we must know how the expected return, variance, and standard deviation of the return for any two-asset portfolio depend on the expected returns of the two assets, their variances, and the correlation between the two assets' returns.

For any portfolio composed of two assets, the expected return to the portfolio, $E(R_p)$, is

$$E(R_p) = w_1 E(R_1) + w_2 E(R_2)$$

where

$E(R_1)$ = the expected return on Asset 1

$E(R_2)$ = the expected return on Asset 2

The portfolio variance of return is

$$\sigma_p^2 = w_1^2\sigma_1^2 + w_2^2\sigma_2^2 + 2w_1w_2\rho_{1,2}\sigma_1\sigma_2$$

where

σ_1 = the standard deviation of return on Asset 1

σ_2 = the standard deviation of return on Asset 2

$\rho_{1,2}$ = the correlation between the two assets' returns

and $\mathrm{Cov}(R_1, R_2) = \rho_{1,2}\sigma_1\sigma_2$ is the covariance between the two returns, recalling the definition of correlation as the covariance divided by the individual standard deviations. The portfolio standard deviation of return is

$$\sigma_p = \left(w_1^2\sigma_1^2 + w_2^2\sigma_2^2 + 2w_1w_2\rho_{1,2}\sigma_1\sigma_2\right)^{1/2}$$

In this case, the expected return to the portfolio is $E(R_p) = w_1(0.15) + w_2(0.05)$, and the portfolio variance is $\sigma_p^2 = w_1^2 0.15^2 + w_2^2 0.10^2 + 2w_1w_2(0.5)(0.15)(0.10)$.

Given our assumptions about the expected returns, variances, and return correlation for the two assets, we can determine both the variance and the expected return of the portfolio as a function of the proportion of assets invested in large-cap stocks and government bonds. Table 2 shows the portfolio expected return, variance, and standard deviation as the weights on large-cap stocks rise from 0 to 1.0.

Table 2 Relation between Expected Return and Risk for a Portfolio of Stocks and Bonds

Expected Return (%)	Portfolio Variance	Portfolio Standard Deviation (%)	Large-Cap Stocks (w_1)	Government Bonds (w_2)
5	100.00	10.00	0	1.0
6	96.75	9.84	0.1	0.9
7	97.00	9.85	0.2	0.8
8	100.75	10.04	0.3	0.7
9	108.00	10.39	0.4	0.6
10	118.75	10.90	0.5	0.5
11	133.00	11.53	0.6	0.4
12	150.75	12.28	0.7	0.3
13	172.00	13.11	0.8	0.2
14	196.75	14.03	0.9	0.1
15	225.00	15.00	1.0	0

As Table 2 shows, when the weight on large-cap stocks is 0.1, the expected portfolio return is 6 percent and the portfolio variance is 96.75.[3] That portfolio has a higher expected return and lower variance than a portfolio with a weight of 0 on stocks—that is, a portfolio fully invested in government bonds. This improvement in risk–return characteristics illustrates the power of diversification: Because the returns to large-cap stocks are not perfectly correlated with the returns to government bonds (they do not have a correlation of 1), by putting some of the portfolio into large-cap stocks, we increase the expected return and reduce the variance of return. Furthermore, there is no cost to improving the risk–return characteristics of the portfolio in this way.

Figure 1 graphs the possible combinations of risk and return for a portfolio composed of government bonds and large-cap stocks. Figure 1 plots the expected portfolio return on the y-axis and the portfolio variance on the x-axis.

3 Note that the 96.75 is in units of percent squared. In decimals, the expected portfolio return is 0.06 and the portfolio variance is 0.009675.

Figure 1 Minimum-Variance Frontier: Large-Cap Stocks and Government Bonds

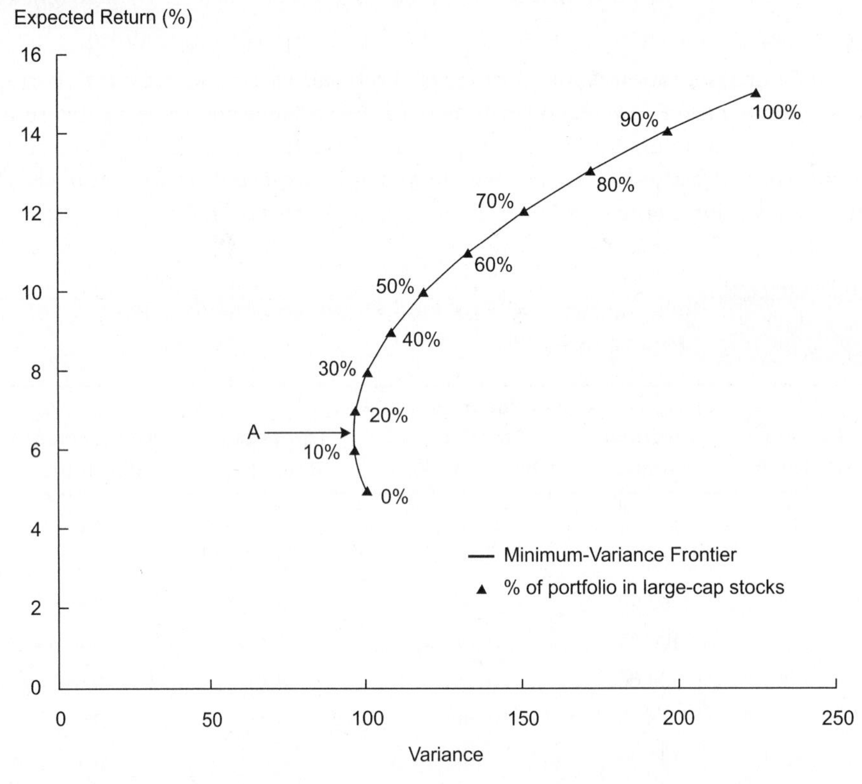

The two-asset case is special because all two-asset portfolios plot on the curve illustrated (there is a unique combination of two assets that provides a given level of expected return). This is the **portfolio possibilities curve**—a curve plotting the expected return and risk of the portfolios that can be formed using two assets. We can also call the curve in Figure 1 the **minimum-variance frontier** because it shows the minimum variance that can be achieved for a given level of expected return. The minimum-variance frontier is a more useful concept than the portfolio possibilities curve because it also applies to portfolios with more than two assets. In the general case of more than two assets, any portfolios plotting on an imaginary horizontal line at any expected return level have the same expected return, and as we move left on that line, we have less variance of return. The attainable portfolio farthest to the left on such a line is the minimum-variance portfolio for that level of expected return and one point on the minimum-variance frontier. With three or more assets, the minimum-variance frontier is a true frontier: It is the border of a region representing all combinations of expected return and risk that are possible (the border of the feasible region). The region results from the fact that with three or more assets, an unlimited number of portfolios can provide a given level of expected return.[4] In the case of three or more assets, if we move to the right from a point on the minimum-variance frontier, we reach another portfolio but one with more risk.

4 For example, if we have three assets with expected returns of 5 percent, 12 percent, and 20 percent and we want an expected return of 11 percent on the portfolio, we would use the following equation to solve for the portfolio weights (using the fact that portfolio weights must sum to 1): $11\% = (5\% \times w_1) + (12\% \times w_2) + [20\% \times (1 - w_1 - w_2)]$. This single equation with two unknowns, w_1 and w_2, has an unlimited number of possible solutions, each solution representing a portfolio.

From Figure 1, note that the variance of the global minimum-variance portfolio (the one with the smallest variance) appears to be close to 96.43 (Point A) when the expected return of the portfolio is 6.43. This global minimum-variance portfolio has 14.3 percent of assets in large-cap stocks and 85.7 percent of assets in government bonds. Given these assumed returns, standard deviations, and correlation, a portfolio manager should not choose a portfolio with less than 14.3 percent of assets in large-cap stocks because any such portfolio will have both a higher variance and a lower expected return than the global minimum-variance portfolio. All of the points on the minimum-variance frontier below Point A are inferior to the global minimum-variance portfolio, and they should be avoided.

Financial economists often say that portfolios located below the global minimum-variance portfolio (Point A in Figure 1) are dominated by others that have the same variances but higher expected returns. Because these dominated portfolios use risk inefficiently, they are inefficient portfolios. The portion of the minimum-variance frontier beginning with the global minimum-variance portfolio and continuing above it is called the **efficient frontier**. Portfolios lying on the efficient frontier offer the maximum expected return for their level of variance of return. Efficient portfolios use risk efficiently: Investors making portfolio choices in terms of mean return and variance of return can restrict their selections to portfolios lying on the efficient frontier. This reduction in the number of portfolios to be considered simplifies the selection process. If an investor can quantify his risk tolerance in terms of variance or standard deviation of return, the efficient portfolio for that level of variance or standard deviation will represent the optimal mean–variance choice.

Because standard deviation is easier to interpret than variance, investors often plot the expected return against standard deviation rather than variance.[5] Figure 2 plots the expected portfolio return for this example on the y-axis and the portfolio standard deviation of return on the x-axis.[6] The curve graphed is still called the minimum-variance frontier.

---

5 Expected return and standard deviation are measured in the same units, percent.

6 For the remainder of this reading, we will plot the expected return against standard deviation of return.

Figure 2 Minimum-Variance Frontier: Large-Cap Stocks and Government Bonds

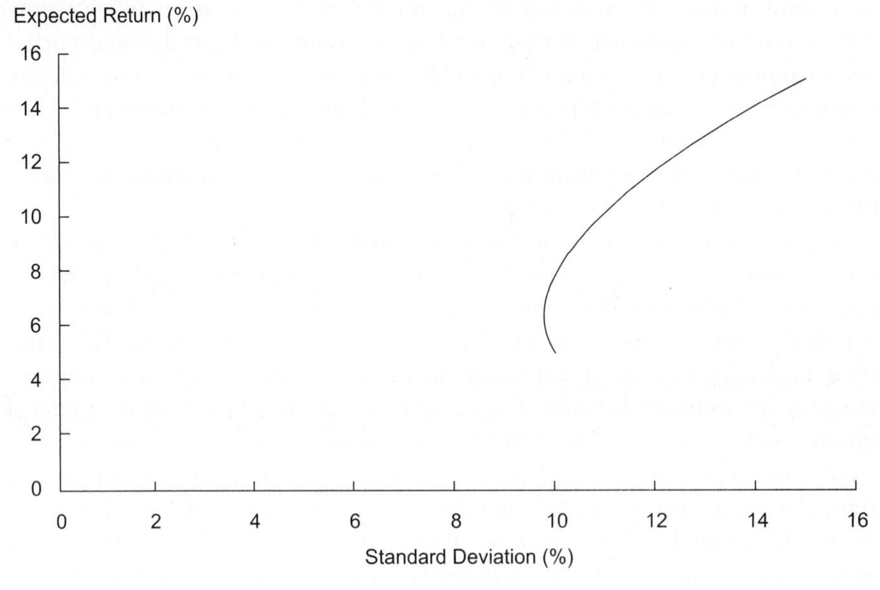

Example 1 illustrates the process of determining a historical minimum-variance frontier.

EXAMPLE 1

A Two-Asset Minimum-Variance Frontier Using Historical U.S. Return Data

Susan Fitzsimmons has decided to invest her retirement plan assets in a U.S. small-cap equity index fund and a U.S. long-term government bond index fund. Fitzsimmons decides to use mean–variance analysis to help determine the fraction of her funds to invest in each fund. Assuming that expected returns and variances can be estimated accurately using monthly historical returns from 1970 through 2002, she computes the average returns, variances of returns, and correlation of returns for the indexes that the index funds attempt to track. Table 3 shows those historical statistics.

Table 3 Average Returns and Variances of Returns (Annualized, Based on Monthly Data, January 1970–December 2002)

Asset Class	Average Return	Variance
U.S. small-cap stocks	14.63%	491.8
U.S. long-term government bonds	9.55%	109.0
Correlation	0.138	

Source: Ibbotson Associates.

Given these statistics, Fitzsimmons can determine the allocation of the portfolio between the two assets using the expected return and variance. To do so, she must calculate

- the range of possible expected returns for the portfolio (minimum and maximum);
- the proportion of each of the two assets (asset weights) in the minimum-variance portfolio for each possible level of expected return; and
- the variance[7] for each possible level of expected return.

Because U.S. government bonds have a lower expected return than U.S. small-cap stocks, the minimum expected return portfolio has 100 percent weight in U.S. long-term government bonds, 0 percent weight in U.S. small-cap stocks, and an expected return of 9.55 percent. In contrast, the maximum expected return portfolio has 100 percent weight in U.S. small-cap stocks, 0 percent weight in U.S. long-term government bonds, and an expected return of 14.63 percent. Therefore, the range of possible expected portfolio returns is 9.55 percent to 14.63 percent.

Fitzsimmons now determines the asset weights of the two asset classes at different levels of expected return, starting at the minimum expected return of 9.55 percent and concluding at the maximum level of expected return of 14.63 percent. The weights at each level of expected return determine the variance for the portfolio consisting of these two asset classes. Table 4 shows the composition of portfolios for various levels of expected return.

Table 4 **Points on the Minimum-Variance Frontier for U.S. Small-Cap Stocks and U.S. Long-Term Government Bonds**

Expected Return (%)	Variance	Standard Deviation (%)	Small-Cap Stocks, w_1	Government Bonds, w_2
9.55	109.0	10.4	0.000	1.000
9.65	106.2	10.3	0.020	0.980
9.95	100.2	10.0	0.079	0.921
10.25	98.0	9.9	0.138	0.862
10.55	99.5	10.0	0.197	0.803
10.75	102.6	10.1	0.236	0.764
14.63	491.8	22.2	1.000	0.000

Table 4 illustrates what happens to the weights in the individual asset classes as we move from the minimum expected return to the maximum expected return. When the expected return is 9.55 percent, the weight for the long-term government bonds is 100 percent. As we increase the expected return, the weight in long-term government bonds decreases; at the same time, the weight for U.S. small stocks increases. This result makes sense because we know that the maximum expected return of 14.63 percent must have a weight of 100 percent

7 In the two-asset case, as previously stated, there is a unique combination of the two assets that provides a given level of expected return, so there is a unique variance for a given level of expected return. Thus the portfolio variance calculated for each level of expected return is trivially the minimum-variance portfolio for that level of expected return.

in U.S. small stocks. The weights in Table 4 reflect that property. Note that the global minimum-variance portfolio (which is also the global minimum-standard-deviation portfolio) contains some of both assets. A portfolio consisting only of bonds has more risk and a lower expected return than the global minimum-variance portfolio because diversification can reduce total portfolio risk, as we discuss shortly.

Figure 3 illustrates the minimum-variance frontier (in the two-asset-class case, merely a portfolio possibilities curve) over the period 1970 to 2002 by graphing expected return as a function of standard deviation.

Figure 3 Minimum-Variance Frontier: U.S. Small-Cap Stocks and Government Bonds

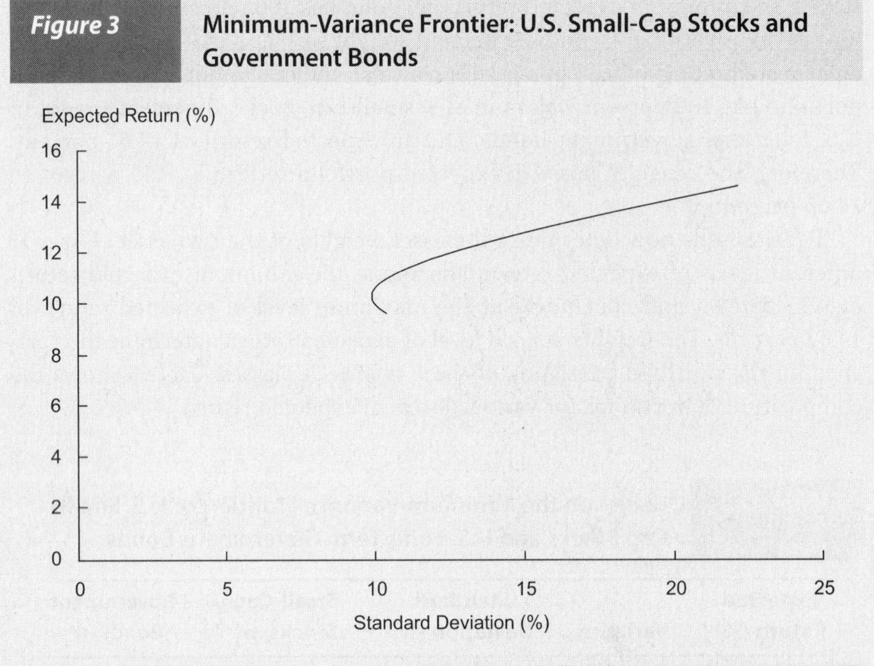

If Fitzsimmons quantifies her risk tolerance as a standard deviation of 10 percent, for example, mean–variance analysis suggests that she choose a portfolio with an approximate weighting of 0.20 in small-cap stocks and 0.80 in long-term government bonds. One major caution that we shall discuss later in this reading is that even small changes in inputs can have a significant effect on the minimum-variance frontier, and the future may obviously be very different from the past. The historical record is only a starting point in developing inputs for calculating the minimum-variance frontier.[8]

The trade-off between risk and return for a portfolio depends not only on the expected asset returns and variances but also on the correlation of asset returns. Returning to the case of large-cap stocks and government bonds, we assumed that the correlation was 0.5. The risk–return trade-off is quite different for other correlation values. Figure 4 shows the minimum-variance frontiers for portfolios containing

8 Note also that the historical data are monthly, corresponding to a monthly investment horizon. The minimum-variance frontier could be quite different if we used data with a different horizon (say quarterly).

large-cap stocks and government bonds for varying weights.[9] The weights go from 100 percent in government bonds and 0 percent in large-cap stocks to 0 percent in government bonds and 100 percent in large-cap stocks, for four different values of the correlation coefficient. The correlations illustrated in Figure 4 are −1, 0, 0.5, and 1.

Figure 4 Minimum-Variance Frontier for Varied Correlations: Large-Cap Stocks and Government Bonds

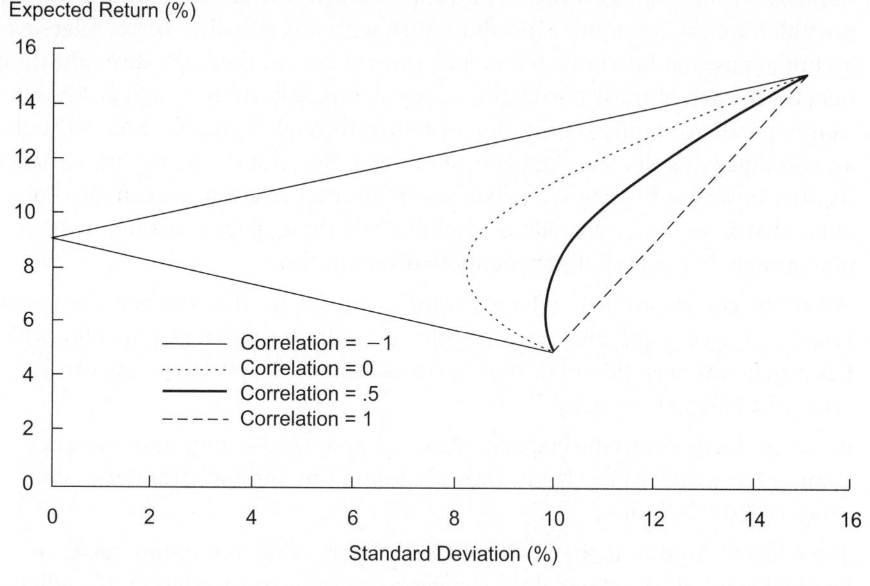

Figure 4 illustrates a number of interesting characteristics about minimum-variance frontiers and diversification:[10]

- The endpoints for all of the frontiers are the same. This fact should not be surprising, because at one endpoint all of the assets are in government bonds and at the other endpoint all of the assets are in large-cap stocks. At each endpoint, the expected return and standard deviation are simply the return and standard deviation for the relevant asset (stocks or bonds).
- When the correlation is +1, the minimum-variance frontier is an upward-sloping straight line. If we start at any point on the line, for each one percentage point increase in standard deviation we achieve the same constant increment in expected return. With a correlation of +1, the return (not just the expected return) on one asset is an exact positive linear function of the return on the other asset.[11] Because fluctuations in the returns on the two assets track each other in this way, the returns on one asset cannot dampen or smooth out the fluctuations in the returns on the other asset. For a correlation of +1, diversification has no potential benefits.

9 Recall from Table 1 that large-cap stocks have an assumed expected return and standard deviation of return of 15 percent, while government bonds have an assumed expected return and standard deviation of return of 5 percent and 10 percent, respectively.

10 We are examining, and our observations generally pertain to, the case in which neither of the two assets is dominated. In mean–variance analysis, an asset A is dominated by an asset B if 1) the mean return on B is equal to or larger than that on A, but B has a smaller standard deviation of return than A; or 2) the mean return on B is strictly larger than that on A, but A and B have the same standard deviation of return. The slope of a straight line connecting two assets, neither of which is dominated, is positive.

11 If the correlation is +1, $R_1 = a + bR_2$, with $b > 0$.

- When we move from a correlation of +1 to a correlation of 0.5, the minimum-variance frontier bows out to the left, in the direction of smaller standard deviation. With any correlation less than +1, we can achieve any feasible level of expected return with a smaller standard deviation of return than for the +1 correlation case. As we move from a correlation of 0.5 to each smaller value of correlation, the minimum-variance frontier bows out farther to the left.
- The frontiers for correlation of 0.5, 0, and −1 have a negatively sloped part.[12] This means that if we start at the lowest point (100 percent in government bonds) and shift money into stocks until we reach the global minimum-variance portfolio, we can get more expected return with less risk. Therefore, relative to an initial position fully invested in government bonds, there are diversification benefits in each of these correlation cases. A diversification benefit is a reduction in portfolio standard deviation of return through diversification without an accompanying decrease in expected return. Because the minimum-variance frontier bows out further to the left as we lower correlation, we can also conclude that as we lower correlation, holding all other values constant, there are increasingly larger potential benefits to diversification.
- When the correlation is −1, the minimum-variance frontier has two linear segments. The two segments join at the global minimum-variance portfolio, which has a standard deviation of 0. With a correlation of −1, portfolio risk can be reduced to zero, if desired.
- Between the two extreme correlations of +1 and −1, the minimum-variance frontier has a bullet-like shape. Thus the minimum-variance frontier is sometimes called the "bullet."
- The efficient frontier is the positively sloped part of the minimum-variance frontier. Holding all other values constant, as we lower correlation, the efficient frontier improves in the sense of offering a higher expected return for a given feasible level of standard deviation of return.

In summary, when the correlation between two portfolios is less than +1, diversification offers potential benefits. As we lower the correlation coefficient toward −1, holding other values constant, the potential benefits to diversification increase.

2.2 Extension to the Three-Asset Case

Earlier we considered forming a portfolio composed of two assets: large-cap stocks and government bonds. For investors in our example who want to maximize expected return for a given level of risk (hold an efficient portfolio), the optimal portfolio combination of two assets contains some of each asset, unless the portfolio is placed entirely in stocks.

Now we may ask, would adding another asset to the possible investment choices improve the available trade-offs between risk and return? The answer to this question is very frequently yes. A fundamental economic principle states that one is never worse off for having additional choices. At worst, an investor can ignore the additional choices and be no worse off than initially. Often, however, a new asset permits us to move to a superior minimum-variance frontier. We can illustrate this common result

12 For positive correlations (between 0 and 1), a negatively sloped part is present when correlation is less than the standard deviation of the less risky asset divided by the standard deviation of the riskier asset. In our case, this ratio is equal to the standard deviation of long-term government bonds to large-cap stocks, or 10/15 = 0.6667. Because 0.5 is less than 0.6667, the minimum-variance frontier for 0.5 has a negatively sloped part. We have not allowed short sales (negative asset weights). If we allow short sales, frontiers for any positive correlation will have a negatively sloped part, which may involve the short sale of the more risky asset. For details, see Elton, Gruber, Brown, and Goetzmann (2003).

by contrasting the minimum-variance frontier for two assets (here, large-cap stocks and government bonds) with the minimum-variance frontier for three assets (large-cap stocks, government bonds, and small-cap stocks).

In our initial two-asset case shown in Table 1, we assumed expected returns, variances, and correlations for large-cap stocks and government bonds. Now suppose we have an additional investment option, small-cap stocks. Can we achieve a better trade-off between risk and return than when we could choose between only two assets, large-cap stocks and government bonds?

Table 5 shows our assumptions about the expected returns of all three assets, along with the standard deviations of the asset returns and their correlations.

Table 5 Assumed Expected Returns, Variances, and Correlations: Three-Asset Case

	Asset 1 Large-Cap Stocks	Asset 2 Government Bonds	Asset 3 Small-Cap Stocks
Expected return	15%	5%	15%
Variance	225	100	225
Standard deviation	15%	10%	15%
Correlations			
Large-cap stocks and bonds	0.5		
Large-cap stocks and small-cap stocks	0.8		
Bonds and small-cap stocks	0.5		

Now we can consider the relation between these statistics and the expected return and variance for the portfolio. For any portfolio composed of three assets with portfolio weights w_1, w_2, and w_3, the expected return on the portfolio, $E(R_p)$, is

$$E(R_p) = w_1 E(R_1) + w_2 E(R_2) + w_3 E(R_3)$$

where

$E(R_1)$ = the expected return on Asset 1 (here, large-cap stocks)
$E(R_2)$ = the expected return on Asset 2 (government bonds)
$E(R_3)$ = the expected return on Asset 3 (small-cap stocks)

The portfolio variance is

$$\sigma_p^2 = w_1^2\sigma_1^2 + w_2^2\sigma_2^2 + w_3^2\sigma_3^2 + 2w_1w_2\rho_{1,2}\sigma_1\sigma_2 + 2w_1w_3\rho_{1,3}\sigma_1\sigma_3 + 2w_2w_3\rho_{2,3}\sigma_2\sigma_3$$

where

σ_1 = the standard deviation of the return on Asset 1
σ_2 = the standard deviation of the return on Asset 2
σ_3 = the standard deviation of the return on Asset 3
$\rho_{1,2}$ = the correlation between returns on Asset 1 and Asset 2
$\rho_{1,3}$ = the correlation between returns on Asset 1 and Asset 3
$\rho_{2,3}$ = the correlation between returns on Asset 2 and Asset 3

The portfolio standard deviation is

$$\sigma_p = \left[w_1^2\sigma_1^2 + w_2^2\sigma_2^2 + w_3^2\sigma_3^2 + 2w_1w_2\rho_{1,2}\sigma_1\sigma_2 + 2w_1w_3\rho_{1,3}\sigma_1\sigma_3 + 2w_2w_3\rho_{2,3}\sigma_2\sigma_3\right]^{1/2}$$

Given our assumptions, the expected return on the portfolio is

$$E(R_p) = w_1(0.15) + w_2(0.05) + w_3(0.15)$$

The portfolio variance is

$$\sigma_p^2 = w_1^2 0.15^2 + w_2^2 0.10^2 + w_3^2 0.15^2 + 2w_1w_2(0.5)(0.15)(0.10) + 2w_1w_3(0.8)(0.15)(0.15) + 2w_2w_3(0.5)(0.10)(0.15)$$

The portfolio standard deviation is

$$\sigma_p = \left[w_1^2 0.15^2 + w_2^2 0.10^2 + w_3^2 0.15^2 + 2w_1w_2(0.5)(0.15)(0.10) + 2w_1w_3(0.8)(0.15)(0.15) + 2w_2w_3(0.5)(0.10)(0.15)\right]^{1/2}$$

In this three-asset case, however, determining the optimal combinations of assets is much more difficult than it was in the two-asset example. In the two-asset case, the percentage of assets in large-cap stocks was simply 100 percent minus the percentage of assets in government bonds. But with three assets, we need a method to determine what combination of assets will produce the lowest variance for any particular expected return. At least we know the minimum expected return (the return that would result from putting all assets in government bonds, 5 percent) and the maximum expected return (the return from putting no assets in government bonds, 15 percent). For any level of expected return between the minimum and maximum levels, we must solve for the portfolio weights that will result in the lowest risk for that level of expected return. We use an **optimizer** (a specialized computer program or a spreadsheet with this capability) to provide these weights.[13]

Notice that the new asset, small-cap stocks, has a correlation of less than +1 with both large-cap stocks and bonds, suggesting that small-cap stocks may be useful in diversifying risk.

Table 6 shows the portfolio expected return, variance, standard deviation, and portfolio weights for the minimum-variance portfolio as the expected return rises from 5 percent to 15 percent.

Table 6 Points on the Minimum-Variance Frontier for the Three-Asset Case

Expected Return (%)	Portfolio Variance	Portfolio Standard Deviation (%)	Large-Cap Stocks (w_1)	Government Bonds (w_2)	Small-Cap (w_3)
5	100.00	10.00	0	1.00	0
6	96.53	9.82	0.05	0.90	0.05
7	96.10	9.80	0.10	0.80	0.10
8	98.72	9.94	0.15	0.70	0.15
9	104.40	10.22	0.20	0.60	0.20
10	113.13	10.64	0.25	0.50	0.25
11	124.90	11.18	0.30	0.40	0.30

13 These programs use a solution method called quadratic programming.

Table 6 (Continued)

Expected Return (%)	Portfolio Variance	Portfolio Standard Deviation (%)	Large-Cap Stocks (w_1)	Government Bonds (w_2)	Small-Cap (w_3)
12	139.73	11.82	0.35	0.30	0.35
13	157.60	12.55	0.40	0.20	0.40
14	178.53	13.36	0.45	0.10	0.45
15	202.50	14.23	0.50	0	0.50

As Table 6 shows, the proportion of the portfolio in large-cap stocks and small-cap stocks is the same in all the minimum-variance portfolios. This proportion results from the simplifying assumption in Table 5 that large-cap stocks and small-cap stocks have identical expected returns and standard deviations of return, as well as the same correlation with government bonds. With a different, more realistic combination of returns, variances, and correlations, the minimum-variance portfolios in this example would contain different proportions of the large-cap stocks and small-cap stocks, but we would reach a similar conclusion about the possibility of improving the available risk–return trade-offs.

How does the minimum variance for each level of expected return in the three-asset case compare with the minimum variance for each level of expected return in the two-asset case? Figure 5 shows the comparison.

Figure 5 Comparing Minimum-Variance Frontiers: Three Assets versus Two Assets

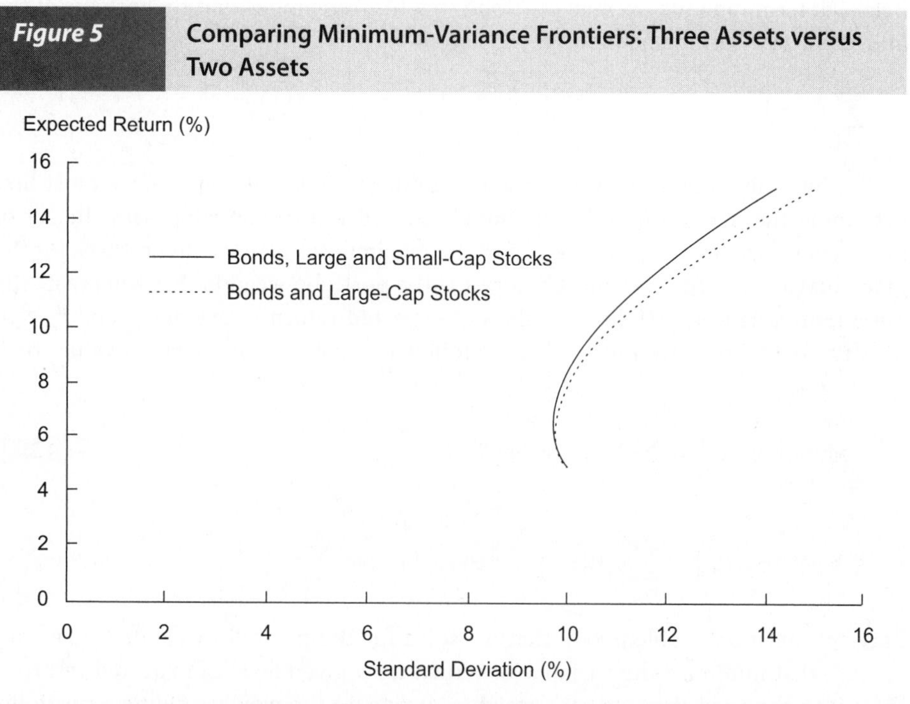

When 100 percent of the portfolio is invested in government bonds, the minimum-variance portfolio has the same expected return (5 percent) and standard deviation (10 percent) in both cases. For every other level of expected return, however, the minimum-variance portfolio in the three-asset case has a lower standard deviation than the minimum-variance portfolio in the two-asset case for the same expected return. Note also that the efficient frontier with three assets dominates the efficient frontier with two assets (we would choose our optimal portfolio from those on the superior efficient frontier).

From this three-asset example, we can draw two conclusions about the theory of portfolio diversification. First, we generally can improve the risk–return trade-off by expanding the set of assets in which we can invest. Second, the composition of the minimum-variance portfolio for any particular level of expected return depends on the expected returns, the variances and correlations of those returns, and the number of assets.

2.3 Determining the Minimum-Variance Frontier for Many Assets

We have shown examples of mean–variance analysis with two and three assets. Typically, however, portfolio managers form optimal portfolios using a larger number of assets. In this section, we show how to determine the minimum-variance frontier for a portfolio composed of many assets.

For a portfolio of n assets, the expected return on the portfolio is[14]

$$E(R_p) = \sum_{j=1}^{n} w_j E(R_j) \quad (1)$$

The variance of return on the portfolio is[15]

$$\sigma_p^2 = \sum_{i=1}^{n}\sum_{j=1}^{n} w_i w_j \mathrm{Cov}(\mathrm{R}_i,\mathrm{R}_j) \quad (2)$$

Before determining the optimal portfolio weights, remember that the weights of the individual assets in the portfolio must sum to 1:

$$\sum_{j=1}^{n} w_j = 1$$

To determine the minimum-variance frontier for a set of n assets, we must first determine the minimum and maximum expected returns possible with the set of assets (these are the minimum, $r_{\min}$, and the maximum, $r_{\max}$, expected returns for the individual assets). Then we must determine the portfolio weights that will create the minimum-variance portfolio for values of expected return between $r_{\min}$ and $r_{\max}$. In mathematical terms, we must solve the following problem for specified values of z, $r_{\min} \le z \le r_{\max}$:

$$\underset{\text{by choice of } w\text{'s}}{\text{Minimize}} \ \sigma_p^2 = \sum_{i=1}^{n}\sum_{j=1}^{n} w_i w_j \mathrm{Cov}(R_i,R_j) \quad (3)$$

$$\text{subject to } E(R_p) = \sum_{j=1}^{n} w_j \mathrm{E}(\mathrm{R}_j) = z \text{ and subject to } \sum_{j=1}^{n} w_j = 1$$

This optimization problem says that we solve for the portfolio weights (w_1, w_2, w_3, . . ., w_n) that minimize the variance of return for a given level of expected return z, subject to the constraint that the weights sum to 1. The weights define a portfolio, and the portfolio is the minimum-variance portfolio for its level of expected return.

14 The summation notation says that we set j equal to 1 through n, and then we sum the resulting terms.
15 The double summation notation says that we set i equal to 1 and let j run from 1 through n, then we set i equal to 2 and let j run from 1 through n, and so forth until i equals n; then we sum all the terms.

Equation 3 shows the simplest case in which the only constraint on portfolio weights is that they sum to 1; this case allows assets to be sold short. A constraint against short sales would require adding a further constraint that $w_j \geq 0$. We trace out the minimum-variance frontier by varying the value of expected return from the minimum to the maximum level. For example, we could determine the optimal portfolio weights for a small set of z values by starting with $z = r_{min}$, then increasing z by 10 basis points (0.10 percent) and solving for the optimal portfolio weights until we reach $z = r_{max}$.[16] We use an optimizer to actually solve the optimization problem. Example 2 shows a minimum-variance frontier that results from using historical data for non-U.S. stocks and three U.S. asset classes.

EXAMPLE 2

A Minimum-Variance Frontier Using International Historical Return Data

In this example, we examine a historical minimum-variance frontier with four asset classes. The three U.S. asset classes are the S&P 500 Index, U.S. small-cap stocks, and U.S. long-term government bonds. To these we add non-U.S. stocks (MSCI World ex-United States). We estimate the minimum-variance frontier based on historical monthly return data from January 1970 to December 2002. Table 7 presents the mean returns, variances, and correlations of these four assets for the entire sample period.

Table 7 shows that the minimum average historical return from these four asset classes was 9.6 percent a year (bonds) and the maximum average historical return was 14.6 percent (U.S. small-cap stocks). To trace out the minimum-variance frontier, we use the optimization model. The optimization program with a short sales constraint solves for the mean–variance frontier using the following equations:

$$\begin{aligned}\text{Min } \sigma_p^2(R) = {} & w_1^2\sigma_1^2 + w_2^2\sigma_2^2 + w_3^2\sigma_3^2 + w_4^2\sigma_4^2 + 2w_1w_2\rho_{1,2}\sigma_1\sigma_2 \\ & + 2w_1w_3\rho_{1,3}\sigma_1\sigma_3 + 2w_1w_4\rho_{1,4}\sigma_1\sigma_4 + 2w_2w_3\rho_{2,3}\sigma_2\sigma_3 \\ & + 2w_2w_4\rho_{2,4}\sigma_2\sigma_4 + 2w_3w_4\rho_{3,4}\sigma_3\sigma_4\end{aligned}$$

subject to $E(R_p) = w_1E(R_1) + w_2E(R_2) + w_3E(R_3) + w_4E(R_4) = z$ (repeated for specified values of z, $0.096 \leq z \leq 0.146$), $w_1 + w_2 + w_3 + w_4 = 1$, and $w_j \geq 0$.

16 There is a shortcut in the case of no constraints against short sales. According to Black's (1972) two-fund theorem, all portfolios on the minimum-variance frontier of risky assets are a linear combination of any two other minimum-variance portfolios, assuming that short sales are allowed. The implication is that we can trace out the minimum-variance frontier if we have calculated the portfolio weights of two minimum-variance portfolios. The procedure in the reading, however, works even when we add the constraint against short sales, which many investors face.

Table 7 **Mean Annual Returns, Standard Deviations, and Correlation Matrix for Four Asset Classes, January 1970–December 2002**

	S&P 500 (%)	U.S. Small-Cap Stocks (%)	MSCI World ex-United States (%)	U.S. Long-Term Government Bonds (%)
Mean Annual Returns	11.6	14.6	11.1	9.6
Standard deviation	15.83	22.18	17.07	10.44
Correlations				
S&P 500	1			
U.S. small-cap stocks	0.731	1		
MSCI World ex-U.S.	0.573	0.475	1	
U.S. long-term bonds	0.266	0.138	0.155	1

Source: Ibbotson Associates.

The weights w_1, w_2, w_3, and w_4 represent the four asset classes in the order listed in Table 7. The optimizer chooses the weights (allocations to the four asset classes) that result in the minimum-variance portfolio for each level of average return as we move from the minimum level (r_{min} = 9.6 percent) to the maximum level (r_{max} = 14.6 percent). In this example, $E(R_j)$ is represented by the sample mean return on asset class j, and the variances and covariances are also sample statistics. Unless we deliberately chose to use these historical data as our forward-looking estimates, we would not interpret the results of the optimization as a prediction about the future.

Figure 6 shows the minimum-variance frontier for these four asset classes based on the historical means, variances, and covariances from 1970 to 2002. The figure also shows the means and standard deviations of the four asset classes separately.

Figure 6 Minimum-Variance Frontier for Four Asset Classes 1970–2002

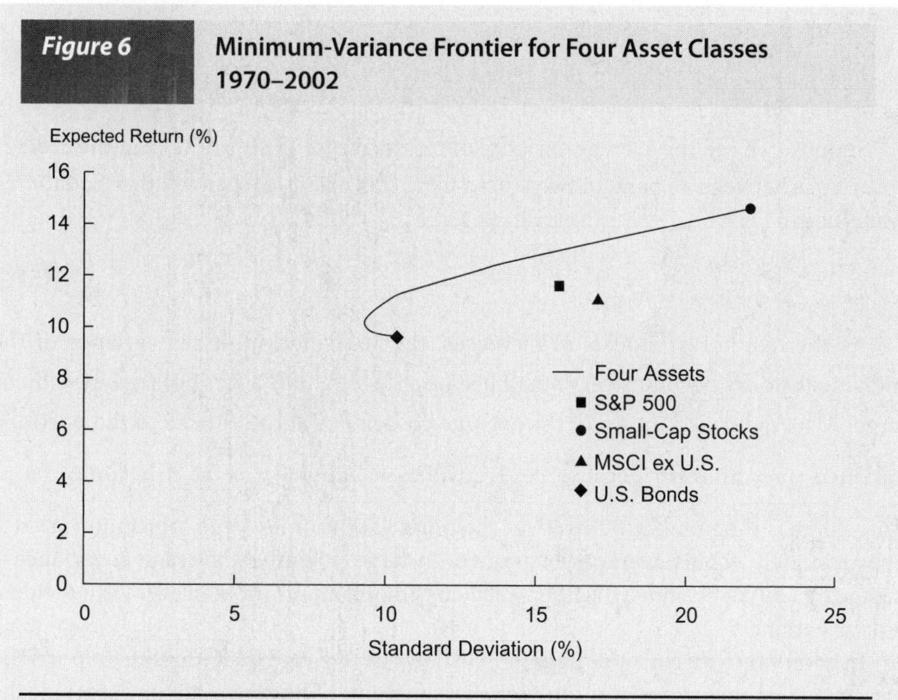

Although U.S. government bonds lie on the minimum-variance frontier, they are dominated by other asset classes that offer a better mean return for the same level of risk. Note that the points representing S&P 500 and the MSCI World ex-U.S. stocks plotted off and to the right of the minimum-variance frontier. If we move directly to the left from either the S&P 500 or MSCI ex-U.S. stock portfolio, we reach a portfolio on the efficient frontier that has smaller risk without affecting the mean return. If we move directly up from either, we reach a portfolio that has greater mean return with the same level of risk. After the fact, at least, these two portfolios were not efficient for an investor who could invest in all four asset classes. Despite the fact that MSCI World ex-U.S. stocks is itself a very broad index, for example, there were benefits to further diversifying. Of the four asset classes, only U.S. small-cap stocks as the highest-mean-return portfolio plotted on the efficient frontier; in general, the highest-mean-return portfolio appears as an endpoint of the efficient frontier in an optimization with a constraint against short sales, as in this case.

In this section, we showed the process for tracing out a minimum-variance frontier. We also analyzed a frontier generated from actual data. In the next section, we address the relationship between portfolio size and diversification.

2.4 Diversification and Portfolio Size

Earlier, we illustrated the diversification benefits of adding a third asset to a two-asset portfolio. That discussion opened a question of practical interest that we explore in this section: How many different stocks must we hold in order to have a well-diversified portfolio? How does covariance or correlation interact with portfolio size in determining a portfolio's risk?

We address these questions using the example of an investor who holds an equally weighted portfolio. Suppose we purchase a portfolio of n stocks and put an equal fraction of the value of the portfolio into each of the stocks ($w_i = 1/n$, $i = 1, 2, \ldots, n$). The variance of return is

$$\sigma_p^2 = \sum_{i=1}^{n}\sum_{j=1}^{n} w_i w_j \text{Cov}(R_i, R_j) = \frac{1}{n^2}\sum_{i=1}^{n}\sum_{j=1}^{n} \text{Cov}(R_i, R_j) \qquad (4)$$

Suppose we call the average variance of return across all stocks $\overline{\sigma}^2$ and the average covariance between all pairs of two stocks $\overline{\text{Cov}}$. It is possible to show[17] that Equation 4 simplifies to

$$\sigma_p^2 = \frac{1}{n}\overline{\sigma}^2 + \frac{n-1}{n}\overline{\text{Cov}} \qquad (5)$$

As the number of stocks, n, increases, the contribution of the variance of the individual stocks becomes very small because $(1/n)\overline{\sigma}^2$ has a limit of 0 as n becomes large. Also, the contribution of the average covariance across stocks to the portfolio variance stays nonzero because $\frac{n-1}{n}\overline{\text{Cov}}$ has a limit of $\overline{\text{Cov}}$ as n becomes large. Therefore, as the number of assets in the portfolio becomes large, portfolio variance approximately equals average covariance. In large portfolios, average covariance—capturing how assets move together—becomes more important than average individual risk or variance.

In addition to this insight, Equation 5 allows us to gauge the reduction in portfolio variance from the completely undiversified position of holding only one stock. If the portfolio contained only one stock, then of course its variance would be the individual stock's variance, which is the position of maximum variance.[18] If the portfolio contained a very large number of stocks, the variance of the portfolio would be close to the average covariance of any two of the stocks, known as the position of minimum variance. How large is the difference between these two levels of variance, and how much of the maximum benefit can we obtain with a relatively small number of stocks?

The answers depend on the sizes of the average variance and the average covariance. Because correlation is easier to interpret than covariance, we will work with correlation. Suppose, for simplicity's sake, that the correlation between the returns for any two stocks is the same and that all stocks have the same standard deviation. Chan, Karceski, and Lakonishok (1999) found that for U.S. NYSE and AMEX stocks over the 1968–98 period, the average correlation of small-stock returns was 0.24, the average correlation of large-stock returns was 0.33, and the average correlation of stock returns across the entire sample of stocks was 0.28. Assume that the common correlation is 0.30, which is in the approximate range for the average correlation of U.S. equities for many time periods. The covariance of two random variables is the correlation of those variables multiplied by the standard deviations of the two variables, so $\overline{\text{Cov}} = 0.30\sigma^2$ (using our assumption that all stocks have the same standard deviation of returns, denoted σ).

Look back at Equation 5 and replace $\overline{\text{Cov}}$ with $0.30\sigma^2$:

17 See Bodie, Kane, and Marcus (2001).

18 For realistic values of correlation, average variance is greater than average covariance.

$$\begin{aligned}\sigma_p^2 &= \frac{1}{n}\sigma^2 + \frac{n-1}{n}\left(0.30\sigma^2\right)\\ &= \frac{\sigma^2}{n}\left[1 + 0.30(n-1)\right]\\ &= \frac{\sigma^2}{n}(0.70 + 0.30n)\\ &= \sigma^2\left(\frac{0.70}{n} + 0.30\right)\end{aligned}$$

which provides an example of the more general expression (assuming stocks have the same standard deviation of returns)

$$\sigma_p^2 = \sigma^2\left(\frac{1-\rho}{n} + \rho\right) \qquad (6)$$

If the portfolio contains one stock, the portfolio variance is σ^2. As n increases, portfolio variance drops rapidly. In our example, if the portfolio contains 15 stocks, the portfolio variance is $0.347\sigma^2$, or only 34.7 percent of the variance of a portfolio with one stock. With 30 stocks, the portfolio variance is 32.3 percent of the variance of a single-stock portfolio. The smallest possible portfolio variance in this case is 30 percent of the variance of a single stock, because $\sigma_p^2 = 0.30\ \sigma^2$ when n is extremely large. With only 30 stocks, for example, the portfolio variance is only approximately 8 percent larger than minimum possible value ($0.323\sigma^2/0.30\sigma^2 - 1 = 0.077$), and the variance is 67.7 percent smaller than the variance of a portfolio that contains only one stock.

For a reasonable assumed value of correlation, the previous example shows that a portfolio composed of many stocks has far less total risk than a portfolio composed of only one stock. In this example, we can diversify away 70 percent of an individual stock's risk by holding many stocks. Furthermore, we may be able to obtain a large part of the risk reduction benefits of diversification with a surprisingly small number of securities.

What if the correlation among stocks is higher than 0.30? Suppose an investor wanted to be sure that his portfolio variance was only 110 percent of the minimum possible portfolio variance of a diversified portfolio. How many stocks would the investor need? If the average correlation among stocks were 0.5, he would need only 10 stocks for the portfolio to have 110 percent of the minimum possible portfolio variance. With a higher correlation, the investor would need fewer stocks to obtain the same percentage of minimum possible portfolio variance. What if the correlation is lower than 0.30? If the correlation among stocks were 0.1, the investor would need 90 stocks in the portfolio to obtain 110 percent of the minimum possible portfolio variance.

One common belief among investors is that almost all of the benefits of diversification can be achieved with a portfolio of only 30 stocks. In fact, Fisher and Lorie (1970) showed that 95 percent of the benefits of diversification among NYSE-traded stocks from 1926 to 1965 were achieved with a portfolio of 32 stocks.

As shown above, the number of stocks needed to achieve a particular diversification gain depends on the average correlation among stock returns: The lower the average correlation, the greater the number of stocks needed. Campbell, Lettau, Malkiel, and Xu (2001) showed that although overall market volatility has not increased since 1963, individual stock returns have been more volatile recently (1986–97) and individual stock returns have been less correlated with each other. Consequently, to achieve the same percentage of the risk-reducing benefits of diversification during the more recent period, more stocks were needed in a portfolio than in the period studied by Fisher and Lorie. Campbell et al. conclude that during the 1963–85 period, "a portfolio of

20 stocks reduced annualized excess standard deviation to about five percent, but in the 1986–1997 subsample, this level of excess standard deviation required almost 50 stocks."[19]

EXAMPLE 3

Diversification at Berkshire Hathaway

Berkshire Hathaway's highly successful CEO, Warren Buffett, is one of the harshest critics of modern portfolio theory and diversification. Buffett has said, for example, that "[I]f you are a know-something investor, able to understand business economics, and find 5 to 10 sensibly priced companies that possess important long-term competitive advantages, conventional diversification makes no sense for you. It is apt simply to hurt your results and increase your risk."[20]

Does Buffett avoid diversification altogether? Certainly his investment record is phenomenal, but even Buffett engages in diversification to some extent. For example, consider Berkshire Hathaway's top three investment holdings at the end of 2002.[21]

American Express Company	\$ 5.6 billion (32%)
The Coca-Cola Company	\$ 8.8 billion (51%)
The Gillette Company	\$ 2.9 billion (17%)
Total	\$ 17.3 billion

How much diversification do these three stocks provide? How much lower is this portfolio's standard deviation than that of a portfolio consisting only of Coca-Cola stock? To answer these questions, assume that the historical mean returns, return standard deviations, and return correlations of these stocks are the best estimates of the future expected returns, return standard deviations, and return correlations. Table 8 shows these historical statistics, based on monthly return data from 1990 through 2002.

Table 8 **Historical Returns, Variances, and Correlations: Berkshire Hathaway's Largest Equity Holdings (Monthly Data, January 1990–December 2002)**

	American Express (%)	Coca-Cola (%)	Gillette (%)
Mean annual return	16.0	16.1	17.6
Standard deviation	29.0	24.7	27.3
Correlations			
American Express and Coca-Cola	0.361		

19 Campbell et al. defined "excess standard deviation" as the standard deviation of a randomly selected portfolio of a given size minus the standard deviation of an equally weighted market index.

20 Buffett (1993).

21 We consider only the top three holdings in order to simplify the computations in this example. Also for simplicity, we rounded the percentage allocations in the portfolio. The weights shown here are the relative weights among these three stocks, not their actual weights in the Berkshire Hathaway portfolio.

Table 8 (Continued)

	American Express (%)	Coca-Cola (%)	Gillette (%)
American Express and Gillette	0.317		
Coca-Cola and Gillette	0.548		

Source: FactSet.

Table 8 shows that for Coca-Cola's stock during this period, the mean annual return was 16.1 percent and the annualized standard deviation of the return was 24.7 percent. In contrast, a portfolio consisting of 32 percent American Express stock, 51 percent Coca-Cola stock, and 17 percent Gillette stock had an expected return of 0.32(0.16) + 0.51(0.161) + 0.17(0.176) = 0.163, or 16.3 percent.

The portfolio's expected standard deviation, based on these weights and the statistics in Table 8, was

$$\sigma_p = \left[w_1^2\sigma_1^2 + w_2^2\sigma_2^2 + w_3^2\sigma_3^2 + 2w_1w_2\rho_{1,2}\sigma_1\sigma_2 + 2w_1w_3\rho_{1,3}\sigma_1\sigma_3 + 2w_2w_3\rho_{2,3}\sigma_2\sigma_3\right]^{1/2}$$

or

$$\begin{aligned}\sigma_p &= \left[\left(0.32^2\right)\left(0.290^2\right) + \left(0.51^2\right)\left(0.247^2\right) + \left(0.17^2\right)\left(0.273^2\right)\right.\\ &\quad + 2(0.32)(0.51)(0.361)(0.290)(0.247)\\ &\quad + 2(0.32)(0.17)(0.317)(0.290)(0.273)\\ &\quad \left. + 2(0.51)(0.17)(0.548)(0.247)(0.273)\right]^{1/2}\\ &= 0.210 \text{ or } 21.0 \text{ percent}\end{aligned}$$

The standard deviation of a portfolio with these three stocks is only 21.0/24.7 = 85.0 percent of the standard deviation of a portfolio composed exclusively of Coca-Cola stock. Therefore, Berkshire Hathaway actually achieved substantial diversification in the sense of risk reduction, even considering only its top three holdings.

2.5 Portfolio Choice with a Risk-Free Asset

So far, we have considered only portfolios of risky securities, implicitly assuming that investors cannot also invest in a risk-free asset. But investors can hold their own government's securities such as Treasury bills, which are virtually risk-free in nominal terms over appropriate time horizons. For example, the purchaser of a one-year Treasury bill knows his nominal return if he holds the bill to maturity. What is the trade-off between risk and return when we can invest in a risk-free asset?

A risk-free asset's standard deviation of return is 0 because the return is certain and there is no risk of default. Suppose, for example, that the return to the risk-free asset is 4 percent a year. If we take the Treasury bill as risk-free, then 4 percent is the actual return, known in advance; it is not an expected return.[22] Because the risk-free

22 We assume here that the maturity of the T-bills is the same as the investment horizon so that there is no interest rate risk.

asset's standard deviation of return is 0, the covariance between the return of the risk-free asset and the return of any other asset must also be 0. These observations help us understand how adding a risk-free asset to a portfolio can affect the mean–variance trade-off among assets.

2.5.1 *The Capital Allocation Line*

The **capital allocation line (CAL)** describes the combinations of expected return and standard deviation of return available to an investor from combining her optimal portfolio of risky assets with the risk-free asset. Thus the CAL describes the expected results of the investor's decision on how to optimally allocate her capital among risky and risk-free assets.

What graph in mean return-standard deviation space satisfies the definition of the CAL? The CAL must be the line from the risk-free rate of return that is tangent to the efficient frontier of risky assets; of all lines we could extend from the risk-free rate to the efficient frontier of risky assets, the tangent line has the maximum slope and best risk–return tradeoff ("tangent" means touching without intersecting). The tangency portfolio is the investor's optimal portfolio of risky assets. The investor's risk tolerance determines which point on the line he or she will choose. Example 4 and the ensuing discussion clarify and illustrate these points.

EXAMPLE 4

An Investor's Trade-Off between Risk and Return with a Risk-Free Asset

Suppose that we want to determine the effect of including a risk-free asset in addition to large-cap stocks and government bonds in our portfolio. Table 9 shows the hypothetical expected returns and correlations for the three asset classes.

Table 9 Expected Returns, Variances, and Correlations: Three-Asset Case with Risk-Free Asset

	Large-Cap Stocks	Government Bonds	Risk-Free Asset
Expected return	15%	5%	4%
Variance	225	100	0
Standard deviation	15%	10%	0%
Correlations			
Large-cap stocks and government bonds		0.5	
Large-cap stocks and risk-free asset		0	
Government bonds and risk-free asset		0	

Suppose we decide to invest the entire portfolio in the risk-free asset with a return of 4 percent. In this case, the expected return to the portfolio is 4 percent and the expected standard deviation is 0. Now assume that we put the entire portfolio into large-cap stocks. The expected return is now 15 percent, and the standard deviation of the portfolio is 15 percent. What will happen if we divide the portfolio between the risk-free asset and large-cap stocks? If the proportion of assets in large-cap stocks is w_1 and the proportion of assets in the risk-free asset is $(1 - w_1)$, then the expected portfolio return is

$$E\left(R_p\right) = w_1(0.15) + (1 - w_1)(0.04)$$

and the portfolio standard deviation is

$$\sigma_p = \left[w_1^2(0.15)^2 + (1 - w_1)^2(0)^2\right]^{1/2} = w_1(0.15)$$

Note that both the expected return and the standard deviation of return are linearly related to w_1, the percentage of the portfolio in large-cap stocks. Figure 7 illustrates the trade-off between risk and return for the risk-free asset and large-cap stocks in this example.

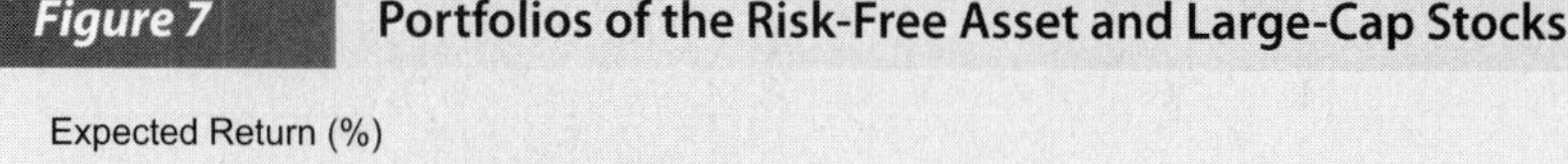

Figure 7 Portfolios of the Risk-Free Asset and Large-Cap Stocks

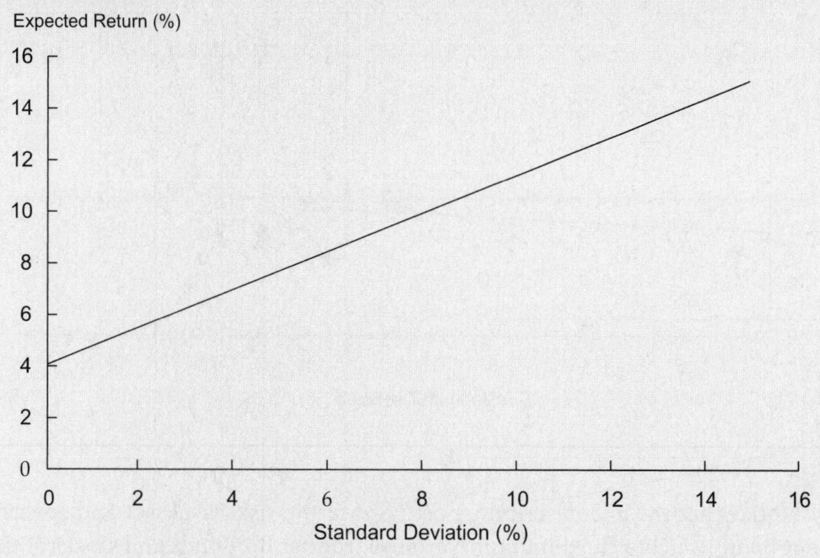

Now let us consider the trade-off between risk and return for a portfolio containing the risk-free asset and U.S. government bonds. Suppose we decide to put the entire portfolio in the risk-free asset. In this case, the expected return to the portfolio is 4 percent and the expected standard deviation of the portfolio is 0. Now assume that we put the entire portfolio into U.S. government bonds. The expected return is now 5 percent, and the standard deviation of the portfolio is 10 percent. What will happen if we divide the portfolio between the risk-free asset and government bonds? If the proportion of assets in government bonds is w_1 and the proportion of assets in the risk-free asset is $(1 - w_1)$, then the expected portfolio return is

$$E\left(R_p\right) = w_1(0.05) + (1 - w_1)(0.04)$$

and the portfolio standard deviation is

$$\sigma_p = \left[w_1^2(0.10)^2 + (1 - w_1)^2(0)^2\right]^{1/2} = w_1(0.10)$$

Note that both the expected return and the standard deviation of return are linearly related to w_1, the percentage of the portfolio in the government bonds. Figure 8 shows the trade-off between risk and return for the risk-free asset and government bonds in this example.

We have just seen the trade-off between risk and return for two different portfolios: one with the risk-free asset and large-cap stocks, the other with the risk-free asset and government bonds. How do these trade-offs between risk and return compare with the original risk–return trade-off between government bonds and large-cap stocks? Figure 9 illustrates the risk–return trade-off for all three portfolios.

Figure 8 Portfolios of the Risk-Free Asset and Government Bonds

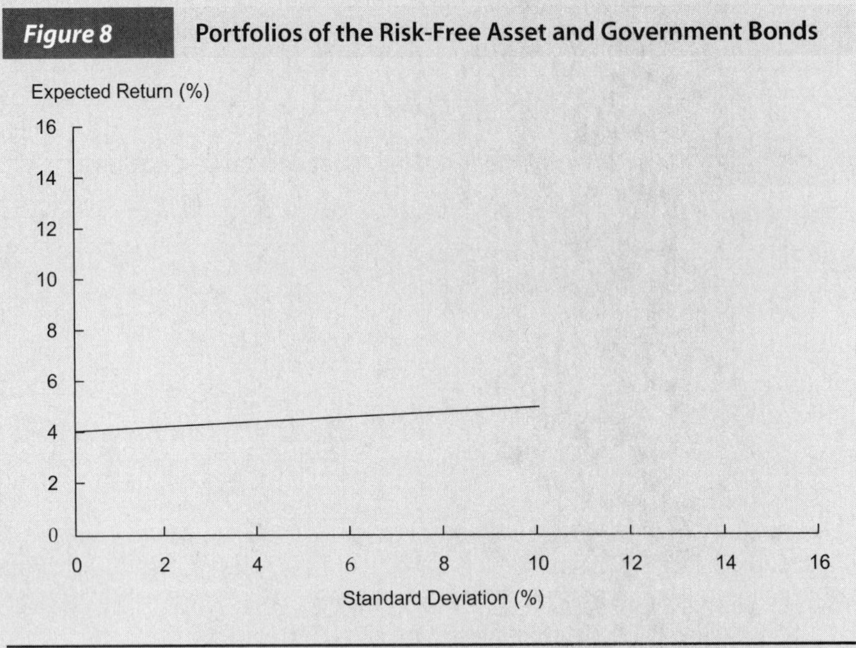

Notice that the line describing portfolios of the risk-free asset and government bonds touches the minimum-variance frontier for bonds and stocks at the point of lowest return on the bond-stock minimum-variance frontier—that is, the point where 100 percent of the portfolio is invested in bonds. Some points on the risk-free asset–bond line have lower risk and return than points on the bond-stock frontier; however, we can find no point where, for a given level of risk, the expected return is higher on the risk-free asset–bond line than on the bond-stock frontier. In this case, if we draw the line with the highest slope from the risk-free asset to the bond-stock frontier, that line is tangent to the bond-stock frontier at a point representing a portfolio 100 percent invested in stocks.[23] This CAL is labeled Risk-Free Asset and Large-Cap Stocks in Figure 9. For given assumptions about expected returns, variances, and covariances, that capital allocation line identifies portfolios with the maximum expected return for a given level of risk, if we can spread our money between an optimal risky portfolio and a risk-free asset. Of all lines we could extend from the risk-free rate to the minimum-variance frontier of risky assets, the CAL has maximum slope. Slope defined as rise (expected return) over run (standard deviation) measures the expected risk–return trade-off. The CAL is the line of maximum slope that touches the minimum-variance frontier; consequently, the capital allocation line offers the best risk–return trade-off achievable, given our expectations.

23 In a typical case with many assets, however, the point where the line with maximum slope from the risk-free asset touches the minimum-variance frontier of risky assets does not represent a portfolio composed of only the highest expected return asset. In such typical cases, the CAL represents combinations of the risk-free asset and a broad combination of risky assets.

Figure 9 Portfolios of the Risk-Free Asset, Large-Cap Stocks, and Government Bonds

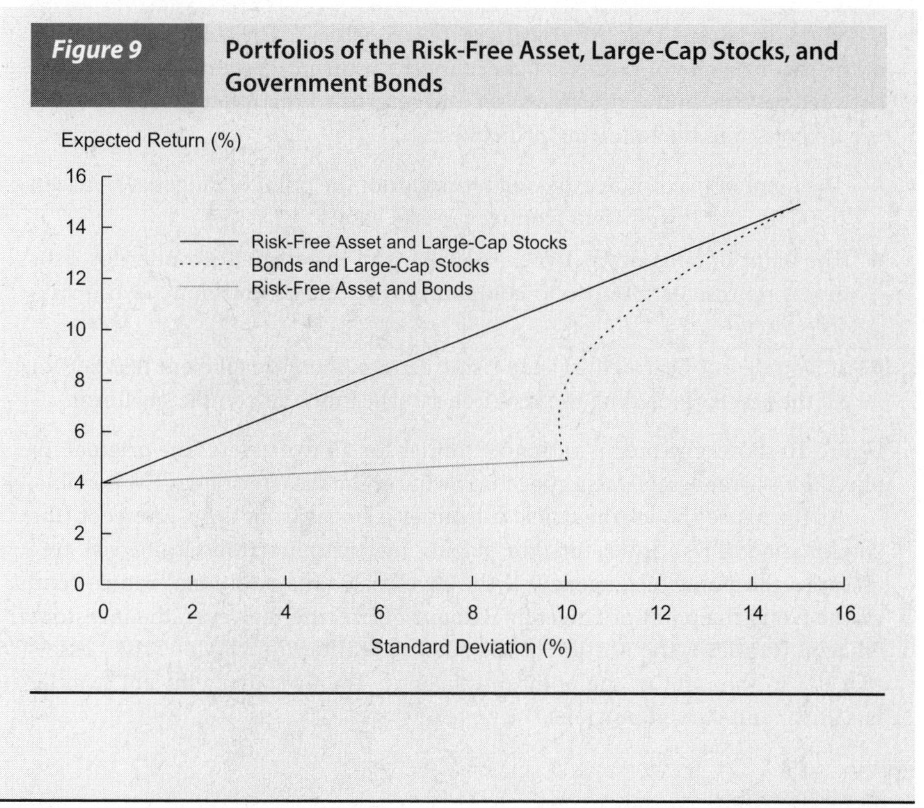

The previous example showed three important general principles concerning the risk–return trade-off in a portfolio containing a risk-free asset:

- If we can invest in a risk-free asset, then the CAL represents the best risk–return trade-off achievable.
- The CAL has a y-intercept equal to the risk-free rate.
- The CAL is tangent to the efficient frontier of risky assets.[24]

EXAMPLE 5A

The CAL with Multiple Assets

In Example 4, the CAL was tangent to the efficient frontier for all risky assets. We now illustrate how the efficient frontier changes depending on the **opportunity set** (the set of assets available for investment) and whether the investor wants to borrow to leverage his investments. We can illustrate this point by reconsidering our earlier example (Example 2) of optimal portfolio choice among the S&P 500, U.S. small-cap stocks, non-U.S. stocks (the MSCI World ex-U.S.), and U.S. government bonds, adding a risk-free asset.

24 Note that when we expand the set of assets to include the risk-free asset, an investor's CAL becomes the efficient frontier defined in relation to the expanded set of assets. The efficient frontier of risky assets is the efficient frontier considering risky assets alone. It is critical to understand that the efficient frontier is always defined in relationship to a specified set of assets.

We now assume that the risk-free rate is 5 percent. The standard deviation of the risk-free rate of return is 0, because the return is certain; the covariance between returns to the risk-free asset and returns to the other assets is also 0. We demonstrate the following principles:

- The point of maximum expected return is not the point of tangency between the CAL and the efficient frontier of risky assets.
- The point of tangency between the CAL and the efficient frontier for risky assets represents a portfolio containing risky assets and none of the risk-free asset.
- If we rule out borrowing at the risk-free rate, then the efficient frontier for all the assets (including the risk-free asset) cannot be completely linear.

Figure 10 shows the mean–variance frontier for all five assets (the original for plus the risk-free assets), assuming borrowing at the risk-free rate is not possible.

As the figure shows, the efficient frontier is linear from the *y*-intercept (the combination of risk and return for placing the entire portfolio in the risk-free asset) to the point of tangency. If the investor wants additional return (and risk) beyond the point of tangency without borrowing, however, the investor's efficient frontier is the portion of the efficient frontier for the four risky assets that lies to the right of the point of tangency. The investor's efficient frontier has linear and curved portions.[25]

Figure 10 **The Effect of Adding a Risk-Free Asset to a Risky Portfolio**

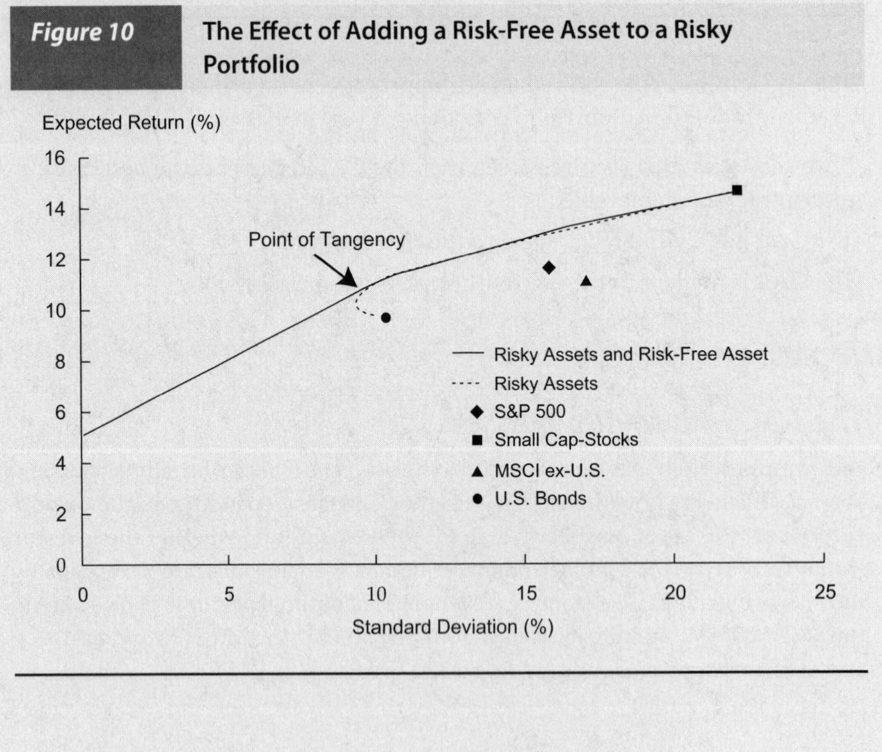

25 If borrowing at the risk-free rate were possible (equivalent to buying on margin at the risk-free rate), the efficient frontier would be the straight line from the risk-free rate, now continued past the point of tangency.

2.5.2 The Capital Allocation Line Equation In the previous section, we discussed the graph of the CAL and illustrated how the efficient frontier can change depending on the set of assets available for investment as well as the portfolio manager's expectations. We now provide the equation for this line.

Suppose that an investor, given expectations about means, variances, and covariances for risky assets, plots the efficient frontier of risky assets. There is a risk-free asset offering a risk-free rate of return, R_F. If w_T is the proportion of the portfolio the investor places in the tangency portfolio, then the expected return for the entire portfolio is

$$E(R_p) = (1 - w_T)R_F + w_T E(R_T)$$

and the standard deviation of the portfolio is

$$\begin{aligned}\sigma_p &= \left[(1 - w_T)^2 \sigma_{R_F}^2 + w_T^2 \sigma_{R_T}^2 + 2(1 - w_T) w_T \sigma_{R_F} \sigma_{R_T} \rho_{R_F,R_T}\right]^{1/2} \\ &= \left[(1 - w_T)^2 (0) + w_T^2 \sigma_{R_T}^2 + 2(1 - w_T) w_T (0)(\sigma_{R_T})(0)\right]^{1/2} \\ &= \left(w_T^2 \sigma_{R_T}^2\right)^{1/2} \\ &= w_T \sigma_{R_T}\end{aligned}$$

An investor can choose to invest any fraction of his assets in the risk-free asset or in the tangency portfolio; therefore, he can choose many combinations of risk and return. If he puts the entire portfolio in the risk-free asset, then

$$\begin{aligned} w_T &= 0 \\ E(R_p) &= (1 - 0)R_F + 0E(R_T) = R_F, \text{ and} \\ \sigma_p &= 0\sigma_{R_T} \\ &= 0 \end{aligned}$$

If he puts his entire portfolio in the tangency portfolio, then

$$\begin{aligned} w_T &= 1 \\ E(R_p) &= (1 - 1)R_F + 1E(R_T) = E(R_T), \text{ and} \\ \sigma_p &= 1\sigma_{R_T} = \sigma_{R_T} \end{aligned}$$

In general, if he puts w_T percent of his portfolio in the tangency portfolio, his portfolio standard deviation will be $\sigma_p = w_T \sigma_{R_T}$.

To see how the portfolio weights, expected return, and risk are related, we use the relationship $w_T = \sigma_p / \sigma_{R_T}$. If we substitute this value of w_T back into the expression for expected return, $E(R_p) = (1 - w_T)R_F + w_T E(R_T)$, we get

$$E(R_p) = \left(1 - \frac{\sigma_p}{\sigma_{R_T}}\right) R_F + \frac{\sigma_p}{\sigma_{R_T}} E(R_T)$$

or

$$E(R_p) = R_F + \frac{E(R_T) - R_F}{\sigma_{R_T}} \sigma_p \qquad (7)$$

This equation shows the best possible trade-off between expected risk and return, given this investor's expectations. The term $\left[E(R_T) - R_F\right] / \sigma_{R_T}$ is the return that the investor demands in order to take on an extra unit of risk. Example 5B illustrates how to calculate the investor's price of risk and other aspects of his investment using the capital allocation line.

EXAMPLE 5B

CAL Calculations

Suppose that the risk-free rate, R_F, is 5 percent; the expected return to an investor's tangency portfolio, $E(R_T)$, is 15 percent; and the standard deviation of the tangency portfolio is 25 percent.

1 How much return does this investor demand in order to take on an extra unit of risk?

2 Suppose the investor wants a portfolio standard deviation of return of 10 percent. What percentage of the assets should be in the tangency portfolio, and what is the expected return?

3 Suppose the investor wants to put 40 percent of the portfolio in the risk-free asset. What is the portfolio expected return? What is the standard deviation?

4 What expected return should the investor demand for a portfolio with a standard deviation of 35 percent?

5 What combination of the tangency portfolio and the risk-free asset does the investor need to hold in order to have a portfolio with an expected return of 19 percent?

6 If the investor has $10 million to invest, how much must she borrow at the risk-free rate to have a portfolio with an expected return of 19%?

Solution to 1:

In this case, $\left[E(R_T) - R_F\right]/\sigma_{R_T} = (0.15 - 0.05)/0.25 = 0.4$The investor demands an additional 40 basis points of expected return of the portfolio for every 1 percentage point increase in the standard deviation of portfolio returns.

Solution to 2:

Because $\sigma_p = w_T\sigma_{R_T}$, then $w_T = 0.1/0.25 = 0.4$, or 40 percent. In other words, 40 percent of the assets are in the tangency portfolio and 60 percent are in the risk-free asset. The expected return for the portfolio is $E(R_p) = R_F + \dfrac{E(R_T) - R_F}{\sigma_{R_T}}\sigma_p = 0.05 + (0.4)(0.1) = 0.09$, or 9 percent.

Solution to 3:

In this case, $w_T = 1 - 0.4 = 0.6$. Therefore, the expected portfolio return is $E(R_p) = (1 - w_T)R_F + w_TE(R_T) = (1 - 0.6)(0.05) + (0.6)(0.15) = 0.11$, or 11 percent. The portfolio standard deviation is $\sigma_p = w_T\sigma_{R_T} = (0.6)(0.25) = 0.15$ or 15 percent.

Solution to 4:

We know that the relation between risk and expected return for this portfolio is $E(R_p) = R_F + \dfrac{E(R_T) - R_F}{\sigma_{R_T}}\sigma_p = 0.05 + \left[(0.15 - 0.05)/0.25\right]\sigma_p = 0.05 + 0.4\sigma_p$

If the standard deviation for the portfolio's returns is 35 percent, then the investor can demand an expected return of $E(R_p) = 0.05 + 0.4\sigma_p = 0.05 + 0.4(0.35) = 0.19$, or 19 percent.

Solution to 5:

With an expected return of 19 percent, the asset allocation must be as follows:

$$E(R_p) = (1 - w_T)R_F + w_T E(R_T) \text{ or}$$
$$0.19 = (1 - w_T)(0.05) + w_T(0.15) = 0.05 + 0.10w_T$$
$$w_T = 1.4$$

How can the weight on the tangency portfolio be 140 percent? The interpretation of $w_T = 1.4$ is that the investment in the tangency portfolio consists of 1) the entire amount of initial wealth and 2) an amount equal to 40 percent of initial wealth that has been borrowed at the risk-free rate. We can confirm that the expected return is $(-0.4)(0.05) + (1.4)(0.15) = 0.19$ or 19 percent.

Solution to 6:

The investor must borrow \$4 million dollars at the risk-free rate to increase the holdings of the tangency-asset portfolio to \$14 million dollars. Therefore, the net value of the portfolio will be \$14 million − \$4 million = \$10 million.

In this section, we have assumed that investors may have different views about risky assets' mean returns, variances of returns, and correlations. Thus each investor may perceive a different efficient frontier of risky assets and have a different tangency portfolio, the optimal portfolio of risky assets which the investor may combine with risk-free borrowing or lending. In the next two sections, we examine the consequences when mean–variance investors share identical expectations.

2.5.3 *The Capital Market Line*

When investors share identical expectations about the mean returns, variance of returns, and correlations of risky assets, the CAL for all investors is the same and is known as the **capital market line (CML)**. With identical expectations, the tangency portfolio must be the same portfolio for all investors. In equilibrium, this tangency portfolio must be a portfolio containing all risky assets in proportions reflecting their market value weights; the tangency portfolio is the market portfolio of all risky assets. The CML is a capital allocation line with the market portfolio as the tangency portfolio. The equation of the CML is

$$E(R_p) = R_F + \frac{E(R_M) - R_F}{\sigma_M}\sigma_p \tag{8}$$

where

$E(R_p)$ = the expected return of portfolio p lying on the capital market line
R_F = the risk-free rate
$E(R_M)$ = the expected rate of return on the market portfolio
σ_M = the standard deviation of return on the market portfolio
σ_p = the standard deviation of return on portfolio p

The slope of the CML, $[E(R_M) - R_F]/\sigma_M,$ is called the **market price of risk** because it indicates the market risk premium for each unit of market risk. As noted, the CML describes the expected return of only efficient portfolios. The implication of the capital market line is that all mean–variance investors, whatever their risk tolerance, can satisfy their investment needs by combining the risk-free asset with a single risky portfolio, the market portfolio of all risky assets.

In the next section we present a mean–variance theory describing the expected return of any asset or portfolio, efficient or inefficient.

2.6 The Capital Asset Pricing Model

The **capital asset pricing model (CAPM)** has played a pivotal role in the development of quantitative investment management since its introduction in the early 1960s. In this section, we review some of its key aspects.

The CAPM makes the following assumptions:[26]

- Investors need only know the expected returns, the variances, and the covariances of returns to determine which portfolios are optimal for them. (This assumption appears throughout all of mean–variance theory.)
- Investors have identical views about risky assets' mean returns, variances of returns, and correlations.
- Investors can buy and sell assets in any quantity without affecting price, and all assets are marketable (can be traded).
- Investors can borrow and lend at the risk-free rate without limit, and they can sell short any asset in any quantity.
- Investors pay no taxes on returns and pay no transaction costs on trades.

The CML represents the efficient frontier when the assumptions of the CAPM hold. In a CAPM world, therefore, all investors can satisfy their investment needs by combining the risk-free asset with the identical tangency portfolio, which is the market portfolio of all risky assets (no risky asset is excluded).

The following equation describes the expected returns on all assets and portfolios, whether efficient or not:

$$E(R_i) = R_F + \beta_i\left[E(R_M) - R_F\right] \quad (9)$$

where

$E(R_i)$ = the expected return on asset i
R_F = the risk-free rate of return
$E(R_M)$ = the expected return on the market portfolio
$\beta_i = \text{Cov}(R_i, R_M)/\text{Var}(R_M)$

Equation 9 itself is referred to as the capital asset pricing model, and its graph is called the **security market line (SML)**. The CAPM is an equation describing the expected return on any asset (or portfolio) as a linear function of its beta, β_i, which is a measure of the asset's sensitivity to movements in the market. The CAPM says that expected return has two components: first, the risk-free rate, R_F, and second, an extra return equal to $\beta_i[E(R_M) - R_F]$. The term $[E(R_M) - R_F]$ is the expected excess return on the market. This amount is the **market risk premium**; if we are 100 percent invested in the market, the market risk premium is the extra return we expect to obtain, on average, compared with the risk-free rate of return.

The market risk premium is multiplied by the asset's beta. A beta of 1 represents average market sensitivity, and we expect an asset with that beta to earn the market risk premium exactly.[27] A beta greater than 1 indicates greater than average market risk and, according to the CAPM, earns a higher expected excess return. Conversely, a beta less than 1 indicates less than average market risk and, according to the CAPM,

26 For a complete list of assumptions, see Elton, Gruber, Brown, and Goetzmann (2003).

27 The market portfolio itself has a beta of 1, as $\beta_M = \text{Cov}(R_M, R_M)/\text{Var}(R_M) = \text{Var}(R_M)/\text{Var}(R_M) = 1$. Because the market portfolio includes all assets, the average asset must have a beta of 1. The same argument applies if we compute the betas of assets in an index, using the index to represent the market.

earns a smaller expected excess return. Expected excess returns are related only to market risk, represented by beta. Sensitivity to the market return is the only source of difference in expected excess returns across assets.[28]

Like all theory-based models, the CAPM comes from a set of assumptions. The CAPM describes a financial market equilibrium in the sense that, if the model is correct and any asset's expected return differs from its expected return as given by the CAPM, market forces will come into play to restore the relationships specified by the model. For example, a stock that offers a higher expected return than justified by its beta will be bid up in price, lowering the stock's expected return; investors would expect that a broad-based portfolio would offset any non-market risk the stock might carry.

Because it is all-inclusive, the market portfolio defined in the CAPM is unobservable. In practice, we must use some broad index to represent it. The CAPM has been used primarily to value equities, so a common choice for the market portfolio is a broad value-weighted stock index or market proxy. The straight-line relationship between expected return and beta results from the efficiency of the market portfolio. As a result, the CAPM theory is equivalent to saying that the unobservable market portfolio is efficient, but not that any particular proxy for the market is efficient.[29] Of more interest to practitioners than the strict truth of CAPM as a theory is whether beta computed using available market proxies is useful for evaluating the expected mean returns to various investment strategies. The evidence now favors the existence of multiple sources of systematic risk affecting the mean returns to investment strategies.

2.7 Mean–Variance Portfolio Choice Rules: An Introduction

In this section, we introduce some of the principles of portfolio choice from a mean–variance perspective. One of the most basic portfolio choice decisions is the selection of an optimal asset allocation starting from a set of permissible asset classes. A second kind of decision involves modifying an existing portfolio. This type of decision is easier because we may be able to conclude that one portfolio represents a mean–variance improvement on another without necessarily establishing that the better portfolio is optimal. We begin with a brief discussion of this second decision type.

2.7.1 *Decisions Related to Existing Portfolios*

We examine two kinds of decisions related to existing portfolios in which mean–variance analysis may play a role.

Comparisons of Portfolios as Stand-Alone Investments The **Markowitz decision rule** provides the principle by which a mean–variance investor facing the choice of putting all her money in Asset A or all her money in Asset B can sometimes reach a decision. This investor prefers A to B if either

- the mean return on A is equal to or larger than that on B, but A has a smaller standard deviation of return than B, or
- the mean return on A is strictly larger than that on B, but A and B have the same standard deviation of return.

28 One intuition for this idea is that the market is the perfectly diversified portfolio. We can cancel out any other risk by holding the market portfolio, and we can costlessly hold the market portfolio (by the no-transaction-costs assumption). Even risk with respect to personal assets such as human capital (representing earning power) can be diversified away (all assets are tradable). Investors should not require extra return for risks they can costlessly hedge.

29 See Bodie, Kane, and Marcus (2001) for more on this topic.

When A is preferred to B by the Markowitz decision rule, we say that A *mean–variance dominates* B: Asset A clearly makes more efficient use of risk than B does. For example, if an investor is presented with a choice between 1) an asset allocation A with a mean return of 9 percent and a standard deviation of return of 12 percent and 2) a second asset allocation B with a mean return of 8 percent and a standard deviation of return of 15 percent, a mean–variance investor will prefer alternative A because it is expected to provide a higher mean return with less risk. A point to note is that when asset allocation has both higher mean return and higher standard deviation, the Markowitz decision rule does not select one asset allocation as superior; rather, the preference depends on the individual investor's risk tolerance.

We can identify an expanded set of mean–variance dominance relationships if we admit borrowing and lending at the risk-free rate. Then we can use the risk-free asset to match risk among the portfolios being compared. The Sharpe ratio (the ratio of mean return in excess of the risk-free rate of return to the standard deviation of return) serves as the appropriate metric.

- If a portfolio p has a higher positive Sharpe ratio than portfolio q, then p mean–variance dominates q if borrowing and lending at the risk-free rate is possible.[30]

Suppose asset allocation A is as before but now B has a mean of 6 percent and a standard deviation of 10 percent. Allocation A has higher mean return than B (9 percent versus 6 percent) but also higher risk (12 percent versus 10 percent), so the Markowitz decision rule is inconclusive about which allocation is better. Suppose we can borrow and lend at a risk-free rate of 3 percent. The Sharpe ratio of A, (9 – 3)/12 = 0.50, is higher than the Sharpe ratio of B, (6 – 3)/10 = 0.30, so we can conclude that A mean–variance dominates B. Note that a portfolio 83.3 percent invested in A and 16.7 percent invested in the risk-free asset has the same standard deviation as B, because 0.833(12) = 10 percent, with mean return of 0.833(9) + 0.167(3) = 8 percent, versus 6 percent for B. In short, we combined the higher Sharpe ratio portfolio p with the risk-free asset to achieve a portfolio with the same risk as portfolio q but with higher mean return. As B was originally defined (mean return of 8 percent and standard deviation of 15 percent), B had a Sharpe ratio of 0.33 and, as expected, the decision based on Sharpe ratios is consistent with that based on the Markowitz decision rule.

Practically, this decision-making approach is most reliable when we are considering choices among well-diversified portfolios and when the return distributions of the choices are at least approximately normal.

The Decision to Add an Investment to an Existing Portfolio We described an approach for choosing between two asset allocations as an either/or proposition. We now discuss an approach to deciding whether to add a new asset class to an existing portfolio, or more generally to further diversify an existing portfolio.

Suppose you hold a portfolio p with expected or mean return $E(R_p)$ and standard deviation of return σ_p. Then you are offered the opportunity to add another investment to your portfolio, for example, a new asset class. Will you effect a mean–variance improvement by expanding your portfolio to include a positive position in the new investment? To answer this question, you need three inputs:

- the Sharpe ratio of the new investment;

30 The reverse of the proposition is also true: If a portfolio p mean–variance dominates a portfolio q, then p has a higher Sharpe ratio than q. The proof of these propositions is in Dybvig and Ross (1985b). Note that we assume a positive Sharpe ratio for the higher Sharpe ratio portfolio to rule out some counterintuitive results when negative-Sharpe-ratio portfolios are compared.

- the Sharpe ratio of the existing portfolio; and
- the correlation between the new investment's return and portfolio p's return, $\text{Corr}(R_{new},R_p)$.

Adding the new asset to your portfolio is optimal if the following condition is met:[31]

$$\frac{E(R_{\text{new}}) - R_F}{\sigma_{\text{new}}} > \left(\frac{E(R_p) - R_F}{\sigma_p}\right)\text{Corr}(R_{\text{new}}, R_p) \quad (10)$$

This expression says that in order to gain by adding the new investment to your holdings, the Sharpe ratio of the new investment must be larger than the product of the Sharpe ratio of your existing portfolio and the correlation of the new investment's returns with the returns of your current portfolio. If Equation 10 holds, we can combine the new investment with the prior holdings to achieve a superior efficient frontier of risky assets (one in which the tangency portfolio has a higher Sharpe ratio). Note that although the expression may indicate that we effect a mean–variance improvement at the margin by adding a positive amount of a new asset, it does not indicate how much of the new asset we might want to add, or more broadly, what the efficient frontier including the new asset may be—to determine it, we would need to conduct an optimization. An insight from Equation 10 is that, in contrast to the case in which we considered investments as stand-alone and needed to consider only Sharpe ratios (from a mean–variance perspective) in choosing among them, in the case in which we can combine two investments, we must also consider their correlation. Example 6 illustrates how to use Equation 10 in deciding whether to add an asset class.

EXAMPLE 6

The Decision to Add an Asset Class

Jim Regal is chief investment officer of a Canadian pension fund invested in Canadian equities, Canadian bonds, Canadian real estate, and U.S. equities. The portfolio has a Sharpe ratio of 0.25. The investment committee is considering adding one or the other (but not both) of the following asset classes:

- Eurobonds: predicted Sharpe ratio = 0.10; predicted correlation with existing portfolio = 0.42.
- Non-North American developed market equities, as represented in the MSCI EAFE (Europe, Australasia, Far East) index: predicted Sharpe ratio = 0.30; predicted correlation with existing portfolio = 0.67.

1 Explain whether the investment committee should add Eurobonds to the existing portfolio.

2 Explain whether the committee should add non-North American developed market equities to the portfolio.

Solution to 1:

(Sharpe ratio of existing portfolio) × (Correlation of Eurobonds with existing portfolio) = 0.25(0.42) = 0.105. We should add Eurobonds if their predicted Sharpe ratio exceeds 0.105. Because the investment committee predicts a Sharpe ratio of 0.10 for Eurobonds, the committee should not add them to the existing portfolio.

31 See Blume (1984) and Elton, Gruber, and Rentzler (1987).

Solution to 2:

(Sharpe ratio of existing portfolio) × (Correlation of new equity class with existing portfolio) = 0.25(0.67) = 0.1675. Because the predicted Sharpe ratio of 0.30 for non-North American equities exceeds 0.1675, the investment committee should add them to the existing portfolio.

In Example 6, even if the correlation between the pension fund's existing portfolio and the proposed new equity class were + 1, so that adding the new asset class had no potential risk reduction benefits, Equation 10 would indicate that the class should be added because the condition for adding the asset class would be satisfied, as 0.30 > 0.25(1.0). For any portfolio, we can always effect a mean–variance improvement at the margin by adding an investment with a higher Sharpe ratio than the existing portfolio. This result is intuitive, because the higher Sharpe ratio investment would mean–variance dominate the existing portfolio in a pairwise comparison. Again, we emphasize that the assumptions of mean–variance analysis must be fulfilled for these results to be reliable.

2.7.2 *Determining an Asset Allocation*

Our objective in this section is to summarize the mean–variance perspective on asset allocation. In a prior section, we gave the mathematical objective and constraints for determining the minimum-variance frontier of risky assets in the simplest case in which the only constraint on portfolio weights is that they sum to 1. Determining the efficient frontier using Equation 3 plus a constraint $w_i \geq 0$ to reflect no short sales is a starting point for many institutional investors in determining an asset allocation.[32] Mean–variance theory then points to choosing the asset allocation represented by the perceived tangency portfolio if the investor can borrow or lend at the risk-free rate. The manager can combine the tangency portfolio with the risk-free asset to achieve an efficient portfolio at a desired level of risk. Because the tangency portfolio represents the highest-Sharpe-ratio portfolio of risky assets, it is a logical baseline for an asset allocation.

This theoretical perspective, however, views the investment in a risk-free asset as a readily available risk-adjustment variable. In practice, investors may be constrained against using margin (borrowing), may face constraints concerning minimum and maximum positive investments in a risk-free asset, or may have other reasons for not adopting the perspective of theory.[33] In such a case, the investor may establish an asset allocation among risky asset classes that differs from the tangency portfolio. Quantifying his risk tolerance in terms of standard deviation of returns, the investor could choose the portfolio on the efficient frontier of risky assets that corresponds to the chosen level of standard deviation.

The CAPM framework provides even more-narrowly focused choices because it adds the assumption that investors share the same views about mean returns, variances of returns, and correlations. Then all investors would agree on the identity of the tangency portfolio, which is the market portfolio of all risky assets held in proportion to their market values. This portfolio represents the highest possible degree of diversification. The exact identity of such an all-inclusive portfolio cannot be established, of

32 See Grinblatt and Titman (1998) and Elton, Gruber, Brown, and Goetzmann (2003) for discussions of solution methods and mechanics. In practice, investors often place additional constraints, such as constraints on maximum percentages, to assure plausible solutions. We discuss this approach further in the section on instability of the minimum-variance frontier.

33 For example, a risk-free asset may not be readily available if the analysis is conducted in real terms. Only short-term inflation-protected securities, if available, are potentially risk free in such a context.

course. Practically, however, investors can own highly diversified passively managed portfolios invested in major asset classes worldwide that approximately reflect the relative market values of the included classes. This asset allocation can be adapted to account for differential expectations. For example, the Black-Litterman (1991, 1992) asset allocation model takes a well-diversified market-value-weighted asset allocation as a neutral starting point for investors. The model incorporates a procedure for deviating from market capitalization weights in directions reflecting an investor's different-from-equilibrium model (CAPM) views concerning expected returns.

Mean–variance theory in relation to portfolio construction and asset allocation has been intensively examined, and researchers have recognized a number of its limitations. We will discuss an important limitation related to the sensitivity of the optimization procedure—the instability of the efficient frontier—in a later section. We must recognize that as a single-period model, mean–variance analysis ignores the liquidity and tax considerations that arise in a multiperiod world in which investors rebalance portfolios. Relatedly, the time horizon associated with the optimization, often one year, may be shorter than an investor's actual time horizon due to difficulties in developing inputs for long horizons.[34] Mean–variance analysis takes into account the correlation of returns across asset classes over single time periods but does not address serial correlation (long-and short-term dependencies) in returns for a given asset class. Monte Carlo simulation is sometimes used in asset allocation to address such multiperiod issues.[35] Despite its limitations, mean–variance analysis provides an objective and fairly adaptable procedure for narrowing the unlimited set of choices we face in selecting an asset allocation.[36]

PRACTICAL ISSUES IN MEAN–VARIANCE ANALYSIS 3

We now discuss practical issues that arise in the application of mean–variance analysis in choosing portfolios. The two areas of focus are:

- estimating inputs for mean–variance optimization, and
- the instability of the minimum-variance frontier, which results from the optimization process's sensitivity to the inputs.

Relative to the first area, we must ask two principal questions concerning the prediction of expected returns, variances, and correlations. First, which methods are feasible? Second, which are most accurate? Relative to sensitivity of the optimization process, we need to ask first, what is the source of the problem, and second, what corrective measures are available to address it.

34 See Swenson (2000). For example, if the investor's time horizon is five years, developing an efficient frontier involves estimating the correlations of five-year returns. Many assets have a limited number of independent five-year observations for correlation that we might use to develop estimates.

35 See the readings on probability distributions for more information about Monte Carlo simulation.

36 For example, Chow (1995) adapted mean–variance optimization to address managers' concerns about performance relative to a benchmark, and Chow, Jacquier, Kritzman, and Lowry (1999) adapted optimization to account for correlations that may change in times of stress.

3.1 Estimating Inputs for Mean–Variance Optimization

In this section, we compare the feasibility and accuracy of several methods for computing the inputs for mean–variance optimization. These methods use one of the following:

- historical means, variances, and correlations;
- historical betas estimated using the market model; or
- adjusted betas.

3.1.1 *Historical Estimates*

This approach involves calculating means, variances, and correlations directly from historical data. The historical method requires estimating a very large number of parameters when we are optimizing for even a moderately large number of assets. As a result, it is more feasible for asset allocation than for portfolio formation involving a large number of stocks.

The number of parameters a portfolio manager needs to estimate to determine the minimum-variance frontier depends on the number of potential stocks in the portfolio. If a portfolio manager has n stocks in a portfolio and wants to use mean–variance analysis, she must estimate

- n parameters for the expected returns to the stocks;
- n parameters for the variances of the stock returns; and
- $n(n - 1)/2$ parameters for the covariances of all the stock returns with each other.

Together, the parameters total $n^2/2 + 3n/2$.

The two limitations of the historical approach involve the quantity of estimates needed and the quality of historical estimates of inputs.

The quantity of estimates needed may easily be very large, mainly because the number of covariances increases in the square of the number of securities. If the portfolio manager wanted to compute the minimum-variance frontier for a portfolio of 100 stocks, she would need to estimate $100^2/2 + 3(100)/2 = 5{,}150$ parameters. If she wanted to compute the minimum-variance frontier for 1,000 stocks, she would need to estimate 501,500 parameters. Not only is this task unappealing, it might be impossible.[37]

The second limitation is that historical estimates of return parameters typically have substantial estimation error. The problem is least severe for estimates of variances.[38] The problem is acute with historical estimates of mean returns because the variability of risky asset returns is high relative to the mean, and the problem cannot be ameliorated by increasing the frequency of observations. Estimation error is also serious with historical estimates of covariances. The intuition in the case of covariances is that the historical method essentially tries to capture every random feature of a historical data set, reducing the usefulness of the estimates in a predictive mode. In a study based on monthly returns for U.S. stocks over the period 1973–1997, Chan, Karceski, and Lakonishok (1999) found that the correlation between past and future sample covariances was 0.34 at the 36-month horizon but only 0.18 at the 12-month horizon.

---

37 The number of time-series observations must exceed the number of securities for the covariances (including variances) to be estimated.

38 See Chan, Karceski, and Lakonishok (1999) for empirical evidence that future variances are relatively more predictable from past variances than is the case for future covariances.

In current industry practice, the historical sample covariance matrix is not used without adjustment in mean–variance optimization. Adjusted values of variance and covariance may be weighted averages of the raw sample values and the average variance or covariance, respectively. For example, if a stock's variance of monthly returns is 0.0210 and the average stock's variance of monthly returns is 0.0098, the procedure might adjust 0.0210 downward, in the direction of the mean. Adjusting values in the direction of the mean reduces the dispersion in the estimates that may be caused by sampling error.[39]

In estimating mean returns, analysts use a variety of approaches. They may adjust historical mean returns to reflect perceived contrasts between current market conditions and past average experience. They frequently use valuation models, such as models based on expected future cash flows, or equilibrium models, such as the CAPM, to develop forward-looking mean return estimates. Their use of these approaches reflects not only the technical issue of estimation error but also the risk in assuming that future performance will mirror past average performance.

3.1.2 *Market Model Estimates: Historical Beta (Unadjusted)*

A simpler way to compute the variances and covariances of asset returns involves the insight that asset returns may be related to each other through their correlation with a limited set of variables or factors. The simplest such model is the market model, which describes a regression relationship between the returns on an asset and the returns on the market portfolio. For asset i, the return to the asset can be modeled as

$$R_i = \alpha_i + \beta_i R_M + \varepsilon_i \quad (11)$$

where

R_i = the return on asset i

R_M = the return on the market portfolio

α_i = average return on asset i unrelated to the market return

β_i = the sensitivity of the return on asset i to the return on the market portfolio

ε_i = an error term

Consider first how to interpret β_i. If the market return increases by one percentage point, the market model predicts that the return to asset i will increase by β_i percentage points. (Recall that β_i is the slope in the market model.)

Now consider how to interpret α_i. If the market return is 0, the market model predicts that the return to asset i will be α_i, the intercept in the market model.

The market model makes the following assumptions about the terms in Equation 11:

- The expected value of the error term is 0, so $E(\varepsilon_i) = 0$.
- The market return (R_M) is uncorrelated with the error term, $\text{Cov}(R_M, \varepsilon_i)$.
- The error terms, ε_i, are uncorrelated among different assets. For example, the error term for asset i is uncorrelated with the error term for asset j. Consequently, $E(\varepsilon_i, \varepsilon_j) = 0$ for all i not equal to j.[40]

39 For more information on this approach, called shrinkage estimators, see Michaud (1998) and Ledoit and Wolf (2004).

40 $\text{Cov}(\varepsilon_i,\varepsilon_j) = E\{[\varepsilon_i - E(\varepsilon_i)][\varepsilon_j - E(\varepsilon_j)]\} = E[(\varepsilon_i - 0)][(\varepsilon_j - 0)] = E(\varepsilon_i\varepsilon_j) = 0$. The assumption of uncorrelated errors is not innocuous. If we have more than one factor that affects returns for assets, then this assumption will be incorrect and single-factor models will produce inaccurate estimates for the covariance of asset returns.

Note that some of these assumptions are very similar to those we made about the single-variable linear regression model in the reading on correlation and regression. The market model, however, does not assume that the error term is normally distributed or that the variance of the error term is identical across assets.

Given these assumptions, the market model makes the following predictions about the expected returns of assets as well as the variances and covariances of asset returns.[41]

First, the expected return for asset i depends on the expected return to the market, $E(R_M)$, the sensitivity of the return on asset i to the return on the market, β_i, and the part of returns on asset i that are independent of market returns, α_i.

$$E(R_i) = \alpha_i + \beta_i E(R_M) \tag{12}$$

Second, the variance of the return to asset i depends on the variance of the return to the market, σ_M^2, the variance of the error for the return of asset i in the market model, $\sigma_{\varepsilon_i}^2$, and the sensitivity, β_i.

$$\text{Var}(R_i) = \beta_i^2 \sigma_M^2 + \sigma_{\varepsilon_i}^2 \tag{13}$$

In the context of a model in which the market portfolio is the only source of risk, the first term in Equation 13, $\beta_i^2 \sigma_M^2$, is sometimes referred to as the systematic risk of asset i. The error variance term in Equation 13, $\sigma_{\varepsilon_i}^2$, is sometimes referred to as the nonsystematic risk of asset i.

Third, the covariance of the return to asset i and the return to asset j depends on the variance of the return to the market, σ_M^2, and on the sensitivities β_i and β_j.

$$\text{Cov}(R_i, R_j) = \beta_i \beta_j \sigma_M^2 \tag{14}$$

We can use the market model to greatly reduce the computational task of providing the inputs to a mean–variance optimization. For each of the n assets, we need to know α_i, β_i, $\sigma_{\varepsilon_i}^2$, as well as the expected return and variance for the market. Because we need to estimate only $3n + 2$ parameters with the market model, we need far fewer parameters to construct the minimum-variance frontier than we would if we estimated the historical means, variances, and covariances of asset returns. For example, if we estimated the minimum-variance frontier for 1,000 assets (say, 1,000 different stocks), the market model would use 3,002 parameters for computing the minimum-variance frontier, whereas the historical estimates approach would require 501,500 parameters, as discussed earlier.

We do not know the parameters of the market model, so we must estimate them. But what method do we use? The most convenient way is to estimate a linear regression using time-series data on the returns to the market and the returns to each asset.

We can use the market model to estimate α_i and β_i by using a separate linear regression for each asset, using historical data on asset returns and market returns.[42] The regression output produces an estimate, $\hat{\beta}_i$, of β_i; we call this estimate an unadjusted beta. Later we will introduce an adjusted beta. We can use these estimates to compute the expected returns and the variances and covariances of those returns for mean–variance optimization.

41 See Elton, Gruber, Brown, and Goetzmann (2003) for derivations of these results.

42 One common practice is to use 60 monthly returns to estimate this model. The default setting on Bloomberg terminals uses two years of weekly data to estimate this model.

EXAMPLE 7

Computing Stock Correlations Using the Market Model

You are estimating the correlation of returns between Cisco Systems (NASDAQ: CSCO) and Microsoft (NASDAQ: MSFT) as of late 2003. You run a market-model regression for each of the two stocks based on monthly returns, using the S&P 500 to represent the market. You obtain the following regression results:

- The estimated beta for Cisco, $\hat{\beta}_{CSCO}$, is 2.09, and the residual standard deviation, $\hat{\sigma}_{\varepsilon_{CSCO}}$, is 11.52.
- The estimated beta for Microsoft, $\hat{\beta}_{MSFT}$, is 1.75, and the residual standard deviation, $\hat{\sigma}_{\varepsilon_{MSFT}}$, is 11.26.

Your estimate of the variance of monthly returns on the S&P 500 is $\hat{\sigma}_M^2 = 29.8$, which corresponds to an annual standard deviation of returns of about 18.9 percent. Using the data given, estimate the correlation of returns between Cisco and Microsoft.

Solution:

We compute $\hat{\sigma}_{\varepsilon_{CSCO}}^2 = 132.71$ and $\hat{\sigma}_{\varepsilon_{MSFT}}^2 = 126.79$. Using the definition of correlation as covariance divided by the individual standard deviations, and using Equations 13 and 14, we have

$$\frac{\text{Cov}(R_{CSCO}, R_{MSFT})}{\text{Var}(R_{CSCO})^{1/2}\,\text{Var}(R_{MSFT})^{1/2}}$$

$$= \frac{\hat{\beta}_{CSCO}\hat{\beta}_{MSFT}\left(\hat{\sigma}_M^2\right)}{\left[\hat{\beta}_{CSCO}^2\left(\hat{\sigma}_M^2\right) + \hat{\sigma}_{\varepsilon_{CSCO}}^2\right]^{1/2}\left[\hat{\beta}_{MSFT}^2\left(\hat{\sigma}_M^2\right) + \hat{\sigma}_{\varepsilon_{MSFT}}^2\right]^{1/2}}$$

$$= \frac{(2.09)(1.75)(29.8)}{\left[(2.09)^2(29.8) + 132.71\right]^{1/2}\left[(1.75)^2(29.8) + 126.79\right]^{1/2}} = 0.4552$$

Thus the market model predicts that the correlation between the two asset returns is 0.4552.

One difficulty with using the market model is determining an appropriate index to represent the market. Typically, analysts who use the market model to determine the risk of individual domestic equities use returns on a domestic equity market index. In the United States, such an index might be the S&P 500 or the Wilshire 5000 Index; in the United Kingdom, the Financial Times Stock Exchange 100 Index might be used. Using returns on an equity market index may create a reasonable market model for equities, but it may not be reasonable for modeling the risk of other asset classes.[43]

43 Using this model to estimate the risk of other asset classes may violate two assumptions of single-factor models discussed earlier: The market return, R_M, is independent of the error term, ε_i; and the error terms, ε_i, are independent across assets. If either of these assumptions is violated, the market model will not produce accurate predictions of expected returns or the variances and covariances of returns.

3.1.3 *Market Model Estimates: Adjusted Beta*

Should we use historical betas from a market model for mean–variance optimization? Before we can answer this question, we need to restate our goal: We want to predict expected returns for a set of assets and the variances and covariances of those returns so that we can estimate the minimum-variance frontier for those assets. Estimates based on historical beta depend on the crucial assumption that the historical beta for a particular asset is the best predictor of the future beta for that asset. If beta changes over time, then this assumption is untrue. Therefore, we may want to use some other measure instead of historical beta to estimate an asset's future beta. These other forecasts are known by the general term **adjusted beta**. Researchers have shown that adjusted beta is often a better forecast of future beta than is historical beta. As a consequence, practitioners often use adjusted beta.

Suppose, for example, we are in period t and we want to estimate the minimum-variance frontier for period $t + 1$ for a set of stocks. We need to use data available in period t to predict the expected stock returns and the variances and covariances of those returns in period $t + 1$. Note, however, that the historical estimate of beta in period t for a particular stock may not be the best estimate we can make in period t of beta in period $t + 1$ for that stock. And the minimum-variance frontier for period $t + 1$ must be based on the forecast of beta for period $t + 1$.

If beta for each stock were a random walk from one period to the next, then we could write the relation between the beta for stock i in period t and the beta for stock i in period $t + 1$ as

$$\beta_{i,t+1} = \beta_{i,t} + \varepsilon_{i,t+1}$$

where $\varepsilon_{i,t+1}$ is an error term. If beta followed a random walk, the best predictor of $\beta_{i,t+1}$ would be $\beta_{i,t}$ because the error term has a mean value of 0. The historical beta would be the best predictor of the future beta, and the historical beta need not be adjusted.

In reality, beta for each stock often is not a random walk from one period to the next, and therefore, historical beta is not necessarily the best predictor of the future beta. For example, if beta can be represented as a first-order autoregression, then

$$\beta_{i,t+1} = \alpha_0 + \alpha_1\beta_{i,t} + \varepsilon_{i,t+1} \tag{15}$$

If we estimate Equation 15 using time-series data on historical betas, the best predictor of $\beta_{i,t+1}$ is $\hat{\alpha}_0 + \hat{\alpha}_1\beta_{i,t}$. In this case, the historical beta needs to be adjusted because the best prediction of beta in the next period is $\hat{\alpha}_0 + \hat{\alpha}_1\beta_{i,t}$, not $\beta_{i,t}$.

Adjusted betas predict future betas better than historical betas do because betas are, on average, mean reverting.[44] Therefore, we should use adjusted, rather than historical, betas. One common method that practitioners use to adjust historical beta is to assume that $\alpha_0 = 0.333$ and $\alpha_1 = 0.667$. With this adjustment,

- if the historical beta equals 1.0, then the adjusted beta will be 0.333 + 0.667(1.0) = 1.0.
- if the historical beta equals 1.5, then adjusted beta will be 0.333 + 0.667(1.5) = 1.333.
- if the historical beta equals 0.5, then adjusted beta will be 0.333 + 0.667(0.5) = 0.667.

44 See, for example, Klemkosky and Martin (1975).

Thus the mean-reverting level of beta is 1.0. If the historical beta is above 1.0, then adjusted beta will be below historical beta; if historical beta is below 1.0, then adjusted beta will be above historical beta.[45]

3.2 Instability in the Minimum-Variance Frontier

Although standard mean–variance optimization, as represented by Equation 3, is a convenient and objective procedure for portfolio formation, we must use care when interpreting its results in practice. In this section, we discuss cautions regarding the use of mean–variance optimization. The problems that can arise have been widely studied, and remedies for them have been developed. With this knowledge, mean–variance optimization can still be a useful tool.

The chief problem with mean–variance optimization is that small changes in input assumptions can lead to large changes in the minimum-variance (and efficient) frontier. This problem is called **instability in the minimum-variance frontier**. It arises because, in practice, uncertainty exists about the expected returns, variances, and covariances used in tracing out the minimum-variance frontier.

Suppose, for example, that we use historical data to compute estimates to be used in an optimization. These means, variances, and covariances are sample quantities that are subject to random variation. Recall that the sample mean has a probability distribution, called its **sampling distribution**. The sample mean is only a point estimate of the underlying or population mean.[46] The optimization process attempts to maximally exploit differences among assets. When these differences are statistically (and economically) insignificant (e.g., representing random variation), the resulting minimum-variance frontiers are misleading and not practically useful. Mean–variance optimization then overfits the data: It does too much with differences that are actually not meaningful. In an optimization with no limitation on short sales, assets can appear with very large negative weights, reflecting this overfitting (a negative weight for an asset means that the asset is sold short). Portfolios with very large short positions are of little practical interest.[47] Because of sensitivity to small changes in inputs, mean–variance optimizations may suggest too-frequent portfolio rebalancing, which is costly. Responses to instability include the following:

- Adding constraints against short sales (which is sometimes an institutional investment policy constraint as well). In Equation 3, we can add a no-short-sales constraint specifying that all asset weights must be positive: $w_j \geq 0$, $j = 1, 2, 3, \ldots, n$.[48]
- Improving the statistical quality of inputs to optimization.
- Using a statistical concept of the efficient frontier, reflecting the fact that the inputs to the optimization are random variables rather than constants.[49]

45 Although practitioners regularly use this method for computing adjusted beta, we are unaware of any published research suggesting that $\alpha_0 = 0.333$ and $\alpha_1 = 0.667$ are the best coefficient values to use in computing adjusted beta. Some researchers suggest an additional adjustment to historical betas called fundamental betas. **Fundamental betas** predict beta based on fundamental data for a company (price–earnings ratio, earnings growth, market capitalization, volatility, and so forth). Consulting firms such as BARRA sell estimates of fundamental betas.

46 The underlying means of asset returns are particularly difficult to estimate accurately. See Luenberger (1998) for an introduction to this problem, as well as Black (1993).

47 In practice, few investors that engage in short sales would take a large short position as a result of an analysis restricted to means, variances, and correlations. Unlimited losses are possible in a short position.

48 In practice, other ad hoc constraints on the size of positions are sometimes used as well.

49 For example, Michaud (1998) defines a region of efficient portfolios that are statistically equivalent at a given confidence level. A portfolio falling in the region is consistent with being efficient and does not need to be rebalanced.

We stated above that mean–variance optimizations can recommend too-frequent portfolio rebalancing. Similarly, we find that the minimum-variance frontier is generally unstable when calculated using historical data for different time periods. One possible explanation is that the different frontiers reflect shifts in the parameters of asset return distribution between sample time periods. Time instability of the minimum-variance frontier can also result from random variation in means, variances, and covariances, when the underlying parameters are actually unchanged. Small differences in sample periods used for mean–variance optimization may greatly affect a model even if the distribution of asset returns is stationary. Example 8 illustrates time instability with the data used for optimization.

EXAMPLE 8

Time Instability of the Minimum-Variance Frontier

In Example 2, we calculated a minimum-variance frontier for four asset classes for the period 1970 through 2002. What variation would we find among minimum-variance frontiers for subperiods of 1970 to 2002? To find out, we take the data for decades within the entire period, calculate the sample statistics, and then trace out the minimum-variance frontier for each decade. Table 10 shows the sample statistics of the monthly asset returns to these four asset classes for 1970 to 1979, 1980 to 1989, 1990 to 2002, and the combined sample period.

Table 10 Average Returns, Standard Deviations, and Correlation Matrixes

	S&P 500	U.S. Small-Cap Stocks	MSCI World Ex-U.S.	U.S. Long-Term Government Bonds
		Average Returns (%)		
Time Period				
1970–1979	7.0	14.4	11.8	5.7
1980–1989	17.6	16.7	21.1	12.9
1990–2002	10.4	13.2	2.7	9.9
Overall period	11.6	14.6	11.1	9.6
		Standard Deviations (%)		
Time Period				
1970–1979	15.93	26.56	16.68	8.25
1980–1989	16.41	19.17	17.32	14.19
1990–2002	15.27	20.71	16.93	8.31
Overall period	15.83	22.18	17.07	10.44
		Correlation Matrixes		
1970–1979				
S&P 500	1			
U.S. Small-cap	0.787	1		
MSCI ex-U.S.	0.544	0.490	1	
U.S. LT Bonds	0.415	0.316	0.218	1
1980–1989				
S&P 500	1			

Table 10 (Continued)

	S&P 500	U.S. Small-Cap Stocks	MSCI World Ex-U.S.	U.S. Long-Term Government Bonds
U.S. Small-cap	0.844	1		
MSCI ex-U.S.	0.512	0.483	1	
U.S. LT Bonds	0.310	0.171	0.229	1
1990–1999				
S&P 500	1			
U.S. Small-cap	0.611	1		
MSCI ex-U.S.	0.647	0.473	1	
U.S. LT Bonds	0.097	−0.047	0.017	1
Overall Period				
S&P 500	1			
U.S. Small-cap	0.731	1		
MSCI ex-U.S.	0.573	0.475	1	
U.S. LT Bonds	0.266	0.138	0.155	1

Source: Ibbotson Associates.

As we might expect, variation occurs within subperiods in the sample means, variances, and covariances for all asset classes. Initially, the correlations offer the impression of relative stability over time. For example, the correlation of the S&P 500 with the MSCI World ex-U.S. was 0.544, 0.512, and 0.647 for 1970 to 1979, 1980 to 1989, and 1990 to 2002, respectively. In contrast to ranking by mean returns, the ranking of asset classes by standard deviation was the same in each decade, with U.S. small-cap stocks the riskiest asset class and bonds the least risky. We could use **statistical inference** to explore interperiod differences. With these initial impressions in mind, however, let us view the decades' minimum-variance frontiers.

Figure 11 shows the minimum-variance frontiers computed using the historical return statistics shown in Table 10 for 1970 to 1979, 1980 to 1989, 1990 to 2002, and the entire sample period. As this figure shows, the minimum-variance frontiers can differ dramatically in different periods. For example, note that the minimum-variance frontiers based on data from 1970 to 1979 and 1980 to 1989 do not overlap at all.

Figure 11 Historical Minimum-Variance Frontier Comparison

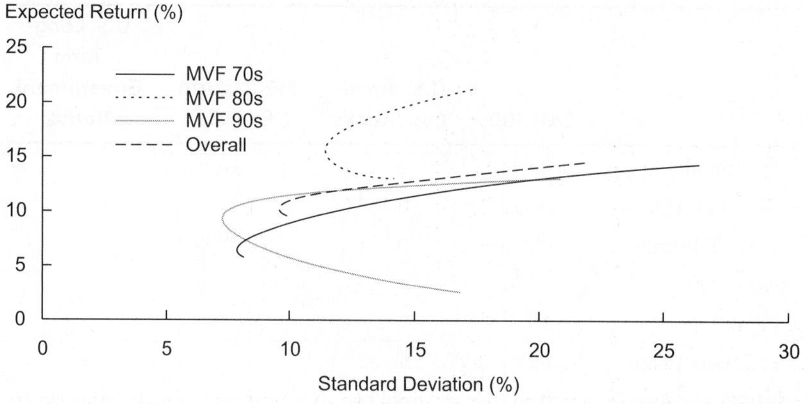

As mentioned, researchers have developed various methods to address portfolio managers' concerns about the issue of instability.

EXAMPLE 9

How Yale University's Endowment Fund Uses Mean–Variance Analysis

David Swensen, Yale University's chief investment officer (who also teaches portfolio management at Yale), wrote that "unconstrained mean–variance [optimization] usually provide[s] solutions unrecognizable as reasonable portfolios... Because the process involves material simplifying assumptions, adopting the unconstrained asset allocation point estimates produced by mean–variance optimization makes little sense."[50]

Swensen's remarks highlight practitioners' concerns about the usefulness of standard mean–variance optimization. Among the most important simplifying assumptions of mean–variance analysis is that the means, variances, and covariances of assets in a portfolio are known. Because the optimization process tries to make much of small differences, and the true values of the means and other parameters are uncertain, this simplifying assumption has a large impact. As mentioned earlier, responses to instability include adding constraints on asset weights and modifying historical sample estimates of the inputs. Despite Swensen's criticism, Yale uses mean–variance analysis for allocating its portfolio; however, the Yale Investment Office adds constraints on weights and does not use raw historical inputs.

4 MULTIFACTOR MODELS

Earlier we discussed the market model, which was historically the first attempt to describe the process that drives asset returns. The market model assumes that all explainable variation in asset returns is related to a single factor, the return to the

50 Swensen (2000).

market. Yet asset returns may be related to factors other than market return, such as interest rate movements, inflation, or industry-specific returns. For many years, investment professionals have used multifactor models in portfolio management, risk analysis, and the evaluation of portfolio performance.

Multifactor models have gained importance for the practical business of portfolio management for two main reasons. First, multifactor models explain asset returns better than the market model does.[51] Second, multifactor models provide a more detailed analysis of risk than does a single factor model. That greater level of detail is useful in both passive and active management.

- *Passive management.* In managing a fund that seeks to track an index with many component securities, portfolio managers may need to select a sample of securities from the index. Analysts can use multifactor models to match an index fund's factor exposures to the factor exposures of the index tracked.
- *Active management.* Multifactor models are used in portfolio formation to model the expected returns and risks of securities and portfolios. Many quantitative investment managers rely on multifactor models in predicting alpha (excess risk-adjusted returns) or relative return (the return on one asset or asset class relative to that of another) as part of a variety of active investment strategies. In evaluating portfolios, analysts use multi-factor models to understand the sources of active managers' returns and assess the risks assumed relative to the manager's **benchmark** (comparison portfolio).

In the following sections, we explain the basic principles of factor models and discuss various types of models and their application. We also present the arbitrage pricing theory developed by Ross (1976), which relates the expected return of investments to their risk with respect to a set of factors.

4.1 Factors and Types of Multifactor Models

To begin by defining terms, a **factor** is a common or underlying element with which several variables are correlated. For example, the market factor is an underlying element with which individual share returns are correlated. We search for **systematic factors**, which affect the average returns of a large number of different assets. These factors represent **priced risk**, risk for which investors require an additional return for bearing. Systematic factors should thus help explain returns.

Many varieties of multifactor models have been proposed and researched. We can categorize most of them into three main groups, according to the type of factor used:

- In **macroeconomic factor models**, the factors are surprises in macroeconomic variables that significantly explain equity returns. The factors can be understood as affecting either the expected future cash flows of companies or the interest rate used to discount these cash flows back to the present.

51 See, for example, Burmeister and McElroy (1988). These authors show that at the 1 percent significance level, the CAPM can be rejected in favor of an arbitrage pricing theory model with several factors. We discuss arbitrage pricing theory later in the reading.

- In **fundamental factor models**, the factors are attributes of stocks or companies that are important in explaining cross-sectional differences in stock prices. Among the fundamental factors that have been used are the book-value-to-price ratio, market capitalization, the price–earnings ratio, and financial leverage.
- In **statistical factor models**, statistical methods are applied to a set of historical returns to determine portfolios that explain historical returns in one of two senses. In factor analysis models, the factors are the portfolios that best explain (reproduce) historical return covariances. In principal-components models, the factors are portfolios that best explain (reproduce) the historical return variances.

Some practical factor models have the characteristics of more than one of the above categories. We can call such models **mixed factor models**.

Our discussion concentrates on macroeconomic factor models and fundamental factor models. Industry use has generally favored fundamental and macroeconomic models, perhaps because such models are much more easily interpreted; nevertheless, statistical factor models have proponents and are used in practical applications.

4.2 The Structure of Macroeconomic Factor Models

The representation of returns in macroeconomic factor models assumes that the returns to each asset are correlated with only the surprises in some factors related to the aggregate economy, such as inflation or real output.[52] We can define **surprise** in general as the actual value minus predicted (or expected) value. A factor's surprise is the component of the factor's return that was unexpected, and the factor surprises constitute the model's independent variables. This idea contrasts to the representation of independent variables as returns (as opposed to the surprise in returns) in fundamental factor models, or for that matter in the market model.

Suppose that K factors explain asset returns. Then in a macroeconomic factor model, the following equation expresses the return of asset i:

$$R_i = a_i + b_{i1}F_1 + b_{i2}F_2 + \ldots + b_{iK}F_K + \varepsilon_i \tag{16}$$

where

R_i = the return to asset i

a_i = the expected return to asset i

F_k = the surprise in the factor k, $k = 1, 2, \ldots, K$

b_{ik} = the sensitivity of the return on asset i to a surprise in factor k, $k = 1, 2, \ldots, K$

ε_i = an error term with a zero mean that represents the portion of the return to asset i not explained by the factor model

What exactly do we mean by the surprise in a macroeconomic factor? Suppose we are analyzing monthly returns for stocks. At the beginning of each month, we have a prediction of inflation for the month. The prediction may come from an econometric model or a professional economic forecaster, for example. Suppose our forecast at the beginning of the month is that inflation will be 0.4 percent during the month. At the end of the month, we find that inflation was actually 0.5 percent during the month. During any month,

Actual inflation = Predicted inflation + Surprise inflation

52 See, for example, Burmeister, Roll, and Ross (1994).

In this case, actual inflation was 0.5 percent and predicted inflation was 0.4 percent. Therefore, the surprise in inflation was 0.5 – 0.4 = 0.1 percent.

What is the effect of defining the factors in terms of surprises? Suppose we believe that inflation and gross domestic product (GDP) growth are priced risk. (GDP is a money measure of the goods and services produced within a country's borders.) We do not use the predicted values of these variables because the predicted values are already reflected in stock prices and thus in their expected returns. The intercept a_i, the expected return to asset i, reflects the effect of the predicted values of the macroeconomic variables on expected stock returns. The surprise in the macroeconomic variables during the month, on the other hand, contains new information about the variable. As a result, this model structure analyzes the return to an asset into three components: the asset's expected return, its unexpected return resulting from new information about the factors, and an error term.

Consider a factor model in which the returns to each asset are correlated with two factors. For example, we might assume that the returns for a particular stock are correlated with surprises in interest rates and surprises in GDP growth. For stock i, the return to the stock can be modeled as

$$R_i = a_i + b_{i1}F_{\text{INT}} + b_{i2}F_{\text{GDP}} + \varepsilon_i \qquad (17)$$

where

R_i = the return to stock i

a_i = the expected return to stock i

b_{i1} = the sensitivity of the return to stock i to interest rate surprises

F_{INT} = the surprise in interest rates

b_{i2} = the sensitivity of the return to stock i to GDP growth surprises

F_{GDP} = the surprise in GDP growth

ε_i = an error term with a zero mean that represents the portion of the return to asset i not explained by the factor model

Consider first how to interpret b_{i1}. The factor model predicts that a one percentage point surprise in interest rates will contribute b_{i1} percentage points to the return to stock i. The slope coefficient b_{i2} has a similar interpretation relative to the GDP growth factor. Thus slope coefficients are naturally interpreted as the factor sensitivities of the asset.[53] A **factor sensitivity** is a measure of the response of return to each unit of increase in a factor, holding all other factors constant.

Now consider how to interpret the intercept a_i. Recall that the error term has a mean or average value of 0. If the surprises in both interest rates and GDP growth are 0, the factor model predicts that the return to asset i will be a_i. Thus a_i is the expected value of the return to stock i.

Finally, consider the error term ε_i. The intercept a_i represents the asset's expected return. The amount $(b_{i1}F_{\text{INT}} + b_{i2}F_{\text{GDP}})$ represents the return resulting from factor surprises, and we have interpreted these as the sources of risk shared with other assets. The term ε_i is the part of return that is unexplained by expected return or the factor surprises. If we have adequately represented the sources of common risk (the factors), then ε_i must represent an asset-specific risk. For a stock, it might represent the return from an unanticipated company-specific event.

We will discuss expected returns further when we present the arbitrage pricing theory. In macroeconomic factor models, the time series of factor surprises are developed first. We use regression analysis to estimate assets' sensitivities to the factors. In our discussion, we assume that you do not estimate sensitivities and intercepts

53 Factor sensitivities are sometimes called **factor betas** or **factor loadings**.

yourself; instead you use estimates from another source (for example, one of the many consulting companies that specialize in factor models).[54] When we have the parameters for the individual assets in a portfolio, we can calculate the portfolio's parameters as a weighted average of the parameters of individual assets. An individual asset's weight in that calculation is the proportion of the total market value of the portfolio that the individual asset represents.

EXAMPLE 10

Factor Sensitivities for a Two-Stock Portfolio

Suppose that stock returns are affected by two common factors: surprises in inflation and surprises in GDP growth. A portfolio manager is analyzing the returns on a portfolio of two stocks, Manumatic (MANM) and Nextech (NXT). The following equations describe the returns for those stocks, where the factors F_{INFL} and F_{GDP} represent the surprise in inflation and GDP growth, respectively:

$$R_{MANM} = 0.09 - 1F_{INFL} + 1F_{GDP} + \varepsilon_{MANM}$$

$$R_{NXT} = 0.12 + 2F_{INFL} + 4F_{GDP} + \varepsilon_{NXT}$$

In evaluating the equations for surprises in inflation and GDP, amounts stated in percent terms need to be converted to decimal form. One-third of the portfolio is invested in Manumatic stock, and two-thirds is invested in Nextech stock.

1 Formulate an expression for the return on the portfolio.
2 State the expected return on the portfolio.
3 Calculate the return on the portfolio given that the surprises in inflation and GDP growth are 1 percent and 0 percent, respectively, assuming that the error terms for MANM and NXT both equal 0.5 percent.

Solution to 1:

The portfolio's return is the following weighted average of the returns to the two stocks:

$$\begin{aligned} R_P = {} & (1/3)(0.09) + (2/3)(0.12) + \left[(1/3)(-1) + (2/3)(2)\right]F_{INFL} \\ & + \left[(1/3)(1) + (2/3)(4)\right]F_{GDP} + (1/3)\,\varepsilon_{MANM} + (2/3)\,\varepsilon_{NXT} \\ = {} & 0.11 + 1F_{INFL} + 3F_{GDP} + (1/3)\,\varepsilon_{MANM} + (2/3)\,\varepsilon_{NXT} \end{aligned}$$

Solution to 2:

The expected return on the portfolio is 11 percent, the value of the intercept in the expression obtained in Part 1.

Solution to 3:

$$\begin{aligned} R_P &= 0.11 + 1F_{INFL} + 3F_{GDP} + (1/3)\,\varepsilon_{MANM} + (2/3)\,\varepsilon_{NXT} \\ &= 0.11 + 1(0.01) + 3(0) + (1/3)(0.005) + (2/3)(0.005) \\ &= 0.125 \text{ or } 12.5 \text{ percent} \end{aligned}$$

54 If you want to estimate your own macroeconomic factor model, follow these steps. First, estimate a time series for each macroeconomic surprise (for example, you could use the residuals from a time-series model for each different macroeconomic series). Then, use time-series data to regress the returns for a particular asset on the surprises to the different macroeconomic factors.

4.3 Arbitrage Pricing Theory and the Factor Model

In the 1970s, Stephen Ross developed the arbitrage pricing theory (APT) as an alternative to the CAPM. APT describes the expected return on an asset (or portfolio) as a linear function of the risk of the asset (or portfolio) with respect to a set of factors. Like the CAPM, the APT describes a financial market equilibrium. However, the APT makes less-strong assumptions than the CAPM. The APT relies on three assumptions:

1 A factor model describes asset returns.
2 There are many assets, so investors can form well-diversified portfolios that eliminate asset-specific risk.
3 No arbitrage opportunities exist among well-diversified portfolios.

Arbitrage is a risk-free operation that earns an expected positive net profit but requires no net investment of money.[55] An **arbitrage opportunity** is an opportunity to conduct an arbitrage—an opportunity to earn an expected positive net profit without risk and with no net investment of money.

In the first assumption, the number of factors is not specified. The second assumption allows us to form portfolios with factor risk but without asset-specific risk. The third assumption is the condition of financial market equilibrium.

Empirical evidence indicates that Assumption 2 is reasonable. When a portfolio contains many stocks, the asset-specific or nonsystematic risk of individual stocks makes almost no contribution to the variance of portfolio returns. Roll and Ross (2001) found that only 1 percent to 3 percent of a well-diversified portfolio's variance comes from the non-systematic variance of the individual stocks in the portfolio, as Figure 12 shows.

According to the APT, if the above three assumptions hold, the following equation holds:[56]

$$E\left(R_p\right) = R_F + \lambda_1\beta_{p,1} + \ldots + \lambda_K\beta_{p,K} \quad (18)$$

55 As we will see, arbitrage typically involves funding the investment in assets with proceeds from the short sale of other assets, so that net, no money is invested. A short sale is the sale of a borrowed asset. Note that the word "arbitrage" is also sometimes used to describe investment operations in which significant risk is present.

56 A risk-free asset is assumed. If no risk-free asset exists, in place of R_F we write λ_0 to represent the expected return on a risky portfolio with zero sensitivity to all the factors. The number of factors is not specified but must be much lower than the number of assets, a condition fulfilled in practice.

Figure 12 Sources of Volatility: The Case of a Well-Diversified Portfolio

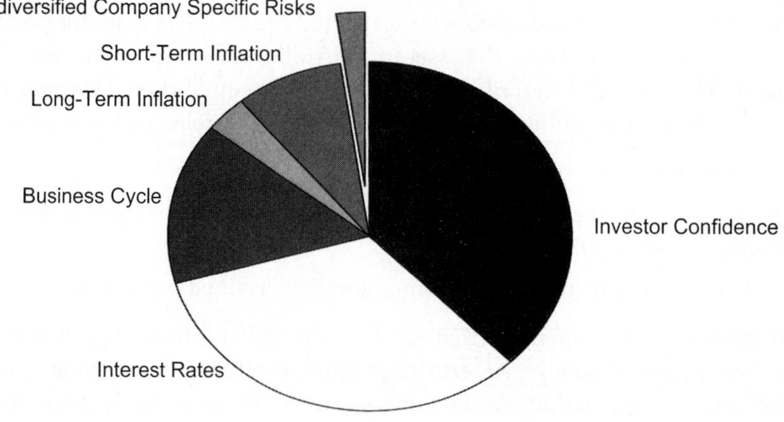

Source: What Is the Arbitrage Pricing Theory. Retrieved May 25, 2001, from the World Wide Web: www.rollross.com/apt.html. Reprinted with permission of Richard Roll.

where

$E(R_p)$ = the expected return to portfolio p
R_F = the risk-free rate
λ_j = the risk premium for factor j
$\beta_{p,j}$ = the sensitivity of the portfolio to factor j
K = the number of factors

The APT equation, Equation 18, says that the expected return on any well-diversified portfolio is linearly related to the factor sensitivities of that portfolio.[57]

The **factor risk premium** (or **factor price**) λ_j represents the expected return in excess of the risk-free rate for a portfolio with a sensitivity of 1 to factor j and a sensitivity of 0 to all other factors. Such a portfolio is called a **pure factor portfolio** for factor j.

For example, suppose we have a portfolio with a sensitivity of 1 with respect to Factor 1 and a sensitivity of 0 to all other factors. With E_1 being the expected return on this portfolio, Equation 18 shows that the expected return on this portfolio is $E_1 = R_F + \lambda_1 \times 1$, so $\lambda_1 = E_1 - R_F$. Suppose that $E_1 = 0.12$ and $R_F = 0.04$. Then the risk premium for Factor 1 is $\lambda_1 = 0.12 - 0.04 = 0.08$ or 8 percent. We obtain an eight percentage point increase in expected return for an increase of 1 in the sensitivity to first factor.

What is the relationship between the APT equation and the equation for a multifactor model, Equation 17? In discussing the multifactor model, we stated that the intercept term is the investment's expected return. The APT equation explains what an investment's expected return is in equilibrium. Thus if the APT holds, it places a restriction on the intercept term in the multifactor model in the sense that the APT model tells us what the intercept's value should be. For instance, in Example 10, the APT would explain the intercept of 0.09 in the model for MANM returns as the expected

57 The APT equation can also describe (at least approximately) the expected return on investments with asset-specific risk, under certain conditions.

return on MANM given the stock's sensitivities to the inflation and GDP factors and the risk premiums of those factors. We can in fact substitute the APT equation into the multifactor model to produce what is known as an APT model in returns form.[58]

To use the APT equation, we need to estimate its parameters. The parameters of the APT equation are the risk-free rate and the factor risk-premiums (the factor sensitivities are specific to individual investments). Example 11 shows how the expected returns and factor sensitivities of a set of portfolios can determine the parameters of the APT model assuming a single factor.

EXAMPLE 11

Determining the Parameters in a One-Factor APT Model

Suppose we have three well-diversified portfolios that are each sensitive to the same single factor. Table 11 shows the expected returns and factor sensitivities of these portfolios. Assume that the expected returns reflect a one-year investment horizon.

Table 11 Sample Portfolios for a One-Factor Model

Portfolio	Expected Return	Factor Sensitivity
A	0.075	0.5
B	0.150	2.0
C	0.070	0.4

We can use these data to determine the parameters of the APT equation. According to Equation 18, for any well-diversified portfolio and assuming a single factor explains returns, we have $E(R_p) = R_F + \lambda_1\beta_{p,1}$. The factor sensitivities and expected returns are known; thus there are two unknowns, the parameters R_F and λ_1. Because two points define a straight line, we need to set up only two equations. Selecting Portfolios A and B, we have

$$E(R_A) = 0.075 = R_F + 0.5\lambda_1$$

and

$$E(R_B) = 0.150 = R_F + 2\lambda_1$$

From the equation for Portfolio A, we have $R_F = 0.075 - 0.5\lambda_1$. Substituting this expression for the risk-free rate into the equation for Portfolio B gives

$$0.15 = 0.075 - 0.5\lambda_1 + 2\lambda_1$$
$$0.15 = 0.075 + 1.5\lambda_1$$

So we have $\lambda_1 = (0.15 - 0.075)/1.5 = 0.05$. Substituting this value for λ_1 back into the equation for the expected return to Portfolio A yields

58 An interesting issue is the relationship between the APT and the CAPM. If the market is the factor in a single-factor model, APT (Equation 18) is consistent with the CAPM. The CAPM can also be consistent with multiple factors in an APT model if the risk premiums in the APT model satisfy certain restrictions; these CAPM-related restrictions have been repeatedly rejected in statistical tests. See Burmeister and McElroy (1988), for example.

$$0.075 = R_F + 0.05 \times 0.5$$
$$R_F = 0.05$$

So the risk-free rate is 0.05 or 5 percent, and the factor premium for the common factor is also 0.05 or 5 percent. The APT equation is

$$E(R_p) = 0.05 + 0.05\beta_{p,1}$$

Portfolio C has a factor sensitivity of 0.4. Accordingly, 0.05 + (0.05 × 0.4) = 0.07 or 7 percent if no arbitrage opportunity exists. The expected return for Portfolio C given in Table 11 is 7 percent. Therefore, in this example no arbitrage opportunity exists.

EXAMPLE 12

Checking Whether Portfolio Returns Are Consistent with No Arbitrage

In this example, we demonstrate how to tell whether a set of expected returns for well-diversified portfolios is consistent with the APT by testing whether an arbitrage opportunity exists. In Example 11, we had three portfolios with expected returns and factor sensitivities that were consistent with the one-factor APT model $E(R_p) = 0.05 + 0.05\beta_{p,1}$. Suppose we expand the set of portfolios to include a fourth well-diversified portfolio, Portfolio D. Table 12 repeats the data given in Table 11 for Portfolios A, B, and C, in addition to providing data on Portfolio D and a portfolio we form using A and C.

Table 12 Sample Portfolios for a One-Factor Model

Portfolio	Expected Return	Factor Sensitivity
A	0.0750	0.50
B	0.1500	2.00
C	0.0700	0.40
D	0.0800	0.45
0.5A + 0.5C	0.0725	0.45

The expected return and factor sensitivity of a portfolio is the weighted average of the expected returns and factor sensitivities of the assets in the portfolio. Suppose we construct a portfolio consisting of 50 percent Portfolio A and 50 percent Portfolio C. Table 12 shows that the expected return of this portfolio is (0.50) (0.0750) + (0.50) (0.07) = 0.0725, or 7.25 percent. The factor sensitivity of this portfolio is (0.50) (0.50) + (0.50) (0.40) = 0.45.

Arbitrage pricing theory assumes that well-diversified portfolios present no arbitrage opportunities. If the initial investment is 0 and we bear no risk, the final expected cash flow should be 0. In this case, the configuration of expected returns in relation to factor risk presents an arbitrage opportunity involving Portfolios A, C, and D. Portfolio D offers too high an expected rate of return given its factor sensitivity. According to the APT model estimated in Example 11, an arbitrage opportunity exists unless $E(R_D) = 0.05 + 0.05\beta_{D,1} = 0.05 + (0.05 \times 0.45) = 0.0725$, so that the expected return on D is 7.25 percent. In fact, the expected return on D is 8 percent. Portfolio D is undervalued relative to its factor risk. We will buy D (hold it long) in the portfolio that exploits the arbitrage opportunity (the **arbitrage portfolio**). We purchase D using the proceeds from selling short a portfolio consisting of A and C with exactly the same 0.45 factor sensitivity as D. As we showed above, an equally weighted portfolio of A and C has a factor sensitivity of 0.45.

The arbitrage thus involves the following strategy: Invest $10,000 in Portfolio D and fund that investment by selling short an equally weighted portfolio of Portfolios A and C; then close out the investment position at the end of one year (the investment horizon for expected returns). Table 13 demonstrates the arbitrage profits to the arbitrage strategy. The final row of the table shows the net cash flow to the arbitrage portfolio.

Table 13 **Arbitrage Opportunity within Sample Portfolios**

	Initial Cash Flow ($)	Final Cash Flow ($)	Factor Sensitivity
Portfolio D	−10,000.00	10,800.00	0.45
Portfolios A and C	10,000.00	−10,725.00	−0.45
Sum	0.00	75.00	0.00

As Table 13 shows, if we buy $10,000 of Portfolio D and sell $10,000 of an equally weighted portfolio of Portfolios A and C, we have an initial net cash flow of $0. The expected value of our investment in Portfolio D at the end of one year is $10,000(1 + 0.08) = $10,800. The expected value of our short position in Portfolios A and C at the end of one year is −$10,000(1.0725) = −$10,725. So the combined expected cash flow from our investment position in one year is $75.

What about the risk? Table 13 shows that the factor risk has been eliminated: Purchasing D and selling short an equally weighted portfolio of A and C creates a portfolio with a factor sensitivity of 0.45 − 0.45 = 0. The portfolios are well diversified, and we assume any asset-specific risk is negligible.

Because the arbitrage is possible, Portfolios A, C, and D cannot all be consistent with the same equilibrium. A unique set of parameters for the APT model does not describe the returns on these three portfolios. If Portfolio D actually had an expected return of 8 percent, investors would bid up its price until the expected return fell and the arbitrage opportunity vanished. Thus arbitrage restores equilibrium relationships among expected returns.

In Example 11, we illustrated how the parameters of a single-factor APT model can be determined from data. Example 13 shows how to determine the model parameters in a model with more than one factor.

EXAMPLE 13

Determining the Parameters in a Two-Factor Model

Suppose that two factors, surprise in inflation (Factor 1) and surprise in GDP growth (Factor 2), explain returns. According to the APT, an arbitrage opportunity exists unless

$$E(R_p) = R_F + \lambda_1\beta_{p,1} + \lambda_2\beta_{p,2}$$

Our goal is to estimate the three parameters of the model, R_F, λ_1, and λ_2. We also have hypothetical data on three well-diversified portfolios, J, K, and L, given in Table 14.

Table 14 Sample Portfolios for a Two-Factor Model

Portfolio	Expected Return	Sensitivity to Inflation Factor	Sensitivity to GDP Factor
J	0.14	1.0	1.5
K	0.12	0.5	1.0
L	0.11	1.3	1.1

If the market is in equilibrium (no arbitrage opportunities exist), the expected returns to the three portfolios should be described by the two-factor APT with the same set of parameters. Using the expected returns and the return sensitivities shown in Table 14 yields

$$E(R_J) = 0.14 = R_F + 1.0\lambda_1 + 1.5\lambda_2$$
$$E(R_K) = 0.12 = R_F + 0.5\lambda_1 + 1.0\lambda_2$$
$$E(R_L) = 0.11 = R_F + 1.3\lambda_1 + 1.1\lambda_2$$

We have three equations with three unknowns, so we can solve for the parameters using the method of substitution. We first want to get two equations with two unknowns. Solving the equation for $E(R_J)$ for the risk-free rate,

$$R_F = 0.14 - 1.0\lambda_1 - 1.5\lambda_2$$

Substituting this expression for the risk-free rate into the equation for $E(R_K)$, we find, after simplification, that $\lambda_1 = 0.04 - \lambda_2$. Using $\lambda_1 = 0.04 - \lambda_2$ to eliminate λ_1 in the equation for $E(R_J)$,

$$0.10 = R_F + 0.5\lambda_2$$

Using $\lambda_1 = 0.04 - \lambda_2$ to eliminate λ_1 in the equation for $E(R_L)$,

$$0.058 = R_F - 0.2\lambda_2$$

Using the two equations in R_F and λ_2 immediately above, we find that $\lambda_2 - 0.06$ (we solved for the risk-free rate in the first of these two equations and used the expression in the second equation). Because $\lambda_1 = 0.04 - \lambda_2$, $\lambda_1 = -0.02$. Finally, $R_F = 0.14 - 1.0 \times (-0.02) - 1.5 \times (0.06) = 0.07$. To summarize:

$$R_F = 0.07 \text{(The risk-free rate is 7 percent.)}$$
$$\lambda_1 = -0.02 \text{ (The inflation risk premium is –2 percent per unit of sensitivity.)}$$
$$\lambda_2 = 0.06 \text{ (The GDP risk premium is 6 percent per unit of sensitivity.)}$$

So, the APT equation for these three portfolios is

$$E(R_p) = 0.07 - 0.02\beta_{p,1} + 0.06\beta_{p,2}$$

This example illustrates the calculations for determining the parameters of an APT model. It also shows that the risk premium for a factor can actually be negative.

In Example 13, we computed a *negative* risk premium for the inflation factor. One explanation for a negative inflation risk premium is that most equities have negative sensitivities to inflation risk (their returns tend to decrease with a positive inflation surprise). An asset with a positive inflation sensitivity would be in demand as an inflation-hedging asset; the premium associated with a factor portfolio for inflation risk could be negative as a result.

4.4 The Structure of Fundamental Factor Models

Earlier we gave the equation of a macroeconomic factor model as

$$R_i = a_i + b_{i1}F_1 + b_{i2}F_2 + \cdots + b_{iK}F_K + \varepsilon_i$$

We can also represent the structure of fundamental factor models with this equation, but we need to interpret the terms differently.

In fundamental factor models, the factors are stated as returns rather than return surprises in relation to predicted values, so they do not generally have expected values of zero. This approach changes the interpretation of the intercept, which we no longer interpret as the expected return.[59]

We also interpret the factor sensitivities differently in most fundamental factor models. In fundamental factor models, the factor sensitivities are attributes of the security. Consider a fundamental model for equities with a dividend yield factor. An asset's sensitivity to the dividend factor is the value of the attribute itself, its dividend yield; the sensitivity is typically standardized. Specifically, an asset *i*'s sensitivity to a given factor would be calculated as the value of the attribute for the asset minus the average value of the attribute across all stocks, divided by the standard deviation of the attribute across all stocks. The **standardized beta** is

$$b_{ij} = \frac{\text{Asset } i\text{'s attribute value} - \text{Average attribute value}}{\sigma(\text{Attribute values})} \quad (19)$$

Continuing with the dividend yield example, after standardization a stock with an average dividend yield will have a factor sensitivity of 0, a stock with a dividend yield one standard deviation above the average will have a factor sensitivity of 1, and a stock with a dividend yield one standard deviation below the average will have a factor sensitivity of −1. Suppose, for example, that an investment has a dividend yield of 3.5 percent and that the average dividend yield across all stocks being considered is 2.5 percent. Further, suppose that the standard deviation of dividend yields across all stocks is 2 percent. The investment's sensitivity to dividend yield is (3.5% − 2.5%)/2% = 0.50, or one-half standard deviation above average. The scaling permits all factor sensitivities to be interpreted similarly, despite differences in units of measure and scale in the variables. The exception to this interpretation is factors for binary variables such as industry membership. A company either participates in an industry or it does

59 If the coefficients were not standardized as described in the following paragraph, the intercept could be interpreted as the risk-free rate, because it would be the return to an asset with no factor risk (zero factor betas) and no asset-specific risk. With standardized coefficients, the intercept is not interpreted beyond being an intercept in a regression included so that the expected asset-specific risk equals 0.

not. The industry factor sensitivities would be 0 – 1 dummy variables; in models that recognize that companies frequently operate in multiple industries, the value of the sensitivity would be 1 for each industry in which a company operated.[60]

A second distinction between macroeconomic multifactor models and fundamental factor models is that with the former, we develop the factor (surprise) series first and then estimate the factor sensitivities through regressions; with the latter, we generally specify the factor sensitivities (attributes) first and then estimate the factor returns through regressions.[61]

4.5 Multifactor Models in Current Practice

In the previous sections, we explained the basic concepts of multifactor models and the APT. We now describe some models in actual industry use.

4.5.1 *Macroeconomic Factor Models*

Chen, Roll, and Ross (1986) pioneered the development of macroeconomic factor models. Following statistically based research suggesting that more than one factor was important in explaining the average returns on U.S. stocks, Chen et al. suggested that a relatively small set of macro factors was the primary influence on the U.S. stock market. The factors in the Chen et al. study were 1) inflation, including unanticipated inflation and changes in expected inflation, 2) a factor related to the term structure of interest rates, represented by long-term government bond returns minus one-month Treasury-bill rates, 3) a factor reflecting changes in market risk and investors' risk aversion, represented by the difference between the returns on low-rated and high-rated bonds, and 4) changes in industrial production.

The usefulness of any factor for explaining asset returns is generally evaluated using historical data. Our confidence that a factor will explain future returns increases if we can give an economic explanation of why a factor should be important in explaining average returns. We can plausibly explain all of Chen et al.'s four factors. For example, inflation affects the cash flows of businesses as well as the level of the discount rate applied to these cash flows by investors. Changes in industrial production affect the cash flows of businesses and the opportunities faced by investors. Example 14 details a current macroeconomic factor model that expanded on the model of Chen et al.

EXAMPLE 14

Expected Return in a Macroeconomic Factor Model

Burmeister, Roll, and Ross (1994) presented a macroeconomic factor model to explain the returns on U.S. equities. The model is known as the BIRR model for short. The BIRR model includes five factors:

1 Confidence risk: the unanticipated change in the return difference between risky corporate bonds and government bonds, both with maturities of 20 years. Risky corporate bonds bear greater default risk than does government debt. Investors' attitudes toward this risk should affect the average returns on equities. To explain the factor's name, when their confidence is high, investors are willing to accept a smaller reward for bearing this risk.

60 To further explain 0 – 1 variables, industry membership is measured on a nominal scale because we can name the industry to which a company belongs but no more. A nominal variable can be represented in a regression by a dummy variable (a variable that takes on the value of 0 or 1).

61 In some models that may be classed as fundamental, the factor sensitivities are regression coefficients and are not specified first.

2 Time horizon risk: the unanticipated change in the return difference between 20-year government bonds and 30-day Treasury bills. This factor reflects investors' willingness to invest for the long term.

3 Inflation risk: the unexpected change in the inflation rate. Nearly all stocks have negative exposure to this factor, as their returns decline with positive surprises in inflation.

4 Business cycle risk: the unexpected change in the level of real business activity. A positive surprise or unanticipated change indicates that the expected growth rate of the economy, measured in constant dollars, has increased.

5 Market timing risk: the portion of the S&P 500's total return that remains unexplained by the first four risk factors.[62] Almost all stocks have positive sensitivity to this factor.

The first four factors are quite similar to Chen et al.'s factors with respect to the economic influences they seek to capture. The fifth factor acknowledges the uncertainty surrounding the correct set of underlying variables for asset pricing; this factor captures influences on the returns to the S&P 500 not explained by the first four factors.

The S&P 500 is a widely used index of 500 U.S. stocks of leading companies in leading industries. Burmeister et al. used the S&P 500 to gauge the influence of their five factors on the mean excess returns (above the Treasury bill rate) to the S&P 500. Table 15 shows their results.

Table 15 Explaining the Annual Expected Excess Return for the S&P 500

Risk Factor	Factor Sensitivity	Risk Premium (%)	Effect of Factor on Expected Return (%)
Confidence risk	0.27	2.59	0.70
Time horizon risk	0.56	−0.66	−0.37
Inflation risk	−0.37	−4.32	1.60
Business cycle risk	1.71	1.49	2.55
Market timing risk	1.00	3.61	3.61
Expected excess return			8.09

Source: Burmeister et al.

The estimated APT model is $E(R_p)$ = T-bill rate + 2.59(Confidence risk) − 0.66(Time horizon risk) − 4.32(Inflation risk) + 1.49(Business cycle risk) + 3.61(Market timing risk). The table shows that the S&P 500 had positive exposure to every risk factor except inflation risk. The two largest contributions to excess return came from market timing risk and business cycle risk. According to the table, this model predicts that the S&P 500 will have an expected excess return of 8.09 percent above the T-bill rate. Therefore, if the 30-day Treasury bill rate were 4 percent, for example, the forecasted return for the S&P 500 would be 4 + 8.09 = 12.09 percent a year.

62 Because of the way the factor is constructed, the S&P 500 itself has a sensitivity of 1 to market timing risk.

In Example 15, we illustrate how we might use the Burmeister et al. factor model to assess the factor bets placed by a portfolio manager managing a U.S. active core equity portfolio (an actively managed portfolio invested in large-cap stocks).

EXAMPLE 15

Exposures to Economy-Wide Risks

William Hughes is the portfolio manager of a U.S. core equity portfolio that is being evaluated relative to its benchmark, the S&P 500. Because Hughes's performance will be evaluated relative to this benchmark, it is useful to understand the active factor bets that Hughes took relative to the S&P 500. With a focus on exposures to economy-wide risk, we use the Burmeister et al. model already presented. Table 16 displays Hughes's data.

Table 16 Excess Factor Sensitivities for a Core Equity

Risk Factor	Core Portfolio's Factor Sensitivity	S&P 500 Factor Sensitivity	Core Portfolio's Excess Factor Sensitivity
Confidence risk	0.27	0.27	0.00
Time horizon risk	0.56	0.56	0.00
Inflation risk	−0.12	−0.37	0.25
Business cycle risk	2.25	1.71	0.54
Market timing risk	1.10	1.00	0.10

We see that the portfolio manager tracks the S&P 500 exactly on confidence and time horizon risk but tilts toward greater business cycle risk. The portfolio also has a small positive excess exposure to the market timing factor.

We can use the excess exposure to business cycle risk to illustrate the numerical interpretation of the excess sensitivities. Ignoring nonsystematic risk and holding the values of the other factors constant, if there is a +1 percent surprise in the business cycle factor, we expect the return on the portfolio to be $0.01 \times 0.54 = 0.0054$ or 0.54 percent higher than the return on the S&P 500. Conversely, we expect the return on the portfolio to be lower than the S&P 500's return by an equal amount for a −1 percent surprise in business cycle risk.

Because of the excess exposure of 0.54, the portfolio manager appears to be placing a bet on economic expansion, relative to the benchmark. If the factor bet is inadvertent, Hughes is perhaps assuming an unwanted risk. If he is aware of the bet, what are the reasons for the bet?

Care must be taken in interpreting the portfolio manager's excess sensitivity of 0.25 to the inflation factor. The S&P 500 has a negative inflation factor exposure. The value of 0.25 represents a smaller negative exposure to inflation for the core portfolio—that is, less rather than more exposure to inflation risk. Note from Table 15 that because the risk premium for inflation risk is negative, Hughes is giving up expected return relative to the benchmark by his bet on inflation. Again, what are his reasons for the inflation factor bet?

The market timing factor has an interpretation somewhat similar to that of the CAPM beta about how a stock tends to respond to changes in the broad market, with a higher value indicating higher sensitivity to market returns, all else equal. But the market timing factor reflects only the portion of the S&P 500's returns not explained by the other four factors, and the two concepts are distinct. Whereas we would expect S&P 500 returns to be correlated with one or more of the first four factors, the market timing factor is constructed to be uncorrelated with the first four factors. Because the market timing factor and the S&P 500 returns are distinct, we would not expect market timing factor sensitivity to be proportional to CAPM beta computed relative to the S&P 500, in general.

Another major macroeconomic factor model is the Salomon Smith Barney U.S. Equity Risk Attribute Model, or Salomon RAM, for short.

EXAMPLE 16

Expected Return in the Salomon RAM

The Salomon RAM model explains returns to U.S. stocks in terms of nine factors: six macroeconomic factors, a residual market factor, a residual size factor, and a residual sector factor:

1 Economic growth: the monthly change in industrial production.
2 Credit quality: the monthly change in the yield of the Salomon Smith Barney High-Yield Market 10 + year index, after removing the component of the change that is correlated with the monthly changes in the yields of 30-year Treasury bonds.
3 Long rates: the monthly change in the yield of the 30-year Treasury bond.
4 Short rates: the monthly change in the yield of the 3-month Treasury bill.
5 Inflation shock: the unexpected component of monthly change in the consumer price index (CPI).
6 Dollar: the monthly change in the trade-weighted dollar.
7 Residual market: the monthly return on the S&P 500 after removing the effects of the six factors above.
8 Small-cap premium: the monthly difference between the return on the Russell 2000 Index and the S&P 500, after removing the effect of the seven factors above.
9 Residual sector: the monthly return on a sector membership index after removing the effect of the eight factors above.

Some noteworthy points concerning this model are as follows:[63]

- In contrast to the BIRR model and the general model (Equation 16), all the factors except inflation are stated in terms of returns rather than surprises.
- Factors 7, 8, and 9 attempt to isolate the net or unique contribution of the factor by removing the component of the factor return that is correlated with the group of preceding factors. Factors 7, 8, and 9 are each uncorrelated among themselves and with the other factors; they are said to be **orthogonal** (uncorrelated) factors. In addition, the credit quality factor is constructed to be uncorrelated with the long-rate factor.

63 See Sorenson, Samak, and Miller (1998) for more information on this model.

- Based on the explanatory power of the model, each stock receives a RAM ranking that reflects its coefficient of determination, with 1 the highest and 5 the lowest rank.
- The factor sensitivities are presented in standardized form.

In Table 17, the factor sensitivities are standardized with the same interpretation as Equation 19.

Table 17 Factor Sensitivities for Four Stocks

	Bank	Cable TV Provider	Department Store	Computer Manufacturer
Economic growth	1.48	−1.30	−0.88	0.88
Credit quality	−1.62	−0.77	−3.19	0.12
Long rates	−0.01	−1.65	1.83	0.78
Short rates	1.00	1.53	1.10	1.17
Inflation shock	−0.97	−1.99	−1.57	0.80
Dollar	0.82	1.47	0.87	−1.63
Residual market	0.06	0.30	0.13	0.26
Small-cap premium	0.13	1.44	0.92	−1.19
Residual sector	0.02	0.00	−0.03	0.00

Note: Entries are standardized factor sensitivities.

The bank and the computer manufacturer have investment-grade debt. The cable TV provider and department store are relatively heavy users of debt that is rated below investment grade. The computer manufacturer uses little debt in its capital structure. Based only on the information given, answer the following questions.

1 Contrast the factor sensitivities of the cable TV provider stock to those of the average stock.

2 State which stocks are expected to do well in an economy showing strong economic growth coupled with an improving credit environment, all else equal.

3 Explain a possible business reason or a reason related to company fundamentals to explain negative sensitivity of the cable TV provider's stock to the credit quality factor.

Solution to 1:

The factor sensitivities to short rates, the trade-weighted dollar, the residual market factor, and the small-cap premium factor are above average, as indicated by positive factor sensitivities. The sensitivity to the residual sector factor is average, as indicated by zero factor sensitivity. By contrast, the cable TV provider's stock has below-average sensitivity to the economic growth, credit quality, long-rate, and inflation factors, as indicated by negative factor sensitivities.

Solution to 2:

Both the bank and the computer manufacturer have positive sensitivity to the economic growth factor, which is the monthly change in industrial production. As the factor and factor sensitivity are defined, the positive sensitivity implies above-average returns for these two stocks in an environment of strong economic growth, all else equal. The bank has a negative coefficient on the credit quality factor, whereas the computer manufacturer has a positive sensitivity. An improving credit environment means that the yields of high-yield bonds are declining. Thus we would observe a negative value for the credit quality factor in that environment. Of the two stocks, we expect that only the bank stock with a negative sensitivity should give above-average returns in an improving credit environment. Thus the bank stock is expected to do well in the stated scenario.

Solution to 3:

The credit quality factor essentially measures the change in the premium for bearing default risk. A negative coefficient on the credit quality factor means that the stock should do well when the premium for bearing default risk declines (an improving credit environment). One explanation for the negative sensitivity of the cable TV provider's stock to the credit quality factor is that the company is a heavy borrower with less than investment-grade debt. The cost of such debt reflects a significant default premium. The cable TV provider's borrowing costs should decline in an improving credit environment; that decline should positively affect its stock price.

4.5.2 *Fundamental Factor Models*

Financial analysts frequently use fundamental factor models for a variety of purposes, including portfolio performance attribution and risk analysis.[64] Fundamental factor models focus on explaining the returns to individual stocks using observable fundamental factors that describe either attributes of the securities themselves or attributes of the securities' issuers. Industry membership, price-earnings ratio, book value-to-price ratio, size, and financial leverage are examples of fundamental factors.

Example 17 reports a study that examined macroeconomic, fundamental, and statistical factor models.

EXAMPLE 17

Alternative Factor Models

Connor (1995) contrasted a macroeconomic factor model with a fundamental factor model to compare how well the models explain stock returns.[65]

Connor reported the results of applying a macroeconomic factor model to the returns for 779 large-cap U.S. stocks based on monthly data from January 1985 through December 1993. Using five macroeconomic factors, Connor was able to explain approximately 11 percent of the variance of return on these stocks.[66] Table 18 shows his results.

64 **Portfolio performance attribution** analyzes the performance of portfolios in terms of the contributions from various sources of risk.

65 We do not discuss results for statistical factor models also reported in Connor (1995).

66 The explanatory power of a given model was computed as 1 − [(Average asset-specific variance of return across stocks) / (Average total variance of return across stocks)]. The variance estimates were corrected for degrees of freedom, so the marginal contribution of a factor to explanatory power can be 0 or negative. Explanatory power captures the proportion of the total variance of return that a given model explains for the average stock.

Table 18 The Explanatory Power of the Macroeconomic Factors

Factor	Explanatory Power from Using Each Factor Alone (%)	Increase in Explanatory Power from Adding Each Factor to All the Others (%)
Inflation	1.3	0.0
Term structure	1.1	7.7
Industrial production	0.5	0.3
Default premium	2.4	8.1
Unemployment	−0.3	0.1
All factors		10.9

Source: Connor (1995).

Connor also reported a fundamental factor analysis of the same companies for which he conducted a macroeconomic factor analysis. The factor model employed was the BARRA US-E2 model (the current version is E3). Table 19 shows these results. In the table, "variability in markets" represents the stock's volatility, "success" is a price momentum variable, "trade activity" distinguishes stocks by how often their shares trade, and "growth" distinguishes stocks by past and anticipated earnings growth.[67]

Table 19 The Explanatory Power of the Fundamental Factors

Factor	Explanatory Power from Using Each Factor Alone (%)	Increase in Explanatory Power from Adding Each Factor to All the Others (%)
Industries	16.3	18.0
Variability in markets	4.3	0.9
Success	2.8	0.8
Size	1.4	0.6
Trade activity	1.4	0.5
Growth	3.0	0.4
Earnings to price	2.2	0.6
Book to price	1.5	0.6
Earnings variability	2.5	0.4
Financial leverage	0.9	0.5
Foreign investment	0.7	0.4
Labor intensity	2.2	0.5
Dividend yield	2.9	0.4
All factors		42.6

Source: Connor (1995).

67 The explanations of the variables are from Grinold and Kahn (1994); Connor did not supply definitions.

As Table 19 shows, the most important fundamental factor is "industries," represented by 55 industry dummy variables. The fundamental factor model explained approximately 43 percent of the variation in stock returns, compared with approximately 11 percent for the macroeconomic factor model. Connor's article does not provide tests of the statistical significance of the various factors in either model; however, Connor did find strong evidence for the usefulness of fundamental factor models, and this evidence is mirrored by the wide use of those models in the investment community. Fundamental factor models are frequently used in portfolio performance attribution, for example. We shall illustrate this use later in the reading. Typically, fundamental factor models employ many more factors than macroeconomic factor models, giving a more detailed picture of the sources of a portfolio manager's results.

We cannot conclude from this study that fundamental factor models are inherently superior to macroeconomic factors, however. Each of the major types of models has its uses. The factors in various macroeconomic factor models are individually backed by statistical evidence that they represent systematic risk (i.e., risk that cannot be diversified away). In contrast, a portfolio manager can easily construct a portfolio that excludes a particular industry, so exposure to a particular industry is not systematic risk. The two types of factors, macroeconomic and fundamental, have different implications for measuring and managing risk, in general. The macroeconomic factor set is parsimonious (five variables). The fundamental factor set is large (67 variables including the 55 industry dummy variables), and at the expense of greater complexity, it can give a more detailed picture of risk in terms that are easily related to company and security characteristics. Connor found that the macroeconomic factor model had no marginal explanatory power when added to the fundamental factor model, implying that the fundamental risk attributes capture all the risk characteristics represented by the macroeconomic factor betas. Because the fundamental factors supply such a detailed description of the characteristics of a stock and its issuer, however, this finding is not necessarily surprising.

We encounter a range of distinct representations of risk in the fundamental models that are currently used in practical applications. Diversity exists in both the identity and exact definition of factors as well as in the underlying functional form and estimation procedures. Despite the diversity, we can place the factors of most fundamental factor models for equities into three broad groups:

- **Company fundamental factors**. These are factors related to the company's internal performance. Examples are factors relating to earnings growth, earnings variability, earnings momentum, and financial leverage.
- **Company share-related factors**. These factors include valuation measures and other factors related to share price of the trading characteristics of the shares. In contrast to the previous category, these factors directly incorporate investors' expectations concerning the company. Examples include price multiples such as earnings yield, dividend yield, and book-to-market. Market capitalization falls under this heading. Various models incorporate variables relating to share price momentum, share price volatility, and trading activity that fall in this category.
- **Macroeconomic factors**. Sector or industry membership factors come under this heading. Various models include factors such as CAPM beta, other similar measures of systematic risk, and yield curve level sensitivity, all of which can be placed in this category.

4.6 Applications

The following sections present some of the major applications of multifactor models in investment practice.

We begin by discussing portfolio performance attribution and risk analysis. We could frame the discussion in terms of raw returns or in terms of returns relative to a portfolio's benchmark. Because they provide a reference standard for risk and return, benchmarks play an important role in many institutional investors' plans for quantitatively risk-controlled returns. We shall thus focus on analyzing returns relative to a benchmark.

Multifactor models can also help portfolio managers form portfolios with specific desired risk characteristics. After discussing performance attribution and risk analysis, we explain the use of multifactor models in creating a portfolio with risk exposures that are similar to those of another portfolio.

4.6.1 *Analyzing Sources of Returns*

Multifactor models can help us understand in detail the sources of a manager's returns relative to a benchmark. For simplicity, in this section we analyze the sources of the returns of a portfolio fully invested in the equities of a single national equity market.[68]

Analysts frequently favor fundamental multifactor models in decomposing (separating into basic elements) the sources of returns. In contrast to statistical factor models, fundamental factor models allow the sources of portfolio performance to be described by name. Also, in contrast to macroeconomic factor models, fundamental models suggest investment style choices and security characteristics more directly, and often in greater detail.

We first need to understand the objectives of active managers. As mentioned, managers are commonly evaluated relative to a specified benchmark. Active portfolio managers hold securities in different-from-benchmark weights in an attempt to add value to their portfolios relative to a passive investment approach. Securities held in different-from-benchmark weights reflect portfolio manager expectations that differ from consensus expectations. For an equity manager, those expectations may relate to common factors driving equity returns or to considerations unique to a company. Thus when we evaluate an active manager, we want to ask questions such as "Did the manager have insights that were valuable in the sense of adding value above a passive strategy?" Analyzing the sources of returns using multifactor models can help answer these questions.

The return on a portfolio, R_p, can be viewed as the sum of the benchmark's return, R_B, and the **active return** (portfolio return minus benchmark return):

$$\text{Active return} = R_p - R_B \quad (20)$$

With a factor model in hand, we can analyze a portfolio manager's active return as the sum of two components. The first component is the product of the portfolio manager's factor tilts (active factor sensitivities) and the factor returns; we may call that component the return from factor tilts. The second component is the part of active return reflecting the manager's skill in individual asset selection; we may call that component asset selection. Equation 21 shows the decomposition of active return into those two components:

68 The assumption allows us to ignore the roles of country selection, asset allocation, market timing, and currency hedging, greatly simplifying the analysis. Even in a more general context, however, we can perform similar analyses using multifactor models.

$$\text{Active return} = \sum_{j=1}^{K} \left[(\text{Portfolio sensitivity})_j - (\text{Benchmark sensitivity})_j \right] \times (\text{Factor return})_j + \text{Asset selection} \quad (21)$$

In Equation 21, we measure the portfolio's and benchmark's sensitivities to each factor in our risk model at the beginning of an evaluation period.

Example 18 illustrates the use of a relatively parsimonious fundamental factor model in decomposing and interpreting returns.

EXAMPLE 18

Active Return Decomposition of an Equity Portfolio Manager

As an equity analyst at a pension fund sponsor, Ronald Service uses the following multifactor model to evaluate U.S. equity portfolios:

$$R_p - R_F = a_p + b_{p1}\text{RMRF} + b_{p2}\text{SMB} + b_{p3}\text{HML} + b_{p4}\text{WML} + \varepsilon_p \quad (22)$$

where

R_p and R_F = the return on the portfolio and the risk-free rate of return, respectively

RMRF = the return on a value-weighted equity index in excess of the one-month T-bill rate

SMB = small minus big, a size (market capitalization) factor. SMB is the average return on three small-cap portfolios minus the average return on three large-cap portfolios.

HML = high minus low, the average return on two high book-to-market portfolios minus the average return on two low book-to-market portfolios

WML = winners minus losers, a momentum factor. WML is the return on a portfolio of the past year's winners minus the return on a portfolio of the past year's losers.[69]

In Equation 22, the sensitivities are interpreted as regression coefficients and are not standardized.

Service's current task is evaluating the performance of the most recently hired U.S. equity manager. That manager's benchmark is the Russell 1000, an index representing the performance of U.S. large-cap stocks. The manager describes herself as a "stock picker" and points to her performance in beating the benchmark as evidence that she is successful. Table 20 presents an analysis based on Equation 21 of the sources of that manager's active return during the year. In Table 20, "A. Return from Factor Tilts," equal to 2.1241 percent, sums the four numbers above it in the column; the return from factor tilts is the first component of Equation 21. Table 20 lists asset selection as equal to –0.05 percent. Active return is found as 2.1241% + (–0.05%) = 2.0741%.

69 WML is an equally weighted average of the stocks with the highest 30 percent 11-month returns lagged 1 month minus the equally weighted average of the stocks with the lowest 30 percent 11-month returns lagged 1 month. The model is based on Carhart (1997); WML is Carhart's PR1YR factor.

From his previous work, Service knows that the returns to growth-style portfolios often have a positive sensitivity to the momentum factor (WML) in Equation 22. By contrast, the returns to certain value-style portfolios, such as those following a contrarian strategy, often have low or negative sensitivity to the momentum factor.

Using the information given, address the following:

1 Determine the manager's investment style mandate.
2 Evaluate the sources of the manager's active return for the year.
3 What concerns might Service discuss with the manager as a result of the return decomposition?

Table 20 Active Return Decomposition

Factor	Factor Sensitivity Portfolio (1)	Factor Sensitivity Benchmark (2)	Factor Sensitivity Difference (3) = (1) – (2)	Factor Return (4)	Contribution to Active Return Absolute (3) × (4)	Contribution to Active Return Proportion of Total Active
RMRF	0.85	0.90	−0.05	5.52%	−0.2760	−13.3%
SMB	0.05	0.10	−0.05	−3.35%	0.1675	8.1%
HML	1.40	1.00	0.40	5.10%	2.0400	98.4%
WML	0.08	0.06	0.02	9.63%	0.1926	9.3%
				A. Return from Factor Tilts =	2.1241	102.4%
				B. Asset Selection =	−0.0500	−2.4%
				C. Active Return (A + B) =	2.0741	100.0%

Solution to 1:

The benchmark's sensitivities reflect the baseline risk characteristics of a manager's investment opportunity set. We can infer the manager's anticipated style by examining the characteristics of the benchmark selected for her. We then confirm these inferences by examining the portfolio's actual factor exposures:

- Stocks with high book-to-market are generally viewed as value stocks. Because the pension sponsor selected a benchmark with a high sensitivity (1.0) to HML (the high book-to-market minus low book-to-market factor), we can infer that the manager has a value orientation. The actual sensitivity of 1.4 to HML indicates that the manager had even more exposure to high book-to-market stocks than the benchmark.
- The benchmark's and portfolio's approximate neutrality to the momentum factor is consistent with a value orientation.
- The benchmark's and portfolio's low exposure to SMB suggests essentially no net exposure to small-cap stocks.

The above considerations as a group suggest that the manager has a large-cap value orientation.

Solution to 2:

The dominant source of the manager's positive active return was her positive active exposure to the HML factor. The bet contributed (1.40 – 1.00)(5.10%) = 2.04% or approximately 98 percent of the realized active return of about 2.07 percent. During the evaluation period, the manager sharpened her value orientation, and that bet paid off. The manager's active exposure to the overall market (RMRF) was unprofitable, but her active exposures to small stocks (SMB) and to momentum (WML) were profitable; however, the magnitudes of the manager's active exposures to RMRF, SMB, and WML were relatively small, so the effects of those bets on active return was minor compared with her large and successful bet on HML.

Solution to 3:

Although the manager is a self-described "stock picker," her active return from asset selection in this period was actually negative. Her positive active return resulted from the concurrence of a large active bet on HML and a high return to that factor during the period. If the market had favored growth rather than value without the manager doing better in individual asset selection, the manager's performance would have been unsatisfactory. Can the manager supply evidence that she can predict changes in returns to the HML factor? Is she overconfident about her stock selection ability? Service may want to discuss these concerns with the manager. The return decomposition has helped Service distinguish between the return from positioning along the value-growth spectrum and return from insights into individual stocks within the investment approach the manager has chosen.

4.6.2 *Analyzing Sources of Risk*

Continuing with our focus on active returns, in this section we explore analysis of active risk. **Active risk** is the standard deviation of active returns. Many terms in use refer to exactly the same concept, so we need to take a short detour to mention them. A traditional synonym is **tracking error** (TE), but the term may be confusing unless *error* is associated by the reader with *standard deviation*; tracking-error volatility (TEV) has been used (where *error* is understood as a *difference*); and **tracking risk** is now in common use (but the natural abbreviation TR could be misunderstood to refer to total return). We will use the abbreviation TE for the concept of tracking risk, and we will refer to it usually as tracking risk:

$$\text{TE} = s\left(R_p - R_B\right) \qquad (23)$$

In Equation 23, $s(R_p - R_B)$ indicates that we take the sample standard deviation (indicated by s) of the time series of differences between the portfolio return, R_p, and the benchmark return, R_B. We should be careful that active return and tracking risk are stated on the same time basis.[70]

As a broad indication of ranges for tracking risk, in U.S. equity markets a well-executed passive investment strategy can often achieve tracking risk on the order of 1 percent or less per annum. A semi-active or enhanced index investment strategy, which makes tightly controlled use of managers' expectations, often has a tracking risk goal of 2 percent per annum. A diversified active U.S. large-cap equity strategy that might be benchmarked on the S&P 500 would commonly have tracking risk in the range of 2 percent to 6 percent per annum. An aggressive active equity manager might have tracking risk in the range of 6 percent to 9 percent or more.

Somewhat analogous to use of the traditional Sharpe measure in evaluating absolute returns, the ratio of mean active return to active risk, the **information ratio** (IR), is a tool for evaluating mean active returns per unit of active risk. The historical or *ex post* IR has the form

$$\text{IR} = \frac{\overline{R}_p - \overline{R}_B}{s\left(R_p - R_B\right)} \qquad (24)$$

In the numerator of Equation 24, $\overline{R}_p$ and $\overline{R}_B$ stand for the sample mean return on the portfolio and the sample mean return on the benchmark, respectively. To illustrate the calculation, if a portfolio achieved a mean return of 9 percent during the same period that its benchmark earned a mean return of 7.5 percent, and the portfolio's tracking risk was 6 percent, we would calculate an information ratio of (9% – 7.5%)/6% = 0.25. Setting guidelines for acceptable active risk or tracking risk is one of the ways that some institutional investors attempt to assure that the overall risk and style characteristics of their investments are in line with those desired.

70 To annualize a daily TE based on daily returns, we multiply daily TE by $(250)^{1/2}$ based on 250 trading days in a year; to annualize a monthly TE based on monthly returns, we multiply monthly TE by $(12)^{1/2}$.

EXAMPLE 19

Communicating with Investment Managers

The framework of active return and active risk is appealing to investors who want to closely control the risk of investments. The benchmark serves as a known and continuously observable reference standard in relation to which quantitative risk and return objectives may be stated and communicated. For example, a U.S. public employee retirement system issued a solicitation (or request for proposal) to prospective investment managers for a "risk-controlled U.S. large-cap equity fund" that included the following requirements:

- Shares must be components of the S&P 500.
- The portfolio should have a minimum of 200 issues. At time of purchase, the maximum amount that may be invested in any one issuer is 5 percent of the portfolio at market value or 150 percent of the issuers' weight within the S&P 500 Index, whichever is greater.
- The portfolio must have a minimum 0.30 percent information ratio either since inception or over the last seven years.
- The portfolio must also have tracking risk of less than 4.0 percent with respect to the S&P 500 either since inception or over the last seven years.

Analysts use multifactor models to understand in detail a portfolio manager's risk exposures. In decomposing active risk, the analyst's objective is to measure the portfolio's active exposure along each dimension of risk—in other words, to understand the sources of tracking risk.[71] Among the questions analysts will want to answer are the following:

- What active exposures contributed most to the manager's tracking risk?
- Was the portfolio manager aware of the nature of his active exposures, and if so, can he articulate a rationale for assuming them?
- Are the portfolio's active risk exposures consistent with the manager's stated investment philosophy?
- Which active bets earned adequate returns for the level of active risk taken?

In addressing these questions, analysts often choose fundamental factor models because they can be used to relate active risk exposures to a manager's portfolio decisions in a fairly direct and intuitive way. In this section, we explain how to decompose or explain a portfolio's active risk using a multifactor model.

We previously addressed the decomposition of active return; now we address the decomposition of active risk. In analyzing risk, it is convenient to use variances rather than standard deviations because the variances of uncorrelated variables are additive. We refer to the variance of active risk as **active risk squared**:

$$\text{Active risk squared} = s^2\left(R_p - R_B\right) \quad (25)$$

71 The portfolio's active risks are weighted averages of the component securities' active risk. Therefore, we may also perform the analysis at the level of individual holdings. A portfolio manager may find this approach useful in making adjustments to his active risk profile.

We can separate a portfolio's active risk squared into two components:

- **Active factor risk** is the contribution to active risk squared resulting from the portfolio's different-than-benchmark exposures relative to factors specified in the risk model.[72]
- **Active specific risk** or **asset selection risk** is the contribution to active risk squared resulting from the portfolio's active weights on individual assets as those weights interact with assets' residual risk.[73]

When applied to an investment in a single asset class, active risk squared has two components. The decomposition of active risk squared into two components is

Active risk squared = Active factor risk + Active specific risk **(26)**

Active factor risk represents the part of active risk squared explained by the portfolio active factor exposures. Active factor risk can be found indirectly as the difference between active risk squared and active specific risk, which has the expression[74]

$$\text{Active specific risk} = \sum_{i=1}^{n} w_i^a \sigma_{\varepsilon_i}^2$$

where w_i^a is the ith asset's active weight in the portfolio (that is, the difference between the asset's weight in the portfolio and its weight in the benchmark) and $\sigma_{\varepsilon_i}^2$ is the residual risk of the ith asset (the variance of the ith asset's returns left unexplained by the factors).[75] Active specific risk identifies the active non-factor or residual risk assumed by the manager. We should look for a positive average return from asset selection as compensation for bearing active specific risk.

EXAMPLE 20

A Comparison of Active Risk

Richard Gray is comparing the risk of four U.S. equity managers who share the same benchmark. He uses a fundamental factor model, the BARRA US-E3 model, which incorporates 13 risk indexes and a set of 52 industrial categories. The risk indexes measure various fundamental aspects of companies and their shares such as size, leverage, and dividend yield. In the model, companies have nonzero exposures to all industries in which the company operates. Table 21 presents Gray's analysis of the active risk squared of the four managers, based on Equation 26.[76] In Table 21, the column labeled "Industry" gives the portfolio's active factor risk associated with the industry exposures of its holdings; the column "Risk Indexes" gives the portfolio's active factor risk associated with the exposures of its holdings to the 13 risk indexes.

72 Throughout this discussion, "active" means "different than benchmark."

73 As we use the terms, "active specific risk" and "active factor risk" refer to variances rather than standard deviations.

74 The direct procedure for calculating active factor risk is as follows. A portfolio's active factor exposure to a given factor j, b_j^a, is found by weighting each asset's sensitivity to factor j by its active weight and summing the terms $b_j^a = \sum_{i=1}^{n} w_j^a b_{ji}$. Then active factor risk equals $\sum_{i=1}^{k}\sum_{j=1}^{k} b_i^a b_j^a \text{Cov}(F_i, F_j)$.

75 The residual returns of the assets are assumed to be uncorrelated with each other and with the factor returns.

76 There is a covariance term in active factor risk, reflecting the correlation of industry membership and the risk indexes, which we assume is negligible in this example.

Table 21 Active Risk Squared Decomposition

	Active Factor				
Portfolio	Industry	Risk Indexes	Total Factor	Active Specific	Active Risk Squared
A	12.25	17.15	29.40	19.60	49
B	1.25	13.75	15.00	10.00	25
C	1.25	17.50	18.75	6.25	25
D	0.03	0.47	0.50	0.50	1

Note: Entries are percent squared.

Using the information in Table 21, address the following:

1 Contrast the active risk decomposition of Portfolios A and B.

2 Contrast the active risk decomposition of Portfolios B and C.

3 Characterize the investment approach of Portfolio D.

Solution to 1:

Table 22 restates the information in Table 21 to show the proportional contributions of the various sources of active risk. In the last column of Table 22, we now give the square root of active risk squared—that is, active risk or tracking risk. To explain the middle set of columns in Table 22, Portfolio A's value of 25 percent under the Industry column is found as 12.25/49 = 0.25. So Portfolio A's active risk related to industry exposures is 25 percent of active risk squared. Portfolio A has assumed a higher level of active risk than B (tracking risk of 7 percent versus 5 percent). Portfolios A and B assumed the same proportions of active factor and active specific risk, but a sharp contrast exists between the two in terms of type of active factor risk exposure. Portfolio A assumed substantial active industry risk, whereas Portfolio B was approximately industry neutral relative to the benchmark. By contrast, Portfolio B had higher active bets on the risk indexes representing company and share characteristics.

Table 22 Active Risk Decomposition (Restated)

	Active Factor (% of Total Active)				
Portfolio	Industry (%)	Risk Indexes (%)	Total Factor (%)	Active Specific (% of Total Active)	Active Risk (%)
A	25	35	60	40	7
B	5	55	60	40	5
C	5	70	75	25	5
D	3	47	50	50	1

Solution to 2:

Portfolios B and C were similar in their absolute amounts of active risk. Furthermore, both Portfolios B and C were both approximately industry neutral relative to the benchmark. Portfolio C assumed more active factor risk related to the risk indexes, but B assumed more active specific risk. We can also infer from the second point that B is somewhat less diversified than C.

Solution to 3:

Portfolio D appears to be a passively managed portfolio, judging by its negligible level of active risk. Referring to Table 21, Portfolio D's active factor risk of 0.50, equal to 0.707 percent expressed as a standard deviation, indicates that the portfolio very closely matches the benchmark along the dimensions of risk that the model identifies as driving average returns.

Example 20 presented a set of hypothetical portfolios with differing degrees of tracking risk in which active factor risk tended to be larger than active specific risk. Given a well-constructed multifactor model and a well-diversified portfolio, this relationship is fairly commonplace. For well-diversified portfolios, managing active factor risk is typically the chief task in managing tracking risk.

Example 20 presented an analysis of active risk at an aggregated level; a portfolio's active factor risks with respect to the multifactor model's 13 risk indexes was aggregated into a single number. In appraising performance, an analyst may be interested in a much more detailed analysis of a portfolio's active risk. How can an analyst appraise the individual contributions of a manager's active factor exposures to active risk squared?

Whatever the set of factors, the procedure for evaluating the contribution of an active factor exposure to active risk squared is the same. This quantity has been called a factor's marginal contribution to active risk squared (FMCAR). With K factors, the marginal contribution to active risk squared for a factor j, FMCAR_j is

$$\text{FMCAR}_j = \frac{b_j^a \sum_{i=1}^{K} b_i^a \text{Cov}\left(\text{F}_j,\text{F}_i\right)}{\text{Active risk squared}} \quad \textbf{(27)}$$

Where b_j^a is the portfolio's active exposure to factor j. The numerator is the active factor risk for factor j.[77] The numerator is similar to expressions involving beta that we encountered earlier in discussing the market model, but with multiple factors, factor covariances as well as variances are relevant. To illustrate Equation 27 in a simple setting, suppose we have a two-factor model:

- The manager's active exposure to the first factor is 0.50; that is, $b_1^a = 0.50$. The other active factor exposure is $b_2^a = 0.15$.
- The variance–covariance matrix of the factors is described by $\text{Cov}(\text{F}_1,\text{F}_1) = \sigma^2(\text{F}_1) = 225$, $\text{Cov}(\text{F}_1,\text{F}_2) = 12$, and $\text{Cov}(\text{F}_2,\text{F}_2) = \sigma^2(\text{F}_2) = 144$.
- Active specific risk is 53.71.

We first compute active factor risk for each factor; that calculation is the numerator in Equation 27. Then we find active risk squared by summing the active factor risks and active specific risk, and form the ratio indicated in Equation 27. For the first factor, we calculate the numerator of FMCAR_1 as

---

77 If we summed the numerator over $j = 1$ to K, we would have the expression for active factor risk given in Footnote 74.

$$b_1^a \sum_{i=1}^{2} b_i^a \mathrm{Cov}(F_1, F_i) = 0.50\left[0.50(225) + 0.15(12)\right] = 57.15$$

For the second factor, we have

$$b_2^a \sum_{i=1}^{2} b_i^a \mathrm{Cov}(F_2, F_i) = 0.15\left[0.50(12) + 0.15(144)\right] = 4.14$$

Active factor risk is 57.15 + 4.14 = 61.29. Adding active specific risk, we find that active risk squared is 61.29 + 53.71 = 115. Thus we have FMCAR_1 = 57.15/115 = 0.497 or 49.7 percent, and FMCAR_2 = 4.14/115 = 0.036 or 3.6 percent. Active factor risk as a fraction of total risk is FMCAR_1 + FMCAR_2 = 49.7% + 3.6% = 53.3%. Active specific risk contributes 100% – 53.3% = 46.7% to active risk squared. Example 21 illustrates the application of these concepts.

EXAMPLE 21

An Analysis of Individual Active Factor Risk

William Whetzell is responsible for a monthly internal performance attribution and risk analysis of a domestic core equity fund managed internally by his organization, a Canadian endowment. In his monthly analyses, Whetzell uses a risk model incorporating the following factors:

- Log of market cap;
- E/P, the earnings yield;
- B/P, the book-to-price ratio;
- Earnings growth;
- Average dividend yield;
- D/A, the long-term debt-to-asset ratio;
- Volatility of return on equity (ROE);
- Volatility of EPS.

The factor sensitivities in the model have the standard interpretation of factor sensitivities in fundamental factor models.

Having determined that he earned an active return of 0.75 percent during the last fiscal year, Whetzell turns to the task of analyzing the portfolio's risk. At the start of the fiscal year, the investment committee made the following decisions:

- to tactically tilt the portfolio in the direction of small-cap stocks;
- to implement an "earnings growth at a reasonable price" (GARP) bias in security selection;
- to keep any active factor risk, expressed as a standard deviation, under 5 percent per annum;
- to keep active specific risk at no more than 50 percent of active risk squared; and
- to achieve an information ratio of 0.15 or greater.

Before Whetzell presented his report, one investment committee member reviewing his material commented that the investment committee should adopt a passive investment strategy for domestic equities if the equity fund continues to perform as it did during the last fiscal year.

Table 23 presents information on the equity fund. The factor returns were constructed to be approximately mutually uncorrelated.

Table 23	Risk Analysis Data		
	Sensitivity		
Factor	Portfolio	Benchmark	Factor Variance
Log of market cap	0.05	0.25	225
E/P	−0.05	0.05	144
B/P	−0.25	−0.02	100
Earnings growth	0.25	0.10	196
Dividend yield	0.01	0.00	169
D/A	0.03	0.03	81
Vol of ROE	−0.25	0.02	121
Vol of EPS	−0.10	0.03	64
		Active specific risk =	29.9406
		Active specific return =	−0.5%
		Active return =	0.75%

Based on the information in Table 23, address the following:

1 For each factor, calculate (A) the active factor risk and (B) the marginal contribution to active risk squared.

2 Discuss whether the data are consistent with the objectives of the investment committee having been met.

3 Appraise the endowment's risk-adjusted performance for the year.

4 Explain two pieces of evidence supporting the committee member's statement concerning a passive investment strategy.

Solution to 1:

(A) Active factor risk for a factor = (Active sensitivity to the factor)^2 (Factor variance) in Equation 27 with zero factor correlations.

$$\text{Log of market cap} = (0.05 - 0.25)^2(225) = 9.0$$

$$E/P = (-0.05 - 0.05)^2(144) = 1.44$$

$$B/P = [-0.25 - (-0.02)]^2(100) = 5.29$$

$$\text{Earnings growth} = (0.25 - 0.10)^2(196) = 4.41$$

$$\text{Dividend yield} = (0.01 - 0.00)^2(169) = 0.0169$$

$$D/A = (0.03 - 0.03)^2(81) = 0.0$$

$$\text{Volatility of ROE} = (-0.25 - 0.02)^2(121) = 8.8209$$

$$\text{Volatility of EPS} = (-0.10 - 0.03)^2(64) = 1.0816$$

(B) The sum of the individual active factor risks equals 30.0594. We add active specific risk to this sum to obtain active risk squared of 30.0594 + 29.9406 = 60. Thus FMCAR for the factors is as follows:

Log of market cap = 9/60 = 0.15
E/P = 1.44/60 = 0.024
B/P = 5.29/60 = 0.0882
Earnings growth = 4.41/60 = 0.0735
Dividend yield = 0.0169/60 = 0.0003
D/A = 0.0/60 = 0.0
Volatility of ROE = 8.8209/60 = 0.1470
Volatility of EPS = 1.0816/60 = 0.0180

Solution to 2:

We consider each investment committee objective in turn. The first objective was *to tactically tilt the portfolio in the direction of small-cap stocks.* A zero sensitivity to the log market cap factor would indicate average exposure to size. An exposure of 1 would indicate a positive exposure to returns to increasing size that is one standard deviation above the mean, given the standard interpretation of factor sensitivities in fundamental factor models. Although the equity fund's exposure to size is positive, the *active* exposure is negative. This result is consistent with tilting toward small-cap stocks.

The second objective was *to implement an "earnings growth at a reasonable price" bias in security selection.* The equity fund has a positive active exposure to earnings growth consistent with seeking companies with high earnings growth rates. It is questionable, however, whether the "reasonable price" part of the approach is being satisfied. The fund's absolute E/P and B/P sensitivities are negative, indicating below-average earning yield and B/P (higher than average P/E and P/B). The active exposures to these factors are also negative. If above-average earnings growth is priced in the marketplace, the fund may need to bear negative active exposures, so we cannot reach a final conclusion. We can say, however, that none of the data positively supports a conclusion that the GARP strategy was implemented.

The third objective was *to keep any active factor risk, expressed as a standard deviation, under 5 percent per annum.* The largest active factor risk was on the log of market cap factor. Expressed as a standard deviation, that risk was $(9)^{1/2}$ = 3 percent per annum, so this objective was met.

The fourth objective was *to keep active specific risk at no more than 50 percent of active risk squared.* Active specific risk as a fraction of active risk squared was 29.9406/60 = 0.4990 or 49.9 percent, so this objective was met.

The fifth objective was *to achieve an information ratio of 0.15 or greater.* The information ratio is active return divided by active risk (tracking risk). Active return was given as 0.75 percent. Active risk is the square root of active risk squared: $(60)^{1/2}$ = 7.7460%. Thus IR = 0.75%/7.7460% = 0.0968 or approximately 0.10, which is short of the stated objective of 0.15.

Solution to 3:

The endowment's realized information ratio of 0.10 means its risk-adjusted performance for the year was inadequate.

Solution to 4:

The active specific return for the year was negative, although the fund incurred substantial active specific risk. Therefore, specific risk had a negative reward. Furthermore, the realized information ratio fell short of the investment committee's objective. With the qualification that this analysis is based on only one year, these facts would argue for the cost-efficient alternative of indexing.

In our discussion of performance attribution and risk analysis, we have given examples related to common stock. Multifactor models have also been used in similar roles for portfolios of bonds and other asset classes.

We have illustrated the use of multifactor models in analyzing a portfolio's active returns and active risk. At least equally important is the use of multifactor models in portfolio construction. At that stage of the portfolio management process, multifactor models permit the portfolio manager to make focused bets or to control portfolio risk relative to her benchmark's risk. In the remaining sections, we discuss these uses of multifactor models.

4.6.3 *Factor Portfolios*

A portfolio manager can use multifactor models to establish a specific desired risk profile for his portfolio. For example, he may want to create and use a factor portfolio. A factor portfolio for a particular factor has a sensitivity of 1 for that factor and a sensitivity of 0 for all other factors. It is thus a portfolio with exposure to only one risk factor and exactly represents the risk of that factor. As a pure bet on a source of risk, factor portfolios are of interest to a portfolio manager who wants to hedge that risk (offset it) or speculate on it. Example 22 illustrates the use of factor portfolios.

EXAMPLE 22

Factor Portfolios

Analyst Wanda Smithfield has constructed six portfolios for possible use by portfolio managers in her firm. The portfolios are labeled A, B, C, D, E, and F in Table 24.

Table 24 Factor Portfolios

	Portfolios					
Risk Factor	**A**	**B**	**C**	**D**	**E**	**F**
Confidence risk	0.50	0.00	1.00	0.00	0.00	0.80
Time horizon risk	1.92	0.00	1.00	1.00	1.00	1.00
Inflation risk	0.00	0.00	1.00	0.00	0.00	–1.05
Business cycle risk	1.00	1.00	0.00	0.00	1.00	0.30
Market timing risk	0.90	0.00	1.00	0.00	0.00	0.75

Note: Entries are factor sensitivities.

1 A portfolio manager wants to place a bet that real business activity will increase.

A Determine and justify the portfolio among the six given that would be most useful to the manager.

B What type of position would the manager take in the portfolio chosen in Part A?

2 A portfolio manager wants to hedge an existing positive exposure to time horizon risk.

A Determine and justify the portfolio among the six given that would be most useful to the manager.

B What type of position would the manager take in the portfolio chosen in Part A?

Solution to 1A:

Portfolio B is the most appropriate choice. Portfolio B is the factor portfolio for business cycle risk because it has a sensitivity of 1 to business cycle risk and a sensitivity of 0 to all other risk factors. Portfolio B is thus efficient for placing a pure bet on an increase in real business activity.

Solution to 1B:

The manager would take a long position in Portfolio B to place a bet on an increase in real business activity.

Solution to 2A:

Portfolio D is the appropriate choice. Portfolio D is the factor portfolio for time horizon risk because it has a sensitivity of 1 to time horizon risk and a sensitivity of 0 to all other risk factors. Portfolio D is thus efficient for hedging an existing positive exposure to time horizon risk.

Solution to 2B:

The manager would take a short position in Portfolio D to hedge the positive exposure to time horizon risk.

The next section illustrates the procedure for constructing a portfolio with a desired configuration of factor sensitivities.

4.6.4 *Creating a Tracking Portfolio*

In the previous section, we discussed the use of multifactor models to speculate on or hedge a specific factor risk. Perhaps even more commonly, portfolio managers use multifactor models to control the risk of portfolios relative to their benchmarks. For example, in a risk-controlled active or enhanced index strategy, the portfolio manager may attempt to earn a small incremental return relative to her benchmark while controlling risk by matching the factor sensitivities of her portfolio to her benchmark. That portfolio would be an example of a tracking portfolio. A **tracking portfolio** is a portfolio having factor sensitivities that are matched to those of a benchmark or other portfolio.

The technique of constructing a portfolio with a target set of factor sensitivities involves the solution of a system of equations using algebra.

- Count the number of constraints. Each target value of beta represents a constraint on the portfolio, and another constraint is that the weights of the investments in the portfolio must sum to one. As *many investments are needed as there are constraints.*
- Set up an equation for the weights of the portfolio's investments reflecting each constraint on the portfolio. We have an equation stating that the portfolio weights sum to 1. We have an equation for each target factor sensitivity; on the left-hand side of the equal sign, we have a weighted average of the factor sensitivities of the investments to the factor, and on the right-hand side of the equal sign we have the target factor sensitivity.
- Solve the system of equations for the weights of the investments in the portfolio.

In Example 23, we illustrate how a tracking portfolio can be created.

EXAMPLE 23

Creating a Tracking Portfolio

Suppose that a pension plan sponsor wants to be fully invested in U.S. common stocks. The plan sponsor has specified an equity benchmark for a portfolio manager, who has decided to create a tracking portfolio for the benchmark. For the sake of using familiar data, let us continue with the three portfolios J, K, and L, as well as the same two-factor model from Example 13.

The portfolio manager determines that the benchmark has a sensitivity of 1.3 to the surprise in inflation and a sensitivity of 1.975 to the surprise in GDP. There are three constraints. One constraint is that portfolio weights sum to 1, a second is that the weighted sum of sensitivities to the inflation factor equals 1.3 (to match the benchmark), and a third is that the weighted sum of sensitivities to the GDP factor equals 1.975 (to match the benchmark). Thus we need three investments to form the portfolio, which we take to be Portfolios J, K, and L. We repeat Table 14 below.

Table 14 Sample Portfolios for a Two-Factor Model (Repeated)

Portfolio	Expected Return	Sensitivity to Inflation Factor	Sensitivity to GDP Factor
J	0.14	1.0	1.5
K	0.12	0.5	1.0
L	0.11	1.3	1.1

As mentioned, we need three equations to determine the portfolio weights w_J, w_K, and w_L in the tracking portfolio.

- *Equation 1.* This equation states that portfolio weights must sum to 1.

$$w_J + w_K + w_L = 1$$

- *Equation 2.* The second equation states that the weighted average of the sensitivities of J, K, and L to the surprise in inflation must equal the benchmark's sensitivity to the surprise in inflation, 1.3. This requirement ensures that the tracking portfolio has the same inflation risk as the benchmark.

$$1.0w_J + 0.5w_K + 1.3w_L = 1.3$$

- *Equation 3.* The third equation states that the weighted average of the sensitivities of J, K, and L to the surprise in GDP must equal the benchmark's sensitivity to the surprise in GDP, 1.975. This requirement ensures that the tracking portfolio has the same GDP risk as the benchmark.

$$1.5w_J + 1.0w_K + 1.1w_L = 1.975$$

We can solve for the weights as follows. From Equation 1, $w_L = (1 - w_J - w_K)$. We substitute this result in the other two equations to find

$$1.0w_J + 0.5w_K + 1.3(1 - w_J - w_K) = 1.3, \text{ simplifying to } w_K = -0.375w_J$$

and

$$1.5w_J + 1.0w_K + 1.1(1 - w_J - w_K) = 1.975,\text{ simplifying to}$$

$$0.4w_J - 0.1w_K = 0.875$$

We next substitute $w_K = -0.375w_J$ into $0.4w_J - 0.1w_K = 0.875$, obtaining $0.4w_J - 0.1(-0.375w_J) = 0.875$ or $0.4w_J + 0.0375w_J = 0.875$, so $w_J = 2$.

Using $w_K = -0.375w_J$ obtained earlier, $w_K = -0.375\times 2 = -0.75$. Finally, from $w_L = (1 - w_J - w_K) = [1 - 2 - (-0.75)] = -0.25$. To summarize,

$$w_J = 0.2$$

$$w_K = -0.75$$

$$w_L = -0.25$$

The tracking has an expected return of $0.14w_J + 0.12w_K + 0.11w_L = 0.14(2) + (0.12)(-0.75) + 0.11(-0.25) = 0.28 - 0.09 - 0.0275 = 0.1625$. In Example 13 using the same inputs, we calculated the APT model as $E(R_p) = 0.07 - 0.02\beta_{p,1} + 0.06\beta_{p,2}$. For the tracking portfolio, $\beta_{p,1} = 1.3$ and $\beta_{p,2} = 1.975$. As $E(R_p) = 0.07 - 0.02(1.3) + 0.06(1.975) = 0.1625$, we have confirmed the expected return calculation.

4.7 Concluding Remarks

In earlier sections, we showed how models with multiple factors can help portfolio managers solve practical tasks in measuring and controlling risk. We now draw contrasts between the CAPM and the APT, providing additional insight into why some risks may be priced and how, as a result, the portfolio implications of a multifactor world differ from those of the world described by the CAPM. An investor may be able to make better portfolio decisions with a multifactor model than with a single-factor model.

The CAPM provides investors with useful and influential concepts for thinking about investments. Considerable evidence has accumulated, however, that shows that the CAPM provides an incomplete description of risk.[78] What is the portfolio advice of CAPM, and how can we improve on it when more than one source of systematic risk drives asset returns? An investor who believes that the CAPM explains asset returns would hold a portfolio consisting only of the risk-free asset and the market portfolio of risky assets. If the investor had a high tolerance for risk, she would put a greater proportion in the market portfolio. But to the extent the investor held risky assets, she would hold them in amounts proportional to their market-value weights, without consideration for any other dimension of risk. In reality, of course, not everyone holds the same portfolio of risky assets. Practically speaking, this CAPM-oriented investor might hold a money market fund and a portfolio indexed on a broad market index.[79]

With more than one source of systematic risk, the average investor might still want to hold a broadly based portfolio and the risk-free asset. Other investors, however, may find it appropriate to tilt away from an index fund after considering dimensions of risk ignored by the CAPM. To make this argument, let us explore why, for example, the business cycle is a source of systematic risk, as in the Burmeister et al. model discussed earlier. There is an economic intuition for why this risk is systematic:[80] Most investors hold jobs and are thus sensitive to recessions. Suppose, for example,

78 See Bodie, Kane, and Marcus (2001) for an introduction to the empirical evidence.

79 Passive management is a distinct issue from holding a single portfolio. There are efficient-markets arguments for holding indexed investments that are separate from the CAPM. An index fund is reasonable for this investor, however.

80 This discussion follows Cochrane (1999a) and (1999b).

that a working investor faces the risk of a recession. If this investor compared two stocks with the same CAPM beta, given his concern about recession risk, he would accept a lower return from the countercyclical stock and require a risk premium on the procyclical one. In contrast, an investor with independent wealth and no job-loss concerns would be willing to accept the recession risk.

If the average investor holding a job bids up the price of the countercyclical stocks, then recession risk will be priced. In addition, procyclical stocks would have lower prices than if the recession factor were not priced. Investors can thus, as Cochrane (1999a) notes, "earn a substantial premium for holding dimensions of risk unrelated to market movements."

This view of risk has portfolio implications. The average investor is exposed to and negatively affected by cyclical risk, which is a priced factor. (Risks that do not affect the average investor should not be priced.) Investors who hold jobs (and thus receive labor income) want lower cyclical risk and create a cyclical risk premium, whereas investors without labor income will accept more cyclical risk to capture a premium for a risk that they do not care about. As a result, an investor who faces lower-than-average recession risk optimally tilts towards greater-than-average exposure to the business cycle factor, all else equal.

In summary, investors should know which priced risks they face and analyze the extent of their exposure. Compared with single-factor models, multifactor models offer a rich context for investors to search for ways to improve portfolio selection.

SUMMARY

In this reading, we have presented a set of concepts, models, and tools that are key ingredients to quantitative portfolio management today.

Mean–Variance Analysis

- Mean–variance analysis is a part of modern portfolio theory that deals with the trade-offs between risk, as represented by variance or standard deviation of return, and expected return.
- Mean–variance analysis assumes the following:
  - Investors are risk averse.
  - Assets' expected returns, variances of returns, and covariances of returns are known.
  - Investors need to know only the expected returns, the variances of returns, and covariances between returns in order to determine which portfolios are optimal.
  - There are no transaction costs or taxes.
- For any portfolio composed of two assets, the expected return to the portfolio, $E(R_p)$, is $E(R_p) = w_1E(R_1) + w_2E(R_2)$, where $E(R_1)$ is the expected return to Asset 1 and $E(R_2)$ is the expected return to Asset 2. In general, the expected return on a portfolio is a weighted average of the expected returns on the individual assets, where the weight applied to each asset's return is the fraction of the portfolio invested in that asset.
- The variance of return on a two-asset portfolio and a three-asset portfolio are, respectively,

$$\sigma_p^2 = w_1^2\sigma_1^2 + w_2^2\sigma_2^2 + 2w_1w_2\rho_{1,2}\sigma_1\sigma_2$$

and

$$\sigma_p^2 = w_1^2\sigma_1^2 + w_2^2\sigma_2^2 + w_3^2\sigma_3^2 + 2w_1w_2\rho_{1,2}\sigma_1\sigma_2 + 2w_1w_3\rho_{1,3}\sigma_1\sigma_3 + 2w_2w_3\rho_{2,3}\sigma_2\sigma_3$$

where

σ_i = the standard deviation of return on asset i, i = 1, 2, 3
$\rho_{i,j}$ = the correlation between the returns on asset i and asset j

- In mean–variance analysis, the investment attributes of individual assets and portfolios are represented by points in a figure having standard deviation or variance of return as the x-axis and expected return as the y-axis.
- The minimum-variance frontier graphs the smallest variance of return attainable for each level of expected return.
- The global minimum-variance portfolio is the portfolio of risky assets having the minimum variance.
- An efficient portfolio is one providing the maximum expected return for a given level of variance or standard deviation of return.
- The efficient frontier represents all combinations of mean return and variance or standard deviation of return that can be attained by holding efficient portfolios (portfolios giving maximum expected return for their levels of standard deviation of return). The efficient frontier is the upper portion of the minimum-variance frontier (the global minimum-variance portfolio and points above).
- According to mean–variance analysis, investors optimally select a portfolio from portfolios that lie on the efficient frontier. By restricting attention to the efficient portfolios, the investor's portfolio selection task is greatly simplified.
- When the correlation between the returns on two assets is less than +1, the potential exists for diversification benefits. Diversification benefits occur when portfolio standard deviation of return can be reduced through diversification without decreasing expected return.
- For the two-asset case, the potential benefits from diversifying increase as we lower the correlation between the two portfolios towards −1, holding all else constant. For a correlation of −1, a portfolio of the two assets exists that eliminates risk. As we lower correlation, the efficient frontier improves in the sense of offering a higher expected return for a given feasible level of standard deviation of return, holding all other values constant.
- In general, to determine the minimum-variance frontier for a set of n assets, we first determine the minimum expected return and the maximum expected return among all the expected returns offered by the n assets. We then choose the individual asset weights that minimize portfolio variance of return for different levels of expected return, subject to the constraint that the individual asset weights sum to 1.
- The introduction of a risk-free asset into the portfolio selection problem results in the efficient frontier having a linear portion that is tangent to the efficient frontier defined using only risky assets. This line is called the capital allocation line (CAL). Portfolios on the CAL represent combinations of the risk-free asset and the tangency portfolio.

- When all investors share identical expectations about mean returns, variance of returns, and correlations, the CAL for all investors is the same and is known as the capital market line (CML). The tangency portfolio is the market portfolio of risky assets held in market value weights. The implication of the CML for portfolio choice is that all mean–variance investors, whatever their risk tolerance, can satisfy their investment needs using the risk-free asset and a single risky portfolio, the market portfolio of all risky assets held in market value weights.
- The assumptions of the capital asset pricing model (CAPM) are that investors have identical views about the expected returns, the variances, and the covariances of assets, and only need to know these characteristics to determine which portfolios are optimal for them. Furthermore, investors can buy and sell assets in any quantity without affecting price, and all assets are marketable (can be traded); they can borrow and lend at the risk-free rate without limit and can sell short any asset in any quantity; and they pay no taxes on returns or transaction costs on trades.
- The CAPM equation describes the expected return on an asset or portfolio (whether efficient or not) as a linear function of its beta (a measure of the sensitivity of an asset's returns to the return on the market portfolio). The CAPM equation is

  $$E(R_i) = R_F + \beta_i\left[E(R_M) - R_F\right]$$

  where

  $E(R_i)$ = the expected return on asset i
  R_F = the risk-free rate of return
  $E(R_M)$ = the expected return on the market portfolio
  $\beta_i = \text{Cov}(R_i, R_M) / \sigma_M^2$, called beta

- The CAPM implies that the expected excess rate of return on an asset is directly proportional to its covariance with the market return.
- The Markowitz decision rule states that an investor should prefer Investment A to Investment B if A's expected return is higher than that of B with no more risk than B, or if A has the same expected return as B with strictly less risk.
- Adding a new asset to a portfolio is optimal if the asset's Sharpe ratio is greater than the product (Sharpe ratio of existing portfolio p) × (Correlation of new investment with p).
- To trace out the minimum-variance frontier with n assets, we need n expected returns, n variances, and $n(n - 1)/2$ covariances. If we use historical values as inputs of mean–variance optimization, then for realistic values of n, the number of parameters that needs to be estimated is very large, owing mostly to the number of covariances needed. Historical estimates are also critically subject to estimation error.
- The market model explains the return on a risky asset as a linear regression with the return on the market as the independent variable.
- According to the market model,

  $$\text{Var}(R_i) = \beta_i^2\sigma_M^2 + \sigma_{\varepsilon_i}^2 \text{ and } \text{Cov}(R_i, R_j) = \beta_i\beta_j\sigma_M^2$$

- We can use the expression for covariance from the market model to greatly simplify the calculational task of estimating the covariances needed to trace out the minimum-variance frontier.

- Using the parameters of the market model, we can express the correlation between the returns on two assets as

$$\text{Corr}(R_1, R_2) = \frac{\beta_1\beta_2\sigma_M^2}{\left(\beta_1^2\sigma_M^2 + \sigma_{\varepsilon_1}^2\right)^{1/2}\left(\beta_2^2\sigma_M^2 + \sigma_{\varepsilon_2}^2\right)^{1/2}}$$

- Adjusted beta is a historical beta adjusted to reflect the tendency of beta to be mean reverting. For example, one common adjustment is

$$\text{Adjusted beta} = 0.33 + 0.67 \text{ Historical beta}$$

  An adjusted beta tends to predict future beta better than historical beta does.
- A problem with standard mean–variance optimization is that small changes in inputs frequently lead to large changes in the weights of portfolios that appear on the minimum-variance frontier. This is the problem of instability. The problem of instability is practically important because the inputs to mean-variance optimization are often based on sample statistics, which are subject to random variation. Relatedly, the minimum-variance frontier is not stable over time. Besides the estimation error in means, variances, and covariance, shifts in the distribution of asset returns between sample time periods can give rise to this time instability of the minimum-variance frontier.

Multifactor Models

- Multifactor models describe the return on an asset in terms of the risk of the asset with respect to a set of factors. Such models generally include systematic factors, which explain the average returns of a large number of risky assets. Such factors represent priced risk, risk which investors require an additional return for bearing.
- Multifactor models are categorized as macroeconomic factor models, fundamental factor models, and statistical factor models, according to the type of factor used.
- In macroeconomic factor models, the factors are surprises in macroeconomic variables that significantly explain equity returns. Surprise is defined as actual minus forecasted value and has an expected value of zero. The factors can be understood as affecting either the expected future cash flows of companies or the interest rate used to discount these cash flows back to the present.
- In fundamental factor models, the factors are attributes of stocks or companies that are important in explaining cross-sectional differences in stock prices. Among the fundamental factors are book-value-to-price ratio, market capitalization, price-earnings ratio, and financial leverage.
- In statistical factor models, statistical methods are applied to a set of historical returns to determine portfolios that explain historical returns in one of two senses. In factor analysis models, the factors are the portfolios that best explain (reproduce) historical return covariances. In principal-components models, the factors are portfolios that best explain (reproduce) the historical return variances.
- Arbitrage pricing theory (APT) describes the expected return on an asset (or portfolio) as a linear function of the risk of the asset with respect to a set of factors. Like the CAPM, the APT describes a financial market equilibrium, but the APT makes less-strong assumptions.

- The major assumptions of the APT are as follows:
  - Asset returns are described by a factor model.
  - There are many assets, so asset-specific risk can be eliminated.
  - Assets are priced so that there are no arbitrage opportunities.
- APT explains the intercept term in the equation of a multifactor model, in which the factors are surprises, as an expected return.
- In contrast to macroeconomic factor models, in fundamental models the factors are stated as returns rather than surprises. In fundamental factor models, we generally specify the factor sensitivities (attributes) first and then estimate the factor returns through regressions, in contrast to macroeconomic factor models, in which we first develop the factor (surprise) series and then estimate the factor sensitivities through regressions. The factors of most fundamental factor models may be classified as company fundamental factors, company share-related factors, or macroeconomic factors.
- Active return is return in excess of the return on the benchmark.
- Active risk is the standard deviation of active returns. Active risk is also called tracking risk. Active risk squared can be decomposed as the sum of active factor risk and active specific risk.
- The information ratio (IR) is mean active return divided by active risk (tracking risk). The IR measures the increment in mean active return per unit of active risk.
- Factor *j*'s marginal contribution to active risk squared is

$$\text{FMCAR}_j = \frac{b_j^a \sum_{i=1}^{K} b_j^a \text{Cov}(F_j, F_i)}{\text{Active risk squared}}$$

  where b_j^a is the portfolio's active exposure to factor *j*. The numerator is the active factor risk for factor *j*. The concept explains how factor tilts away from the benchmark explain a portfolio's tracking risk.
- A factor portfolio is a portfolio with unit sensitivity to a factor and zero sensitivity to other factors. A tracking portfolio is a portfolio with factor sensitivities that match those of a benchmark portfolio or other portfolio. Factor and tracking portfolios can be constructed using as many assets as there are constraints on the portfolio.
- Multifactor models permit a nuanced view of risk that may contrast with a single-factor perspective. From a CAPM perspective, investors should allocate their money between the risk-free asset and a broad-based index fund. With multiple sources of systematic risk, when an investor's factor risk exposures to other sources of income and risk aversion differ from the average investor's, a tilt away from an indexed investment may be optimal.

PRACTICE PROBLEMS

Mean–Variance Analysis

1 Given the large-cap stock index and the government bond index data in the following table, calculate the expected mean return and standard deviation of return for a portfolio 75 percent invested in the stock index and 25 percent invested in the bond index.

Assumed Returns, Variances, and Correlations

	Large-Cap Stock Index	Government Bond Index
Expected return	15%	5%
Variance	225	100
Standard deviation	15%	10%
Correlation	0.5	

For Problems 2 and 3, assume the following:

- Each stock has the same variance of return, denoted σ^2.
- The correlation between all pairs of stocks is the same, ρ.
- Stocks are equally weighted.

2 Suppose 0.3 is the common correlation of returns between any two stocks in a portfolio containing 100 stocks. Also, suppose the average variance of stocks in the portfolio is 625 (corresponding to a standard deviation of return of 25 percent). Calculate the portfolio standard deviation of return.

3 Suppose the average variance of return of all stocks in a portfolio is 625 and the correlation between the returns of any two stocks is 0.3. Calculate the variance of return of an equally weighted portfolio of 24 stocks. Then state that variance as a percent of the portfolio variance achievable given an unlimited number of stocks, holding stock variance and correlation constant.

4 Suppose a risk-free asset has a 5 percent return and a second asset has an expected return of 13 percent with a standard deviation of 23 percent. Calculate the expected portfolio return and standard deviation of a portfolio consisting 10 percent of the risk-free asset and 90 percent of the second asset.

5 Suppose you have a \$100,000 investment in an S&P 500 index fund. You then replace 10 percent of your investment in the index fund with an investment in a stock having a beta of 2 with respect to the index. Why is it impossible for your new portfolio, consisting of the index fund and the stock, to have a lower standard deviation of return than the original portfolio?

6 Suppose that the risk-free rate is 6 percent and the expected return on the investor's tangency portfolio is 14 percent, with a standard deviation of 24 percent.

A Calculate the investor's expected risk premium per unit of risk.

B Calculate the portfolio's expected return if the portfolio's standard deviation of return is 20 percent.

7 Eduardo Martinez is evaluating the following investments:

Portfolio A: $E(R_A)$ = 12 percent, $\sigma(R_A) = 15$

Portfolio B: $E(R_B)$ = 10 percent, $\sigma(R_B) = 8$

Portfolio C: $E(R_C)$ = 10 percent, $\sigma(R_C) = 9$

A Explain the choice among Portfolios A, B, and C using the Markowitz decision rule.

B Explain the choice among Portfolios A, B, and C assuming that borrowing and lending at a risk-free rate of R_F = 2 percent is possible.

8 Gita Subramaniam is the chief investment officer of an Indian pension scheme invested in Indian equities, Indian government bonds, and U.S. equities. Her current portfolio has a Sharpe ratio of 0.15, and she is considering adding U.S. bonds to this portfolio. The predicted Sharpe ratio of U.S. bonds is 0.10, and their predicted correlation with the existing portfolio is 0.20. Explain whether Subramaniam should add U.S. bonds to the pension fund.

9 Suppose that the risk-free rate is 5 percent and the expected return on the market portfolio of risky assets is 13 percent. An investor with $1 million to invest wants to achieve a 17 percent rate of return on a portfolio combining a risk-free asset and the market portfolio of risky assets. Calculate how much this investor would need to borrow at the risk-free rate in order to establish this target expected return.

10 Two assets have betas of 1.5 and 1.2, respectively. The residual standard deviation from the market model is 2 for the first asset and 4 for the second. The market standard deviation is 8. What is the correlation between the two assets?

11 Suppose that the best predictor for a stock's future beta is determined to be Expected beta = 0.33 + 0.67 (Historical beta). The historical beta is calculated as 1.2. The risk-free rate is 5 percent, and the market risk premium is 8.5 percent. Calculate the expected return on the stock using expected (adjusted) beta in the CAPM.

Multifactor Models

12 Suppose that the expected return on the stock in the following table is 11 percent. Using a two-factor model, calculate the stock's return if the company-specific surprise for the year is 3 percent.

Variable	Actual Value (%)	Expected Value (%)	Stock's Factor Sensitivity
Change in interest rate	2.0	0.0	−1.5
Growth in GDP	1.0	4.0	2.0

13 A portfolio manager plans to create a portfolio from two stocks, Manumatic (MANM) and Nextech (NXT). The following equations describe the returns for those stocks:

$$R_{MANM} = 0.09 - 1F_{INFL} + 1F_{GDP} + \varepsilon_{MANM}$$
$$R_{NXT} = 0.12 + 2F_{INFL} + 4F_{GDP} + \varepsilon_{NXT}$$

You form a portfolio with market value weights of 50 percent Manumatic and 50 percent Nextech. Calculate the sensitivity of the portfolio to a 1 percent surprise in inflation.

14 Suppose we have the three portfolios with factor sensitivities given in the table below. Using the information in the following table, create an arbitrage portfolio using a short position in A and B and a long position in C. Calculate the expected cash flow on the arbitrage portfolio for a $10,000 investment in C.

Expected Returns and Factor Sensitivities (One-Factor Model)

Portfolio	Expected Return	Factor Sensitivity
A	0.1500	2.00
B	0.0700	0.40
C	0.0800	0.45

15 Suppose that an institution holds Portfolio K. The institution wants to use Portfolio L to hedge its exposure to inflation. Specifically, it wants to combine K and L to reduce its inflation exposure to 0. Portfolios K and L are well diversified, so the manager can ignore the risk of individual assets and assume that the only source of uncertainty in the portfolio is the surprises in the two factors. The returns to the two portfolios are

$$R_K = 0.12 + 0.5F_{INFL} + 1.0F_{GDP}$$
$$R_L = 0.11 + 1.5F_{INFL} + 2.5F_{GDP}$$

Calculate the weights that a manager should have on K and L to achieve this goal.

16 Portfolio A has an expected return of 10.25 percent and a factor sensitivity of 0.5. Portfolio B has an expected return of 16.2 percent and a factor sensitivity of 1.2. The risk-free rate is 6 percent, and there is one factor. Determine the factor's price of risk.

17 A portfolio manager uses the multifactor model shown in the following table:

Risk Factor	Portfolio A Factor Sensitivity	Portfolio B Factor Sensitivity	S&P 500 Factor Sensitivity	Portfolio A Excess Factor Sensitivity
Confidence risk	0.27	0.27	0.27	0.00
Time horizon risk	0.56	0.56	0.56	0.00
Inflation risk	−0.12	−0.45	−0.37	0.25
Business cycle risk	2.25	1.00	1.71	0.54
Market timing risk	1.00	1.00	1.00	0.00

The S&P 500 is the benchmark Portfolios A and B. Calculate the weights the manager would put on Portfolios A and B to have zero excess business cycle factor sensitivity (relative to the business cycle sensitivity of the S&P 500). Then calculate the inflation factor sensitivity of the resulting portfolio.

18 A wealthy investor has no other source of income beyond her investments. Her investment advisor recommends that she tilt her portfolio to cyclical stocks and high-yield bonds because the average investor holds a job and is recession sensitive. Explain the advisor's advice.

Questions 19 through 26 relate to the STAR Foundation.[1]

Amy White is a portfolio manager at Andes Management. A new client, the STAR Foundation, has been assigned to White. The STAR Foundation investment portfolio is valued at $10 million. The Foundation's current asset allocation is $6 million in government bonds and $4 million in large-cap stocks. White has been asked to evaluate the existing portfolio and consider investment alternatives, including expanding the number of asset classes for STAR Foundation. The research department at Andes Management estimates the expected return for the market portfolio as 8.4%, and provides White with risk and return characteristics for various asset classes in Exhibit 1 and Exhibit 2.

White believes the adjusted beta, calculated as β_{adj} = 0.33 + 0.67 (historical beta), is a better predictor of a stock's future beta.

Exhibit 1 Expected Asset Risks & Returns

	Government Bonds	Large-Cap. Stocks	Small-Cap. Stocks	Risk-Free Asset
Expected return	5.00%	10.00%	15.00%	2.00%
Variance	100	400	625	
Standard deviation	10.00%	20.00%	25.00%	
Historical Beta		1.25	2.03	

1 This item set was developed by Michael Whitehurst, CFA (San Diego, CA, USA).

Exhibit 2 Asset Correlation Matrix

	Government Bonds	Large-Cap. Stocks	Small-Cap. Stocks	Risk-Free Asset
to Govt. Bonds	1.00	0.05	-0.05	0.00
to Large-Cap Stocks	0.05	1.00	0.80	0.00
to Small-Cap Stocks	-0.05	0.80	1.00	0.00
to Risk-Free Asset	0.00	0.00	0.00	1.00

White discusses her findings with her colleagues at Andes Management and asks for recommendations to improve the available tradeoffs between risk and return for the Foundation's portfolio. White receives a recommendation from Mark Adams, senior portfolio manager.

Specifically, Adams states:

> "I recommend reducing the Foundation portfolio's allocation to large-cap stocks, increasing exposure to government bonds, and adding some exposure to small-cap stocks. Specifically, rebalance the current portfolio to have \$2 million invested in small-cap stocks, \$1 million in large-cap stocks, and \$7 million invested in government bonds."

Sarah Trip, research analyst, provides White with the data in Exhibit 3 for two funds managed internally by Andes Management. Fund A is a large-cap stock fund, and Fund B is a small-cap stock fund.

Exhibit 3 Expected Returns and Sensitivity Factors

Fund	Expected Return	Sensitivity to Inflation Factor	Sensitivity to GDP Factor
A	10.0%	1.2	1.0
B	15.0%	0.5	2.5

Note: The expected value of all regression error terms is assumed to be zero.

White also receives a recommendation from Trip. Specifically, Trip states:

> "I recommend selling all the large-cap stocks currently held in the Foundation's portfolio and reinvesting \$1,333,333 into Fund A, and \$2,666,667 into Fund B."

White is forecasting a surprise in inflation that is 5% higher than expected, and a surprise in GDP growth that is 3% lower than expected. White believes that the returns of Fund A and Fund B will be impacted by these surprises in inflation and GDP growth.

19 Based upon Exhibit 1 and the current asset allocation, the expected return of the Foundation's investment portfolio is *closest* to:

A 7.0%.

B 7.5%.

C 8.0%.

20 Based upon Exhibits 1 and 2, and the current asset allocation, the expected standard deviation of the Foundation's investment portfolio is *closest* to:

A 10.24%.

B 12.16%.

C 14.99%.

21 Based upon Exhibit 1, the asset allocation recommended by Adams would *most likely* cause the Foundation's investment portfolio's expected return to:

A increase.

B decrease.

C remain unchanged.

22 Based upon Exhibits 1 and 2, the asset allocation recommended by Adams would *most likely* cause the Foundation's investment portfolio's standard deviation to:

A increase.

B decrease.

C remain the same.

23 Based upon Exhibit 1, the expected return for large-cap stocks using the adjusted beta in the capital asset pricing model (CAPM) *is closest to:*

A 9.5%.

B 10.0%.

C 11.8%.

24 Based upon Exhibit 1, the asset class with the *highest* Sharpe ratio is:

A large-cap stocks.

B small-cap stocks.

C government bonds.

25 Based upon Exhibit 3 and assuming White implements Trip's recommendation, the total return for the portion of the Foundation's portfolio invested in Fund A and Fund B, given White's forecast, is *closest* to:

A 11.0%

B 13.3%.

C 23.0%

26 Assuming White implements Trip's recommendation, for the portion of the Foundation's portfolio invested in Fund A and Fund B, the *most appropriate* allocation to Fund A and Fund B to fully hedge GDP risk is to short:

A \$0.40 of Fund B for every \$1.40 invested in Fund A.

B \$0.67 of Fund B for every \$1.67 invested in Fund A.

C \$0.71 of Fund B for every \$1.71 invested in Fund A.

SOLUTIONS

1 The expected return is $0.75E$(return on stocks) + $0.25E$(return on bonds)

$$= 0.75(15) + 0.25(5)$$
$$= 12.5 \text{ percent}$$

The standard deviation is

$$\sigma = \left[w_{\text{stocks}}^2\sigma_{\text{stocks}}^2 + w_{\text{bonds}}^2\sigma_{\text{bonds}}^2 + 2w_{\text{stocks}}w_{\text{bonds}}\right.$$
$$\left.\text{Corr}\left(R_{\text{stocks}}, R_{\text{bonds}}\right)\sigma_{\text{stocks}}\sigma_{\text{bonds}}\right]^{1/2}$$
$$= \left[0.75^2(225) + 0.25^2(100) + 2(0.75)(0.25)(0.5)(15)(10)\right]^{1/2}$$
$$= (126.5625 + 6.25 + 28.125)^{1/2}$$
$$= (160.9375)^{1/2}$$
$$= 12.69\%$$

2 Use the expression

$$\sigma_p^2 = \sigma^2\left(\frac{1-\rho}{n} + \rho\right)$$

The square root of this expression is standard deviation. With variance equal to 625 and correlation equal to 0.3,

$$\sigma_p = \sqrt{625\left(\frac{1-0.3}{100} + 0.3\right)}$$
$$= 13.85\%$$

3 Find portfolio variance using the following expression

$$\sigma_p^2 = \sigma^2\left(\frac{1-\rho}{n} + \rho\right)$$
$$\sigma_p^2 = 625\left[(1-0.3)/24 + 0.3\right] = 205.73$$

With 24 stocks, variance of return is 205.73 (equivalent to a standard deviation of 14.34 percent). With an unlimited number of securities, the first term in square brackets is 0 and the smallest variance is achieved:

$$\sigma_{\min}^2 = \sigma^2\rho = 625(0.30) = 187.5$$

This result is equivalent to a standard deviation of 13.69 percent. The ratio of the variance of the 24-stock portfolio to the portfolio with an unlimited number of securities is

$$\frac{\sigma_p^2}{\sigma_{\min}^2} = \frac{205.73}{187.5} = 1.097$$

The variance of the 24-stock portfolio is approximately 110 percent of the variance of the portfolio with an unlimited number of securities.

4 Define

R_p = return on the portfolio

R_1 = return on the risk-free asset

R_2 = return on the risky asset

w_1 = fraction of the portfolio invested in the risk-free asset

w_2 = fraction of the portfolio invested in the risky asset

Then the expected return on the portfolio is

$$E(R_p) = w_1 E(R_1) + w_2 E(R_2)(R_2)$$
$$= 0.10(5\%) + 0.9(13\%) = 0.5 + 11.7 = 12.2\%$$

To calculate standard deviation of return, we calculate variance of return and take the square root of variance:

$$\sigma^2(R_p) = w_1^2\sigma^2(R_1) + w_2^2\sigma^2(R_2) + 2w_1w_2\text{Cov}(R_1, R_2)$$
$$= 0.1^2(0^2) + 0.9^2(23^2) + 2(0.1)(0.9)(0)$$
$$= 0.9^2(23^2)$$
$$= 428.49$$

Thus the portfolio standard deviation of return is $\sigma(R_p) = (428.49)^{1/2}$ = 20.7 percent.

5 According to the market model, $\text{Var}(R_p) = \beta_p^2\sigma_M^2 + \sigma_{\varepsilon_p}^2$. The S&P 500 index fund should have a beta of 1 with respect to the S&P 500. By moving 10 percent of invested funds from the index fund to a security with a beta of 2, we necessarily will increase $\beta_p^2\sigma_M^2$ (systematic risk) for the portfolio. An individual asset will also have higher nonsystematic risk (residual risk) than the highly diversified index fund, so $\sigma_{\varepsilon_p}^2$ will increase as well. Thus the new portfolio cannot have a lower standard deviation of return than the old portfolio.

6 **A** With R_T the return on the tangency portfolio and R_F the risk-free rate, Expected risk premium per unit of risk $= \dfrac{E(R_T) - R_F}{\sigma(R_T)} = \dfrac{14 - 6}{24} = 0.33$

B First, we find the weight w of the tangency portfolio in the investor's portfolio using the expression $\sigma(R_p) = w\sigma(R_T)$,

so

$$w = (20/24) = 0.8333$$

Then

$$E(R_p) = wE(R_T) + (1 - w)R_F = 0.833333(14\%) + 0.166667(6\%)$$
$$= 12.67\%$$

7 **A** According to the Markowitz decision rule, Martínez should prefer Portfolio B to Portfolio C because B has the same expected return as C with lower standard deviation of return than C. Thus he can eliminate C from consideration as a stand-alone portfolio. The Markowitz decision rule is inconclusive concerning the choice between A and B, however, because although A has higher mean return, it also has higher standard deviation of return.

B With a risk-free asset, we can evaluate portfolios using the Sharpe ratio (the ratio of mean return in excess of the risk-free rate divided by standard deviation of return). The Sharpe ratios are

Portfolio A: $(12 - 2)/15 = 0.67$

Portfolio B: $(10 - 2)/8 = 1.00$

Portfolio C: $(10 - 2)/9 = 0.89$

With risk-free borrowing and lending possible, Martínez will choose Portfolio B because it has the highest Sharpe ratio.

8 The quantity (Sharpe ratio of existing portfolio) × (Correlation of U.S. bonds with existing portfolio) = 0.15(0.20) = 0.03. Because U.S. bonds' predicted Sharpe ratio of 0.10 exceeds 0.03, it is optimal to add them to the existing portfolio.

9 With R_M the return on the market portfolio, and all the other terms as defined in previous answers, we have

$$E(R_p) = wE(R_M) + (1 - w)R_F$$
$$17 = 13w + 5(1 - w) = 8w + 5$$
$$12 = 8w$$
$$w = 1.5$$

Thus 1 – 1.5 = –0.5 of initial wealth goes into the risk-free asset. The negative sign indicates borrowing: –0.5($1 million) = –$500,000, so the investor borrows $500,000.

10 We start from the definition of correlation (first line below). In the numerator, we substitute for covariance using Equation 14; in the denominator we use Equation 13 to substitute for the standard deviations of return.

$$\begin{aligned}\text{Corr}(R_1,R_2) &= \frac{\text{Cov}(R_1,R_2)}{\sigma_1\sigma_2}\\ &= \frac{\beta_1\beta_2\sigma_M^2}{\sqrt{\beta_1^2\sigma_M^2 + \sigma_{\epsilon_1}^2}\sqrt{\beta_2^2\sigma_M^2 + \sigma_{\epsilon_2}^2}}\\ &= \frac{1.5(1.2)(8)^2}{\sqrt{1.5^2(8^2) + 2^2}\sqrt{1.2^2(8^2) + 4^2}}\\ &= 0.91\end{aligned}$$

11

$$\begin{aligned}\beta_{adj} &= 0.33 + (0.67)(1.2)\\ &= 0.33 + 0.80\\ &= 1.13\end{aligned}$$

$$\begin{aligned}E(R_p) = E(R_i) &= R_F + \beta_i[E(R_M) - R_F]\\ &= 5\% + 1.13(8.5\%)\\ &= 14.6\%\end{aligned}$$

12 The surprise in a factor equals actual value minus expected value. For the interest rate factor, the surprise was 2 percent; for the GDP factor, the surprise was – 3 percent.

$$R = \text{Expected return} - 1.5(\text{Interest rate surprise}) + 2(\text{GDP surprise}) + \text{Company-specific surprise}$$
$$= 11\% - 1.5(2\%) + 2(-3\%) + 3\%$$
$$= 5\%$$

13 Portfolio inflation sensitivity is the weight on Manumatic stock multiplied by its inflation sensitivity, plus the weight on Nextech stock multiplied by its inflation sensitivity: 0.5(−1) + 0.5(2) = 0.5. So a 1 percent interest rate surprise increase in inflation is expected to produce a 50 basis point increase in the portfolio's return.

14 The arbitrage portfolio must have zero sensitivity to the factor. We first need to find the proportions of A and B in short position that combine to produce a factor sensitivity equal to 0.45, the factor sensitivity of C, which we will hold long. Using *w* as the weight on A in the short position,

$$2w + 0.4(1 - w) = 0.45$$
$$2w + 0.4 - 0.4w = 0.45$$
$$1.6w = 0.05$$
$$w = 0.05/1.6 = 0.03125$$

Hence, the weights on A and B are −0.03125 and −0.96875, respectively. These sum to −1. The arbitrage portfolio has zero net investment. The weight on C in the arbitrage portfolio must be 1, so that combined with the short position, the net investment is 0. The expected return on the arbitrage portfolio is 1(0.08) − 0.03125(0.15) − 0.96875(0.07) = 0.08 − 0.0725 = 0.0075 or 0.75 percent. For $10,000 invested in C, this represents a $10,000 × 0.0075 = $75 arbitrage profit.

15 We need to combine Portfolios K and L in such a way that sensitivity to the inflation factor is zero. The inflation sensitivities of Portfolios K and L are 0.5 and 1.5, respectively. With *w* the weight on Portfolio L, we have

$$0 = 0.5(1 - w) + 1.5w$$
$$0 = 0.5 - 0.5w + 1.5w$$
$$0 = 0.5 + w$$
$$w = -0.5$$

The weight on Portfolio L in the new portfolio is −0.5, and the weight on Portfolio K is 1.5 (−0.5 + 1.5 = 1). For every $1.50 invested on Portfolio K, the institution shorts $0.50 of Portfolio L. The new portfolio's return is

$$R = 0.125 + 0.25F_{\text{GDP}}$$

The intercept is computed as (1.50 × 0.12) + (−0.5 × 0.11) = 0.125, and the sensitivity to the GDP factor is computed as (1.50 × 1.0) + (−0.5 × 2.5) = 0.25.

16 $E(R_A) = 6 + 0.5\lambda = 10.25$

$$E(R_B) = 6 + 1.2\lambda = 16.2$$

Using either equation, we can calculate the price of factor risk as

$$\lambda = \frac{10.25 - 6}{0.5} = \frac{16.2 - 6}{1.2} = 8.5$$

The risk premium for each unit of factor risk, or price of risk, is 8.5 percent.

17 With *w* the weight on Portfolio A, (1 − *w*) the weight on Portfolio B, and 1.71 the sensitivity of the S&P 500 to the business cycle factor, we have

$$2.25w + 1.00(1 - w) = 1.71$$
$$2.25w + 1 - w = 1.71$$
$$1.25w = 0.71$$

Thus

$w = 0.568$, weight on Portfolio A

$1 - w = 0.432$, weight on Portfolio B

With a weight of 0.568 on A and 0.432 on B, the resulting inflation factor sensitivity is $0.568(-0.12) + 0.432(-0.45) = -0.263$.

18 If the average investor has income from employment, then this income makes this investor recession sensitive. Hence, the average investor requires a risk premium to hold recession-sensitive securities. The average investor's need for a risk premium for these stocks influences their prices. Cyclical stocks and high-yield bonds are both very sensitive to economic conditions. For example, the debt-paying ability of high-yield bond issuers is strongly affected by recessions. The wealthy investor with no labor income can take the recession risk for which she would receive a premium (pay a lower price than would be the case if the average investor were not recession sensitive). The high-wealth investor can afford to take the risk because she does not face recession risk from labor income.

19 A is correct. The expected return of a portfolio, $E(R_p)$, is the sum of individual asset weights multiplied by the expected return of those assets: $E(R_p) = \omega_1 E(R_1) + \omega_2 E(R_2)$

ω_1 = current portfolio weighting of government bonds = 60%
$E(R_1)$ = expected return of government bonds = 5%
ω_2 = current portfolio weighting of large-cap stocks = 40%
$E(R_2)$ = expected return of large-cap stocks = 10%

$$E(R_p) = (0.60 \times 0.05) + (0.40 \times 0.10)$$
$$E(R_p) = 0.03 + 0.04$$
$$E(R_p) = 7.0\%$$

20 A is correct. The portfolio standard deviation of returns, σ_p, is:

$$\sigma_p = (\omega_1^2\sigma_1^2 + \omega_2^2\sigma_2^2 + 2\omega_1\omega_2\rho_{1,2}\sigma_1\sigma_2)^{1/2}$$

ω_1 = portfolio weighting of government bonds = 60%
σ_1 = standard deviation of returns of government bonds = 10%
ω_2 = portfolio weighting of large-cap stocks = 40%
σ_2 = standard deviation of returns of large-cap stocks = 20%
$\rho_{1,2}$ = correlation of returns between government bonds and large-cap stocks = 0.05

$$\sigma_p = \left\{\left[(0.60)^2 \times (0.10)^2\right] + \left[(0.40)^2 \times (0.2)^2\right] + [2 \times 0.60 \times 0.40 \times 0.05 \times 0.10 \times 0.20]\right\}^{1/2}$$

$$\sigma_p = (0.0036 + 0.0064 + 0.00048)^{1/2}$$

$$\sigma_p = (0.01048)^{1/2}$$

$$\sigma_p = 10.2372\%, \text{ or } 10.24\%$$

21 A is correct. The current portfolio has an expected return of 7% and the recommended portfolio allocation will change the expected return to 7.5%.

The expected return of a portfolio, $E(R_p)$, is the sum of individual asset weights multiplied by the expected return of those assets: $E(R_p) = \omega_1 E(R_1) + \omega_2 E(R_2)$
Expected return of current portfolio allocation:

ω_1 = current portfolio weighting of government bonds = 60%
$E(R_1)$ = expected return of government bonds = 5%
ω_2 = current portfolio weighting of large-cap stocks = 40%
$E(R_2)$ = expected return of large-cap stocks = 10%

$$E(R_p) = (0.60 * 0.05) + (0.40 * 0.10)$$

$$E(R_p) = 0.03 + 0.04$$

$$E(R_p) = 7.0\%$$

Expected return of recommended portfolio allocation:

ω_1 = current portfolio weighting of government bonds = 70%
$E(R_1)$ = expected return of government bonds = 5%
ω_2 = current portfolio weighting of large-cap stocks = 10%
$E(R_2)$ = expected return of large-cap stocks = 10%
ω_3 = current portfolio weighting of small-cap stocks = 20%
$E(R_3)$ = expected return of small-cap stocks = 15%

$$E(R_p) = \omega_1 E(R_1) + \omega_2 E(R_2) + \omega_3 E(R_3)$$

$$E(R_p) = (0.70 \times 0.05) + (0.10 \times 0.10) + (0.20 \times 0.15)$$

$$E(R_p) = 0.035 + 0.01 + 0.03$$

$$E(R_p) = 7.5\%$$

22 B is correct. The current portfolio has an expected standard deviation of 10.24% and the recommended portfolio allocation will lower the expected standard deviation to 9.59%.

The portfolio standard deviation of return, σ_p, of a 2-asset portfolio is:

$$\sigma_p = (\omega_1^2\sigma_1^2 + \omega_2^2\sigma_2^2 + 2\omega_1\omega_2\rho_{1,2}\sigma_1\sigma_2)^{1/2}$$

The portfolio standard deviation of return, σ_p, of a 3-asset portfolio is:

$$\sigma_p = (w_1^2\sigma_1^2 + w_2^2\sigma_2^2 + w_3^2\sigma_3^2 + 2\omega_1\omega_2\rho_{1,2}\sigma_1\sigma_2 + 2\omega_1\omega_3\rho_{1,3}\sigma_1\sigma_3 + 2\omega_2\omega_3\rho_{2,3}\sigma_2\sigma_3)^{1/2}$$

Expected standard deviation given current portfolio allocation:

ω_1 = portfolio weighting of government bonds = 60%
σ_1 = standard deviation of returns of government bonds = 10%

ω_2 = portfolio weighting of large-cap stocks = 40%
ω_2 = standard deviation of returns of large-cap stocks = 20%
$\rho_{1,2}$ = correlation of returns between government bonds and large-cap stocks = 0.05

$$\sigma_P = \left\{\left[(0.60)^2 \times (0.10)^2\right] + \left[(0.40)^2 \times (0.2)^2\right] + [2 \times 0.60 \times 0.40 \times 0.05 \times 0.10 \times 0.20]\right\}$$

$$\sigma_P = (0.0036 + 0.0064 + 0.00048)^{1/2}$$

$$\sigma_P = (0.01048)^{1/2}$$

$$\sigma_P = 10.2372\%, \text{ or } 10.24\%$$

Expected standard deviation of recommended portfolio allocation:

ω_1 = portfolio weighting of government bonds = 60%
σ_1 = standard deviation of returns of government bonds = 10%
ω_2 = portfolio weighting of large-cap stocks = 40%
σ_2 = standard deviation of returns of large-cap stocks = 20%
ω_3 = portfolio weighting of small-cap stocks = 40%
σ_3 = standard deviation of returns of small-cap stocks = 20%
$r_{1,2}$ = correlation of returns between government bonds and large-cap stocks = 0.05
$r_{1,3}$ = correlation of returns between government bonds and small-cap stocks = −0.05
$r_{2,3}$ = correlation of returns between large-cap stocks and small-cap stocks = 0.80

$$\sigma_P = \left\{ [(0.70)^2 \times (0.10)^2] + [(0.10)^2 \times (0.20)^2] + [(0.20)^2 \times (0.25)^2] + [2 \times 0.70 \times 0.10 \times 0.05 \times 0.10 \times 0.2] + [2 \times 0.70\ 0.20 \times -0.05 \times 0.10 \times 0.25] + [2 \times 0.10 \times 0.20 \times 0.80 \times 0.20 \times 0.25]\right\}^{1/2}$$

$$\sigma_P = (0.0049 + 0.0004 + 0.0025 + 0.00014 - 0.00035 + 0.0016)^{1/2}$$

$$\sigma_P = (0.00919)^{1/2}$$

$$\sigma_P = 9.5864\%, \text{ or } 9.59\%$$

23 A is correct. The expected return based upon the CAPM with an adjusted beta is 9.5%. The first step is to calculate adjusted beta for large-cap stocks using the given beta adjustment formula:

$$b_{adj} = 0.33 + (0.67) \times (1.25)$$

$$b_{adj} = 0.33 + 0.8375$$

$$b_{adj} = 1.1675$$

The next step is to insert adjusted beta into the CAPM defined by the equation:

$$E(R_{adj}) = R_F + b_{adj}[E(R_M) - R_F]$$

Substituting R_F = 2.0%, b_{adj} = 1.1675, and $E(R_M)$ = 8.4%, solve for the expected return for large-cap stocks $E(R_{adj})$:

$$E(R_{adj}) = 0.02 + 1.1675 * (0.084 - 0.02)$$
$$E(R_{adj}) = 0.02 + 0.0747$$
$$E(R_{adj}) = 0.947\text{, or } 9.5\%$$

24 B is correct. Small-cap stocks have the highest Sharpe ratio at 0.52. The Sharpe ratio is calculated as:

$$\text{Sharpe ratio} = [E(R_i) - R_F] / \sigma_i$$

For small-cap stocks, the Sharpe ratio is:

Sharpe ratio (small-cap) = (0.15 – 0.02) / 0.25 = 0.52

For large-cap stocks, the Sharpe ratio is:

Sharpe ratio (large-cap) = (0.10 – 0.02) / 0.20 = 0.40

For government bonds, the Sharpe ratio is:

Sharpe ratio (government bonds) = (0.05 – 0.02) / 0.10 = 0.30

25 A is correct because the return for that portion of the Foundation portfolio is 11%.

The return for Fund A is 10% + $1.2F_{INFL}$ + $1.0F_{GDP}$

The return for Fund B is 15% + $0.5F_{INFL}$ + $2.5F_{GDP}$.

Based upon an asset weighting of 1/3 in Fund A and 2/3 in Fund B, and given that regression error terms are expected to be zero, the return given the surprise factors is:

$$R_p = [(1/3)\times(0.10) + (2/3)\times(0.15)] + [(1/3)\times(1.2) + (2/3)\times(0.5)]F_{INFL} + [(1/3)\times(1.0) + (2/3)\times(2.5)]F_{GDP}.$$
$$R_p = (0.1333) + (0.7333)F_{INFL} + (2)F_{GDP}.$$
$$R_p = (0.1333) + [0.7333\times 0.05] - [2 \times 0.03].$$
$$R_p = 0.11 = 11\%.$$

26 B is correct. The data in Exhibit 3 shows Fund A has factor sensitivity to GDP of 1.0 while Fund B has a factor sensitivity of 2.5. To fully hedge GDP risk, set the combined weighting in Fund A and Fund B equal to 0 and solve for the portfolio weights, ω_A and

$$\omega_B = (1 - \omega_A).$$
$$0 = 1.0\times(\omega_A) + 2.5\times(1-\omega_A)$$
$$0 = \omega_A + 2.5 - 2.5\omega_A$$
$$0 = 2.5 - 1.5\omega_A$$
$$\omega_A = 1.67\text{, and}$$
$$\omega_B = (1-\omega_A) = -0.67$$

Thus, the allocation should consist of a short position of \$0.67 of Fund B for every \$1.67 invested in Fund A.

LOFT
68

READING

58

Residual Risk and Return: The Information Ratio

by Richard C. Grinold and Ronald N. Khan

LEARNING OUTCOMES

Mastery	The candidate should be able to:
☐	**a.** define the terms "alpha" and "information ratio" in both their ex post and ex ante senses;
☐	**b.** compare the information ratio and the alpha's T-statistic;
☐	**c.** explain the objective of active management in terms of value added;
☐	**d.** calculate the optimal level of residual risk to assume for given levels of manager ability and investor risk aversion;
☐	**e.** justify why the choice for a particular active strategy does not depend on investor risk aversion.

INTRODUCTION

The theory of investments is based on the premise that assets are fairly valued. This is reassuring for the financial economist and frustrating to the active manager. The active manager needs theoretical support. In the next four chapters[1] we will provide a structure, if not a theory, for the active manager.

This chapter starts the process by building a strategic context for management of residual risk and return. Within that context, we will develop some concepts and rules of thumb that we find valuable in the evaluation and implementation of active strategies.

The reader is urged to *rise above the details.* Do not worry about transactions costs, restrictions on holdings, liquidity, short sales, or the source of the alphas. We will deal with those questions in later chapters. At this point, we should free ourselves

1 Throughout this reading, references to other chapters refer to the source material: *Active Portfolio Management: A Quantitative Approach for Providing Superior Returns and Controlling Risk*, by Richard C. Grinold and Ronald N. Khan.

from the clutter and look at active management from a strategic perspective. Later chapters on implementation will focus on the details and indicate how we might adjust our conclusions to take these important practical matters into consideration.

There is no prior theory. We must pull ourselves up by our bootstraps. Economists are good at this. Recall the parable of the engineer, the philosopher, and the economist stranded on a South Sea island with no tools, very little to eat on the island, and a large quantity of canned food. The engineer devises schemes for opening the cans by boiling them, dropping them on the rocks, etc. The philosopher ponders the trifling nature of food and the ultimate futility of life. The economist just sits and gazes out to sea. Suddenly, he jumps up and shouts, "I've got it! Assume you have a can opener."

The active manager's can opener is the assumption of success. The notion of success is captured and quantified by the information ratio. The information ratio says how good you think you are. The assumption of future success is used to open up other questions. If our insights are superior to those of other investors, then how we should use those insights?

We proceed with can opener and analysis. The results are insights, rules of thumb, and a formal procedure for managing residual risk and return. Some of the highlights are:

- The *information ratio* measures achievement ex post (looking backward) and connotes opportunity ex ante (looking forward).
- The information ratio defines the *residual frontier*, the opportunities available to the active manager.
- Each manager's information ratio and residual risk aversion determine his or her level of aggressiveness (residual risk).
- *Intuition* can lead to reasonable values for the information ratio and residual risk aversion.
- *Value added* depends on the manager's opportunities and aggressiveness.

The chapter starts with the definition of the information ratio, which is one of the book's central characters. In this chapter we use the information ratio in its ex ante (hope springs eternal) form. The ex ante information ratio is an indication of the opportunities available to the active manager; it determines the residual frontier. In Chap. 4 we defined an objective for the active manager that considers both risk and return. The main results of this chapter flow from the interaction of our opportunities (information ratio) with our objectives.

In Chap. 4 we showed that a manager could add value through either benchmark timing or stock selection. We postpone the discussion of benchmark timing to Chap. 19 and will concentrate on stock selection until that point. This means that we are concerned about the trade-off between residual risk and alpha. Recall that when portfolio beta is equal to 1, residual risk and active risk coincide.

A technical appendix considers the information ratio in merciless detail.

THE DEFINITION OF ALPHA

Looking forward (ex ante), alpha is a forecast of residual return. Looking backward (ex post), alpha is the average of the realized residual returns.

The term *alpha*, like the term *beta*, arises from the use of linear regression to break the return on a portfolio into a component that is perfectly correlated with the benchmark and an uncorrelated or residual component. If $r_P(t)$ are portfolio excess returns in periods $t = 1,2, \ldots T$ and $r_B(t)$ are benchmark excess returns over those same periods, then the regression is

$$r_P(t) = \alpha_P + \beta_P \cdot r_B(t) + \varepsilon_P(t) \tag{1}$$

The estimates of β_p and α_p obtained from the regression are the *realized* or *historical* beta and alpha. The residual returns for portfolio P are

$$\theta_P(t) = \alpha_P + \varepsilon_P(t) \tag{2}$$

where α_p is the average residual return and $\varepsilon_p(t)$ is the mean zero random component of residual return.

This chapter concentrates on forecast alphas. In Chap. 12, "Information Analysis," we'll learn how to evaluate the quality of the alpha forecasts. We'll consider realized alphas in Chap. 17, "Performance Analysis." Realized alphas are for keeping score. The job of the active manager is to score. To do that, we need good forecast alphas.

When we are looking to the future, alpha is a forecast of residual return. Let θ_n be the residual return on stock n. We have

$$\alpha_n = E\{\theta_n\} \tag{3}$$

Alpha has the portfolio property, since both residual returns and expectations have the portfolio property. Consider a simple case with two stocks whose alphas are α_1 and α_2. If we have a two-stock portfolio with holdings $h_p(1)$ in stock 1 and $h_p(2)$ in stock 2, then the alpha of the portfolio will be

$$\alpha_P = h_P(1) \cdot \alpha_1 + h_P(2) \cdot \alpha_2 \tag{4}$$

This is consistent with the notion that α_p is the forecast of expected residual return on the portfolio.

By definition, the benchmark portfolio will always have a residual return equal to 0; i.e., $\theta_B = 0$ with certainty. Therefore, the alpha of the benchmark portfolio must be 0; $\alpha_B = 0$. The requirement that $\alpha_B = 0$ is the restriction that the alphas be benchmark-neutral.

Recall that the risk-free portfolio also has a zero residual return, and so the alpha for cash α_F is always equal to 0. Thus any portfolio made up of a mixture of the benchmark and cash will have a zero alpha.

THE EX POST INFORMATION RATIO: A MEASURE OF ACHIEVEMENT

An *information ratio*,[2] denoted *IR*, is a ratio of (annualized) residual return to (annualized) residual risk. If we consider the information ratio for some realized residual return (ex post), we have realized residual return divided by the residual risk taken to obtain that return. Thus we may have an average of 2.3 percent residual return per year with residual risk of 3.45 percent. That is an information ratio of 2.3/3.45 = 0.67.

A realized information ratio can (and frequently will) be negative. Don't forget that the information ratio of the benchmark must be exactly zero. If our residual return has averaged a poor −1.7 percent per year with the same residual risk level of 3.45 percent, then the realized information ratio is (−1.7)/3.45 = −0.49.

We will say more about ex post information ratios at the end of this chapter and in Chap. 17, "Performance Analysis." We offer one teaser: The ex-post information ratio is related to the t statistic one obtains for the alpha in the regression [Eq. (1)]. If the data in the regression cover Y years, then the information ratio is approximately the alpha's t statistic divided by the square root of Y.

2 Treynor and Black (1973) refer to this quantity as the appraisal ratio.

THE EX ANTE INFORMATION RATIO: A MEASURE OF OPPORTUNITY

Now we look to the future. The information ratio is the expected level of annual residual return per unit of annual residual risk. There is an implication that information is being used efficiently. Thus, the more precise definition of the information ratio is the highest ratio of annual residual return to residual risk that the manager can obtain.

Let's begin with the analysis for a start-up investment manager with no track record. We will then compare results with some empirical observations.

We first need a plausible value for the information ratio. Recall that this is an assumed can opener. Don't get carried away—we are making this number up; we don't need to be terribly precise.

This new manager must develop target expectations for residual risk and return. The risk target is less controversial. We will assume that the manager is aiming for the 5 to 6 percent residual risk range. We will use 5.5 percent for concreteness.

Now what about the expected residual return target? The answer here involves a struggle between those two titans: hope and humility. A truly humble (no better than average) active manager would say zero. That's not good enough. You can't be an active manager with that much humility. A very hopeful manager, indeed a dreamer, might say 10 percent. This quixotic manager is confusing what is possible with what can be expected.

In the end, the manager must confront both hope and humility. Let's say the manager is assuming between 3 and 4 percent, or 3.5 percent, to pick a number.

Our ex ante information ratio is 3.5/5.5 = 0.64. We have found our way to a sensible number. This analysis is intentionally vague. We don't care if the answer came out 0.63 or 0.65. This is not the time for spurious precision. Our analysis produced residual risk in the 5 to 6 percent range and expected (hoped-for) residual returns in the 3 to 4 percent range. In the extreme cases, we could have obtained an answer between 0.8 = 4/5 and 0.5 = 3/6.

So far, we have not revealed any empirically observed information ratios. The empirical results will vary somewhat by time period, by asset class, and by fee level. But overall, before-fee information ratios typically fall close to the distribution in Table 1.

Table 1

Percentile	Information Ratio
90	1.0
75	0.5
50	0.0
25	−0.5
10	−1.0

A top-quartile manager has an information ratio of one-half. That's a good number to remember. Ex ante, investment managers should aspire to top-quartile status. Our analysis of a start-up investment manager's information ratio, which we estimated at 0.64, provided a reasonable ballpark estimate, consistent with Table 1.

Table 1 displays a symmetric distribution of information ratios, centered on zero. This is consistent with our fundamental understanding of active management as a zero-sum game.

Table 1 also implies that if IR = 0.5 is good, then IR = 1.0 is exceptional. We will further define IR = 0.75 as very good and use that simple classification scheme throughout the book. Later in this chapter, we will provide more details on empirical observations of information ratios, as well as on active returns and active risk.

We will now define the information ratio in a more formal manner. Given an alpha for each stock, any (random) portfolio *P* will have a portfolio alpha α_P and a portfolio residual risk ω_P. The *information ratio for portfolio P* is

$$IR_P = \frac{\alpha_P}{\omega_P} \tag{5}$$

Our personal "information ratio" is the maximum information ratio that we can attain over all possible portfolios:

$$IR = \text{Max}\{IR_P|P\} \tag{6}$$

So we measure our information ratio based on portfolios optimized to our alphas.

The notation IR hides the fact that the information ratio depends on the alphas. Indeed, one of the uses of the information ratio concept is to scale the alphas so that a reasonable value of IR is obtained through Eq. (6).

Our definition of the information ratio says that a manager who can get an expected residual return of 2 percent with 4 percent residual risk can also get an expected residual return of 3 percent with 6 percent residual risk. The ratio of risk to return stays constant and equal to the information ratio even as the level of risk changes. A small example will indicate that this is indeed the case.

We consider four stocks, cash, and a benchmark portfolio that is 25 percent in each of the stocks. Table 2 summarizes the situation. The alphas for both the benchmark portfolio (the weighted sum of the stock alphas) and cash are, of course, equal to zero. This is no accident.

Table 2

Stock	Alpha	Benchmark Weight	Portfolio *P* Total Weight	Portfolio *P* Active Weight	Portfolio *L* Total Weight	Portfolio *L* Active Weight
1	1.50%	25.00%	35.00%	10.00%	40.00%	15.00%
2	−2.00%	25.00%	10.00%	−15.00%	2.50%	−22.50%
3	1.75%	25.00%	40.00%	15.00%	47.50%	22.50%
4	−1.25%	25.00%	15.00%	−10.00%	10.00%	−15.00%
Benchmark	0.00%					
Cash	0.00%					

The last four columns describe two possible portfolios, *P* and *L*. For each portfolio, we have shown the portfolio's total and active holdings. The active holdings are simply the portfolio holdings less the benchmark holdings. In portfolio *P*, we have positive active positions for the two stocks with positive alphas, and negative active positions for the stocks with negative alphas. Since the alpha for the benchmark is zero, we can calculate the alpha for the portfolio using only the active holdings.[3] The alpha for portfolio P is

$$\begin{aligned}\alpha_P &= (1.50\%)\cdot(0.10)+(-2.00\%)\cdot(-0.15)+(1.75\%)\cdot(0.15)+(-1.25\%)\cdot(-1.10)\\ &= 0.84\end{aligned}$$

The risk of this active position is 2.04 percent.[4]

Notice that portfolio L is just a more aggressive version of portfolio P. This isn't clear when we look at the holdings in portfolio L, but it is obvious when we look at the active holdings. The active holdings of portfolio L are 50 percent greater than the active holdings of portfolio P. For stock 1, our active position goes from +10 percent to +15 percent. For stock 2, our active position goes from −15 percent to −22.5 percent. In both cases, the active position increases by 50 percent. This means that the alpha for portfolio L must be 50 percent larger as well, and that the active risk is also 50 percent higher.[5] If both the portfolio alpha and the residual risk increase by 50 percent, the ratio of the two will remain the same.

The information ratio is independent of the manager's level of aggressiveness.

We will consistently assume that the information ratio is independent of the level of risk. This relationship eventually breaks down in real-world applications, because of constraints. So in Table 2, if there is a constraint on short selling, we have little additional room to bet against stock 2 beyond portfolio L. Chapter 15, "Long/Short Investing," expands on this idea, estimating a cost for the no short selling constraint based on the effective reduction in information ratio.

Although the information ratio is independent of the level of aggressiveness, it does depend on the time horizon. In order to avoid confusion, we standardize by using a 1-year horizon. The reason is that expected returns and variances both tend to grow with the length of the horizon. Therefore risk, standard deviation, will grow as the square root of the horizon, and the ratio of expected return (growing with time) to risk (growing as the square root of time) will increase with the square root of time. That means that the quarterly information ratio is half as large as the annual information ratio. The monthly information ratio would be $1/\sqrt{12} = 0.288$ the size of the annual information ratio.

THE RESIDUAL FRONTIER: THE MANAGER'S OPPORTUNITY SET

The choices available to the active manager are easier to see if we look at the alpha versus residual risk trade-offs. The residual frontier will describe the opportunities available to the active manager. The ex ante information ratio determines the manager's residual frontier.

3 The portfolio holdings are $\mathbf{h}_P = \mathbf{h}_B + \mathbf{h}_{PA}$, where $\mathbf{h}_B$ and $\mathbf{h}_{PA}$ are benchmark and active holdings. If $\boldsymbol{\alpha}$ is a vector of alphas, then $\boldsymbol{\alpha}^T \cdot \mathbf{h}_B = 0$ implies $\boldsymbol{\alpha}^T \cdot \mathbf{h}_P = \boldsymbol{\alpha}^T \cdot \mathbf{h}_{PA}$.

4 Table 2 doesn't contain the information necessary to calculate this. But see Chap. 4 for the definition of active risk and the procedure for calculating active risk. If $\mathbf{V}$ is the covariance matrix, and h_P and h_B are the holdings in the managed and benchmark portfolios, respectively, then $\mathbf{h}_{PA} = h_P - h_B$ contains the active holdings and $\psi_P^2 = \mathbf{h}_{PA}^T \cdot \mathbf{V} \cdot \mathbf{h}_{PA}$ is the active variance.

5 If the active holdings change from h_{PA} to $\phi \cdot \mathbf{h}_{PA}$, then the active risk changes from ψ_P to $\phi \cdot \psi_P = \sqrt{(\phi \cdot \mathbf{h}_{PA})^T \cdot \mathbf{V} \cdot (\phi \cdot \mathbf{h}_{PA})}$.

In Fig. 1 we have the residual frontier for an exceptional manager with an information ratio of 1. This residual frontier plots expected residual return α_P, against residual risk ω_P. The residual frontier is a straight line through the origin. Notice that portfolio *Q* is on the frontier. Portfolio *Q* is a solution to Eq. (6); i.e., IR = IR_Q. Portfolio *Q* is not alone on the residual frontier. The portfolios P_1, P_2, up to P_6 are also on the residual frontier. The manager can attain any expected residual return and residual risk combination below the frontier line. Portfolios P_1 through P_6 have (respectively) 1 percent to 6 percent expected residual return and residual risk.

Figure 1 The Residual Frontier

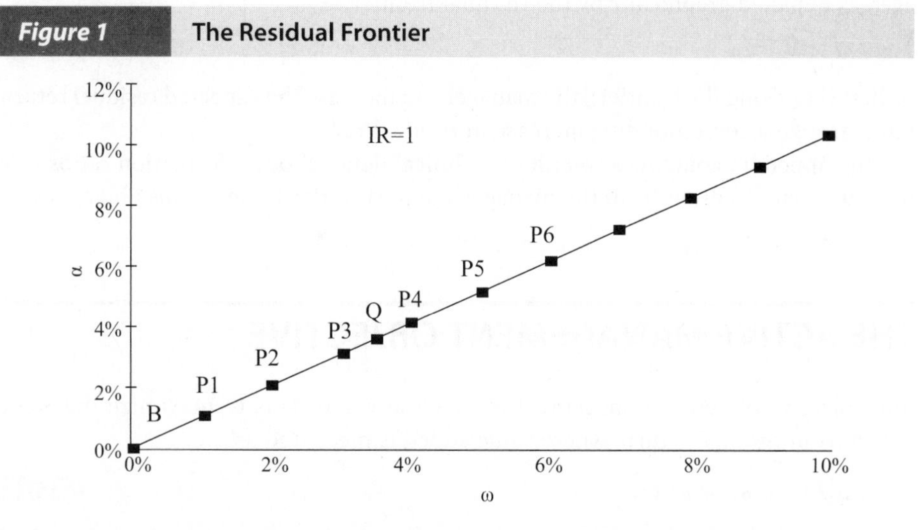

The origin, designated *B*, represents the benchmark portfolio. The benchmark, by definition, has no residual return, and thus both α_B and ω_B are equal to zero. Likewise, the risk-free asset will reside at the origin, since the risk-free asset also has a zero residual return.

In Fig. 2 we show the residual frontiers of three different managers. The good manager has an information ratio of 0.5, the very good manager has an information ratio of 0.75, and the exceptional manager has an information ratio of 1.00.

Figure 2 Opportunities

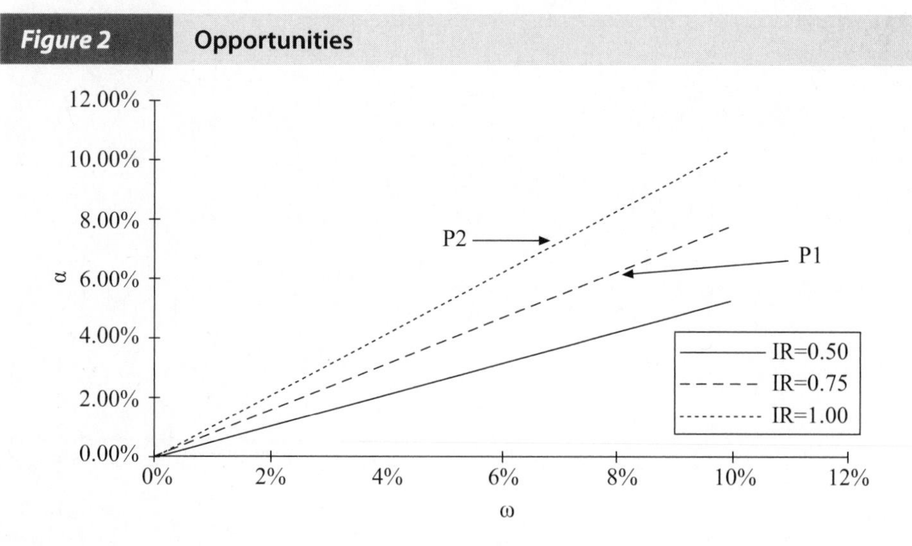

We can see from Fig. 2 that the information ratio indicates opportunity. The manager with an information ratio of 0.75 has choices—portfolio P_1, for example—that are not available to the manager with an information ratio of 0.5. Similarly, the exceptional manager has opportunities—at point P_2, for example—that are not available to the very good manager. This doesn't mean that the very good manager cannot hold the stocks in portfolio P_2. It does mean that this very good manager's information will not lead him or her to that portfolio; it will, instead, lead this manager to a portfolio like P_1 that is on his or her residual frontier.

Effectively, the information ratio defines a "budget constraint" for the active manager, as depicted graphically by the residual frontier:

$$\alpha_P = \text{IR} \cdot \omega_P \tag{7}$$

At best (i.e., along the frontier), the manager can increase the expected residual return only through a corresponding increase in residual risk.

The appendix contains a wealth of technical detail about information ratios. We now turn our attention from the manager's opportunities to her or his objectives.

THE ACTIVE MANAGEMENT OBJECTIVE

The objective of active management (derived in Chap. 4) is to maximize the value added from residual return, where value added is measured as[6]

$$\text{VA}[P] = \alpha_P - \lambda_R \cdot \omega_P^2 \tag{8}$$

This objective awards a credit for the expected residual return and a debit for residual risk. The parameter λ_R measures the aversion to residual risk; it transforms residual variance into a loss in alpha. In Fig. 3 we show the loss in alpha for different levels of residual risk. The three curves show high ($\lambda_R = 0.15$), moderate ($\lambda_R = 0.10$), and low ($\lambda_R = 0.05$) levels of residual risk aversion. In each case, the loss increases with the square of the residual risk ω_P. For a residual risk of $\omega_P = 5\%$, the losses are 3.75 percent, 2.5 percent, and 1.25 percent, respectively, for the high, moderate, and low levels of residual risk aversion.

6 We are ignoring benchmark timing, so active return equals residual return and active risk equals residual risk.

Figure 3 Loss In Alpha

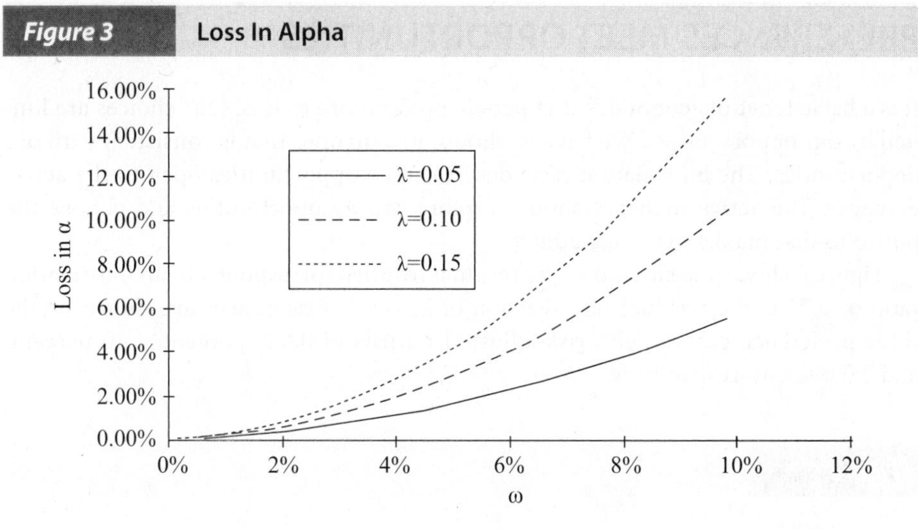

The lines of equal value added, plotted as functions of expected residual return α_P and residual risk ω_P, are parabolas. In Fig. 4 we have plotted three such parabolas for value added of 2.5 percent, 1.4 percent, and 0.625 percent. These curves are of the form $\alpha_P = 2.5 + \lambda_R \cdot \omega_P^2$, $\alpha_P = 1.4 + \lambda_R \cdot \omega_P^2$, and $\alpha_P = 0.625 + \lambda_R \cdot \omega_P^2$. The figure shows the situation when we have a moderate level of residual risk aversion $\lambda_R = 0.10$. The three parabolas are parallel and increasing to the right. Every point along the top curve has a value added of 2.5 percent. The point {α = 2.5 percent, ω = 0 percent} and the point {α = 4.1 percent, ω = 4 percent} are on this curve. At the first point, with zero residual risk and an alpha of 2.5 percent, we have a value added of 2.5 percent. At the second point, the value added is still 2.5 percent, although we have risk. Thus, with ω = 4 percent and α = 4.1 percent, we have $VA = 2.5 = 4.1 - (0.1) \cdot 4^2$.

Figure 4 Constant Value Added Lines

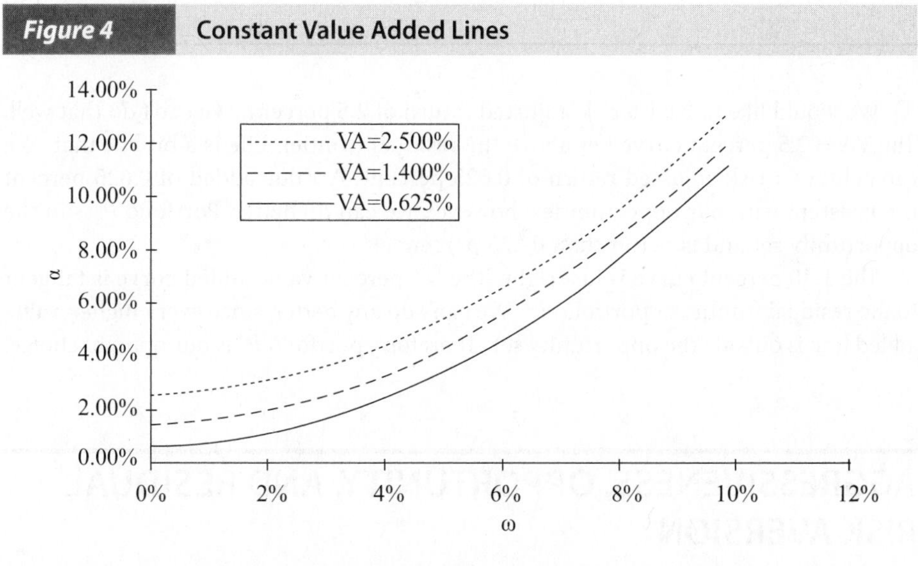

We sometimes refer to the value added as the *certainty equivalent return.* Given a risk aversion λ_R, the investor will equate return α_P and risk ω_P with a certain return $\alpha_P - \lambda_R \cdot \omega_P^2$ to a (residual) risk-free investment.

PREFERENCES MEET OPPORTUNITIES

It is a basic tenet of economics that people prefer more to less. Our choices are limited by our opportunities. We have to choose in a manner that is consistent with our opportunities. The information ratio describes the opportunities open to the active manager. The active manager should explore those opportunities and choose the portfolio that maximizes value added.

Figure 5 shows the situation. The residual frontier corresponds to an information ratio of 0.75 and a residual risk aversion of $\lambda_R = 0.1$. Preferences are shown by the three preference curves, with risk-adjusted returns of 0.625 percent, 1.40 percent, and 2.5 percent, respectively.

Figure 5

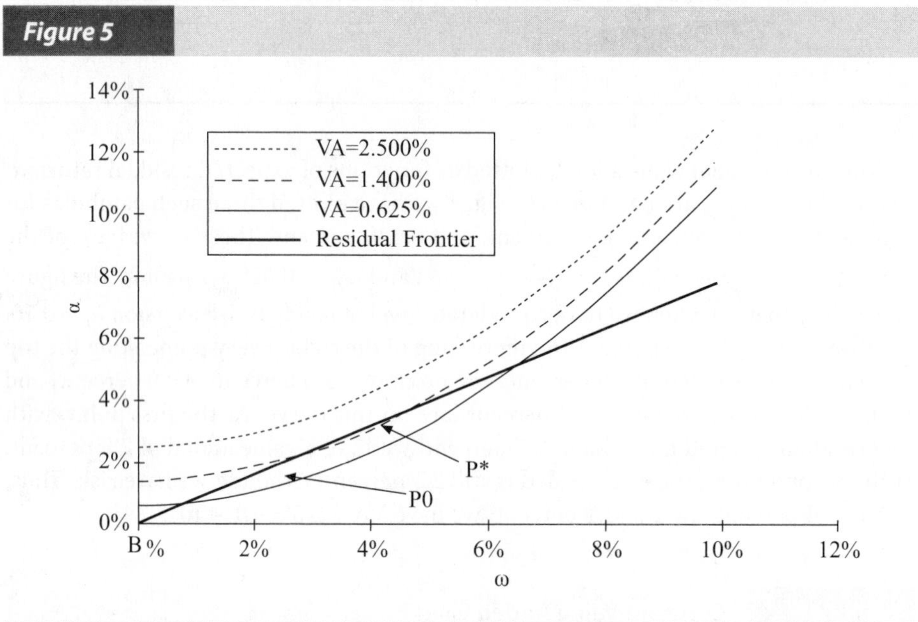

We would like to have a risk-adjusted return of 2.5 percent. We can't do that well. The VA = 2.5 percent curve lies above the residual frontier. Life is a bit like that. We can achieve a risk-adjusted return of 0.625 percent. A value added of 0.625 percent is consistent with our opportunities; however, we can do better. Portfolio P_0 is in the opportunity set and is better than 0.625 percent.

The 1.40 percent curve is just right. The 1.4 percent value added curve is tangent to the residual frontier at portfolio P^*. We can't do any better, since every higher-value added line is outside the opportunity set. Therefore, portfolio P^* is our optimal choice.

AGGRESSIVENESS, OPPORTUNITY, AND RESIDUAL RISK AVERSION

The manager's information ratio and residual risk aversion determine a simple rule that links those concepts with the manager's optimal level of residual risk or aggressiveness. We can discover the rule through a more formal examination of the graphical analysis carried out in the last section.

The manager will want to choose a portfolio[7] on the residual frontier. The only question is the manager's level of aggressiveness. Using the "budget constraint" [Eq. (7)] in the manager's objective, Eq. (8), we find

$$VA[\omega_P] = \omega_P \cdot IR - \lambda_R \cdot \omega_P^2 \quad (9)$$

Now we have completely parameterized the problem in terms of risk. As we increase risk, we increase expected return and we increase the penalty for risk. Figure 6 shows the situation, representing the median case with IR = 0.75 and $\lambda_R = 0.10$.

Figure 6

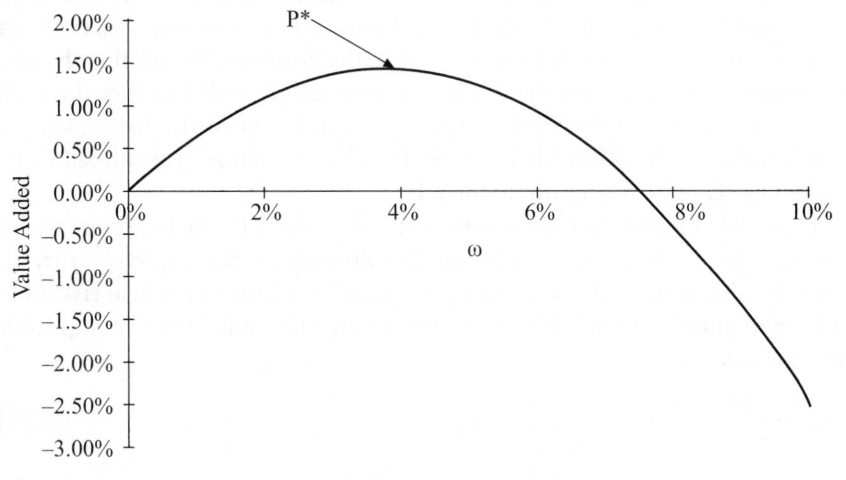

The optimal level of residual risk, ω^*, which maximizes VA $[\omega_p]$ is

$$\omega^* = \frac{IR}{2\lambda_R} \quad (10)$$

This is certainly a sensible result. Our desired level of residual risk will increase with our opportunities and decrease with our residual risk aversion. Doubling the information ratio will double the optimal risk level. Doubling the risk aversion will halve the optimal risk level.

Table 3 shows how the residual risk will vary for reasonable values of the information ratio and residual risk aversion. The information ratio has three possible levels: 0.50 (good), 0.75 (very good), and 1.0 (exceptional). The residual risk aversion also has three possible levels: 0.05 (aggressive), 0.1 (moderate), and 0.15 (restrained).

7 The formal problem is to maximize $\alpha - \lambda \cdot \omega^2$, subject to the constraint $\alpha/\omega \leq IR$. Since we know that the constraint will be binding at the optimal solution, we can use it to eliminate α from the objective.

Table 3 Residual Risk

IR	Risk Aversion λ		
	Aggressive (0.05)	**Moderate (0.10)**	**Restrained (0.15)**
Exceptional (1.00)	10.00%	5.00%	3.33%
Very good (0.75)	7.50%	3.75%	2.50%
Good (0.50)	5.00%	2.50%	1.67%

The highest level of aggressiveness is 10 percent, corresponding to the low residual risk aversion ($\lambda_R = 0.05$) and the high information ratio (IR = 1.00). At the other corner, with fewer opportunities (IR = 0.50) and more restraint ($\lambda_R = 0.15$), we have an annual residual risk of 1.67 percent. Table 3 is quite useful; it allows a manager to link two alien concepts, the information ratio and residual risk aversion, to the more specific notion of the amount of residual risk in the portfolio. We see that the greater our opportunities, the higher the level of aggressiveness, and the lower the residual risk aversion, the greater the level of aggressiveness. The table also helps us calibrate our sensibilities as to reasonable levels of IR and λ_R. Equation (10) will tell us if any suggested levels of IR and λ_R are reasonable.

It is possible to turn the question around and use Eq. (10) to determine a reasonable level of residual risk aversion. Recall the information ratio analysis earlier in the chapter. We determined that the manager wanted 5.5 percent residual risk and had an information ratio of 0.64. We can rearrange Eq. (10) and extract an implied level of residual risk aversion:

$$\lambda_R = \frac{\text{IR}}{2 \cdot \omega^*} \tag{11}$$

For our example, we have $0.64/(2 \cdot 5.5) = 0.058$. The manager is aggressive, with risk aversion at the lower end of the spectrum.

VALUE ADDED: RISK-ADJUSTED RESIDUAL RETURN

We have located the optimal portfolio P^* at the point where the residual frontier is tangent to a preference line, and we have found a simple expression for the level of residual risk for the optimal portfolio. In this section, we will go one step further and determine the risk-adjusted residual return of the optimal portfolio P^*.

If we substitute the optimal level of residual risk [Eq. (10)] into Eq. (9), we find the relationship between the value added as measured by utility and the manager's opportunity as measured by the information ratio IR:

$$\text{VA}^* = \text{VA}\left[\omega^*\right] = \frac{\text{IR}^2}{4\lambda_R} = \frac{\omega^* \cdot \text{IR}}{2} \tag{12}$$

This says that the ability of the manager to add value increases as the *square* of the information ratio and decreases as the manager becomes more risk-averse. So a manager's information ratio determines his or her potential to add value.

Equation (12) states a critical result. Imagine we are risk-verse investors, with high λ_R. According to Equation (12), given our λ_R, we will maximize our value added by choosing the investment strategy (or manager) with the highest IR. But a very risk-tolerant investor will make exactly the same calculation. In fact, every investor seeks the strategy or manager with the highest information ratio. Different investors will differ only in how aggressively they implement the strategy.

The Information Ratio Is the Key to Active Management

Table 4 shows the value added for the same three choices of information ratio and residual risk aversion used in Table 3. In our best case, the value added is 5.00 percent per year. That is probably more than one could expect. In the worst case, the value added is 42 basis points per year. A good manager (IR = 0.50) with a conservative implementation ($\lambda_R = 0.15$, so $\omega^* = 1.66$) will probably not add enough value to justify an active fee.

In our initial analysis of a manager's information ratio, we found IR = 0.64 and $\lambda_R = 0.058$, and so the value added is 1.77 percent per year.

Table 4 Value Added

	Risk Aversion λ_R		
IR	**Aggressive (0.05)**	**Moderate (0.10)**	**Restrained (0.15)**
Exceptional (1.00)	5.00%	2.50%	1.67%
Very good (0.75)	2.81%	1.41%	0.94%
Good (0.50)	1.25%	0.63%	0.42%

THE β = 1 FRONTIER

How do our residual risk/return choices look in the total risk/total return picture? The portfolios we will select (in the absence of any benchmark timing) will lie along the $\beta = 1$ *frontier*. This is the set of all portfolios with beta equal to 1 that are efficient; i.e., they have the minimum risk for a specified level of expected return. They are not necessarily fully invested. We develop this concept more fully in the technical appendix.

Figure 7 compares different efficient frontiers. The efficient frontier is the straight line through *F* and *Q*. The efficient frontier for fully invested portfolios starts at *C* and runs through *Q*. The efficient frontier for portfolios with beta equal to 1 starts at the benchmark, *B*, and runs through *P*.

Figure 7

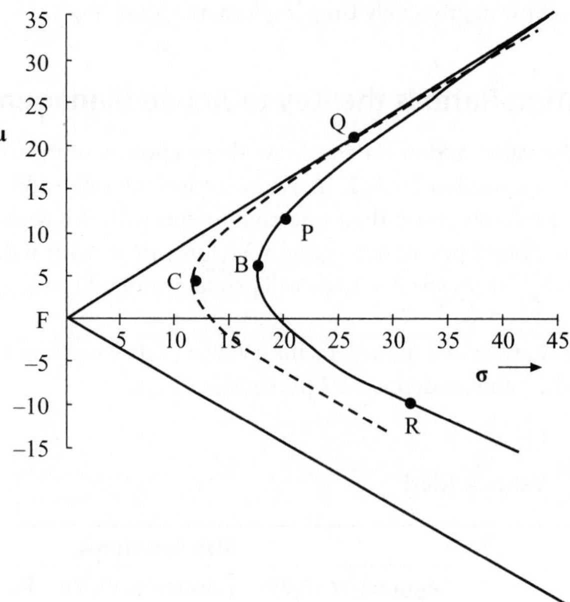

The benchmark is the minimum-risk portfolio with β = 1, since it has zero residual risk. All other β = 1 portfolios have the same systematic risk, but more residual risk.

A glance at Fig. 7 may make us rethink our value added objective. There are obviously portfolios that dominate the β = 1 frontier. However, these portfolios have a large amount of active risk, and therefore expose the manager to the business risk of poor *relative* performance.

These two frontiers cross at the point along the fully invested frontier with β = 1. This crossing point will typically involve high levels of residual risk.

If we require our portfolios to satisfy a no active cash condition, then we have the situation shown in Fig. 8. The β = 1 no active cash frontier is the parabola centered on the benchmark portfolio *B* and passing through the portfolio *Y*. This efficient frontier combines the restriction to full investment (assuming that the benchmark is fully invested) with the β = 1 restriction. The opportunities without the no active cash restriction dominate those with the restriction. A constraint reduces our opportunities.

Figure 8

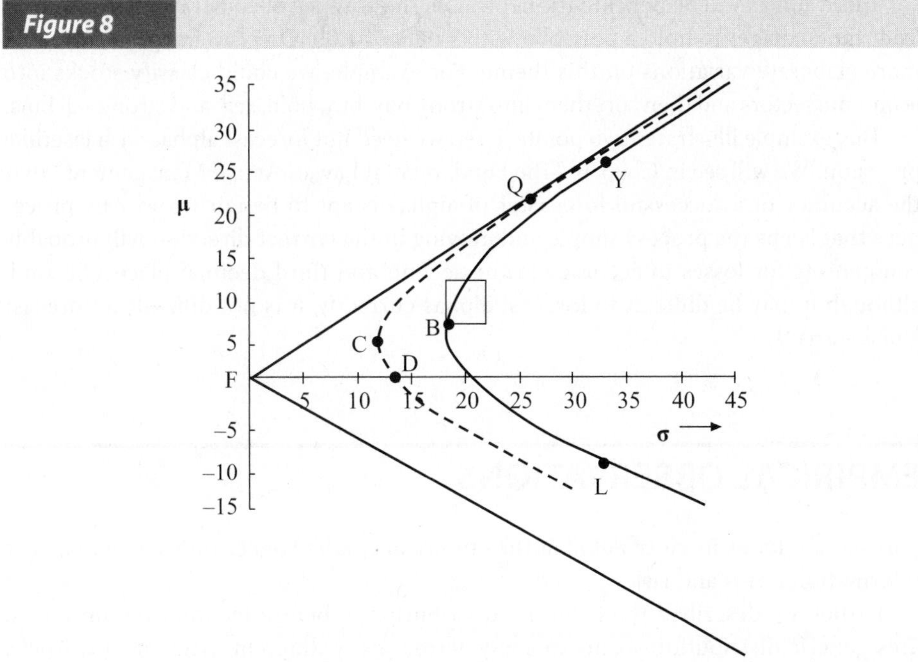

FORECAST ALPHAS DIRECTLY!

We have decided to manage relative to a benchmark and (at least until Chap. 19) to forgo benchmark timing. We have a need for alphas. We will discuss this topic at great length in the remainder of the book. However, we would like to show at this early stage that it isn't very hard to produce a rudimentary set of alphas with a small amount of work. One way to get these alphas is to start with expected returns and then go through the complicated procedure described in Chap. 4. An alternative is to skip the intermediate steps and forecast the alphas directly. In fact, one of the goals of developing the active management machinery is to avoid having to forecast several quantities (like the expected return to the benchmark) which probably will not ultimately influence our portfolio. Here, then, is a reasonable example of what we mean, converting a simple ranking of stocks into alpha forecasts. To start, sort the assets into five bins: strong buy, buy, hold, sell, and strong sell. Assign them respective alphas of 2.00 percent, 1.00 percent, 0.00 percent, −1.00 percent, and −2.00 percent. Then find the benchmark average alpha. If it is zero, we are finished. If it isn't zero (and there is no guarantee that it will be), modify the alphas by subtracting the benchmark average times the stock's beta from each original alpha.

These alphas will be benchmark-neutral. In the absence of constraints, they should lead[8] the manager to hold a portfolio with a beta of 1.00. One can imagine more and more elaborate variations on this theme. For example, we could classify stocks into economic sectors and then sort them into strong buy, buy, hold, sell, and strong sell bins.

This example illustrates two points. First, we need not forecast alphas with laserlike precision. We will see in Chap. 6, "The Fundamental Law of Active Management," that the accuracy of a successful forecaster of alphas is apt to be fairly low. Any procedure that keeps the process simple and moving in the correct direction will probably compensate for losses in accuracy in the second and third decimal places. Second, although it may be difficult to forecast alphas correctly, it is not difficult to forecast alphas directly.

EMPIRICAL OBSERVATIONS

This section looks in more detail at the empirical results concerning active manager information ratios and risk.

Earlier, we described the "generic" distribution of before-fee information ratios. This generic distribution seems to apply across many different asset classes, stocks to bonds to international. Here we will present some of the empirical observations underlying the generic result.

These results were produced and partly described in Kahn and Rudd (1995, 1997). They arise from analysis of active U.S. domestic equity and bond mutual funds and institutional portfolios. These empirical studies utilized style analysis, which we describe in Chap. 17, "Performance Analysis." Suffice it to say that this analysis allows us to estimate several empirical distributions of interest here. Table 5 briefly describes the data underlying the results that follow. The time periods involved are admittedly short, in part because style analysis requires an extensive in-sample period to determine a custom benchmark for each fund. The good news is that these are out-of-sample results. The bad news is that they do not cover an extensive time period.

Table 5

Study	Number of Funds	Calculation Time Period
U.S. active equity mutual funds	300	January 1991–December 1993
U.S. active equity institutional portfolios	367	October 1995–December 1996
U.S. active bond mutual funds	195	April 1993–September 1994
U.S. active bond institutional portfolios	215	October 1995–December 1996

8 The manager's objective is to maximize $\mathbf{h}_{PA}^T \cdot \alpha - \lambda_R \cdot \mathbf{h}_{PA}^T \cdot \mathbf{V} \cdot \mathbf{h}_{PA}$. In the absence of constraints, the optimal solution, call it $\mathbf{h}_{PA}^*$, will satisfy $\alpha - 2 \cdot \lambda_R \cdot \mathbf{V} \cdot \mathbf{h}_{PA}^* = 0$. If we multiply these first-order conditions by the benchmark weights $\mathbf{h}_B$, and recall that $\mathbf{h}_B^T \cdot \mathbf{V} = \sigma_B^2 \cdot \beta^T$ and $\alpha_B = 0$, we find

$$\begin{aligned} \mathbf{h}_B^T \cdot \alpha &= \alpha_B = 0 \\ &= 2 \cdot \lambda_R \cdot \mathbf{h}_B^T \cdot \mathbf{V} \cdot \mathbf{h}_{PA}^* = 2 \cdot \lambda_R \cdot \sigma_B^2 \cdot \beta^T \cdot \mathbf{h}_{PA}^* \\ &= 2 \cdot \lambda_R \cdot \sigma_B^2 \cdot \beta_{PA}^* \end{aligned}$$

The short time period will not bias the median estimates, but the large sample errors associated with the short time period will broaden the distributions.[9] The problem is more severe for institutional portfolios, where we have only quarterly return data, and hence a smaller number of observations.

Tables 6 and 7 display empirical distributions of information ratios for equity and bond investors, respectively. These tables generally support the generic distribution of Table 1, especially considering that all empirical results will depend on time period, analysis methodology, etc.

Table 6 Information Ratios, U.S. Active Equity Investments

	Mutual Funds		Institutional Portfolios	
Percentile	**Before Fees**	**After Fees**	**Before Fees**	**After Fees**
90	1.33	1.08	1.25	1.01
75	0.78	0.58	0.63	0.48
50	0.32	0.12	−0.01	−0.15
25	−0.08	−0.33	−0.56	−0.72
10	−0.47	−0.72	−1.03	−1.25

Table 7 Information Ratios, U.S. Active Bond Investments

	Mutual Funds		Institutional Portfolios	
Percentile	**Before Fees**	**After Fees**	**Before Fees**	**After Fees**
90	1.14	0.50	1.81	1.29
75	0.50	−0.22	0.89	0.38
50	−0.11	−0.86	0.01	−0.57
25	−0.61	−1.50	−0.62	−1.37
10	−1.22	−2.21	−1.50	−2.41

For equity investors, the empirical data show that top-quartile investors achieve information ratios of 0.63 to 0.78 before fees and 0.58 to 0.48 after fees. Given the standard errors for these results of roughly 0.05, and the fact that estimation errors tend to broaden the distribution, these empirical results are roughly consistent with Table 1.

The before-fee data on bond managers look roughly similar to the equity results, with top-quartile information ratios ranging from 0.50 to 0.89. The after-fee results differ strikingly from the equity manager results. For more on this phenomenon, see Kahn (1998).

Overall, given these empirical results, Table 1 appears to be a very good ex ante distribution of information ratios, before fees.

---

9 In the extreme, imagine a sample of 300 funds, each with true IR = 0. We will observe a distribution of sample information ratios. It may well center on IR = 0, but that distribution will shrink toward zero only as we increase our observation period.

We can also look at distributions of active risk. Tables 8 and 9 show the distributions. Active managers should find this risk information useful: It helps define manager aggressiveness relative to the broad universe of active managers.

Table 8 Annual Active Risk, U.S. Active Equity Investments

Percentile	Mutual Funds	Institutional Portfolios
90	9.87%	9.49%
75	7.00%	6.47%
50	4.76%	4.39%
25	3.66%	2.85%
10	2.90%	1.93%

Table 9 Annual Active Risk, U.S. Active Bond Investments

Percentile	Mutual Funds	Institutional Portfolios
90	3.44%	1.89%
75	2.01%	0.98%
50	1.33%	0.61%
25	0.96%	0.41%
10	0.74%	0.26%

For equity managers, median active risk falls between 4 and 5 percent. Mutual fund risk resembles institutional portfolio risk, except at the low-risk end of the spectrum, where institutional managers offer lower-risk products.

For active domestic bond managers, the risk distributions vary between mutual funds and institutional portfolios, although both are well below the active equity risk distribution. Median active risk is 1.33 percent for bond mutual funds and only 0.61 percent for institutional bond portfolios.

SUMMARY

We have built a simple framework for the management of residual risk and return. There are two key constructs in this framework:

- The information ratio as a measure of our opportunities
- The residual risk aversion as a measure of our willingness to exploit those opportunities

These two constructs determine our desired level of residual risk [Eq. (10)] and our ability to add value [Equation (12)]. In the next chapter, we will push this analysis further to uncover some of the structure that leads to the information ratio.

REFERENCES

Ambachtsheer, Keith. 1977. "Where are the Customer's Alphas?" *Journal of Portfolio Management*, vol. 4, no. 1 (Fall):52–56.

Goodwin, Thomas H. 1998. "The Information Ratio." *Financial Analysts Journal*, vol. 54, no. 4 (July/August):34–43.

Kahn, Ronald N. 1998. "Bond Managers Need to Take More Risk." *Journal of Portfolio Management*, vol. 24, no. 3 (Spring):70–76.

Kahn, Ronald N., and Andrew Rudd. 1995. "Does Historical Performance Predict Future Performance?" *Financial Analysts Journal*, vol. 51, no. 6 (November/December):43–52.

______. "The Persistence of Equity Style Performance: Evidence from Mutual Fund Data." In *The Handbook of Equity Style Management*, 2d ed., edited by Daniel T. Coggin, Frank J. Fabozzi, and Robert Arnott (New Hope, PA: Frank J. Fabozzi Associates), 1997, pp. 257–267.

_____. "The Persistence of Fixed Income Style Performance: Evidence from Mutual Fund Data." In *Managing Fixed Income Portfolios*, edited by Frank J. Fabozzi (New Hope, PA: Frank J. Fabozzi Associates), 1997, pp. 299–307.

Roll, Richard. 1992. "A Mean/Variance Analysis of Tracking Error." *Journal of Portfolio Management*, vol. 18, no. 4 (Summer):13–23.

Rosenberg, Barr. 1976 "Security Appraisal and Unsystematic Risk in Institutional Investment." *Proceedings of the Seminar on the Analysis of Security Prices* (Chicago: University of Chicago Press), November, pp. 171–237.

Rudd, Andrew, and Henry K. Clasing, Jr.. 1988 *Modern Portfolio Theory*, 2d ed. (Orinda, Calif.: Andrew Rudd).

Sharpe, William F. 1994. "The Sharpe Ratio." *Journal of Portfolio Management*, vol. 21, no. 1 (Fall):49–59.

Treynor, Jack, and Fischer Black. 1973. "How to Use Security Analysis to Improve Portfolio Selection." *Journal of Business*, vol. 46, no. 1 (January):66–86.

LOFT
68

READING

59

The Fundamental Law of Active Management

by Richard C. Grinold and Ronald N. Khan

LEARNING OUTCOMES

Mastery	The candidate should be able to:
☐	a. define the terms "information coefficient" and "breadth" and describe how they combine to determine the information ratio;
☐	b. describe how the optimal level of residual risk of an investment strategy changes with information coefficient and breadth, and how the value added of an investment strategy changes with information coefficient and breadth;
☐	c. contrast market timing and security selection in terms of breadth and required investment skill;
☐	d. describe how the information ratio changes when the original investment strategy is augmented with other strategies or information sources;
☐	e. describe the assumptions on which the fundamental law of active management is based.

INTRODUCTION

In Chap. 5,[1] the information ratio played the role of the "assumed can opener" for our investigation of active strategies. In this chapter, we will give that can opener more substance by finding the attributes of an investment strategy that will determine the information ratio.

1 Throughout this reading, references to other chapters refer to the source material: *Active Portfolio Management: A Quantitative Approach for Providing Superior Returns and Controlling Risk*, by Richard C. Grinold and Ronald N. Khan.

The insights that we gain will be useful in guiding a research program and in enhancing the quality of an investment strategy. Major points in this chapter are:

- A strategy's breadth is the number of independent, active decisions available per year.
- The manager's skill, measured by the information coefficient, is the correlation between forecasts and results.
- The fundamental law of active management explains the information ratio in terms of breadth and skill.
- The additivity of the fundamental law allows for an attribution of value added to different components of a strategy.

THE FUNDAMENTAL LAW

The information ratio is a measure of a manager's opportunities. If we assume that the manager exploits those opportunities in a way that is mean/variance-efficient, then the value added by the manager will be proportional to the information ratio squared. As we saw in Chap. 5, all investors seek the strategies and managers with the highest information ratios. In this chapter, we investigate how to achieve high information ratios.

A simple and surprisingly general formula called the *fundamental law of active management* gives an approximation to the information ratio. We derive the result in the technical appendix. The law is based on two attributes of a strategy, breadth and skill. The breadth of a strategy is the number of independent investment decisions that are made each year, and the skill, represented by the information coefficient, measures the quality of those investment decisions. The formal definitions are as follows:

> BR is the strategy's *breadth*. Breadth is defined as the number of independent forecasts of exceptional return we make per year.
>
> IC is the manager's *information coefficient*. This measure of skill is the correlation of each forecast with the actual outcomes. We have assumed for convenience that IC is the same for all forecasts.

The law connects breadth and skill to the information ratio through the (approximately true) formula:

$$\mathrm{IR} = \mathrm{IC} \cdot \sqrt{\mathrm{BR}} \tag{1}$$

The approximation underlying Eq. (1) ignores the benefits of reducing risk that our forecasts provide. For relatively low values of IC (below 0.1), this reduction in risk is extremely small. We consider the assumptions behind the law in detail in a later section.

To increase the information ratio from 0.5 to 1.0, we need to either double our skill, increase our breadth by a factor of 4, or do some combination of the above.

In Chap. 5, we established a relationship [Eq. (5.10)] between the level of residual risk and the information ratio. With the aid of the fundamental law, we can express that relationship in terms of skill and breadth:

$$\omega^* = \frac{\mathrm{IR}}{2\lambda_R} = \frac{\mathrm{IC} \cdot \sqrt{\mathrm{BR}}}{2\lambda_R} \tag{2}$$

We see that the desired level of aggressiveness will increase directly with the skill level and as the square root of the breadth. The breadth allows for diversification among the active bets so that the overall level of aggressiveness ω^* can increase. The skill increases the possibility of success; thus, we are willing to incur more risk, since the gains appear to be larger.

The value a manager can add depends on the information ratio [Eq. (5.12)]. If we express the manager's ability to add value in terms of skill and breadth, we see

$$VA^* = \frac{IR^2}{4\lambda_R} = \frac{IC^2 \cdot BR}{4\lambda_R} \tag{3}$$

The value added by a strategy (the risk-adjusted return) will increase with the breadth and with the square of the skill level.

The fundamental law is designed to give us insight into active management. It isn't an operational tool. A manager needs to know the trade-offs between increasing the breadth of the strategy BR—by either covering more stocks or shortening the time horizons of the forecasts—and improving skill IC. Thus we can see that a 50 percent increase in the strategy breadth (with no diminution in skill) is equivalent to a 22 percent increase in skill (maintaining the same breadth). A quick calculation of this sort may be quite valuable before launching a major research project. Operationally, it will prove difficult in particular to estimate BR accurately, because of the requirement that the forecasts be independent.

Figure 1 shows the trade-offs between breadth and skill for two levels of the information ratio.

Figure 1

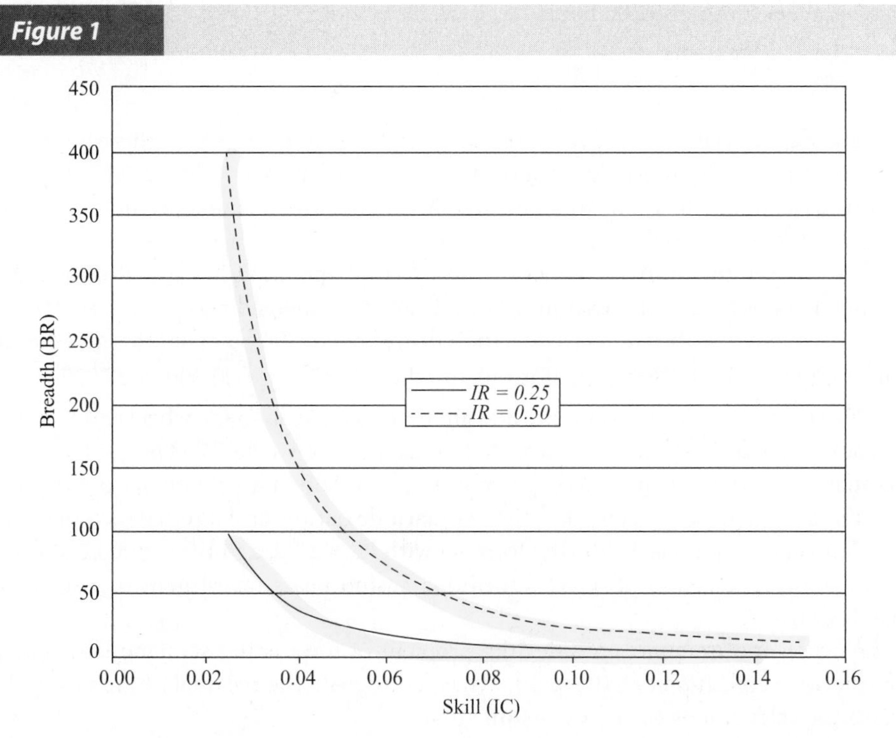

We can see the power of the law by making an assessment of three strategies. In each strategy, we want an information ratio of 0.50. Start with a market timer who has independent information about market returns each quarter. The market timer needs an information coefficient of 0.25, since $0.50 = 0.25 \cdot \sqrt{4}$. As an alternative, consider a stock selecter who follows 100 companies and revises the assessments each quarter. The stock selecter makes 400 bets per year; he needs an information coefficient of 0.025, since $0.50 = 0.025 \cdot \sqrt{400}$. As a third example, consider a specialist who follows two companies and revises her bets on each 200 times per year. The specialist will make 400 bets per year and require a skill level of 0.025. The stock selecter achieves breadth by looking at a large number of companies intermittently, and the specialist achieves it by examining a small group of companies constantly. We can see from these examples that strategies with similar information ratios can differ radically in the requirements they place on the investor.

EXAMPLES

We can give three very straightforward examples of the law in action. First, consider a gambling example. Since we want to be successful active managers, we will play the role of the casino. Let's take a roulette game where bettors choose either red or black. The roulette wheel has 18 red spots, 18 black spots, and 1 green spot. Each of the 37 spots has probability 1/37 of being selected at each turn of the wheel. The green spot is our advantage.

If the bettor chooses black, the casino wins if the wheel stops on green or red. If the bettor chooses red, the casino wins if the wheel stops on green or black. Consider a \$1.00 bet. The casino puts up a matching \$1.00; that's the casino's investment. The casino will end up with \$2.00 (a plus 100 percent return) with probability 19/37, and with zero (a minus 100 percent return) with probability 18/37. The casino's expected percentage return per \$1.00 bet is

$$\left(\frac{19}{37}\right) \cdot (100\%) + \left(\frac{18}{37}\right) \cdot (-100\%) = 2.7027\%$$

The standard deviation of the return on that single bet is 99.9634%.[2] If there is one bet of \$1.00 in a year, the information ratio for the casino will be 0.027038 = 2.7027/99.9634. In this case, our skill is 1/37 and our breadth is one. The formula predicts an information ratio of 0.027027. That's pretty close.

We can see the dramatic effect breadth has by operating like a real casino and having 1 million bets of \$1.00 in a year. Then the expected return will remain at 2.7027 percent, but the standard deviation drops to 0.09996 percent. This gives us an information ratio of 27.038. The formula predicts $(1/37) \cdot \sqrt{1{,}000{,}000} = 27.027$.

We could (American casinos do) add another green spot on the wheel and increase our advantage to 2/38. Then our expected return per bet will be 5.263 percent, and the standard deviation will be 99.861 percent. For 1 million plays per year, the expected return stays at 5.263 percent, and the standard deviation drops to 0.09986 percent. The information ratio is 52.70. The formula with IC = 2/38, and BR = 1,000,000 leads to an information ratio of 52.63. Owning a casino beats investment management hands down.

As a second example, consider the problem of forecasting semiannual residual returns on a collection of 200 stocks. We will designate the residual returns as θ_n. To make the calculations easier, we assume that

- The residual returns are independent across stocks.

2 The variance is $(19/37) \cdot (100\% - 100\%/37)^2 + (18/37) \cdot (-100\% - 100\%/37)^2 = 9992.696\%^2$, and therefore the standard deviation is 99.9634.

- The residual returns have an expected value of zero.
- The standard deviation of the semiannual residual return is 17.32 percent—that's 24.49 percent annual for each stock.

Our information advantage is an ability to forecast the residual returns. The correlation between our forecasts and the subsequent residual returns is 0.0577. One way to picture our situation is to imagine the residual return itself as the sum of 300 independent terms for each stock, $\theta_{n,j}$ for $j = 1, 2, \ldots, 300$:

$$\theta_n = \sum_j \theta_{n,j} \tag{4}$$

where each $\theta_{n,j}$ is equally likely to be +1.00 percent or −1.00 percent. Each $\theta_{n,j}$ will have a mean of 0 and standard deviation of 1.00 percent. The standard deviation of 300 of these added together will be $\sqrt{300} = 17.32$.

Our forecasting procedure tells us $\theta_{n,1}$ and leaves us in the dark about $\theta_{n,2}$ through $\theta_{n,300}$. The correlation of $\theta_{n,1}$ with θ_n will be 0.0577.[3] There are 300 equally important things that we might know about each stock, and we know only 1 of them. We don't know very much.

Since we are following 200 stocks, we will have 200 pieces of information twice a year, for a total of 400 per year. Our information coefficient, the correlation of $\theta_{n,1}$ and $\theta_{n'}$ is 0.0577. According to the fundamental law, the information ratio should be $0.0577 \cdot \sqrt{400} = 1.154$.

Can we fashion an investment strategy that will achieve an information ratio that high? In order to describe a portfolio strategy to exploit this information and calculate its attributes easily, we need a simplifying assumption. Assume that the benchmark portfolio is an equal-weighted portfolio of the 200 stocks (0.50 percent each). In each 6-month period, we expect to have about 100 stocks with a forecasted residual return for the quarter of +1.00 percent and 100 stocks with a forecasted residual return of −1.00 percent. This is akin to a buy list and a sell list. We will equal-weight the buy list (at 1.00 percent each), and not hold the sell list.

The expected *active* return will be 1.00 percent per 6 months with an active standard deviation of 1.2227 percent per 6 months.[4] The 6-month information ratio is 0.8179. To calculate an annual information ratio, we multiply the 6-month information ratio by the square root of 2, to find $\sqrt{2} \cdot 0.8179 = 1.1566$. This is slightly greater than the 1.154 predicted by the formula, since the formula does not consider the slight reduction in uncertainty resulting from the knowledge of $\theta_{n,1}$.[5]

We can also consider a third example, to put the information coefficient in further context. Suppose we want to forecast the direction of the market each quarter. In this simple example, we care only about forecasting direction. We will model the market direction as a variable $x(t) = \pm 1$, where x has mean 0 and standard deviation 1. Our forecast is $y(t) = \pm 1$, also with mean 0 and standard deviation 1. Then the information coefficient—the correlation of $x(t)$ and $y(t)$—depends on the covariance of $x(t)$ and $y(t)$:

---

3 The covariance of $\theta_{n,1}$ with θ_n is 1, since $\theta_{n,1}$ is uncorrelated with $\theta_{n,j}$ for $j \geq 2$. Since the standard deviations of $\theta_{n,1}$ and θ_n are 1.0 and 17.32, respectively, their correlation is 0.0577. (The correlation is the covariance divided by the two standard deviations. See Appendix C.)

4 The active holdings are 1/200 for 100 stocks and −1/200 for another 100 stocks. The expected active return is $100 \cdot (1/200) \cdot (1\%) + 100 \cdot (-1/200) \cdot (-1\%) = 1\%$. The residual variance of each asset (conditional on knowing $\theta_{n,1}$) is 299. The active variance of our position is $\sum_n \left(1/200\right)^2 \cdot 299 = \frac{299}{200} = (1.2227)^2$.

5 We can go one step further with this example. In each half year, about 50 of the stocks will move from the buy list to the sell list, and another 50 will move from the sell list to the buy list. To implement the change will require about 50 percent turnover per 6 months, or 100 percent turnover per year. If round-trip transactions costs are 0.80 percent, then we lose 0.80 percent per year in transactions costs. The information ratio drops to 0.70, since the annual alpha net of costs is 1.21 percent and the annual residual risk stays at 1.729 percent.

$$IC = \text{Cov}\{x(t), y(t)\} = \frac{1}{N} \cdot \sum_{t=1}^{N} x(t) \cdot y(t) \quad (5)$$

where we observe N bets on market direction.

If we correctly forecast market direction ($x = y$) N_1 times, and incorrectly forecast market direction ($x = -y$) $N - N_1$ times, then the information coefficient is

$$IC = \frac{1}{N} \cdot [N_1 - (N - N_1)] = 2 \cdot \left(\frac{N_1}{N}\right) - 1 \quad (6)$$

Equation (6) provides some further intuition into the information coefficient. For example, we saw that an information coefficient of 0.0577 can lead to an information ratio above 1.0 (top decile, according to Chap. 5). Using Eq. (6), an IC = 0.0577 corresponds to correctly forecasting direction only 52.885 percent of the time—a small edge indeed.

These examples not only show the formula at work, but also show how little information one needs in order to be highly successful. In fact, an information coefficient of 0.02 between forecasted stock return and realized return over 200 stocks each quarter [with an implied accuracy of only 51 percent according to Eq. (6)] will produce a highly respectable information ratio of 0.56.

ADDITIVITY

The fundamental law is additive in the squared information ratios. Suppose there are two classes of stocks. In class 1 you have BR_1 stocks and a skill level of IC_1. Class 2 has BR_2 stocks and a skill level IC_2. The information ratio for the aggregate will be

$$IR^2 = BR_1 \cdot IC_1^2 + BR_2 \cdot IC_2^2 \quad (7)$$

assuming optimal implementation of the alphas across the combined set of stocks.[6] Notice that this is the sum of the squared information ratios for the first class and second class combined. Suppose the manager currently follows 200 stocks with semiannual forecasts; the breadth is 400. The information coefficient for these forecasts is 0.04. The information ratio will be $0.8 = 0.04 \cdot \sqrt{400}$. How would the information ratio and value added increase if the manager was to follow an additional 100 stocks (again with two forecasts per year) with information coefficient 0.03? The manager's value added will be proportional to $0.64 + (0.03)^2 \cdot 200 = 0.64 + 0.18 = 0.82$. There will be a 28 percent increase in the manager's ability to add value. The information ratio will increase from 0.8 to $0.906 = \sqrt{0.82}$.

The additivity works along other dimensions as well. Suppose a manager follows 400 equities and takes a position on these on the average of once per year. The manager's information coefficient is 0.03. This yields an information ratio of $0.6 = 0.03 \cdot \sqrt{400}$. In addition, the manager makes a quarterly forecast on the market. The information coefficient for the market forecasts is 0.1. The information ratio for the market timing is $0.2 = 0.1 \cdot \sqrt{4}$. The overall information ratio will be the square root of the sum of the squared information ratios for stock selection and market timing: 0.63.

We can even carry this notion to an international portfolio. Figure 2 shows the breakdown of return on an international portfolio. The active return comes from three main sources: active currency positions, active allocations across countries, and active allocations within country markets.

6 For example, if you index the second set of stocks, the combined information ratio will be only IR_1.

Figure 2

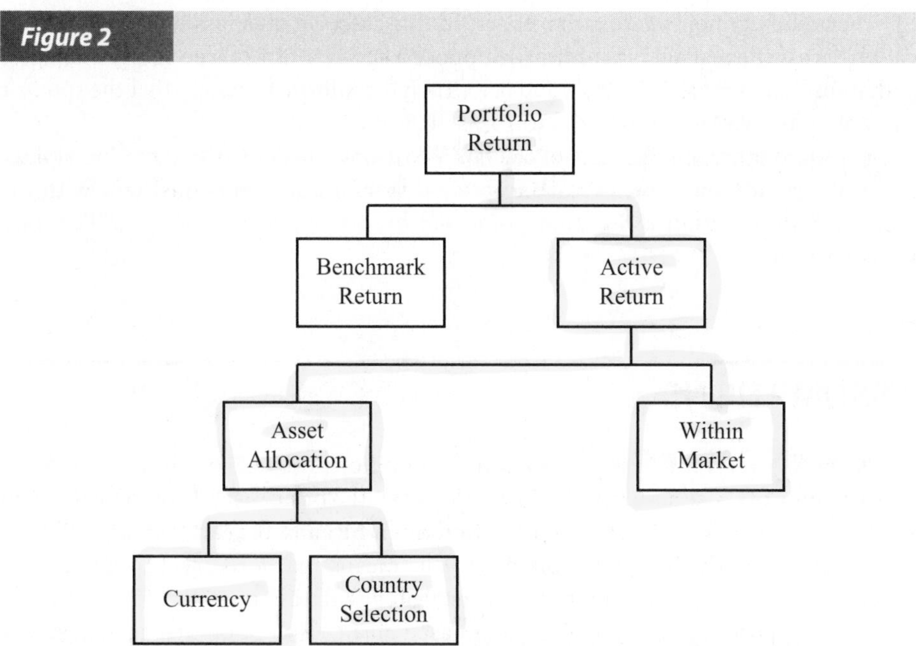

Assume that we are based in London, and that we invest in four countries: the United States, Japan, Germany, and the United Kingdom. There are three currency bets available to us;[7] we revise our currency position each quarter, and so we make 12 independent bets per year. We also make active bets across countries. These bet on the local elements of market return (separated from the currency component). We revise these market allocations each quarter. In addition we select stocks in each of the markets. We follow 400 stocks in the United States, 300 in Japan, 200 in the United Kingdom, and 100 in Germany. We revise our forecasts on these stocks once a year. Suppose our skill levels are IC_C for currency, IC_M for market allocation, and IC_{US}, IC_J, IC_{UK}, and IC_G for the national stocks. The overall information ratio will be

$$IR = \sqrt{\begin{array}{l} IC_C^2 \cdot 12 + IC_M^2 \cdot 12 + IC_{US}^2 \cdot 400 + IC_J^2 \cdot 300 + \\ IC_{UK}^2 \cdot 200 + IC_G^2 \cdot 100 \end{array}} \tag{8}$$

To make things simple, suppose that $IC_{US} = IC_J = IC_{UK} = IC_G = 0.02$. Then the squared information ratio contribution from the stocks will be $0.40 = 1000 \cdot (0.02)^2$. For the timing component to contribute equally, we would need $IC_C = IC_M = 0.129$, since $0.40 = 24 \cdot (0.129)^2$. Consider a more realistic (although still optimistic) information coefficient of 0.075 for the currency and market allocation decisions. That would make the contribution from currency and market allocation 0.135. The total squared information ratio would be $0.535 = 0.40 + 0.135$. The total information ratio is $0.73 = \sqrt{0.535}$.

7 With only one country, we would have no currency bet. Two countries would allow one currency bet, etc. The total active currency position must be zero.

The additivity holds across managers. In this case, we must assume that the allocation across the managers is optimal. Suppose a sponsor hires three equity managers with information ratios 0.75, 0.50, and 0.30. Then the information ratio that the sponsor can obtain is 0.95,[8] since $(0.95)^2 = (0.75)^2 + (0.50)^2 + (0.30)^2$.

There are other applications of the law. Most notable is its use in scaling alphas; i.e., making sure that forecasts of exceptional stock returns are consistent with the manager's information ratio. That point will be discussed in Chap. 14, "Portfolio Construction."

ASSUMPTIONS

The law, like everything else, is based on assumptions that are not quite true. We'll discuss some of those assumptions later. However, the basic insight we can gain from the law is clear: It is important to play often (high BR) and to play well (high IC).

The forecasts should be independent. This means that forecast 2 should not be based on a source of information that is correlated with the sources of forecast 1. For example, suppose that our first forecast is based on an assumption that growth stocks will do poorly, and our second is based on an assumption that high-yield stocks will do well. These pieces of information are not independent; growth stocks tend to have very low yields, and not many high-yield stocks would be called growth stocks. We've just picked out two ways to measure the same phenomenon. An example of independent forecasts is a quarterly adjustment of the portfolio's beta from 1.00 to either 1.05 or 0.95 as a market timing decision based on *new* information each quarter.

In a situation where analysts provide recommendations on a firm-by-firm basis, it is possible to check the level of dependence among these forecasts by first quantifying the recommendations and then regressing them against attributes of the firms. Analysts may like all the firms in a particular industry: Their stock picks are actually a single industry bet. All recommended stocks may have a high earnings yield: The analysts have made a single bet on earnings-to-price ratios. Finally, analysts may like all firms that have performed well in the last year; instead of a firm-by-firm bet, we have a single bet on the concept of momentum. More significantly, the residuals of

8 Suppose manager n has information ratio IR_n and active risk ω_n. The sponsor's utility is

$$\sum_n y_n \cdot IR_n \cdot \omega_n - \lambda_{SA} \cdot \sum_n (y_n \cdot \omega_n)^2$$

assuming independent active risks and a sponsor's active risk aversion of λ_{SA}. The optimal allocation to manager n is

$$y_n^* = \frac{IR_n}{2\lambda_{SA} \cdot \omega_n}$$

The overall alpha will be

$$\alpha = \sum_n y_n^* \cdot \omega_n \cdot IR_n = \left(\frac{1}{2\lambda_{SA}}\right) \cdot \sum_n IR_n^2$$

The active variance will be

$$\omega^2 = \sum_n \left(y_n^* \cdot \omega_n\right)^2 = \left(\frac{1}{2\lambda_{SA}}\right)^2 \cdot \sum_n IR_n^2$$

and so the ratio of the alpha to the standard deviation will be

$$IR = \sqrt{\sum_n IR_n^2}$$

the regression will actually be independent forecasts of individual stock return. Thus the regression analysis gives us the opportunity both to uncover consistent patterns in our recommendations and to remove them if we choose.

The same masking of dependence can occur over time. If you reassess your industry bets on the basis of new information each year, but rebalance your portfolios monthly, you shouldn't think that you make 12 industry bets per year. You just make the same bet 12 times.

We can see how dependence in the information sources will lower our overall skill level with a simple example. Consider the case where there are two sources of information. Separately, each has a level of skill IC; that is, the forecasts have a correlation of IC with the eventual returns. However, if the two information sources are dependent, then the information derived from the second source is not entirely new. Part of the second source's information will just reinforce what we knew from the first source, and part will be new or incremental information. We have to discover the value of the incremental information. As one can imagine, the greater the dependence between the two information sources, the lower the value of the incremental information. If γ is the correlation between the two information sources, then the skill level of the combined sources, IC(com), will be

$$IC(com) = IC \cdot \sqrt{\frac{2}{1+\gamma}} \tag{9}$$

If there is no correlation between sources ($\gamma = 0$), then $IC^2(com) = 2 \cdot IC^2$—the two sources will add in their ability to add value. As γ increases toward 1, the value of the second source diminishes.

For example, recall the case earlier in this chapter where the residual return θ_n on stock n was made up of 300 nuggets of return $\theta_{n,j}$ for $j = 1,2, \ldots, 300$. Suppose we have two information sources on the stocks. Source 1 knows $\theta_{n,1}$ and $\theta_{n,2}$ and source 2 knows $\theta_{n,2}$ and $\theta_{n,3}$. The information coefficient of each source is 0.0816. In this situation, the information coefficient of the combined sources will be 0.0942, since the information supplied by source 2 is correlated with that supplied by source 1; $\gamma = 0.5$. The formula gives $0.0816 \cdot \sqrt{2/1.5} = 0.0942$, which you can confirm by a direct calculation.

The law is based on the assumption that each of the BR active bets has the same level of skill. In fact, the manager will have greater skills in one area than another. We can see from the additivity principle, Eq. (7), that the square of the information ratio is the sum of the squares of the information ratios for the particular sources. Figure 3 demonstrates this phenomenon. If we order the information sources from highest skill level to lowest, then the total value added is just the area under the "skill" curve. Notice that the law assumes that the skill curve is horizontal; i.e., we replace the sum of the skill levels by an average skill level.

Figure 3

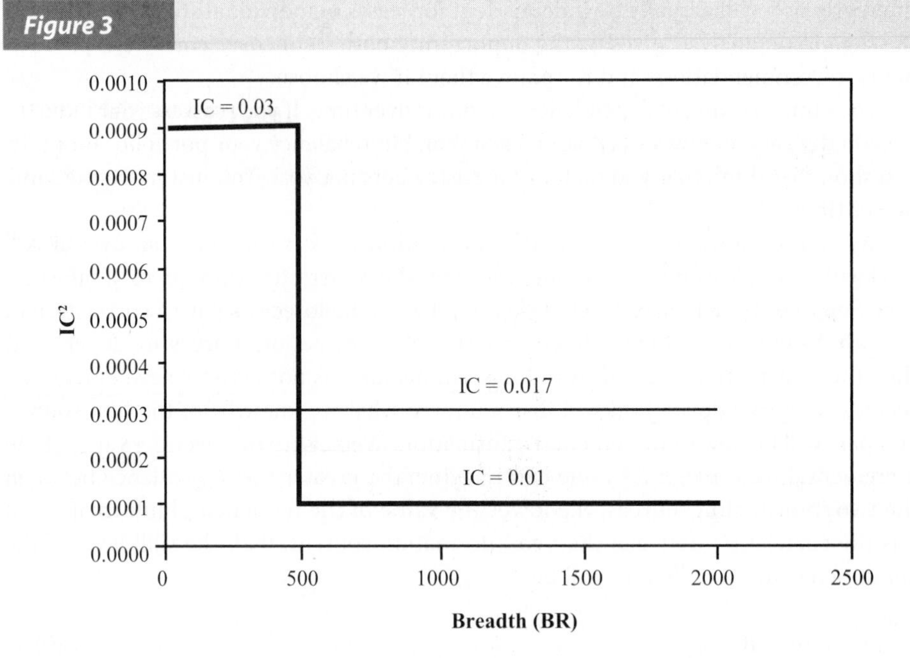

The strongest assumption behind the law is that the manager will accurately gauge the value of information and build portfolios that use that information in an optimal way. This requires insight and humility, a desirable combination that is not usually found in one individual.

NOT THE LAW OF LARGE NUMBERS

A few investment professionals interpret the fundamental law of active management as a version of the statistical law of large numbers. This is a misinterpretation of one law or both. The law of large numbers says that sample averages for large samples will be very close to the true mean, and that our approximation of the true mean gets better and better as the sample gets larger.

The fundamental law says that more breadth is better if you can maintain the skill level. However, the law is just as valid with a breadth of 10 as with a breadth of 1000. The information ratio is still $IR = IC \cdot \sqrt{BR}$.

This confusion stems from the role of breadth. More breadth at the same skill level lets us diversify the residual risk. This is analogous to the role of large sample sizes in the law of large numbers, where the large sample size allows us to diversify the sampling error.

TESTS

The fundamental law is a guideline, not an operational tool. It is desirable that we have some faith in the law's ability to make reasonable predictions. We have conducted some tests of the law and found it to be excellent in its predictions.

The tests took the following form: Each year we supply alphas for BR stocks. The alphas are a mixture of the residual return on the stock over the next year and some random noise. The mixture can be set[9] so that the correlation of the forecasts with the residuals will be IC. That gives us a prediction of the information ratio that we should realize with these alphas.

The realized information ratios for optimal portfolios based on these forecasts are statistically indistinguishable from the forecasts of the fundamental law. When we then impose institutional constraints limiting short sales, the realized information ratios drop somewhat.

INVESTMENT STYLE

The law encourages managers to have an eclectic style. If a manager can find some independent source of information that will be of use, then he or she should exploit that information. It is the manager's need to present a clear picture of his or her style to clients that inhibits the manager from adopting an eclectic style. At the same time, the sponsor who hires a stable of managers has an incentive to diversify their styles in order to ensure that their bets are independent. The way investment management is currently organized in the United States, the managers prepare the distinct ingredients and the sponsor makes the stew.

SUMMARY

We have shown how the information ratio of an active manager can be explained by two components: the skill (IC) of the investment manager and the breadth (BR) of the strategy. These are related to the value added by the strategy by a simple formula [Eq. (3)].

Three main assumptions underlie this result. First and foremost, we assumed that the manager has an accurate measure of his or her own skills and exploits information in an optimal way. Second, we assumed that the sources of information are independent; i.e., the manager doesn't bet twice on a repackaged form of the same information. Third, we assumed that the skill involved in forecasting each component, IC, is the same. The first assumption, call it competence or hypercompetence, is the most crucial. Investment managers need a precise idea of what they know and, more significantly, what they don't know. Moreover, they need to know how to turn their ideas into portfolios and gain the benefits of their insights. The second two assumptions are merely simplifying approximations and can be mitigated by some of the devices mentioned above.

The message is clear: you must play often and play well to win at the investment management game. It takes only a modest amount of skill to win as long as that skill is deployed frequently and across a large number of stocks.

9 The forecast is

$$\alpha = \text{IC} \cdot \left[\text{IC} \cdot \theta + \omega \cdot \sqrt{1 - \text{IC}^2} \cdot z \right]$$

where z is a random number with mean 0 and variance 1. We see that $\text{Var}\{\alpha\} = \text{IC}^2 \cdot \text{Var}\{\theta\}$ and $\text{Cov}\{\alpha,\theta\} = \text{IC}^2 \cdot \text{Var}\{\theta\}$, and so $\text{Corr}\{\alpha,\theta\} = \text{IC}$.

REFERENCES

Divecha, Arjun, and Richard C. Grinold. 1989. "Normal Portfolios: Issues for Sponsors, Managers and Consultants." *Financial Analysts Journal*, vol. 45, no. 2:7–13.

Ferguson, Robert. 1975. "Active Portfolio Management." *Financial Analysts Journal*, vol. 31, no. 3:63–72.

———. 1986. "The Trouble with Performance Measurement." *Journal of Portfolio Management*, vol. 12, no. 3.

Fisher, Lawrence. 1975. "Using Modern Portfolio Theory to Maintain an Efficiently Diversified Portfolio." *Financial Analysts Journal*, vol. 31, no. 3:73–85.

Grinold, Richard. 1989. "The Fundamental Law of Active Management." *Journal of Portfolio Management*, vol. 15, no. 3:30–37.

Jacobs, Bruce I., and Kenneth N. Levy. 1995. "The Law of One Alpha." *Journal of Portfolio Management*, vol. 21, no. 4:78–79.

Rosenberg, Barr. 1976 "Security Appraisal and Unsystematic Risk in Institutional Investment." *Proceedings of the Seminar on the Analysis of Security Prices* (Chicago: University of Chicago Press, November), pp. 171–237.

Rudd, Andrew. 1987 "Business Risk and Investment Risk." *Investment Management Review*, November-December, pp. 19–27.

Sharpe, William F. 1966. "Mutual Fund Performance." *Journal of Business*, vol. 39, no. 1 (January):66–86.

Treynor, Jack, and Fischer Black. 1973. "How to Use Security Analysis to Improve Portfolio Selection." *Journal of Business*, vol. 46, no. 1:66–86.

READING

60

The Portfolio Management Process and the Investment Policy Statement

by John L. Maginn, CFA, Donald L. Tuttle, CFA, Dennis W. McLeavey, CFA, and Jerald E. Pinto, CFA

LEARNING OUTCOMES

Mastery	*The candidate should be able to:*
☐	a. explain the importance of the portfolio perspective;
☐	b. describe the steps of the portfolio management process and the components of those steps;
☐	c. explain the role of the investment policy statement in the portfolio management process, and describe the elements of an investment policy statement;
☐	d. explain how capital market expectations and the investment policy statement help influence the strategic asset allocation decision and how an investor's investment time horizon may influence the investor's strategic asset allocation;
☐	e. define investment objectives and constraints, and explain and distinguish among the types of investment objectives and constraints;
☐	f. contrast the types of investment time horizons, determine the time horizon for a particular investor, and evaluate the effects of this time horizon on portfolio choice;
☐	g. justify ethical conduct as a requirement for managing investment portfolios.

INTRODUCTION

1

In setting out to master the concepts and tools of portfolio management, we first need a coherent description of the portfolio management process. The portfolio management process is an integrated set of steps undertaken in a consistent manner to create and maintain an appropriate portfolio (combination of assets) to meet clients' stated goals. The process we present in this reading is a distillation of the shared elements of current practice.

Because it serves as the foundation for the process, we also introduce the investment policy statement through a discussion of its main components. An investment policy statement (IPS) is a written document that clearly sets out a client's return objectives and risk tolerance over that client's relevant time horizon, along with applicable constraints such as liquidity needs, tax considerations, regulatory requirements, and unique circumstances.

The portfolio management process moves from planning, through execution, and then to feedback. In the planning step, investment objectives and policies are formulated, capital market expectations are formed, and strategic asset allocations are established. In the execution step, the portfolio manager constructs the portfolio. In the feedback step, the manager monitors and evaluates the portfolio compared with the plan. Any changes suggested by the feedback must be examined carefully to ensure that they represent long-run considerations.

The investment policy statement provides the foundation of the portfolio management process. In creating an IPS, the manager writes down the client's special characteristics and needs. The IPS must clearly communicate the client's objectives and constraints. The IPS thereby becomes a plan that can be executed by any advisor or portfolio manager the client might subsequently hire. A properly developed IPS disciplines the portfolio management process and helps ensure against ad hoc revisions in strategy.

When combined with capital market expectations, the IPS forms the basis for a strategic asset allocation. Capital market expectations concern the risk and return characteristics of capital market instruments such as stocks and bonds. The strategic asset allocation establishes acceptable exposures to IPS-permissible asset classes to achieve the client's long-run objectives and constraints.

The portfolio perspective underlies the portfolio management process and IPS. The next sections illustrate this perspective.

2 INVESTMENT MANAGEMENT

Investment management is the service of professionally investing money. As a profession, investment management has its roots in the activities of European investment bankers in managing the fortunes created by the Industrial Revolution. By the beginning of the 21st century, investment management had become an important part of the financial services sector of all developed economies. By the end of 2003, the United States alone had approximately 15,000 money managers (registered investment advisors) responsible for investing more than $23 trillion, according to Standard & Poor's *Directory of Registered Investment Advisors* (2004). No worldwide count of investment advisors is available, but looking at another familiar professionally managed investment, the number of mutual funds stood at about 54,000 at year-end 2003; of these funds only 15 percent were U.S. based.[1]

The economics of investment management are relatively simple. An investment manager's revenue is fee driven; primarily, fees are based on a percentage of the average amount of assets under management and the type of investment program run for the client, as spelled out in detail in the investment management contract or

1 These facts are based on statistics produced by the Investment Company Institute and the International Investment Funds Association.

other governing document. Consequently, an investment management firm's size is judged by the amount of assets under management, which is thus directly related to manager's revenue, another measure of size. Traditionally, the value of an investment management business (or a first estimate of value) is determined as a multiple of its annual fee income.

To understand an investment management firm or product beyond its size, we need to know not only its investment disciplines but also the type or types of investor it primarily serves. Broadly speaking, investors can be described as institutional or individual. Institutional investors are entities such as pension funds, foundations and endowments, insurance companies, and banks that ultimately serve as financial intermediaries between individuals and financial markets. The investment policy decisions of institutional investors are typically made by investment committees or trustees, with at least some members having a professional background in finance. The committee members or trustees frequently also bear a fiduciary relationship to the funds for which they have investment responsibility. Such a relationship, if it is present, imposes some legal standards regarding processes and decisions, which is reflected in the processes of the investment managers who serve that market segment.

Beginning in the second half of the 20th century, the tremendous growth of institutional investors, especially defined benefit pension plans, spurred a tremendous expansion in investment management firms or investment units of other entities (such as bank trust divisions) to service their needs.[2] As the potentially onerous financial responsibilities imposed on the sponsors by such plans became more evident, however, the 1980s and 1990s saw trends to other types of retirement schemes focused on participant responsibility for investment decisions and results. In addition, a long-lasting worldwide economic expansion created a great amount of individual wealth. As a result, investment advisors oriented to serving high-net-worth individuals as well as mutual funds (which serve the individual and, to a lesser extent, the smaller institutional market) gained in relative importance.

Such individual-investor-oriented advisors may incorporate a heavy personal financial planning emphasis in their services. Many wealthy families establish family offices to serve as trusted managers of their finances. Family offices are entities, typically organized and owned by a family, that assume responsibility for services such as financial planning, estate planning, and asset management, as well as a range of practical matters from tax return preparation to bill paying. Some family offices evolve such depth in professional staff that they open access to their services to other families (multi-family offices). In contrast to family offices, some investment management businesses service both individual and institutional markets, sometimes in separate divisions or corporate units, sometimes worldwide, and sometimes as part of a financial giant (American Express and Citigroup are examples of such financial supermarkets). In such cases, wrap-fee accounts packaging the services of outside investment managers may vie for the client's business with in-house, separately managed accounts, as well as in-house mutual funds, external mutual funds, and other offerings marketed by a brokerage arm of the business.

Investment management companies employ portfolio managers, analysts, and traders, as well as marketing and support personnel. Portfolio managers may use both outside research produced by **sell-side analysts** (analysts employed by brokerages) and research generated by in-house analysts—so-called **buy-side analysts** (analysts employed by an investment manager or institutional investor). The staffing of in-house research departments depends on the size of the investment management firm, the variety of investment offerings, and the investment disciplines employed. An example

---

2 A defined benefit pension plan specifies the plan sponsor's obligations in terms of benefit to plan participants. The plan sponsor bears the investment risk of such plans.

may illustrate the variety of talent employed: The research department of one money manager with $30 billion in assets under management employs 34 equity analysts, 23 credit analysts, 3 hedge fund analysts, 12 quantitative analysts, 4 risk management professionals, 1 economist, and 1 economic analyst. That same company has a trading department with 8 equity and 8 bond traders and many support personnel. CFA charterholders can be found in all of these functions.

3 THE PORTFOLIO PERSPECTIVE

The portfolio perspective is our focus on the aggregate of all the investor's holdings: the portfolio. Because economic fundamentals influence the average returns of many assets, the risk associated with one asset's returns is generally related to the risk associated with other assets' returns. If we evaluate the prospects of each asset in isolation and ignore their interrelationships, we will likely misunderstand the risk and return prospects of the investor's total investment position—our most basic concern.

The historical roots of this portfolio perspective date to the work of Nobel laureate Harry Markowitz (1952). Markowitz and subsequent researchers, such as Jack Treynor and Nobel laureate William Sharpe, established the field of modern portfolio theory (MPT)—the analysis of rational portfolio choices based on the efficient use of risk. Modern portfolio theory revolutionized investment management. First, professional investment practice began to recognize the importance of the portfolio perspective in achieving investment objectives. Second, MPT helped spread the knowledge and use of quantitative methods in portfolio management. Today, quantitative and qualitative concepts complement each other in investment management practice.

In developing his theory of portfolio choice, Markowitz began with the perspective of investing for a single period. Others, including Nobel laureate Robert Merton, explored the dynamics of portfolio choice in a multiperiod setting. These subsequent contributions have greatly enriched the content of MPT.

If Markowitz, Merton, and other researchers created the supply, three developments in the investment community created demand for the portfolio perspective. First, institutional investing emerged worldwide to play an increasingly dominant role in financial markets. Measuring and controlling the risk of large pools of money became imperative. The second development was the increasing availability of ever-cheaper computer processing power and communications possibilities. As a result, a broader range of techniques for implementing MPT portfolio concepts became feasible. The third related development was the professionalization of the investment management field. This professionalization has been reflected in the worldwide growth of the professional accreditation program leading to the Chartered Financial Analyst (CFA®) designation.

4 PORTFOLIO MANAGEMENT AS A PROCESS

The unified presentation of portfolio management as a process represented an important advance in the investment management literature. Prior to the introduction of this concept in the first edition of this book, much of the traditional literature reflected an approach of selecting individual securities without an overall plan. Through the eyes of the professional, however, portfolio management is a *process*, an integrated set of activities that combine in a logical, orderly manner to produce a desired product. The process view is a *dynamic* and *flexible* concept that applies to all types of portfolio investments—bonds, stocks, real estate, gold, collectibles; to various organizational types—trust company, investment counsel firm, insurance company, mutual fund; to a full range of investors—individuals, pension plans, endowments, foundations, insurance companies, banks; and is independent of manager, location, investment philosophy, style, or approach. Portfolio management is a continuous and systematic process complete with feedback loops for monitoring and rebalancing. The process can be as loose or as disciplined, as quantitative or as qualitative, and as simple or as complex as its operators desire.

The portfolio management process is the same in every application: an integrated set of steps undertaken in a consistent manner to create and maintain appropriate combinations of investment assets. In the next sections, we explore the main features of this process.

THE PORTFOLIO MANAGEMENT PROCESS LOGIC 5

Three elements in managing any business process are planning, execution, and feedback. These same elements form the basis for the portfolio management process as depicted in Figure 1.

5.1 The Planning Step

The planning step is described in the four leftmost boxes in Figure 1. The top two boxes represent investor-related input factors, while the bottom two factors represent economic and market input.

5.1.1 *Identifying and Specifying the Investor's Objectives and Constraints*

The first task in investment planning is to identify and specify the investor's objectives and constraints. **Investment objectives** are desired investment outcomes. In investments, objectives chiefly pertain to return and risk. Constraints are limitations on the investor's ability to take full or partial advantage of particular investments. For example, an investor may face constraints related to the concentration of holdings as a result of government regulation, or restrictions in a governing legal document. Constraints are either internal, such as a client's specific liquidity needs, time horizon, and unique circumstances, or external, such as tax issues and legal and regulatory requirements. In Section 6, we examine the objective and constraint specification process.

5.1.2 *Creating the Investment Policy Statement*

Once a client has specified a set of objectives and constraints, the manager's next task is to formulate the investment policy statement. The IPS serves as the governing document for all investment decision-making. In addition to objectives and constraints, the IPS may also cover a variety of other issues. For example, the IPS generally details reporting requirements, rebalancing guidelines, frequency and format of investment communication, manager fees, investment strategy, and the desired investment style or styles of investment managers. A typical IPS includes the following elements:

- a brief client description;
- the purpose of establishing policies and guidelines;
- the duties and investment responsibilities of parties involved, particularly those relating to fiduciary duties, communication, operational efficiency, and accountability. Parties involved include the client, any investment committee, the investment manager, and the bank custodian;

Figure 1 The Portfolio Construction, Monitoring, and Revision Process

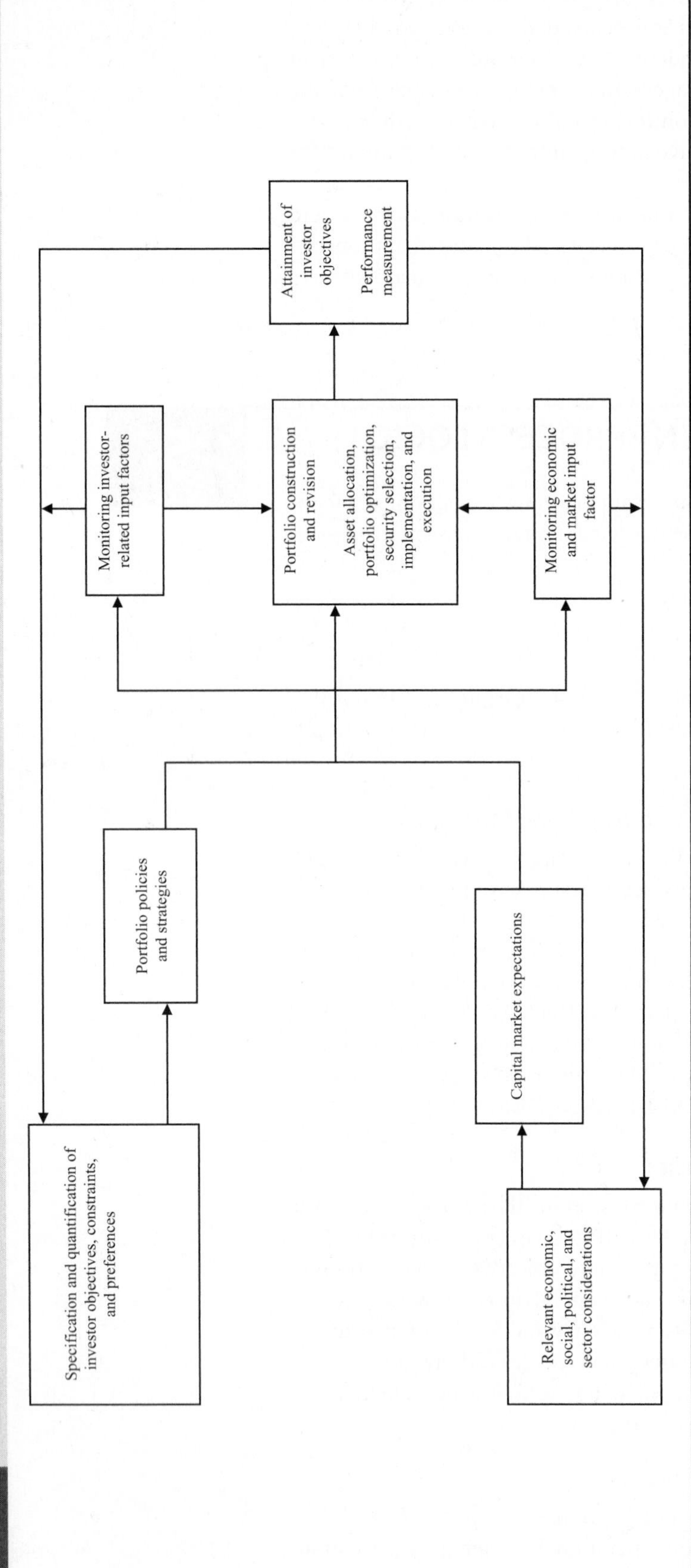

- the statement of investment goals, objectives, and constraints;
- the schedule for review of investment performance as well as the IPS itself;
- performance measures and benchmarks to be used in performance evaluation;
- any considerations to be taken into account in developing the strategic asset allocation;
- investment strategies and investment style(s); and
- guidelines for rebalancing the portfolio based on feedback.

The IPS forms the basis for the strategic asset allocation, which reflects the interaction of objectives and constraints with the investor's long-run capital market expectations. When experienced professionals include the policy allocation as part of the IPS, they are implicitly forming capital market expectations and also examining the interaction of objectives and constraints with long-run capital market expectations. In practice, one may see IPSs that include strategic asset allocations, but we will maintain a distinction between the two types.

The planning process involves the concrete elaboration of an **investment strategy**—that is, the manager's approach to investment analysis and security selection. A clearly formulated investment strategy organizes and clarifies the basis for investment decisions. It also guides those decisions toward achieving investment objectives. In the broadest sense, investment strategies are passive, active, or semiactive.

- In a passive investment approach, portfolio composition does not react to changes in capital market expectations (*passive* means *not reacting*). For example, a portfolio indexed to the MSCI-Europe Index, an index representing European equity markets, might add or drop a holding in response to a change in the index composition but not in response to changes in capital market expectations concerning the security's investment value. **Indexing**, a common passive approach to investing, refers to holding a portfolio of securities designed to replicate the returns on a specified index of securities. A second type of passive investing is a strict buy-and-hold strategy, such as a fixed, but non-indexed, portfolio of bonds to be held to maturity.
- In contrast, with an active investment approach, a portfolio manager will respond to changing capital market expectations. Active management of a portfolio means that its holdings differ from the portfolio's **benchmark** or comparison portfolio in an attempt to produce positive excess risk-adjusted returns, also known as positive **alpha**. Securities held in different-from-benchmark weights reflect expectations of the portfolio manager that differ from consensus expectations. If the portfolio manager's differential expectations are also on average correct, active portfolio management may add value.
- A third category, the semiactive, risk-controlled active, or enhanced index approach, seeks positive alpha while keeping tight control over risk relative to the portfolio's benchmark. As an example, an index-tilt strategy seeks to track closely the risk of a securities index while adding a targeted amount of incremental value by tilting portfolio weightings in some direction that the manager expects to be profitable.

Active investment approaches encompass a very wide range of disciplines. To organize this diversity, investment analysts appeal to the concept of investment style. Following Brown and Goetzmann (1997), we can define an investment style (such as an emphasis on growth stocks or value stocks) as a natural grouping of investment disciplines that has some predictive power in explaining the future dispersion in returns across portfolios.

5.1.3 *Forming Capital Market Expectations*

The manager's third task in the planning process is to form capital market expectations. Long-run forecasts of risk and return characteristics for various asset classes form the basis for choosing portfolios that maximize expected return for given levels of risk, or minimize risk for given levels of expected return.

5.1.4 *Creating the Strategic Asset Allocation*

The fourth and final task in the planning process is determining the strategic asset allocation. Here the manager combines the IPS and capital market expectations to determine target asset class weights; maximum and minimum permissible asset class weights are often also specified as a risk-control mechanism. The investor may seek both single-period and multiperiod perspectives in the return and risk characteristics of asset allocations under consideration. A single-period perspective has the advantage of simplicity. A multiperiod perspective can address the liquidity and tax considerations that arise from rebalancing portfolios over time, as well as serial correlation (long- and short-term dependencies) in returns, but is more costly to implement.

This reading focuses on the creation of an IPS in the planning step and thereby lays the groundwork for the discussion in other readings of tailoring the IPS to individual and institutional investors' needs. The execution and feedback steps in the portfolio management process are as important as the planning step. For now, we merely outline how these steps fit in the portfolio management process.

5.2 The Execution Step

The execution step is represented by the "portfolio construction and revision" box in Figure 1. In the execution step, the manager integrates investment strategies with capital market expectations to select the specific assets for the portfolio (the portfolio selection/composition decision). Portfolio managers initiate portfolio decisions based on analysts' inputs, and trading desks then implement these decisions (portfolio implementation decision). Subsequently, the portfolio is revised as investor circumstances or capital market expectations change; thus the execution step interacts constantly with the feedback step.

In making the portfolio selection/composition decision, portfolio managers may use the techniques of portfolio optimization. Portfolio optimization—quantitative tools for combining assets efficiently to achieve a set of return and risk objectives—plays a key role in the integration of strategies with expectations and appears in Figure 1 in the portfolio construction and revision box.

At times, a portfolio's actual asset allocation may purposefully and temporarily differ from the strategic asset allocation. For example, the asset allocation might change to reflect an investor's current circumstances that are different from normal. The temporary allocation may remain in place until circumstances return to those described in the IPS and reflected in the strategic asset allocation. If the changed circumstances become permanent, the manager must update the investor's IPS and the temporary asset allocation plan will effectively become the new strategic asset allocation. A strategy known as tactical asset allocation also results in differences from the strategic asset allocation. Tactical asset allocation responds to changes in short-term capital market expectations rather than to investor circumstances.

The portfolio implementation decision is as important as the portfolio selection/composition decision. Poorly managed executions result in transaction costs that reduce performance. Transaction costs include all costs of trading, including explicit transaction costs, implicit transaction costs, and missed trade opportunity costs. Explicit transaction costs include commissions paid to brokers, fees paid to exchanges, and taxes. Implicit transaction costs include bid–ask spreads and market price impacts of large trades. Missed trade opportunity costs can arise due to price changes that prevent trades from being filled.

In sum, in the execution step, plans are turned into reality—with all the attendant real-world challenges.

5.3 The Feedback Step

In any business endeavor, feedback and control are essential elements in reaching a goal. In portfolio management, this step has two components: monitoring and rebalancing, and performance evaluation.

5.3.1 *Monitoring and Rebalancing*

Monitoring and rebalancing involve the use of feedback to manage ongoing exposures to available investment opportunities so that the client's current objectives and constraints continue to be satisfied. Two types of factors are monitored: investor-related factors such as the investor's circumstances, and economic and market input factors.

One impetus for portfolio revision is a change in investment objectives or constraints because of changes in investor circumstances. Portfolio managers need a process in place to stay informed of changes in clients' circumstances. The termination of a pension plan or death of a spouse may trigger an abrupt change in a client's time horizon and tax concerns, and the IPS should list the occurrence of such changes as a basis for appropriate portfolio revision.

More predictably, changes in economic and market input factors give rise to the regular need for portfolio revision. Again, portfolio managers need to systematically review the risk attributes of assets as well as economic and capital market factors. A change in expectations may trigger portfolio revision. When asset price changes occur, however, revisions can be required even without changes in expectations. The actual timing and magnitude of rebalancing may be triggered by review periods or by specific rules governing the management of the portfolio and deviation from the tolerances or ranges specified in the strategic asset allocation, or the timing and magnitude may be at the discretion of the manager. For example, suppose the policy allocation calls for an initial portfolio with a 70 percent weighting to stocks and a 30 percent weighting to bonds. Suppose the value of the stock holdings then grows by 40 percent, while the value of the bond holdings grows by 10 percent. The new weighting is roughly 75 percent in stocks and 25 percent in bonds. To bring the portfolio back into compliance with investment policy, it must be rebalanced back to the long-term policy weights. In any event, the rebalancing decision is a crucial one that must take into account many factors, such as transaction costs and taxes (for taxable investors). Disciplined rebalancing will have a major impact on the attainment of investment objectives. Rebalancing takes us back to the issues of execution, as is appropriate in a feedback process.

5.3.2 *Performance Evaluation*

Investment performance must periodically be evaluated by the investor to assess progress toward the achievement of investment objectives as well as to assess portfolio management skill.

The assessment of portfolio management skill has three components. Performance measurement involves the calculation of the portfolio's rate of return. Performance attribution examines why the portfolio performed as it did and involves determining the sources of a portfolio's performance. **Performance appraisal** is the evaluation of whether or not the manager is doing a good job based on how the portfolio did relative to a benchmark (a comparison portfolio).

Often, we can examine a portfolio's performance, in terms of absolute returns, through three sources: decisions regarding the strategic asset allocation, **market timing** (returns attributable to shorter-term tactical deviations from the strategic asset allocation), and security selection (skill in selecting individual securities within an asset class). However, portfolio management is frequently conducted with reference to a benchmark, or for some entities, with reference to a stream of projected liabilities or a specified target rate of return. As a result, relative portfolio performance evaluation, in addition to absolute performance measurement, is often of key importance.

With respect to relative performance we may ask questions such as, "Relative to the investment manager's benchmark, what economic sectors were underweighted or overweighted?" or "What was the manager's rationale for these decisions and how successful were they?" Portfolio evaluation may also be conducted with respect to specific risk models, such as multifactor models, which attempt to explain asset returns in terms of exposures to a set of risk factors.

Concurrent with evaluation of the manager is the ongoing review of the benchmark to establish its continuing suitability. For some benchmarks, this review would include a thorough understanding of how economic sectors and subsectors are determined in the benchmark, the classification of securities within them, and how frequently the classifications change. For any benchmark, one would review whether the benchmark continues to be a fair measuring stick given the manager's mandate.

As with other parts of the portfolio management process, performance evaluation and performance presentation are critical. These topics play a central role in the portfolio management process.

5.4 A Definition of Portfolio Management

In sum, the process logic is incorporated in the following definition, which is the cornerstone for this book. Portfolio management is an ongoing process in which

- investment objectives and constraints are identified and specified;
- investment strategies are developed;
- portfolio composition is decided in detail;
- portfolio decisions are initiated by portfolio managers and implemented by traders;
- portfolio performance is measured and evaluated;
- investor and market conditions are monitored; and
- any necessary rebalancing is implemented.

Although we have provided general insights into the portfolio management process, we make no judgments and voice no opinions about how the process should be organized, who should make which decisions, or any other process-operating matter. How well the process works is a critical component of investment success. In a survey of pension fund chief operating officers, Ambachtsheer, Capelle, and Scheibelhut (1998) found that 98 percent of the respondents cited a poor portfolio management process as a barrier to achieving excellence in organizational performance. The organization of the portfolio management process of any investment management company should be the result of careful planning.

INVESTMENT OBJECTIVES AND CONSTRAINTS

6

As previously discussed, the IPS is the cornerstone of the portfolio management process. Because of the IPS's fundamental importance, we introduce its main components in this reading. In this section, we return to the tasks of identifying and specifying the investor's objectives and constraints that initiate the planning step.

Although we discuss objectives first and then constraints, the actual process of delineating these for any investor may appropriately start with an examination of investor constraints. For example, a short time horizon affects the investor's ability to take risk.

6.1 Objectives

The two objectives in this framework, risk and return, are interdependent—one cannot be discussed without reference to the other. The risk objective limits how high the investor can set the return objective.

6.1.1 *Risk Objective*

The first element of the risk–return framework is the risk objective because it will largely determine the return objective. A 10 percent standard deviation risk objective, for example, implies a different asset allocation than a 15 percent standard deviation risk objective, because expected asset risk is generally positively correlated with expected asset return. In formulating a risk objective, the investor must address the following questions:

1 *How do I measure risk?* Risk measurement is a key issue in investments, and several approaches exist for measuring risk. In practice, risk may be measured in absolute terms or in relative terms with reference to various risk concepts. Examples of absolute risk objectives are a specified level of standard deviation or variance of total return. The **variance** of a random variable is the expected value of squared deviations from the random variable's mean. Variance is often referred to as volatility. **Standard deviation** is the positive square root of variance. An example of a relative risk objective is a specified level of tracking risk. Tracking risk is the standard deviation of the differences between a portfolio's and the benchmark's total returns.

   Downside risk concepts, such as **value at risk (VAR)**, may also be important to an investor. Value at risk is a probability-based measure of the loss that one anticipates will be exceeded only a specified small fraction of the time over a given horizon—for example, in 5 percent of all monthly holding periods. Besides statistical measures of risk, other risk exposures, such as exposures to specific economic sectors, or risk with respect to a factor model of returns, may be relevant as well.

2 *What is the investor's willingness to take risk?* The investor's stated willingness to take risk is often very different for institutional versus individual investors. Managers should try to understand the behavioral and, for individuals, the personality factors behind an investor's willingness to take risk. In the reading on individual investors, we explore behavioral issues in reference to the investor's willingness to take risk.

3 *What is the investor's ability to take risk?* Even if an investor is eager to bear risk, practical or financial limitations often limit the amount of risk that can be prudently assumed. For the sake of illustration, in the following discussion we talk about risk in terms of the volatility of asset values.

- In terms of spending needs, how much volatility would inconvenience an investor who depends on investments (such as a university in relationship to its endowment fund)? Or, how much volatility would inconvenience an investor who otherwise cannot afford to incur substantial short-term losses? Investors with high levels of wealth relative to probable worst-case short-term loss scenarios can take more risk.
- In terms of long-term wealth targets or obligations, how much volatility might prevent the investor from reaching these goals? Investors with high levels of wealth relative to long-term wealth targets or obligations can take more risk.
- What are the investor's liabilities or pseudo liabilities? An institution may face legally promised future payments to beneficiaries (liabilities) and an individual may face future retirement spending needs (pseudo liabilities).
- What is the investor's financial strength—that is, the ability to increase the savings/contribution level if the portfolio cannot support the planned spending? More financial strength means more risk can be taken.

4 *How much risk is the investor both willing and able to bear?* The answer to this question defines the investor's risk tolerance. Risk tolerance, the capacity to accept risk, is a function of both an investor's willingness and ability to do so. Risk tolerance can also be described in terms of risk aversion, the degree of an investor's inability and unwillingness to take risk. The investor's specific risk objectives are formulated with that investor's level of risk tolerance in mind. Importantly, any assessment of risk tolerance must consider both an investor's willingness and that investor's ability to take risk. When a mismatch exists between the two, determining risk tolerance requires educating the client on the dangers of excess risk taking or of ignoring inflation risk, depending on the case. In our presentation in this book, we assume that such education has taken place and that we are providing an appropriate risk objective in the IPS proposed to the client. When an investor's willingness to accept risk exceeds ability to do so, ability prudently places a limit on the amount of risk the investor should assume. When ability exceeds willingness, the investor may fall short of the return objective because willingness would be the limiting factor. These interactions are shown in Table 1.

An investor with an above-average ability to assume risk may have legitimate reasons for choosing a lower risk strategy. As well, an investor may face the pleasant situation of having an excess of wealth to meet financial needs for a long period of time. In these cases, the investor needs to have a clear understanding of the eventual consequences of the decision to effectively spend down excess wealth over time. As with any strategy, such a decision must be reevaluated periodically. In the case of a high-net-worth investor who has earned substantial wealth from entrepreneurial risk taking, such an investor may now simply not want to lose wealth and may desire only liquidity to spend in order to maintain her current lifestyle.

5 *What are the specific risk objective(s)?* Just as risk may be measured either absolutely or relatively, we may specify both absolute risk and relative risk objectives. In practice, investors often find that quantitative risk objectives are easier to specify in relative than in absolute terms. Possibly as a consequence, absolute risk objectives in particular are frequently specified in qualitative rather than quantitative terms.

What distinguishes the risk objective from risk tolerance is the level of specificity. For example, the statement that a person has a "lower than average risk tolerance" might be converted operationally into "the loss in any one year is not to exceed *x* percent of portfolio value" or "annual volatility of the portfolio is not to exceed *y* percent." Often, clients—particularly individual investors—do not understand or appreciate this level of specificity, and more-general risk-tolerance statements substitute for a quantitative risk objective.

6 *How should the investor allocate risk?* This is how some investors frame capital allocation decisions today, particularly when active strategies will play a role in the portfolio. The question may concern the portfolio as a whole or some part of it. Risk budgeting disciplines address the above question most directly. After the investor has determined the *measure* of risk of concern to him (e.g., VAR or tracking risk) and the *desired total quantity of risk* (the overall risk budget), an investor using risk budgeting would allocate the overall risk budget to specific investments so as to maximize expected overall risk-adjusted return. The resulting optimal risk budgets for the investments would translate to specific allocations of capital to them.

Table 1 Risk Tolerance

	Ability to Take Risk	
Willingness to Take Risk	**Below Average**	**Above Average**
Below Average	Below-average risk tolerance	Resolution needed
Above Average	Resolution needed	Above-average risk tolerance

6.1.2 *Return Objective*

The second element of the investment policy framework is the return objective, which must be consistent with the risk objective. Just as tension may exist between willingness and ability in setting the risk objective, so the return objective requires a resolution of return desires versus the risk objective. In formulating a return objective, the investor must address the following four questions:

1 *How is return measured?* The usual measure is total return, the sum of the return from price appreciation and the return from investment income. Return may be stated as an absolute amount, such as 10 percent a year, or as a return relative to the benchmark's return, such as benchmark return plus 2 percent a year. Nominal returns must be distinguished from real returns. Nominal returns are unadjusted for inflation. Real returns are adjusted for inflation and sometimes simply called inflation-adjusted returns. Also, pretax returns must be distinguished from post-tax returns. Pretax returns are returns before taxes, and post-tax returns are returns after taxes are paid on investment income and realized capital gains.

2 *How much return does the investor say she wants?* This amount is the stated return desire. These wants or desires may be realistic or unrealistic. For example, an investor may have higher than average return desires to meet high consumption desires or a high ending wealth target: for instance, "I want a 20 percent annual return." The advisor or portfolio manager must continually evaluate the desire for high returns in light of the investor's ability to assume risk and the reasonableness of the stated return desire, especially relative to capital market expectations.

3 *How much return does the investor need to achieve, on average?* This amount is the required return or return requirement. Requirements are more stringent than desires because investors with requirements typically must achieve those returns, at least on average. An example of a return requirement is the average return a pension fund projects it must earn to fund liabilities to current and future pensioners, based on actuarial calculations. The compound rate of return that an individual investor must earn to attain the asset base needed for retirement is another example of a return requirement. A third example would be the return that a retired investor must earn on his investment portfolio to cover his annual living expenses. We illustrate these last two cases.

Suppose that a married couple needs £2 million in 18 years to fund retirement. Their current investable assets total £1,200,000. The projected future need (£2 million) incorporates expected inflation. The couple would need to earn $(£2{,}000{,}000/£1{,}200{,}000)^{1/18} - 1.0 = 2.88$ percent per year after-tax to achieve their goal. Every cash flow needs to be accounted for in such calculations. If the couple needed to liquidate £25,000 from the portfolio at the end of each year (keeping all other facts unchanged), they would need to earn 4.55 percent per year on an after-tax basis to have £2 million in 18 years (a financial calculator is needed to confirm this result). If all investment returns were taxed at 35 percent, 4.55 percent after tax would correspond to a 7 percent pretax required return $[4.55/(1 - 0.35) = 7\%]$.

A retiree may depend on his investment portfolio for some or all of his living expenses. That need defines a return requirement. Suppose that a retiree must achieve a 4 percent after-tax return on his current investment portfolio to meet his current annual living expenses. Thus, his return requirement on a real, after-tax basis is 4 percent per year. If he expects inflation to be 2 percent per year and a 40 percent tax rate applies to investment returns from any source, we could estimate his pretax nominal return requirement as (After-tax real return requirement + Expected inflation rate)/(1 – Tax rate) = $(4\% + 2\%)/(1 - 0.40) =$ 10 percent.

In contrast to desired returns, which can be reduced if incongruent with risk objectives, large required returns are an important source of potential conflict between return and risk objectives. Other required return issues that are relevant to specific situations include the following:

- What are the needs and desires for current spending versus ending wealth?
- How do nominal total return requirements relate to expected rates of price inflation? If assets fund obligations subject to inflation, the return requirements should reflect expected rates of inflation.

4 *What are the specific return objectives?* The return objective incorporates the required return, the stated return desire, and the risk objective into a measurable annual total return specification. For example, an investor with a 5 percent after-tax, required, inflation-adjusted annual rate of return but above-average risk tolerance might reasonably set a higher than 5 percent after-tax, inflation-adjusted annual rate of return objective to maximize expected wealth.

An investor's return objective should be consistent with that investor's risk objective. A high return objective may suggest an asset allocation with an expected level of risk that is too great in relation to the risk objective, for example. In addition, the anticipated return from the portfolio should be sufficient to meet wealth objectives or liabilities that the portfolio must fund.

For investors with current investment income needs, the return objective should be sufficient to meet spending needs from capital appreciation and investment income: When a well-considered return objective is not consistent with risk tolerance, other adjustments may need to take place, such as increasing savings or modifying wealth objectives.

An investor delegating portfolio management to an investment manager will communicate a mandate—a set of instructions detailing the investment manager's task and how his performance will be evaluated—that includes a specification of the manager's benchmark. Because the manager's performance will be evaluated against the benchmark, the benchmark's total return is an effective return objective for the investment manager. These instructions may be part of the investment policy statement or, in the case of a portfolio with multiple managers, outlined in separate instructions for each mandate to each manager.

Although an absolute return objective is sometimes set (e.g., 8 percent), the reality of the markets suggests that a relative return objective may be more plausible. A relative return objective is stated as a return relative to the portfolio benchmark's total return (e.g., 1 percent higher than the benchmark).

Table 2 illustrates the variation in return requirement and risk tolerance among various categories of investors.

Table 2 Return Requirements and Risk Tolerances of Various Investors

Type of Investor	Return Requirement	Risk Tolerance
Individual	Depends on stage of life, circumstances, and obligations	Varies
Pension Plans (Defined Benefit)	The return that will adequately fund liabilities on an inflation-adjusted basis	Depends on plan and sponsor characteristics, plan features, funding status, and workforce characteristics
Pension Plans (Defined Contribution)	Depends on stage of life of individual participants	Varies with the risk tolerance of individual participants
Foundations and Endowments	The return that will cover annual spending, investment expenses, and expected inflation	Determined by amount of assets relative to needs, but generally above-average or average
Life Insurance Companies	Determined by rates used to determine policyholder reserves	Below average due to factors such as regulatory constraints
Non-Life-Insurance Companies	Determined by the need to price policies competitively and by financial needs	Below average due to factors such as regulatory constraints
Banks	Determined by cost of funds	Varies

6.2 Constraints

The investor's risk and return objectives are set within the context of several constraints: liquidity, time horizon, tax concerns, legal and regulatory factors, and unique circumstances. Although all of these factors influence portfolio choice, the first two constraints bear directly on the investor's ability to take risk and thus constrain both risk and return objectives.

6.2.1 *Liquidity*

A liquidity requirement is a need for cash *in excess of new contributions* (for pension plans and endowments, for example) or *savings* (for individuals) at a specified point in time. Such needs may be anticipated or unanticipated, but either way they stem from liquidity events. An example of a liquidity event is planned construction of a building in one year.

The liquidity requirement may reflect nonrecurring needs or the desire to hold cash against unanticipated needs (a safety or reserve fund). This requirement may be met by holding cash or cash equivalents in the portfolio or by converting other assets into cash equivalents. Any risk of economic loss because of the need to sell relatively less liquid assets to meet liquidity requirements is **liquidity risk**. (An asset that can be converted into cash only at relatively high total cost is said to be relatively less liquid.) Liquidity risk, therefore, arises for two reasons: an asset-side reason (asset liquidity) and a liability-side reason (liquidity requirements). Portfolio managers control asset selection but not liquidity requirements; as a result, in practice, managers use asset selection to manage liquidity risk. If the portfolio's asset and income base are large relative to its potential liquidity requirements, relatively less liquid assets can be held. A distinct consideration is liquidity requirements in relation to price risk of the asset—the risk of fluctuations in market price. Assets with high price risk are frequently less liquid, especially during market downturns. If the timing of an investor's liquidity requirements is significantly correlated with market downturns, these requirements can influence asset selection in favor of less risky assets. In many cases, therefore, consideration of both liquidity risk and price risk means that an investor will choose to hold some part of the portfolio in highly liquid and low-price-risk assets in anticipation of future liquidity requirements. Investors may also modify the payoff structure of a risky portfolio to address liquidity requirements using derivative strategies, although such modifications often incur costs. (**Derivatives** are contracts whose payoffs depend on the value of another asset, often called the underlying asset.)

6.2.2 *Time Horizon*

Time horizon most often refers to the time period associated with an investment objective. Investment objectives and associated time horizons may be short term, long term, or a combination of the two. (A time horizon of 10 years or more is often considered to be long term. Investment performance over the long term should average results over several market and business cycles.) A multistage horizon is a combination of shorter term and longer term horizons. An example of a multistage horizon is the case of funding children's education shorter term and the investor's retirement longer term.

Other constraints, such as a unique circumstance or a specific liquidity requirement, can also affect an investor's time horizon. For example, an individual investor's temporary family living arrangement can dictate that his time horizon constraint be stated in multistage terms. Similarly, an institutional investor's need to make an imminent substantial disbursement of funds for a capital project can necessitate a multistage approach to the time horizon constraint.

In general, relevant time horizon questions include the following:

- *How does the length of the time horizon modify the investor's ability to take risk?* The longer the time horizon the more risk the investor can take. The longer the time horizon, the greater the investor's ability to replenish investment resources by increasing savings. A long-term investor's labor income may also be an asset sufficiently stable to support a higher level of portfolio risk.[3] Cash may be safe for a short-term investor but risky for a long-term investor who will be faced with continuously reinvesting.

- *How does the length of the time horizon modify the investor's asset allocation?* Many investors allocate a greater proportion of funds to risky assets when they address long-term as opposed to short-term investment objectives. Decreased risk-taking ability with shorter horizons can thus constrain portfolio choice.
- *How does the investor's willingness and ability to bear fluctuations in portfolio value modify the asset allocation?* With a focus on risk, even an investor with a long-term objective may limit risk taking because of sensitivity to the possibility of substantial interim losses. The chance of unanticipated liquidity needs may increase during market downturns, for instance, because a market downturn may be linked to a decline in economic activity affecting income or other sources of wealth. An investor that often faces unanticipated short-term liquidity needs will usually favor investments with a shorter time horizon so as to limit the risk of loss of value.
- *How does a multistage time horizon constrain the investor's asset allocation?* The investment policy must be designed to accommodate all time horizons in a multistage horizon case. Such design will probably entail some compromise in the setting of objectives to attain short-, medium-, and long-term goals.

6.2.3 *Tax Concerns*

A country's tax policy can affect important aspects of investment decision-making for investors who reside there. Tax concerns arise for taxable investors because tax payments reduce the amount of the total return that can be used for current needs or reinvested for future growth. Differences between the tax rates applying to investment income and capital gains will influence taxable investors' choice of investments and their timing of sales. Estate taxes on wealth triggered by the investor's death can also affect investment decisions. Finally, tax policy changes that affect security prices affect both taxable and tax-exempt investors.

6.2.4 *Legal and Regulatory Factors*

Legal and regulatory factors are external factors imposed by governmental, regulatory, or oversight authorities to constrain investment decision-making. In the United Kingdom, for example, regulations issued by the Financial Services Authority (FSA) limit the concentration of holdings in debt and equity securities for U.K. mutual funds. Another example is the United States' Employee Retirement Income Security Act (ERISA) of 1974, as interpreted by regulatory agencies and the courts. ERISA limits the acquisition and holding of employer securities by certain pension plans. Some countries limit the use of certain asset classes in retirement accounts.

6.2.5 *Unique Circumstances*

Unique circumstances are internal factors (other than a liquidity requirement, time horizon, or tax concern) that may constrain portfolio choices. For example, a university endowment may be constrained to avoid certain investments against which there may be ethical objections or social responsibility considerations. Similarly, an individual investor's portfolio choices may be constrained by circumstances focusing on health needs, support of dependents, and other circumstances unique to the particular individual. Investors may specify avoidance of nondomestic shares or

3 See Campbell and Viceira (2002) for a discussion of this and the following point.

derivatives. Portfolio choices may also be constrained by investor capability in terms of both human resources and financial resources such as time, interest, background, and technical expertise.

7 THE DYNAMICS OF THE PROCESS

One of the truly satisfying aspects of portfolio management as a professional activity is the underlying logic and the dynamism of the portfolio process concept. In a broad sense, the work of analysts, economists, and market strategists is all a matter of "getting ready." The work of portfolio management is the action: taking the inputs and moving step by step through the orderly process of converting this raw material into a portfolio that maximizes expected return relative to the investor's ability to bear risk, that meets the investor's constraints and preferences, and that integrates portfolio policies with expectational factors and market uncertainties. Portfolio management is where the payoff is, because this is where it all comes together. Of course, it is the end result of this process that is judged: the performance of the portfolio relative to expectations and comparison standards.

Professionalism is enhanced and practice improved by managing portfolios as a process that

- consists of the steps outlined in this volume;
- flows logically and systematically through an orderly sequence of decision-making; and
- is continuous once put into motion with respect to a given investor.

This view approaches portfolio management not as a set of separate elements operating by fits and starts as intuition or inspiration dictates but rather as an integrated whole in which every decision moves the portfolio down the process path and in which no decision can be skipped without sacrificing functional integrity.

8 THE FUTURE OF PORTFOLIO MANAGEMENT

In the last few decades, portfolio management has become a more science-based discipline somewhat analogous to engineering and medicine. As in these other fields, advances in basic theory, technology, and market structure constantly translate into improvements in products and professional practices.

Among the most significant recent theoretical advances in investments is the recognition that the risk characteristics of the nontradable assets owned by an individual client, such as future earnings from a job, a business, or an expected inheritance, should be included in the definition of that client's portfolio. In the institutional area also, there is an increasing awareness and use of multifactor risk models and methods of managing risk.

Among the most significant market developments is the emergence of a broad range of new standardized derivative contracts—swaps, futures, and options. As active trading in these standardized products continues to develop, they make possible the creation of an infinite variety of customized investment products tailored to the needs of specific clients. As analysts continue to develop a more comprehensive view of risk, they also command a wider set of tools with which to manage it.[4]

THE ETHICAL RESPONSIBILITIES OF PORTFOLIO MANAGERS

9

In this reading, we have initiated a course of study that we hope will further the reader in his or her career as an investment professional. We select the term investment *professional* advisedly. The dictionary defines professional as "conforming to the standards of a profession." Every thoughtful person who has explored the subject has concluded that professional standards are of two types: standards of competence and standards of conduct. Merely drawing a livelihood from managing or advising on the investment of client monies is insufficient in itself to make an investment professional.

But verbal distinctions are not the most important point. The conduct of a portfolio manager affects the well-being of clients and many other people. The connection to individuals and their welfare is always present; it is no less important in those institutional contexts in which the portfolio manager may never meet the client. In the first years of the 21st century press attention focused on abuses in the U.S. mutual fund industry such as late trading, abusive market timing, selective disclosure of information on portfolio holdings, and undisclosed payments for "shelf space" to gain placement on brokers' preferred lists.[5] Certain fund executives facilitated or participated in these activities for personal enrichment, at the expense of the well-being of their clients, mutual fund shareholders. In truth, the docket of cases of professional misconduct is never empty, but the profession can and must work towards minimizing it. The portfolio manager must keep foremost in mind that he or she is in a position of trust, requiring ethical conduct towards the public, client, prospects, employers, employees, and fellow workers. For CFA Institute members, this position of trust is reflected in the Code of Ethics and Standards of Professional Conduct to which members subscribe, as well as in the Professional Conduct Statement they submit annually. Ethical conduct is the foundation requirement for managing investment portfolios.

SUMMARY

In this reading, we have presented the portfolio management process and the elements of the investment policy statement.

- According to the portfolio perspective, individual investments should be judged in the context of how much risk they add to a portfolio rather than on how risky they are on a stand-alone basis.
- The three steps in the portfolio management process are the planning step (objectives and constraint determination, investment policy statement creation, capital market expectation formation, and strategic asset allocation creation);

4 This section on the future of portfolio management was contributed by Dr. Zvi Bodie.

5 The listing follows the enumeration of William H. Donaldson, CFA, chair of the U.S. Securities and Exchange Commission, in a speech to the Mutual Fund Directors Forum on 7 January 2004.

the execution step (portfolio selection/composition and portfolio implementation); and the feedback step (performance evaluation and portfolio monitoring and rebalancing).

- Investment objectives are specific and measurable desired performance outcomes, and constraints are limitations on the ability to make use of particular investments. The two types of objectives are risk and return. The two types of constraints are internal (posed by the characteristics of the investor) and external (imposed by outside agencies).
- An investment policy statement is a written planning document that governs all investment decisions for the client. This document integrates a client's needs, preferences, and circumstances into a statement of that client's objectives and constraints.
- A policy or strategic asset allocation establishes exposures to IPS-permissible asset classes in a manner designed to satisfy the client's long-run objectives and constraints. The plan reflects the interaction of objectives and constraints with long-run capital market expectations.
- In a passive investment strategy approach, portfolio composition does not react to changes in expectations; an example is indexing, which involves a fixed portfolio designed to replicate the returns on an index. An active approach involves holding a portfolio different from a benchmark or comparison portfolio for the purpose of producing positive excess risk-adjusted returns. A semiactive approach refers to an indexing approach with controlled use of weights different from the benchmark.
- The portfolio selection/composition decision concerns portfolio construction and often uses portfolio optimization to combine assets efficiently to achieve return and risk objectives. The portfolio implementation decision concerns the trading desk function of implementing portfolio decisions and involves explicit and implicit transaction costs.
- The elements of performance evaluation are performance measurement, attribution, and appraisal. Performance measurement is the calculation of portfolio rates of return. Performance attribution is the analysis of those rates of return to determine the factors that explain how the return was achieved. Performance appraisal assesses how well the portfolio manager performed on a risk-adjusted basis, whether absolute or relative to a benchmark.
- Portfolio monitoring and rebalancing use feedback to manage ongoing exposures to available investment opportunities in order to continually satisfy the client's current objectives and constraints.
- Portfolio management is an ongoing process in which the investment objectives and constraints are identified and specified, investment policies and strategies are developed, the portfolio composition is decided in detail, portfolio decisions are initiated by portfolio managers and implemented by traders, portfolio performance is evaluated, investor and market conditions are monitored, and any necessary rebalancing is implemented.
- To determine a risk objective, there are several steps: specify a risk measure (or measures) such as standard deviation, determine the investor's willingness to take risk, determine the investor's ability to take risk, synthesize the investor's willingness and ability into the investor's risk tolerance, and specify an objective using the measure(s) in the first step above.
- To determine a return objective, there are several steps: specify a return measure such as total nominal return, determine the investor's stated return desire, determine the investor's required rate of return, and specify an objective in terms of the return measure in the first step above.

- A liquidity requirement is a need for cash in excess of the contribution rate or the savings rate at a specified point in time. This need may be either anticipated or unanticipated.
- A time horizon is the time period associated with an investment objective. Investment objectives and associated time horizons may be short term, long term, or a combination of these two. A multistage horizon is a combination of shorter term and longer term horizons. A time horizon can be considered a constraint because shorter time horizons generally indicate lower risk tolerance and hence constrain portfolio choice, making it more conservative.
- A tax concern is any issue arising from a tax structure that reduces the amount of the total return that can be used for current needs or reinvested for future growth. Tax concerns constrain portfolio choice. If differences exist between the tax rates applying to investment income and capital gains, tax considerations will influence the choice of investment.
- Legal and regulatory factors are external considerations that may constrain investment decision making. For example, a government agency may limit the use of certain asset classes in retirement portfolios.
- Unique circumstances are internal factors (other than a liquidity requirement, time horizon, or tax concerns) that may constrain portfolio choices. For example, an investor seeking to avoid investments in tobacco companies will place an internal constraint on portfolio choice.

PRACTICE PROBLEMS

1 A An individual expects to save €50,000 during the coming year from income from non-portfolio sources, such as salary. She will need €95,000 within the year to make a down payment for a house purchase. What is her liquidity requirement for the coming year?

B Endowments are funds that are typically owned by non-profit institutions involved in educational, medical, cultural, and other charitable activities. Classified as institutional investors, endowments are almost always established with the intent of lasting into perpetuity.

The Wilson-Fowler Endowment was established in the United States to provide financial support to Wilson-Fowler College. An endowment's spending rate defines the fraction of endowment assets distributed to the supported institution. The Wilson-Fowler Endowment has established a spending rate of 4 percent a year; the endowment follows the simple rule of spending, in a given year, an amount equal to 4% × (Market value of the endowment at the end of the prior year). This amount is committed to the budgetary support of the college for the coming year. At the end of the prior year, the market value of the Wilson-Fowler Endowment's assets stood at $75,000,000. In addition, the Wilson-Fowler Endowment has committed to contribute $1,000,000 in the coming year to the construction of a new student dormitory. Planners at the endowment expect the endowment to receive contributions or gifts (from alumni and other sources) of $400,000 over the coming year. What is the anticipated liquidity requirement of the Wilson-Fowler Endowment for the coming year?

2 The Executive Director of the Judd University Endowment estimates that the capital markets will provide a 9 percent expected return for an endowment portfolio taking above-average risk, and a 7 percent expected return for an endowment portfolio taking average risk. The Judd Endowment provides tuition scholarships for Judd University students. The spending rate has been 4 percent, and the expected tuition inflation rate is 3 percent. Recently university officials have pressured the endowment to increase the spending rate to 6 percent. The endowment has an average to below-average ability to accept risk and only an average willingness to take risk, but a university official claims that the risk tolerance should be raised because higher returns are needed. Discuss an appropriate return objective and risk tolerance for the Judd Endowment.

3 Stux (1994) describes a country allocation strategy across five major equity markets: the United States, the United Kingdom, Germany, France, and Japan. In this strategy, a measure of relative attractiveness among the five equity markets is used as a factor in determining the weights of the five equity markets in the overall portfolio. The investment in each country, however, whatever the country's weight, is an indexed investment in the equity market of that country. The weights of the five equity markets in the overall portfolio generally are expected to differ from benchmark weights (the weights of the countries in an appropriate benchmark for the international equity market), within limits.

A Characterize the two components (portfolio weights and within-country investments) of the country allocation strategy using the text's framework for classifying investment strategies.

Practice Problems and Solutions: 1–4 taken from *Managing Investment Portfolios: A Dynamic Process*, Third Edition, John L. Maginn, CFA, Donald L. Tuttle, CFA, Jerald E. Pinto, CFA, and Dennis W. McLeavey, CFA, editors.

B Characterize the country allocation strategy overall.

4 Characterize each of the investment objectives given below as one of the following: an absolute risk objective, a relative risk objective, an absolute return objective, or a relative return objective.

A Achieve a rate of return of 8 percent a year.

B Limit the standard deviation of portfolio returns to 20 percent a year or less.

C Achieve returns in the top quartile of the portfolio's peer universe (the set of portfolios with similar investment objectives and characteristics).

D Maintain a 10 percent or smaller probability that the portfolio's return falls below the threshold level of 5 percent per annum over a one-year time horizon.

E Achieve a tracking risk of no more than 4 percent per annum with respect to the portfolio's benchmark.

The following information relates to Questions 5–10

James Stephenson, age 55 and single, is a surgeon who has accumulated a substantial investment portfolio without a clear long-term strategy in mind. Two of his patients who work in financial markets comment as follows:

James Hrdina:	"My investment firm, based on its experience with investors, has standard investment policy statements in five categories. You would be better served to adopt one of these standard policy statements instead of spending time developing a policy based on your individual circumstances."
Charles Gionta:	"Developing a long-term policy can be unwise given the fluctuations of the market. You want your investment advisor to react continuously to changing conditions and not be limited by a set policy."

Stephenson hires a financial advisor, Caroline Coppa. At their initial meeting, Coppa compiles the following notes:

> Stephenson currently has a $2.0 million portfolio that has a large concentration in small-capitalization U.S. equities. Over the past five years, the portfolio has averaged 20 percent annual total return on investment. Stephenson hopes that, over the long term, his portfolio will continue to earn 20 percent annually. When asked about his risk tolerance, he described it as "average." He was surprised when informed that U.S. small-cap portfolios have experienced extremely high volatility.
>
> He does not expect to retire before age 70. His current income is more than sufficient to meet his expenses. Upon retirement, he plans to sell his surgical practice and use the proceeds to purchase an annuity to cover his post-retirement cash flow needs.

Both his income and realized capital gains are taxed at a 30 percent rate. No pertinent legal or regulatory issues apply. He has no pension or retirement plan but does have sufficient health insurance for post-retirement needs.

5 The comments about investment policy statements made by Stephenson's patients are *best* characterized as:

	Hrdina	Gionta
A	Correct	Correct
B	Incorrect	Correct
C	Incorrect	Incorrect

6 In formulating the return objective for Stephenson's investment policy statement, the *most* appropriate determining factor for Coppa to focus on is:

A return desires.

B ability to take risk.

C return requirement.

7 Stephenson's willingness and ability to accept risk can be *best* characterized as:

	Willingness to accept risk	Ability to accept risk
A	Below average	Above average
B	Above average	Below average
C	Above average	Above average

8 Stephenson's tax and liquidity constraints can be *best* characterized as:

	Tax constraint	Liquidity constraint
A	Significant	Significant
B	Significant	Insignificant
C	Insignificant	Insignificant

9 Stephenson's time horizon is *best* characterized as:

A short-term and single-stage.

B long-term and single-stage.

C long-term and multistage.

10 Stephenson's return objective and risk tolerance are *most* appropriately described as:

	Return Objective	Risk Tolerance
A	Below average	Above average
B	Above average	Below average
C	Above average	Above average

The following information relates to Questions 11–16

Gina Benedetti, a trust officer at an Italian bank, interviewed Alessandro Santalucia, a new client. A summary of her interview appears in Exhibit 1.

Exhibit 1 Interview Summary for Client Alessandro Santalucia

Age	45
Family	Married but divorce is pending; three children ages 16, 17, and 18
Hobbies	Speed boat racing, mountain climbing
Business	Real estate speculation, buying firms with turn-around potential
Assets	€1 million in his private business and real estate and €500,000 in a nondiversified investment portfolio
Retirement plans	None; wishes to continue working until physically unable to do so
Current income	Spending modestly exceeds income
Spending plans/ Requirements	Children's college education (estimated at €30,000/year per child); divorce settlement may be up to one-half of his assets

Benedetti develops an investment policy statement and recommended asset allocation for Santalucia and puts the following notes in Santalucia's file:

1 I met with our staff economist to review his thinking on short-term trends in the economy and financial markets. I relied greatly on his forecast to draft an investment policy statement for Santalucia.

2 Santalucia's situation is very similar to that of another client from several years ago. I used that client's asset allocation as a basis for my portfolio recommendations for Santalucia.

Benedetti next meets with her firm's research analyst, Kurt Westerlund, to discuss changes to the firm's recommended list. One company of interest is an upcoming initial public offering (IPO) for Palladio Corp. To analyze this IPO, Westerlund used data from 20 publicly traded peer companies with business lines similar to Palladio's. He combined them into an equally weighted portfolio to approximate the anticipated behavior of Palladio's stock once it becomes publicly traded. Some of this information is presented in Exhibit 2.

During their conversation, Westerlund makes several statements about Palladio and the capital markets:

Statement #1 "I estimated the Palladio proxy portfolio's beta over several different time periods, and this portfolio beta has always been stable, with the high and low estimates within 5 percent of each other. However, Palladio's estimated beta will be more volatile over time than that of the proxy portfolio."

Statement #2 "The estimation of beta is affected by several factors, including regression to the mean, volume of trading, and the market proxy used."

Statement #3 "The capital market line (CML) uses a measure of total risk, and the SML uses a standardized measure of systematic risk."

Statement #4 "The SML is the equation that specifies the required/expected return for a security that is implied by the CML when the market is in equilibrium."

Exhibit 2 **Data for Palladio Peer Firms Monthly Data, May 2000–May 2006 (Returns Measured as Decimal; 1% = 0.01)**

	Palladio Proxy Portfolio	Market
Average monthly return	0.0051	0.0025
Variance of returns	0.0033	0.0021
Covariance with market return	0.0015	0.0021
Correlation with market return	0.5697	1.000

Benedetti notes that the current short-term government bill rate offers 2.5 percent annually and her firm's economist anticipates a market risk premium of 7.0 percent on stock market investments.

In addition to her consideration of Palladio, Benedetti wants to review Borgonovo, Inc., and decide whether it should remain on the bank's recommended list or be removed. Borgonovo has a beta of 1.2, and a forecasted return of 9.0 percent.

11 Which of the following *best* describes Santalucia's current risk tolerance and liquidity constraint? Santalucia's risk tolerance is:

A below average, and his liquidity constraint is significant.

B above average, and his liquidity constraint is significant.

C above average, and his liquidity constraint is insignificant.

12 Do Benedetti's two notes for Santalucia's file describe the correct process for constructing an investment policy statement and for developing portfolio recommendations?

	Note #1 on investment policy statement process	Note #2 on developing portfolio recommendations
A	No	No
B	Yes	No
C	Yes	Yes

13 Are Westerlund's statements #1 and #2 correct regarding the:

	Palladio systematic risk?	factors affecting beta estimation?
A	No	Yes
B	Yes	No
C	Yes	Yes

14 Are Westerlund's statements #3 and #4 correct regarding:

	types of risk measures?	equilibrium?
A	No	No
B	Yes	No
C	Yes	Yes

15 Based on Exhibit 2, the estimated beta for Palladio is *closest* to:

A 0.40.

B 0.57.

C 0.71.

16 Based on the relationship of Borgonovo's stock to the SML, what is the *most* appropriate decision Benedetti should make regarding the Borgonovo stock?

A Keep Borgonovo on the recommended list because it plots below the SML.

B Keep Borgonovo on the recommended list because it plots above the SML.

C Remove Borgonovo from the recommended list because it plots below the SML.

SOLUTIONS

1 A The liquidity requirement for this individual is her need for cash in excess of her savings during the coming year. Therefore, her liquidity requirement is €95,000 − €50,000 = €45,000.

B The Wilson-Fowler Endowment's anticipated liquidity requirement is $600,000, calculated as $1,000,000 (the planned contribution to the construction of the new dormitory) minus $400,000 (the anticipated amount of new contributions to the endowment). Note that the amount of 4% × $75,000,000 = $3,000,000, as provided for in the spending rule, is fully committed to budgetary support; thus this amount is not available to help meet the endowment's planned contribution to the building project.

2 The Judd Endowment's risk tolerance is limited by its ability and willingness to accept risk. Risk tolerance is *not* a function of a need for higher returns. The return objective should be consistent with risk tolerance, so an appropriate return objective for the Judd Endowment is 7 percent. A spending rate of 6 percent is too high for this endowment; raising the return objective to 9 percent would only compound the problem created by a 6 percent spending rate, which is inappropriately high for this endowment.

3 A The country allocation strategy as described mixes elements of active and passive investment approaches. The portfolio weights are actively determined and differ from benchmark weights, within limits. However, the investments in individual countries are passive, indexed investments.

B Overall, we can classify the country allocation strategy as a semiactive or controlled-active investment approach.

4 A This is an absolute return objective because it does not reference a comparison to the performance of another portfolio but rather is stated in terms of a fixed number (an 8 percent annual return).

B This is an absolute risk objective because it does not reference a comparison to the performance of another portfolio but rather is stated in terms of a fixed number (a standard deviation of return of 20 percent a year).

C This is a relative return objective because it references a comparison to the performance of other portfolios.

D This is an absolute risk objective because it addresses the risk that a portfolio's return will fall below a minimum acceptable level over a stated time horizon.

E This is a relative risk objective because it references a comparison to the performance of another portfolio, the benchmark.

5 C is correct. The comments about investment policy statements made by Stephenson's patients are incorrect. The IPS should identify pertinent investment objectives and constraints for a *particular* investor. Clearly identified objectives and constraints ensure that the policy statement is accurate and relevant to the investor's specific situation and desires. The result should be an optimal balance between return and risk for that investor. The IPS provides a long-term plan for an investor and a basis for making disciplined investment decisions over time. The absence of an investment policy statement reduces decision making to an individual-event basis and often leads to pursuing short-term opportunities that may not contribute to, or may even detract from, reaching long-term goals.

6 B is correct. An investor's ability to take risk puts an upper limit on a reasonable return objective.

7 C is correct. Even though Stephenson describes his risk tolerance as "average," his present investment portfolio and his desire for large returns indicate an above-average willingness to take risk. His financial situation (large asset base, ample income to cover expenses, lack of need for liquidity, and long time horizon) indicates an above-average ability to accept risk.

8 B is correct. Stephenson has adequate income to cover his living expenses and has no major outlays for which he needs cash, so his liquidity needs are minimal. He is not a tax-exempt investor (both income and capital gains are taxed at 30%), so taxes should play a considerable role in his investment decisions.

9 C is correct. Stephenson's time horizon is long—he is currently only 55 years old. The time horizon consists of two stages: the first stage extends to his retirement in 15 years; the second stage may last for 20 years or more and extends from retirement until his death.

10 C is correct.

Risk: Stephenson has an above-average risk tolerance based on both his ability and willingness to assume risk. His large asset base, long time horizon, ample income to cover expenses, and lack of need for liquidity or cash flow indicate an above-average ability to assume risk. His concentration in U.S. small-capitalization stocks and his desire for high returns indicate substantial willingness to assume risk.

Return: Stephenson's financial circumstances (long time horizon, sizable asset base, ample income, and low liquidity needs) and his risk tolerance warrant an above-average total return objective. His expressed desire for a continued return of 20 percent, however, is unrealistic. Coppa should counsel Stephenson on what level of returns to reasonably expect from the financial markets over long periods of time and to define an achievable return objective.

11 A is correct. Santalucia's lifestyle and business career (speedboats, mountain climbing, real estate speculation, turnarounds) show a *willingness* to take risks. His current *ability* to take risks is diminished, given his total assets and his expected divorce settlement, his current income/spending situation, and upcoming college bills. When an investor's willingness to accept risk exceeds the ability to do so, ability prudently places a limit on the amount of risk the investor should assume. Santalucia's pending divorce and college education bills create a significant liquidity constraint.

12 A is correct. Neither note describes the correct process. The IPS process requires that members first identify and specify the investor's objectives and constraints and then create the investment policy statement. Incorporating short-term economic trends into the policy statement is inappropriate. Only after the IPS has been created should members form capital market expectations and then create the strategic asset allocation. Using another client's asset allocation from several years earlier is inappropriate because it does not include current capital market expectations.

13 C is correct. Westerlund's first statement is correct: Beta is more stable for portfolios than for individual stocks. The second statement is also correct: Beta estimation is affected by all the listed items.

14 C is correct. The first statement is correct: Variance, or total risk, is the relevant risk measure for the CML; the SML uses beta, the asset's risk standardized by the market's risk. The second statement is also correct: The SML is based on the CML and both are equilibrium relationships.

15 C is correct. The estimated beta is the covariance of Palladio's returns with the market's returns divided by the variance of the market's returns, or 0.0015/0.0021 = 0.714.

16 C is correct. The SML required return for Borgonovo is 2.5% + 1.2(7%) = 10.9%. With a forecasted return of 9.0%, Borgonovo lies below the SML (indicating it is overvalued) and should be removed from the bank's recommended list.

Glossary

Abandonment option The ability to terminate a project at some future time if the financial results are disappointing.
Abnormal earnings See *residual income.*
Abnormal return The return on an asset in excess of the asset's required rate of return; the risk-adjusted return.
Absolute convergence The idea that developing countries, regardless of their particular characteristics, will eventually catch up with the developed countries and match them in per capita output.
Absolute valuation model A model that specifies an asset's intrinsic value.
Absolute version of PPP The extension of the law of one price to the broad range of goods and services that are consumed in different countries.
Accounting estimates Estimates of items such as the useful lives of assets, warranty costs, and the amount of uncollectible receivables.
Accrual basis Method of accounting in which the effect of transactions on financial condition and income are recorded when they occur, not when they are settled in cash.
Acquirer The company in a merger or acquisition that is acquiring the target.
Acquiring company The company in a merger or acquisition that is acquiring the target.
Acquisition The purchase of some portion of one company by another; the purchase may be for assets, a definable segment of another entity, or the purchase of an entire company.
Active factor risk The contribution to active risk squared resulting from the portfolio's different-than-benchmark exposures relative to factors specified in the risk model.
Active return The return on a portfolio minus the return on the portfolio's benchmark.
Active risk The standard deviation of active returns.
Active risk squared The variance of active returns; active risk raised to the second power.
Active specific risk The contribution to active risk squared resulting from the portfolio's active weights on individual assets as those weights interact with assets' residual risk.
Add-on interest A procedure for determining the interest on a bond or loan in which the interest is added onto the face value of a contract.
Adjusted R^2 A measure of goodness-of-fit of a regression that is adjusted for degrees of freedom and hence does not automatically increase when another independent variable is added to a regression.
Adjusted beta Historical beta adjusted to reflect the tendency of beta to be mean reverting.
Adjusted funds from operations Funds from operations (FFO) adjusted to remove any non-cash rent reported under straight-line rent accounting and to subtract maintenance-type capital expenditures and leasing costs, including leasing agents' commissions and tenants' improvement allowances.
Adjusted present value (APV) As an approach to valuing a company, the sum of the value of the company, assuming no use of debt, and the net present value of any effects of debt on company value.
Administrative regulations or administrative law Rules issued by government agencies or other regulators.
Agency costs Costs associated with the conflict of interest present when a company is managed by non-owners. Agency costs result from the inherent conflicts of interest between managers and equity owners.
Agency costs of equity The smaller the stake that managers have in the company, the less is their share in bearing the cost of excessive perquisite consumption or not giving their best efforts in running the company.
Agency issues Conflicts of interest that arise when the agent in an agency relationship has goals and incentives that differ from the principal to whom the agent owes a fiduciary duty. Also called *agency problems* or *principal–agent problems.*
Agency problem A conflict of interest that arises when the agent in an agency relationship has goals and incentives that differ from the principal to whom the agent owes a fiduciary duty.
Alpha The return on an asset in excess of the asset's required rate of return; the risk-adjusted return.
American Depositary Receipt A negotiable certificate issued by a depositary bank that represents ownership in a non--U.S. company's deposited equity (i.e., equity held in custody by the depositary bank in the company's home market).
American option An option that can be exercised at any time until its expiration date.
Amortizing and accreting swaps A swap in which the notional principal changes according to a formula related to changes in the underlying.
Analysis of variance (ANOVA) The analysis of the total variability of a dataset (such as observations on the dependent variable in a regression) into components representing different sources of variation; with reference to regression, ANOVA provides the inputs for an F-test of the significance of the regression as a whole.
Arbitrage 1) The simultaneous purchase of an undervalued asset or portfolio and sale of an overvalued but equivalent asset or portfolio, in order to obtain a riskless profit on the price differential. Taking advantage of a market inefficiency in a risk-free manner. 2) The condition in a financial market in which equivalent assets or combinations of assets sell for two different prices, creating an opportunity to profit at no risk with no commitment of money. In a well-functioning financial market, few arbitrage opportunities are possible. 3) A risk-free operation that earns an expected positive net profit but requires no net investment of money.
Arbitrage opportunity An opportunity to conduct an arbitrage; an opportunity to earn an expected positive net profit without risk and with no net investment of money.
Arbitrage portfolio The portfolio that exploits an arbitrage opportunity.

Arrears swap A type of interest rate swap in which the floating payment is set at the end of the period and the interest is paid at that same time.

Asset beta The unlevered beta; reflects the business risk of the assets; the asset's systematic risk.

Asset purchase An acquisition in which the acquirer purchases the target company's assets and payment is made directly to the target company.

Asset selection risk The contribution to active risk squared resulting from the portfolio's active weights on individual assets as those weights interact with assets' residual risk.

Asset-backed securities A type of bond issued by a legal entity called a *special purpose vehicle* (SPV), on a collection of assets that the SPV owns. Also, securities backed by receivables and loans other than mortgage loans.

Asset-based approach Approach that values a private company based on the values of the underlying assets of the entity less the value of any related liabilities.

Asset-based valuation An approach to valuing natural resource companies that estimates company value on the basis of the market value of the natural resources the company controls.

Asymmetric information The differential of information between corporate insiders and outsiders regarding the company's performance and prospects. Managers typically have more information about the company's performance and prospects than owners and creditors.

At-the-money An option in which the underlying value equals the exercise price.

Autocorrelation The correlation of a time series with its own past values.

Autoregressive model (AR) A time series regressed on its own past values, in which the independent variable is a lagged value of the dependent variable.

Available-for-sale investments Debt and equity securities not classified as either held-to-maturity or fair value through profit or loss securities. The investor is willing to sell but not actively planning to sell. In general, available-for-sale securities are reported at fair value on the balance sheet.

Backward integration A merger involving the purchase of a target ahead of the acquirer in the value or production chain; for example, to acquire a supplier.

Backwardation A condition in the futures markets in which the benefits of holding an asset exceed the costs, leaving the futures price less than the spot price.

Balance-sheet-based accruals ratio The difference between net operating assets at the end and the beginning of the period compared to the average net operating assets over the period.

Balance-sheet-based aggregate accruals The difference between net operating assets at the end and the beginning of the period.

Bankruptcy A declaration provided for by a country's laws that typically involves the establishment of a legal procedure that forces creditors to defer their claims.

Basic earnings per share (EPS) Net earnings available to common shareholders (i.e., net income minus preferred dividends) divided by the weighted average number of common shares outstanding during the period.

Basis swap 1) An interest rate swap involving two floating rates. 2) A swap in which both parties pay a floating rate.

Basis trade A trade based on the pricing of credit in the bond market versus the price of the same credit in the CDS market. To execute a basis trade, go long the "underpriced" credit and short the "overpriced" credit. A profit is realized when the price of credit between the short and long position converges.

Bear hug A tactic used by acquirers to circumvent target management's objections to a proposed merger by submitting the proposal directly to the target company's board of directors.

Benchmark A comparison portfolio; a point of reference or comparison.

Benchmark value of the multiple In using the method of comparables, the value of a price multiple for the comparison asset; when we have comparison assets (a group), the mean or median value of the multiple for the group of assets.

Bill-and-hold basis Sales on a bill-and-hold basis involve selling products but not delivering those products until a later date.

Binomial model A model for pricing options in which the underlying price can move to only one of two possible new prices.

Binomial tree The graphical representation of a model of asset price dynamics in which, at each period, the asset moves up with probability p or down with probability $(1 - p)$.

Blockage factor An illiquidity discount that occurs when an investor sells a large amount of stock relative to its trading volume (assuming it is not large enough to constitute a controlling ownership).

Bond indenture A legal contract specifying the terms of a bond issue.

Bond option An option in which the underlying is a bond; primarily traded in over-the-counter markets.

Bond yield plus risk premium method An estimate of the cost of common equity that is produced by summing the before-tax cost of debt and a risk premium that captures the additional yield on a company's stock relative to its bonds. The additional yield is often estimated using historical spreads between bond yields and stock yields.

Bond-equivalent yield The yield to maturity on a basis that ignores compounding.

Bonding costs Costs borne by management to assure owners that they are working in the owners' best interest (e.g., implicit cost of non-compete agreements).

Book value Shareholders' equity (total assets minus total liabilities) minus the value of preferred stock; common shareholders' equity.

Book value of equity Shareholders' equity (total assets minus total liabilities) minus the value of preferred stock; common shareholders' equity.

Book value per share The amount of book value (also called carrying value) of common equity per share of common stock, calculated by dividing the book value of shareholders' equity by the number of shares of common stock outstanding.

Bottom-up approach With respect to forecasting, an approach that usually begins at the level of the individual company or a unit within the company.

Bottom-up investing An approach to investing that focuses on the individual characteristics of securities rather than on macroeconomic or overall market forecasts.

Breakup value The value derived using a sum-of-the-parts valuation.

Breusch–Pagan test A test for conditional heteroskedasticity in the error term of a regression.

Broker 1) An agent who executes orders to buy or sell securities on behalf of a client in exchange for a commission. 2) *See* Futures commission merchants.

Brokerage The business of acting as agents for buyers or sellers, usually in return for commissions.

Buy-side analysts Analysts who work for investment management firms, trusts, and bank trust departments, and similar institutions.

CDS spread A periodic premium paid by the buyer to the seller that serves as a return over LIBOR required to protect against credit risk.

Call An option that gives the holder the right to buy an underlying asset from another party at a fixed price over a specific period of time.

Cannibalization Cannibalization occurs when an investment takes customers and sales away from another part of the company.

Cap 1) A contract on an interest rate, whereby at periodic payment dates, the writer of the cap pays the difference between the market interest rate and a specified cap rate if, and only if, this difference is positive. This is equivalent to a stream of call options on the interest rate. 2) A combination of interest rate call options designed to hedge a borrower against rate increases on a floating-rate loan.

Cap rate See *capitalization rate.*

Capital allocation line (CAL) A graph line that describes the combinations of expected return and standard deviation of return available to an investor from combining the optimal portfolio of risky assets with the risk-free asset.

Capital asset pricing model (CAPM) An equation describing the expected return on any asset (or portfolio) as a linear function of its beta relative to the market portfolio.

Capital charge The company's total cost of capital in money terms.

Capital deepening An increase in the capital-to-labor ratio.

Capital market line (CML) The line with an intercept point equal to the risk-free rate that is tangent to the efficient frontier of risky assets; represents the efficient frontier when a risk-free asset is available for investment.

Capital rationing A capital rationing environment assumes that the company has a fixed amount of funds to invest.

Capital structure The mix of debt and equity that a company uses to finance its business; a company's specific mixture of long-term financing.

Capitalization of earnings method In the context of private company valuation, valuation model based on an assumption of a constant growth rate of free cash flow to the firm or a constant growth rate of free cash flow to equity.

Capitalization rate The divisor in the expression for the value of perpetuity. In the context of real estate, the divisor in the direct capitalization method of estimating value. The cap rate equals net operating income divided by value.

Capitalized cash flow method In the context of private company valuation, valuation model based on an assumption of a constant growth rate of free cash flow to the firm or a constant growth rate of free cash flow to equity. Also called *capitalized cash flow model.*

Capitalized cash flow model In the context of private company valuation, valuation model based on an assumption of a constant growth rate of free cash flow to the firm or a constant growth rate of free cash flow to equity. Also called *capitalized cash flow method.*

Capitalized income method In the context of private company valuation, valuation model based on an assumption of a constant growth rate of free cash flow to the firm or a constant growth rate of free cash flow to equity.

Caplet Each component call option in a cap.

Capped swap A swap in which the floating payments have an upper limit.

Carried interest A share of any profits that is paid to the general partner (manager) of an investment partnership, such as a private equity or hedge fund, as a form of compensation designed to be an incentive to the manager to maximize performance of the investment fund.

Carrying costs The costs of holding an asset, generally a function of the physical characteristics of the underlying asset.

Cash available for distribution Funds from operations (FFO) adjusted to remove any non-cash rent reported under straight-line rent accounting and to subtract maintenance-type capital expenditures and leasing costs, including leasing agents' commissions and tenants' improvement allowances.

Cash basis Accounting method in which the only relevant transactions for the financial statements are those that involve cash.

Cash offering A merger or acquisition that is to be paid for with cash; the cash for the merger might come from the acquiring company's existing assets or from a debt issue.

Cash settlement A procedure used in certain derivative transactions that specifies that the long and short parties engage in the equivalent cash value of a delivery transaction.

Cash-flow-statement-based accruals ratio The difference between reported net income on an accrual basis and the cash flows from operating and investing activities compared to the average net operating assets over the period.

Cash-flow-statement-based aggregate accruals The difference between reported net income on an accrual basis and the cash flows from operating and investing activities.

Cash-generating unit The smallest identifiable group of assets that generates cash inflows that are largely independent of the cash inflows of other assets or groups of assets.

Catalyst An event or piece of information that causes the marketplace to re-evaluate the prospects of a company.

Chain rule of forecasting A forecasting process in which the next period's value as predicted by the forecasting equation is substituted into the right-hand side of the equation to give a predicted value two periods ahead.

Cheapest-to-deliver The debt instrument that can be purchased and delivered at the lowest cost yet has the same seniority as the reference obligation.

Clean surplus accounting Accounting that satisfies the condition that all changes in the book value of equity other than transactions with owners are reflected in income. The bottom-line income reflects all changes in shareholders' equity arising from other than owner transactions. In the absence of owner transactions, the change in shareholders' equity should equal net income. No adjustments such as translation adjustments bypass the income statement and go directly to shareholders equity.

Clean surplus relation The relationship between earnings, dividends, and book value in which ending book value is equal to the beginning book value plus earnings less dividends, apart from ownership transactions.

Clientele effect The preference some investors have for shares that exhibit certain characteristics.

Club convergence The idea that only rich and middle-income countries sharing a set of favorable attributes (i.e., are members of the "club") will converge to the income level of the richest countries.

Cobb–Douglas production function A function of the form $Y = K^{\alpha} L^{1-\alpha}$ relating output (Y) to labor (L) and capital (K) inputs.

Cointegrated Describes two time series that have a long-term financial or economic relationship such that they do not diverge from each other without bound in the long run.

Commercial mortgage-backed securities Securities backed by commercial mortgage loans.

Commercial real estate properties Income-producing real estate properties, properties purchased with the intent to let, lease, or rent (in other words, produce income).

Common size statements Financial statements in which all elements (accounts) are stated as a percentage of a key figure such as revenue for an income statement or total assets for a balance sheet.

Company fundamental factors Factors related to the company's internal performance, such as factors relating to earnings growth, earnings variability, earnings momentum, and financial leverage.

Company share-related factors Valuation measures and other factors related to share price or the trading characteristics of the shares, such as earnings yield, dividend yield, and book-to-market value.

Comparables Assets used as benchmarks when applying the method of comparables to value an asset. Also called *comps*, *guideline assets*, or *guideline companies*.

Compiled financial statements Financial statements that are not accompanied by an auditor's opinion letter.

Comprehensive income All changes in equity other than contributions by, and distributions to, owners; income under clean surplus accounting; includes all changes in equity during a period except those resulting from investments by owners and distributions to owners; comprehensive income equals net income plus other comprehensive income.

Comps Assets used as benchmarks when applying the method of comparables to value an asset.

Conditional convergence The idea that convergence of per capita income is conditional on the countries having the same savings rate, population growth rate, and production function.

Conditional heteroskedasticity Heteroskedasticity in the error variance that is correlated with the values of the independent variable(s) in the regression.

Conglomerate discount The discount possibly applied by the market to the stock of a company operating in multiple, unrelated businesses.

Conglomerate merger A merger involving companies that are in unrelated businesses.

Consolidation The combining of the results of operations of subsidiaries with the parent company to present financial statements as if they were a single economic unit. The assets, liabilities, revenues and expenses of the subsidiaries are combined with those of the parent company, eliminating intercompany transactions.

Constant dividend payout ratio policy A policy in which a constant percentage of net income is paid out in dividends.

Constant maturity swap A swap in which the floating rate is the rate on a security known as a constant maturity treasury or CMT security.

Constant maturity treasury (CMT) A hypothetical U.S. Treasury note with a constant maturity. A CMT exists for various years in the range of 2 to 10.

Constant returns to scale The condition that if all inputs into the production process are increased by a given percentage, then output rises by that same percentage.

Contango A situation in a futures market where the current futures price is greater than the current spot price for the underlying asset.

Contingent consideration Potential future payments to the seller that are contingent on the achievement of certain agreed on occurrences.

Continuing earnings Earnings excluding nonrecurring components.

Continuing residual income Residual income after the forecast horizon.

Continuing value The analyst's estimate of a stock's value at a particular point in the future.

Continuous time Time thought of as advancing in extremely small increments.

Control premium An increment or premium to value associated with a controlling ownership interest in a company.

Convenience yield The nonmonetary return offered by an asset when the asset is in short supply, often associated with assets with seasonal production processes.

Conventional cash flow A conventional cash flow pattern is one with an initial outflow followed by a series of inflows.

Conversion factor An adjustment used to facilitate delivery on bond futures contracts in which any of a number of bonds with different characteristics are eligible for delivery.

Core earnings Earnings excluding nonrecurring components.

Corporate governance The system of principles, policies, procedures, and clearly defined responsibilities and accountabilities used by stakeholders to overcome the conflicts of interest inherent in the corporate form.

Corporate raider A person or organization seeking to profit by acquiring a company and reselling it, or seeking to profit from the takeover attempt itself (e.g., greenmail).

Corporation A legal entity with rights similar to those of a person. The chief officers, executives, or top managers act as agents for the firm and are legally entitled to authorize corporate activities and to enter into contracts on behalf of the business.

Correlation analysis The analysis of the strength of the linear relationship between two data series.

Cost approach Approach that values a private company based on the values of the underlying assets of the entity less the value of any related liabilities. In the context of real estate, this approach estimates the value of a property based on what it would cost to buy the land and construct a new property on the site that has the same utility or functionality as the property being appraised.

Cost of carry The cost associated with holding some asset, including financing, storage, and insurance costs. Any yield received on the asset is treated as a negative carrying cost.

Cost of debt The cost of debt financing to a company, such as when it issues a bond or takes out a bank loan.

Cost of equity The required rate of return on common stock.

Cost-of-carry model A model for pricing futures contracts in which the futures price is determined by adding the cost of carry to the spot price.

Covariance stationary Describes a time series when its expected value and variance are constant and finite in all periods and when its covariance with itself for a fixed number of periods in the past or future is constant and finite in all periods.

Covered interest arbitrage A transaction executed in the foreign exchange market in which a currency is purchased (sold) and a forward contract is sold (purchased) to lock in the exchange rate for future delivery of the currency. This transaction should earn the risk-free rate of the investor's home country.

Covered interest rate parity Relationship among the spot exchange rate, forward exchange rate, and the interest rates in two currencies that ensures that the return on a hedged (i.e., covered) foreign risk-free investment is the same as the return on a domestic risk-free investment.

Credit correlation The correlation of credits contained in an index CDS.

Credit curve The credit spreads for a range of maturities of a company's debt; applies to non-government borrowers and incorporates credit risk into each rate.

Credit default swap A derivative contract between two parties in which the buyer makes a series of cash payments to the seller and receives a promise of compensation for credit losses resulting from the default.

Credit derivative A derivative instrument in which the underlying is a measure of the credit quality of a borrower.

Credit event The outcome that triggers a payment from the credit protection seller to the credit protection buyer.

Credit protection buyer One party to a credit default swap; the buyer makes a series of cash payments to the seller and receives a promise of compensation for credit losses resulting from the default.

Credit protection seller One party to a credit default swap; the buyer makes a series of cash payments to the seller and receives a promise of compensation for credit losses resulting from the default.

Credit ratings Ordinal rankings of the credit risk of a company, government (sovereign), quasi-government, or asset-backed security.

Credit risk The risk that the borrower will not repay principal and interest. Also called *default risk*.

Credit scoring Ordinal rankings of a retail borrower's credit riskiness. It is called an *ordinal ranking* because it only orders borrowers' riskiness from highest to lowest.

Credit spreads The difference between the yields on default-free and credit risky zero-coupon bonds.

Currency option An option that allows the holder to buy (if a call) or sell (if a put) an underlying currency at a fixed exercise rate, expressed as an exchange rate.

Current credit risk The risk associated with the possibility that a payment currently due will not be made.

Current exchange rate For accounting purposes, the spot exchange rate on the balance sheet date.

Current rate method Approach to translating foreign currency financial statements for consolidation in which all assets and liabilities are translated at the current exchange rate. The current rate method is the prevalent method of translation.

Curve trade Buying a CDS of one maturity and selling a CDS on the same reference entity with a different maturity.

Cyclical businesses Businesses with high sensitivity to business- or industry-cycle influences.

DOWNREIT A variation of the UPREIT structure under which the REIT owns more than one partnership and may own properties at both the REIT level and the partnership level.

Daily settlement See *marking to market*.

Data mining The practice of determining a model by extensive searching through a dataset for statistically significant patterns.

Day trader A trader holding a position open somewhat longer than a scalper but closing all positions at the end of the day.

"Dead-hand" provision A poison pill provision that allows for the redemption or cancellation of a poison pill provision only by a vote of continuing directors (generally directors who were on the target company's board prior to the takeover attempt).

Debt covenants Agreements between the company as borrower and its creditors.

Debt ratings An objective measure of the quality and safety of a company's debt based upon an analysis of the company's ability to pay the promised cash flows, as well as an analysis of any indentures.

Decision rule With respect to hypothesis testing, the rule according to which the null hypothesis will be rejected or not rejected; involves the comparison of the test statistic to rejection point(s).

Deep-in-the-money Options that are far in-the-money.

Deep-out-of-the-money Options that are far out-of-the-money.

Default intensity Gives the probability of default over the next instant $[t, t + \Delta]$ when the economy is in state X_t.

Default probability See *probability of default*.

Default risk See *credit risk*.

Deferred revenue A liability account for money that has been collected for goods or services that have not yet been delivered; payment received in advance of providing a good or service.

Definition of value A specification of how "value" is to be understood in the context of a specific valuation.

Definitive merger agreement A contract signed by both parties to a merger that clarifies the details of the transaction, including the terms, warranties, conditions, termination details, and the rights of all parties.

Delivery A process used in a deliverable forward contract in which the long pays the agreed-upon price to the short, which in turn delivers the underlying asset to the long.

Delivery option The feature of a futures contract giving the short the right to make decisions about what, when, and where to deliver.

Delta The relationship between the option price and the underlying price, which reflects the sensitivity of the price of the option to changes in the price of the underlying.

Dependent variable The variable whose variation about its mean is to be explained by the regression; the left-hand-side variable in a regression equation.

Depository Trust and Clearinghouse Corporation A U.S.-headquartered entity providing post-trade clearing, settlement, and information services.

Depreciated replacement cost In the context of real estate, the replacement cost of a building adjusted different types of depreciation.

Derivative A financial instrument whose value depends on the value of some underlying asset or factor (e.g., a stock price, an interest rate, or exchange rate).

Descriptive statistics The study of how data can be summarized effectively.

Diff swaps A swap in which the payments are based on the difference between interest rates in two countries but payments are made in only a single currency.

Diluted earnings per share (diluted EPS) Net income, minus preferred dividends, divided by the number of common shares outstanding considering all dilutive securities (e.g., convertible debt and options); the EPS that would result if all dilutive securities were converted into common shares.

Dilution A reduction in proportional ownership interest as a result of the issuance of new shares.

Diminishing marginal productivity When each additional unit of an input, keeping the other inputs unchanged, increases output by a smaller increment.

Direct capitalization method In the context of real estate, this method estimates the value of an income-producing property based on the level and quality of its net operating income.

Direct financing leases A type of finance lease, from a lessor perspective, where the present value of the lease payments (lease receivable) equals the carrying value of the leased asset. The revenues earned by the lessor are financing in nature.

Discount To reduce the value of a future payment in allowance for how far away it is in time; to calculate the present value of some future amount. Also, the amount by which an instrument is priced below its face value.

Discount for lack of control An amount or percentage deducted from the pro rata share of 100 percent of the value of an equity interest in a business to reflect the absence of some or all of the powers of control.

Discount for lack of marketability An amount of percentage deducted from the value of an ownership interest to reflect the relative absence of marketability.

Discount interest A procedure for determining the interest on a loan or bond in which the interest is deducted from the face value in advance.

Discount rate Any rate used in finding the present value of a future cash flow.

Discounted abnormal earnings model A model of stock valuation that views intrinsic value of stock as the sum of book value per share plus the present value of the stock's expected future residual income per share.

Discounted cash flow (DCF) analysis In the context of merger analysis, it is an estimate of a target company's value found by discounting the company's expected future free cash flows to the present.

Discounted cash flow method Income approach that values an asset based on estimates of future cash flows discounted to present value by using a discount rate reflective of the risks associated with the cash flows. In the context of real estate, this method estimates the value of an income-producing property based by discounting future projected cash flows.

Discounted cash flow model A model of intrinsic value that views the value of an asset as the present value of the asset's expected future cash flows.

Discrete time Time thought of as advancing in distinct finite increments.

Discriminant analysis A multivariate classification technique used to discriminate between groups, such as companies that either will or will not become bankrupt during some time frame.

Diversified REITs REITs that own and operate in more than one type of property; they are more common in Europe and Asia than in the United States.

Divestiture The sale, liquidation, or spin-off of a division or subsidiary.

Dividend coverage ratio The ratio of net income to dividends.

Dividend discount model (DDM) A present value model of stock value that views the intrinsic value of a stock as present value of the stock's expected future dividends.

Dividend displacement of earnings The concept that dividends paid now displace earnings in all future periods.

Dividend imputation tax system A taxation system which effectively assures that corporate profits distributed as dividends are taxed just once, at the shareholder's tax rate.

Dividend payout ratio The ratio of cash dividends paid to earnings for a period.

Dividend policy The strategy a company follows with regard to the amount and timing of dividend payments.

Dividend rate The most recent quarterly dividend multiplied by four.

Double taxation system Corporate earnings are taxed twice when paid out as dividends. First, corporate earnings are taxed regardless of whether they will be distributed as dividends or retained at the G-13 corporate level, and second, dividends are taxed again at the individual shareholder level.

Downstream A transaction between two related companies, an investor company (or a parent company) and an associate company (or a subsidiary) such that the investor company records a profit on its income statement. An example is a sale of inventory by the investor company to the associate or by a parent to a subsidiary company.

Due diligence Investigation and analysis in support of a recommendation; the failure to exercise due diligence may sometimes result in liability according to various securities laws.

Dummy variable A type of qualitative variable that takes on a value of 1 if a particular condition is true and 0 if that condition is false.

Duration A measure of an option-free bond's average maturity. Specifically, the weighted average maturity of all future cash flows paid by a security, in which the weights are the present value of these cash flows as a fraction of the bond's price. A measure of a bond's price sensitivity to interest rate movements.

Dutch disease A situation in which currency appreciation driven by strong export demand for resources makes other segments of the economy (particularly manufacturing) globally uncompetitive.

Dynamic hedging A strategy in which a position is hedged by making frequent adjustments to the quantity of the instrument used for hedging in relation to the instrument being hedged.

Earnings expectations management Attempts by management to encourage analysts to forecast a slightly lower number for expected earnings than the analysts would otherwise forecast.

Earnings game Management's focus on reporting earnings that meet consensus estimates.

Earnings management activity Deliberate activity aimed at influencing reporting earnings numbers, often with the goal of placing management in a favorable light; the opportunistic use of accruals to manage earnings.

Earnings surprise The difference between reported earnings per share and expected earnings per share.

Earnings yield Earnings per share divided by price; the reciprocal of the P/E ratio.

Economic growth The expansion of production possibilities that results from capital accumulation and technological change.

Economic obsolescence In the context of real estate, a reduction in value due to current economic conditions.

Economic profit See *residual income.*

Economic sectors Large industry groupings.

Economic value added (EVA®) A commercial implementation of the residual income concept; the computation of EVA® is the net operating profit after taxes minus the cost of capital, where these inputs are adjusted for a number of items.

Economies of scale A situation in which average costs per unit of good or service produced fall as volume rises. In reference to mergers, the savings achieved through the consolidation of operations and elimination of duplicate resources.

Edwards–Bell–Ohlson model A model of stock valuation that views intrinsic value of stock as the sum of book value per share plus the present value of the stock's expected future residual income per share.

Efficient frontier The portion of the minimum-variance frontier beginning with the global minimum-variance portfolio and continuing above it; the graph of the set of portfolios offering the maximum expected return for their level of variance of return.

Efficient portfolio A portfolio offering the highest expected return for a given level of risk as measured by variance or standard deviation of return.

Enterprise value (EV) Total company value (the market value of debt, common equity, and preferred equity) minus the value of cash and investments.

Enterprise value multiple A valuation multiple that relates the total market value of all sources of a company's capital (net of cash) to a measure of fundamental value for the entire company (such as a pre-interest earnings measure).

Entry price The price paid to buy an asset.

Equilibrium The condition in which supply equals demand.

Equity REIT A REIT that owns, operates, and/or selectively develops income-producing real estate.

Equity carve-out A form of restructuring that involves the creation of a new legal entity and the sale of equity in it to outsiders.

Equity charge The estimated cost of equity capital in money terms.

Equity forward A contract calling for the purchase of an individual stock, a stock portfolio, or a stock index at a later date at an agreed-upon price.

Equity options Options on individual stocks; also known as stock options.

Error autocorrelation The autocorrelation of the error term.

Error term The portion of the dependent variable that is not explained by the independent variable(s) in the regression.

Estimated parameters With reference to a regression analysis, the estimated values of the population intercept and population slope coefficient(s) in a regression.

Eurodollar A dollar deposited outside the United States.

European option An option that can only be exercised on its expiration date.

Ex ante version of PPP Hypothesis that expected changes in the spot exchange rate are equal to expected differences in national inflation rates. An extension of relative purchasing power parity to expected future changes in the exchange rate.

Ex-dividend Trading ex-dividend refers to shares that no longer carry the right to the next dividend payment.

Ex-dividend date The first date that a share trades without (i.e., "ex") the dividend.

Ex-dividend price The price at which a share first trades without (i.e., "ex") the right to receive an upcoming dividend.

Excess earnings method Income approach that estimates the value of all intangible assets of the business by capitalizing future earnings in excess of the estimated return requirements associated with working capital and fixed assets.

Exchange for physicals (EFP) A permissible delivery procedure used by futures market participants, in which the long and short arrange a delivery procedure other than the normal procedures stipulated by the futures exchange.

Exchange ratio The number of shares that target stockholders are to receive in exchange for each of their shares in the target company.

Exercise The process of using an option to buy or sell the underlying. Also called *exercising the option.*

Exercise price The fixed price at which an option holder can buy or sell the underlying. Also called *strike price, striking price,* or *strike.*

Exercise rate The fixed rate at which the holder of an interest rate option can buy or sell the underlying. Also called *strike rate.*

Exercise value The value of an asset given a hypothetically complete understanding of the asset's investment characteristics; the value obtained if an option is exercised based on current conditions. Also called *intrinsic value.*

Exercising the option The process of using an option to buy or sell the underlying. Also called *exercise.*

Exit price The price received to sell an asset or transfer a liability.

Expanded CAPM An adaptation of the CAPM that adds to the CAPM a premium for small size and company-specific risk.

Expected holding-period return The expected total return on an asset over a stated holding period; for stocks, the sum of the expected dividend yield and the expected price appreciation over the holding period.

Expected loss The probability of default multiplied by the loss given default; the full amount owed minus the expected recovery.

Expenses Outflows of economic resources or increases in liabilities that result in decreases in equity (other than decreases because of distributions to owners); reductions in net assets associated with the creation of revenues.

Expiration date The date on which a derivative contract expires.

Exposure to foreign exchange risk The risk of a change in value of an asset or liability denominated in a foreign currency due to a change in exchange rates.

External growth Company growth in output or sales that is achieved by buying the necessary resources externally (i.e., achieved through mergers and acquisitions).

External sustainability approach An approach to assessing the equilibrium exchange rate that focuses on exchange rate adjustments required to ensure that a country's net foreign-asset/GDP ratio or net foreign-liability/GDP ratio stabilizes at a sustainable level.

Externalities Spillover effects of production and consumption activities onto others who did not consent to participate in the activity.

FX carry trade An investment strategy that involves taking on long positions in high-yield currencies and short positions in low-yield currencies.

Factor A common or underlying element with which several variables are correlated.

Factor betas An asset's sensitivity to a particular factor; a measure of the response of return to each unit of increase in a factor, holding all other factors constant.

Factor loadings See *factor betas*.

Factor price The expected return in excess of the risk-free rate for a portfolio with a sensitivity of 1 to one factor and a sensitivity of 0 to all other factors.

Factor risk premium The expected return in excess of the risk-free rate for a portfolio with a sensitivity of 1 to one factor and a sensitivity of 0 to all other factors. Also called *factor price*.

Factor sensitivity See *factor betas*.

Failure to pay When a borrower does not make a scheduled payment of principal or interest on any outstanding obligations after a grace period.

Fair market value The market price of an asset or liability that trades regularly.

Fair value The amount at which an asset (or liability) could be bought (or incurred) or sold (or settled) in a current transaction between willing parties, that is, other than in a forced or liquidation sale; the price that would be received to sell an asset or paid to transfer a liability in an orderly transaction between market participants at the measurement date.

Fiduciary call A combination of a European call and a risk-free bond that matures on the option expiration day and has a face value equal to the exercise price of the call.

Finance lease Essentially, the purchase of some asset by the buyer (lessee) that is directly financed by the seller (lessor). Also called *capital lease*.

Financial contagion A situation where financial shocks spread from their place of origin to other locales; in essence, a faltering economy infects other, healthier economies.

Financial distress Heightened uncertainty regarding a company's ability to meet its various obligations because of lower or negative earnings.

Financial futures Futures contracts in which the underlying is a stock, bond, or currency.

Financial reporting quality The accuracy with which a company's reported financials reflect its operating performance and their usefulness for forecasting future cash flows.

Financial risk The risk that environmental, social, or governance risk factors will result in significant costs or other losses to a company and its shareholders; the risk arising from a company's obligation to meet required payments under its financing agreements.

Financial transaction A purchase involving a buyer having essentially no material synergies with the target (e.g., the purchase of a private company by a company in an unrelated industry or by a private equity firm would typically be a financial transaction).

First-differencing A transformation that subtracts the value of the time series in period $t-1$ from its value in period t.

First-in, first-out (FIFO) The first in, first out, method of accounting for inventory, which matches sales against the costs of items of inventory in the order in which they were placed in inventory.

First-order serial correlation Correlation between adjacent observations in a time series.

Fitted parameters With reference to a regression analysis, the estimated values of the population intercept and population slope coefficient(s) in a regression.

Fixed-rate perpetual preferred stock Nonconvertible, noncallable preferred stock with a specified dividend rate that has a claim on earnings senior to the claim of common stock, and no maturity date.

Flip-in pill A poison pill takeover defense that dilutes an acquirer's ownership in a target by giving other existing target company shareholders the right to buy additional target company shares at a discount.

Flip-over pill A poison pill takeover defense that gives target company shareholders the right to purchase shares of the acquirer at a significant discount to the market price, which has the effect of causing dilution to all existing acquiring company shareholders.

Floor A combination of interest rate put options designed to hedge a lender against lower rates on a floating-rate loan.

Floor traders Market makers that buy and sell by quoting a bid and an ask price. They are the primary providers of liquidity to the market.

Floored swap A swap in which the floating payments have a lower limit.

Floorlet Each component put option in a floor.

Flotation cost Fees charged to companies by investment bankers and other costs associated with raising new capital.

Foreign currency transactions Transactions that are denominated in a currency other than a company's functional currency.

Forward P/E A P/E calculated on the basis of a forecast of EPS; a stock's current price divided by next year's expected earnings.

Forward contract An agreement between two parties in which one party, the buyer, agrees to buy from the other party, the seller, an underlying asset at a later date for a price established at the start of the contract.

Forward dividend yield A dividend yield based on the anticipated dividend during the next 12 months.

Forward integration A merger involving the purchase of a target that is farther along the value or production chain; for example, to acquire a distributor.

Forward price or forward rate The fixed price or rate at which the transaction scheduled to occur at the expiration of a forward contract will take place. This price is agreed on at the initiation date of the contract.

Forward rate agreement (FRA) A forward contract calling for one party to make a fixed interest payment and the other to make an interest payment at a rate to be determined at the contract expiration.

Forward swap A forward contract to enter into a swap.

Franking credit A tax credit received by shareholders for the taxes that a corporation paid on its distributed earnings.

Free cash flow The actual cash that would be available to the company's investors after making all investments necessary to maintain the company as an ongoing enterprise (also referred to as free cash flow to the firm); the internally generated funds that can be distributed to the company's investors (e.g., shareholders and bondholders) without impairing the value of the company.

Free cash flow hypothesis The hypothesis that higher debt levels discipline managers by forcing them to make fixed debt service payments and by reducing the company's free cash flow.

Free cash flow method Income approach that values an asset based on estimates of future cash flows discounted to present value by using a discount rate reflective of the risks associated with the cash flows.

Free cash flow to equity The cash flow available to a company's common shareholders after all operating expenses, interest, and principal payments have been made, and necessary investments in working and fixed capital have been made.

Free cash flow to equity model A model of stock valuation that views a stock's intrinsic value as the present value of expected future free cash flows to equity.

Free cash flow to the firm The cash flow available to the company's suppliers of capital after all operating expenses (including taxes) have been paid and necessary investments in working and fixed capital have been made.

Free cash flow to the firm model A model of stock valuation that views the value of a firm as the present value of expected future free cash flows to the firm.

Friendly transaction A potential business combination that is endorsed by the managers of both companies.

Functional currency The currency of the primary economic environment in which an entity operates.

Functional obsolescence In the context of real estate, a reduction in value due to a design that differs from that of a new building constructed for the intended use of the property.

Fundamental beta A beta that is based at least in part on fundamental data for a company.

Fundamental factor models A multifactor model in which the factors are attributes of stocks or companies that are important in explaining cross-sectional differences in stock prices.

Fundamentals Economic characteristics of a business such as profitability, financial strength, and risk.

Funds available for distribution Funds from operations (FFO) adjusted to remove any non-cash rent reported under straight-line rent accounting and to subtract maintenance-type capital expenditures and leasing costs, including leasing agents' commissions and tenants' improvement allowances.

Funds from operations Accounting net earnings excluding (1) depreciation charges on real estate, (2) deferred tax charges, and (3) gains or losses from sales of property and debt restructuring.

Futures commission merchants (FCMs) Individuals or companies that execute futures transactions for other parties off the exchange.

Futures contract A variation of a forward contract that has essentially the same basic definition but with some additional features, such as a clearinghouse guarantee against credit losses, a daily settlement of gains and losses, and an organized electronic or floor trading facility.

Gamma A numerical measure of how sensitive an option's delta is to a change in the underlying.

Generalized least squares A regression estimation technique that addresses heteroskedasticity of the error term.

Going-concern assumption The assumption that the business will maintain its business activities into the foreseeable future.

Going-concern value A business's value under a going-concern assumption.

Goodwill An intangible asset that represents the excess of the purchase price of an acquired company over the value of the net assets acquired.

Gross domestic product A money measure of the goods and services produced within a country's borders over a stated time period.

Gross lease A lease under which the tenant pays a gross rent to the landlord who is responsible for all operating costs, utilities, maintenance expenses, and real estate taxes relating to the property.

Growth accounting equation The production function written in the form of growth rates. For the basic Cobb–Douglas production function, it states that the growth rate of output equals the rate of technological change plus α times the growth rate of capital plus $(1 - \alpha)$ times the growth rate of labor.

Growth capital expenditures Capital expenditures needed for expansion.

Growth option The ability to make additional investments in a project at some future time if the financial results are strong. Also called *expansion option.*

Guideline assets Assets used as benchmarks when applying the method of comparables to value an asset.

Guideline companies Assets used as benchmarks when applying the method of comparables to value an asset.

Guideline public companies Public-company comparables for the company being valued.

Guideline public company method A variation of the market approach; establishes a value estimate based on the observed multiples from trading activity in the shares of public companies viewed as reasonably comparable to the subject private company.

Guideline transactions method A variation of the market approach; establishes a value estimate based on pricing multiples derived from the acquisition of control of entire public or private companies that were acquired.

Harmonic mean A type of weighted mean computed by averaging the reciprocals of the observations, then taking the reciprocal of that average.

Hazard rate The probability that an event will occur, given that it has not already occurred.

Hazard rate estimation A technique for estimating the probability of a binary event, such as default/no default, mortality/no mortality, and prepay/no prepay.

Health care REITs REITs that invest in skilled nursing facilities (nursing homes), assisted living and independent residential facilities for retired persons, hospitals, medical office buildings, or rehabilitation centers.

Hedge ratio The relationship of the quantity of an asset being hedged to the quantity of the derivative used for hedging.

Hedging A general strategy usually thought of as reducing, if not eliminating, risk.

Held for trading investments Debt or equity securities acquired with the intent to sell them in the near term.

Held-to-maturity investments Debt (fixed-income) securities that a company intends to hold to maturity; these are presented at their original cost, updated for any amortization of discounts or premiums.

Herfindahl–Hirschman Index (HHI) A measure of market concentration that is calculated by summing the squared market shares for competing companies in an industry; high HHI readings or mergers that would result in large HHI increases are more likely to result in regulatory challenges.

Heteroskedastic With reference to the error term of regression, having a variance that differs across observations.

Heteroskedasticity The property of having a nonconstant variance; refers to an error term with the property that its variance differs across observations.

Heteroskedasticity-consistent standard errors Standard errors of the estimated parameters of a regression that correct for the presence of heteroskedasticity in the regression's error term.

Historical exchange rates For accounting purposes, the exchange rates that existed when the assets and liabilities were initially recorded.

Holding period return The return that an investor earns during a specified holding period; a synonym for total return.

Homoskedasticity The property of having a constant variance; refers to an error term that is constant across observations.

Horizontal merger A merger involving companies in the same line of business, usually as competitors.

Hostile transaction An attempt to acquire a company against the wishes of the target's managers.

Hotel REITs REITs that own hotel properties but, similar to health care REITs, in many countries they must refrain from operating their properties themselves to maintain their tax-advantaged REIT status.

Human capital The accumulated knowledge and skill that workers acquire from education, training, or life experience.

Hybrid REITs REITs that own and operate income-producing real estate and invest in mortgages as well; REITs that have positions in both real estate assets and real estate debt.

Hybrid approach With respect to forecasting, an approach that combines elements of both top-down and bottom-up analysis.

ISDA Master Agreement A standard or "master" agreement published by the International Swaps and Derivatives Association. The master agreement establishes the terms for each party involved in the transaction.

Illiquidity discount A reduction or discount to value that reflects the lack of depth of trading or liquidity in that asset's market.

Impairment Diminishment in value as a result of carrying (book) value exceeding fair value and/or recoverable value.

Impairment of capital rule A legal restriction that dividends cannot exceed retained earnings.

Implied repo rate The rate of return from a cash-and-carry transaction implied by the futures price relative to the spot price.

Implied volatility The volatility that option traders use to price an option, implied by the price of the option and a particular option-pricing model.

In-process research and development Research and development costs relating to projects that are not yet completed, such as have been incurred by a company that is being acquired.

In-sample forecast errors The residuals from a fitted time-series model within the sample period used to fit the model.

In-the-money Options that, if exercised, would result in the value received being worth more than the payment required to exercise.

Income approach Valuation approach that values an asset as the present discounted value of the income expected from it. In the context of real estate, this approach estimates the value of a property based on an expected rate of return; the estimated value is the present value of the expected future income from the property, including proceeds from resale at the end of a typical investment holding period.

Incremental cash flow The cash flow that is realized because of a decision; the changes or increments to cash flows resulting from a decision or action.

Indenture A written contract between a lender and borrower that specifies the terms of the loan, such as interest rate, interest payment schedule, maturity, etc.

Independent projects Independent projects are projects whose cash flows are independent of each other.

Independent regulators Regulators recognized and granted authority by a government body or agency. They are not government agencies per se and typically do not rely on government funding.

Independent variable A variable used to explain the dependent variable in a regression; a right-hand-side variable in a regression equation.

Index CDS A type of credit default swap that involves a combination of borrowers.

Index amortizing swap An interest rate swap in which the notional principal is indexed to the level of interest rates and declines with the level of interest rates according to a predefined schedule. This type of swap is frequently used to hedge securities that are prepaid as interest rates decline, such as mortgage-backed securities.

Indexing An investment strategy in which an investor constructs a portfolio to mirror the performance of a specified index.

Industrial REITs REITs that hold portfolios of single-tenant or multi-tenant industrial properties that are used as warehouses, distribution centers, light manufacturing facilities, and small office or "flex" space.

Industry structure An industry's underlying economic and technical characteristics.

Information ratio (IR) Mean active return divided by active risk; or alpha divided by the standard deviation of diversifiable risk.

Informational frictions Forces that restrict availability, quality, and/or flow of information and its use.

Initial margin requirement The margin requirement on the first day of a transaction as well as on any day in which additional margin funds must be deposited.

Initial public offering (IPO) The initial issuance of common stock registered for public trading by a formerly private corporation.

Instability in the minimum-variance frontier The characteristic of minimum-variance frontiers that they are sensitive to small changes in inputs.

Interest rate call An option in which the holder has the right to make a known interest payment and receive an unknown interest payment.

Interest rate cap A series of call options on an interest rate, with each option expiring at the date on which the floating loan rate will be reset, and with each option having the same exercise rate. A cap in general can have an underlying other than an interest rate.

Interest rate collar A combination of a long cap and a short floor, or a short cap and a long floor. A collar in general can have an underlying other than an interest rate.

Interest rate floor A series of put options on an interest rate, with each option expiring at the date on which the floating loan rate will be reset, and with each option having the same exercise rate. A floor in general can have an underlying other than the interest rate. Also called *floor*.

Interest rate option An option in which the underlying is an interest rate.

Interest rate parity A formula that expresses the equivalence or parity of spot and forward rates, after adjusting for differences in the interest rates.

Interest rate put An option in which the holder has the right to make an unknown interest payment and receive a known interest payment.

Interest rate risk Risk that interest rates will change such that the return earned is not commensurate with returns on comparable instruments in the marketplace.

Internal rate of return (IRR) Rate of return that discounts future cash flows from an investment to the exact amount of the investment; the discount rate that makes the present value of an investment's costs (outflows) equal to the present value of the investment's benefits (inflows).

Internal ratings Credit ratings developed internally and used by financial institutions or other entities to manage risk.

International Fisher effect Proposition that nominal interest rate differentials across currencies are determined by expected inflation differentials.

Intrinsic value The value of an asset given a hypothetically complete understanding of the asset's investment characteristics; the value obtained if an option is exercised based on current conditions. The difference between the spot exchange rate and the strike price of a currency.

Inverse price ratio The reciprocal of a price multiple, e.g., in the case of a P/E ratio, the "earnings yield" E/P (where P is share price and E is earnings per share).

Investment objectives Desired investment outcomes; includes risk objectives and return objectives.

Investment strategy An approach to investment analysis and security selection.

Investment value The value to a specific buyer, taking account of potential synergies based on the investor's requirements and expectations.

Judicial law Interpretations of courts.

Justified (fundamental) P/E The price-to-earnings ratio that is fair, warranted, or justified on the basis of forecasted fundamentals.

Justified price multiple The estimated fair value of the price multiple, usually based on forecasted fundamentals or comparables.

***k*th order autocorrelation** The correlation between observations in a time series separated by *k* periods.

Labor force Everyone of working age (ages 16 to 64) that either is employed or is available for work but not working.

Labor force participation rate The percentage of the working age population that is in the labor force.

Labor productivity The quantity of real GDP produced by an hour of labor. More generally, output per unit of labor input.

Labor productivity growth accounting equation States that potential GDP growth equals the growth rate of the labor input plus the growth rate of labor productivity.

Lack of marketability discount An extra return to investors to compensate for lack of a public market or lack of marketability.

Last-in, first-out (LIFO) The last in, first out, method of accounting for inventory, which matches sales against the costs of items of inventory in the reverse order the items were placed in inventory (i.e., inventory produced or acquired last are assumed to be sold first).

Law of one price Hypothesis that (1) identical goods should trade at the same price across countries when valued in terms of a common currency, or (2) two equivalent financial instruments or combinations of financial instruments can sell for only one price. The latter form is equivalent to the principle that no arbitrage opportunities are possible.

Leading P/E A P/E calculated on the basis of a forecast of EPS; a stock's current price divided by next year's expected earnings.

Leading dividend yield Forecasted dividends per share over the next year divided by current stock price.

Legal risk The risk that failures by company managers to effectively manage a company's environmental, social, and governance risk exposures will lead to lawsuits and other judicial remedies, resulting in potentially catastrophic losses for the company; the risk that the legal system will not enforce a contract in case of dispute or fraud.

Legislative and regulatory risk The risk that governmental laws and regulations directly or indirectly affecting a company's operations will change with potentially severe adverse effects on the company's continued profitability and even its long-term sustainability.

Lessee The party obtaining the use of an asset through a lease.

Lessor The owner of an asset that grants the right to use the asset to another party.

Leveraged buyout (LBO) A transaction whereby the target company management team converts the target to a privately held company by using heavy borrowing to finance the purchase of the target company's outstanding shares.

Leveraged recapitalization A post-offer takeover defense mechanism that involves the assumption of a large amount of debt that is then used to finance share repurchases; the effect is to dramatically change the company's capital structure while attempting to deliver a value to target shareholders in excess of a hostile bid.

Limit down A limit move in the futures market in which the price at which a transaction would be made is at or below the lower limit.

Limit move A condition in the futures markets in which the price at which a transaction would be made is at or beyond the price limits.

Limit up A limit move in the futures market in which the price at which a transaction would be made is at or above the upper limit.

Linear association A straight-line relationship, as opposed to a relationship that cannot be graphed as a straight line.

Linear regression Regression that models the straight-line relationship between the dependent and independent variable(s).

Linear trend A trend in which the dependent variable changes at a constant rate with time.

Liquidation To sell the assets of a company, division, or subsidiary piecemeal, typically because of bankruptcy; the form of bankruptcy that allows for the orderly satisfaction of creditors' claims after which the company ceases to exist.

Liquidation value The value of a company if the company were dissolved and its assets sold individually.

Liquidity risk The risk that a financial instrument cannot be purchased or sold without a significant concession in price due to the size of the market.

Local currency The currency of the country where a company is located.

Locals Market makers that buy and sell by quoting a bid and an ask price. They are the primary providers of liquidity to the market.

Locational obsolescence In the context of real estate, a reduction in value due to decreased desirability of the location of the building.

Locked limit A condition in the futures markets in which a transaction cannot take place because the price would be beyond the limits.

Log-linear model With reference to time-series models, a model in which the growth rate of the time series as a function of time is constant.

Log-log regression model A regression that expresses the dependent and independent variables as natural logarithms.

Logit model A qualitative-dependent-variable multiple regression model based on the logistic probability distribution.

London interbank offered rate (Libor or LIBOR) Collective name for multiple rates at which a select set of banks believe they could borrow unsecured funds from other banks in the London interbank market for different currencies and different borrowing periods ranging from overnight to one year.

Long The buyer of a derivative contract. Also refers to the position of owning a derivative.

Long-term equity anticipatory securities (LEAPS) Options originally created with expirations of several years.

Long/short trade A long position in one CDS and a short position in another.

Look-ahead bias A bias caused by using information that was not available on the test date.

Loss given default The amount that will be lost if a default occurs.

Lower bound The lowest possible value of an option.

Macroeconomic balance approach An approach to assessing the equilibrium exchange rate that focuses on exchange rate adjustments needed to close the gap between the medium-term expectation for a country's current account balance and that country's normal (or sustainable) current account balance.

Macroeconomic factor A factor related to the economy, such as the inflation rate, industrial production, or economic sector membership.

Macroeconomic factor model A multifactor model in which the factors are surprises in macroeconomic variables that significantly explain equity returns.

Maintenance capital expenditures Capital expenditures needed to maintain operations at the current level.

Maintenance margin requirement The margin requirement on any day other than the first day of a transaction.

Managerialism theories Theories that posit that corporate executives are motivated to engage in mergers to maximize the size of their company rather than shareholder value.

Margin The amount of money that a trader deposits in a margin account. The term is derived from the stock market practice in which an investor borrows a portion of the money required to purchase a certain amount of stock. In futures markets, there is no borrowing so the margin is more of a down payment or performance bond.

Marginal investor An investor in a given share who is very likely to be part of the next trade in the share and who is therefore important in setting price.

Mark-to-market The revaluation of a financial asset or liability to its current market value or fair value.

Market approach Valuation approach that values an asset based on pricing multiples from sales of assets viewed as similar to the subject asset.

Market efficiency A finance perspective on capital markets that deals with the relationship of price to intrinsic value. The **traditional efficient markets formulation** asserts that an asset's price is the best available estimate of its intrinsic value. The **rational efficient markets formulation** asserts that investors should expect to be rewarded for the costs of information gathering and analysis by higher gross returns.

Market price of risk The slope of the capital market line, indicating the market risk premium for each unit of market risk.

Market risk premium The expected excess return on the market over the risk-free rate.

Market timing Asset allocation in which the investment in the market is increased if one forecasts that the market will outperform T-bills.

Market value The estimated amount for which a property should exchange on the date of valuation between a willing buyer and a willing seller in an arm's-length transaction after proper marketing wherein the parties had each acted knowledgeably, prudently, and without compulsion.

Market value of invested capital The market value of debt and equity.

Marking to market A procedure used primarily in futures markets in which the parties to a contract settle the amount owed daily. Also known as the *daily settlement.*

Markowitz decision rule A decision rule for choosing between two investments based on their means and variances.

Mature growth rate The earnings growth rate in a company's mature phase; an earnings growth rate that can be sustained long term.

Mean reversion The tendency of a time series to fall when its level is above its mean and rise when its level is below its mean; a mean-reverting time series tends to return to its long-term mean.

Mean–variance analysis An approach to portfolio analysis using expected means, variances, and covariances of asset returns.

Merger The absorption of one company by another; two companies become one entity and one or both of the pre-merger companies ceases to exist as a separate entity.

Method based on forecasted fundamentals An approach to using price multiples that relates a price multiple to forecasts of fundamentals through a discounted cash flow model.

Method of comparables An approach to valuation that involves using a price multiple to evaluate whether an asset is relatively fairly valued, relatively undervalued, or relatively overvalued when compared to a benchmark value of the multiple.

Minimum-variance frontier The graph of the set of portfolios that have minimum variance for their level of expected return.

Minimum-variance portfolio The portfolio with the minimum variance for each given level of expected return.

Minority Interest The proportion of the ownership of a subsidiary not held by the parent (controlling) company.

Mispricing Any departure of the market price of an asset from the asset's estimated intrinsic value.

Mixed factor models Factor models that combine features of more than one type of factor model.

Mixed offering A merger or acquisition that is to be paid for with cash, securities, or some combination of the two.

Model specification With reference to regression, the set of variables included in the regression and the regression equation's functional form.

Modified duration A measure of a bond's price sensitivity to interest rate movements. Equal to the Macaulay duration of a bond divided by one plus its yield to maturity.

Molodovsky effect The observation that P/Es tend to be high on depressed EPS at the bottom of a business cycle, and tend to be low on unusually high EPS at the top of a business cycle.

Momentum indicators Valuation indicators that relate either price or a fundamental (such as earnings) to the time series of their own past values (or in some cases to their expected value).

Monetary assets and liabilities Assets and liabilities with value equal to the amount of currency contracted for, a fixed amount of currency. Examples are cash, accounts receivable, accounts payable, bonds payable, and mortgages payable. Inventory is not a monetary asset. Most liabilities are monetary.

Monetary/non-monetary method Approach to translating foreign currency financial statements for consolidation in which monetary assets and liabilities are translated at the current exchange rate. Non-monetary assets and liabilities are translated at historical exchange rates (the exchange rates that existed when the assets and liabilities were acquired).

Monetizing The conversion of the value of a financial transaction into currency.

Moneyness The relationship between the price of the underlying and an option's exercise price.

Monitoring costs Costs borne by owners to monitor the management of the company (e.g., board of director expenses).

Mortgage REITs REITs that invest the bulk of their assets in interest-bearing mortgages, mortgage securities, or short-term loans secured by real estate.

Mortgage sector The mortgage-backed securities sector.

Mortgage-backed securities Asset-backed securitized debt obligations that represent rights to receive cash flows from portfolios of mortgage loans.

Mortgages Loans with real estate serving as collateral for the loans.

Multi-family/residential REITs REITs that invest in and manage rental apartments for lease to individual tenants, typically using one-year leases.

Multicollinearity A regression assumption violation that occurs when two or more independent variables (or combinations of independent variables) are highly but not perfectly correlated with each other.

Multiple linear regression Linear regression involving two or more independent variables.

Multiple linear regression model A linear regression model with two or more independent variables.

Mutually exclusive projects Mutually exclusive projects compete directly with each other. For example, if Projects A and B are mutually exclusive, you can choose A or B, but you cannot choose both.

NTM P/E Next twelve months P/E: current market price divided by an estimated next twelve months EPS.

Naked credit default swap A position where the owner of the CDS does not have a position in the underlying credit.

Negative serial correlation Serial correlation in which a positive error for one observation increases the chance of a negative error for another observation, and vice versa.

Net asset balance sheet exposure When assets translated at the current exchange rate are greater in amount than liabilities translated at the current exchange rate. Assets exposed to translation gains or losses exceed the exposed liabilities.

Net asset value The difference between assets and liabilities, all taken at current market values instead of accounting book values.

Net asset value per share Net asset value divided by the number of shares outstanding.

Net lease A lease under which the tenant pays a net rent to the landlord as well as an additional amount based on the tenant's pro rata share of the operating costs, utilities, maintenance expenses, and real estate taxes relating to the property.

Net liability balance sheet exposure When liabilities translated at the current exchange rate are greater assets translated at the current exchange rate. Liabilities exposed to translation gains or losses exceed the exposed assets.

Net operating assets The difference between operating assets (total assets less cash) and operating liabilities (total liabilities less total debt).

Net operating income Gross rental revenue minus operating costs, but before deducting depreciation, corporate overhead, and interest expense. In the context of real estate, a measure of the income from the property after deducting operating expenses for such items as property taxes, insurance, maintenance, utilities, repairs, and insurance but before deducting any costs associated with financing and before deducting federal income taxes. It is similar to earnings before interest, taxes, depreciation, and amortization (EBITDA) in a financial reporting context.

Net operating profit less adjusted taxes (NOPLAT) A company's operating profit with adjustments to normalize the effects of capital structure.

Net present value (NPV) The present value of an investment's cash inflows (benefits) minus the present value of its cash outflows (costs).

Net realisable value Estimated selling price in the ordinary course of business less the estimated costs necessary to make the sale.

Net regulatory burden The private costs of regulation less the private benefits of regulation.

Net rent A rent that consists of a stipulated rent to the landlord and a further amount based on their share of common area costs for utilities, maintenance, and property taxes.

Netting When parties agree to exchange only the net amount owed from one party to the other.

Network externalities The impact that users of a good, a service, or a technology have on other users of that product; it can be positive (e.g., a critical mass of users makes a product more useful) or negative (e.g., congestion makes the product less useful).

No-growth company A company without positive expected net present value projects.

No-growth value per share The value per share of a no-growth company, equal to the expected level amount of earnings divided by the stock's required rate of return.

Node Each value on a binomial tree from which successive moves or outcomes branch.

Non-cash rent An amount equal to the difference between the average contractual rent over a lease term (the straight-line rent) and the cash rent actually paid during a period. This figure is one of the deductions made from FFO to calculate AFFO.

Non-convergence trap A situation in which a country remains relative poor, or even falls further behind, because it fails to t implement necessary institutional reforms and/or adopt leading technologies.

Non-monetary assets and liabilities Assets and liabilities that are not monetary assets and liabilities. Non-monetary assets include inventory, fixed assets, and intangibles, and non-monetary liabilities include deferred revenue.

Non-renewable resources Finite resources that are depleted once they are consumed; oil and coal are examples.

Nonconventional cash flow In a nonconventional cash flow pattern, the initial outflow is not followed by inflows only, but the cash flows can flip from positive (inflows) to negative (outflows) again (or even change signs several times).

Nondeliverable forwards (NDFs) Cash-settled forward contracts, used predominately with respect to foreign exchange forwards.

Nonearning assets Cash and investments (specifically cash, cash equivalents, and short-term investments).

Nonlinear relation An association or relationship between variables that cannot be graphed as a straight line.

Nonstationarity With reference to a random variable, the property of having characteristics such as mean and variance that are not constant through time.

Normal EPS The earnings per share that a business could achieve currently under mid-cyclical conditions.

Normal backwardation The condition in futures markets in which futures prices are lower than expected spot prices.

Normal contango The condition in futures markets in which futures prices are higher than expected spot prices.

Normalized EPS The earnings per share that a business could achieve currently under mid-cyclical conditions.

Normalized P/E P/Es based on normalized EPS data.

Normalized earnings The expected level of mid-cycle earnings for a company in the absence of any unusual or temporary factors that affect profitability (either positively or negatively).

Notional amount The amount of protection being purchased in a CDS.

***n*-Period moving average** The average of the current and immediately prior $n - 1$ values of a time series.

Off-market FRA A contract in which the initial value is intentionally set at a value other than zero and therefore requires a cash payment at the start from one party to the other.

Off-the-run A series of securities or indexes that were issued/created prior to the most recently issued/created series.

Office REITs REITs that invest in and manage multi-tenanted office properties in central business districts of cities and suburban markets.

Offsetting A transaction in exchange-listed derivative markets in which a party re-enters the market to close out a position.

On-the-run The most recently issued/created series of securities or indexes.

Operating lease An agreement allowing the lessee to use some asset for a period of time; essentially a rental.

Operating risk The risk attributed to the operating cost structure, in particular the use of fixed costs in operations; the risk arising from the mix of fixed and variable costs; the risk that a company's operations may be severely affected by environmental, social, and governance risk factors.

Operational risk The risk of loss from failures in a company's systems and procedures, or from external events.

Opportunity cost The value that investors forgo by choosing a particular course of action; the value of something in its best alternative use.

Opportunity set The set of assets available for investment.

Optimal capital structure The capital structure at which the value of the company is maximized.

Optimizer A specialized computer program or a spreadsheet that solves for the portfolio weights that will result in the lowest risk for a specified level of expected return.

Option A financial instrument that gives one party the right, but not the obligation, to buy or sell an underlying asset from or to another party at a fixed price over a specific period of time. Also referred to as contingent claims.

Option premium The amount of money a buyer pays and seller receives to engage in an option transaction.

Option price The amount of money a buyer pays and seller receives to engage in an option transaction.

Orderly liquidation value The estimated gross amount of money that could be realized from the liquidation sale of an asset or assets, given a reasonable amount of time to find a purchaser or purchasers.

Organic growth Company growth in output or sales that is achieved by making investments internally (i.e., excludes growth achieved through mergers and acquisitions).

Orthogonal Uncorrelated; at a right angle.

Other comprehensive income Changes to equity that bypass (are not reported in) the income statement; the difference between comprehensive income and net income.

Out-of-sample forecast errors The differences between actual and predicted value of time series outside the sample period used to fit the model.

Out-of-the-money Options that, if exercised, would require the payment of more money than the value received and therefore would not be currently exercised.

Overnight index swap (OIS) A swap in which the floating rate is the cumulative value of a single unit of currency invested at an overnight rate during the settlement period.

PEG The P/E-to-growth ratio, calculated as the stock's P/E divided by the expected earnings growth rate.

Pairs trading An approach to trading that uses pairs of closely related stocks, buying the relatively undervalued stock and selling short the relatively overvalued stock.

Parameter instability The problem or issue of population regression parameters that have changed over time.

Partial regression coefficients The slope coefficients in a multiple regression. Also called *partial slope coefficients*.

Partial slope coefficients The slope coefficients in a multiple regression. Also called *partial regression coefficients*.

Partnership A business owned and operated by more than one individual.

Payer swaption A swaption that allows the holder to enter into a swap as the fixed-rate payer and floating-rate receiver.

Payoff The value of an option at expiration.

Payout amount The payout ratio times the notional.

Payout policy The principles by which a company distributes cash to common shareholders by means of cash dividends and/or share repurchases.

Payout ratio An estimate of the expected credit loss.

Pecking order theory The theory that managers take into account how their actions might be interpreted by outsiders and thus order their preferences for various forms of corporate financing. Forms of financing that are least visible to outsiders (e.g., internally generated funds) are most preferable to managers and those that are most visible (e.g., equity) are least preferable.

Perfect capital markets Markets in which, by assumption, there are no taxes, transactions costs, or bankruptcy costs, and in which all investors have equal ("symmetric") information.

Performance appraisal The evaluation of risk-adjusted performance; the evaluation of investment skill.

Periodic inventory system An inventory accounting system in which inventory values and costs of sales are determined at the end of the accounting period.

Perpetual inventory system An inventory accounting system in which inventory values and costs of sales are continuously updated to reflect purchases and sales.

Perpetuity A perpetual annuity, or a set of never-ending level sequential cash flows, with the first cash flow occurring one period from now.

Persistent earnings Earnings excluding nonrecurring components.

Pet projects Projects in which influential managers want the corporation to invest. Often, unfortunately, pet projects are selected without undergoing normal capital budgeting analysis.

Physical deterioration In the context of real estate, a reduction in value due to wear and tear.

Physical settlement Involves actual delivery of the debt instrument in exchange for a payment by the credit protection seller of the notional amount of the contract.

Plain vanilla swap An interest rate swap in which one party pays a fixed rate and the other pays a floating rate, with both sets of payments in the same currency.

Poison pill A pre-offer takeover defense mechanism that makes it prohibitively costly for an acquirer to take control of a target without the prior approval of the target's board of directors.

Poison puts A pre-offer takeover defense mechanism that gives target company bondholders the right to sell their bonds back to the target at a pre-specified redemption price, typically at or above par value; this defense increases the need for cash and raises the cost of the acquisition.

Pooling of interests method A method of accounting in which combined companies were portrayed as if they had always operated as a single economic entity. Called pooling of interests under U.S. GAAP and uniting of interests under IFRS. (No longer allowed under U.S. GAAP or IFRS).

Portfolio balance approach A theory of exchange rate determination that emphasizes the portfolio investment decisions of global investors and the requirement that global investors willingly hold all outstanding securities denominated in each currency at prevailing prices and exchange rates.

Portfolio performance attribution The analysis of portfolio performance in terms of the contributions from various sources of risk.

Portfolio possibilities curve A graphical representation of the expected return and risk of all portfolios that can be formed using two assets.

Position trader A trader who typically holds positions open overnight.

Positive serial correlation Serial correlation in which a positive error for one observation increases the chance of a positive error for another observation, and a negative error for one observation increases the chance of a negative error for another observation.

Potential GDP The maximum amount of output an economy can sustainably produce without inducing an increase in the inflation rate. The output level that corresponds to full employment with consistent wage and price expectations.

Potential credit risk The risk associated with the possibility that a payment due at a later date will not be made.

Premise of value The status of a company in the sense of whether it is assumed to be a going concern or not.

Premium The amount of money a buyer pays and seller receives to engage in an option transaction.

Premium leg The series of payments the credit protection buyer promises to make to the credit protection seller.

Present value model A model of intrinsic value that views the value of an asset as the present value of the asset's expected future cash flows.

Present value of growth opportunities The difference between the actual value per share and the nogrowth value per share. Also called *value of growth*.

Present value of the expected loss Conceptually, the largest price one would be willing to pay on a bond to a third party (e.g., an insurer) to entirely remove the credit risk of purchasing and holding the bond.

Presentation currency The currency in which financial statement amounts are presented.

Price limits Limits imposed by a futures exchange on the price change that can occur from one day to the next.

Price momentum A valuation indicator based on past price movement.

Price multiples The ratio of a stock's market price to some measure of value per share.

Price-setting option The operational flexibility to adjust prices when demand varies from forecast. For example, when demand exceeds capacity, the company could benefit from the excess demand by increasing prices.

Priced risk Risk for which investors demand compensation for bearing (e.g., equity risk, company-specific factors, macroeconomic factors).

Principal-agent problem A conflict of interest that arises when the agent in an agency relationship has goals and incentives that differ from the principal to whom the agent owes a fiduciary duty.

Prior transaction method A variation of the market approach; considers actual transactions in the stock of the subject private company.

Private market value The value derived using a sum-of-the-parts valuation.

Probability of default The probability that a bond issuer will not meet its contractual obligations on schedule.

Probability of survival The probability that a bond issuer will meet its contractual obligations on schedule.

Probit model A qualitative-dependent-variable multiple regression model based on the normal distribution.

Procedural law The body of law that focuses on the protection and enforcement of the substantive laws.

Production-flexibility The operational flexibility to alter production when demand varies from forecast. For example, if demand is strong, a company may profit from employees working overtime or from adding additional shifts.

Project sequencing To defer the decision to invest in a future project until the outcome of some or all of a current project is known. Projects are sequenced through time, so that investing in a project creates the option to invest in future projects.

Prospective P/E A P/E calculated on the basis of a forecast of EPS; a stock's current price divided by next year's expected earnings.

Protection leg The contingent payment that the credit protection seller may have to make to the credit protection buyer.

Protective put An option strategy in which a long position in an asset is combined with a long position in a put.

Proxy fight An attempt to take control of a company through a shareholder vote.

Proxy statement A public document that provides the material facts concerning matters on which shareholders will vote.

Prudential supervision Regulation and monitoring of the safety and soundness of financial institutions to promote financial stability, reduce system-wide risks, and protect customers of financial institutions.

Purchased in-process research and development costs Costs of research and development in progress at an acquired company; often, part of the purchase price of an acquired company is allocated to such costs.

Purchasing power gain A gain in value caused by changes in price levels. Monetary liabilities experience purchasing power gains during periods of inflation.

Purchasing power loss A loss in value caused by changes in price levels. Monetary assets experience purchasing power loss during periods of inflation.

Purchasing power parity (PPP) The idea that exchange rates move to equalize the purchasing power of different currencies.

Pure factor portfolio A portfolio with sensitivity of 1 to the factor in question and a sensitivity of 0 to all other factors.

Put An option that gives the holder the right to sell an underlying asset to another party at a fixed price over a specific period of time.

Put–call parity An equation expressing the equivalence (parity) of a portfolio of a call and a bond with a portfolio of a put and the underlying, which leads to the relationship between put and call prices.

Put–call–forward parity The relationship among puts, calls, and forward contracts.

Qualitative dependent variables Dummy variables used as dependent variables rather than as independent variables.

Quality of earnings analysis The investigation of issues relating to the accuracy of reported accounting results as reflections of economic performance; quality of earnings analysis is broadly understood to include not only earnings management, but also balance sheet management.

Random walk A time series in which the value of the series in one period is the value of the series in the previous period plus an unpredictable random error.

Rational efficient markets formulation See *market efficiency*.

Real estate investment trusts (REITS) Tax-advantaged entities (companies or trusts) that typically own, operate, and—to a limited extent—develop income-producing real estate property.

Real estate operating companies Regular taxable real estate ownership companies that operate in the real estate industry in countries that do not have a tax-advantaged REIT regime in place or are engaged in real estate activities of a kind and to an extent that do not fit within their country's REIT framework.

Real exchange rate The relative purchasing power of two currencies, defined in terms of the *real* goods and services that each can buy at prevailing national price levels and nominal exchange rates. Measured as the ratio of national price levels expressed in a common currency.

Real interest rate parity The proposition that real interest rates will converge to the same level across different markets.

Real options Options that relate to investment decisions such as the option to time the start of a project, the option to adjust its scale, or the option to abandon a project that has begun.

Receiver swaption A swaption that allows the holder to enter into a swap as the fixed-rate receiver and floating-rate payer.

Recovery rate The percentage of the loss recovered.

Reduced form models Models of credit analysis based on the outputs of a structural model but with different assumptions. The model's credit risk measures reflect changing economic conditions.

Reference entity The borrower on a single-name CDS.

Reference obligation A particular debt instrument issued by the borrower that is the designated instrument being covered.

Regime With reference to a time series, the underlying model generating the times series.

Regression coefficients The intercept and slope coefficient(s) of a regression.

Regulatory arbitrage Entities identify and use some aspect of regulations that allows them to exploit differences in economic substance and regulatory interpretation or in foreign and domestic regulatory regimes to their (the entities) advantage.

Regulatory burden The costs of regulation for the regulated entity.

Regulatory capture Theory that regulation often arises to enhance the interests of the regulated.

Regulatory competition Regulators may compete to provide a regulatory environment designed to attract certain entities.

Relative valuation models A model that specifies an asset's value relative to the value of another asset.

Relative version of PPP Hypothesis that changes in (nominal) exchange rates over time are equal to national inflation rate differentials.

Relative-strength indicators Valuation indicators that compare a stock's performance during a period either to its own past performance or to the performance of some group of stocks.

Renewable resources Resources that can be replenished, such as a forest.

Rental price of capital The cost per unit of time to rent a unit of capital.

Replacement cost In the context of real estate, the value of a building assuming it was built today using current construction costs and standards.

Replacement value The market value of a swap.

Reporting unit An operating segment or one level below an operating segment (referred to as a component).

Reputational risk The risk that a company will suffer an extended diminution in market value relative to other companies in the same industry due to a demonstrated lack of concern for environmental, social, and governance risk factors.

Required rate of return The minimum rate of return required by an investor to invest in an asset, given the asset's riskiness.

Residential mortgage-backed securities Securities backed by residential mortgage loans.

Residential properties Properties that provide housing for individuals or families. Single-family properties may be owner-occupied or rental properties, whereas multi-family properties are rental properties even if the owner or manager occupies one of the units.

Residual autocorrelations The sample autocorrelations of the residuals.

Residual dividend policy A policy in which dividends are paid from any internally generated funds remaining after such funds are used to finance positive NPV projects.

Residual income Earnings for a given time period, minus a deduction for common shareholders' opportunity cost in generating the earnings. Also called *economic profit* or *abnormal earnings*.

Residual income method Income approach that estimates the value of all intangible assets of the business by capitalizing future earnings in excess of the estimated return requirements associated with working capital and fixed assets.

Residual income model (RIM) A model of stock valuation that views intrinsic value of stock as the sum of book value per share plus the present value of the stock's expected future residual income per share. Also called *discounted abnormal earnings model* or *Edwards–Bell–Ohlson model*.

Residual loss Agency costs that are incurred despite adequate monitoring and bonding of management.

Restructuring Reorganizing the financial structure of a firm.

Retail REITs REITs that invest in such retail properties as regional shopping malls or community/neighborhood shopping centers.

Return on capital employed Operating profit divided by capital employed (debt and equity capital).

Return on invested capital A measure of the after-tax profitability of the capital invested by the company's shareholders and debt holders.

Revenue The amount charged for the delivery of goods or services in the ordinary activities of a business over a stated period; the inflows of economic resources to a company over a stated period.

Reviewed financial statements A type of non-audited financial statements; typically provide an opinion letter with representations and assurances by the reviewing accountant that are less than those in audited financial statements.

Rho The sensitivity of the option price to the risk-free rate.

Risk reversal An option position that consists of the purchase of an out-of-the-money call and the simultaneous sale of an out-of-the-money put with the same "delta," on the same underlying currency or security, and with the same expiration date.

Risk-neutral probabilities Weights that are used to compute a binomial option price. They are the probabilities that would apply if a risk-neutral investor valued an option.

Risk-neutral valuation The process by which options and other derivatives are priced by treating investors as though they were risk neutral.

Robust standard errors Standard errors of the estimated parameters of a regression that correct for the presence of heteroskedasticity in the regression's error term.

Roll When an investor moves from one series to a new one.

Root mean squared error (RMSE) The square root of the average squared forecast error; used to compare the out-of-sample forecasting performance of forecasting models.

Sales comparison approach In the context of real estate, this approach estimates value based on what similar or comparable properties (comparables) transacted for in the current market.

Sales-type leases A type of finance lease, from a lessor perspective, where the present value of the lease payments (lease receivable) exceeds the carrying value of the leased asset. The revenues earned by the lessor are operating (the profit on the sale) and financing (interest) in nature.

Sampling distribution The distribution of all distinct possible values that a statistic can assume when computed from samples of the same size randomly drawn from the same population.

Scaled earnings surprise Unexpected earnings divided by the standard deviation of analysts' earnings forecasts.

Scalper A trader who offers to buy or sell futures contracts, holding the position for only a brief period of time. Scalpers attempt to profit by buying at the bid price and selling at the higher ask price.

Scatter plot A two-dimensional plot of pairs of observations on two data series.

Scenario analysis Analysis that involves changing multiple assumptions at the same time.

Screening The application of a set of criteria to reduce a set of potential investments to a smaller set having certain desired characteristics.

Seats Memberships in a derivatives exchange.

Sector neutralizing Measure of financial reporting quality by subtracting the mean or median ratio for a given sector group from a given company's ratio.

Securities offering A merger or acquisition in which target shareholders are to receive shares of the acquirer's common stock as compensation.

Security market line (SML) The graph of the capital asset pricing model.

Self-regulating organizations Private, non-governmental organizations that both represent and regulate their members. Some self-regulating organizations are also independent regulators.

Sell-side analysts Analysts who work at brokerages.

Sensitivity analysis Analysis that shows the range of possible outcomes as specific assumptions are changed; involves changing one assumption at a time.

Serially correlated With reference to regression errors, errors that are correlated across observations.

Settlement In the case of a credit event, the process by which the two parties to a CDS contract satisfy their respective obligations.

Settlement date The date on which the parties to a swap make payments. Also called *payment date*.

Settlement period The time between settlement dates.

Settlement price The official price, designated by the clearinghouse, from which daily gains and losses will be determined and marked to market.

Shareholders' equity Total assets minus total liabilities.

Shark repellents A pre-offer takeover defense mechanism involving the corporate charter (e.g., staggered boards of directors and supermajority provisions).

Shopping center REITs that invest in such retail properties as regional shopping malls or community/neighborhood shopping centers.

Short The seller of a derivative contract. Also refers to the position of being short a derivative.

Single-name CDS Credit default swap on one specific borrower.

Sole proprietorship A business owned and operated by a single person.

Special purpose vehicle A non-operating entity created to carry out a specified purpose, such as leasing assets or securitizing receivables; can be a corporation, partnership, trust, limited liability, or partnership formed to facilitate a specific type of business activity. Also called *special purpose entity* or *variable interest entity*.

Speculative value The difference between the market price of the option and its intrinsic value, determined by the uncertainty of the underlying over the remaining life of the option. Also called *time value*.

Spin-off A form of restructuring in which shareholders of a parent company receive a proportional number of shares in a new, separate entity; shareholders end up owning stock in two different companies where there used to be one.

Split-off A form of restructuring in which shareholders of the parent company are given shares in a newly created entity in exchange for their shares of the parent company.

Split-rate tax system In reference to corporate taxes, a split-rate system taxes earnings to be distributed as dividends at a different rate than earnings to be retained. Corporate profits distributed as dividends are taxed at a lower rate than those retained in the business.

Spurious correlation A correlation that misleadingly points toward associations between variables.

Stabilized NOI In the context of real estate, the expected NOI when a renovation is complete.

Stable dividend policy A policy in which regular dividends are paid that reflect long-run expected earnings. In contrast to a constant dividend payout ratio policy, a stable dividend policy does not reflect short-term volatility in earnings.

Standard deviation The positive square root of the variance; a measure of dispersion in the same units as the original data.

Standard of value A specification of how "value" is to be understood in the context of a specific valuation.

Standardized beta With reference to fundamental factor models, the value of the attribute for an asset minus the average value of the attribute across all stocks, divided by the standard deviation of the attribute across all stocks.

Standardized unexpected earnings (SUE) Unexpected earnings per share divided by the standard deviation of unexpected earnings per share over a specified prior time period.

Static trade-off theory of capital structure A theory pertaining to a company's optimal capital structure; the optimal level of debt is found at the point where additional debt would cause the costs of financial distress to increase by a greater amount than the benefit of the additional tax shield.

Statistical factor models A multifactor model in which statistical methods are applied to a set of historical returns to determine portfolios that best explain either historical return covariances or variances.

Statistical inference Making forecasts, estimates, or judgments about a larger group from a smaller group actually observed; using a sample statistic to infer the value of an unknown population parameter.

Statistically significant A result indicating that the null hypothesis can be rejected; with reference to an estimated regression coefficient, frequently understood to mean a result indicating that the corresponding population regression coefficient is different from 0.

Statutes Laws enacted by legislative bodies.

Statutory merger A merger in which one company ceases to exist as an identifiable entity and all its assets and liabilities become part of a purchasing company.

Steady state rate of growth The constant growth rate of output (or output per capita) which can or will be sustained indefinitely once it is reached. Key ratios, such as the capital–output ratio, are constant on the steady-state growth path.

Sterilized intervention A policy measure in which a monetary authority buys or sells its own currency to mitigate undesired exchange rate movements and simultaneously offsets the impact on the money supply with transactions in other financial instruments (usually money market instruments).

Stock purchase An acquisition in which the acquirer gives the target company's shareholders some combination of cash and securities in exchange for shares of the target company's stock.

Storage REITs REITs that own and operate self-storage properties, sometimes referred to as mini-warehouse facilities.

Storage costs The costs of holding an asset, generally a function of the physical characteristics of the underlying asset.

Straight-line rent The average annual rent under a multi-year lease agreement that contains contractual increases in rent during the life of the lease. For example if the rent is \$100,000 in Year 1, \$105,000 in Year 2, and \$110,000 in Year 3, the average rent to be recognized each year as revenue under straight-line rent accounting is (\$100,000 + \$105,000 + \$110,000)/3 = \$105,000.

Straight-line rent adjustment See *non-cash rent*.

Strategic transaction A purchase involving a buyer that would benefit from certain synergies associated with owning the target firm.

Strike See *exercise price*.

Strike price See *exercise price*.

Strike rate The fixed rate at which the holder of an interest rate option can buy or sell the underlying. Also called *exercise rate*.

Striking price See *exercise price*.

Structural models Structural models of credit analysis build on the insights of option pricing theory. They are based on the structure of a company's balance sheet.

Subsidiary merger A merger in which the company being purchased becomes a subsidiary of the purchaser.

Substantive law The body of law that focuses on the rights and responsibilities of entities and relationships among entities.

Succession event A change of corporate structure of the reference entity, such as through a merger, divestiture, spinoff, or any similar action, in which ultimate responsibility for the debt in question is unclear.

Sum-of-the-parts valuation A valuation that sums the estimated values of each of a company's businesses as if each business were an independent going concern.

Sunk cost A cost that has already been incurred.

Supernormal growth Above average or abnormally high growth rate in earnings per share.
Surprise The actual value of a variable minus its predicted (or expected) value.
Survivorship bias Bias that may result when failed or defunct companies are excluded from membership in a group.
Sustainable growth rate The rate of dividend (and earnings) growth that can be sustained over time for a given level of return on equity, keeping the capital structure constant and without issuing additional common stock.
Swap spread The difference between the fixed rate on an interest rate swap and the rate on a Treasury note with equivalent maturity; it reflects the general level of credit risk in the market.
Swaption An option to enter into a swap.
Synthetic CDO Created by combining a portfolio of default-free securities with a combination of credit default swaps undertaken as protection sellers.
Synthetic call The combination of puts, the underlying, and risk-free bonds that replicates a call option.
Synthetic forward contract The combination of the underlying, puts, calls, and risk-free bonds that replicates a forward contract.
Synthetic lease A lease that is structured to provide a company with the tax benefits of ownership while not requiring the asset to be reflected on the company's financial statements.
Synthetic put The combination of calls, the underlying, and risk-free bonds that replicates a put option.
Systematic factors Factors that affect the average returns of a large number of different assets.
Systemic risk The risk of failure of the financial system.
Takeover A merger; the term may be applied to any transaction, but is often used in reference to hostile transactions.
Takeover premium The amount by which the takeover price for each share of stock must exceed the current stock price in order to entice shareholders to relinquish control of the company to an acquirer.
Tangible book value per share Common shareholders' equity minus intangible assets from the balance sheet, divided by the number of shares outstanding.
Target The company in a merger or acquisition that is being acquired.
Target capital structure A company's chosen proportions of debt and equity.
Target company The company in a merger or acquisition that is being acquired.
Target payout ratio A strategic corporate goal representing the long-term proportion of earnings that the company intends to distribute to shareholders as dividends.
Technical indicators Momentum indicators based on price.
Temporal method A variation of the monetary/non-monetary translation method that requires not only monetary assets and liabilities, but also non-monetary assets and liabilities that are measured at their current value on the balance sheet date to be translated at the current exchange rate. Assets and liabilities are translated at rates consistent with the timing of their measurement value. This method is typically used when the functional currency is other than the local currency.
Tender offer A public offer whereby the acquirer invites target shareholders to submit ("tender") their shares in return for the proposed payment.
Terminal price multiples The price multiple for a stock assumed to hold at a stated future time.
Terminal share price The share price at a particular point in the future.
Terminal value of the stock The analyst's estimate of a stock's value at a particular point in the future. Also called *continuing value of the stock.*
Termination date The date of the final payment on a swap; also, the swap's expiration date.
Theta The rate at which an option's time value decays.
Time series A set of observations on a variable's outcomes in different time periods.
Time to expiration The time remaining in the life of a derivative, typically expressed in years.
Time value The difference between the market price of the option and its intrinsic value, determined by the uncertainty of the underlying over the remaining life of the option. Also called *speculative value.*
Time value decay The loss in the value of an option resulting from movement of the option price towards its payoff value as the expiration day approaches.
Tobin's *q* The ratio of the market value of debt and equity to the replacement cost of total assets.
Top-down approach With respect to forecasting, an approach that usually begins at the level of the overall economy. Forecasts are then made at more narrowly defined levels, such as sector, industry, and market for a specific product.
Top-down investing An approach to investing that typically begins with macroeconomic forecasts.
Total factor productivity (TFP) A multiplicative scale factor that reflects the general level of productivity or technology in the economy. Changes in total factor productivity generate proportional changes in output for any input combination.
Total invested capital The sum of market value of common equity, book value of preferred equity, and face value of debt.
Total return swap A swap in which one party agrees to pay the total return on a security. Often used as a credit derivative, in which the underlying is a bond.
Tracking error The standard deviation of the differences between a portfolio's returns and its benchmark's returns; a synonym of active risk. Also called *tracking risk.*
Tracking portfolio A portfolio having factor sensitivities that are matched to those of a benchmark or other portfolio.
Tracking risk The standard deviation of the differences between a portfolio's returns and its benchmark's returns; a synonym of active risk. Also called *tracking error.*
Trailing P/E A stock's current market price divided by the most recent four quarters of earnings per share. Also called *current P/E.*
Trailing dividend yield Current market price divided by the most recent quarterly per-share dividend multiplied by four.
Tranche CDS A type of credit default swap that covers a combination of borrowers but only up to pre-specified levels of losses.
Transaction exposure The risk of a change in value between the transaction date and the settlement date of an asset of liability denominated in a foreign currency.
Trend A long-term pattern of movement in a particular direction.
Triangular arbitrage An arbitrage transaction involving three currencies which attempts to exploit inconsistencies among pair wise exchange rates.

UPREITs An umbrella partnership REIT under which the REIT owns an operating partnership and serves as the general partner of the operating partnership. All or most of the properties are held in the operating partnership.

Unconditional heteroskedasticity Heteroskedasticity of the error term that is not correlated with the values of the independent variable(s) in the regression.

Uncovered interest rate parity The proposition that the expected return on an uncovered (i.e., unhedged) foreign currency (risk-free) investment should equal the return on a comparable domestic currency investment.

Underlying An asset that trades in a market in which buyers and sellers meet, decide on a price, and the seller then delivers the asset to the buyer and receives payment. The underlying is the asset or other derivative on which a particular derivative is based. The market for the underlying is also referred to as the spot market.

Underlying earnings Earnings excluding nonrecurring components.

Unearned revenue A liability account for money that has been collected for goods or services that have not yet been delivered; payment received in advance of providing a good or service.

Unexpected earnings The difference between reported earnings per share and expected earnings per share.

Unit root A time series that is not covariance stationary is said to have a unit root.

Uniting of interests method A method of accounting in which combined companies were portrayed as if they had always operated as a single economic entity. Called pooling of interests under U.S. GAAP and uniting of interests under IFRS. (No longer allowed under U.S. GAAP or IFRS).

Unlimited funds An unlimited funds environment assumes that the company can raise the funds it wants for all profitable projects simply by paying the required rate of return.

Unsterilized intervention A policy measure in which a monetary authority buys or sells its own currency to mitigate undesired exchange rate movements and does not offset the impact on the money supply with transactions in other financial instruments.

Upfront payment The difference between the credit spread and the standard rate paid by the protection if the standard rate is insufficient to compensate the protection seller. Also called *upfront premium.*

Upfront premium See *upfront payment.*

Upstream A transaction between two related companies, an investor company (or a parent company) and an associate company (or a subsidiary company) such that the associate company records a profit on its income statement. An example is a sale of inventory by the associate to the investor company or by a subsidiary to a parent company.

Valuation The process of determining the value of an asset or service on the basis of variables perceived to be related to future investment returns, or on the basis of comparisons with closely similar assets.

Value at risk (VAR) A money measure of the minimum value of losses expected during a specified time period at a given level of probability.

Value of growth The difference between the actual value per share and the nogrowth value per share.

Variance The expected value (the probability-weighted average) of squared deviations from a random variable's expected value.

Variation margin Additional margin that must be deposited in an amount sufficient to bring the balance up to the initial margin requirement.

Vega The relationship between option price and volatility.

Venture capital investors Private equity investors in development-stage companies.

Vertical merger A merger involving companies at different positions of the same production chain; for example, a supplier or a distributor.

Visibility The extent to which a company's operations are predictable with substantial confidence.

Weighted average cost An inventory accounting method that averages the total cost of available inventory items over the total units available for sale.

Weighted average cost of capital (WACC) A weighted average of the after-tax required rates of return on a company's common stock, preferred stock, and long-term debt, where the weights are the fraction of each source of financing in the company's target capital structure.

Weighted harmonic mean See *harmonic mean.*

White knight A third party that is sought out by the target company's board to purchase the target in lieu of a hostile bidder.

White squire A third party that is sought out by the target company's board to purchase a substantial minority stake in the target—enough to block a hostile takeover without selling the entire company.

White-corrected standard errors A synonym for robust standard errors.

Winner's curse The tendency for the winner in certain competitive bidding situations to overpay, whether because of overestimation of intrinsic value, emotion, or information asymmetries.

Write-down A reduction in the value of an asset as stated in the balance sheet.

Zero-cost collar A transaction in which a position in the underlying is protected by buying a put and selling a call with the premium from the sale of the call offsetting the premium from the purchase of the put. It can also be used to protect a floating-rate borrower against interest rate increases with the premium on a long cap offsetting the premium on a short floor.

Index

R